BRANDS, CONSUMERS, SYMBOLS,  RESEARCH

—For Bobette, Joyce, Chris, and Leslie Ann —
— In memory of Bruce —

BRANDS, CONSUMERS, SYMBOLS, & RESEARCH

Sidney J. Levy on Marketing

Compiled by
Dennis W. Rook

Sage Publications, Inc.
International Educational and Professional Publisher
Thousand Oaks   London   New Delhi

For information:

Sage Publications, Inc.
2455 Teller Road
Thousand Oaks, California 91320
E-mail: order@sagepub.com

Sage Publications Ltd.
6 Bonhill Street
London EC2A 4PU
United Kingdom

Sage Publications India Pvt. Ltd.
M-32 Market
Greater Kailash I
New Delhi 110 048 India

Printed in the United States of America

Library of Congress Cataloging-in-Publication Data

Levy, Sidney J., 1921–
    Brands, consumers, symbols, and research: Sidney J. Levy on
marketing / edited by Dennis W. Rook; authored by Sidney J. Levy.
        p.   cm.
    Includes bibliographical references and index.
    ISBN 0-7619-1696-2 (cloth: acid-free paper)
    ISBN 0-7619-1697-0 (pbk.: acid-free paper)
    1. Marketing—United States.   2. Advertising—United States.
3. Consumer behavior—United States.   I. Rook, Dennis W.
II. Title.
HF5415.1 .L48   1999
658.8'243—dc21   99-6225

This book is printed on acid-free paper.

99   00   01   02   03   04   05   7   6   5   4   3   2   1

Acquiring Editor:	Harry Briggs
Editorial Assistant:	MaryAnn Vail
Production Editor:	Astrid Virding
Editorial Assistant:	Stephanie Allen
Designer/Typesetter:	Janelle LeMaster/Lynn Miyata
Indexer:	Juniee Oneida
Cover Designer:	Candice Harman

CONTENTS

FOREWORD

Now and then, master craftsmen enter a domain, and it is never the same again. They cast a new habit of mind on a field that can't be ignored. Master craftsmen are very interesting people. They dare to be different, and the difference in their thinking is not in their taking sides so much as it is in creating a new one. To be a master of any craft, marketing included, requires a seamless blending of science and art. Master craftsmen know better than to even make such a distinction. Impressionist painters, for instance, made very sophisticated use of a science of color vision that was ahead of its time. Similarly, there is considerable poetry and artistic vision in the works of great scientists. Indeed, the drafting of anything involves advancing and exploiting tacit and explicit understandings of the basic nature of things and the ability to represent them in ways others can appreciate.

Another quality of master craftsmen is that they produce masterpieces. A number of widely shared defining characteristics of masterpieces are worth noting here. First, it is a critical audience (usually a sizable one) rather than the producer of a work that judges something a masterpiece. Once produced, the craftsman has little or no control over the ultimate pronouncements made about his or her opus. Masterpiece status is conferred by a public audience. Second, these judgments are usually made over successive generations of professional and lay critics whose criteria and historical perspectives may differ. The test of time is not inherently friendly, and few works survive it. Third, to stand a chance of being a masterpiece, a work—be it a play, novel, theory, or experiment; a visual, gustatory, or auditory representation; or whater—has to meet two conditions. The first condition is that everything that is necessary is present. The second condition, as stringent as the first, is that everything that is unnecessary is absent. These are the qualities a craftsman can control. If there is anything magical about creating a masterpiece, it is to be found in how a master meets these two conditions.

Another reason master craftsmen are interesting lies beyond what they do and how they do it. They can be interesting because of who they are as spouses, parents, and friends, as well as the roles they play in the lives of others in their trade. Here, the history of science and art is illuminating. People who produce masterpieces can be, for lack of a better term, jerks. They may even have more of a knack for this than those producing lesser works. But sometimes, too, master craftsmen can be wonderfully human and enriching of the lives of those around them. They provide what loved ones and colleagues need while being careful to not provide what isn't needed. Moreover, they do this by nature, not by plan.

So, being a master craftsman, especially one whose personal values and sensitivity to others create another set of high standards, is no easy thing. Which beings me to Sidney J. Levy. The 54 collected works in this volume provide an opportunity for the reader to determine whether Sidney's works, individually and/or collectively, qualify as a masterpiece. For me, Sidney has created more individual pieces of work that merit this status than any other marketing scholar I know. Collectively, the work in this volume is a masterpiece of insight into the social enterprise that is marketing. Again, I don't know anyone whose career-long program of thought is so extraordinarily rich in imagination and practical value. He challenges, provokes, excites, soothes, and supports us with one or another of his writings. Does he walk on water? No. (After all, he once convinced me to fly with him in a tiny plane in Costa Rica in which we nearly met the Grim Reaper.) Does he come close? As close as anyone could. Professional life is very personal, too, and it is rare that people who are so adept in the creation of master works can forge a professional life that also expresses who they are in the more private world as mate, parent, and friend.

This volume contains two feasts: the ideas themselves and the style of mind that has produced them. The first feast requires less of the reader's energy. The second should encourage those who don't know Sidney Levy to do some sleuthing to figure out what blend of intellectual spices a mind must have to produce such provocative ideas. *Bon appetit!*

Gerald Zaltman
Harvard Business School

INTRODUCTION
Ideas of a Major Marketing Man

To the best of my knowledge, this book is a first of its kind in the marketing field. More than a few corporate marketing and advertising executives have provided biographical and philosophical perspectives on their marketplace successes and failures. This volume is a different breed of book. Specifically, it is the first comprehensive collection of significant scholarly essays and studies in the field of marketing by a single author—Sidney J. Levy—and his collaborators. And what a compendium this is. Sidney Levy is a prolific, seminal, internationally recognized, award-winning writer whose ideas began to influence marketing executives in the late 1940s and today continue to have an impact on how

we think about marketing's role in management, how managers develop products and brands, how they understand their consumers, and how corporate and academic researchers investigate marketplace concerns. The breadth, longevity, and influence of Sidney Levy's thinking are unique. His contribution to marketing thought and practice is extraordinary, and his stature among his colleagues today, to Sidney's embarrassment, verges on that of a venerated guru. In addition to the general dissemination of his ideas throughout the field of marketing, his 36-year teaching career at Northwestern University's Kellogg Graduate School of Management has directly influenced several generations of marketing managers. Although fewer in number, Sidney Levy's Ph.D. students are faculty at the world's leading business schools today.

In November 1997, Sid Levy was inducted as the first "Living Legend of Marketing" at the HEC-Montreal School of Business in Montreal, Canada. In the parlance of my Southern California subculture, Sid is a big star whose gentle and generous brilliance has defined marketing's professional borders, content, technology, and ethos for over 50 years. The 54 articles in this volume document the emergence and evolution of many core marketing concepts, and they also illuminate compelling, contemporary topics such as brand-image equity, product symbolism, consumer motivation, marketing ethics, sex appeal, focus groups, and global marketing. Levy's writings span five decades, and they reveal his fascinating perspective on marketing's fertile mix of products, companies, and consumers. Together, this material constitutes a remarkable and exciting intellectual history of the field of marketing. Serious marketing students, managers, marketing researchers, and academic scholars should all find many interesting and useful ideas in this volume.

PROSPECTIVE READERS

From the late 1940s on, Sid Levy has shared his ideas and observations throughout the world in classrooms and boardrooms and at academic symposia and governmental conferences. Sidney is a Gemini, so naturally his professional life has multiple aspects and audiences, for whom this volume likely offers different benefits. From 1961 to 1997, Sid Levy taught thousands of budding managers at Northwestern University (and he now heads the marketing department at the University of Arizona); his past students might value this book as an indepth refresher course whose relevance is enhanced by their own professional experiences. For the larger population of today's marketing managers, this collection of articles represents an invigorating educational opportunity to understand marketing and consumer behavior at an advanced, sophisticated level. A cursory examination of the contents reveals that this is not a Crown Book flavor of the month. Rather, it includes serious and lively discussions of important and enduring marketing issues.

From my own observations, academics tend to think of Sid Levy as a professor and as a consumer behavior theorist. True enough, but relatively few grasp his long and distinguished career in marketing research and consulting or its relationship to his academic writings. Many of the articles in this collection provide excellent examples of how his mind abstracts from particular commercial needs, for example, to sell more milk or wine, to a general theory of beverage behavior (see Chapter 39, "Synchrony and Diachrony in Product Perceptions"). Levy's theories and their practical applications should inform the recurring and often contentious academic debate about the merits of particular versus universal research in marketing.

Finally, marketing researchers should find the section on qualitative research methods fascinating, useful, and perhaps even inspiring. Today, there is much misunderstanding and misuse of .qualitative research, and the material in this section presents key issues and historical facts in perspective. These readings should assist both marketing managers and researchers in designing and fielding qualitative studies with more confidence and creativity.

MARKETING TOPICS

The articles in this volume are organized into six sections. The first includes Sid Levy's most recent contribution to the *Journal of Consumer Research*, the field's premier scholarly journal. Not only is this Levy's most recent publication, it is his most autobiographical, which makes it a great place to begin. Accompanying this 1996 publication is a talk—"The Exemplary Research"—that then Ph.D. student Sidney Levy gave to the faculty and students of the Committee on Human Development at the University of Chicago in January 1953. Together, these two articles will help ground the reader in Levy's intellectual origins, orientation, and style. Following these introductory essays, the remaining articles concentrate on these five topics:

Marketing

Products and brands

The symbolic nature of marketing

Consumer analyses and observations

Qualitative methods of marketing study

Clearly, these are among the most important issues in marketing today, and each section contains articles that suggest how to think about and cope with them. Also, each begins with a historically significant lead article that introduces Levy's intellectual breakthroughs and provides a useful entry point to relevant topics. The accompanying articles appear in chronological order, but the reader may want to explore things differently and pursue particular interests. To facilitate this, in each of the volume's major sections, I have written an introduction that provides information about the origins, applications, evolution, and contribution of Levy's main ideas.

THEMES AND QUALITIES IN SJL'S WRITING

Ultimately, readers will make their own decisions about these issues, but as editor of this compendium, I would like to point out several qualities that characterize and span Sid Levy's writings. First, whereas his scholarship in marketing is *nonpareil*, his writing is highly accessible; and it is always interesting, engaging, provocative, and fun to read. A second important element that distinguishes his work from most others is its interdisciplinary nature. Levy's thinking eclectically dances and weaves across behavioral disciplines, and by mixing things up, he offers original, polyfocal perspectives to marketing situations that are commonly construed much too narrowly. Another enduring quality of his work is an emphasis on the role of interpretive analysis in marketing management. This idea materialized in his 1950s landmark *Harvard Business Review* articles about products, brands, and symbols, and it is forcefully reiterated in this volume's opening article, "Stalking the Amphisbaena."

Looking at Sid Levy's achievements from the perspective of 1997, the reader might erroneously conclude that his accomplishments were akin to anointments. This is historically incorrect, as another key quality of his work is the intellectual conflict it had to overcome. This aspect is prominent in Part II (Marketing), but it also applies to his work on symbols, consumers, and qualitative research. In each arena, Sidney had to confront literal minded and sometimes mean-spirited critics who derided his nuanced analyses, his emphasis on noneconomic variables, and his use of "touchy-feely" research methods. Yet, one advantage of a 1999 retrospective is the opportunity to observe how his ideas have prevailed.

Finally, Sid Levy's work is characterized by both prescience and timelessness. Reading several of the articles in this collection, I am struck by how many developments that Levy predicted years ago have come true. A particularly striking example of this visionary quality can be found in "Cigarette Smoking and the Public Interest," which was published in 1963 and which anticipates many of the specific developments that have occurred in this controversial arena. Not only prescient, Sid Levy's writings have a timeless quality. As an example, I would refer the reader to "Symbols for Sale," the lead article to Part IV. Except for minor details (e.g., now defunct brands), this material is strikingly contemporary, despite its publication date, 1959. This timelessness, I believe, is a measure of work that has enduring impact and utility.

Quite a few of Sid Levy's articles have been anthologized in various marketing "classics" collections. Thus, in some cases, readers will note that he has added comments to original articles at the request of a particular collection editor. For the present volume, he has added reminiscences about the genesis of certain articles. The materials in this volume are not the complete collected works of Sidney J. Levy. Some early writings have been, as Sidney describes it, "lost in the mists of time;" not represented are the five books that he has written. The first, *Living With Television* (with Ira O. Glick), was published in 1961. In its Foreword, W. Lloyd Warner describes this work as "an exciting contribution to our body of knowledge about the meanings

and function of the symbol systems commonly shared by most Americans."

Levy has published two books about marketing communications and promotion: *Promotion: A Behavioral View* (with Harper W. Boyd, Jr.) in 1967 and his own *Promotional Behavior* in 1971. In response to the social turmoil of the late 1960s and early 1970s, and its inevitable spillover into the marketing arena, Levy collaborated with Gerald Zaltman on *Marketing, Society, and Conflict,* which appeared in 1975. His fifth book, a consumer behavior text titled *Marketplace Behavior: Its Meaning for Management,* was published in 1978.

A PERSONAL NOTE

I hope the reader is now eager to "get on with it" and begin reading. Let me end this introduction with a few comments about how I came to know Sidney Levy, and to study and work with him. I first met him in his Northwestern University office in the Spring of 1979. I was a burned-out social services administrator in Evanston, Illinois, who in my community activities had met a few Northwestern faculty wives. Outstanding among them was Bobette Adler Levy, who encouraged me to talk with her husband about Northwestern's MBA program as an escape route from the welfare office and an entree to a more gratifying and creative career . . . possibly in "marketing." I made an appointment with Dr. Levy and approached his office with trepidation and some ambivalence about going back to school. He couldn't have been nicer. We talked about a lot of different things, and an hour passed in what seemed like minutes.

I was really enjoying the meeting until Sidney suggested that, in his opinion, I was not an ideal candidate for an MBA. My psyche crashed, and I thought, "Oh well, back to the welfare office." In my gloom, I barely heard his follow-up recommendation that I might consider Northwestern's doctoral program in marketing. Within 6 months I began graduate studies there and completed my dissertation, *The Ritual Dimension of Consumer Behavior,* under Sid Levy's supervision, in 1983. Along the way, I learned a huge amount from Sidney about marketing, brands, consumers, and research; I am still learning from him; and I use the ideas and tools he taught me daily in my professional life as a professor and management consultant.

I am lucky that much of my learning from Sidney Levy was in person, in class, through collaborative research and writing, at formal academic occasions, and in casual talk at his home or mine. Obviously, this volume provides a vicarious Levy experience, yet, it is very much alive with Sidney's compelling ideas and lively presentation. I hope readers will enjoy this intellectual adventure as much as I have, and take away learning that will enhance their professional lives.

—Dennis W. Rook

Critics customarily characterize qualitative and introspective works as self-indulgent, so let me be the first to say it. This collection is a gracious compliment to me from my friends Dennis Rook, Gerry Zaltman, editor Harry Briggs, and the Editorial Board of Sage Publications, Inc. I appreciate their indulging me by putting together these 54 pieces of my writing (alone and with colleagues) from 1953 to 1996. These articles will show that, as part of the marketing scene from 1948 to the present, I have consistently built on my excellent University of Chicago liberal arts education, my experience as a research worker at Social Research, Inc., and my work as an educator at Northwestern University. Although still active as head of the marketing department at the University of Arizona, I see this book as a summing up of what I have offered the marketing field and hope that it may afford readers useful food for thought.

—Sidney J. Levy

PART
ONE

A LIFE IN THE
MARKETPLACE

——— •◆• ———

Dennis Rook: This section is the shortest in this volume, as it includes only two papers, and its introduction will be correspondingly brief. The first article, "Stalking the Amphisbaena," appeared in the *Journal of Consumer Research* in 1996. The Journal recently instituted a policy of occasionally inviting an eminent consumer researcher to submit a manuscript that would not undergo the typical publication review process. This enlightened editorial innovation was designed to encourage selected authors to be more reflective, philosophical, and critical. And the policy appears to have worked: thoughtful and influential pieces have been published in *JCR* by invited authors Bill Wells, Hal Kassarjian, and Kent Monroe over the past several years. During his editorship, Kent Monroe invited Sidney Levy to prepare a manuscript for publication in the Journal: Brian Sternthal repeated the invitation, and Sidney completed the article in 1996.

Stalking the Amphisbaena (*Journal of Consumer Research*, 1996)
The Exemplary Research (Ph.D. student speech, 1953)

The result is a fascinating, complex, eclectic, and provocative article. It is a good place to begin examining Levy's collected works because it is biographical and personal in ways that academic journals do not normally tolerate. Also, it provides an intellectual preview of material in the subsequent sections on consumers, brands, research, and other matters. Particularly delightful is Levy's realistic, frank, and amusing analysis of the consumers' consumption *sensorium*. Also, the article addresses some fundamental research methodology issues by illustrating how introspection pervades the research process, whether it involves lab experiments, surveys, or picture drawing. Levy reminds us that data do not speak for themselves and that researchers add value by providing creative, persuasive, and sound analyses of complex behavioral problems.

The second article in this section, *The Exemplary Research* (1953), is Sidney Levy's first major graduate academic presentation. Qualities that characterize his subsequent work are apparent here: an interdisciplinary orientation, engaging and sophisticated ideas, masterful writing, and a sense of humor. In 1953, Levy's seminal work, "The Product and the Brand," was only 2 years away from appearing in the *Harvard Business Review* (see Chapter 13), yet in "The Exemplary Research," we see Levy the pure behavioral scientist and student of the University of Chicago's Committee on Human Development, making a sort of intellectual debut.

———— •◆• ————

## Chapter 1

STALKING THE AMPHISBAENA

Sidney J. Levy

AMPHISBAENA: A fabulous animal, keeper of the "Great Secret," according to a 16th-century Italian manuscript which belonged to Count Pierre V. Piobb. It is a symbol which occurs with some frequency in heraldic images, marks, and signs. It was known to the Greeks, and it owes its name to the belief that, having a head at both ends, it could move forward or backward with equal ease. Sometimes it is depicted with the claws of a bird and the pointed wings of a bat (Piobb, 1950). According to Diel (1952), it was probably intended to express the horror and anguish associated with ambivalent situations. Like all fabulous animals, it instances the ability of the human mind to reorder aspects of the real world, according to supra-logical laws, blending them into patterns expressive of man's motivating psychic forces (Cirlot, 1962).

HAPPY BIRTHDAY, JCR!

I appreciate the chance to celebrate the twenty-second and a half anniversary of the founding of this periodical and ask your indulgence of an old-timer's nostalgic essay. The *Journal of Consumer Research, An Interdisciplinary Quarterly,* first appeared in June 1974. Having reached its maturity, the journal may serve as a marker for our inquiries into consumer behavior, perhaps a marker that looks both backward and forward. People's time-binding ability to remember and record the past, to evaluate

This chapter was first published in the *Journal of Consumer Research*, 23(3), December 1996, pp. 163-176. © 1996 by the Journal of Consumer Research, Inc. All rights reserved. Reprinted by permission of the *Journal of Consumer Research* and the University of Chicago Press.

the present, and to conceive of and plan for the future enables us to do consumer research. Lacking memory and aspiration, we would have nothing to study, nor the capacity to study it. To symbolize our time-ranging awareness and the consequent complexities of our lives and the study of them, I chose a mythic animal, the amphisbaena. It is a legendary two-headed creature that stands for our ability to look in all directions, to see where we have been and where we are going. These and other implications will be taken up in this paper, as vehicles for expressing the work of the Journal and the field in which it operates.

In the first issue, editor Ron Frank indicated his fear that an interdisciplinary journal could be regarded as a second-best journal, but also his determination that *JCR* should become the "first journal in which professionals sharing an interest in consumer behavior" report their material. It is apparent that this goal has been achieved for a core group: *JCR* is well-rooted, and its stature as the journal of choice for consumer researchers is flourishing. Since 1974, the original 10 sponsoring associations have been joined by Division 8 of the American Psychological Association and the American Anthropological Association, and the editorial board has expanded from 25 to 75 people representing a broad array of institutions and fields. The interest in consumer research is international, with links to personnel in several other countries who conduct studies and report their work in the various consumer conferences every year and submit manuscripts to *JCR*. These facts support the statement by Brian Sternthal, the editor at this writing, that *JCR* is a multidisciplinary journal whose submissions reflect a diversity in disciplines, paradigms, and methods.

The importance of *JCR* for all disciplines is not equal, as is evident by the prominence of researchers from the field of marketing. They naturally have a strong interest in consumers and of course represent a large constituency in the schools of business and management that support their inquiries into the consumer. They form something of an ingroup whose devotion has created and sustained the consumer research field. For example, on the present policy and editorial boards, we benefit from the presence of Jim Bettman, Hal Kassarjian, Jerry Kernan, and Bill Wells, who were on the original boards. It is also striking to note that 73 of the 75 members of the editorial board are members of the Association for Consumer Research. That association is a small one of under 1,500 members, most of whom teach at schools of business and who represent the fundamental constituency of *JCR*.

Despite the gains, then, as the Journal has generally avoided becoming a narrow marketing practitioner's review and has sought to encourage participation by scholars from diverse areas, a challenge remains to reach out to other groups who ought to be sharing the consumer research enterprise. One way to do that is to continue the Journal's tradition of receptivity to fresh areas of inquiry, to novel theoretical formulations, and to variations in methodology. Recently, Bill Wells (1993) offered a perspective on this matter and made several suggestions. There may be value in making more fully known the large definition of what a consumer is or what consuming is about that underlies this interdisciplinary receptivity. The Journal's 22nd birthday, plus its closeness to my own 75th last May, leads me to ruminations about the nature of consumers and aspects of researching them that have evolved in my mind since I started noticing consumers in 1930 and studying them formally in 1948. This essay has the character of a potpourri, but I trust the reader will observe its underlying structure and how it represents the paper's guiding concepts: You will see a progression in my thinking about products as commodities to noting the importance of branding them; and a preoccupation with the inherent ambivalence that characterizes and energizes our cognitive and emotional lives. As part of its privileged perspectives, the amphisbaena represents this ambivalence—our uncertainties, indecisions, split personalities, public and private selves, and layered psycho dynamics—and thus, consumer choice-making as well as researcher conflicts.

MY EARLY BEGINNINGS

I began to take a professional interest in marketing and the importance to consumers of products and brands when I was nine years old and worked in my father's produce store. (Food has remained a central topic of study for me, especially also as food companies have been leaders in sponsoring marketing research.) At first, I noticed commodities because of the general low amount of branding that typified the old-fashioned produce store. It was apparent that some products were more favored than others—e.g., that fruits had higher status than vegetables, that names like rutabaga, squash, and radish were not as exalted as peas, carrots, and sweet corn. That seemed natural, taken for granted, just part of everyday life. I observed this hierarchy among fruits in general and among their specific forms. Apples and pears were relatively ordinary, available throughout the

year, some varieties regarded as better than others, with the apple being a touch Biblical and healthy for daily consumption. Oranges were more special. As one consumer said in a later marketing research study, "Oranges are a God-packaged juice." Oranges were rare, seasonal, and expensive. Then I became aware that oranges had names. Among them were the Florida kind, those that were pale, juicy, and somewhat tart. The greatest oranges had a more specific and evocative name: Sunkist. They were big, a bright orange, and sweet, and sort of amazing as they had navels and no seeds. Their bellybuttons made them look kind of sexy, while the absence of seeds suggested a scientific miracle, although one that had been kissed by the sun. The work by Deborah Heisley sixty years later (Heisley, 1990) on the mundane status distinctions we make among fruits and vegetables, as well as their gender meanings and other symbolic issues, illustrates how we had to wait until this self-conscious era for such anthropological and semiotically oriented study.

Thinking about basic commodities such as fruits and vegetables, particularly those that may be eaten raw, returns us to the primitive roots of consuming. The first definition of the word *consume* is usually to eat, to ingest, followed by other meanings also derived from the Latin origins of the word—to take completely, to use up, to destroy, and to waste. As consuming organisms, we take food, use it, and make waste. As our needs and desires move beyond food, consuming includes all the other products we use and everywhere that we lay waste. Of course, we are ambivalent about doing that, worrying ("getting and spending we lay waste our powers") and holding in; and also being excited by the life-affirming aspects of consuming, the enjoyment of eating, wearing costumes, furnishing our homes, driving cars, wearing sports shoes, making and feeling music, dancing, and all the other arts, and going out.

STIMULATING THE SENSORIUM

At a fundamental level, our consuming involves all our senses in the casual ways they are needed to enable us to discern and apprehend our consumer choices and in the profound ways they are used to achieve levels of satisfaction. Despite the many ways that consuming requires the involvement of the sensorium in the creation of preferences, primary study of sensory experiences is usually left to laboratory specialists who do not often appear in *JCR* and whose work may seem too technical to interest our readers. Also, tastes, textures, smells, sights, and sounds are so richly and subtly interwoven in our experiences to form such complex gestalts that taking hold of them in a fully relevant manner is a major research challenge. How do we compare the loud pounding sounds and amazing sights of *Batman Forever* or *Mortal Kombat* in a theater redolent with popcorn and full of rapt contemporaries to the impact of a Prince or Madonna video (or for that matter, of Hootie and the Blowfish, the drums of the Kodo group, the Lyric Opera performance of *Mephistopheles,* the astonishing, wondrous effects of the Cirque du Soleil), and how capture in an insightful research these profitable offerings for consumption (Levy, Rook, & Czepiel, 1980). How can we relate these excitements to the vague interior apprehensions of hunger, nausea, loss, or lonesome yearnings, to say nothing of the surging energies felt by

Stephen Gould (1991) or the epiphanies described by Celsi, Rose, and Leigh (1993) and Arnould and Price (1993)?

Study of the human organism at the physiological level can include all we do to maintain health and to restore it, including the everyday nitty-gritty, as well as dramas of butt-tucks, rhinoplasties, breast enhancements, and hair transplants. Our society is able to afford an obsession with the consumption of wellness programs, Nautilus equipment, nutrition, and supplementary vitamins, aimed at enhancing our potency and sense of *élan vital,* warding off aging, living longer—perhaps we imagine forever? What do we know about consuming the products, regimens, and regimes that sustain our ordinary bodily existence? The studies we report tend to be about the consumption of nice things among the foods, beverages, clothes, packaged goods, and durables of our material world. Work on materialism and possessions (Belk, 1985; Richins, 1994), the dark side of gifting (Sherry, McGrath, & Levy, 1993), and addiction (Hirschman, 1990) shows that there are grosser aspects of consuming that we can study for a more well-rounded and realistic view. I once wondered what a field of "abnormal consumer behavior" might be like: obeying *Consumer Reports* or flouting it?—and Morris Holbrook (1995) refers to consumer *mis*behavior.

We might benefit from exploring more fully and systematically in the direction Dennis Rook (1985) went to examine the rituals of grooming, into the realms of tooth brushing and flossing, using toilet tissue, shampoo, lotions, and endless varieties of medication and equipment to ease our discomforts, pains, and disorders and enable our pleasures. Through life we smear Vitamin A&D ointment on babies' bottoms to alleviate rashes, agonize with

Oxy 10 and Clearasil for teenage acne, keep after the athlete's foot and warts we bring home from the health club, squeeze out oceans of sexual lubricants and don millions of condoms, take Tums or Beano for burps and farts, coat our bodies with a high level of sun screen, rub in Rogaine, ingest tons of pain-killers, and wind up with IVs, dialysis, and oxygen tanks.

A lot of this is a drag, not something we want to talk about or study unless doing a marketing research project for an interested company. My work of that kind for many factors in industry focused me on the idea that people are ambivalent about their animal nature. On the one hand, they aspire to be socialized and self-controlled, to be virtuous and to rise above their base animalistic selves. But they also want to be free to be gross, passionate, and natural, free to be evil by consuming things animals never would (Levy, 1992). They (we) want to satisfy our base lusts, gratifying the senses in an elemental way by smearing, by slurping, by eating to satiation, by masturbating and rubbing against another person, by getting intoxicated, by lying in the sun and soaking in a hot tub. All this may seem innocent and enjoyable, and a desirable part of being a natural being; and/or it may arouse feelings of shame and guilt. In any event, these satisfactions are often kept personal and private; and in good Maslovian fashion, consumers generally strive by various methods to elevate themselves toward being less animal and more human.

To avoid or restrain sensuous and sensual experience some people become ascetic, abstinent, or participate sparingly. Another way is to transform brutish experience by symbolizing it, giving it transcendence via idealization, stylization, obsession, and/or artistic metamorphosis. Thus,

consumers gain greater distance from "primitive" eating, drinking, dressing, and housing by getting older and more sophisticated and by gaining higher status. Their experiences become less spontaneous and more ritualistic, more intellectual and deliberate; they read about doing things rather than doing them, or they do them with flair and imaginative elaboration. They appreciate qualities regarded as peculiarly human: respect for tradition, humor, and empathy. They throng to view art exhibitions of bland Monet pastel paintings of peaceful scenery or of haystacks that would otherwise not interest them at all. Eating then encompasses sensitivity to subtle flavors, appreciation of novelty, concern with manners and proper use of utensils, and a context of social interaction about exotic eating locales and interesting foods one has eaten; and gourmets join the American Wine and Food Society. The obsessive interests may be exalted as a high level kind of animality, a superior reaction against the robotic depersonalization of a technological civilization; as being a part of nature that is available to those who can truly appreciate it—or they may be seen as psychological complexities to which the flesh is enslaved (O'Guinn & Faber, 1989) or nostalgic about (Holbrook, 1995).

Smoking might be regarded as an aberrant kind of eating. Putting cigarettes in one's mouth is an odd form of ingestion and inhalation. On the one hand, to smoke is a strange and singularly human thing to invent doing, while also being crude, dangerous, and physiologically enslaving. Its symbolism is engaging, elaborated early in its history with ideas of mysticism, spirit life, and peace pipe; and later as being sophisticated and virile. High status cigarettes were made longer, tipped, and filtered to show one's distance from the base

Figure 1.1. The amphisbaena as an elegiraffe by George Zinkhan

tobacco and fire. Handling burning cigarettes is also a subtle kind of violence, shown in the movies of the 1930s and 1940s as elegant and mannered, part of a tradition that says violence in entertainment is okay if it is esthetically and exquisitely portrayed by an *auteur* film director and intense actors such as Bette Davis and Humphrey Bogart. In the film *Smoke,* smoke seems like the human soul made visible, as the actors struggle with the implacable vicissitudes of life. Now our society has turned against smoking as part of a wave of virtue enhancement and an obsession with health and fitness that is inconceivable in any other species (except perhaps for fastidious cats).

But not everyone abstains from smoking; a segment of almost a fourth of the population smokes. And marketing attends to the needs of this segment by luring them away with nicotine patches and chewing gum. In fact, every one of our actions declares a degree of membership among some user or nonuser group, categorized demographically or psychographically in marketing research studies as VALS subgroups or lifestyle segments. And, if only analogously, our kinship with animals remains. Morris Holbrook (1995) has classified researchers as individualistic cats or obsequious dogs, and Dominique Bouchet (1991) amusingly distinguishes among consumers as ants, snails, and chameleons. Or perhaps one's genes, one's environment, and one's choices may result in a smart but ponderous elephantine person or a quiet, aloof, ruminant giraffe, or both, depending on the occasion and the stimulation, as depicted by George Zinkhan in Figure 1.1.

"'Lord save us!' cried the duck. 'How does it make up its mind?'"

Figure 1.2. Hugh Lofting's Pushme-Pullya

Thus, from dawn to dawn, there is a stream of consciousness that expresses the busy amphisbaena of routine decision making, especially notable in how people decide what, where, when, and how to eat and with whom. At the level of body care, there are those preoccupying thoughts about whether to have coffee regular or decaf and what snacks are tolerable, given their sugar, fat, salt, chocolate, and calories. In addition are the concerns for the group, for the family and its proper eating, eating out with friends at interesting ethnic restaurants, or saving the body, the environment, and the animals through vegetarianism. How shall one decide? Hugh Lofting's (1920) version of the amphisbaena is the pushme-pullya, shown being introduced in Figure 1.2 by Dr. Doolittle while the duck wonders about the basic issue: "How does it make up its mind?"

Maybe the consumer amphisbaena chooses to have a meal that is egocentric, gorging, delicious—perhaps a double cheeseburger and a triple-dip banana split with chocolate syrup, whipped cream, nuts, and maraschino cherries; or one that is socially and morally uplifting—perhaps a tofu burger and spinach salad? That may be caricature, but our lives are made up of an accumulation of such decisions; and general trends are visible and captured through examining changing consumer behavior via the ups and downs of hot dogs, hamburgers, pizzas, spicy chicken wings, kiwi fruit, pasta, French nicoise olives, tacos, Snapple, Starbuck's, and fat-free fats, to say nothing of melatonin and chromium picolinate.

FROM COMMODITIES TO BRANDS

In " 'We Gather Together': Consumption Rituals of Thanksgiving," Melanie Wallendorf and Eric J. Arnould (1991) discuss the way consumers "decommodify" manufactured, commercially produced and packaged, branded goods by unbranding them, so to speak, using them to prepare dishes at home that are then considered to be made more or less from scratch. The commercial products are said to be decommodified, because they are reclaimed from the manufacturer's production and labeling process, restored to the cook's control, and made sacred by family ritual use. I would say that in actuality the branded products are not being decommodified, but are being recommodified, being returned to the commodity state, as commodities are the non-branded ingredients that cooks historically used when they made dishes from scratch. As used by Wallendorf and Arnould, the term decommodification refers to the viewpoint that sees commercially produced goods as somehow bad, part of the exploitation and impersonalization of people, treating people as commodities as well. Here, the assumption is that there is a better, more natural world, that of the Noble Savage or, like Robinson Crusoe's, one in which people grew their own foodstuffs, were independent and self-reliant and thus more worthy people because of it. Of course, people give up that world when they can, in general because they find that such a life is arduous and inefficient and that division of labor in society provides goods in greater variety and quantity. They flock or commute to the city, abandoning the commodity life in pursuit of the brand life.

It seems that decommodification should more literally mean creating branded items so they are no longer just commodities, thus referring to the change from distributing homogeneous bulk commodities in sacks, barrels, and tubs to distributing them in small tins, jars, and boxes with brand names on them. It is interesting that then the acceptance of brands implies a movement *toward* personalization, toward products being manufactured, packaged, and promoted in more discriminating and value-added ways. In depression days, *Consumers Reports* used to recommend buying baking soda in quantity to use as a dentifrice instead of wasteful and expensive tubes of branded toothpaste; but it does not do that sort of thing any more. Instead, it fosters the branding process by offering increasingly refined tests of discrimination among the brands. And in general people do prefer the kind of decommodification that brings them brand choices over the recommodification that returns them to nonbranded goods. Perhaps the movement that Wallendorf and Arnould refer to might be termed debranding, unbranding, or decommercialization, wherein the brand remains desirable as an object of choice and a convenient way of obtaining food, but its commercial origin and identity are concealed in the service of the homey, creative motives they describe. Also, the motivation to escape brands is often driven by thrift, as consumers move down the continuum from costlier national brands to top store brands, to ordinary store brands, or to supposedly anonymous less expensive generic brands, even while wishing they could afford the better labels.

Still, the nostalgia remains, the amphisbaena looking back, as Holbrook (1995) delineated in his article about nostalgia, fueling ambivalence about past ways. Consumers may go so far as to grow their own tomatoes and herbs, or seek out organically grown produce, or go to a butcher shop to buy meat that seems closer to its slaughter. As growing your own in the city has definite limits, other people just prefer to buy unlabeled chicken at the supermarket as more real and more economical than the packaged cuts; and there is widespread liking for the idea of produce freshly brought to the farmers' market in the summer or spread in bulk on stands rather than in pre-measured plastic-wrapped units.

In true amphisbaena fashion, this desire to prepare one's own food from scratch is accompanied by the vastly increased use of foods prepared by other people. Growth has occurred on several fronts: (a) eating out—especially at fast food outlets, ethnic, and theme restaurants; (b) using home delivery or take out of prepared dishes; and (c) using frozen and shelf-stable meals and pre-prepared dishes.

IS DINNER DEAD?

Although much is said about the deterioration of family values, the ambivalence about harking to the past or embracing the future is notable. For example, the evening dinner remains a defining aspiration of everyday family unity and virtue. The ideal vision is of the family members coming together every evening from their diverse and separate activities to affirm their relatedness and love. There they are to act out the important roles of mother, father, and child or children, in the ways they esteem, expressed in face-to-face fashion. An item in the *Chicago Sun-Times,* August 25, 1991, reports the following:

FAMILY DINNER: A survey of National Merit Scholars turned up an interesting common thread: outstanding students reported having a daily, uninterrupted family dinner hour that was full of conversation. Parent Action Network in Rockford says family mealtime is a bonding experience. To make the time together count, the group recommends: Keep the conversation positive; encourage everyone to help prepare the meal; schedule mealtime so everyone can be there; don't turn mealtime into an etiquette drill; make conversation—not eating—the focus of the meal.

We see here the many values of unity, mid-American substance, the sharing of responsibility and equality of self-expression, being affirmative, upbeat, noncritical, exchanging ideas and social interaction, training by example and practice rather than instruction and drill; overall, that is, exalting symbolic experience over mere nutrition and sustenance.

Such affirmation of the importance of the united dinner was demonstrated also in the *Evanston Review,* a Chicago North Shore community newspaper. In response to an earlier column by Carol Mueller headed, "Is Dinner Dead?" there was a flood of letters denying that dinner was dead and relating examples of its vitality among the writers' families, with the usual litanies about the warmth of the occasion and its importance for teaching, sharing, and maintaining family values. Dinner together may even create a family before there is one. One writer said, "My husband and I have been married for three years but we 'lived in sin' for several years before that and I have always made a point of having dinner together."

At the same time, the denials that dinner is dead were couched in ways that showed family dinners were not actually possible or even desirable every evening and that the dinners were almost a last remnant or holdout against dissolution of the family's togetherness. It is noticeable that family dinners are a tradition being clung to self-consciously. Lest she be thought out of step with modern ways, one woman qualified her appreciation of the unified family dinner by saying "Believe me, I'm no 'Mrs. Brady Bunch.' But I do believe in establishing some traditions." And another noted that she was "sometimes aware of having my own time warp . . . My daughter's boyfriend has actually called me Mrs. Cleaver.

Actually, I don't even like to cook, but I work at it anyway." Another writer felt the need to defend herself, saying that despite the family's eating dinner together most nights, she considers herself "a person of the '90s and my family does all kinds of trendy things."

The falling away from the idealized version is also visible in the excuse that the family dinners are hard to sustain every night: as one woman said, "To answer your question—yes, we eat dinner together every night unless my husband and I are going out." A woman who had given up on the whole idea explained, "My husband, kids, and I eat apart for many reasons." She lists her husband working overtime a lot and his dietary restrictions, the daughter's many lessons at odd times, and the fact that her son "is always hungry around 4:30 p.m." Then he can't sit still at dinner and makes eating together a power struggle. When they tried eating together, having to jump up for kids' needs and conflict about what constitutes good behavior meant that "my fantasy of a lovely meal together is always shattered." For many families, just one of these reasons is enough to prevent regular, harmonious family dinners.

A family dinner is generally beneficial, but it is optimal if the meal is homemade by the wife and mother. Many women insist on that even when they say they do not like to cook or that their other responsibilities make it hard to be a cook too.

We have dinner together nightly and it is homemade. Am I tired of cooking? You bet! Will I stop? Probably not! Why? As the wife and mother, I feel it's my job (I know this is not a popular view) . . . I know my kids will always remember dinner when they're on their own.

Most nights I cook. (Gasp, shudder!).

I'd like to respond, and proudly so, that I cook dinner every night.

The side comments indicate that women who make homemade meals feel they are bucking the times, doing something no longer conventional. The various degrees of falling away from preparing homemade meals are visible among respondents who value family dinner together. Many of those meals turn out not to be homemade but are eaten away from the home or involve frozen dinners, carry out, or delivery. One woman commented, "If TV trays in the den qualify as 'putting our feet under the same table,' then my husband and I (who are 40 something) eat dinner together every night." The woman who said she believed in establishing traditions and sense of wholeness as a family also slipped in that "one of the simplest ways to do that is to break bread (or pizza) together."

So, is dinner dead or not? Surely not, as many comments illustrate that there is a holding action going on that clings to the past. Still, even while defending the homemade family dinner, some respondents thought they saw where things are going. "As a clinical psychologist in independent practice, I too have noted a trend toward individually-eaten 'nuked' meals, TV dinners eaten in front of the television, etc." A single male who usually eats out looked way down the road:

In a few years you might be asking 'Is the Kitchen Dead?' I now know two couples (not trendy Yuppies in their 30s) who are late 50s with no kids and they remodeled their kitchen into another work/study area. They have a wet bar in the rec room with a mini

Figure 1.3. Fridolf Johnson's amphisbaena

microwave *in case* they want to cook, but they eat out so much they decided to get rid of the kitchen.

Also, when questions are put differently, in just talking about food and eating and how things are changing, and discussing the pros and cons of using foods prepared by restaurants and packagers (rather than putting respondents on the defensive about the survival of dinner), a somewhat different picture emerges. One then hears how hectic life is, how many contending demands there are, how little time there is, what great advantages there are to the microwave oven and the huge variety of quite

edible dishes available from Healthy Choice, Budget Gourmet, Lean Cuisine, Stouffer's, etc., etc. Nostalgic fixations and regressions to old-fashioned skills and foods may be reserved to Thanksgiving, Christmas, Passover, and Hanukkah, to making salads and sometimes baking bread; while people otherwise yield to forward-looking pursuits of modernity, freedom, cosmopolitanism, adeptness, technology, and recreation.

Perhaps contemplating Pliny's version of the amphisbaena, as rendered by Fridolf Johnson (1976) in Figure 1.3, will help sort out one's own uncertainties, if one feels that life is like chasing one's tail. It shows that despite our ambivalence, our being of two minds may be reconciled or unified, demonstrating our ability to be flexible and roll along, even, like that formidable bird, coping well with a wintry setting. That is, we can cook hot soup from scratch when the spirit moves and otherwise rely on catering, delivering, taking out, and eating out.

THE VALUE OF BRANDS

As noted, in practice, most urbanized people do not want to live the simple or arduous make-it-from-scratch life and would rather satisfy their ambivalence by growing houseplants and making occasional forays into canning fruit picked in someone else's orchard. There is also the recognition of the logic and value of branding. Despite the criticisms of branding, it is seen as an expression of merit, of providing products that are worth more money. The common-sense and financial values placed on the reputation of an established name, traditionally called "goodwill" and sold as an intangible asset, have been restored to prominence by recent emphasis on the concept of brand equity (Aaker, 1991; Kapferer, 1992).

In the process of moving away from mass homogeneity of persons and products, branding is a specific extension of the idea of identity, which to my mind combines *id* with *entity,* meaning the vitality of a thing. Branding cannot basically be distinguished from identifying or naming anything that we believe is available for sale or exchange—whether ideas, objects, or persons. Commodities are lower case brands when no one speaks up to claim them; but identities quickly arise. Japanese rice, Norwegian salmon, amber from the Baltics, diamonds from Africa, cotton grown in Egypt, are differentiated from other rice, salmon, amber, diamonds, and cotton.

Brands with proper names belong to someone and appear to come from a source with some pride. The fact of a label implies features that distinguish brands from the nameless mass. Even if no special claim is made, we are still inclined to think that the least brand may be better than a product that does not boast of its source. We do buy some things without brand labels or store names, such as pumpkins in November and fir trees in December, and various things at flea and farmers' markets, where the risk seems high but the cost low, and when we have reason to be unusually confident in our ability to judge what we are buying. But few people would be willing to buy a nameless make of car in a vacant lot. They take for granted the amazing thousands of brands in the huge supermarket and shopping mall—and an experienced shopper knows the names of a vast number of them. A recent sales slip from my shopping had printed on it: Lifesavers, Ben & Jerry, Gold Medal, Hersheys, Motts, Pompeian, Green Giant, Campbells, Progresso, Hunts, Sun-Maid, Dole, Stouffers, Mounds, Milky Way, Ore-Ida, Jiffy, Pringles, Libbys, Swanson, Pepperidge Farm, Scotchbrite, McCormick, etc., etc. Like other shoppers I am familiar with those names, and innumerable others, and have preferences among them because of their particular patterns of meaning, trivial as some may seem. These choices are revelatory; as in the classic Mason Haire study, other people can tell a lot about me or my household from examining this list.

A brand is originally a piece of burning wood (I wrote a poem for my high school yearbook in 1938, praising education and referring to youth advancing "with knowledge as a burning brand"); its animation arises from the vitality and passion that come to us in its presentation, the qualities we attribute to it, and the emotions we feel. I saw a teenage girl weeping a bit at a Pepsi commercial that assured her that Pepsi knew she had "a lot to live," just as Pepsi had "a lot to give," although she could not articulate why she was moved at this vague expression of sympathy from a cola beverage. Nevertheless, in her mind whatever it is that the name Pepsi stands for was more than just a tasty liquid which in itself would presumably not make her cry, but also its posture of understanding and responsiveness.

Personality characteristics such as being obsessive, displayed in commercials for the perfume, Obsession; being reliable and supportive as Allstate claims in its slogan, "You're in good hands with Allstate;" being a good old-fashioned home baker like the Pepperidge Farm geezer driving a horse and carriage; or being radically socially conscientious like Benetton; all these serve useful functions for consumers. What would otherwise be merely an odor, an insurance policy, a loaf of bread, or a shirt gains meanings that help people to decide whether such personalities and images fit their own. Given personality differences among consumers, differences in brand personalities make choices simpler when there are clear one-to-one correspondences. But in a larger sense, branding combines technical realities with symbolism, to make for more alternatives, more choices, and greater complexity in life. It fosters competition, status distinctions, personal awareness, refined sensory and judgmental discriminations. From the consumers' viewpoints, given enough variety, there are brands that one would like to be able to use; brands that one ought to use; brands

that one would never use; and brands that one does use, some often, some occasionally. Because products and brands have personalities that are good, bad, and indifferent, simple, complex, subtle, and obvious, etc., they enable consumers to express their aspirations, virtues, vices, aversions, realities, and fantasies. Nested among one's own configuration of brands is a unique individual.

We can envision a continuum or a hierarchy, then, from bulk commodities through big brands to small brands to brands that are so custom designed, elite, and individual as to be unknown to the general population. At the huge bulk end are the movements of grain to feed starving masses, as in Somalia. As the commodities are turned into competitive brands, they offer choices to segments with preferences—large segments that share their preferences for famous brands, smaller segments for lesser brands, and ultimately individuals choosing something almost or literally unique. Thus, we may go from the commodity of corn flour to the widely eaten Kellogg's Corn Flakes to a picky segment wanting corn flour as Martha White Yellow Corn Muffin Mix, up to the elite who order Bert Lily's catered fresh baked corn pone. This hierarchy also correlates with prices moving from (ideally) perfectly competitive lowest prices for the commodities to the most expensive individualized products and services at the top. Therefore, as brands compete through price promotion they move down the hierarchy toward reducing their symbolic differences; they move up the hierarchy via advertising and other marketing activities designed to create distinction. Articles in *Advertising Age* over time boringly attest to the waxing and waning of awareness of this fact. A recent example:

TABLE 1.1 The Continua of Research

Economics	*Anthropology*	*Sociology*	*Psychology*	*Aesthetics*
Commodities	Societies	Subgroups	Individuals	Inner Lives
Prices	Cultures	Members	Selves	Feelings
Models	Ethnographies	Surveys	Projectives	Introspections

MarkeTrends Brands are back
by Pat Sloan

Two years after Marlboro Friday, a watershed event widely viewed as an omen of doom for many national brands, corporate America has a new mantra: Stand by your brands. In boardrooms across the country—from Unilever's Elizabeth Arden Co. to Eastman Kodak Co. and Johnson & Johnson—there's a reborn reverence for brands as the matters of brand building and brand loyalty are increasingly seen as sound business policy, not just the province of package-goods marketing departments.

THE CONTINUA OF RESEARCH

There is a continuum of disciplinary and research focus that represents the preferred perspective of thinkers about consumers and the marketplace. As noted, the flow from commodities to brands entails a general parallel movement from large quantities to small, from masses of people being provided for to subgroups, to small groups, to individuals. Parallel to that are prices ranging from low for anonymous commodities to high for custom made products and services, accompanied by social statuses going from low to high. Similarly, price competition generally forces products down the scale, so that sales, deals, coupons, and price wars reduce the value of

branding while advertising and publicity add distinctiveness to brands.

If we see these continua in terms of disciplines of study, narrated spatially (not ideologically, but perhaps in keeping with brain lateralization) from the left to the right, at the far left is economics, so strongly addressed to the market in an impersonal, commodity, and price-oriented way, through anthropology to sociology to psychology, in their varying and typical attention to the larger groups of society, cultures, subgroups, or individuals, and ultimately to aesthetics and its concern with the most sensitive, subjective, ineffable aspects of human sensory experience (see Table 1.1).

Of course, ambivalence and ambiguity afflict the researchers as well as their subjects. In methodologies, we must similarly choose within the continua from the general to the specific, the large to the small, and the outer to the inner, depending on our goals. These clusters of ways of perceiving and thinking, roughly depicted here, become contending methods of research. To the left lies Behaviorism, the world of surface actions, demand curves, stimulus-response, trial and error, and behavior modification through conditioning; in the middle are inferences about the black box of the mind; and to the right is Depth Theory with its interest in genesis, layering, conflict, and symbolism. Commonly, laboratory experiments seek basic principles with broad application, surveys sweep for frequencies across groups, ethnographies live with the group, focus groups inquire into segments, and projective methods look within individuals. External methods measure, internal methods introspect. The devotees of these theories and methods are commonly arrogant and self-righteous, jealous of their scientific faiths, all believe their part of the amphisbaena is the right one, and because they fear the possible threat of domination or displacement by the other methods, at times they foolishly become vicious in attacking each other, instead of recognizing the need for all the methods, that the shared research enterprise requires more than one head. *JCR* has made progress in including more work on the right side of these continua, even to the degree of showing pictures and drawings. Too bad it could not yet bring itself to the acceptance of poetry as a vehicle for expressing insights into consumers or research. Perhaps one might not be amiss here.

Awash in Ideas

> Freud used metaphors from hydraulics and theory electric
> With talk of damming instincts and of charges cathectic.
> Now we folks of *JCR,* with images and IP, are into other lore,
> With fuzzy concepts, Lisrel and Bayes, and much to explore.
> Will we go into the field and do something ethnographic
> Or skip the specifics and stick with caution stochastic?
> Well, my thoughts here are from old and medieval myth,
> Ruminating about consuming with the amphisbaena's pith.

INTROSPECTION

Because of the desire to examine consumers' actions, motivations, and perceptions more closely and richly than the usual surveys, statistical regressions, and cognitive experiments, the use of qualitative methods to study consumer behavior has recently grown. (Actually, I have been making that remark optimistically for fifty years.) Use of the more obvious or candid introspections of the researchers at work using ethnography, discursive interviewing, or interpretation of projective techniques arouses anxiety and controversy, with disparagement and defensiveness on all sides. Some of this noise sounds like the verbal flailing that went on in the 1950s when qualitative methods (then termed *motivation research*) became visible and threatening to the entrenched surveyor. The issue of introspection is especially controversial, although as K. Spence (1944) pointed out— also over 50 years ago—verbal report (by subjects and researchers) is so ever-present and of such unavoidable significance that everyone must find some sort of accommodation to it. Despite the efforts of behaviorism to kill introspection, it has a long history as a method of study.

In a casual sense, introspection is an inevitable part of consumer research, used by all research workers, as it merely means looking within one's self to know one's ideas and feelings. That is, introspection is another word for being self-conscious, aware, thoughtful, having ideas and knowing what they are. I thought it would be a useful exercise to observe how that kind of introspection shows itself even in the work that would be respectfully regarded as following classical objective procedures. Dipping into a handy issue of the *Journal of Marketing Research* for a presumably non-introspective example, the initial article I came upon was by Vicki G. Morwitz and David Schmittlein (1992), "Using Segmentation to Improve Sales Forecasts Based on Purchase Intent: Which 'Intenders' Actually Buy?" This article starts with an observation about a well-known fact: "Purchase intentions are used routinely in consumer research" as a predictor of subsequent behavior. The authors' introspection on the matter, however, tells them that "some key questions about the predictive validity of intention measures remain." Their article reports on their study. It is a story, a reminiscence about this doubt they had and what they did to find out whom, whether, and/or to what degree we should believe when people give us their introspections about their intentions to make purchases. All along, the authors show the need to reassure us persuasively that they have acted in ways that researchers should approve, showing they are knowledgeable about what other researchers have done, saying "Several approaches can be used to predict sales from stated intentions," "One popular example is . . . " Having introspected on their thinking, they urge that they are following suitable, logical modes of thought, saying "It therefore seems reasonable to assume . . . " and offer that they are making modest claims, that the process they are following merely or at least "sheds light on these questions." They learn that the consumers' introspections—intentions to buy cars and computers—are generally believable, but are in themselves rather weak reeds to lean on. Forecasts of sales are improved when other methods of segmentation are taken into account. They are kind to the respondents whose introspections did not predict their own behavior, saying, "Among nonintenders, 8% of those who have previously used a PC at work or

school actually do buy within the year. Perhaps (the authors speculate) because of their job an unanticipated need for the product arises, and they are already familiar with the technology and are able to actually purchase within the year." That is a meager introspection; of course, there could be many other reasons that Morwitz and Schmittlein did not introspect about— perhaps a financial windfall, an unusual bargain, a persuasive friend, a technical advance, new excitement in the market, and so on.

This example suggests that although we often strive for the appearance and security of objectivity, this should not obscure the fact that all our thoughts are introspective, are comments and stories about what we observed, what we did, what we thought, and why we thought it. For all the objectivity and methodological externalization, including "nonparametric methods, such as AID or CART," we don't have to believe Morwitz and Schmittlein other than when what they say seems plausible. After all, even they themselves sound a bit wistful about their results, saying "Though the findings are specific to these data, they are interesting and not, perhaps, intuitively obvious." We are still free to think their introspection is wrong, that the results are not satisfactorily generalizable; they do seem rather obvious, and are not especially interesting as no one should be surprised at people not predicting their behavior very well, which seems mainly what they found out.

This example is shored up with extensive methodological care and precision relating to samples and their measurement. Researchers who want to insist more deliberately and centrally on the use of introspection may not bother with such concern about samples and precision. But they, too, ultimately rely on whether the results are interesting and not, perhaps, intuitively obvious, as no one will care if they are both obvious and uninteresting. We are always left with the problem of findings "being specific to these data," as all sample data are "dead" as soon as they have been gathered and may say nothing about the future behavior of larger populations. For various reasons, that seems to bother people only when they don't like the findings. If findings are just specific to these data, the question arises as to why we want to know about it. Is it to know for knowing's sake? Or do we always assume some kind of generalization, that this specificity must represent some generality within some margin of error? Are we planning to act on it? If so, we want a correspondence to reality that we can rely on.

Deliberate introspectionists are more forthcoming about their claims; they seem to want to give special philosophical weight to *their* broodings, in keeping with Heidegger, who says that authenticity comes with self-reflection. Then, again, why should insisting on the value of the subjectivity, as if it were a deep affirmation of the way we know things, support any greater claim to truth. Popper (1934/1959) noted this:

> There is a widespread belief that the statement, "I see this table here is white," possesses some profound advantage over the statement, "This table here is white," from the point of view of epistemology. But from the point of view of evaluating its possible objective tests, the first statement, in speaking about me, does not appear more secure than the second statement, which speaks about the table here. (p. 99)

Of course, he continues to discuss the many aspects of how empirical science goes about testing its statements about reality. But what are these tests worth if we are not convinced? What seems more evident is that we tend to honor the assertions of people we think are smarter and more capable, no matter what methods they use, if they seem validated by something or other, whether the usual scientific trappings, the plausibility of their inferences, the weight of their experience, the support of a respected peer group, or the vividness of their insights—as per the big bang, black holes, quarks, or the existence of the unconscious.

As noted above, on a continuum in research philosophies Behaviorists ostensibly ignore the role of introspection, preferring to stick to external stimuli and responses, seeming to avoid all the problems of what one does with introspection, although it is not clear how they cope with the fact that their Behaviorism is itself an assertion of somebody's introspection. (Research questions: How do behaviorists live with the evident occurrence of introspection in their everyday lives and why do they want to exclude it as a significance phenomenon from their professional work? To do so because studies by Nisbet and others show that humans are complex and often cannot explain themselves completely and accurately is a poor excuse).

At the other extreme, phenomenologists or ostensible solipsists give introspection a central place in their work. If they carry doing that far enough, being totally egocentric and fanatical, denying that there is an external objective reality to be known, or that all interpretations of it have equal standing, it is not clear if they truly believe that. If any such persons read or write for this journal, why would they seek to communicate with anyone else, or attend a conference to annoy the rest of us if there is no one else out there. Perhaps they cannot escape the belief that there is a real audience, to whom they wish to bring the special insights in their introspections. Or perhaps we are not really here, but are just epiphenomena of their fantasies.

What weight one gives to facing up to the role of introspection is also observable on a continuum in marketing research. It ranges from studies at the behavioristic end, using facts derived from impersonal or mechanical records of behavior, such as scanner data, as if to avoid any introspection at all or to bury it in the research process by using the passive voice in telling about it. Along the way are surveyors who ask questions of large random samples of respondents about facts of behavior and then use the responses as if they were hard facts rather than ethereal introspections. Some surveyors ask people how they think and feel about their behavior (or their intentions, as with Morwitz and Schmittlein); they may report the responses as realities to be explained or as if these feelings and thoughts are suspicious data to be checked on. Then there are research analysts who are explicit about making interpretations of what people say. At the other extreme are those who look within themselves for the significance of experience, reporting an ultimate existential reality as intuitive knowledge with transcendental merit.

These methodological variations raise many questions of large philosophical sorts concerning the nature of reality and how we know it. Susanne K. Langer (1967), in her extended exploration of the mind, takes note of related issues.

Intuition is the basic intellectual function . . . "intuition" is direct logical or semantic perception; the perception of (1) relations,

(2) forms, (3) instances, or exemplifications of forms, and (4) meaning . . . (pp. 128-129)

Reasoning is the use of logic to make implicitly given conditions explicit; and logic is a fundamentally simple yet powerful machinery for getting from one intuition to another, systematically, successively, without losing any member of the series. The sort and degree of complex relational pattern which can be understood directly, without discursive analysis and technical process of reasoning varies widely from one individual to another. There are, for instance, persons to whom numerical relations are immediately apparent which other people have to deduce by a long train of concatenated intuitive judgments. Both procedures are equally intellectual. (p. 146)

John D. Barrow (1992) provides a nice corrective to those who exaggerate the obvious shortcomings of introspection in favor of quantification as the savior of objectivity. His book is a pleasant history of mathematics, framed as a rumination on whether mathematics is discovered or invented. He starts with the statement that

A mystery lurks beneath the magic carpet of science, something that scientists have not been telling, something too shocking to mention except in rather esoterically refined circles: that at the root of the success of twentieth century science there lies a deeply "religious" belief—a belief in an unseen and perfect transcendental world that controls us in an unexplained way, yet upon which we seem to exert no influence whatsoever . . . (p. 1)

There seems a surprising amount of room for human preference and intuitive feeling regarding the foundations of the subject [of mathematics]. (p. 198)

Joining feelings and mathematics sounds oxymoronic or contradictory, perhaps along the lines of praying to a two-headed god of atheists.

Kurt Gödel's (1943) introspections and intuitions about mathematical reality have had powerful consequences, and he has been regarded as the greatest logician of all time. (Unfortunately, his brilliance did not keep him from dying of starvation due to his fatal paranoid introspections.) Gödel is credited with discovering the limitations of formal reasoning, by showing how certain mathematical statements are unprovable or undecidable by being inconsistent with the systems to which they refer. Gödel did believe that there was a reality out there to be discovered; he also believed that "The idea that everything in the world has a meaning is an exact analogue of the principle that everything has a cause, on which rests all of science." Ever since I was taught that everything that exists must exist in some quantity and therefore may be measured, I also thought that if it exists it must have meaning and therefore may be studied for that meaning.

The friction that arises when research is made an issue of quantitative versus qualitative is an old one. Workers who emphasize the quantitative approaches often derogate other methods as nonscientific, to which defensive responses are made, as shown in this example from *Science News* (1940):

> I am surprised that Frazier quotes the statement . . . that the only way to solve these problems . . . is by large computers. A man as experienced as Frazier should know what every scientist knows, namely that no scientific problem is ever solved by computers. Problems are solved by human patience and imagination and nothing else. A computer comes in when it is a matter of getting quantitative information once a problem has been qualitatively understood. I think it is fair to say that the problem which Frazier reports has not yet been solved. Nothing could be more useless in this state of affairs than a computer. (p. 448)

E. J. Hobsbawm (1970) makes the point more generally:

> There are some things for which the prevailing scientific orthodoxy can more plausibly be blamed . . . it deliberately narrows the scope of what we can "know" to what we can measure and state quantitatively, reproduce or falsify experimentally, or formulate mathematically . . . The results of this distinction between "hard" and "soft" knowledge, the former being regarded as in some sense more real when it is only more manageable, are perhaps most dangerously absurd in the social and life sciences . . . If human beings and societies were reducible to a limited bundle of quantifiable motivations and aims, as corporations can be reduced to rational profit maximizers . . . it would eliminate precisely those problems to which the solution purports to apply, those of men in societies. (p. 15)

My introspection tells me that we move back and forth between the freedoms and the confinements provided to our intellects by both the ultimately inductive nature of our observed and accumulated experience and the ultimately deductive nature of the structures of our sensorium and our minds. The research continuum noted here has been more fully delineated by Gareth Morgan and Linda Smircich (1980) and variously explored by Shelby Hunt (1991). Underneath all research methods that merit attention are the intellectual facts that Alice

Tybout pointed out in her 1994 Association for Consumer Research Presidential Address on the necessity of theory: at heart are the essential thoughts about those ideas we postulate as dependent or independent and the rival hypotheses we entertain about them in our search for parsimonious explanations. In doing such thinking, the different conceptualizations of reality tolerate the expression of different degrees of introspection, so that researchers' preferences fit together their philosophies of science, research methods, and their personalities, including their tolerance for ambiguity. There may be linkages even among researchers' political ideologies and whether they prefer to emphasize conditioned response, trial and error, and behavior modification rather than insight, depth analysis, and radical personal expression, whether they look for the wonderful variable that accounts for the greatest amount of variation or search for the inner complexity.

A while ago, Beth Hirschman (1985) pigeon-holed me as a particular humanist, a sensing-feeling kind of researcher, and more recently Fuat Firat and Alladi Venkatesh (1995) decided I was an interpretivist and a strict structuralist, and not a postmodernist. I think fondly of these friends, each has a piece of the truth, but I must tell them they do not know the whole body of my work and should not overly interpret specific articles. The piece by Firat and Venkatesh is about postmodernism but is itself an old-fashioned modernist article; are they then still just modernists? My article about Levi-Strauss did not make me a structuralist. (In a working paper at Odense University, Denmark, Per Østergaard says the broadened concept of marketing is a manifestation of the postmodern condition.) I claim to be only an eclectic social scientist wandering around in search of insights, whether they come from watching people, living with them, reading about them, talking to them, interviewing them, measuring them, dreaming about them, photographing them, learning their dreams and their stories, and constructing fantasies about them that I think correspond for the while to versions of their realities, always using and testing against that dear old nomological network that says what reality is. Perhaps future hindsight will show that the era of Postmodernism was really the Age of PreTension, given the struggles to come and the exaggeration of the claims made on its behalf.

So, I attest, we all need our introspections, whether we hide them behind the rules of science, call them heuristics, see them as useful interpretations of real stimuli, or assert them center stage as individualism triumphant. Fundamentally, we all stalk the amphisbaena and are haunted and hunted by it.

REFERENCES

Aaker, D. (1991). *Managing brand equity: Capitalizing on the value of a brand name.* New York: Free Press.

Arnould, E. J., & Price, L. (1993). River magic: extraordinary experience and the extended service encounter. *Journal of Consumer Research, 20,* 24-45.

Barrow, J. D. (1992). *Pi in the sky: Counting, thinking, and being.* Oxford, UK: Clarendon Press.

Belk, R. W. (1985). Materialism: Trait aspects of living in the material world. *Journal of Consumer Research, 12,* 265-280.

Bouchet, D. (1991). Marketing as a specific form of communication. In C. A. Alsted, H. H. Larsen, & D. Mick (Eds.), *Semiotic approaches, marketing, and semiotics: The Copenhagen symposium* (pp. 31-51). Copenhagen, DK: Nyt Nordisk Frolag, Arnold Busck.

Celsi, R. L., Rose, R. L., & Leigh, T. W. (1993). An exploration of high-risk leisure consumption through skydiving. *Journal of Consumer Research, 20,* 1-23.

Cirlot, J. E. (1962). *A dictionary of symbols.* London: Routledge & Kegan Paul.

Diel, P. (1952). *Le symbolisme dans la mythologie grecque.* Paris: Elsasser.

Firat, A. F., & Venkatesh, A. (1995). Liberatory postmodernism and the re-enchantment of consumption. *Journal of Consumer Research, 22,* 239-267.

Gödel, K. (1943). *On undecidable propositions of formal mathematical systems.* Princeton, NJ: Princeton University Press.

Gould, S. J. (1991). The self-manipulation of my pervasive, vital energy through product use: An introspective-praxis approach. *Journal of Consumer Research, 18,* 194-207.

Heisley, D. D. (1990). *Gender symbolism in food.* Ph.D. dissertation, Northwestern University, Evanston, IL.

Hirschman, E. C. (1985). Scientific style and the conduct of consumer research. *Journal of Consumer Research, 12,* 225-239.

Hirschman, E. C. (1990). Secular mortality and the dark side of consumer behavior: Or how semiotics saved my life. In R. H. Holman & M. R. Solomon (Eds.) *Advances in consumer research* (Vol. 18, pp. 1-4). Provo, UT: Association for Consumer Research.

Hobsbawm, E. J. (1970, November). Is science evil? *The New York Review.*

Holbrook, M. B. (1995). *Consumer research: Introspective essays on the study of consumption.* Thousand Oaks, CA: Sage.

Hunt, S. (1991). *Modern marketing theory: Critical issues in the philosophy of marketing science.* Cincinnati: Southwestern.

Johnson, F. (1976). *Mythical beasts coloring book* (Vol. 3). Mineola, NY: Dover Publications.

Kapferer, J. (1992). *Strategic brand management: New approaches to creating and evaluating brand equity.* New York: Free Press.

Langer, S. K. (1967). *Mind: An essay on human feeling.* Baltimore: Johns Hopkins University Press.

Levy, S. J., Rook, D. W., & Czepiel, J. (1980). Social division and aesthetic specialization: The middle class and musical events. In *Symbolic consumer behavior* (pp. 38-45). Ann Arbor, MI: Association for Consumer Research.

Levy, S. J. (1992). Constructing consumer behavior: A grand template. *Advances in Consumer Research, 19,* 1-6.

Lofting, H. (1920). *The story of doctor Doolittle.* New York: Dell.

Morgan, G., & Smircich, L. (1980). The case for qualitative research. *Academy of Management Review, 5,* 491-500.

Morwitz, V. G., & Schmittlein, D. (1992). Using segmentation to improve sales forecasts based on purchase intent: Which "intenders" actually buy? *Journal of Marketing Research, 29,* 391-405.

O'Guinn, T. C., & Faber, R. J. (1989). Compulsive buying: A phenomenological exploration. *Journal of Consumer Research, 16,* 147-157.

Piobb, P. V. (1950). *Clef universelle des sciences secrètes.* Paris.

Popper, K. R. (1959). *The logic of scientific discovery.* New York: Basic Books. (Original work published 1934)

Richins, M. L. (1994). Special possessions and the expression of material values. *Journal of Consumer Research, 21,* 522-533.

Rook, D. W. (1985). The ritual dimension of consumer behavior. *Journal of Consumer Research, 12,* 251-264.

Sherry, J., McGrath, M. A., & Levy, S. J. (1993). The dark side of the gift. *Journal of Business Research, 28*(3), 225-244.

Spence, K. (1994). The nature of theory construction in contemporary psychology. *Psychological Review,* 49-68.

Wallendorf, M., & Arnould, E. J. (1991). "We gather together": Consumption rituals of Thanksgiving Day. *Journal of Consumer Research, 18,* 13-31.

Wells, W. D. (1993). Discovery-oriented consumer research. *Journal of Consumer Research, 19,* 489-504.

Chapter 2

THE EXEMPLARY RESEARCH

Sidney J. Levy

Sidney J. Levy: Each year, a dinner was held by the Committee on Human Development at the University of Chicago. There were three speakers: an invited guest, a member of the faculty, and a doctoral student. I was invited to give the student talk, which follows, on January 31, 1953.

Mr. Havighurst, Ladies and Gentlemen:

When I was asked to speak to you this evening on behalf of the doctoral students of the Committee on Human Development, I shrank from the enormity of the task. I pondered long as to what function I could serve here, how best fulfill the heavy obligation to my peers, my teachers, our guests. I was told that the best thing was to be funny—as though that were the simplest thing. But I am not easily given to jokes, and my natural austerity combined with the grandeur of the occasion to insist that—No, this is a time for solemnity, not jokes. So let us break with the pleasant traditions and be serious.

I felt that the best thing I could do was to show an example of what Human De-

velopment is about. Consequently, in the best spirit of our committee and our goals, I bring you not a speech, but a scientific paper describing a research project in the field of Human Development. The title of the investigation is as follows: A Qualitative Analysis of Developmental Variables in the Genesis, Proliferation, and Stultification of Human Risibilities.

PURPOSE

The goal of the study was to observe and analyze in what manner human beings develop, maintain, and decline in their special abilities to engage in wit, laughter, and humor, to act in those ways particularly defined as silly, ridiculous, and foolish, to say nothing of risque and shaggy dog—without of course being any of these things.

It was felt necessary to study this topic in an encompassing way. Those who enter the Committee on Human Development have one distinctive characteristic—they want to know everything. Since the faculty claim to be slightly more modest and refuse to solve all problems in the lecture hall, it is necessary to do research to find out All. We therefore need to study thoroughly and insatiably the wit of wisdom, the fun of folklore, the satire of savants, the irony of intellect. Few other students have such a thirst to learn so much.

All good research normally requires a specific theoretical framework for reasons too obscure to be gone into here. However, this is not true of research in Human Development. The reason is that when the area of study is basically everything, essentially unconfined—like joy—it is obvious that any framework will do—or consequently none. In Human Development we need only gather data and fit it into the great All. This is the secret of our distinction, the source of our pride and our strength in conflicts with students of less catholic dimensions.

However, for the un-emancipated, for those who are not yet fully integrated, who are still enmeshed in the departmentalizations of our society, whose personalities bind them to some particular academic discipline, there are the following theoretical considerations.

1. It has been observed that few animals besides cats drink milk after being weaned. People are one of them.

2. It has also been observed that hyenas don't really laugh.

These two facts have an intricate relation. The study will not make clear what that is, but it serves as the keystone of the research framework and should stimulate discussion. With these concrete theoretical considerations in mind, and probably others to come, *ipso ergo sum*, the basic question of the research may be stated:

What the hell are you laughing at?

We will now state the main hypotheses of the investigation.

First, all humor is a recognition and acceptance of being human. (The inclusiveness of the proposition is what makes it an ideal topic for Human Development.) This recognition and acceptance point the way to the inner content of humor. Tragedy differs, not only because of the emotions it relieves, as Aristotle noted, but because it is the submission to being human, a giving in. It is clear that tragic people focus on the facts—they do not deny their guilt. Second, all humor derives from an assessment of reality, that is to say, a determination whether something is true or not true. This questioning is a basic disbelief that fuses with the acceptance of being human and makes for the humor triad; it is a doubt that rescues fact from tragedy. The bottom layer of the triad is "It's really true (or false) as I well know." In itself this is a fact and not funny. It is the basic recognition. The second layer of the triad is "But it isn't really, or perhaps it's not, or we can pretend it's not." This is denial or doubt, in itself not funny.

People who observe only the first layer of humor are humorless and literal people who are afraid reality will scoot away if they don't keep a sharp eye on it. They are often scientists and accountants. People who stop at the second level tend to be obsessive, not sure when a joke is a joke. They laugh hesitantly, uncertain in their view of reality and its nuances. They are often well-meaning philosophers and some kinds of psychologists, given to writing papers on epistemology and the nature of humor.

Truly humorous people fuse the two layers to form the triad, "It's a joke, son." Their awareness of and skepticism of reality is at once sure, spontaneous, and astute. They know it is all real, but they don't believe it. They know it hurts only when they laugh, but it doesn't keep them from laughing. Only truly humorous people know that everything is potentially funny, given sufficient objectivity. They are thus likely to be schizoid types and have no occupations, as such.

SURVEY OF THE LITERATURE

First, see last year's Human Development Bulletin listing recent articles by members of the faculty. Otherwise, the author of this paper begs to take a rather iconoclastic view of surveys of literature. These are dreadfully monotonous things to prepare and ultimately serve no useful purpose. They are assumed to demonstrate how one builds on the past and advances beyond it. Now, this is clearly a pious hope. If one is going to build on the past, the plagiarism is best kept quiet; and there is little point in driving students to the tortuous logic and semantic inventions that are served up as contributions to the field. If a research is an advance beyond its predecessors, it should be apparent to anyone who cares, and it is unfortunate that an author need point it out by belittling the supposedly lesser efforts of fallen giants. This is known as the "We owe a great debt to Freud, but . . . "

school. Why should one rise to new heights by snidely noting (in the passive voice) that it has been observed that Mr. Havighurst was remiss in not listing the acquisition of a sense of humor as a developmental task of infancy? Why force Miss Koch to defend herself all the way from Frankfurt because in a 1935 article, an analysis of certain forms of so-called "nervous habits" in young children, she did not clarify the role of sibling tickling?

These are perhaps academic questions best dealt with by an ad hoc committee, hereby delegated to Martin Loeb. It would probably be advisable to move along, noting only that several sources may be consulted for bibliographic guidance to the topic at hand. Burton's *Anatomy of Melancholy* is a useful beginning for those who do not wish to plunge headlong into the subject. More advanced students will find profitable materials in the *Congressional Record* and the works of an obscure author named James Thurber.

METHOD

In carrying out the aims of this research, the investigator was intensely motivated by his desire to prove his hypotheses. There seems little doubt that this is the case with most investigators who know their hypotheses are true. As a matter of fact, one might question the integrity and earnestness of a research worker who sets small store by his hypotheses. Scientific treatises need some relief from preoccupations with such pseudo-objective devices as the null hypothesis. We should accept our devotion to our ideas, since small minus correlations are not likely to sway us away from them anyway. Also, we are then more likely to establish our own School of Thought; and soon numerous other researchers and suggestible assistants will join in to prove the dogmas our persistence creates. As a consequence of this burning desire to make the study come out right, as the saying goes, it was determined to use every possible method that would support the basic proposition and which the incredible technical armament of the Social Sciences could provide. Of course, it so happened that many usual techniques had to be ruled out.

The Murray Thematic Apperception Test was omitted as still protected by Harvard's copyright and the bookstore's price. No other pictures were available for substitution as the study was begun while William E. Henry, keeper of the analysis of fantasy, was on one of his trips to Europe. The Rorschach was also not used since the research worker felt he should be even more incompetent with it to really profit from using it in the study. One gains much more from using unfamiliar projective techniques, as this allows wider latitude for interpretation. In this sense, a little knowledge is a liberating thing. Also not applied were statistical measures since these required computing, which is a mode of intellectual functioning indulged in by an exclusive and mystic elite that excludes the writer from its community of ideation.

Deprived of these methods, the main instrument used was the Self. The Self is a little known device despite its age and fascination. Its complexity makes it difficult for even experts to handle. Selves are kept at the Counseling Center, and a Rockefeller grant made the Center permissive enough to check one out for this study. The main facilities of the Self found useful in the study of human risibilities turned out to be Intuiting, Thinking, and Imagining, with some subsidiary uses of Seeing and Hearing. There were of course some real prob-

lems in using this marvelous instrument; ordinarily it does not organize data as systematically as an IBM; also it develops Pride and Scatomas and shows Bias coming around voluptuous curves. However, the Self makes up for all such inadequacies by possessing that unique attribute found in no other research invention—the capacity for the judgment of intangibles. The Self was sent out into the primordial habitat of research workers, the Field, there to do battle with the recalcitrant subject matter of the study. To demonstrate the hypotheses a variety of observations were gathered, mostly on people. This phase of the research went smoothly enough, except for a brief interval when the Self was charged with voyeurism, an embarrassing episode that had to be charged off to the hazards of a very Sociable Science.

When all the data were in, they were manipulated. How this was done is of course in the Public Domain of true Science and available to all but the representatives of Pravda. Free copies may be obtained by anyone with a microfilm projector and the nerve to ask.

THE RESULTS

It so happens that the hypotheses were borne out. The author vouches for this since he bore them out himself. He can also call for witness and evidence three judges who should have been mentioned in the method. These three people were used for Validity and Reliability. Actually, they turned out to be more valid than they were reliable. They came from different Schools of Thought—the client-centered one could never get away from his client, a tavern owner named Jimmy; and the Psychoanalytic one was always contemplating a libido just when needed most. The rare Behaviorist was found after 30 years in the Harper Stacks. He spoke only to the Rogers man, and the Freudian had great fun analyzing them both.

The excellent results achieved came about in the following remarkable way. The first observation was made on a pre-natal pre-infant. This object was supplied, mother and all, by 312-A, a course that is devoted to conceptions, abstract and concrete, and the fine beginnings of things. Here we found the first display of amusement in the process of Human Development. About to enter the world, and in sublime comment on the nature of this imminent reality, the child was found to be standing on its head! Actually, this is only reported by the Self and the Freudian. The Behaviorist had misplaced his glasses and couldn't see the baby very well, so naturally could not admit the phenomenon. The Counselor did not regard the activity as a true expression of felt feeling and was unwilling to reflect on it. Considering that this datum is best appreciated by pregnant research workers it was consequently discarded as having limited application. For the sake of brevity, the next phase may be readily condensed, or evaporated, as you will. For the sake of honesty, it should also be said, the very young children did not turn out to be very funny. They were in the serious process of acquiring their basic traumas and neuroses and trying like the devil not to accept a reality adults make so unpleasant. Besides there were mechanical problems. The kiddies were closely guarded by a legal firm named Erikson, Gesell, Dennis, Spitz, and Goldfarb; and Margaret Mead kept dropping in to take photographs. In a well-tailored fit of pique we forthwith established our own kinder-neugarten (reference to Professor Bernice Neugarten), and astonishing achievements are expected daily. Now, having noted that humor has its genesis in a pre-natal Perception of the Incredibility of Reality, we may observe how this develops further. Skipping rapidly along, we arrived at middle childhood. This is a period one of the judges—it is not certain which one—insisted on calling latency. During this time children are quite tragic in their outlook. They find life very earnest and real; they collect furiously and consider members of the opposite sex to be products of malevolence. The main difficulty with children at this stage is that they know more than adults do, including grammar school teachers. Adults become superfluous; they are silly creatures, beneath contempt, knowing nothing of stamps, outer space, or the secrets that sustain the gang. They are the only funny things on the horizon; that is, they are in this instance objects clearly observed as Counter to Reality and horrible portents of Things to Come. In this somewhat chill atmosphere where the only way to get along is to know more woodcraft than an Eagle Scout, the researchers felt more blatant than latent and hastened off to more provocative confines.

While not quite out of the woods, still feeling rather earnest and haggard (reference to Professor Ernest Haggard), they passed an interesting-looking establishment for children who were being taught how to laugh. This unique place, known as the Hansel and Gretelheim (reference to Professor Bruno Bettelheim) was obviously engaged in good works, appropriately perhaps, near an abandoned church. The tin woodsman, otherwise known as the Behaviorist, inquired, "Which doctor works here?"—to which the Counselor assented "Yes." The next observation elevated the study to new heights, revealed unusual profundity, and illuminated many dynamics. (Like all contemporary exemplary researches, this one is of course dynamic, full of flux, conflict, and causes.) Almost before the Behaviorist had measured the growth spurt on the Wetzel-Grid Graph, for another study in Human Development, data began to come in on that paragon phase of growth, that interminably American process, Adolescence.

American adolescence (see cross-cultural index for comparative data) is essentially the funniest time in human existence, except for whichever age you happen to be. Adolescence is the most ridiculous, the most satirical, the most rudely humorous time, for a great variety of reasons. If it didn't happen, it would have to be invented, for anything else to happen. Only at this stage do human beings, to generalize from a small sample, contain the concentrated diversity of forces, the emotional and intellectual fluidity to vie at once with all other ages and complex mental states. Here, at the age-graded crossroads of growing up, the Human Comedy is enacted in all its flashing facets. Now humor is compounded of new richness; reality becomes marvelously coruscating and kaleidoscopic in its nuance and complication. The Self was astounded, not being a proper scientist, to see the blazing dramatic exhibitionism of adolescence, the horrendous depth of agonized despair, and the cloud-like, ethereal, shimmering swoonings of ecstasy. Observe the self-consciousness, the childish lack of self-control, alternating with the reserve and elegance of supposed fruition. Fantasy and abstraction ride high to create the delicate poem and the profound intellect. Embodying all in one the child and the adult, the dreams and ideas of age and philosophy, the wallowing affects of all times, adolescence is the Big Laugh, the Doubt of all Reality combined with its ardent embrace.

At this point it became necessary to conclude the research. For one thing, it was too many martinis too late to go on to the greater absurdities of maturity and old age. The Self was fascinated by adolescence and fixated there. Also there were other objections. The Psychology Department (AFL) got jealous and claimed the research subject for its clinical implications—jurisdiction is now being debated by the University Senate and the Hyde Park-Woodlawn Community Conference. Even more fatal is the fact that when the subjects of the study were measured for social class placement, they turned out to be Upper Outer and without Evaluated Participation. The only fortunate result is that the study findings cannot then apply to me—and only possibly to thee.

Nevertheless, we must take heart; for students there is always more research. After today, we can all concur that we need further research if only to reaffirm our faith that it is the laughing skeptic who designs the best experiments and cuts the neatest capers in the congenial dance of academic life.

finis.

PART
TWO

MARKETING

——— •◆• ———

Dennis Rook: Marketing practitioners and scholars often differ in how they see things. Yet, one area of general agreement is an almost normative belief about the broad and malleable applicability of basic marketing concepts and tools in ever more diverse management settings and situations. Over the past half century, marketing thought and practice have grown from their contemporary origins in packaged goods manufacturers to a current prominent presence in the economy's service sectors, nonprofit organizations, arts and entertainment enterprises, health care providers, religious organizations, the professions, and political campaigns. Marketing seems to be "at work" almost everywhere today and, in fact, is a successful American export. Managers throughout the world share similar concerns that are expressed in a common marketing language and focus on a common core of strategic issues about consumers, targets, positioning, the competition, and the marketing environment. Historically, this diffusion transpired steadily and rapidly, which might lead one to believe that marketing's acceptance, adoption, and growth were inevitable, a preordained progression. Not exactly. The current widely received view about marketing's broad mission did not materialize from beneficent thin air. Rather, fundamental ideas about marketing that we now share matter-of-factly emerged from a fierce intellectual battle that took place over 25 years ago. Sidney J. Levy was a principal combatant in this war, and he led the forces who favored broadening over restricting marketing's definition and domain. To note the obvious, Levy's views prevailed, and modern enterprise generally exhibits a more expansive concept of marketing. Yet, flare-ups of this core debate reappear occasionally and reintroduce various sources of mental and organizational resistance to marketing, and the battle is resumed. For example, extensive focus group research in well-funded political campaigns often attracts criticism that candidates are pandering to research findings; and today's telemarketers are derided as intrusive spies, or worse. Even many advertising creative people hate market-testing their copy; and fine arts sensibilities are prone to find the very idea of marketing vulgar and unappealing. As the title of a *Newsweek* magazine feature on the Jacqueline Kennedy Onassis estate auction proclaimed last Spring: "Jacky, How Tacky!" These examples illustrate an important point. Although marketing's intellectual paradigm shift occurred when today's prototypic 45-year-old marketing executive was finishing high school, aftershocks from this debate can introduce powerful ideas into his or her professional life today. For example, a corporate mission that prioritizes an expanded marketing orientation has profound consequences for managers' activities, budgets, resource requirements, and performance evaluation. Thus, ideas about the nature of marketing are not merely historical, and modern marketers and scholars can benefit from better understanding their evolution and dissemination. Levy's writings in this section address a variety of core issues. First, two articles propose basic philosophical ideas about marketing. The centerpiece here is "Broadening the Concept of Marketing," written with Levy's Northwestern colleague, Philip Kotler. When the article appeared in the *Journal of Marketing* in January 1969, it quickly attracted vehement, if somewhat hysterical criticism for its perceived "potential to diminish social order." Articles in academic journals are rarely recognized as having this kind of potential. Today's reader, however, is unlikely to perceive this article as revolutionary pamphleteering, because its ideas are now mainstream. To provide some historical context, we have included "Toward a Broader Concept of Marketing's Role in Social Order," which was a response to criticisms published in the *Journal of Academy of Marketing Science* 10 years later, in 1979.

Equally important are the underlying ideas that elaborate and extend Levy's primary premise about the encompassing nature of marketing. "Marcology 101 or the Domain of Marketing" (1976) is a delightful and thought-provoking article that examines historical sources of ambivalence and hostility toward marketing and proposes more neutral, objective grounds for marketing theory and practice. "What Kind of Corporate Objectives?," co-authored 10 years earlier with Northwestern colleague Harper Boyd, is a useful companion piece that illustrates how marketing's role in a particular corporate setting will vary according to a company's relative focus on material resources and fabrication processes, or on consumers' traits and activities. Finally, another collaboration with Philip Kotler, "Demarketing, Yes, Demarketing," highlights Levy's zen-like creative thinking in arguing that the marketer's task is more complex than just to blindly engineer increases in sales. This article appeared in 1971 in the *Harvard Business Review* and served managers who in subsequent years would be challenged to cope with product shortages and overheated demand in numerous categories (e.g., oil, Cabbage Patch dolls, tourism) or to reduce demand from specific market segments.

In 1970, "Broadening the Concept of Marketing" was selected to receive the Alpha Kappa Psi award for best theoretical article in the *Journal of Marketing*. Although this represents an intellectual victory for Levy and other proponents of a broadened marketing concept, an equally important aspect of this paradigm shift lies in the actual extensions of marketing concepts to professional arenas that were unfamiliar with and often hostile to marketing's promise. Three articles included here illustrate marketing's interactions with aesthetics, ethics, government, education, and health. "Marketing and Aesthetics," co-authored in 1974 with New York University's John Czepiel, offers insights into the role of aesthetics in marketing management and shows the mutuality between the two fields. Arguably, the recent emphasis on product design and, more generally, the growth of marketing in both fine and commercial arts reflect the seminal qualities of this article. A more recent discussion, "Absolute Ethics, Relatively Speaking," considers the renewed emphasis on ethical issues in marketing. If one had to select a topic that is rife with such issues, cigarette smoking would be a good candidate. In an article published almost 35 years ago in *Business Horizons*, "Cigarette Smoking and the Public Interest," Levy and colleague Harper Boyd explore this issue with a breadth of perspective and a prescience that is striking. Many of the remedies they identify have been adopted or are the subject of contemporary dialogue.

——— •◆• ———

Sidney J. Levy: My work with Philip Kotler was precipitated by the change in character of the Northwestern University Graduate School of Business. Many students were applying to the program to study business management although their aim was to work in nonbusiness settings, so the faculty voted to change the name of the school to the Graduate School of Management. The marketing department was asked for its adaptation, whereupon we met to discuss our plans. I brought to that meeting a memorandum headed "Broadening the Concept of Marketing" in which I pointed out that we had been doing marketing research at Social Research, Inc. for over 20 years for all sorts of organizations, not just businesses, and that it was apparent that marketing functions are essential to all individuals and organizations. Although initially dubious, Philip became intrigued with this broader idea of marketing, and we jointly prepared the article, "Broadening the Concept of Marketing." The impact of this article was notable. It swept the field and was embraced in time by numerous nonbusiness fields; it also created controversy along the way. The 1970 American Marketing Association Summer Educators' Conference was titled "Broadening the Concept of Marketing," and Philip and I received an award for Best Article in the *Journal of Marketing* of 1969. At the meeting, an irritated colleague mentioned to me that he didn't see what all the fuss was about, as he had always thought marketing applied to all individuals and organizations. I airily suggested to him that he should have written an article. In fact, the article was a stimulus to much work on activities called social marketing and nonprofit marketing; and in 1974 I published (with John Czepiel) "Marketing and Aesthetics," which encouraged activities within the field of marketing the arts. "Beyond Marketing: the Furthering Concept" was written as a variation on the Broadening article, recasting it to suggest the magnitude of the change in thinking that was needed to embrace the larger view of marketing—to the point of renaming it Furthering—but too late, Broadening had taken flight.

"Demarketing, Yes, Demarketing" was titled by the editors of the *Harvard Business Review.* The article was conceived when I met Philip Kotler for lunch at a conference in Boston; (although we both lived and worked in Evanston, we were glad of a chance to get together out of town). Something was said that reminded me that most people think of marketing as meaning the wooing of customers, which also reminded me that too often I did not feel wooed but actually denied what I might be seeking in the marketplace, as if the sellers were "demarketing" their offerings. Philip and I discussed some of the complexities of not wooing customers, or of doing so in subtle or indirect ways, which led to the drafting of the article. I sent it to the *Harvard Business Review,* suggesting it might be illustrated with amusing drawings of customers being warded off. The editor told me the latest issue of the journal was almost in press but that they liked this piece and were going to include it.

"Marcology 101, or the Domain of Marketing" served several purposes in my mind when I wrote it. For one, I wanted to explore why it is that marketing has been looked down on and derogated throughout the centuries. Second, the recurring conflict between the theoretical and applied aspects of marketing seemed to warrant some attention, perhaps to be dramatized by suggesting a stronger separation of them by distinguishing between the activity of marketing and the study of it.

———— •◆• ————

## Chapter 3

BROADENING THE CONCEPT OF MARKETING

Philip Kotler

Sidney J. Levy

The term *marketing* connotes to most people a function peculiar to business firms. Marketing is seen as the task of finding and stimulating buyers for the firm's output. It involves product development, pricing, distribution, and communication, and in the more progressive firms, continuous attention to the changing needs of customers and the development of new products, with product modifications and services to meet these needs. But whether marketing is viewed in the old sense of "pushing" products or in the new sense of "customer satisfaction engineering," it is almost always viewed and discussed as a business activity.

It is the authors' contention that marketing is a pervasive societal activity that goes considerably beyond the selling of toothpaste, soap, and steel. Political contests remind us that candidates are marketed as well as soap; student recruitment by colleges reminds us that higher education is marketed; and fund raising reminds us that "causes" are marketed. Yet these areas of marketing are typically ignored by the student of marketing. Or they are treated

This chapter was first published in the *Journal of Marketing, 33,* July 1969, pp. 10-15. Reprinted by permission of the American Marketing Association.

cursorily as public relations or publicity activities. No attempt is made to incorporate these phenomena in the body proper of marketing thought and theory. No attempt is made to redefine the meaning of product development, pricing, distribution, and communication in these newer contexts to see if they have a useful meaning. No attempt is made to examine whether the principles of "good" marketing in traditional product areas are transferable to the marketing of services, persons, and ideas.

The authors see a great opportunity for marketing people to expand their thinking and to apply their skills to an increasingly interesting range of social activity. The challenge depends on the attention given to it; marketing will either take on a broader social meaning or remain a narrowly defined business activity.

THE RISE OF ORGANIZATIONAL MARKETING

One of the most striking trends in the United States is the increasing amount of society's work being performed by organizations other than business firms. As a society moves beyond the stage where shortages of food, clothing, and shelter are the major problems, it begins to organize to meet other social needs that formerly had been put aside. Business enterprises remain a dominant type of organization, but other types of organizations gain in conspicuousness and in influence. Many of these organizations become enormous and require the same rarefied management skills as traditional business organizations. Managing the United Auto Workers, Defense Department, Ford Foundation, World Bank,

Catholic Church, and University of California has become every bit as challenging as managing Procter and Gamble, General Motors, and General Electric. These nonbusiness organizations have an increasing range of influence, affect as many livelihoods, and occupy as much media prominence as major business firms.

All of these organizations perform the classic business function. Every organization must perform a financial function insofar as money must be raised, managed, and budgeted according to sound business principles. Every organization must perform a production function in that it must conceive of the best way of arranging inputs to produce the output of the organization. Every organization must perform a personnel function in that people must be hired, trained, assigned, and promoted in the course of the organization's work. Every organization must perform a purchasing function in that it must acquire materials in an efficient way through comparing and selecting sources of supply.

When we come to the marketing function, it is also clear that every organization performs marketing-like activities whether or not they are recognized as such. Several examples can be given. The police department of a major U.S. city, concerned with the poor image it has among an important segment of its population, developed a campaign to "win friends and influence people." One highlight of this campaign is a "visit your police station" day in which tours are conducted to show citizens the daily operations of the police department, including the crime laboratories, police lineup, and cells. The police department also sends officers to speak at public schools and carries out a number of other activities to improve its community relations.

Most museum directors interpret their primary responsibility as "the proper preservation of an artistic heritage for posterity" (Lee, 1968, p. 66). As a result, for many people, museums are cold marble mausoleums that house miles of relics that soon give way to yawns and tired feet. Although museum attendance in the United States advances each year, a large number of citizens are uninterested in museums. Is this indifference due to failure in the manner of presenting what museums have to offer?

This nagging question led the new director of the Metropolitan Museum of Art to broaden the museum's appeal through sponsoring contemporary art shows and "happenings." His marketing philosophy of museum management led to substantial increases in the Met's attendance.

The public school system in Oklahoma City sorely needed more public support and funds to prevent a deterioration of facilities and exodus of teachers. It recently resorted to television programming to dramatize the work the public schools were doing to fight the high school dropout problem, to develop new teaching techniques, and to enrich the children. Although an expensive medium, television quickly reached large numbers of parents whose response and interest were tremendous.

Nations also resort to international marketing campaigns to get across important points about themselves to the citizens of other countries. The junta of Greek colonels who seized power in Greece in 1967 found the international publicity surrounding their cause to be extremely unfavorable and potentially disruptive of international recognition. They hired a major New York public relations firm, and soon full-page newspaper ads appeared carrying the headline "Greece Was Saved From Commu-

nism," detailing in small print why the takeover was necessary for the stability of Greece and the world ("PR for the Colonels," 1968).

An anti-cigarette group in Canada is trying to press the Canadian legislature to ban cigarettes on the grounds that they are harmful to health. There is widespread support for this cause, but the organization's funds are limited, particularly measured against the huge advertising resources of the cigarette industry. The group's problem is to find effective ways to make a little money go a long way in persuading influential legislators of the need for discouraging cigarette consumption. This group has come up with several ideas for marketing anti-smoking to Canadians, including television spots, a paperback book featuring pictures of cancer and heart disease patients, and legal research on company liability for the smoker's loss of health.

What concepts are common to these and many other possible illustrations of organizational marketing? All of these organizations are concerned about their "product" in the eyes of certain "consumers" and are seeking to find "tools" for furthering their acceptance. Let us consider each of these concepts in general organizational terms.

Products

Every organization produces a product of at least one of the following types:

Physical products. Product first brings to mind everyday items like soap, clothes, and food and extends to cover millions of tangible items that have a market value and are available for purchase.

Services. Services are intangible goods that are subject to market transaction such as tours, insurance, consultation, hairdos, and banking.

Persons. Personal marketing is an endemic human activity, from the employee trying to impress his boss to the statesman trying to win the support of the public. With the advent of mass communications, the marketing of persons has been turned over to professionals. Hollywood stars have their press agents, political candidates their advertising agencies, and so on.

Organizations. Many organizations spend a great deal of time marketing themselves. The Republican Party has invested considerable thought and resources in trying to develop a modern look. The American Medical Association decided recently that it needed to launch a campaign to improve the image of the American doctor themselves ("Doctors Try," 1968). Many charitable organizations and universities see selling their organization as their primary responsibility.

Ideas. Many organizations are mainly in the business of selling ideas to the larger society. Population organizations are trying to sell the idea of birth control, and the Women's Christian Temperance Union is still trying to sell the idea of prohibition. Thus the product can take many forms, and this is the first crucial point in the case for broadening the concept of marketing.

Consumers

The second crucial point is that organizations must deal with many groups that are interested in their product and can make a difference in its success. It is vitally important to the organization's success that it be sensitive to, serve, and satisfy these groups. One set of groups can be called the suppliers. Suppliers are those who provide the management group with the inputs necessary to perform its work and develop its product effectively. Suppliers include employees, vendors of the material, banks, advertising agencies, and consultants.

The other set of groups is the consumers of the organization's product, of which four subgroups can be distinguished. The clients are those who are the immediate consumers of the organization's product. The clients of a business firm are its buyers and potential buyers; of a service organization, those receiving the services, such as the needy (from the Salvation Army) or the sick (from County Hospital); and of a protective or a primary organization, the members.

The second group is the trustees or directors, those who are vested with the legal authority and responsibility for the organization, oversee the management, and enjoy a variety of benefits from the product. The third group is the active publics that take a specific interest in the organization. For a business firm, the active publics include consumer rating groups, governmental agencies, and pressure groups of various kinds. For a university, the active publics include alumni and friends of the university, foundations, and city fathers. Finally, the fourth consumer group is the general public. These are the people who might develop attitudes toward the organization that might affect its conduct in some way. Organizational marketing concerns the programs designed by management to create satisfactions and favorable attitudes in the organization's four consuming groups: clients, trustees, active publics, and general public.

Marketing Tools

Students of business firms spend much time studying the various tools under the firm's control that affect product acceptance: product improvement, pricing, distribution, and communication. All of these tools have counterpart applications to nonbusiness organizational activity.

Nonbusiness organizations to various degrees engage in product improvement, especially when they recognize the competition they face from other organizations. Thus, over the years churches have added a host of nonreligious activities to their basic religious activities to satisfy members seeking other bases of human fellowship. Universities keep updating their curricula and adding new student services in an attempt to make the educational experience relevant to the students. Where they have failed to do this, students have sometimes organized their own courses and publications or have expressed their dissatisfaction in organized protest. Government agencies such as license bureaus, police forces, and taxing bodies are often not responsive to the public because of monopoly status; but even here citizens have shown an increasing readiness to protest mediocre services, and more alert bureaucracies have shown a growing interest in reading the user's needs and developing the required product services.

All organizations face the problem of pricing the products and services so that they cover costs. Churches charge dues, universities charge tuition, governmental agencies charge fees, fund-raising organizations send out bills. Very often specific product charges are not sufficient to meet the organization's budget, and it must rely on gifts and surcharges to make up the difference. Opinions vary as to how much the users should be charged for the individual services and how much should be made up through general collection. If the university increases its tuition, it will have to face losing some students and putting more students on scholarship. If the hospital raises its charges to cover rising costs and additional services, it may provoke a reaction from the community. All organizations face complex pricing issues although not all of them understand good pricing practice.

Distribution is a central concern to the manufacturer seeking to make his goods conveniently accessible to buyers. Distribution also can be an important marketing decision area for nonbusiness organizations. A city's public library has to consider the best means of making its books available to the public. Should it establish one large library with an extensive collection of books or several neighborhood branch libraries with duplication of books? Should it use bookmobiles that bring the books to the customers instead of relying exclusively on the customers coming to the books? Should it distribute through school libraries? Similarly, the police department of a city must think through the problem of distributing its protective services efficiently through the community. It has to determine how much protective service to allocate to different neighborhoods; the respective merits of squad cars, motorcycles, and foot patrolmen; and the positioning of emergency phones.

Customer communication is an essential activity of all organizations although many nonmarketing organizations often fail to accord it the importance it deserves. Managements of many organizations think they have fully met their communication responsibilities by setting up advertising and/or public relations departments. They fail to realize that everything about an organization talks. Customers form impressions of an organization from its physical facilities, employees, officers, stationery, and a hundred other company surrogates. Only when this is appreciated do the members of the organization recognize that they all are in marketing, whatever else they do. With this understanding they can assess realistically the impact of their activities on consumers.

CONCEPTS FOR EFFECTIVE MARKETING MANAGEMENT IN NONBUSINESS ORGANIZATIONS

Although all organizations have products, markets, and marketing tools, the art and science of effective marketing management have reached their highest state of development in the business type of organization. Business organizations depend on customer goodwill for survival and have generally learned how to sense and cater to their needs effectively. As other types of organizations recognize their marketing roles, they will turn increasingly to the body of marketing principles worked out by business organizations and adapt them to their own situations.

What are the main principles of effective marketing management as they appear in most forward-looking business organizations? Nine concepts stand out as crucial in guiding the marketing effort of a business organization.

Generic Product Definition

Business organizations have increasingly recognized the value of placing a broad definition on their products, one that emphasizes the basic customer need(s) being served. A modern soap company recognizes that its basic product is cleaning, not soap; a cosmetics company sees its basic product as beauty or hope, not lipsticks and makeup; a publishing company sees its basic product as information, not books.

The same need for a broader definition of its business is incumbent on nonbusiness organizations if they are to survive and grow. Churches at one time tended to define their product narrowly as that of producing religious services for members. Recently, most churchmen have decided that their basic product is human fellowship. There was a time when educators said that their product was the three Rs. Now most of them define their product as education for the whole man. They try to serve the social, emotional, and political needs of young people in addition to intellectual needs.

Target Groups Definition

A generic product definition usually results in defining a very wide market, and it is then necessary for the organization, because of limited resources, to limit its product offering to certain clearly defined groups within the market. Although the generic product of an automobile company is transportation, the company typically sticks to cars, trucks, and buses, and stays away from bicycles, airplanes, and steamships. Furthermore, the manufacturer does not produce every size and shape of car but concentrates on producing a few major types to satisfy certain substantial and specific parts of the market.

In the same way, nonbusiness organizations have to define their target groups carefully. For example, in Chicago, the YMCA defines its target groups as men, women, and children who want recreational opportunities and are willing to pay $20 or more a year for them. The Chicago

Boys Club, on the other hand, defines its target group as poorer boys within the city boundaries who are in want of recreational facilities and can pay $1 a year.

Differentiated Marketing

When a business organization sets out to serve more than one target group, it will be maximally effective by differentiating its product offerings and communications. This is also true for nonbusiness organizations. Fund-raising organizations have recognized the advantage of treating clients, trustees, and various publics in different ways. These groups require differentiated appeals and frequency of solicitation. Labor unions find that they must address different messages to different parties rather than one message to all parties. To the company they may seem unyielding, to the conciliator they may appear willing to compromise, and to the public they seek to appear economically exploited.

Customer Behavior Analysis

Business organizations are increasingly recognizing that customer needs and behavior are not obvious without formal research and analysis; they cannot rely on impressionistic evidence. Soap companies spend hundreds of thousands of dollars each year researching how Mrs. Housewife feels about her laundry; how, when, and where she does her laundry; and what she desires of a detergent.

Fund raising illustrates how an industry has benefitted by replacing stereotypes of donors with studies of why people contribute to causes. Fund raisers have learned that people give because they are getting something. Many give to community chests to relieve a sense of guilt because of their elevated state compared to the needy. Many give to medical charities to relieve a sense of fear that they may be struck by a disease whose cure has not yet been found, or because of the illness of a family member. Some give to feel pride or a sense of nobility. Fund raisers have stressed the importance of identifying the motives operating in the marketplace of givers as a basis for planning drives.

Differential Advantages

In considering different ways of reaching target groups, an organization is advised to think in terms of seeking a differential advantage. It should consider what elements in its reputation or resources can be exploited to create a special value in the minds of its potential customers. In the same way that Zenith has built a reputation for quality and International Harvester a reputation for service, a nonbusiness organization should base its case on some dramatic value that competitive organizations lack. The small island of Nassau can compete against Miami for the tourist trade by advertising the greater dependability of its weather; the Heart Association can compete for funds against the Cancer Society by advertising the amazing strides made in heart research.

Multiple Marketing Tools

The modern business firm relies on a multitude of tools to sell its product, including product improvement, consumer and dealer advertising, salesman incentive programs, sales promotions, contests, multiple-size offerings, and so forth. Likewise nonbusiness organizations can reach their audiences in a variety of ways. A church can sustain the interest of its members through discussion groups, news-letters, news releases, campaign drives, an-nual reports, and retreats. Its "salesmen" include the religious head, the board mem-bers, and the present members in terms of attracting potential members. Its advertis-ing includes announcements of weddings, births, and deaths, religious pronounce-ments, and newsworthy developments.

Integrated Marketing Planning

The multiplicity of available marketing tools suggests the desirability of overall coordination so that these tools do not work at cross-purposes. Over time, busi-ness firms have placed under a marketing vice president activities that were pre-viously managed in a semi-autonomous fashion, such as sales, advertising, and mar-keting research. Nonbusiness organizations typically have not integrated their market-ing activities. Thus, no single officer in the typical university is given total responsibil-ity for studying the needs and attitudes of clients, trustees, and various publics and undertaking the necessary product devel-opment and communication programs to serve these groups. The university admin-istration instead includes a variety of mar-keting positions, such as dean of students, director of alumni affairs, director of public relations, and director of development; co-ordination is often poor.

Continuous Marketing Feedback

Business organizations gather continu-ous information about changes in the envi-ronment and about their own perfor-mance. They use their salesmen, research department, specialized research services,

and other means to check on the movement of goods, actions of competitors, and feel-ings of customers to make sure they are progressing along satisfactory lines. Non-business organizations typically are more casual about collecting vital information on how they are doing and what is happening in the marketplace. Universities have been caught off guard by underestimating the magnitude of student grievance and unrest, and so have major cities underestimated the degree to which they were failing to meet the needs of important minority constitu-encies.

Marketing Audit

Change is a fact of life, although it may proceed almost invisibly on a day-to-day basis. Over a long stretch of time it might be so fundamental as to threaten organiza-tions that have not provided for periodic reexaminations of their purposes. Organi-zations can grow set in their ways and unresponsive to new opportunities or problems. Some great American companies are no longer with us because they did not change definitions of their businesses, and their products lost relevance in a changing world. Political parties become unrespon-sive after they enjoy power for a while and every so often experience a major upset. Many union leaders grow insensitive to new needs and problems until one day they find themselves out of office. For an orga-nization to remain viable, its management must provide for periodic audits of its ob-jectives, resources, and opportunities. It must reexamine its basic business, target groups, differential advantage, communi-cation channels, and messages in the light of current trends and needs. It might rec-ognize when change is needed and make it before it is too late.

IS ORGANIZATIONAL MARKETING A SOCIALLY USEFUL ACTIVITY?

Modern marketing has two different meanings in the minds of people who use the term. One meaning of marketing conjures up the terms selling, influencing, persuading. Marketing is seen as a huge and increasingly dangerous technology, making it possible to sell persons on buying things, propositions, and causes they either do not want or which are bad for them. This was the indictment in Vance Packard's *Hidden Persuaders* and numerous other social criticisms, with the net effect that a large number of persons think of marketing as immoral or entirely self-seeking in its fundamental premises. They can be counted on to resist the idea of organizational marketing as so much "Madison Avenue."

The other meaning of marketing unfortunately is weaker in the public mind; it is the concept of sensitively serving and satisfying human needs. This was the great contribution of the marketing concept that was promulgated in the 1950s, and that concept now counts many business firms as its practitioners. The marketing concept holds that the problem of all business firms in an age of abundance is to develop customer loyalties and satisfaction, and the key to this problem is to focus on the customer's needs. Perhaps the short-run problem of business firms is to sell people on buying the existing products, but the long-run problem is clearly to create the products that people need. By this recognition that effective marketing requires a consumer orientation instead of a product orientation, marketing has taken a new lease on life and tied its economic activity to a higher social purpose.

It is this second side of marketing that provides a useful concept for all organizations. All organizations are formed to serve the interest of particular groups: hospitals serve the sick, schools serve the students, governments serve the citizens, and labor unions serve the members. In the course of evolving, many organizations lose sight of their original mandate, grow hard, and become self-serving. The bureaucratic mentality begins to dominate the original service mentality. Hospitals may become perfunctory in their handling of patients, schools treat their students as nuisances, city bureaucrats behave like petty tyrants toward the citizens, and labor unions try to run instead of serve their members.

All of these actions tend to build frustration in the consuming groups. As a result some withdraw meekly from these organizations, accept frustration as part of their condition, and find their satisfactions elsewhere. This used to be the common reaction of ghetto Negroes and college students in the face of indifferent city and university bureaucracies. But new possibilities have arisen, and now the same consumers refuse to withdraw so readily. Organized dissent and protest are seen to be an answer, and many organizations thinking of themselves as responsible have been stunned into recognizing that they have lost touch with their constituencies. They had grown unresponsive.

Where does marketing fit into this picture? Marketing is that function of the organization that can keep in constant touch with the organization's consumers, read their needs, develop products that meet these needs, and build a program of communications to express the organization's purposes. Certainly selling and influencing will be large parts of organizational marketing; but, properly seen, selling follows rather than precedes the organization's drive to create products to satisfy its consumers.

CONCLUSION

It has been argued here that the modern marketing concept serves very naturally to describe an important facet of all organizational activity. All organizations must develop appropriate products to serve their sundry consuming groups and must use modern tools of communication to reach their consuming publics. The business heritage of marketing provides a useful set of concepts for guiding all organizations.

The choice facing those who manage nonbusiness organizations is not whether to market or not to market, for no organization can avoid marketing. The choice is whether to do it well or poorly, and on this necessity the case for organizational marketing is basically founded.

REFERENCES

Doctors try an image transplant. (1968). *Business Week, 2025*, 64.

Lee, S. (1968). *Newsweek, 71*, 66.

PR for the colonels. (1968). *Newsweek, 71*, 70.

Chapter 4

CIGARETTE SMOKING
AND THE PUBLIC INTEREST

Harper W. Boyd, Jr.
Sidney J. Levy

What constitutes the responsibility of a business organization to the society of which it is a part? This question is not easily answered. Certainly, large corporations' conceptions of their duties and obligations have been modified to some degree in the transition from "robber baron" days to the present era of wider public stock ownership. Obvious reflections of this modification are increased dependence on buyers' goodwill and the growth of government regulation. In many cases, the increase of government control has been invited by business refusal to show the kind of leadership that would make federal intervention unnecessary. A striking example is afforded by the current situation regarding cigarettes.

This chapter was first published as "Cigarette Smoking and the Public Interest: Opportunity for Business Leadership," in *Business Horizons,* Fall 1963, pp. 37-44. © 1963 by the Foundation for the Kelley School of Business at Indiana University. Reprinted with permission.

THE DANGERS OF SMOKING

The habit of using tobacco in one form or another has been around for some 400 years. There have always been taboos against smoking, some of them based on assumptions regarding tobacco usage and health. In the opinion of many doctors these assumptions have recently become facts. Studies conducted over the past 10 years or so leave little doubt in the minds of a substantial number of scientists and doctors that cigarette smokers have a higher death rate than nonsmokers. What makes this so frightening is that smoking is quite widespread. The U.S. Public Health Service estimates that 78% of American men have a history of tobacco use and that, while the percentage of men smokers has in recent years been relatively stable, the percentage of women smokers has shown a steady increase.

The American public has been continuously exposed to these findings and to the warnings of leading medical researchers on the subject of smoking and health. In 1959, Dr. Leroy E. Barney, Surgeon General of the U.S. Public Health Service, stated in the *Journal of the American Medical Association* that "The weight of evidence at present implicates smoking as the principal . . . factor in the increased incidence of lung cancer."

E. H. Hammond, a well-known medical researcher, goes further in concluding that "after reviewing the evidence, the mildest statement I can make is that, in my opinion, the inhalation of tobacco smoke produces a number of very harmful effects and shortens the life span of human beings." In a 1962 report entitled *Smoking and Health,* the Royal College of Physicians of London concluded that cigarette smoking is an important cause of lung cancer and that if the habit ceased, the number of deaths from the disease would decline significantly. The report goes on to say,

> The chance of dying in the next 10 years for a man aged 35 who is a heavy cigarette smoker is 1 in 23 whereas the risk for a nonsmoker is only 1 in 90. Only 15 per cent (one in six) of men of this age who are nonsmokers but 33 per cent (one in three) of heavy smokers will die before the age of 65.

A study conducted by Hammond and Daniel Horn of 187,783 men between the ages of 50 and 69 led to the conclusion that the total death rate from all causes was 1.57 times higher among men with a history of regular cigarette smoking and that death rates rose progressively as the numbers of cigarettes consumed daily increased. The relative death rate from lung cancer among regular cigarette smokers was 10.73 times greater than for nonsmokers.

Deaths from lung cancer among males in the United States (36,000 in 1960) have increased 600% since 1935. Lung cancer (a most unpleasant way to die) accounted for 2% of all deaths in 1960 in the United States, but for about 6% of deaths among men in their late 50s and early 60s. Cigarette smoking has also been linked to coronary heart disease, cancer of the male bladder, and cancer of the mouth, throat, and gullet.

If there were a way to treat tobacco or filter the smoke to overcome or even minimize the effects of smoking, the solution of the problem would be relatively simple. But to date, no method of treatment or filtering has been demonstrated to have any material effect. The best solution is to stop smoking; the evidence is that this action reduces the death rate substantially, even after long exposure. If one cannot stop smoking, the danger can be somewhat lessened by switching to pipes or cigars, which, because of infrequent inhalation, are reported to be less harmful.

Amazingly enough, despite the mass media's extensive coverage of the findings of the studies quoted earlier, not too many people (only 16%, according to a recent American Cancer Society survey) believe that there is a correlation between cigarette smoking and lung cancer. This may be selective perception at work; that is, because the facts of the situation are totally unpleasant and affect a basic habit, the mind rejects the message or, in effect, never receives it. Domestic sales of cigarettes in 1963 hit a record 512 billion, well over 100 billion in the past 10 years. Cigarette consumption per capita according to the U.S. Department of Agriculture was about 4,025 in 1961, up 3% over 1960 and 17% over 1956. Decreases have occurred in only 2 years since 1935: 1953 and 1954, the years following the publicity given the earlier cancer studies. The increase since 1954 can no doubt be attributed in part to filters, which now account for over 50% of all cigarette sales. While the filter has never been conclusively shown to be a health safeguard, it does permit smokers to rationalize the habit.

SOLVING THE PROBLEM

We are actually concerned with two overriding questions: First, how can we prevent future generations from starting to smoke cigarettes, and second, how can we get people who are now cigarette smokers to terminate the habit or at least switch to cigars or pipes? The need for a solution to the first question is apparent in the fact that

persons who begin to smoke do so at an ever younger age. It has been reported that 20% of all boys have started smoking by the ninth grade and that almost 30% of all girls smoke before they graduate from high school.

In attempting to solve these problems, we must recognize and understand that smoking is widespread and deeply entrenched and that it satisfies deep-seated human needs that have existed for a long period of time. Its existence is the direct result of strong forces operating in our culture. How else could the habit continue to exist when so many smokers classify it as being unhealthy, wasteful, dirty, and immoral? Certainly, powerful motivations must be operating to sustain cigarette smoking in the face of these negative attitudes.

Psychologists point out that cigarette smoking signifies energy and accomplishment and is deemed necessary to relieve tension. Thus, it is justified on the basis of its value as a reward or a means of self-gratification, and even as quasi-therapeutic. Social Research, Inc., in a rather elaborate study entitled *Cigarettes, Their Role and Function,* divided the reasons why people smoke into two categories, personal and social. Under "personal," they note that cigarette smoking has many uses.

1. It is an intimate function and has the quality of a personal ritual. Like all rituals, it gives a sense of well-being, a feeling of security.

2. The process of smoking provides a variety of sensuous pleasures, including oral indulgence.

3. It provides a perverse pleasure that many people derive from punishing or endangering themselves in masochistic fashion.

4. It helps smokers tell what kind of people they are. Important here are the ideas of maturity, virility, and aggressiveness among men and poise, sophistication, and liberation, especially for women.

Under social meanings, the study reports that cigarettes can be equated with sociability, that they serve as gestures of affiliation or instruments of social interaction, and that they represent conformity. For the teenager, cigarette smoking serves as an initiation into the ranks of adults. Not to smoke is to be stigmatized as weak, prudish, or timid.

Whatever the reasons for smoking, it is clear that they are sufficiently powerful to make the habit difficult to break. So long as cigarettes have high personal and cultural values, individuals who now smoke them or who can be induced to smoke them will find the habit attractive. Thus, any remedial action must attempt to minimize the psychological and social values of cigarettes.

RESPONSIBLE PARTIES

The Federal Government

Given the above evidence, many persons would conclude that cigarettes should be classed as a harmful drug and so treated by the federal government, that is, their sale to the public should be prohibited. But such a solution ignores the facts that most adults smoke, that the habit is a strong one, and that cigarettes can be made from tobacco designed to be used for other forms of smoking. Extreme government action would probably end up worse than the

diseases associated with cigarette smoking. Shades of the Volstead Act!

To be sure, the government has a distinct responsibility to protect the health and welfare of its citizens. To date, it has delayed action pending a "facts and recommendations" report from an advisory committee named by the U.S. Surgeon General. Perhaps some insight into possible action can be gleaned from the suggestions made to the British government by the Royal College of Physicians. These include: (a) preventing or at least restricting cigarette advertising, (b) more effectively regulating the sale of tobacco to children, (c) curtailing smoking in public places to alter its social acceptability, (d) placing a differential tax on cigarettes while reducing the tax on pipe tobacco and cigars, (e) organizing anti-smoking clinics, (f) informing purchasers of cigarettes of the tar and nicotine content of cigarette smoke, and (g) drawing the attention of the public to the dangers of smoking, with special care being taken to the education of school children.

It goes without saying that the government should continue and even expand its expenditures for research on cancer and other diseases to which smoking has been linked, which are currently only about $100 million annually. (In comparison, the government's tobacco price support program for the period from June 1, 1960 to April 30, 1961, totaled $42.8 million.) Any additional research costs could easily be financed by a special "medical research" tax per package; for example, at present consumption rates, a tax of $.05 per package would provide over $1 billion annually, even allowing for a tax reduction on cigars and smoking tobacco. Not all of this money would have to be spent on medical research. Some could be allocated to an intensive propaganda campaign designed to educate the public regarding the ill effects of cigarette smoking. The effectiveness of the tax could be increased by placing a tax stamp on each package with the statement, "Proceeds from this special tax are used to support cancer research." Hopefully, the additional tax (which would substantially raise the cost of a package of cigarettes) would cause some persons to quit or reduce their smoking because of the higher cost.

Certainly the government has the responsibility for issuing a definitive statement on smoking and health in a form that can easily be understood by the layman. In addition, the government could ban all cigarette advertising (as Italy has done) and could even use federal funds to "advertise" the ill effects of cigarette smoking. Such a campaign might include the use of scare posters similar to those issued by the British Ministry of Health. One poster shows the rise in lung cancer deaths from 5,303 in 1940 to 25,288 in 1961. The figures are printed in gray on the lids of five coffins, which presumably will increase in size as the lung cancer death figures go up. This poster says: "The more cigarettes you smoke the greater risk. You have been warned."

In an effort to head off youngsters who might fall victims of the habit, the government could issue educational materials for use by the school. New York State has released a pamphlet warning youngsters of the "serious health hazard." The American Cancer Society has increased its showings of educational films to teenagers on cancer and cigarettes and claims that they are having a considerable impact. But the likely response of many youths to such educational materials is, "Why worry about a disease that won't hit for 30 or 40 years?" Youngsters' smoking could be restricted by the enforcement of laws already on the

books of most states that prohibit the sale of cigarettes to minors. Enforcement is difficult, however, because automatic vending machines are left unattended and cigarettes are readily available through casual adults.

The federal government has a unique role to play in helping to solve the cigarette problem, but its actions cannot get at the basic question of how to destroy the favorable image possessed by the cigarette in our culture. These actions can be important or even drastic, but much will depend on the consensus developed through cooperation from the industries involved.

The Tobacco Industry

This embattled industry with some 65,000 employees and annual sales of nearly $8 billion has shown much anxiety over the cigarette problem but little tendency to accept any responsibility for solving it. In fact, many would argue that the industry has deliberately attempted to minimize or mask the various research findings regarding the harmful effects of cigarette smoking. It has played up the contention that other factors such as gas and industrial fumes are more likely causes of lung cancer than cigarettes and has argued that to date there is no proof that cigarettes are linked to cancer.

In 1954, in response to the initial research releases citing evidence of the dangers of cigarette smoking, the industry set up the Tobacco Industry Research Committee (TIRC) to finance scientific inquiry into the relationship, if any, between smoking and such maladies as lung cancer and heart disease. Through 1962, total research expenditures made by TIRC have been only $5.5 million, considerably less than 1% of the industry's approximately $170 million annual advertising expenditures. The tobacco industry could easily afford a larger research expenditure. Annual net profits of the "big five" (R. J. Reynolds Tobacco Co., Philip Morris, Inc., P. Lorillard Company, Liggett & Myers Tobacco Co., and The American Tobacco Co.) exceed $262 million and are thus in excess of twice the total yearly expenditures for cancer research in this country.

Although the storm warnings have been flying for some 10 years, the major tobacco companies have done little to diversify. They are thus vulnerable to drastic outside action and reluctant to show initiative in facing up to the challenges of business statesmanship. Philip Morris has diversified into flexible packaging materials, chewing gum, chemicals and adhesives, and razor blades and shaving supplies to the extent that the sales of these products account for about 25% of total sales. Reynolds, the only other major tobacco company to do much by way of diversification, has acquired Pacific Hawaiian Products Company with annual sales of under $30 million in fruit juice and cake mixes. Reynolds's Archer Aluminum Division is expanding and increased sales are expected, and U.S. Tobacco is now in the candy business.

For the most part, the tobacco companies have tried to meet the health issue on their own ground, that is, by launching new filter and king size brands. The filter tip market now represents 55% of the total market, in contrast to about 1% a decade ago. The nonfilter king size has about 20% of the total, not because of its economy appeal, but because many smokers have apparently been attracted by the argument that the extra length serves as a natural filter.

The marketing of these new brands of cigarettes has been an expensive undertaking—over $10 million is often expended to introduce a new brand. The industry's attempt to solve its problems by more aggressive marketing is reflected, in part, by its substantial advertising expenditures. The cost per carton, as estimated by *Advertising Age,* varies widely among brands, ranging in 1961 from $.028 per carton for Camel and Lucky Strike to $.669 for Belair.

An ironical twist to the advertising situation is that from the late 1940s through 1954 the industry literally spent a small fortune creating doubts about the healthfulness of its products. Most of the advertising during this period featured doctors and filters that "really worked." Ads were filled with tars and resins presented so graphically as to convince some smokers that these were agents of destruction, as indeed they may well be. The Federal Trade Commission's rulings in 1955 and again in 1960 that, in effect, health cannot be dealt with in any cigarette advertising account for the present emphasis on pleasure. Perhaps the contrast suggests that the themes of health or pleasure affect smoking habits less than their widespread presentation, which lends public approval and acceptance to smoking. It seems clear that, although cigarette manufacturers should have a sense of public responsibility, they have given no evidence that they feel any real obligation to the public interest. This is not the case in other countries. Two Canadian cigarette manufacturers, following the example set in England, recently agreed to limit TV advertising to the hours after 9 p.m., when children are supposedly in bed.

The Advertising Agency

The executives of many advertising agencies have long been defensive and insecure about the value to society of their role. They have often stated that the public doesn't understand their important contribution to "keeping the economy moving." And presumably they have reason to be on the defensive, given the public image of advertising executives as portrayed in the movies, in the popular literature, and on television.

It would surely contradict that image if the advertising industry could be persuaded to make a significant contribution to solving the cigarette problem. After all, it has been partially responsible for giving cigarette smoking a virile, socially acceptable, sensuous image. Certainly it would be difficult for an advertising agency executive to claim that the billions of dollars spent in advertising cigarettes over the past 30 years had made no impact on demand. An example of early cigarette advertising is the 1932 Lucky Strike ad in which the question was asked, "Do you inhale?" followed by the statement "What's there to be afraid of?" An earlier "Reach for a Lucky" campaign (circa 1930) described cigarettes as safe and even attributed medicinal values to them. In 1934, a Camel ad suggested that cigarettes would alleviate jangled nerves, while a 1936 Camel ad identified smoking with doctors.

But to place the argument in this frame of reference is probably not fair. According to Neil Borden's classic study entitled *Economic Effects of Advertising,* advertising's part in expanding the market for cigarettes has been no more than an acceleration of a habit that has its roots in our culture. As our social environment has changed— especially in the breakdown of social restrictions upon personal behavior, the forces or prejudices against smoking have all but disappeared. Advertising men early perceived that smoking is a social habit and, as such, could be stimulated by making it

socially acceptable, or by accelerating the forces already at work through emulation of well-known personages.

Now that smoking's link to cancer has been established, however, shouldn't this principle of emulation be dropped as the basis of advertising copy? At least one medical research authority on cancer believes that it should. Dr. Michael B. Shimkin, one of the senior directors of the National Cancer Institute of Bethesda, Md., has pleaded, "In fairness to our children the least the industry and the government should do is eliminate some of the shameful appeals from tobacco advertising such as those which equate smoking with bravery, sexual virility, and social status." Some of the present cigarette advertising unquestionably appeals to our youth—despite denials of the tobacco industry. The TV advertising in the fall of 1961 that featured Paul Hornung is but one example.

To be sure, advertising men until recently didn't know, or suspect, the potential harm in cigarettes when they created their advertising claims. But they know it now, or at least should have strong doubts about the healthfulness of cigarette smoking. Yet they go on behaving as though cigarette smoking were harmless and even therapeutic. A few advertising agencies, all large, handle the bulk of all cigarette advertising. Each could survive the resignation of their cigarette accounts. (Collectively, these accounts represent an income of about $30 million to the agencies involved.)

Imagine the furor that would follow the announcement of such a resignation, especially one accompanied by the statement, "We can no longer in good conscience continue to attempt to increase the demand for a product that possesses such potentially dangerous effects on users." It might even be argued that such leadership would be rewarded by its attraction of new accounts from business executives who admired such a stand.

Responsible agency leaders could go further and spark action by the Advertising Council, a nonprofit organization that marshals the forces of advertising for the social good. The council's unique and successful history of proven service is exemplified in the campaign to prevent forest fires (featuring Smokey the Bear) and the promotion of U.S. Savings Bonds. Leading advertising agencies could organize their talents behind an educational campaign designed to inform the public of the dangers of smoking and to play down the social role of cigarettes.

Advertising Media

Resignation of the cigarette advertising accounts by agencies would not, of course, shut off the flow of advertising. The tobacco companies could hire other agencies, or, assuming an industry-wide boycott, set up "house agencies." Only if the mass media act collectively to refuse such advertising is there any chance of a really effective blackout action.

At least one industry representative has spoken out about the responsibility of the mass media with regard to cigarette smoking. Leroy Collins, President of the National Association of Broadcasters, stated in November 1962 that radio and TV codes

> should be much more than sets of legalistic standards and delineations of good taste and estimated public tolerance. I think the codes should serve as a broadcast conscience as well. Under them and to them, the individual broadcaster and all related enterprises should be able to look for, and find, ethical and unbiased leadership. For example, if we

are honest with ourselves, we cannot ignore the mounting evidence that tobacco provides a serious hazard to health. Can we either in good conscience ignore the fact that progressively more and more of our high school age—and lower—children are now becoming habitual cigarette smokers? . . . We also know that this condition is being made continuously worse under the promotional impact of advertising designed primarily to influence young people.

As might be expected, the tobacco manufacturers accused Collins of having made a final judgment on a medical question that is still under study. They also denied advertising to American youth, although, according to Senator Maurine Neuberger (D., Oregon), some 40% of all national advertising placed in college newspapers was sponsored by the tobacco companies. Only in recent months did the big five cigarette companies stop all campus advertising and promotion. This action was taken after a number of American universities banned cigarette advertising, largely at the urging of the American Cancer Society. Also within broadcasting's own ranks, many tried to minimize Collins's statements and publicly assured tobacco sponsors that the broadcast media were eager for their advertising dollars.

It would be a gigantic step forward to refuse cigarette advertising; it would be an even bigger step to provide free time to the Advertising Council for anti-smoking propaganda. But one is forced to conclude that, despite the fact that radio and TV networks and stations have by their own admission unique social responsibilities, it is unlikely that they, as a group, will ban cigarette advertising.

At least four major groups in our society have a responsibility for making a sincere effort to help solve the problem of cigarette smoking. Given the dimensions and roots of the problem, all four working together could accomplish more than any one working alone. It would be refreshing if the business groups were the first to act, for in so doing they would demonstrate that they were responsible agents of a free society. Too frequently, business is victimized by its inability to assume leadership. Thus, it falls into the position of criticizing action by the government without having an alternative offer. Businessmen could justify their actions by understanding that, in reality, they are acting only in their own interests and in the long-run interests of the free enterprise system that they claim is being continually eroded by the growth in power of the federal government. The opportunity afforded by the magnitude of the problem should excite, rather than inhibit, the relatively small group of men who can exercise effective leadership in this situation.

The last paragraph is likely to be misunderstood by many business leaders. The grounds on which the points advanced here will be repudiated are predictable:

The link between cigarette smoking and lung cancer has not yet been proven.

Advertising agencies act as agents for their clients; they work within regulations handed down by others.

If we turn down the advertising, somebody else will accept it.

Unfortunately, the authors are forced to conclude that only the federal government will take action and that business in general as well as many of those who consume or will consume cigarettes will be the losers. Intervention by the federal government into the problem of cigarette smoking will inevitably involve the various groups mentioned in this article, and any such intervention will be likely to serve as a precedent in cases of other products that can be shown to be potentially harmful. If the federal government acts in a way that is either not effective in solving the problem or that invades the domain of the agency or the media, then no one can be counted as the winner—least of all the cigarette smoker.

Chapter **5**

WHAT KIND OF CORPORATE OBJECTIVES?

Harper W. Boyd, Jr.
Sidney J. Levy

An overriding objective is critical to the successful functioning of a business enterprise. Lack of specificity in objectives often causes management to fall back on vague, overgeneralized statements. When this happens, the decisions relating to such major strategies as product and product line, pricing, personal selling, advertising, channels, research and development, and plant location are poorly coordinated. Too often the decisions are made by merely following industry practice ("all companies have their own sales force"), by historical precedent ("we have always had exclusive dealers"),

and by tradition, uncertainty, and imitation, as well as by sound precedent and experienced insight.

As corporations have grown in size, executive problems have increased in complexity. Consider the desires of certain departments with respect to length of product line. The marketing group wants a long product line because it means a better position in the marketplace. But the production people want long production runs in order to minimize manufacturing costs. And the financial executives want to minimize capital investments in inventory and

This chapter was first printed in *Journal of Marketing, 30,* October 1966, pp. 63-68. Reprinted by permission of the American Marketing Association.

the extra production equipment needed to produce the longer line.

Reference to the firm's overall objectives is the only effective way of resolving such differences (Churchman, Ackoff, & Arnoff, 1957). Operations researchers long have been interested in the setting of objectives, both from the point of view of individual executives and the organization as a whole. Some have documented both the need and the difficulty of specifying objectives and conclude that most organizations are unable to describe their specific goals satisfactorily (Miller & Starr, 1960).

Multiple objectives can be stated in terms of departmental objectives or area responsibilities, such as those suggested by Peter F. Drucker (1965)—market standing, innovation, productivity, physical and financial resources, profitability, manager performance and development, worker performance and attitudes, and public responsibility.

Such objectives, often conflicting, raise the question of suboptimization. A "best" solution to such a problem requires assigning relative weights to the objectives involved and determining their substitutability (Ackoff, 1953). Clearly the presence of a governing objective would increase greatly the efficiency of solutions to the problems of suboptimization. Thus, despite the conclusions drawn by some operation researchers, continuation of the search for some way to set forth an overriding objective is needed.

There have been a number of attempts to get at this problem. Typically the "procedures" center around the kind of businesses in which the firm should be engaged, what market niche the company should attempt to occupy, what product or products the company should produce, and where the company wants to be in the next 5 to 10 years. All have one thing in common:

lack of the precision necessary if the firm is to have a true rationale for existence.

CATEGORIES OF OBJECTIVES

Our purpose here is to discuss only the overriding or "broader" corporate objective, in contrast with the subobjectives which would be used to accomplish the larger objective (Grander, 1964). Although there is no simple solution and no easy formula available by which to accomplish our task, it should be helpful to discuss those aims an enterprise might have—growing out of what it has to sell, the utilization of its products or services, and its relationships to its customers.

Study of more than 200 statements received from a research inquiry which pertained to corporate objectives, many discussions with corporate executives, and results from numerous research projects suggest different sources of objectives which have the potential of generating goals from which relatively specific plans can be developed. Here are six for consideration:

1. Focus on material resources

2. Concern with fabricated objects

3. Major interest in events and activities, requiring certain products or services

4. Emphasis on kind of person whose needs are to be met

5. Catering to specific physical parts of a person

6. Examining wants and needs and seeking to adapt to them

These categories are not mutually exclusive and do not include such nondifferentiating objectives as the making of profits, the generating of increased sales, the desire to perpetuate the firm, and other such management-centered aims. Also, the discussion of the six categories centers largely around firms producing consumer goods, although the principles apply for the most part to industrial goods firms.

FOCUS ON
MATERIAL RESOURCES

Many modern companies owe their origin and continued existence to having owned or been granted rights to drill, mine, and hew. Still others were founded to process certain natural resources, including those derived from agriculture, for example, grain crops, meats, and milk. Earlier, the main problems were to get the raw materials and to overcome the transportation difficulties in bringing them to an expanding market.

The companies that were founded to process agricultural products were the first to change, or else die. The very efficiency of the American farmer "choked" many to death. The growth of standardized processing methods, the development of substitute products via the laboratory, and the difficulty and cost of marketing also took their toll.

The milling and dairy industries are but two examples of the evolution that took place in the growth of large diversified companies. In natural fibers, the growth of the man-made synthetics altered substantially the viewpoints of those in the carpeting and clothing industries.

The metal, oil, and gas industries have not escaped the technological revolution. The competition among metals and between metals and plastics has been intense, with important effects on the management philosophies of the firms involved. The attention paid to the market and its needs by basic plastics producers and by the aluminum

companies has forced some of the old-line companies to accelerate their R & D efforts and do a better job of satisfying customer needs, as an example, through the development of certain metal alloys. The plastic companies rely on chemical research and recognize the inevitability of a product life cycle, with the superseding of one plastic by another. In order to capitalize on innovations they engage heavily in market- development programs. Thus, to promote its polystyrene, the Dow Chemical Company established a product evaluation program designed to evaluate end products on the following basis: (a) General plastics application—should an plastic material be used? (b) Specific material application—should Dow Styron be used, and if so, what formulation? (c) Product design, (d) Workmanship.

In recent years many producers of raw materials have devoted considerable effort to increasing demand by finding new and attractive uses for their products. Thus, the producers of raw asbestos fibers have expanded their market by producing asbestos woven sheets which will withstand extremely high temperatures and which can be used by a variety of industries. Such producers have been led from merely supplying industry to thinking about ultimate consumption. They often start with the need to sell byproducts of raw materials, and as they think about how to foster consumption of their products, they may start to use and sell other products in conjunction with their own. The fact that the oil companies typically sell certain chemical products as well as tires, batteries, accessories, mechanical repairs, soft drinks, travel items, and food is a case in point.

Although raw material-oriented companies have come to be highly concerned about their markets, many tend to remain heavily preoccupied with the discovery of new supplies, new techniques for shipping, automated processing, negotiations with governments, geopolitical problems of extracting minerals, large-scale effects of laws, fiscal policies, and economic patterns.

Thus, the attempt to be market-oriented centers mainly on helping the customer to sell, and the customer's customer to sell. Personal selling and the heavy use of consumer advertising are the means used. But while these activities may have a beneficial effect on market share, they rarely solve the long-range problems of finding new and better ways to satisfy the needs and wants of the ultimate consumer. Individuals who manage raw-materials companies probably are more tough-minded, more dedicated to a single-minded purpose, and more centered on inner-oriented activities of the company than those managers who, at the other extreme, are concerned with examining human wants and needs and seeking to adapt to them. The latter survive not by battling nature but by ingratiation and catering to whims. Compare, if you will, the food company to an oil company.

The danger of being materials-oriented in objectives is obvious. Given the fast pace of technological change, a company that concentrates narrowly on its materials power can easily be rendered obsolete. The management of such a company would find it difficult to change successfully the company's mission. The very attributes which make for a successful manager of a raw- materials company would serve as liabilities, given a set of objectives that are market-oriented.

CONCERN WITH FABRICATED OBJECTS

A significant center of energy and attention is the manufactured object. It has been and remains a major source of interest and dedication to many company executives. The main objective of many companies is the production of a "thing" (or things). Attention focuses on what it is, what its characteristics are, how it gets made, its contents and specifications, and how it works. Questions dealing with who uses it, what is done with it, and why people might or might not want it may be left unanswered.

Clearly, product orientation and concern with production problems are uppermost in the minds of such managements. This preoccupation with production restricts the horizons of company thinking. This means that the urge to perfect the product may be greater than the willingness to change it radically, or to make variations that might lead to a product line, or to develop alternatives to replace it. As an example, the president of a large and well-known quality producer of men's suits reacted to synthetic fibers by indicating that they did not fit into his way of doing business. He said that his buyers were wool buyers, not synthetic buyers.

It is also likely that a company's interest in just selling more of a product can become the main goal of management, since the channeling of energy into production makes increased productivity the only apparent avenue to profits. Given a stable history and growing demand for the product, such a production orientation is likely to build a strong feeling of security and confidence. On the other hand, when market changes occur that affect the demand for the product, such managements are vulnerable. The area where they exert the greatest control—within the plant—is least helpful in modifying their relationship to the external environment. Many traditionally minded small businessmen often find themselves in such difficult situations.

The focus on material resources and the concern with fabricated objects are basically oriented away from the consumer, or at least are not specifically aimed at him. He is largely taken for granted. The sources of objectives which follow tend to develop an awareness of the consumer; there is some more or less direct concern with meeting his needs and wants, and gratifying him or stimulating him.

MAJOR INTEREST IN
EVENTS AND ACTIVITIES

If the major interest of the management of a company is to sell products or services which fit into a consumer's life in a special way, then this will serve as a useful source of company vitality. If a management perceives its objective as that solely of producing a golf ball, then it is likely to be less flexible and responsive to change than a management which thinks of itself as making products which are to be used in golfing, or in sports activities, or in recreation. This larger definition, which deals with what people are doing in the sporting world, or in the changing world of recreation, enlarges the scope of management's thinking about what the company should be trying to accomplish. Management will be more likely to search out new lines and to anticipate or foster new trends.

Events and activities can be a useful way of segmenting the market. Emery Air Freight developed a unique service "to handle emergencies" through the use of a complex network of air carriers and delivery trucks. Emery even took into account the psychological aspects of an emergency by offering, at extra cost, a time of delivery service which informed the buyer exactly where his shipment was and when it would be delivered.

Events and activities which tie to style considerations tend to generate flexibility and sensitivity to change in the management of those companies which cater to

such objectives, for example, clothing for holidays or vacations. When the consumer's goals transcend the significance of the product itself and management recognizes the fact, then the firm is also likely to be more sensitive to the external environment and the opportunities inherent in the process of change.

In recent years the American public has taken up in increasing numbers "new" sporting activities—including skiing, surfing, and skin diving. Golf is more popular than ever. These changes in our avocations have provided many manufacturers with new and lucrative markets. Another illustration has to do with high school graduation. This used to be an occasion celebrated with the gift of a watch. But today fewer watches are given if only because the new graduate is likely already to possess one.

EMPHASIS ON
KIND OF PERSON

Through various historical circumstances, the managers of some companies have come to think of themselves as serving the needs and wants of a particular kind of person. They are focused on a certain market segment, rather than on supplying a product line to different kinds of people. This makes a great difference in what policies are pursued. Gerber advertises "Babies Are Our Business—Our Only Business." If Gerber were to extend this policy (and it has done so to some extent) it might end up with a diversified line of clothing, furniture, and other articles—all designed solely for babies.

This targeting on a certain kind of person, depending on how the kind is defined, can make a great deal of sense. Many small specialized retailers or service establishments build business around such an objective—for instance, a quality haberdasher. But if the objective centers on a disappearing kind of person, then the firm will experience trouble. A publisher who caters to the education and amusement of the wives of blue-collar workers might, over the next decade or two, experience a substantial reduction in his potential market.

The ability to be successful in serving people, as contrasted with producing things for people, has merit, of course, since the executives of a firm must understand what is different about "their kind of people" as compared with other kinds. And a preoccupation with a type of person may induce great sensitivity to any changes in such individuals, as retailers who have catered successfully to college students over the past decade can testify. The behavioral sciences have provided some insightful information about certain groups of individuals. For example, knowledge of how social classes differ with respect to their lifestyle and buying behavior is helpful in the establishment of market segments (Fisher, 1955; Martineau, 1968).

CATERING TO SPECIFIC PHYSICAL PARTS OF A PERSON

Consider the concern of companies as to eyes (Maybelline), teeth (Dr. West), feet (Florsheim), skin (Noxzema), hair (Alberto Culver), beard (Gillette), and legs (Hanes).

However, the physical part of a person for which concern is expressed is merely part of a person's total gestalt. The use of lip rouge and hair dye and the colors involved are affected by cultural norms as well as by the lifestyle to which a woman aspires.

Still, the parts objective has considerable appeal. By focusing on a relatively small

and specialized part of a person, a firm can build a relatively secure market. But it may be difficult to build up sufficient sales to compete against a larger and more diversified seller. A related problem has been experienced in the channels of distribution. Companies producing products having to do with the feet and legs, that is, shoes and stockings, have had difficulty in obtaining specialty-type selling without setting up their own outlets or leased departments. Only the larger firms have been able to afford such expenditures.

EXAMINATION OF WANTS AND NEEDS

To have real meaning, an objective must be specific—as to what wants and needs of what parts of the market are to be satisfied. This objective can be accomplished with some probability of success if the management of a firm considers (a) what generic use is to be satisfied, and (b) what consumption systems are operating to satisfy these generic uses.

Generic use. A broad affirmation of corporate intentions provides some guidance to planning. It makes considerable difference whether a company defines its goals as being primarily financial and sets about acquiring divisions chosen for their tax advantages rather than for their product fit; whether it aims to cater to, say, the textbook market and develop academic contacts to attract authors; or whether it wants to provide a congenial environment for bright and inventive engineers. In a large sense, companies sell transportation, nutrition, energy, comfort, self-expression, escape, intellectual development, and conformity—rather than cars, bread, gasoline, pillows, pens, novels, textbooks, and uniforms. Transportation can be served by objects other than cars, and bread serves other functions than nutrition, and so on.

This means that objectives can be phrased and interpreted in different ways by companies in the very same industry. A company that centers its objectives on helping people to express their individual styles of communication might do better with the market by creating a new, more malleable pen, rather than by devising a cigarette lighter just because it happens to have the equipment to turn out small gadgets.

A logical starting point in the setting of need objectives would be to state the end uses to which the product applies and the basic needs that the end use is attempting to satisfy. For example, a manufacturer of wristwatches might state that the basic need for the product is to measure time. The human outlook here rests in compulsive attention to precision and accuracy. Less literally, there is the definition of the wearer as mature enough to control the organization of his timed activities, and to relate to other people in a "socially synchronized" way. If precision and accuracy are to be the main factors, then the necessity for fineness and quality of workmanship follows. If control of timed activities is given precedence, the company may begin to develop activating mechanisms and miscellaneous automatic timing devices. If social relationship and synchronization are emphasized, the company may turn toward making watches for children, for cocktail wear, and for jewelry adornment.

The petroleum industry will take quite different courses—depending on whether company managers see themselves as providing power, automotive service, and transportation or as being a conveniently located channel of distribution for a variety of products.

Generic use refers to the satisfaction of fairly general consumer needs and wants. But how they are gratified can vary and change through time. People need food, shelter, and sex if they and their kind are to survive; but overweight people, "high-rise" dwellers, and contraceptive users have made some significant modifications in their diet, environmental control, and sensual gratifications. It is necessary to keep abreast of changing social, cultural, and psychological situations and what they imply for product variation and innovation.

Consumption Systems

It is useful to think of the consumer as a decision maker who individually or in conjunction with others controls the operation of a system comprising products, effort (labor), and machines (Churchman et al., 1957). Every product is, therefore, by definition a part of some consumption system. The totality of the system exists to satisfy some basic need or want—that is, to solve a problem. This "solving a problem"—or goal-directedness—is critical. A failure to understand the nature of the goals and the standards set by the consumer will inevitably result in difficulties. Typically, there are a constellation of goals; for example, the housewife cleans a floor to remove dirt, to show that she is a competent housewife, to demonstrate to her family that she loves them, and so on. The housewife uses many systems as she goes about her household tasks. Cleaning house, preparing food, washing clothes, caring for the baby, and getting ready to go out provide examples of consumption systems in operation.

Here the consumer is like an economic entity—engaged in buying, transporting, and changing raw materials into finished products in a sequence of events that is more or less efficient and more or less satisfying to the participants. A manufacturer wishing her business has to produce and sell a product that will "fit." He has to understand what she is doing in behavioristic (her actions), as well as teleological (her goals) terms.

Knowledge of the consumption system, more fully and carefully dissected, can alert the manufacturer to the fact that the housewife is acting in an orderly or purposeful way, according to her likes and dislikes; that there is a series of interrelated steps which require decision making based on knowledge, expectations, standards (as well as ignorance, surprise, and uncertainty); and that the product is used with other products with which it must be compatible.

When the manufacturer knows these systems in detail and keeps his knowledge current, then he is in a position to assess opportunities (perhaps he can meet the standards of a housewife better with a new or modified product) as well as threats (for example, the development of a new washing machine which cleans by vibration). We can also assume that a knowledge of the more important systems will help him to innovate, or at least provide him with a better understanding of the opportunities to do so. Certainly he has a point of reference, since time as well as the actions of competitors no doubt will change the system, thereby providing him with new opportunities.

A seller of industrial equipment or supplies should easily be able to perceive the usefulness of the systems approach to objectives. Manufacturing systems are more precise and logical in their operation than are consumer systems. They center around a flow, so that a manufacturer can predict with a fair degree of accuracy what he must do to "plug into" a given system at a specific point.

REFERENCES

Ackoff, R. L. (1953). *The design of social research.* Chicago: The University of Chicago Press.

Churchman, C. W., Ackoff, R. L., & Arnoff, E. L. (1957). *Introduction to operations research.* New York: John Wiley.

Drucker, P. F. (1965). *The practice of management.* New York: Harper & Brothers.

Fisher, J. (1955). Family life cycle analysis in research on consumer behavior. In L. H. Clark (Ed.), *Consumer behavior: The life cycle and consumer behavior* (Vol. 2, pp. 28-35). New York: New York University Press.

Grander, C. H. (1964). The hierarchy of objectives. *Harvard Business Review, 42,* 63-74.

Martineau, P. (1968). Social classes and spending behavior. *Journal of Marketing, 23,* 121-130.

Miller, D. M., & Starr, M. K. (1960). *Executive decisions and operations research.* Englewood Cliffs, NJ: Prentice Hall.

## Chapter 6

BEYOND MARKETING
The Furthering Concept

Sidney J. Levy

Philip Kotler

As modern marketing grows and evolves, some stock taking may be useful to see the direction of this activity and what it encompasses. As Eugene J. Kelley (1967) points out, "marketing is a discipline which can be researched and analyzed from different viewpoints; it has significant managerial, social, legal, institutional, and interdisciplinary dimensions" (p. 11). Various attempts are being made to view this fact with some generality, to define the structure and province of marketing thought (Bartels, 1968).

As such attempts seek to develop general theories of marketing, they must become increasingly encompassing. The boundaries of marketing continue to grow: marketing executives are required to take account of more and more variables in a field that John Howard has termed "fantastically complex." In addition, the scope of marketing is extended by the widening realization that marketing-like activities are not confined to the traditional economic units that have held them as their function.

This chapter is reprinted from the *California Management Review,* 7(2), Winter 1969, pp. 67-73. © 1969, by The Regents of the University of California. Reprinted by permission of the Regents.

The basic goal of this article is to show that marketing is an activity that is being increasingly redefined to include organizations and relationships that have traditionally been less talked about as part of marketing. A second goal is to indicate that basic nature of marketing when its breadth is recognized.

WHAT ARE THE REASONS FOR THE GROWING SCOPE OF MARKETING?

1. *The selling of intangibles.* Insurance, mutual funds, travel, memberships, new credit arrangements, leasing, consultation, consortium plans of various kinds, and so on, require fresh viewpoints and perspectives on markets and an understanding of consumer groups and their evolving motivations.

2. *International marketing,* with its novel demands for cultural sensitivity. Despite those who claim marketing is basically the same the world over, the international marketer is often forced to adapt to widely different circumstances, governments, laws, customs, and product and media mixes (Donnelly & Ryans, 1969).

3. *The growing role of government,* both as a force affecting companies' marketing actions and as an organization with marketing functions, modifies the commercial nexus of marketing. In obvious and subtle ways, the government as regulator, as seller and customer, constantly changes the character of the market and the marketing methods.

4. *A fast-moving environment* of intense competition, mergers, jolting technology, and social changes creates a strong pressure for product innovation and innovation in the techniques of marketing.

5. *The "tribalizing" effects* of rapid communications give marketplace a quick sense of success or failure. The feeling of shared knowledge induces bandwagon effects, makes possible consumerism, and uses up ideas omnivorously.

6. *The growing incidence of organized social protest* against business firms, city governments, schools, and other institutions increases interest in reviewing the organization's basic purpose, its offerings, and the effectiveness of its communication with the institution's clients.

NEW DEMANDS ON THE MARKETING MANAGER

Marketing management has come a great distance since its early history when its content was fairly narrowly concerned with firing line problems of salesmanship, retailing, distribution, and pricing. Now it is more taken for granted that the marketing managers will have a legitimate and urgent interest in products and their development—although there are still companies where production and technological research units guard themselves jealously from marketing "interference."

As advertising expertise grows, the marketing manager who does not as yet give full and active thought to consumer behavior feels that he should be doing so. The rise of the concept of image (for all its abuses) gives managers a handle for expressing their general communication aims. Marketing research as an entrenched activity and tool adds a powerful intellectual dimension to those marketing managers who have mastered its administration and use.

???????
MARKETING
Using varied means to
effect economic transactions

SELLING
Face-to-face exchange of goods and money

BARTERING
Face-to-face exchange of goods

Figure 6.1. Marketing encompasses selling and bartering

Those who have not yet achieved this competence are coming to aspire to it.

The marketing manager finds his way to conferences, seminars, evening schools, books, and consultants. Where effective progress has been made, he has come a long way from the early marketer who worked close to his intuition and his interpersonal, face-to-face skills. He moves toward being less the genial seller and more the engineer of market forces.

Recognition of the need for an enlarged perspective is reflected in the recent attention directed toward the concept of interface (Berenson, 1968), in which marketing personnel are confronted with their relations to technology, government, and other company departments and social units. The demands for social awareness and company responsibilities in the public sector eventuate in such activities as U.S. Gypsum's housing program and market research aimed at problems of poverty and the ghetto (Lamale, 1968; Sturdivant, 1968).

The marketer is urged to look toward distant horizons. Walt W. Rostow (1966)

has discussed the challenge to efficient marketing institutions posed by developing countries. He points to information diffusion, the growth of consumer goods incentives, the modernization of rural marketing, and other needs in the development of national markets—all calling for a new and significant role for marketing.

This enlargement and vitality in marketing raise the possibility that some new perspectives on the nature of marketing are needed. The persuasive presentation of goods grew beyond the perspective of the traditional sales manager as the need for an advertising manager, research manager, a brand manager, and so on, pointed to the overarching necessity of a marketing manager. Earlier, the selling function, with its exchange of product and dollar, meant an enlargement that went beyond bartering. Possibly, the growth of marketing activities necessitates a reconceptualization at another level. As selling was extended beyond the sales force, perhaps marketing is extended above the marketing staff to replace the question marks in Figure 6.1.

MARKETING IS EVERYONE'S BUSINESS

There is a growing awareness that all organizations (as well as individuals) are confronted with certain basic marketing-like
tasks. Marketing-like responsibility is inherent in all management units. This is
true for hospitals, foundations, unions, associations, libraries, museums, government
agencies, media, professional groups,
schools, churches, politicians, welfare
agencies, and whole countries. From the
individual who has to struggle with what
Erving Goffman has called "the management of impressions in everyday life" to the
nation that is concerned about the quality
reputation of its exports and attracting its
tourist traffic, people and organizations are
confronted with common marketing necessities. It is a truism that "everyone sells
something"—that is, he has wishes or goals
defining how he would like to be received
and responded to, whether as a private
person or as a manager in an organization.
The librarian wants to enhance his institution, to increase the level of book with-
drawals or the use of other library facilities.
The hospital administrator may want to
increase cooperation and the support he
gets, to reduce interference from the
Women's Board, or to gain more contributions from the medical staff. A professional
association wants to improve the status of
its members.

Francis Keppel points to the marketing
problem of interesting youth in new self-
concepts, and he partly poses this as a
communications problem.

> Leadership in society must obviously amount
> to more than just holding corporate office—
> it implies being in the forefront of society,
> not trailing in its wake; and hence it means

the alertness to advance fresh ideas and the
courage to espouse unpopular causes and the
ability to subordinate self-interest to community interest. The problem is to get across to
those not of our generation the fact that in
all walks of American life the same definition
of leadership applies. I wonder whether we
might encourage . . . in this new enterprise
system, the notion of multiple careers . . . for
example, would it be possible for reasonably
normal young men and women to think
about in their lifetime serving in business,
some branch of government, and perhaps in
the academic world, maybe all three at some
point in their working lives? (*AACSB Bulletin,* 1967).

What makes this an extended marketing
problem? Keppel does not want to communicate a new idea just to express himself.
He does not wish to foster an intellectual
investigation for its own sake or to encourage students in autonomous career fulfillment. He wants to promote a new state of
mind, to sell young men and women on the
suitability to themselves of multiple careers. He eventually wants a return, a response of accord, a reorientation. To the
extent that he is successful, the young men
and women will spend their career-building
money differently to become consumers of
multiple careers. To "get across the fact"
and to "encourage the notion" will require
essential marketing techniques of identifying appropriate audience segments, studying their present attitudes, choosing proper
channels of communication, and determining what kinds of messages will foster receptivity to this proposed social good.

The goal of marketing one's career in a
successful manner may elicit cynical or satirical advice, but recently Walter B. Simon
took the time to instruct young psychologists in the prerequisites for acclaim.

Maybe the most important one is to have the "right attitude." This has nothing to do with one's scientific knowledge but concerns "knowing what the score is" and acting accordingly. Currently one of the more important elements is to bring not only credit to the employing organization but also cash. This is sometimes known as "grantsmanship." The importance attached to grants is attested by the lectures, colloquia and brochures devoted to obtaining and renewing them. The more staff or equipment colleges, hospitals or other employing organizations can obtain without paying their own money for it, the better they like it. This has been more true of colleges than of hospitals and clinics but the latter are catching up. With various federal laws appropriating funds for health in general and for mental health in particular, the obtaining of grants will become more rather than less important for mental health institutions (Simon, 1968).

The wish to impress publics (students, governments, professional colleagues, etc.) in order to capture a larger share of the market in grants, esteem, participation, and so on, seems to exempt no one. In a provocative essay James H. Billington (1968), professor of history at Princeton University, complains that liberal education is largely dead, its humanistic heartbeat failed. He blames especially the commercialization, competition, and compartmentalization of higher education, the search for money and public imagery that goes on in what he calls the market-versity. He seems not to recognize that kinds of knowledge (even the humanities which can so ennoble us) have to compete for their audiences. Or perhaps he does recognize this and, on the brink of bankruptcy, decided to do some marketing on behalf of the humanities. Feeling driven to compete in this way, he uses many tactics

that are familiar to marketers. He complains that the competition is too big (like a grocer who cannot withstand the supermarket). He is incensed at the universities' "relentless search for money" and then complains that "a paltry one out of every thousand dollars of government funds given for basic research in 1966 went to the humanities" (p. 34). He is not against the search for money after all, he just wants a larger share. He is contemptuous of the university's concern with its image and its relations with the outside world, but he writes an article in *Life* magazine, presumably hoping to stir a wide public audience. And fearing that the large product benefits he offers for the humanities may not be persuasive enough appeals, he seeks to develop more innocuous and pragmatic-sounding satisfactions, saying that "humanistic scholarship is fun" and that reviving the humanities may provide useful occupational therapy for a disturbed humanity. It is not a bad sales pitch, after all, complete with an illustration of Aristotle.

This example shows that it is misleading to say that the alternatives are to market or not to market; rather, they are to market well or to market poorly. The humanities cannot escape their responsibility to sell the "stockholders (alumni), the management (administration), the professional staff (faculty) and the consumers (students)" on doing better by the humanities, as any product manager may need to do for a product he believes in.

In the various examples described above, the tasks facing Keppel, young psychologists, and Billington have common elements that are recognized in marketing. The basic character of the process is not altered by the fact that we would prefer that all be done in the service of noble goals, that the means of persuasion should fit our ethics, and that the images which audiences inevitably use to guide their response should accord with realities.

To accomplish nonbusiness objectives (or even unbusinesslike ones) requires definition and analysis of the audiences or publics one wants to address and of the content that is to be dealt with to gain the desired response. As in marketing products, the manager (of association, union, society, agency, etc.) has to think about more than immediate sales. He also wants to create customers, to develop loyalties, to build lines, even to change the nature of the audience. What makes all such planning kin is the orientation to communications and persuasion. Marketing moved beyond clerking as it was realized that thought needed to be given to intervening aims and activities, to becoming known, to learning about values of the audience, to determining messages of appropriate symbolic character, and to offering imagery compatible with the buyer's and the seller's aims. Actions thus became more than the retailing face-to-face exchange of coin and product; now they are a long-term teaching process producing new or sustained behaviors grounded in complex perceptions of the price one pays in money, time, devotion, and change of self.

Nonbusiness groups, institutions, and organizations resist the term *marketing* applied to their activities, feeling that it stigmatizes them by implying they value and seek money or success instead of less meretricious goals of social and professional kinds. This means there is a semantic and conceptual problem. The term marketing might be suitable if it were more objectively defined to include the kinds of selling of views and values described here; but emotional reactions work against it. *Public relations* would be a useful general name if it

had not already been preempted to refer to a subcategory of marketing activity that is also frequently derogated.

Perhaps the overall concepts encompassing the determination of audience needs and the generating of audience interest and supportive response to one's aims might use the term *furthering* instead of marketing. Marketing might then remain reserved to those interactions and forms of furthering that have a more specific money fulcrum. Since to *further* means "to help forward (a work, undertaking, cause, etc.); promote, advance, forward," it accurately subsumes marketing, while seeming less invidious for those who want to further less immediately economic aims. An organization could have a Furthering Department or a director of Furthering to candidly face the tasks of advancement and promotion of the cause.

The progression of concepts can be seen in the second box by noting that, with increased complexity, bartering became a special, more limited form subsumed under selling. In turn, the sales function eventually became a special, more limited form subsumed under marketing as the complexity of offering products and services grew. As the breadth of marketing becomes extended into more intangible areas and its relevance for nonbusiness organizations is explored, marketing may be seen to be a special, more limited form of a general process of furthering, as depicted in Figure 6.2.

THE RESPONSIBILITY FOR FURTHERING

In advancing any concept that seeks to be a higher-order generalization of previous concepts, one justifies it by showing that it

FURTHERING

Forwarding, advancing work, undertaking cause

MARKETING

Using varied means to effect economic transactions

SELLING

Face-to-face exchange of goods and money (intentions)

BARTERING

Face-to-face exchange of goods

Figure 6.2. Furthering encompasses marketing, selling, and bartering

illuminates converging areas of management behavior and responsibility not completely articulated at the present time. There are many indications that organizations, both business and nonbusiness, are searching for a new concept that would cover a variety of marketing-like responsibilities. Recently the General Electric Company announced the appointment of Douglas S. Moore as vice president of marketing and public affairs. He "will be responsible for all corporate activities in advertising, public affairs and public relations. He will also handle corporate marketing, including research and personnel development." General Electric has been a leader in organizational innovation and was among the first firms in the early 1950s to articulate and promulgate the marketing concept. This recent appointment indicates a sensing by General Electric of the need for a still higher-level integration of several responsibilities that all serve to further the goals of the company and its groups.

Most business firms have pondered the question of what relation to establish between such activities as corporate marketing, public relations, and public affairs. Corporate marketing typically deals with product-related questions and new areas of business opportunity; public relations deals with maintaining and promoting the overall public image of the corporation; and public affairs, a more recent development, deals with positive programs of the company to serve the general welfare. Although these three responsibilities can be handled in different departments, they tend to become highly intertwined in aims and specific issues facing the company and require some steps toward positive coordination. Public affairs would involve the company in activities that have public relations overtones such as air pollution control, Negro training programs, and urban redevelopment; public relations would develop campaigns to promote the public image of the company which will affect the sale of its products and thus concern the marketing department; and corporate marketing might develop product marketing philosophies, such as hard sell, product obsolescence, or premium pricing which also affect public relations. In hundreds of ways, these activities touch each other and may call for conflict resolution. The usual solution is to coordinate by committee; General Electric signals a newer solution where the three activities are coordinated as the responsibility of one man.

Nonbusiness organizations also show a growing sense of the interrelation of many marketing-like responsibilities. The American Chemical Society is a professional society of chemists and is organized in several divisions. One of its major divisions is the Division of Public, Professional, and Member Relations. This division is a recognition of the multiple groups being served by the Society and the need for coordinating the interests of these groups.

A similar need is beginning to dawn in American universities, stimulated largely by the recent campus troubles and their reverberations among students, faculty, alumni, and the general public. A typical university has several officers pursuing and promoting the interest of different university groups: vice presidents in charge of faculty, student affairs, development (alumni affairs and fund raising), and public relations. Each one is in charge of furthering (and thereby defining) the interests of the university in a particular way, but no one is in charge of furthering them in general. As a result, on one of the campuses during a recent student building takeover, the vice presidents took quite different positions on what should be done to resolve flare-up. The positions included calling in the police (development and alumni affairs), sitting it out (faculty affairs), and making several concessions in recognition of "just" grievances (student affairs). The officers interpreted the furthering of the university's interests in different ways, each reflecting his own involvement in a local

portion of the total university. There was no officer responsible for the general furthering of the university who could advise a sound course of action based on his expertise on students, faculty, alumni, and public. This job falls de facto to the president and board of trustees. Perhaps this defines the basic nature of the job of company president: he is the furthering officer. But as a philosophy and a set of skills these competencies may not exist expertly in the person of the president. The expertise of furthering (which is a generalization of marketing expertise) might better be located one step below the president, just as other expertises such as finance, production, and personnel are located one step below.

THE EXPERTISE OF FURTHERING

To define furthering as an expertise, it is necessary to differentiate it from other expertises. We start with the premise that all management positions, regardless of their names, are multifaceted in the activities that have to be performed by the position holder. The sales manager, for example, manages men, money, equipment, goods, and information. This means he ties into systems that go under the name of personnel, finance, production, selling, and accounting. At the same time, the sales manager has a primary charge, the development and cultivation of customers, which defines his needed competence. In the same vein, the furthering officer has a primary charge that will define his needed competencies. His primary charge is to mesh the organization's aims with those of the groups it serves in a way that will advance both. His primary orientation is toward groups that the organization relates to and toward skills in promoting either the common aims of the organization and its groups or their exchange of values.

Every organization, no matter whether it is a business organization, service organization (orphanage, foundation, university), protective organization (labor union, cooperative), or primary organization (clubs, churches, lodges), deals with a number of groups that it affects and that vitally affect it. The management group of the organization has to deal with two basic types of groups—suppliers and consumers. Suppliers consist of all those persons and organizations that furnish the goods and services required by the management group to effectively pursue the organization's goals. Included as suppliers are the employees, banks, advertising agencies, and vendors of various kinds. The selection and management of these suppliers is a major responsibility area for the organization and will be called the supply management function.

The consumers of the organization represent those persons and organizations who are affected by the product of the organization. Here four basic groups can be distinguished:

1. *Clients.* Those who immediately consume the organization's product. The clients of a business firm are its buyers and potential buyers: of a service organization, those receiving the service, such as the needy (Salvation Army) or the sick (County Hospital); and of a protective or a primary organization, the members themselves.

2. *Trustees.* Those who are vested with the legal authority and responsibility for the organization, oversee the management, and enjoy a variety of benefits from the product. This group goes by the name of board of directors or trustees and must be dealt with imaginatively by the management group.

3. *Active publics.* Those who take a specific interest in the organization. For a business firm, the active publics include consumer rating groups, governmental agencies, and pressure groups of various kinds. For a university, the active publics include alumni and friends of the university, foundations, city fathers, and so on.

4. *The general public.* This group, which potentially affects every organization, consists of the people who are potential audience for the organization, who develop images of the organization, a climate of public opinion, and attitudes toward it that might affect its product in some way.

When we talk about the furthering function of organizations, we are talking about the management of the organization's four consuming groups: clients, trustees, active publics, and general public. Effective management of these groups rests on three basic skills: scanning, planning, and communicating.

1. *Scanning is vital to any organization* if it is to remain sensitive and responsive to the groups it serves. Military and business organizations are probably the most advanced in the gathering of continuous intelligence about events in the environment that affect them. Business firms annually spend hundreds of millions of dollars each year on marketing research and intelligence to keep management informed of customer attitudes and purchasing behavior, competitive maneuvers, new technology, and legal developments. Other types of organizations have generally done less to formalize the intelligence operation. We continue to hear of universities caught by surprise by student rebellion, city governments falling out of touch with minority groups who revolt out of frustration against an unresponsive government machinery,

state political organizations that suddenly find themselves challenged by party members when they ignore primary preferences, and so on. An intelligence operation is essential for those organizations that wish to be responsive to and responsible for their consumers' interests.

2. *Furthering also calls for planning skills.* For example, the American Chemical Society set the following goal as a result of a study conducted for them by Social Research, Inc., a behavioral marketing research company: "To help improve professional status, a majority of the members favor such Society activities as seeking greater publicity for chemists and chemical engineering, encouraging discussion of professional topics among college students" ("What ACS Members Think," 1969). Given these goals, the Society must develop annual and long-run plans that will promote these goals. In a similar vein, church groups must develop plans for membership drives, hospitals must develop plans for raising money among active donors, and nations must develop plans for attracting tourists and favorable public opinion.

3. *The third, and perhaps central skill involved in furthering is that of communicating.* It is clear from what has been said that everything about an organization talks—its products, leaders, employees, innovation, social commitment, letterhead,

physical plant, and so on. All of these have an actual or potential influence on various consumer groups. Yet the typical organization lacks anyone concerned with the totality of the impact of the company's actions on all of its consumers. The seeds of this skill are in the marketing department and the public relations department but unfortunately are too often without the breadth that takes the whole organization into account.

CONCLUSION

It is our contention that furthering is a basic management function carried out in some fashion by all organizations. It is rooted in the work done by the marketing department, public relations, public affairs, the president's office, and so on. Too often, however, no one formally pays attention to the conflicts and tradeoffs among these activities. We propose the concept of furthering as a higher order generalization of the older concepts. Its recognition will take time, much as did the concept of planning responsibility where few firms saw the need for a planning department since every management group planned. This is the main point about the need for a furthering concept: everyone in the organization is seeking to further the goals of the organization and its consumer groups, but no one has the overall responsibility.

REFERENCES

AACSB Bulletin, 3, 26 (1967).

Bartels, R. (1968). The general theory of marketing. *Journal of Marketing, 32*(1), 29-33.

Berenson, C. (1968). The r&d: marketing interface—a general analogue model for technology diffusion. *Journal of Marketing, 32*(2), 8-15.

Billington, J. H. (1968). The humanistic heartbeat has failed. *Life, 60*(21), 32-35.

Donnelly, J. H., Jr., & Ryans, J. K., Jr. (1969). Standardized global advertising, a call as yet unanswered. *Journal of Marketing, 33*(2), 57-60.

Kelley, E. J. (1967). From the editor. *Journal of Marketing, 31,* 11.

Lamale, H. H. (1968). How the poor spend their money. In H. P. Miller (Ed.), *Poverty American style* (pp. 150-161). Belmont, CA: Wadsworth.

Rostow, W. W. (1966). The concept of a national market and its economic growth implications. In P. D. Benett (Ed.), *Marketing and economic development* (pp. 11-20). Chicago: American Marketing Association.

Simon, W. B. (1968). What every young psychologist should know. *Journal of Social Issues, 24,* 21, 115.

Sturdivant, F. D. (1968). Better deal for ghetto shoppers. *Harvard Business Review, 56*(2), 130-139.

What ACS members think about professional status. (1969). *Chemical and Engineering News, 39,* 78.

## Chapter 7

DEMARKETING, YES, DEMARKETING

Philip Kotler

Sidney J. Levy

The popular conception of marketing is that it deals with the problem of furthering or expanding demand. Whether one takes the traditional view that marketing is finding customers for existing products, or the more recent view that it is developing new products for unmet consumer wants, it is seen as the technology of bringing about increases in company sales and profits. The marketer is a professional builder of sales volume who makes deft use of product, price, place, and promotion variables.

This is a narrow concept of marketing and the potential applications of marketing technology. It is a concept that arose in a period of goods oversupply. It also reflects a widespread tendency to define marketing in terms of what marketers ought to do rather than to analyze what they actually do under various circumstances. Much marketing literature approaches marketing with exhortations: define your objectives, know your market, meet consumer needs, and so on, all underlaid with the implied

This chapter was first published in the *Harvard Business Review,* November-December 1971, pp. 74-80. Copyright © 1971 by President and Fellows of Harvard College. Reprinted by permission of *Harvard Business Review.*

promise that then you will sell more. As a result, marketing has been too closely identified with the problem of buyer markets.

But suppose that an economy were suddenly plunged into a state of widespread product shortages. What would be the role of marketing management then? Would it evolve into a minor business function? Would it disappear altogether? Or would it continue to perform critical functions for the company? Most production, financial, and marketing men who are asked this question opine that marketing's role would be greatly reduced in a scarcity economy. They see marketing as a "fair weather" profession, one that seems to be important chiefly in periods of excess supply. In this respect marketing differs from manufacturing, accounting, and other business functions that are critical in all stages of the economy.

But this is an untenable position. True, if marketers are narrowly seen as responsible primarily for finding customers or increasing demand, then they would seem superfluous when demand becomes unmanageably great. However, in practice excess demand is as much a marketing problem as excess supply. A company faces a host of difficult customer-mix and marketing-mix decisions in periods of excess demand. It has to find ways of reducing total demand or certain classes of demand to the level of supply without damaging long-run customer relations.

Our name for this kind of activity is *creative demarketing*. More formally, we define demarketing as that aspect of marketing that deals with discouraging customers in general or a certain class of customers in particular on either a temporary or permanent basis. The tasks of coping with shrinking demand or deliberately discouraging segments of the market call for the use of all the major marketing tools. As such, marketing thinking is just as relevant to the problem of reducing demand as it is to the problem of increasing demand.

Once this view is appreciated, the true character of marketing's mission becomes clearer. Marketing is the business function concerned with controlling the level and composition of demand facing the company. Its short-run task is to adjust the demand to a level and composition that the company can, or wishes to, handle. Its long-run task is to adjust the demand to a level and composition that meets the company's long-run objectives. In this article we will describe three different types of demarketing:

1. General demarketing, which is required when a company wants to shrink the level of total demand

2. Selective demarketing, which is required when a company wants to discourage the demand coming from certain customer classes

3. Ostensible demarketing, which involves the appearance of trying to discourage demand as a device for actually increasing it

(A fourth type, unintentional demarketing, is also important but does not need to be considered here. So many abortive efforts to increase demand, resulting actually in driving customers away, have been reported in recent years that the dreary tale does not need to be told again.)

GENERAL DEMARKETING

At times excess demand can characterize a whole economy and at other times, only a limited number of firms. Even in the absence of a general scarcity economy, there are always individual sellers who are facing excess demand for one or more of their products. While most other companies may be looking for customers, these sellers face the need to discourage customers, at least temporarily. Their marketing stance may become one of indifference or of arrogance. In a responsible organization, however, attempts are made to act in a framework that respects the marketing concept, that is, the long-run aim of developing satisfied customers.

It is possible to distinguish at least three different situations that may give rise to general demarketing by a company. Let us consider each situation briefly.

Temporary Shortages

Many companies have the periodic fortune—or misfortune—of finding particular products in excess demand. Management underestimated demand, overestimated production, or did both. The following cases illustrate:

Eastman Kodak introduced its Instamatic camera in the early 1960s and found itself facing runaway demand. A few years passed before Kodak achieved enough capacity to handle demand.

Anheuser-Busch underestimated the rate of growth in demand for its popular Budweiser beer and found itself in the late 1960s having to ration supplies to its better dealers and markets while it was making a crash effort to expand its plants.

Savings and loan associations in 1970-1971 faced an oversupply of savings relative to

their ability to invest the funds and sought means to discourage the savings customers. They were willing to encourage small accounts but refused large depositors.

These cases reflect temporary shortages of products that are corrected as the company manages to bring about sufficient plant expansion. In the interim, management must carry out two distinct tasks. The first is that of demand containment, that is, curbing the growth of total demand. The second is that of product allocation, that is, deciding which dealers and customers will receive the available product.

Steps to Encourage Deconsuming

Demand containment is the attempt to stabilize or reduce demand so that the product shortage is not further aggravated. This is largely accomplished by using the classic marketing instruments in reverse. To bring about deconsuming, management can:

Curtail advertising expenditures for the product, modifying the content of the messages

Reduce sales promotion expenditures, investing less in trade exhibits, point-of-purchase displays, catalog space, and so on

Cut back salesmen's selling time on the product and their entertainment budgets, asking them to concentrate on other products, spend more time in service and intelligence work ("No Sales Force," 1970), and learn to say no in a way that customers find acceptable

Increase the price and other conditions of sale to the advantage of the marketing company (this may include eliminating freight allowances, trade discounts, and so on)

Add to the time and expense necessary for the buyer to procure the product or service—what might be called his "effort and psychological costs"—as a means of discouraging demand

Reduce product quality or content, either to encourage deconsuming or to make more of the product available and thus demarket at a slower rate

Curtail the number of distribution outlets, using the product shortage as an opportunity to eliminate undesirable dealers and/or customers

Marketing management does not usually take these steps in isolation but rather as part of a demarketing mix. It should make judicious estimates of the elasticity and cross-elasticities of the different instruments, that is, their impact on demand when employed with varying intensity, both individually and in combination. Otherwise, the demarketing program may overinhibit demand, and the company may find itself facing a shortage of customers.

Alternatives in Allocation

While these demarketing steps are being undertaken, marketing management should also develop a sound plan of product allocation. It must decide how, to whom, and in what quantities to allocate existing supply. There are four plausible solutions to this problem:

1. Management can allocate the product on a *first-come, first-served basis.* This is a standard method regarded as fair by almost everyone except new customers. Dealers and customers get their stock in the order of their ordering.

2. Management can allocate the product on a *proportional demand* basis. This means determining that the company can satisfy x% of total demand and then supplying each customer with x% of its original order level. This is also held to be a fair solution.

3. A company can allocate supply on a *favored customer* basis. It determines its most valuable customers and satisfies their demand levels completely; the remaining customers may receive some fraction of their original order levels, with the rest being back-ordered. This is held to be a discriminatory solution, even if an understandable one.

4. A company can allocate products on a *highest bid* basis. The supply goes to those customers who offer the highest premium for early delivery. While many people consider this an exploitative strategy, economists typically argue that it makes the most sense since the product flows to those who presumably need it most.

Policies for allocating supply should be made by top management with marketing executives playing a central role in advising what impact the alternatives would have on long-run customer relations. If it assumes that the shortage is temporary, management should estimate customer feeling toward the company in the post-shortage period when the demand-supply balance is reestablished. Each general solution involves some amount and distribution of customer disappointment. If the company seeks to maximize its long-run, rather than short-run profits, it should choose solutions that minimize the total disappointment of customers during the period in question.

Chronic Overpopularity

There are some real, although perhaps rare, situations where an organization is faced with chronic overpopularity, and it wishes for one reason or another to bring demand down to a permanently lower level. Two situations can be distinguished:

In the first, the product's present popularity may be seen as posing a serious threat to the long-run quality of the product. For example, the island of Bali in the South Pacific has long been a tourist's dream. In recent years, it has attracted a larger number of tourists than can be handled comfortably with its facilities. The island is in danger of becoming overcrowded and spoiled. If tourism goes unchecked, Bali faces the same fate as Hawaii, which has lost its pristine appeal because of teeming crowds and soaring prices. The authorities in Bali are aware of this danger and are considering measures to reduce demand. Their demarketing strategy is to reduce the island's attractiveness to middle-income tourists while maintaining or increasing its appeal to high-income tourists. They prefer fewer higher-spending tourists to a larger number of lower-spending tourists (in contrast to the savings and loan example cited earlier). To accomplish this, they will build luxury hotels and restaurants, place their advertising in media reaching the rich, and build a distinct image of catering to the affluent class.

Also because of fear that the area's natural beauty will be spoiled by congestion, officials in the state of Oregon are demarketing to prospective settlers. But the state does promote tourist trade; the governor encourages people to visit so long as they do not stay.

In the second situation, overpopularity is a problem because management does not want the strain of handling all of the demand. For example, there is an exceptionally fine restaurant in London that can seat only 30 persons. Word-of-mouth advertising has been so good that the restaurant is fully booked for months in advance. Nevertheless, tourists without reservations crowd around in the hope of cancellations. They add noise and detract from the intended atmosphere of leisurely dining.

The two men who run the restaurant enjoyed their role as managers of a small, intimate restaurant noted for its fine cuisine. For this reason, they decided on demarketing. They added a doorman who discouraged people from waiting for cancellations and from phoning about the availability of reservations. They also raised the prices. They were able to do all this without creating increased demand as a result of scarce resources, the reverse phenomenon to be described later in our discussion of ostensible demarketing.

Product Elimination

Deft demarketing is called for when a company would like to eliminate a product or service that some loyal customers still require or desire, for example, a superseded model. Demand at any point in time can be considered as temporarily excessive in relation to the level at which the company prefers to see demand. So as not to create customer ill will, the company's task is not only to reduce production and inventory as soon as possible but also to reduce demand. Among the demarketing strategies available are: informing the customer as to why the product is being dropped, offering partial or full compensation to important customers who are hurt by the disappearance of the product, and maintaining a minimal stock of the product to satisfy the hard-core customers. These strategies are warranted where the same customers purchase other items from the company and their goodwill must be maintained.

SELECTIVE DEMARKETING

Often an organization does not wish to contain or reduce the level of total demand but rather the demand coming from specific segments of the market. These segments or customer classes may be considered relatively unprofitable in themselves or undesirable in terms of their impact on other segments of demand. The company is not free to refuse sales outright, either as a matter of law or of public opinion. So it searches for other means to discourage demand from the unwanted customers. To illustrate:

> A luxury hotel catering to middle-aged, conservative people has recently attracted rich hippies who come wearing long hair and odd clothes and who sit on the lobby floor making a good deal of noise. This has turned off the hotel's main clientele, and the management must rapidly take steps to discourage further reservations by hippies.

An automobile manufacturer of a luxury car purchased mainly by affluent whites as a status symbol has discovered that an increasing number of sales are going to newly rich members of the black community. As a result, affluent whites are switching to another well-known luxury automobile. The automobile manufacturer has to decide whether to let the market take its natural course, attempt to market to both groups, or to demarket to the new customer class.

> A small appliance manufacturer wants to keep one of its popular brands in selective distribution, but it receives continuous pressure from marginal channels that want to carry the product. Not wanting to put his product through these channels, the manufacturer faces the problem of depriving them without alienating them.

The common problem faced by management in such cases is that the main clientele is threatened by the emergence of a new clientele. The organization does not find it possible to maintain both clienteles simultaneously. Gresham's Law seems to operate: the cheaper segment appears to drive the dearer segment from circulation. For one reason or another, the organization expects a higher risk and/or lower return (whether financial or psychological) from the new clientele. The alternative is to demarket selectively to the new clientele.

Methods and Implications

How is this done? When a company markets to one segment of the public, it may discourage other prospects who are unresponsive to, or alienated by, the appeals employed. For instance, advertising which plays up the joys of conventional home life demarkets the product to singles. In this sense, demarketing is the negative of marketing.

Selective demarketing refers to (a) the deliberate choice of segments that are to be avoided and (b) the specific means chosen to ward off the undesired customers. Management decreases the benefit/cost ratio which the wanted segment receives from patronage.

In examples like those cited, the marketer is typically not free to charge a discriminatory price to the undesirable segment. The demarketing mix has to be built out of other elements. Activities like these may be pursued:

The company discourages hope for product availability. The hotel fears it will be out of rooms, or the automobile company indicates that the customer must wait a long time for delivery.

The salesmen do not make calls on small organizations.

The company provides poor service to the undesirable segment. The undesirable customers receive poorer hotel rooms, slower service, insolent treatment—all suggesting that their business is not welcome.

The company makes it harder for the undesirable segment to find product channels or information. Auto companies are careful to locate dealerships away from changing neighborhoods, and hotels are selective about where they advertise and who receives their information.

To describe these steps is not to approve them. They are cited as familiar examples of what companies may do to discourage demand from certain classes of customers.

The steps may raise thorny issues in social ethics. On the one hand, it seems understandable that an organization should have the right to choose or protect its major clientele, especially if its long-run profits are at stake. On the other hand, it is unjust to discriminate against buyers who have long hair, black skin, lower status, or small orders. The injustice seems especially intolerable if the discriminated buyers are left without equivalent alternatives. In that case demarketing becomes entwined with the social, legal, and political problems relating to unacceptable forms of discriminatory demarketing.

OSTENSIBLE DEMARKETING

Sometimes an establishment goes through the motions of demarketing in the hope of achieving the opposite effect. By creating the appearance of not wanting more customers, it hopes to make the product even more desirable to people. The marketer works on the principle that people want what may be hard to get and may even masochistically "enjoy" being neglected by the seller. Consider the following possibilities:

An artist operates a small gallery in which hang some of his own and other artists' paintings. He works in the back room and seems to resent the intrusion of would-be buyers. A buyer has to wait for the artist to emerge from the back room, and even then is treated brusquely. But the sales are good; many persons enjoy being mistreated and buying on the artist's terms.

An antique dealer keeps his store in relative disarray with very good objets d'art buried in dust-laden clusters of junk. Patrons often comment that he would attract more customers by cleaning up his store, eliminating the junk, and thus achieve better presentation. But they may be mistaken. The owner feels he attracts more customers this way, reasoning that people love a bargain and dream of discovering a Rembrandt buried among the ancient cracking canvases of third-rate painters.

A department store arranges very carefully a stock of new blouses on a counter to make sure all sizes are represented. Then, a few minutes before the first customers arrive, the sales personnel pull the blouses out of their boxes and mix them about in chaotic fashion, ostensibly making the goods less attractive. But the customers spot the blouses and are attracted in large crowds to the counter in search of a bargain.

The managers of a rock concert advertise it on the radio in a discouraging way, saying the crowds will be too large and that seats are practically sold out. The hidden intention is to increase the number of attendees by attracting those who hate to feel left out.

QUESTIONS FOR STUDY

Marketers have dealt with the problem of increasing demand for so long that they have overlooked a host of situations where the problem is to reduce demand or cope with inability to meet it. Whether the task is to reduce the level of total demand without alienating loyal customers, to discourage the demand coming from certain segments of the market that are either unprofitable or possess the potential of injuring loyal buyers, or to appear to want

less demand for the sake of actually increasing it, the need is for creative demarketing.

It is easy to assume that demarketing is only marketing in reverse—product, price, place, and promotion policies can also be used to discourage demand. Yet the optimal demarketing mix is not obvious. First, there is the danger of overreducing short-run demand, which can be more serious than increasing it too much. Second, there is the danger of doing irreparable harm to long-run demand through indelicate handling of current customers. This means that there is a need for careful research into the phenomenon of demarketing. Some important issues are:

1. When do companies face demarketing situations? What are the major types of situations and how extensive are they?

2. What demarketing policies and instruments are commonly used by these companies? How do companies reduce total demand and selective demand? How do they allocate scarce products?

3. What are optimal marketing policies for different demarketing situations?

4. What role is played by marketing management in advising or deciding on appropriate demarketing policies? Does top management recognize that specialized marketing skill is as essential in demarketing situations as in marketing situations?

5. What are the public policy issues and needs with respect to company demarketing practices, especially discriminatory demarketing?

Research into these questions should help clarify the important and neglected phenomenon of demarketing. Of equal importance, it should help establish a more objective and realistic conception of marketing. Marketing's task is not blindly to engineer increases in demand; that view came about because marketing developed during a period of economic growth and surpluses, and it is too casually related to "hard sell" tactics and pervasive advertising. Rather, marketing functions to regulate the level and shape of demand so that it

conforms to the organization's current supply situation and to its long-run objectives.

When this view is accepted, it is not necessary to contrast marketing and demarketing. We have used the term demarketing to dramatize semantically a neglected phenomenon, but this would not be necessary if all marketing situations were recognized. Marketing inevitably has a role to play in the face of excess demand: the challenge is to demarket thoughtfully and skillfully.

REFERENCE

No sales force for sale. (1970). *Sales Management, 43.*

Chapter 8

MARKETING AND AESTHETICS

Sidney J. Levy
John Czepiel

Marketing managers give aesthetics a lot of practical attention because they frequently make decisions about products, packages, logos, and advertisements and inevitably take account of form, color, sound, composition, and other sensory elements. Nevertheless, outside of specialized circles, the aesthetic motive as a matter for deliberate consideration has been relatively neglected. Managers' decisions are often made on grounds of personal preference alone, or on clichéd beliefs about what people will like. As a field of study, aesthetics has been left largely to artists, teachers of humanities, critics, and some psychologists. Nevertheless, the relationship between business and aesthetics is growing vigorously on several fronts.

THE UTILITARIAN OUTLOOK

In its short history, from the early 1900s when it was separated out and defined as a business function, marketing has successively shifted its focus and has grown in

This chapter first appeared in R. C. Curhan (Ed.), *Combined Proceedings, Series 36, 1974,* pp. 386-391. Reprinted by permission of the American Marketing Association.

subject matter. Its early focus was on the product and its distribution. The main problem was to make things that worked or served their function, to make enough of them, and to get them shipped out. Essential topics were of the production line, pricing, transportation and delivery difficulties, and means of motivating salesmen to do a more effective job. The pragmatism of the times was summed up in the famous Ford dictum concerning autos: one could get any color desired as long as it was black. There was a general marketing aesthetic, that is, but it brooked no exceptions, choices, or self-expression. (In fact, of course, there were white cars and flamboyantly decorated jalopies, as the determined aesthetic of the rich and young will emerge.)

When concern with such utilities as performance, price, and place is central, it is natural for marketers to think most about physical, structural features of products, their numbers and schedules, and to pursue the values of more and faster. Primary goals are efficiency and profit. Of course, the aesthetics of past times were also operating, each moment having its style, its fashions, its looks, its ideas of beauty, its preferred colors; and some sought for comfort and a brighter spirit. But the force of aesthetic motivation was hardly part of deliberate marketing planning in product design, appeals to customers, or the marketer's conception of his responsibility to the environment.

THE SOCIAL PSYCHOLOGICAL PHASE

The shift to a higher productive gear during World War II, and the resulting buyers' market after the war, led to an upsurge of competition, with new brands rising to challenge the dominating old mainstays. The marketing concept that evolved, with its great emphasis on learning about the customer and seeking to meet his needs, brought forward the need to communicate with him. In the area of consumer goods, the growth of large modern self-service retailing units increasingly removed the customer from the immediate influence of sellers. As a consequence the role of intervening mass media communications came into its own.

Pressure built up to understand customers in their varied segmentations, to research their views, interpret their motives, analyze their perceptions. Recognizing a new market, the behavioral sciences offered their wares, sending personnel, research techniques, and ideas. In 1955, the concept of brand image was introduced (Gardner & Levy, 1955) and widely seized upon because it aptly summed up the idea that consumers buy a brand for the meanings it has, not only for its physical attributes. Consumer behavior became a new field of study. Although the new era of behavioral study added richness to marketing analysis, the aesthetic portion of the psyche continued in relative neglect. The marketing motives that were given special attention were those of blatant sexual aims, status striving, and fear, along with the usual appeals to self-esteem and sociability.

THE BEAUTIFUL AND THE UGLY

While the marriage of traditional or technical marketing with the behavioral sciences was going on, there was a certain flirting with the humanities along the way. Art directors and copywriters with English majors created the content of advertising; industrial design became a recognized field dominated by the names of Walter Teague, Raymond Loewy, Henry Dreyfuss, and Walter Gropius; and some

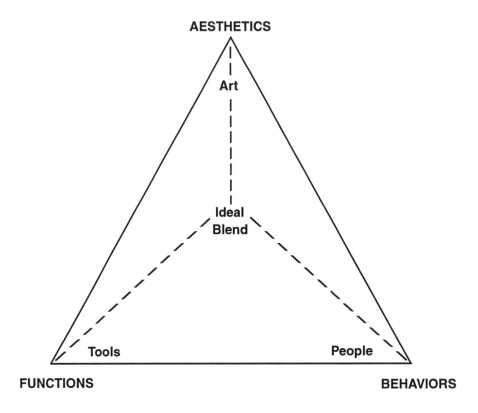

Figure 8.1. The functional-psychosocial-aesthetic pyramid

definite, if sporadic attention was given to the role of fashion as an economic and marketing force (Carruth, 1967; Clerget, 1914; Robinson, 1958b).

As managers become more explicitly aware of the importance of aesthetics, it seems timely to discuss the nature of the aesthetic motive and its pervasiveness. Such discussion can encourage use of a marketing model that vigorously joins aesthetic values to the pragmatic utilitarian values and psychosocial values that have predominated in marketing thinking. Figure 8.1 suggests this model as a simple pyramid; objects and services are judged for the extent to which they represent the interacting values of each category.

For example, a plain furnace or an unadorned truck may in some eyes have the inherent beauty of "form that follows function" but is more apt to be regarded as sheerly practical and at the negative end of an aesthetic continuum or social dimension (in the basement or garage, not the living room). Similarly, paintings need merely exist for aesthetic enjoyment and are not normally thought to perform efficiently, even if some are used to cover wall cracks (presumably to serve an aesthetic aim, anyway) or to attest to one's social stature. Social and psychological goals are also mixed in the marketing of many products and services but are pronounced in their behavioral meanings, often at a sacrifice of practical function or the consumer's idea of beauty. Conforming by wearing uncomfortable or even precarious shoes or being a reluctant "social drinker" are examples.

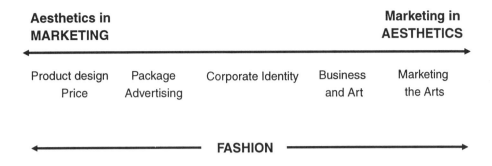

Figure 8.2. The aesthetic continuum

At the apex of the model might be located ideal objects or services that are optimal blends of function, aesthetics, and psychosocial meaning. But this seems to interfere with the purity of experience. Art that is useful is crass, and social considerations make for inefficiency; the tendency is to polarize toward pure Love, Beauty, or the Perpetual Motion machine.

PERVASIVE AESTHETICS

Aesthetics is usually related to the field of the fine arts, and many subtle distinctions have been made in the struggle to define the various degrees of art. These will not be wrestled with here. Rather, aesthetics is taken to refer to the entire realm in which people feel interest, pleasure, and emotion at the presence or absence of beauty. Aesthetic feelings can be stirred by many varieties of experience—pictures, words, music, colors, shapes, movements. Obviously, the elements for aesthetic reaction are always present; aesthetics is pervasive.

Although aesthetics is pervasive, it does not always prevail. Among human needs and motives there appears a hierarchy, as Maslow (1954) and others have discussed. Subsistence, security, and other psychologi-cal and social needs seem to take precedence, requiring adequate satisfaction before one can progress to the higher levels of self-actualization and aesthetic need. Thus, aesthetic motivation has been associated with leisure, and concern with the quantity of life tends to come before concern with the quality of life. It seems apparent that this hierarchy operates generally, although among some individuals and groups aesthetic activities occur despite great poverty and insecurity. The latter phenomenon is noticeable enough that the contrary hypothesis also exists, that deprivation and suffering are essential to artistic creativity. Perhaps both theories are correct (if too simple) with deprivation being conducive to the originality and individuality of the producer of art, while leisure and affluence make for its consumption—with exceptions galore.

How the aesthetic issue is interwoven with marketing problems depends on the people involved, the nature of their motives, and the product or services they are dealing with. A continuum (Figure 8.2) can be drawn to highlight the character of different situations, ranging from a focus on the role of *aesthetics in marketing* to a focus on the role of *marketing in aesthetics*.

Figure 8.3. A meat grinder designed for sheer utility

AESTHETICS IN MARKETING

The problem of attention to aesthetics in marketing is boldly posed by the need for product design. From the great diversity of products, industries, and the mixed pace of historical development, a sequence of steps may be adduced.

1. The product's design is dictated by its function.

2. The product is decorated for aesthetic stimulation.

3. The design is reshaped to fit some aesthetic effect.

4. The design is aimed at a psychology of market segmentation.

5. The product design becomes (or claims to be) a work of art.

Initially, a product is likely to take the form and color dictated by its function and basic materials. Whatever aesthetic the object has is governed less by the intention of the creator than by the appeal it happens to find in the eyes of its contemporaries. Apart from interest in the purpose of the invention, its very novelty could be regarded as an aesthetic element that will attract customers. Figure 8.3 shows an example of a product that struggled mainly to come into bare being in order to grind meat, much less to be concerned with how it looked (regardless of its 1830s' charm in modern eyes).

Many modern kitchen utensils still stick close to their basic necessity with a kind of "minimal design."

A second step is shown in Figure 8.4 where the basic design of a coffee grinder has been modified slightly with the addition of hatching and floral curves in the cast iron top. A general aesthetic aim has been introduced; "prettying" the top has no effect on the performance of the grinder. A frequent early step toward deliberate aes-

Figure 8.4. A touch of aesthetics added

Figure 8.5. Design may override function

thetics is the addition of color, as in the case of a truck interior.

Colored telephones became widely available not many years ago, and most people are probably still unaware of the growing vogue for colored condoms. Japanese condoms have been sold in a wide range of colors for several years; pale green and black do well in Sweden.

The dicing knife shown in Figure 8.5 has been reshaped and cased with marked attention to the product's visual characteristics to fit a designer's aesthetic. It is hardly recognizable as a knife. Not infrequently, the importance given to beauty can even override efficiency of performance. Streamlined cars with bumpers that do not protect the chassis, or with opera windows providing inadequate visibility, are examples. These elements of decoration or design may mainly reflect the designer's urge to express himself, or they may aim at making the product more generally attractive.

As awareness grows that taste varies among groups in the population, aesthetics becomes a basis for deliberately segmenting the market. For example, study shows that upper middle class people tend to prefer the qualities of angularity and texture, compared to the greater preference by people of lower status for the opposite qualities of smoothness and curves. Color preferences are consistently related to various psychological and personality traits: for example, blue to conservatism, yellow to austerity, red to aggressiveness. Adding color may not affect the function of the product itself, but it can alter the user. A pink telephone may help a woman feel more feminine in her boudoir, and colored condoms may improve the user's performance, although there is no firm evidence yet. What used to be called "white goods" has lost out to the highly decorated bed linen that is mainly appreciated when people are asleep. In modern marketing, where the elements are complexly and richly interwoven, it is a challenge to design, interpret, and research the relative forces of utility, psychosocial symbolism, and aesthetic appeal.

In moving from bare function through varying degrees of integration of artistic design, aesthetic self-consciousness increases until pride in the beauty of the object may take precedence over its utility. It is no longer a practical object that happens also to look good, but it has become an art object that happens also to work.

Note, for example the copy in Figure 8.6 where Braun makes this idea explicit: "The Braun museum piece. The Braun Table Lighter is in the permanent collection of the New York Museum of Modern Art. No wonder. It is magnificent sculpture that works." Similarly, Olivetti typewriters and Volkswagen cars are on exhibition as objects of sheer beauty (Figures 8.7 and 8.8).

Antiques are often utilitarian products that have become transformed into art objects, traversing the product continuum described above. The 1830s meat grinder is now worthy of an honored place on a pedestal in the living room, never again to touch hamburger.

THE CURRENT OF FASHION

Concern with the contemporary and imminent preferences for product aesthetics means a focus on fashion—not just in clothing, but in all spheres. Basic product function has fashion, as even technology comes into vogue in different societies at different times. Changes in taste are often dramatic, rapid phenomena, especially in modern times, that tantalize the marketer because he is drawn to participate in the success of a fashion and to avoid the threat of being left behind or abandoned by it. A constant challenge is to analyze where fashion comes from. Theories of fashion are profuse. Herbert Blumer (1968) has pointed to several of them that he thinks are basically erroneous.

1. Fashion is not restricted to costume and adornment, nor to any narrow human sphere.

2. Fashion is not an inconsequential minor influence shaping social life.

Figure 8.6. The product shown as beautiful to own

The olivetti collection

Figure 8.7. Typewriters as works of art

3. Fashion is not merely an abnormal, irrational, bizarre affair.

4. Fashion is not merely the expression of such psychological aims as escape from existing social forms, exhibitionism, or daring.

5. Fashion is not something that originates in the elite's distinction and prestige, with imitation from below.

While elements of these ideas are readily visible, Blumer believes they all are part of a basic fashion process of a somewhat mysterious sort. In it the designers, the alleged tastemakers, are seen as immersing themselves in the central expression of modernity, developing a common body of sensitivities. They "embody within themselves some effective anticipation of what the fashion-consuming public is going to adopt and to this extent they are operating as a surrogate, a kind of unwitting agent of the public." It is basically a matter of the leaders discerning where the followers are going. The situation is complicated because in its working out there is constant competition among available and potential choices; and locating the process too strongly in "the public" may underestimate the force of specific influences or individuals. Nevertheless, the key to the process is interaction, and the more the manager immerses himself in the currents of events at various cultural levels, the better he can sense their character and then find the means of relating to their direction.

The search for such patterns can take the form of examining likely trends, as forecast by experts. Recently, Jack Denst, Chicago artist-designer, related home decor colors to significant social and news events.

In 1969, a Volkswagen was named one of the world's most beautiful things.

Figure 8.8. The Volkswagen on display at the Museum of Art

The religious aspects of the baroque period in the late 17th century resulted in the introduction of soft tones of pink, white, and gold.

The Edwardian era, placid and prosperous, encouraged the use of white, soft green, and black.

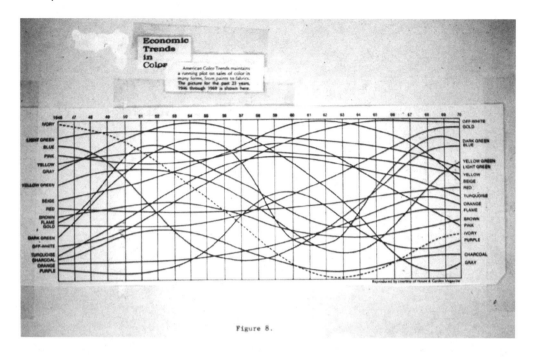

Figure 8.

Figure 8.9. The ebb and flow of color preferences

A decade rampant with riots, drug scenes, and social revolution, the 1960s also saw space and lunar exploration. Thus, in the middle of mind-boggling reds, yellows, intense blues, and gold green, came the clear gleam of silver, inspired by technical advancements.

Pastels of the 70's will cool the scene, and before long the earth colors will take over, reflecting the public's serious involvement with ecology.

Another set of relationships is suggested between clothing and music, pointing to nuances that are visible to those close to the rock scene. These influences may be exaggerated, especially as no broader sense of explanation or trend is provided. Taking even broader sweeps of time pitches the problem at another level, ignoring what individuals like Alice Cooper or Mick Jagger are doing, to track more generally characteristic cycles and phenomena. The curves in Figure 8.9, with their long fundamental character, flow past the overtones of seasons and jogs of certain years, suggesting only a coming and going of color preferences, unrelated to other events. The relationship between lengths of women's skirts and economic depression indicated in Figure 8.10 shows another reason for trying to avoid the latter as long skirts and bad times seem to go together. Similarly, there are attempts to integrate the aesthetic manifestations of fashion among women's fashions, appliances, and cars summed up in Figure 8.11. Dwight Robinson (1958a) has discussed style and era from this viewpoint, and many cultural histories deal with the topic: one of the most absorbing is Russell Lynes's (1949) *The Tastemakers*.

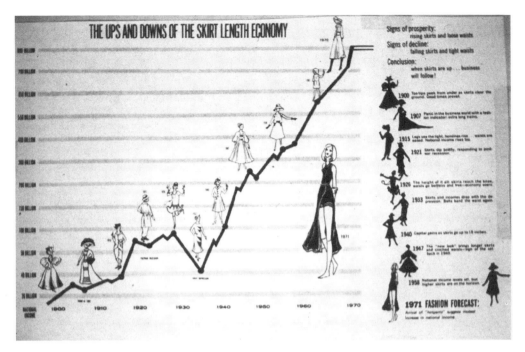

Figure 8.10. Long skirts go with economic depression

CORPORATE POLICY AND AESTHETICS

A company can show its aesthetic orientation via products and all the other means of presenting itself in its packaging, advertising, buildings, and community participation. But some have led and not all others have followed. Lynes, tracing history, notes the uneasiness of American business with artistic matters; and Robinson (1968) explains this in terms of America's social dynamism and special interest in changing the shape of objects, "far less from our studious efforts to become connoisseurs of the traditional niceties, or what are known as the fine arts."

Nevertheless, the classic Kleenex box showed the influence of Mondrian, and the Container Corporation of America amazed the skeptical trade with its abstract art advertisements (Figure 8.12). Developing and designing logograms flourish with the growing awareness of the charm and power of visual symbols (Rosen, 1970). The idea that buildings and their landscaping are dramatic statements of an aesthetic sort in addition to their value as housing and income-producing investments shows itself in the bold displays by Rockefeller Center, Lever House, the Hancock Center, and the First National Bank of Chicago with its popular plaza and colorful Chagall mosaic. In June 1973, Shell boasted of its program of service station renovation across the country in an advertisement (Figure 8.13) that put forth an aesthetic appeal as a contribution to civic betterment. Concern with the aesthetic quality of life is taken as one contemporary means of ameliorating consumerist criticisms. Even the government is not exempt from the new aesthetic currents. The First Federal Design Assembly was funded in 1973 to consider the question "How can the arts and artists be of help to your agency and to its pro-

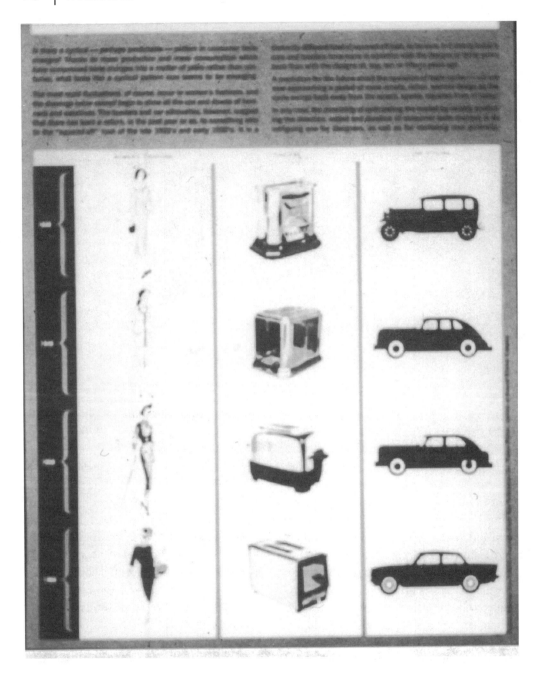

Figure 8.11. Matching clothes, toasters, and cars

grams?" A $100,000 program was initiated, "said to represent the first time that the Government—the country's largest planner, builder, landlord and printer—has recognized its responsibility to provide the country with the best possible design environment" (*New York Times,* February 12, 1973, p. 22).

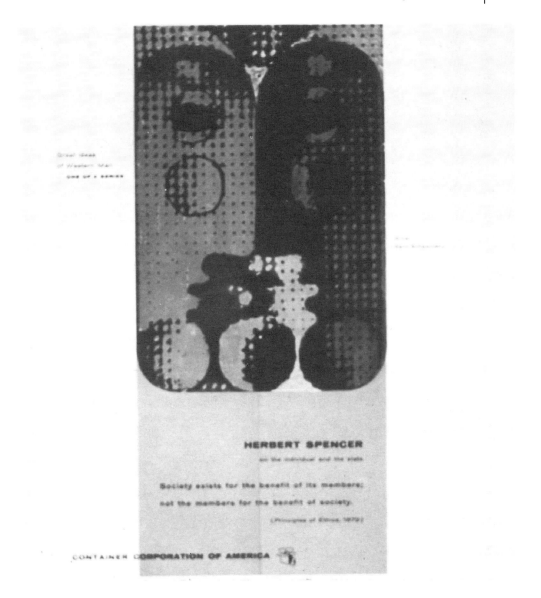

Figure 8.12. Modern art in a corporate advertisement

BUSINESS AND THE ARTS

Vigorous aesthetic activity by a corporation is often associated with the name of a prime mover—Adriano Olivetti, David Rockefeller, Walter Paepcke, Charles Coiner— people who have an interest in fine art as well as in making their enterprise more attractive. Unlike some of the early mag-nates who mainly built private collections, they were instrumental in bringing business and art closer. Leonard Rubin of Fidelity World Arts, Inc., estimates that one in five companies has an art collection or commissions art and that corporations bought about as much original art in 1972 as museums did. The corporate obligation is becoming increasingly institutionalized,

Figure 8.13. Improving appearance in the channel of distribution

urged along by the Business Committee for the Arts, currently chaired by Frank Stanton. Corporations are supporting symphonies and museums in the traditional manner, and with the outstanding long-term example of Texaco's opera sponsorship, making possible special theatrical events, the Summergarden program at the Museum of Modern Art (Mobil Oil Corporation), and urban wall murals.

Such activities go beyond the use of art for sheer commercial purposes in advertisements, packages, or even the corporate imagery and self-expression effected by office furnishings and landscaping. Social aims are cultivated, greater emphasis is given to the idea that people need art for art's sake and corporations have a duty to help provide it. Functional considerations are less apparent, being quite intangible and "institutional," with the payoff hard to measure; although marketing motives probably still require some satisfaction. Controversy continues over whether it is a business's business to display social responsibility and spend shareholder wealth on aesthetic "frills." The suspicion that business motives are always mercenary and the American businessman is by nature an aesthetic dullard has elicited some defense. The *Saturday Review of the Arts* (before it failed, perhaps due to some aesthetic or marketing shortcomings) quoted George Weissman, President of Philip Morris, "Businessmen are human, you know. They do actually enjoy the arts," and cited a study that found graduate students of business "listed art, music, entertainment, and the presence of intellectual stimulation high on the list of requirements for communities to which they planned to move their families" (*Saturday Review of the Arts,* April 1973, p. 26).

At this point in the continuum, the move toward marketing more aesthetically goes beyond adornment and making company communications attractive, to a focus on the aesthetic product itself and its consumer. The artist is the seller, and a new vantage point arises.

MARKETING THE ARTS

The relationship of the arts to the economic life of the community is a thorny one, involving questions and controversies that certainly cannot be resolved here. But some will be examined. The flow of money in the direction of the humanities has lately much increased. From business, government, and the consumer, support has grown to the point of being fashionable. Irving Kristol (1973), who points out that the Humanities Endowment, the Arts Endowment, and Public Broadcasting will spend some $200 million in 1973, is dubious about the relevance of the outlay, as psychosocial aims often seem more involved than those of the humanities. Whether the arts should be "marketed" is a troublesome issue. Those devoted to High Culture see the market mechanism as one that debases and distorts cultural values to pander to a mass taste (Macdonald, 1961). Harold Rosenberg (1973) writes that art (painting, sculpture) has lost its rationale as art because the market has taken over. He sees the collaboration between dealers, collectors, and exhibitors so defining opinion and fashion that the artist's achievement is a financial one that can no longer be judged in aesthetic terms. He rather bitterly concludes that it may be time to abandon his field, art criticism, "which has anyway become little more than a shopping guide" (p. 77).

Brian Dixon (1970), an artist and a professor of administrative studies at Canada's York University, says that "Any attempts to superimpose business criteria on artistic activities involves trying to have the arts follow a set of values and assumptions about economic maximizing behavior, which have no particular relevance for artistic goals" (p. 29). He considers it unreasonable that the arts should be arbitrated in any substantial way by the dictates of the market. He favors much greater subsidy support to free the arts from the market mechanism, with "efficiency" provided separately by arts administrators.

Nevertheless, where there are audiences, customers, consumers, whether they be corporations, government, or individuals, there is a marketplace of some sort. J. H. Plumb points out the way Hogarth combined aesthetic genius and marketing skills in exploiting the rising middle class market of 18th century England.

> Hogarth, however, had a very keen market sense and he was as ready as Josiah Wedgewood to exploit any trick that might enlarge his market or protect what he has captured. He used advertisement extensively, organized the Engravers' Copyright Act, tried auctioning his own pictures (Plumb, 1971).

The market is there, it is growing, and many recognize a need for the arts to be more effective in the use of marketing methods. Noting the small audience for a concert of The Chamber Series of the Chicago Symphony Orchestra, Robert Marsh of the *Chicago Sun-Times* commented, "The failure is not one of art but of salesmanship." Chairman of the Ravinia Festival, Stanley Freehling said, "We're a retail merchant trying to sell our wares to all age groups and areas. We don't want to be the plaything of the North Shore." Bernard Lefort of the Paris Opera similarly believes, "You can't wait for the public to come to you, you have to go to them." Much fanfare attended the publication of the report *Arts and the People* by the American Council for the Arts in Education (1973), in which perhaps too much comfort was taken from the willingness of great numbers of people to tell an interviewer that they have a positive interest in arts and sculpture, but there is little doubt of the upsurge at art auctions, the burgeoning of craft activity, the crowds at museums, and the vitality of the community theaters in many locales. The opportunities for market segmentation are great, a fact that provides some satisfaction as a solution to avowed elitists such as Dwight Macdonald in recognizing that "The mass audience is divisible, we have discovered— and the more it is divided, the better. Even television . . . might be improved by this approach."

The use of marketing methods to increase sales and attendance is having its impact. Museums are reaching out to the community with special exhibits, publicity, advertising, and sale of memberships to a wide audience. Sotheby Parke Bernet offers a 5-year guarantee of the authenticity of any art object it sells. Numerous mail order catalogs offer prints and reproductions; discount stores sell inexpensive original paintings. Dominick's Food Stores offer copies of famous art works as popular premiums. The Houston Opera House advertises "Tannhauser Is Hot Stuff!"

The success thus far in marketing of the arts falls far short of being purely aesthetic. Functional and social considerations are important in motivating people to be consumers. Collecting is faddish, a way of participating in some socially exhibitionistic manner. Pleasant design is justified as making people more efficient workers; and the value of art as an investment (Figure 8.14) is often its most attractive appeal. It may be

Figure 8.14. Art advertised as an investment

that therapy and profit, education and so-cial pressures, combine to give aesthetics a foot in the door. Then beauty can do its work, gratifying that motive as well, continuing to reduce the antagonism to the arts that Kristol attributes to the traditional "populist-philistine" temper of the American peo-ple." All along the marketing-aesthetic con-tinuum, the marketer has roles to play:

Improving the product, package, their appeal and segmentation, via design

Fostering his organization's identity and public relations with advertising, logo, landscape

Serving as patron, consumer, collector, audience

Managing the marketing function of theaters, galleries, museums

Studying these contents and processes

Marketing and marketing study have grown by their increased awareness of the impact of technology on product develop-ment and innovation; of the sciences of be-havior on segmentation and communication. Fresh opportunities for research are being found in its relations with the humanities.

REFERENCES

Blumer, H. (1968). Sociological analysis of fash-ion. In *Proceedings,* Conference of College Teachers of Textiles and Clothing.

Carruth, E. (1967). The great fashion explo-sion. *Fortune.*

Clerget, P. (1914). The economic and social role of fashion. In *Annual Report of the Smith-sonian Institution.* Washington, DC: Gov-ernment Printing Office.

Dixon, B. (1970, Summer). Should the arts be businesslike? *The Business Quarterly,* p. 29.

Gardner, B. B., & Levy, S. J. (1955, March-April). The product and the brand. *Harvard Business Review,* pp. 33-39.

Kristol, I. (1973, March 14). The misgivings of a philanthropist. *Wall Street Journal.*

Lynes, R. (1949). *The tastemakers.* New York: Harper.

Macdonald, D. (1961). Masscult and midcult. *Partisan Review Series,* No. 4.

Maslow A. (1954). *Motivation and personality.* New York: Harper & Row.

Plumb, J. H. (1971, December 16). Hogarth's progress. *New York Review of Books,* p. 28.

Robinson, D. W. (1958a). Fashion memory and product design. *Harvard Business Review.*

Robinson, D. E. (1958b). Fashion theory and product design. *Harvard Business Review.*

Robinson, D. E. (1968). U.S. style invades Europe. *Harvard Business Review.*

Rosen, B. (1970). *The corporate search for visual identity.* New York: Van Nostrand Reinhold.

Rosenberg, H. (1973, August 20). The art world: Adding up. *The New Yorker,* p. 77.

## Chapter 9

MARCOLOGY 101, OR THE DOMAIN OF MARKETING

Sidney J. Levy

Sidney J. Levy: The paper, "Marcology 101, or the Domain of Marketing," came about in the following way. The immediate spur to writing it was an invitation from Keith Hunt to participate in the program of the 1976 AMA Educators' Conference in a session that he was to chair on *The Domain of Marketing.* I took the opportunity to write down some thoughts that had been in my mind for some time. The marketing department at Northwestern University in the 1960s and early 1970s was (and still is) an enjoyable and stimulating environment. A group of faculty of diverse backgrounds and views had been brought together, and we had an exciting time exploring ideas. To the eager curiosity of Harper Boyd, the intellectual integrity of Ralph Westfall, and the careful, open-minded attention of Richard Clewett, already established there, were joined the pioneering interdisciplinary experience of Steuart Henderson Britt, the encompassing mind of Philip Kotler, the broad understanding and vitality of Gerald Zaltman, the rich mind and urgency of Louis Stern, and the brilliance and discipline of Brian Sternthal and Bobby Calder.

This chapter was first published in K. L. Bernhardt (Ed.), *Marketing: 1776-1976 and Beyond,* 1976, pp. 577-581. Reprinted by permission of the American Marketing Association.

Whether like adolescents or like mature philosophers, some of us spent endless hours ruminating on the nature of things, becoming intently absorbed in thinking about the question What is marketing? As Spinoza was said to be a God-intoxicated philosopher. we were marketing intoxicated. Some people find that foolish, immature, and futile—an early outside reviewer of "Marcology 101" dismissed it as just another impractical and useless essay on the nature of marketing. But out of such conversations, hoping to get at the heart of the matter, came such works as "Broadening the Concept of Marketing," "Social Marketing," and *Marketing, Society, and Conflict,* which examined ideas about marketing as exchange, as a pervasive phenomenon, and as theoretically controversial. Not least of the results of these conversations was a stream of award-winning doctoral dissertations by Alice Tybout, Louis Chandon, Richard Bagozzi, and several others.

This experience indicates to me the value of raising what may seem simple-minded questions about phenomena that are otherwise taken for granted or pursued at superficial levels in our attempts to get at the deeper roots of meaning in our professional field. I have not changed the essay because it still seems very much to the point in justifying the distinction between the marcological level of inquiry and analysis and the level of marketing actions.

There seems to be a great amount of conflict and brooding going on over the state of marketing, reflecting both old problems and new ones. Discerning a crisis in one's field is a common ploy, but some times do appear to be more critical than others, and the recent agitation is unusually lively. It may help in the search for clarity to discuss some main controversial ideas. There are three central issues that are here cast in the form of three major criticisms of marketing:

1. Marketing is a general evil.

2. Marketing trespasses on other fields.

3. Marketing theory is irrelevant.

These three negative ideas generate a noticeable degree of heat and challenge all marketing educators to examine their field and its basic nature, and to clarify response to these criticisms. The endeavor may be foolish—perhaps unnecessary for thoughtful and reasonable people and futile for others. Still, these ideas have repercussions, they repel good students, affect the support of marketing scholars, and hamper the free expression of inquiry seeking to understand the human actions, structures, and processes called marketing. These three problems radiate in many directions and involve numerous subissues and segments of society. They indicate that marketing is a controversial subject and source of conflict between marketers and nonmarketers, among marketing thinkers, and between marketing thinkers and marketing doers.

The first proposition affects marketing in all its relations, stigmatizing it for existing in society; the second restricts its definition and application in a mean-minded and territorial fashion; and the third complaint denies the value of serious advanced study of marketing. The conflicts entailed are perhaps so deep and encompassing that they are ultimately irreconcilable, but they will probably gain from airing and dialogue, as Boris Becker (1975) has pointed out, in our search for truth. Differences due to real opposed interests will undoubtedly continue, but those due to misunderstanding or confusion might be mitigated. It is not the purpose of this discussion to defend specific marketing actions against all comers, but to explore the issues and to suggest an ameliorative approach.

MARKETING STIGMATIZED

The general understanding of what constitutes marketing is both self-confident and negative. That is, most people do not doubt they know that marketing is the selling of goods and that the selling is conducted in a manner deserving of censure. This knowledge is ancient, going back to traditional attitudes toward those who sell. The root ideas of *mercari,* to trade, *mereri,* to serve for hire, and *merere,* to earn may seem neutral enough (or even positive, as in merit), but the use of these roots to form words such as *meretricious,* meaning like a prostitute, and *mercenary,* to indicate one who will do anything for money shows the early attachment of negative value judgments to ideas of selling. Aristotle agreed with the opinion of the day when he wrote that "retail trade . . . is justly censured; for it is unnatural and a mode by which men gain from one another."

BASIC MOTIVES

It is interesting to speculate on the sources of the degradation of marketing. They are presumably deep-rooted in being so pervasive and enduring. A common assumption in condemning marketing is that the buyer is taken advantage of by the seller. Even when the marketing exchange is supposed to be equal in value to both participants, dissatisfaction often remains. The many reasons for this go on at various levels. One problem is that the equation is composed of units whose values are either not easily determined or compared. If the buyer receives the product and satisfaction of his need and the seller receives the payment for his cost and markup (P + S = C + M), how can the two sides of the equation be judged truly equal? Even in a trade of goods where both parties are clearly buyer *and* seller, mutual suspicion may arise that one has yielded up a greater value than that received.

A second great source of difficulty relates to the perceived purposes of the seller, especially when a middleman exists and when money is involved. The distributor becomes divorced from basic production and is associated more narrowly with the goals of gaining and accumulating money, supposedly as much as possible. This motive is taken as unusually egocentric and damaging to other people, and therefore deserving of less admiration than other vocational aims. Those who grow or craft goods, whose work is healing, study, salvation, artistry, appear to have a commitment that is direct and socially valuable—although they, too, become suspect if money looms too large in their aims. Because the professions are supposedly self-denying in this respect, they have been ennobled. If the merchant, the paradigm of the marketer, sought only to provide, to be the selfless, dedicated quartermaster to the community, then his endeavor too might be exalted.

But even the most loving provider (e.g., the nursing mother) thwarts the fundamental desire to receive without return. Resist as one may, society insists on *quid pro quo* and socializes the young to believe it is more blessed to give than to receive, a precept that would not be needed if it were self-evident in one's feelings. But some giving becomes gratifying, a source of pride, sociability, greater receiving, and other benefits, so that not all exchange is condemned. Ideas of fair return become possible, as well as intellectual recognition of economic necessities relative to profit and accumulation of capital.

THE SYNECHDOCHIC MECHANISM

Learning to adapt to the requirements of an elaborate system of giving and receiving, as society demands (Firth, 1973), leads to many complexities of outlook. In given economies, haggling may come to be admired, and bribery a way of life. In attempts to deny their own persistent desire to get, people do much blaming of others. Marketing is blamed for fostering materialism; and in case consumers seem overly fertile ground for its attractions and too eager to embrace it, the products are deemed shoddy, and the seduction credited to lies and aggressive selling. Implying that in some state of nature (sans marketing) one would have only virtuous spontaneous needs and wants, marketing is accused of brainwashing, forcing, and manipulating people to want things they do not need and to buy things they do not want.

Certainly, there are marketers who make inferior goods, sell aggressively, and tell lies in their advertising. And it is no defense of them to cite equally culpable quack physicians, destructive politicians, cheating customers, faithless ministers, and ignorant teachers. But it is worth noting the overgeneralizing that occurs when all marketing is stigmatized and the term becomes synonymous with doing bad things. All group prejudice is a form of this overgeneralizing, or fallacy of composition. To identify it here, the way a part of marketing is taken for the whole is called the synechdochic mechanism. A *synechdoche* is a rhetorical device wherein the singular is substituted for the plural: here the disapproved marketer is being used to define the category, substituted for those others who strive to make a fine product, offer an excellent service, price fairly, sell helpfully, and communicate honestly.

To refer to such positive marketing probably arouses cynical reactions even in an audience identified with marketing. It illustrates the deep-rooted nature of the problem to observe within the marketing professions signs of self-hatred, acceptance of the stigma, and casual use of the rhetoric that makes marketing a bad word. For example, W. T. Tucker (1974) cites critics of the marketing viewpoint who equate marketing activities with exploiting motives, and "more gimmickry and packaging than substantive change." He seems to accept their criticism and the verb *marketed* as a negative one when he says that the student is a special person who "must not be marketed into doing what the organizations want" (p. 31).

Thus it is that marketing is stigmatized because it is associated with the many frustrations of wanting and giving—with material things and guilt over the desire for them, with money and its deflection of direct interest in providing goods and services—leading to the projection of these frustrations onto marketing and marketers and to the synechdochic equation of the whole field with its worst manifestations.

THE DOMAIN OF MARKETING

Another level of explanation of marketing's poor reputation may lie in confusion or misunderstanding as to what marketing actually is. Perhaps the conventional notion of marketing is not a good or accurate one, and redefinition could assist in making some useful distinctions. Partly, this is an academic exercise. As Robert Oliver says, in trying to offer a definition of the field of speech,

> Knowledge does not lend itself readily to segmentalization. Departmentalization is decreed on our campuses not for investigative, but administrative, convenience. The boundaries established around the various academic specialties are not strong enough to contain human curiosity. (Oliver, 1967)

In the field of speech, Oliver finds the heart of the matter in one purpose: to deal with influence as exerted through oral discourse. He clings to this, despite his qualms.

> Like other professions, ours has been highly introspective, defensive, self-critical, and uncertain of its goals. its methods, and its boundaries . . . When we replace the term "language" with the much more inclusive term "speech," the boundaries of our field tend to disappear. Yet within this complexity we must somehow establish our own identity of goals and methods. The task is appalling. (Oliver, 1967, p. 265)

TERRITORIALITY

The marketing literature shows that marketing thinkers have trouble with finding their consistent locus, also, because their subject matter radiates so readily into and across other disciplines and ways of thinking about human behavior. In his discussion of "the identity crisis in marketing," Bartels (1974) raises this basic question:

> The crux of the issue is this: Is the identity of marketing determined by the *subject matter* dealt with or by the technology with which the subject is handled?. . . . Marketing has initially and generally been associated exclusively with the distributive part of the economic institution and function. In this capacity, marketing is identified by the *substance* and the *subject* of its area of concern. (p. 76)

Bartels (1974) seems open-minded about the issue, perhaps preferring the substantive definition rather than the methodological application one. He thinks the fresh interest in physical distribution, or *logistics,* may allow the word marketing to go on to refer to both economic and non-economic fields of application. Still, he sees marketing as but a species of generic behavioral activity, and one that is trying to trespass on someone else's territory: "From this standpoint, too, the idea that the fields of political campaigns, religious evangelism, or Red Cross solicitation are the province of marketers, rather than of social scientists, may also be questionable" (p. 76).

David Luck (1974) also expresses his concern over the confusion of terminology and conceptualization created by the idea that "every sort of organization is engaged in marketing" (p. 71), and hopes that an authoritative definition of marketing might come from a commission created for the purpose. These territorial considerations are probably basically irrelevant. As Karl Popper (1963) says, "All this classification and distinction is a comparatively unimportant and superficial affair. We are not students of some subject matter but students of problems. And problems may cut right across the borders of any subject matter or discipline" (p. 67).

That is, no one has any special right to a problem. Intellectual territoriality is not like the ownership of a piece of physical geography. Voting behavior may seem the province of political scientists, but that does not prevent sociologists from studying the behavior and need not inhibit marketers. That people like a particular food can be studied by biologists as a process of osmosis or hormonal secretions, by psychologists as a conditioned response or fixation due to trauma, by anthropologists as a cultural imperative, and by speech scholars as a reaction to the oral discourse, "Come and get it!" What makes sex political and politics sexual is the determined attention, analysis, and actions of feminists. To dismiss this as a "Feminist supremacy syndrome" (à la Luck's reference to those "with a sort of marketing supremacy syndrome") seems pointless and ostrich-like. To perceive or study the marketing content of a problem is not to say it is the marketer's province *rather than* the social scientist's, but that it is *also* the marketer's province.

Tucker (1974) implies that Kotler and Levy sought to broaden the boundaries of marketing in 1969 in a desire to follow "the action" of important problems growing elsewhere; but Levy studied such problems at Social Research, Inc., since starting his marketing research career in 1948. It may

more properly be said that the action came to marketing for help rather than the other way around, as nonbusiness managers recognized that the marketing point of view might be useful with their problems. In some ways, to resist or resent this fact is further agreement that marketing is an evil that socially virtuous causes ought not to turn to for help.

EXCHANGE

It has been suggested above that the core issues in marketing arise from the coming together of *providing* and *needing* or *wanting*. That is, *exchange* comes about because one must always give something to get something one wants. The paradigm is the infant, reaching for anything available and trying to incorporate it. But experience soon teaches two conditions: one can't have everything, and one must give something in return. The first is the condition for making choices, and the second creates exchanges.

The issue of exchange has been much discussed—views have been presented by many, including Alderson (1957), Kotler (1972), and Levy and Zaltman (1975), and two excellent recent articles by Bagozzi (1974, 1975). These will not be gone into here, except to reiterate and emphasize the latter's statement that marketing is "a general function of universal applicability. It is the discipline of exchange behavior, and it deals with problems related to this behavior." (Bagozzi, 1975, p. 39).

It seems important to insist on the issue of universal applicability, mainly because there seems no adequately consistent way to define marketing exchange that limits it short of universality. What is a marketing exchange as different from any other exchange? Some try to restrict marketing to the exchange of money for products, a distinction that fails immediately with consideration of markets in which money is exchanged for money, products for products, and money or product are exchanged for services. Then is there any way to limit which moneys, products, or services will be considered elements of marketing exchange, and which will not? Some use the word *economic* as the limiting adjective. But what is economic and what is noneconomic? Economics texts wrestle with such definitions and mainly retreat to notions of scarce resources, utilities, production, and consumption, usually trying to stay as close to money as possible. But again, universality of reference is hard to avoid, as what is not a scarce resource, what is not a utility? These concepts are all interwoven. Money is a measure and surrogate for value for one's labor; labor is a form of energy, skill, and service. Anything can be a commodity. All utility is a form of satisfaction. In a world in which there is no truly free air (although optimistically cited by Samuelson as a noneconomic good in his classic text on economics), in which all exchanges are economic choices and all are exchanges of satisfactions, there can be no nonmarketing exchanges. What is being exchanged may sometimes be hard to analyze, but marketing cannot be limited to being the science of *simple* exchanges.

It may be convenient, of course, to make distinctions between marketing exchanges that are culturally defined as commercial or economic and other types. Some educators and most marketing practitioners in everyday business are more comfortable then.

But that should not lead to the exclusion from marketing theory of the exchanges of goods and services in marriages, churches, politics, aesthetics, schools, government, and social causes.

MARKETING THEORY AND PRACTICE

Theorists and practitioners often develop tensions due to conflict of aims, procedures, concepts of scientific and professional standards, relevance, and so on. Academic psychologists and clinical psychologists show this tension, and its recent flare-up in the marketing field is notable. For some time, marketing people have thought about the development of marketing as a science. Certainly, that ultimate state has not fully arrived; but various workers have been striving in that direction. The establishment of the Marketing Science Institute is one indication, as well as numerous conferences, symposia, and articles, fretting over marketing as a science, an art, a pseudo science, as having theory, metatheory, and so on (Bartels, 1970; Dawson, 1971; Tucker, 1974; Zaltman et al., 1973)

In the classical extreme, practitioners see theorists (viz., academicians) as ivory tower thinkers, impractical people who do not know the realities of the marketplace, who have "never met a payroll," who teach because they can't do. The theorists return the compliment by regarding practitioners as concrete-minded people who are overly specialized and vocational, unable to generalize their experience, who want to know how-to-do-it rather than to understand why it works as it does. If a science is to work toward understanding, predicting, and controlling, the researcher and teacher tend to emphasize the first two aims, and the practitioner the last two.

The extremists write accusations about the uselessness of academic research or defend the validity and importance of the intellectual enterprise. Outstanding examples from the *Marketing News* are Newton Frank's rude and vituperative letter (March 14, 1975) on the uselessness of academic research, as well as the letter (December 1, 1974) from James F. Engel in which he says that marketing is not a pure science and that publications should face this fact and judge their contents only by their practical value to the applied marketer. He defines marketing as akin to an engineering discipline that draws upon several underlying disciplines; and he regards the proposal of Randall Schultz (November 1, 1974) that there be separate journals of study and practice as a perpetuation of the travesty of educators talking to themselves.

Between the extremes are such moderating, judicious suggestions as a broader dialogue, by Professor Becker (*Marketing News,* March 31, 1975) who, however, also believes that if practitioners are determined to be so ignorant, then it is time to go our separate ways. Richard E. Homans (August 15, 1975) offers an accommodating discussion explaining the benefits of academic research. Thomas Lea Davidson's (1975) article shows alarm.

A schism exists today within the marketing community—with marketing academicians lined up on one side and marketing practitioners on the other. The continued growth of that schism—and it is growing—can only be detrimental to both sides.

His solution is indicated in the headline above his article:

One businessman's comments on marketing educators:

EDUCATORS MUST SEE MARKETING AS A "DOING PROFESSION" AND ADD "CLINICAL EXPERIENCE" TO "CLASSROOM VACUUM"

The pressure is to get more practice into the classroom by inviting businessmen to talk to classes, by urging practitioners to write for the *Journal of Marketing.*

THE SCIENCE OF MARCOLOGY

It is evident that many of the problems discussed above are real ones that will not easily be solved. Marketing will always be regarded as an evil by those who refuse to recognize its universality or do not want to countenance its demands for a return and often a profit. There are manipulative marketers, deceptive ads, and high pressure salesmen. There are sincere disagreements about discipline boundaries and preferred definitions and about the value of theory. All solutions are partial—the calls for dialogue, a commission to define marketing, an article giving business persons 10 guidelines to follow when invited to speak to students, and another by a young man exhorting marketers to be honest.

One source of these problems and the struggles with them lies in the idea of marketing as an activity. It is not surprising that educators are urged to see marketing as a "doing profession" when *marketing* is a *doing*. When one is a seller and markets, one is a marketer who *does* marketing; a buyer *goes* marketing. Thus, if educators teach marketing, they should teach how to do it and how to go to it: then no wonder Engel says they are acting as engineers of the marketplace. Then it is reasonable that textbooks tend to be prescriptive writing, oriented to helping students to be profitable, successful marketers, good marketers who apply the marketing concept or virtuous marketers who consider their social responsibility in accordance with the latest ideas of how marketing ought to be done. Such prescriptions and applications are indeed not a "pure science," but the teaching of particular sets of marketing values, and they produce the faddishness and biases that Robert F. Agne (1974) deplores.

A marketing science should be demarcated that does not do *marketing research* but that does *research into marketing.* It should be a pursuit of knowledge, as distinguished from its application, candidly and proudly so. It should exist in relation to marketing as physics or chemistry are to their respective engineering, as psychology is to counseling. Some have thought that marketing is applied economics, but economics shows little interest in marketing and marketing draws on economics mainly as it might on any other discipline, as sociology and economics draw on psychology and mathematics.

Marketing needs its own parent discipline and theoretical roots, its area of basic study. Despite being hampered by the confusions of being called marketers when they are trying to be teachers and researchers into marketing, such professionals have nevertheless been developing concepts, models, and a theoretical literature and have doctoral students carrying out theoretical inquiries.

The name of such a science might draw on some appropriate linguistic roots and be called Marcology. Marcology could be the discipline of exchanges, operating at various levels of abstraction and in whatever contexts are of interest to the scholars. It could have its own focus and its interdisciplinary character, as all the behavioral sciences do. Marcology could study the history of exchanges, why marketing is evil, the various types of exchange, and such divisions of activity as commercial marketing, family or intimate marketing, social and political marketing—or their various marcologies. Abnormal or deviant marcology might study "unusual payments," as a study group recently called large-scale foreign bribery, without having to moralize about them. As *scientists,* marcologists should not teach their opinions about whether television or consumerism or emotional appeals or premiums or unit pricing are good or bad, but rather what these are, and how and why they affect which participants in the exchange. They can study what is exchanged, by whom, where, when, and why, with what consequences personally, socially, nationally. They can do this like other scientists, *just to know,* and for those who wish, in order to share that knowledge without being condemned for having a journal that is not practical in character. And if they wish, like other scientists, marcologists can try to say what is likely to happen under given circumstances, so that practical people can learn from that and apply it as physics is applied to manufacturing and biology to medicine.

If there is to be a commission, let it convene marcologists to define their discipline and its curriculum. In this way, both marcology and the engineering activity that is marketing could be clarified, as well as the role identities that accompany the distinctions between research, teaching, and application.

REFERENCES

Agne, R. F. (1974, August 15). Businessman proposes conduct code for academicians. *Marketing News*, p. 4.

Alderson, W. (1957). *Marketing behavior and executive action*. Homewood, IL: Richard D. Irwin.

Bagozzi, R. P. (1974, October). Marketing as an organized behavioral system of exchange. *Journal of Marketing, 38*, 77-81.

Bagozzi, R. P. (1975, October). Marketing as exchange. *Journal of Marketing, 39*, 32-39.

Bartels, R. (1970). *Marketing theory and metatheory*. Homewood, IL: Richard D. Irwin.

Bartels, R. (1974, October). The identity crisis in marketing. *Journal of Marketing, 38*.

Becker, B. W. (1975, April 25). Letters. *Marketing News*, p. 2.

Davidson, T. L. (1975, August 15). *Marketing News*, p. 1.

Dawson, L. M. (1971, July). Marketing science in the age of Aquarius. *Journal of Marketing, 35*, 66-72.

Firth, R. (1973). Symbolism in giving and getting. In *Symbols public and private* (pp. 368-402). London: George Allen & Unwin.

Kotler, P. (1972, April). A generic concept of marketing. *Journal of Marketing, 36*, 46-54.

Kotler, P., & Levy, S. J. (1969, January). Broadening the concept of marketing. *Journal of Marketing, 33*, 10-15.

Levy, S. J., & Zaltman, G. (1975). *Marketing, society, and conflict*. Englewood Cliffs, NJ: Prentice Hall.

Luck, D. J. (1974, October). Social marketing: Confusion compounded. *Journal of Marketing, 38*, 71.

Oliver, R. T. (1967). Contributions of the speech profession to the study of human communication. In F. E. X. Dance (Ed.), *Human communication theory*. New York: Holt, Rinehart & Winston.

Popper, K. R. (1963). *Conjectures and refutations*. New York: Harper & Row.

Tucker, W. T. (1974, April). Future directions in marketing theory. *Journal of Marketing, 38*, 30-35.

Zaltman, G., et al. (1973). *Metatheory and consumer Research*. New York: Holt, Rinehart & Winston.

## Chapter 10

A REJOINDER
Toward a Broader Concept of Marketing's Role in Social Order

Sidney J. Levy

Philip Kotler

It strikes us that the article by Laczniak and Michie (1979) is a welter of misunderstandings and fears concerning the nature of social order, science, and marketing; and a somewhat astonishing approach to criticism of the broadened concept of marketing. We will respond to a few of the main issues raised there.

First, let us take up the central thrust of the article that distinguishes it from their repetition of the usual criticisms of the broadened concept: "the importance of social order in society" and its significant relation to language. No doubt language is important for social order, and for most anything else social. But it does not follow that therefore language must be precise and unambiguous. All language has varying degrees of ambiguity because denotations are always accompanied by connotations; and

This chapter was first published in *Journal of the Academy of Marketing Science,* 7(3) 1979, pp. 233-237. Reprinted by permission of Sage Publications, Inc.

knowledge of the former differs among members of society, and the latter can never have total consensus due to the variety of experiences within a society and between societies. Also, language changes constantly, the clarity of concepts is argued in all disciplines, except perhaps where—only temporarily—tradition, authority, and oppression manage to create a static situation by forbidding new ideas (the Church and Galileo), insisting on official ideology (Stalin and Lysenko), and other warnings of social danger. This is not to place "broadening" on such an august conceptual level, but to point to the need for intellectual freedom for all.

Language changes because ideas change and social orders change. The features cited by Laczniak and Michie (1979) as prerequisite for social order have famous sponsors in Lawrence Frank and Talcott Parsons, among others, but lack an important ingredient. Their ideas reflect the thinking of consensus-oriented sociologists and philosophers and neglect the counterbalancing thinking about conflict and change as inevitable (and desirable?) mechanisms in social affairs (Hodges, 1974; Levy & Zaltman, 1975). In the main portion of the paper they make a blanket plea for stability with no allowance for social change, even an improved social order that may require some intervening social disorder. Toward the end, as a kind of afterthought, they retreat from their earlier position and grant the necessity of some social change. We are glad that they modified their ideas toward sounding more reasonable; and perhaps with further thought and discussion they will come even closer to agree with us. However, despite their urging that marketing take responsibility for these changes, their conclusion shows they clearly do not want them at all. Also, they give little real-

istic recognition of how social institutions are modified. They refer to adaptation and balance, but the adaptation seems mainly a criterion of efficiency, and the balance is another rigidity "fastened together in the long run by an iron law" which apparently threatens the intrepid marketing broadeners. The language of the article overflows with "traditional conception," "institutional direction and control," "harmonious interaction," "the demand of law," sounding more like a political treatise than a scientific discussion of the validity of recent definitions of marketing. They fear increased regulation and urge more of it themselves (e.g., a public review board to oversee broadened marketing, horrendous as that sounds).

Laczniak and Michie (1979) are kind enough to deny that broadened marketing will "undermine the entire social fabric," for which we must be thankful; but they brought up that idea, too, and to be accused of the "potential to diminish social order and ultimately damage the reputation of the discipline of marketing" is no small matter, either. It smacks surprisingly of threats against the expression of ideas. In the November 9, 1978, issue of the *New York Review of Books,* the arrest warrant issued against the novelist Jiri Grusa by the Czech authorities reads: "Jiri Grusa . . . is accused of the crime of initiating disorder" (p. 35).

The rest may be commented upon summarily. As we have noted, the relationships among activities, ideas, and words is in constant flux. As scientists we study these phenomena. Words are not forever defined precisely. Even the definition of marketing "sanctioned"(!) by the American Marketing Association of which Laczniak and Michie (1979) approve is not the same as the AMA definition that preceded it. Also, it is not precise and unambiguous as they claim. Does the definition refer to process or content? Like *exchange,* the words *performance* and *direct* imply process; *business activities* and *goods and services* imply content. But how are these precise and unambiguous? Is there a list of the AMA-sanctioned businesses? There are clearly business activities that are illegal. Should they be allowed to be studied, even theoretically? Are there any goods and services that are excluded from this definition? The government is involved in the flow of goods and services. Business activities are involved in the raising of political campaign funds and paying for candidates' commercials, and so on. Why, then exclude the political arena from marketing attention—or pretend it isn't happening or that the people who are doing it are not marketers or are not practicing marketing? Like the U.S. Constitution, properly interpreted, even the AMA definition includes the broadened marketing concept.

At the outset (Philip & Levy, 1969), we too referred to "marketing-like" activities. But it became necessary to give up that usage when it became apparent that there was no realistic difference between marketing activities and marketing-like activities. None of the attempts to distinguish business marketing and marketing in any other setting in a fundamental way hold water. The ground has been gone over elsewhere and will not be detailed here, other than to repeat that not even Samuelson is able to give a precise and unambiguous definition of economic goods that excludes anything that is being offered or received in human exchanges.

Laczniak and Michie (1979) struggle with this at one point by talking about the application of sophisticated marketing methods to the dissemination of ethically charged ideas such as neofascism, euthanasia, pornographic entertainment, gay rights, and other controversial concepts. They mix up the two issues of whether such application is marketing in the first place and whether responsible marketers should do it. Clearly, they think not, in both cases, warning marketers away from the "marketing of ideas." This is superficial reasoning. They do not seem to be aware that all products and services are "ethically charged" and that we are always "marketing an idea," whether it is the idea of Campbell's soup, Pinto cars, or guns, drugs, abortions, or X-rated films. These are all "traditional economic goods." Laczniak and Michie (1979) fail to recognize the basic issue, that all individuals and organizations are inevitably marketing their goods, services, and ideas, whether the marketing professionals choose to acknowledge that and assist it or not.

Another main area of misconception lies in the field of Venn diagrams, where anyone may play. Laczniak and Michie (1979) depict marketing first as properly nestled away in Economics, Behavioral Science, and Law, with perhaps a touch less Mathematics than many would like to see. They contrast this with the megalomaniac picture of Imperial Marketing lording it over all the other disciplines, and with just a handful of recent Ph.D.s to run the empire. Still, the second diagram is accurate in implying that marketing thinking and activity may be applied to all those other fields. What is not shown is that a similar diagram could be drawn for each of the fields of thought. Each field can be applied reciprocally to each other. There is a sociology of law and of theology, everyone uses mathematics, everything is either legal or illegal, political scientists may study power struggles in law, marketing, or the church, and a good theologian knows that despite the separation of church and state God is everywhere. This is not "egotistic arrogance" but the recognition that any scholar may think "universally" in observing how his discipline permeates human activities. So there is law in marketing and marketing in and of law, aesthetics in marketing and marketing of aesthetics, education in marketing and marketing of education, and so forth. The broadened concept was merely calling attention to this fact that academic domains are conveniences and blinkered specializations; and as Laczniak and Michie (1979) note, many marketing scholars have been glad to free themselves from this artificial limitation and make themselves more useful to the social order.

It is an odd idea that marketing personnel who assist in the offering of the goods and services of which Laczniak and Michie (1979) disapprove—or which are disapproved by any other groups in the society—are irresponsible. Marketing personnel who foster a "controversial and ultimately dysfunctional message" (whoever decides that?) are responsible as individuals who are willing to foster that cause and will suffer from the conflict with other groups, the government, and so on, just as Kellogg's and Leo Burnett are suffering from opposition to their advertising of sugared cereals. Whether the First Amendment protects or not has to be decided for anyone's message, not just sellers of "ideas." The idea of cigarettes is banned from broadcast media, but the sale of cigarettes is not banned.

The irony is that the broadened concept of marketing, rather than contributing to social disorder, is making an increasingly important contribution to social order. Hospitals, colleges, social agencies, museums, churches, and other troubled social institutions are receiving the help of profes-sional marketers to better understand their changing markets and take constructive steps to survive and grow. These nonbusiness institutions for many years operated without a sufficient sensitivity to market and consumer concerns and only now are becoming aware of the vital connection between their survival and their market-orientated-ness.

Finally, it is unfortunate for marketing educators to foster a monolithic identification of marketing activities, one that means bad practices are generalized to all marketing. Too many people foolishly do that already. It makes no sense to say there will be evil consequences "if marketing denies responsibility for its action when problems and abuses occur." Marketing is not an entity, "it" has no collective responsibility. Everyone engages in it, perforce, and whatever else they may be, all exchanges are also marketing exchanges. Each conscience, in and out of tradition, controls its own responsibility. The "severe regulation" of marketing due to abuse is probably less likely to come about because of the conceptualization and application of marketing thought in broadened spheres than due to the unfortunate abuses that have plagued traditional marketing.

There is probably a limit to the social order that humans find acceptable, given the propensities to seek change, development, improvement, excitement, and novelty and to create as well as to avoid complications. Marketers should not fear change, other disciplines, "society," or the power of their ideas. A higher concept of social order has to take account of the uses of disorder (Sennett, 1970), the disturbances of tradition and of those complacently precise and unambiguous definitions that we hope will yield to the search for truth.

REFERENCES

Hodges, H. M., Jr. (1974). *Conduct and consensus*. New York: Harper & Row.

Kotler, P., & Levy, S. J. (1969, January). Broadening the concept of marketing. *Journal of Marketing, 33*, 10-15.

Laczniak, G. R., & Michie, D. A. (1979). The social disorder of the broadened concept of marketing. *Journal of the Academy of Marketing Science, 7*(3), 214-232.

Levy, S. J., & Zaltman, G. (1975). *Marketing, society, and conflict*. Englewood Cliffs, NJ: Prentice Hall.

Sennett, R. (1970). *The uses of disorder*. New York: Knopf.

Chapter 11

THE HEART OF QUALITY SERVICE

Sidney J. Levy

In discussing the topic of quality, it is customary to talk about what might be done to increase the excellence of products and services, how to make things better. Of course, not everyone wants or can afford the same level of excellence, so there are degrees of quality and service. Figure 11.1 shows a ladder of service quality, to suggest such degrees. To explore what lies behind this ladder, I will take a semiotic approach to the topic by exploring thoughts about the core meanings of the terms *quality* and *service*.

Quality is a central issue in marketing. The word is used casually and frequently.

It is such a common claim that we might expect its ability to discriminate among products and services to be lost. Yet its use persists, and we continue to strive to understand what it refers to and how customers identify it. Quality is such a common claim because it is an attribute that people desire. But what is that attribute and when do we know that we have it? The root of quality is *qua*. When we say this is a desk *qua* desk, we are referring to its essential being, to that Platonic Ideal Desk that exists in heaven and invests the particular desk with its inherent identity. Quality is the basic nature of a thing. Real life versions are

This chapter was first presented as a paper at the *International Institute on Marketing Meaning*, July 19, 1989, Indianapolis.

A LADDER OF SERVICE QUALITY			
Rungs	*Description*	*Characterization*	*Reaction*
Top Rung	Eager to serve Accommodating Go out of the way Energetic in redress Positive attitude Extras, care about you	High quality	Enjoyment Enthusiasn Surprise
Third Rung	Friendly/Impersonal Reasonably pleasant	Fine, good No problems	Expectancy Hope
Second Rung	Accurate Impersonal Standardized	Not special I don't mind It's okay	Tolerance
Bottom Rung	Serious mistakes Slow to remedy Active rudeness to unpleasant attitude	Terrible service	Aversion

Figure 11.1 A ladder of service quality

sometimes so prototypical that they seem to meet the Ideal—perhaps Heinz catsup docs this. But most things fall naturally short. Therefore, high quality refers to the degree to which the purity and perfection of the object *qua* object is approached, the extent to which it can be said to be the absolute thing in itself—perhaps as Absolut vodka seeks to imply for itself.

In some cases we are so uncertain about how much quality there is in what we buy that we substitute other variables or judgments that are presumed to correlate with it. We then rely on price or sheer reputation to inform us. When price is used as a guide, people can determine how much quality they have access to, the ratio of quality to resources they can afford. Value is the best quality for the money; as the ladder shows, different acceptable values indicate the standards to which individuals aspire in given areas of product and service.

Sometimes we reason from the contrary: That is, rarity or small quantity is often taken as one of the hallmarks of high quality. On the logic that good things must be difficult to come by, quantity is seen as inversely related to quality. Also, quantity implies substance, weight, numerous units, thus having the character of grossness, potentially of excess or glut, whereas quality seems to be something intangible and ineffable. Some quantity of quality is desirable, but it is usually perceived to be less a matter of amount than one of level. Quality should be high rather than middling or low. Also, quality is to be experienced, not counted.

Quality is relative to the object. Customarily, there is exaltation of the fragile, refined, or slow painstaking versions that have as little substance or grossness as possible to achieve the result, using the paradox of "less is more," perhaps even the renunciation of material life to reach quality *qua* quality. Assessing quality may then be based on the perceived ratio of the aesthetic to the functional, whereby even a furnace may be deemed higher quality if it is thought beautiful as well as efficient. But in everyday life quality is seen in practical assets such as durability or speed, where those are especially desirable. Further, to complicate matters, there can be high quality in sheer excess when having that is the point: An example might be the sense of "it's all too much" as necessary to experiencing the exquisite rarification of boredom suggested by Fellini in the film *La Dolce Vita.*

The concept of quality contains diverse social values. It implies approval of basic virtues, so that "a quality person" is a good person, reliable and sincere. Then again, the old expressions referring to certain people as "The Quality," and "a Lady of Quality" imply higher social position, people who can live an elevated style of life with money, gracious manners, and refined clothing.

If quality is ultimately the idea of perfection, what is the marriage of quality and service? In everyday understanding, service refers to the situations in which people provide something to other people—give them a haircut, insure them, lodge them, transport them, and so on. Service takes various forms and has various meanings; different settings give different emphases. The expressions, *to service, to serve a meal, the military services, financial services, church services,* differ in their implications of what it is they provide.

At the root of these activities lies the word *servus,* a slave, a serf. Slavery implies total and involuntary obligation and an uneven relationship wherein the inferior must serve a superior. One should be "your obedient servant" and do whatever is re-

quired. In a casual sense, one can provide service to an equal, although probably at the moment the one who is being served is raised up. Religious services show deference to God; the military services enable us to show our obedience to the larger patriotic cause. At one level, the idea of this relationship is an impersonal one, as suggested by the use of *servicing* to describe a male animal being brought to copulate with a female, or a prostitute offering to service a client, or the putting of gasoline in an automobile. As many servers and servants are well aware, there are people who take great advantage of their power (political, economic, physical, etc.) to command service that is extreme in its compliance, with marked indifference to the feelings of the servers: Below service is *subservience.* It is evident that commonly there is a desire to receive not only the service actions themselves but also various emotions or feelings. Some service recipients look for visible deference to accompany the actions; they want bootlickers and lackeys, fawning and obsequiousness, evidence of a desire to please as well to be dutiful.

Some of this attitude is more general, reflected in the desire for "service with a smile." This desire also implies that the service should seem to be provided willingly. The slaves should give the appearance of loving their chains and their masters; and many masters—and servers—come to believe that they do. Many servers, of course, do feel positive about providing service. Serving others can be a source of satisfaction; it makes people feel good. They are variously motivated by their pride in the nature of their service, their skill in giving it, outdoing competitive servers, grateful for the rewards they receive in money, admiration, and thanks, and so on (and perhaps, like serfs, the protection of the lord).

Customarily, they identify with the status of their clientele, so that serving a higher group increases the stature of the servers.

Those who are egalitarian minded or too sensitive to the servers' true attitudes, which their skepticism might suspect, or who have low self-esteem, may not be able to tolerate high degrees of personal service. Further, the service relationship is an exchange situation. It is often not enough to lord it over the servers, nor to be satisfied with paying them. The emotions of the servers draw reciprocation from the served; they want to be loved and to love back and may thus become paternalistic, give extra rewards to show their appreciation and that they are deserving of good service. Thus, some people are bribers, overgenerous tippers, or givers of gifts to suppliers of service.

But generally, signs of the willingness and the love become something extra that distinguishes good service; they imply the worthiness of the receiver as an individual to be prized and given special rather than routine attention. The devotion is something that continues beyond the minimum, as with "sales and service—we don't stop with sales, but continue to take care of you."

However, service situations are intense ones, by involving these complexities of interpersonal relationships. They are likely, therefore, to be hard to sustain at a given level. This leads to the common phenomenon of "service wearout." Customers tend to come to take the service and the servers more for granted, to treat them either more impersonally, or, conversely, to presume on the "friendship" they want to believe has arisen so that they seem more demanding. At the same time, the server's enthusiasm and dedication decline; the appeal of new customers looms larger. The service is carried out less well; in some instances the client is stood up, neglected, and the excuses proliferate: There are the excuses about illness, other projects or customers with greater needs, the demands of relatives, illness, the transportation problems (borrowed, stolen vehicles, accidents), the failure of equipment, the unreliability of other suppliers, and so on. The bloom is off the rose, and one feels it may be time to find another client or vendor. This situation points to the life cycle of service relationships and raises issues of how to pitch service at a level that is sustainable and of finding ways to renew motivation.

In sum, ordinary service is often understood as merely providing people with marketplace objects and activities; and most people are glad to settle for a level of quality that is not too demanding on either side. But service qua service, or service in its quintessential character, is Quality Service. Quality Service is providing not only what is needed but giving the emotional gratification that we more deeply wish for as well. It exalts the receiver and, if only in its facade, says that both the giver and the receiver are highly valued. At heart, Quality Service is the dream of Perfect Love.

## Chapter 12

ABSOLUTE ETHICS,
RELATIVELY SPEAKING

Sidney J. Levy

Marketing education has become increasingly enriched by the need to consider a variety of modern additions to the curriculum. In a discipline sensitive to contemporary currents—and in a time when sensitivity itself has become one of the currents—it is incumbent on marketing, marketers, and marketing study to pay attention to what is happening. This is a form of self-consciousness, because whatever is happening *is* marketing in the first place. For example, as marketing becomes more international in character, marketers are expected to engage in

it and schools are urged to give it academic attention. That is, we not only engage in more international marketing but we also engage in marketing the idea of international marketing. The same process has historically occurred with the issues of marketing competition, innovation, marketing research, qualitative research, entrepreneurship, concern with social change, the environment, diversity, quality, and lately ethics. Of course, these subjects and the necessity to deal with them were there earlier, in some form and in some instances

This chapter was first published in *Journal of Public Policy & Marketing,* 12(1), Spring 1993, pp. 137-139. Reprinted by permission of the American Marketing Association.

importantly so, but the great self-conscious scanning mechanisms of awareness and public emphasis had not come sufficiently into play.

Various efforts have been made to bring the problems of ethics in marketing to the attention of marketing professionals, as shown by contributors to the *Journal of Business Ethics* and to the recent volume on *The Frontier of Research in the Consumer Interest* (Maynes, 1988) and by the writings of Patrick Murphy, Gene Laczniak, Shelby Hunt, O. C. Ferrell, Larry Gresham, and too many others to list. There are the more fervent among us, crusaders like Rick Pollay and Alan Andreasen, as well as the compliant, the indifferent, and the unethical. The topic and debate about ethics are ancient, going back to the Bible and the Greeks at least, like so much else. At the heart of the contention is usually criticism of the desire for monetary gain and the corruption it produces. This is what so many see as the fundamental fault of marketing—not merely the desire to provide goods and services for others in exchange for the same, but to make money in doing so and thereby being led to take undue advantage of other people. It is easy to believe that exchanges are not even ones, but that others are benefitting to an unfair degree. In John Ruskin's (1880) polemic, "Usury," he sneers that the commercial phrase "interest" has been adopted supposedly to distinguish an open and unoppressive rate of usury from a surreptitious and tyrannical one, but that the debate has never turned seriously on that distinction. He says that usury in any degree is asserted by the Doctors of the early Church to be sinful, were the interest even only a penny. His view is contested by the Bishop of Manchester, who finds no sin in an agreeable exchange, with profit to both parties.

But how do we judge when this condition will obtain, given the complexity of many decisions that face modern marketing managers, when the agreeable exchange involves not only money but the quality of goods, information, and service treatment? Conflict in the marketplace is inevitable, as I have elsewhere discussed in detail (Levy & Zaltman, 1975), and many disagreeable instances arise.

The current interest in ethics has grown to the point that the marketplace needs a comprehensive textbook that examines ethics issues commonly encountered by marketing managers. As a result, such a textbook has appeared, in the form of *Ethics in Marketing* by N. Craig Smith and John A. Quelch (1992). The book is an edited collection of chapters, following a scheme that provides a rich and varied body of material. Organized around the major realms of marketing activity, the volume takes up the many problems posed for marketing managers by society and the environment, marketing research, product policy, pricing policy, distribution policy, communications, sales, advertising and sales promotion, and marketing strategy. The chapters include overall discussion of the main ethical issues, several written by the editors and others by these authors: E. Raymond Corey, Lynn Sharp Paine, Melvyn A. J. Menezes, Fred W. Morgan, Gwendolyn K. Ortmeyer, Jeffrey Sonnenfeld, Paul R. Lawrence, Frank V. Cespedes, Patrick J. Kaufmann, Robert J. Kopp, Diana C. Robertson, Erin Anderson, Minette E. Drumwright, and Ivan L. Preston. Each chapter includes several Harvard cases and a section, "In the News," of examples drawn from newspaper articles. The volume ends with "A General Theory of Marketing Ethics" with a retrospective and revision, by Shelby D. Hunt and Scott J.

Vitell. The Appendix includes examples of codes of conduct (Apple Computer, Inc., Quaker Oats Company, and the American Marketing Association), exercises to challenge discussion, and an extensive bibliography.

This plan thus ranges from the abstractions of theory, philosophy, and setting of contexts, to the concrete instances of cases and news items, a most useful compendium for anyone interested in exploring ethics problems facing marketing managers. Faculty are usually asked to include some aspects of important issues in their courses, so that every course should have some attention to international, to quality, to ethics, and so on; thus, anyone might take note of relevant portions of this book as a supplement to other course content. Also, whole courses devoted to ethics have come into being, which would clearly find this book helpful, whether as a text for the course, or as a valuable resource, given its many examples that involve famous names from the contemporary marketing scene, such as McDonald's, Reebok, Gallo, Black & Decker, Procter & Gamble, Suzuki, and so on, to capture the students' attention.

The publication of this book raises some curious questions. Does it signify that the ethics of marketers, suspect since ancient times, are getting worse (epitomized in the self-seeking, greedy 1980s), so that the ethically minded find it necessary to intensify their efforts to reverse this deterioration in the conduct of business? Is there a pendulum in these matters, whereby we are due for an ethical swing? Perhaps the book is a manifestation of a growth of general virtue in society, in keeping with an historic movement away from the old attitude of the "public be damned" that led to the muckrakers, the Consumers Union, and recently to the surge in concern for the

environment. Maybe this concern with ethics expresses realignments of power in society, as the retailers struggle for distribution control against the manufacturers, as litigation and legislation soar, with the consumer groups (patients, drivers, etc.) exercising their ability to boycott and bring class action suits. Then, too, there is the desire to be healthy and long-lived, fit and bodily perfect, with exercise and plastic surgery, plus the recent preoccupation with making food ideally nutritious, acting as an obsessive drive toward virtuous behavior.

In any event, the contest between good and evil is likely to be eternal, given the widespread persistence of atrocious behavior; and the ethical issues will remain. Society has a continuum of prescriptions for positive behavior, ranging from being nice to behaving properly, to acting in an ethical way, to obeying the moral and ethical principles that have been enacted into law. But while we may distinguish between what we must or must not do, by law, and the greyer areas of what we ought or ought not do, short of law, we live in such litigious times that almost any disapproved behavior may be cause for court action.

The first chapter of *Ethics and the Marketing Manager*, by N. Craig Smith, is a thoughtful introduction to the topic, aiming to limit the focus of the book, to sort out its intention from the larger ethical philosophies and frameworks. Basing his normative approach on a 2-year research project at Harvard, he wants to help marketing managers to think in a way that answers their common question, "How do I know my marketing is ethical?" This posture does not advance ethical relativism, but it does recognize an ethical continuum that ranges in emphasis from caveat emptor to caveat venditor—a kind of relativism within the absolutism of an ethics that says we all know that we should be doing the good and right thing. But what should be our emphasis? Smith recommends the consumer sovereignty goal, promoting as a first priority the interests of the consumer. The text materials give ample opportunity to debate this premise, since a broad guide to behavior leaves much open to individual interpretation and expression of values. Many people have trouble with general guides and want to be told what to do in specific situations. The December 1992 issue of the *American Psychologist* prints the "Ethical Principles of Psychologists and Code of Conduct:" This document is 13½ pages long! It must be as hard to be an ethical psychologist (I am one, and I know it) as to be an ethical marketing manager. The Apple Computer Company Code of Conduct is nine pages long. At the same time, lying behind these specificities are general principles, attitudes, motives, that cannot be ignored, given their force and influence; and the Smith and Quelch book ranges through and across them via the sheer heterogeneity of the readings and cases.

A last question: Will this text help students become more ethical managers, to "handle ethically questionable marketing practices with courage and conviction," as it hopes? We can suppose that fostering classroom discussion both creates and teaches ethics, in the sense that some participants lead and assert positions that others follow, benefitting from hearing the contention of views and the articulation of what the average person should do. Certainly some clarification will occur that pushes many people in the direction of a popular or common position. After all, that is what *mores* and *ethos* are—the prevailing customs and beliefs of the group, so the results should seem successful.

"Prevailing" seems an important aspect of the situation. Twenty years ago, I tried to involve students in an environmental case about the cutting of trees, and they were quite uninterested. Nowadays, they discuss it with intensity. Similarly, a few years ago, Amitai Etzioni wrote a piece about his visit to the Harvard Business School to teach a course in ethics. He apparently found the students so recalcitrant that he considered his course (and his visit) a failure. Perhaps he would have better luck now—or perhaps the ethics he wanted to teach were not the ethics the students wanted to learn. Recently, I had a lively discussion with a graduate class about whether they would rather ban cigarette advertising, as the *New Yorker* magazine has for many years, or liquor ads, considering the great evils created by alcohol consumption. The overwhelming consensus was against cigarettes. When I asked why, one student sent the class into gales of laughter by asserting, "Because we none of us smoke, but we all drink!"

Ethics in Marketing will probably not do well with the more egocentric, the cynics, and the skeptics; and those who are negativistic about the holier-than-thou and self-righteous folks who claim to know what is good for everyone else. As it happens (unfortunately?), there are lots of these people, some who put freedom before virtue, others who believe that they "should do unto others before they do unto you," who think the worst sin is getting caught, or who are ethical relativists. The latter suffer from not being able to hold the moral and ethical high ground; they are disparaged and put down as "guilty" of sophistry. However, these various dissidents will have to debate their positions or keep their peace, and that might have some therapeutic value. For the rest, the use of *Ethics in Marketing* should do very well, as it makes public in classes, and informs students who want to conform, what the contemporary governing sentiments should be. It will do this in some ultimate sense, because its posture implies that there is a good and right way of doing things; but with provocations that are lively, examples that are varied, opportunities for the airing of contentious positions and a range of values.

REFERENCES

Levy, S. J., & Zaltman, G. (1975). *Marketing, society, and conflict.* Englewood Cliffs, NJ: Prentice Hall.

Maynes, E. S. (Ed.). (1988). *The frontier of research in the consumer interest.* Columbia, MO: American Council on Consumer Interests.

Ruskin, J. (1880). Usury. *Contemporary Review, 37,* 316-333.

Smith, N. C., & Quelch, J. A. (1992). *Ethics in marketing.* Burr Ridge, IL: Irwin.

PART
THREE

PRODUCTS AND
BRANDS

— •◆• —

Dennis Rook: Consumers in postindustrial economies reside in "branded" cultures, where markets are increasingly populated by an expanding universe of brand offerings, and companies strive to gain visibility and attract customers to their brands. The economic significance of brands receives frequent press attention, and over the past several years experts have variously debated whether brands are "on the run" or are "the main thing." In the 1980s, dramatic decreases in advertising, the growth of private and store brands, and recessionary pressures

---

The Product and the Brand (*Harvard Business Review*, 1955)

Brands, Trademarks, and the Law (*Review of Marketing*, 1981)

The Two Tiers of Marketing (*Marketing 2000 and Beyond*, 1990)

Marketing Stages in Developing Nations (*Proceedings*, International Conference on Marketing and Development, 1991)

Defending the Dowager: Communication Strategies for Declining Main Brands (Manuscript, 1993)

on consumers encouraged some business writers to declare the end of the great American brand era. Obviously, this epitaph was premature and, also, oblivious to the cyclical nature of such things. Today, brands are on the upswing, and both managers and scholars pay more attention to the idea of *brand equity*. Despite the current emphasis on brands, an enduring blind spot is the concept of the *brand image*.

This idea was first introduced over 40 years ago, in the lead article in this section, "The Product and the Brand," which appeared in the *Harvard Business Review* in 1955. This work grew out of Sid Levy's experience at Social Research, Inc. (SRI), which began in 1948 and involved numerous research studies of how consumers perceived products and brands. Across these diverse studies, Levy discovered the explanatory power of the concept of imagery, and he characterized a brand as a *complex symbol* that incorporates consumers' motives, feelings, logic, and attitudes. Consequently, consumers think of brands not merely as bundles of features and obvious benefits, but as more richly complex entities with different personalities, public personas, and other, often nonobvious symbolic qualities and implications.

This new, sophisticated thinking attracted immediate attention, particularly from advertising agencies and their clients. Industry pioneer David Ogilvy admiringly cited "The Product and the Brand" in a 1955 speech to the American Association of Advertising Agencies. The article's historical impact rests not only in its seminal articulation of brand imagery, but in its understanding of the need to integrate all marketing mix efforts to support "long-term investment in the reputation of the brand." Many managers today probably view *integrated marketing* as a recent innovation, yet its basic foundations were detailed long ago, in this article. Another contribution of this work comes from its recognition of the distinctive advantages of qualitative research methods for discovering the depth and subtlety of consumers' brand images. This thinking is elaborated in the final section of this volume, "Qualitative Methods of Marketing Study." Finally, brand imagery is one of many expressions of the symbolic nature of marketing. Other aspects of this, along with their theoretical sources, are covered in the next section, "The Symbolic Nature of Marketing." This cross-referencing points not only to the centrality of brands in marketing management but also to a theoretical and operational interconnectedness between how marketers think about brands and how effectively they research consumers' brand images.

The other articles in this section extend Levy's thinking about brands to several key arenas, including intellectual property law, competitive strategy, and global economic and marketing development. Today, there is much emphasis on developing brands as part of the new product development process; somewhat less dialogue about managing a brand's image as it grows toward maturity; and very little said about what to do when a brand seems past its prime and headed downhill. One factor that discourages more vigorous dialogue about postmaturity brands is the pessimistic assumption that their marketing decline is inevitable. (In Chapter 30, in his article on "Phases in Changing Interpersonal

Relations," Levy explains why this pessimism is commonly warranted.) In "Defending the Dowager: Communications Strategies for Declining Main Brands," Levy and I propose a framework for understanding the reasons for consumers' movements away from a once top brand, and we suggest procedures for designing communication strategies to win some of them back.

The relationship between brands and their intellectual property concerns is an area of growing interest. Trademark rights and infringement disputes are big ticket, strategic concerns for many companies today. In "Brands, Trademarks, and the Law (1981)," Levy and I emphasize the need to interpret a brand's meaning broadly in order to make realistic and fair assessments in trademark infringement and loss of rights litigation.

Consumers who pay attention to the "made in" sections of product labels are well aware how many different countries are represented. This country-of-origin information provides new levels of stimulation and meaning; a typical department store sportswear section, for example, is a virtual United Nations of garments, inviting consumers to ponder differences between a pair of shorts from India versus Sri Lanka . . . and where exactly is Gabon? In "Marketing Stages in Developing Nations" (1991), Levy provides an analysis of how countries acquire brand images, and how these change as countries move from being viewed as sources of cheap labor and shoddy goods toward images as providers of higher quality, more creative, and more refined products and services. In "The Two Tiers of Marketing" (1990), Levy interprets these global marketing movements as part of a larger interplay between the forces of what he characterizes as obligatory versus permissive marketing.

———— •◆• ————

## Chapter 13

THE PRODUCT AND THE BRAND

Burleigh B. Gardner
Sidney J. Levy

Basic to many of the problems of advertising and selling is the question of consumers' attitudes toward the product and particularly their conception of the brand. Qualitative research, especially of the kind which has so recently come to the fore as "consumer motivation" research, promises to add substantially to our knowledge in this area. The quantitative approach, which we used to have to rely on, only brings us part way to finding the kind of answers we need; now we can take a distinct step forward. Inquiry has taken a direct route in the past, oriented toward finding out the number of people who use the product, the main reasons they offer for doing so, the advantages and disadvantages they find in the brand, and so forth. The users have been counted; their reasons have been listed in order of frequency (and assumed to be the most potent); and their praises and complaints have been aired and duly registered. This information is important and useful for many purposes. But it leaves a great deal untouched and hence can be misleading.

This chapter first appeared in the *Harvard Business Review,* March-April 1955, pp. 33-39. Copyright 1955 by President and Fellows of Harvard College. Reprinted by permission of *Harvard Business Review.*

SUPERFICIAL REASONS

For one thing, the reasons people usually give for using a product are inclined to be either strongly rationalized or related to the product's most obvious purposes. Thus, most surveys tend to show that consumers want products to be, in one form or another, effective: to get clothes white, groom the hair, quench thirst, prevent tooth decay, taste good, and so on.

When such goals as these are taken at their face value and considered to be the end of the matter, they lead up many blind alleys. The belief that people are fretting over those minute differences presumed to provide the best quality results in such affairs as blindfold tests that try to find an otherwise indiscernible superiority on the part of one brand over other brands, in advertisements constantly claiming "more," and sometimes in a shrill focus on product merits beyond all proportion and sensible differentiation.

STEREOTYPED CLAIMS

The consumer, who generally believes that well-known brands will quite adequately perform their intended functions, gets a glazed feeling at the scholarly astuteness required to distinguish between insistently repetitive claims. A striking example of the stereotypes into which competitive brands can fall is this list of soap and detergent themes, each from a different brand's advertisement:

No detergent under the sun gets clothes whiter, brighter

Washes more kinds of clothes whiter and brighter

Beats the sun for getting clothes whiter and brighter

Washes clothes whiter without a bleach

Gives you a whiter wash without bleaching than any other "no rinse" suds with bleach added

Alone gets clothes whiter than bleach

Presumably little else can be done if the advertisers have the fixed idea that housewives are preoccupied solely with the whiteness of their laundry—because that is the most frequent, conscious, immediate notion women can muster up to explain their use of detergents and to justify the use of any preferred brand. But surely there is more to the matter than that.

What are some of the more fundamental issues a manufacturer and his advertising people should face in getting beyond such apparent aims, and what can they do about them?

NEW INSIGHTS

Answering this question calls for a greater awareness of the social and psychological nature of products—whether brands, media, companies, institutional figures, services, industries, or ideas. New conceptions and orientations are needed for a sensible understanding of the communication process that goes on in offering an object to the public.

COMPLEX MOTIVES

Many current ideas about human psychology are overly simple and nonoperational in definition. Gross assumptions are made about what people want and what motivates their wanting. Quick generalizations are made and arbitrarily transferred from one situation to another, often inappropriately.

For example, two very common motives that are belabored (when specific product substances and effects are not made the main issue) are (a) the striving to be economical and (b) the desire to emulate people of higher status. Undoubtedly consumers do pursue bargains, and many people do have social aspirations. In given instances these ideas may have to be given crucial consideration. Nevertheless, there is a tremendous range of other variables that may totally negate, or even reverse, the direction of these strivings—and the complications in any single situation should be specifically studied.

Thus, as far as economy is concerned, with many kinds of products low cost is not intently sought, or there may be a subtle assessment of "good value" being made. Indeed, consumers may have a definite figure in mind (arrived at in some curious way) which they believe is the price the object should cost. Hence elasticity of demand can vary in strange patterns.

Again, with the mobility of our society, millions of Americans do want to make progress, but not necessarily upward. They simply may not want to be like, or to live like, people of a different social status. While sometimes a "woman's point of view" may prevail in management councils, and the manufacturer's wife may then be a good source of information, all too often lower middle-class and upper lower-class housewives (most of the housewives) do not think like Mrs. Management, do not share many of her needs, her values, her esthetics, or her ways of solving problems.

Thus, one of the first things a manufacturer and his advertising people need to explore is the particular constellation of goals and attitudes most pertinent to their product and brand situation, rather than applying blindly the one that seemed so useful to Listerine 15 years ago, to Ford last year, or to Kraft this year.

PRODUCT DIMENSIONS

Such explorations must take into account the character of the product (the human needs it serves and the particular way it does so), the dimensions employed in evaluating brands of such a product, and where the particular brand stands on these dimensions. At the literal level, a newspaper, for example, is supposed to be "a printed publication issued at regular intervals, usually daily or weekly, and commonly containing news, comment, features, and advertisements" (according to the *American College Dictionary*). These are common expectations, and a newspaper will be measured as to how well or poorly it is printed, how regularly it appears, whether it distinguishes its news, comments, features, and ads, and so on.

However, in our society other dimensions will emerge, perhaps of greater importance, to differentiate the papers in influential ways. The definition does not show (as qualitative research does) that the public tends to feel that a sense of public responsibility is a major ingredient in the character of a newspaper; and this factor will be very important to the image of any given paper, in itself and in how it compares with its competitors.

Furthermore, anyone can readily observe that different papers generally have what we can call different personalities.

Thus, *The New York Times* is quite a different thing from the New York *Daily News,* or the *Chicago Tribune* is different from the *Chicago Sun-Times*. These differences appear in many ways: selection of news, handling of particular stories, choice of headlines, types of facts reported, and editorial content. Thus they represent complex systems of values and of judgments, applied to the daily process of getting out a paper.

PUBLIC IMAGE

In similar fashion, a brand name is more than the label employed to differentiate among the manufacturers of a product. It is a complex symbol that represents a variety of ideas and attributes. It tells the consumers many things, not only by the way it sounds (and its literal meaning if it has one) but, more important, via the body of associations it has built up and acquired as a public object over a period of time. A well-chosen brand name may have a rhythmic quality (like Jell-O for desserts) or an apt air (like Bell for telephones). It will also convey meanings which advertising, merchandising, promotion, publicity, and even sheer length of existence have created.

The net result is a public image, a character or personality that may be more important for the overall status (and sales) of the brand than many technical facts about the product. Conceiving of a brand in this way calls for a rethinking of brand advertising and of the kinds of judgments that have to be made by an informed management about its communications to the public.

CRUCIAL SYMBOLS

The image of a product associated with the brand may be clear-cut or relatively vague; it may be varied or simple; it may be intense or innocuous. Sometimes the notions people have about a brand do not even seem very sensible or relevant to those who know what the product is "really" like. But they all contribute to the customer's deciding whether or not the brand is the one "for me."

These sets of ideas, feelings, and attitudes that consumers have about brands are crucial to them in picking and sticking to ones that seem most appropriate. How else can they decide whether to smoke Camels or Marlboro; to use Nescafe or Maxim's instant coffee; to drive a Ford or a Chevrolet or a Plymouth.

Justifying choice is easier with the cars; there at least the products have clearly visible differences. But the reasons people give for choosing a brand of cigarettes (and soap and bread and laxatives) are pretty much the same. Thus you find drinkers of any brand of beer justifying their preference in identical terms: "Millers is better because it's dry." "I like a dry beer, so I prefer Bud to Millers."

Something must make a greater difference; the conceptions of the different brands must be compounded of subtle variations in feelings about them, not necessarily in product qualities. A big problem in this area, then, is what kind of symbol a given brand is to consumers.

RESEARCH IN DEPTH

A variety of concepts and methods are being applied to this type of problem. Procedures first developed to explore the complex facets of attitudes and motives in clinical and academic research are finding new adaptations. They are especially useful for arriving at an understanding of the attitudes and feelings which make up the image of a product and a brand.

Uncovering Attitudes

Rather than interviewing a large number of respondents in a terse, question-and-answer fashion, researchers take smaller samples and interview them at some length. The subjects are allowed to express themselves with a relatively large degree of individuality, to give their views in their own words. Hence, the interview usually proceeds in a conversational fashion rather than being held to a tightly circumscribed framework. In addition, various kinds of more or less vague and ambiguous stimuli are introduced into the interview. They present an issue or a task that the respondent must handle in his or her own way, thereby "projecting" assumptions and evaluations that might not otherwise be made explicit. An example of one of these projective techniques is thematic analysis of storytelling.

Interviewees are shown a picture that makes some reference to use of the product or a particular brand. Although respondents might not be willing to say, for instance, that they are relatively indifferent to the object, it may be apparent from their stories. Perhaps the stories are unusually brief, limited in variety of ideas, lacking in liveliness, or extremely repetitive. By contrast, another object being studied might elicit stories expressed enthusiastically and

with a good deal of individu ciations and experiences.

Discerning Differences

Where the various brands of a product are largely indistinguishable as to quality, cost, effectiveness, and so on—or, what is about the same thing, each user group claims that its brand is outstanding on the same points—how can the consumers' varying brand evaluations be discerned? Sometimes matching techniques show public views that consumers have difficulty in stating—or that they even deny. When consumers are presented with a list of kinds of people and asked to name those most likely to choose each of the brands, many resist the task as meaningless, since presumably all the brands are basically comparable. Nevertheless, random patterns of these evaluations rarely emerge, as would be expected if consumers' responses were taken at their face value. Instead, definite dimensions do show up. In other words, consumers really believe there are differences among the brands. To illustrate:

On one device, Brand A may turn out to be regarded as the most suitable for wives of doctors, lawyers, office managers, and company presidents, while Brand B is attributed to the wives of electricians, carpenters, taxi drivers, and grocery clerks. Clearly, there is a social status differentiation between the two brands that helps a woman determine which is more suited for her own needs. (Remember, it does not mean that Brand B will be rejected, either; many consumers do not want to emulate members of other social groups.) It may also turn out that on another device Brand A is named as especially used

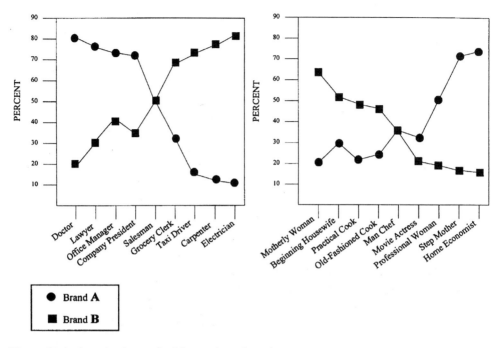

Figure 13.1. A projective method for studying brands

by home economists, stepmothers, professional women, and movie actresses, while Brand B is regarded as suitable for motherly women, beginning housewives, practical cooks, and old-fashioned cooks. The image of Brand A is more austere, less friendly; the consumers see it not only as of higher status but also somewhat remote. On the other hand, Brand B has a warmer sound to it, a down-to-earth quality; it is regarded as a more ordinary brand, one for everyday people (see Figure 13.1).

By the use of such approaches, including incomplete sentences, word association, forced choices, and role playing, the main dimensions of a brand or product character can be drawn out. The important ideas may not be mysterious, or even profound psychological constructions; they are more likely to be similar in quality to the way human personalities show themselves. The

techniques used are not the crux of the matter; they are only avenues to understanding. The emphasis in such research must necessarily be given to skill in interpretation and to reaching a coherent picture of the brand. The researchers must allow their respondents sufficient self-expression so that the data are rich in complex evaluations of the brand. In this way, the consumers' thoughts and feelings are given precedence rather than the preconceptions of the researchers, although these are present too in hypotheses and questions.

MANAGEMENT'S TASK

Having discovered how the product and brand are organized in consumers' minds, management's problem is what to do about it.

Setting Goals

First of all, management must take into account these two basic points:

1. *A reputable brand persists as a stable image through time.* The ideas people have about it are not completely malleable, not idly swayed by one communication and then another. If the public believes that a certain brand is of inferior quality or that another is "on the skids," or that some other has all the latest improvements, these beliefs are not usually modified very rapidly. Such reputations are built through time, frequently in ways that management is not aware of.

2. *It is rarely possible for a product or brand to be all things to all people.* It may be most desirable to sell to the most people, but hardly anyone can sell to everyone. Some brands have very skillfully built up reputations of being suitable for a wide variety of people, but in most areas audience groupings will differ, if only because there are deviants who refuse to consume the same way other people do.

More significantly, there are different age, sex, social class, personality groupings, to say nothing of special interest groups, ethnic groups, and occupational groups. It is not easy for a brand to appeal to stable lower middle-class people and at the same time to be interesting to sophisticated, intellectual upper middle-class buyers.

Accordingly, management has to determine what kind of brand it wants to present. Does it wish to be very dignified (and forgo the teen-age, dime-store customers), does it want to be smart and individual (and latch onto *The New Yorker* readers), or does it want to seem a bit daring and frivolous (and skip a lot of moral middle-class housewives)?

Decision Making

Basically, although advertising and research people can contribute a great deal toward making the judgment most realistic, this is a management decision. A great deal can stand or fall on the direction taken—such as whether the company stakes its success on winning a larger part of a smaller market, or moving more goods at a lower margin, or whatever the long-range strategy may be.

Knowingly or not, management makes this decision. Thus, some companies do it by refusing to sponsor certain radio or television shows because they believe they are undignified, and (by making these and other such decisions) may wind up in the public eye as a rather stuffy outfit with a too-expensive product. Other managements insist on "hard sell" until they discover to their dismay that their market has become predominantly lower class.

Deciding about each campaign or action may not require a session on the razor's edge, but the most fruitful approach is one that involves an awareness of long-range goals for the character of the product as well as some attempt to be consistent with the chosen course.

Preparing for Action

It is not enough for management to say to itself, "Of course we want a favorable brand image. So having decided we want one that will appeal to all groups, that will have all good qualities and no negative ones, let's tell the world this is what we are." The management that takes this approach to developing an effective brand image is no more likely to succeed than the management that tries to convince its employees it is benevolent and only concerned with their good by merely telling them loud and often about its benevolent intentions.

For management to be able to handle this problem effectively it should evaluate its brand's current public image, the differences seen by different important consumer groups, and the images of competitive brands. Otherwise, it does not know just what it is working against, what limitations in image must be overcome, and what strengths it has to build on.

Basic attitudes toward products may set limits on the kind of image that might be developed or in the kinds of satisfactions that the product image may imply. Or a given brand may have such a strong image in some respects that it is more feasible to accept these than to change them. For example, if a product has a strong image of high quality and special-occasion use, it might be disastrous to try to reduce it rapidly to more prosaic everyday use.

By knowing the possible directions in which it might go, management is in a position to judge the specific moves or campaigns designed to reach the goals it has set.

THE AGENCY'S ROLE

Once the current public view of a brand has been explored and an image to be aimed at for the future has been determined, the major problems are assumed by the company's advertising agency. It is the business of advertising to assist in the creation of brand images, to give them structure and content, to develop a pattern of consumer attitudes likely to lead to brand purchase. How can the advertising agency go about this? What is its role?

Professional Standards

As a profession, advertising has many possible roles: Should it be creative, businesslike, or sociable; should it nursemaid the client (and maybe his family) or strike out for independence and professional integrity. Advertising has been subject to pressures from the whims and presumed knowledge of its clients in a way that well-established professions refuse to tolerate—and for several reasons:

- Advertising has been an occupation of creativity and individual personalities.
- The effects of advertising campaigns are often difficult to measure.
- Single accounts can mean life or death to an agency.
- Everyone believes he knows what an advertisement should be like.

However, as advertising builds up a body of principles, an increased understanding of audience composition and reactions, and a wide-ranging familiarity with procedures and techniques—plus a sense of responsibility and pride in good performance—management should recognize these developments and take advantage of them.

Having set the goals for its product, management ideally should leave to the skills and know-how of the advertising people the job of implementing them. A layman (with reference to any profession) is frequently not in a position to understand how a particular process or step—or advertising layout—is conducive to the desired goals.

Building the Brand

In creating, developing, or modifying a brand image, the advertising people must have a good understanding of the situation that confronts them. This includes a nuanced appreciation of the brand image as it already exists—with an awareness that the momentary sales position of the brand may be less important for its future than the danger that people may think of it as getting increasingly passé, perhaps.

Advertising men must think about such problems as:

1. In a lively product area, is the brand thought of as dull?

2. In a conservative product area, is the brand too frivolously presented?

3. Does it involve anxious connotations?

4. Does its use pattern seem increasingly circumscribed?

5. Is it an "unfriendly" brand, an overly masculine brand, a weak-seeming brand, and so on?

Understanding the brand problems and the manufacturer's goals (and remember that his objective is not always just to sell the most goods the quickest) is a basic requirement. Then a thorough knowledge of how to move ahead is needed. What are the kinds of valuables that have to be dealt with? How can they be got across to the public?

The truly sophisticated advertising man realizes that communications are subtle, that many an advertisement says things about the product that were never intended by the copywriter. To illustrate: Some time ago a less sophisticated advertising man wanted to know why it was that instant coffee had come to be regarded as an inferior substitute when it was originally thought of as an expensive concentrate. It did not occur to him that his own agency

had for a long time been instrumental in offering a brand of instant coffee with constant emphasis on savings, bargains, deals, economies.

Brand images do not grow in a vacuum. A newspaper advertisement that employed a heavy black border to demarcate it from its neighbors was noted by consumers as dead-looking, and the product was thought impure. An advertisement that showed the fine texture of the product under a microscope made people think of disease bacteria.

Long-Term Investment

In themselves, such instances of individual advertisements may not be crucial; certainly a product image is the result of many varied experiences. They all make their contributions, for good or for bad, and will do so best when the long-range goals are kept in mind during their creation. Too many advertisements are built as individual units, with a conglomeration of elements to satisfy different agency and client tastes rather than with reference to a guiding, governing product and brand personality that is unified and coherently meaningful.

In many advertising conferences someone will ask: "Which of these campaigns will sell the most packages?" This is not an irrelevant question, certainly, since presumably advertising that does not sell is unproductive. Nevertheless, a single campaign is not the manufacturer's only salesman, and he usually intends to remain in business for many following years. From this point of view it is more profitable to think of an advertisement as a contribution to the complex symbol which is the brand image—as part of the long-term investment in the reputation of the brand.

This point of view has many implications. It means that:

- Copy should be thought about in terms of its symbolic and indirect meanings as well as its literal communication.
- Color and illustration are not merely aesthetic problems since they also have social and psychological implications.
- Media selection should be related to a brand image plan and not merely geared to circulation figures.
- Research should seek out ideas and meanings as well as audience statistics.

CONCLUSION

We have sought to highlight some ideas that seem to be important in the thoughtful presentation of products and brands. Products and brands have interwoven sets of characteristics and are complexly evaluated by consumers. Hence, advertising a product is not a matter of isolated messages. It calls for analyses of attitudes and motives. It also calls for a differentiated knowledge and judgment on the part of management and advertising people; in a sense, their tasks become richer, and the division of responsibility more meaningful.

With the findings of qualitative research, management can see its product in a clearer perspective. Advertising people can increase their awareness of the social-scientific nature of the communication process and the way in which their actions influence it. Those on the creative side of advertising, particularly, can find new sources of stimulation and inspiration in breaking away from the preconceptions and conventions that have fixed so much advertising in set molds.

Chapter 14

BRANDS, TRADEMARKS, AND THE LAW

Sidney J. Levy
Dennis W. Rook

Entertainer Johnny Carson failed recently to stop a suburban Detroit outhouse manufacturer from calling its portable toilets "Here's Johnny." A U.S. District Court Judge ruled in the case that use of the phrase, "Here's Johnny" on portable outhouses does not constitute trademark infringement. (Carson later won on appeal.)

In St. Louis last year a Federal Appeals Court upheld a lower court decision prohibiting the Seven-Up Company from using *Quirst* as the name for a new noncarbon-ated lemon drink. The court concluded that the Quirst name trespassed upon the Squirt Company's *Squirt* mark for its carbonated grapefruit beverage.

In Boston, a U.S. District Judge barred the sale of T-shirts emblazoned with a big yellow M similar to McDonald's logo and the saying "Marijuana—over 10 billion stoned." The hamburger chain said the T-shirts infringed on its trademarked arches and detracted from its image of quality, cleanliness, and wholesomeness.

This chapter was first published in B. Enis & K. J. Roering (Eds.), *Review of Marketing*, 1981, pp. 185-194. Reprinted by permission of the American Marketing Association.

Parker Brothers has initiated trademark litigation against the manufacturers of a table game named *Anti-Monopoly,* which they claim infringes upon their *Monopoly* product. The defendant in this case has counterargued that *Monopoly* has assumed a generic existence and can no longer be deemed a private trademark.

These examples partially illustrate the extent and metaphysical nature of the conflicts that characterize the trademark arena. Although state and federal trademark laws (notably the Lanham Act, 1946) have been enacted to protect legitimate proprietary rights and to safeguard consumers from confusion and deception—poaching and counterfeiting are today widespread. Playboy Enterprises' legal department handles almost two trademark infringement cases a week. Recently the International Anticounterfeiting Coalition was formed by 25 multinational companies that considered themselves principal victims of trademark violations, to the tune of $100 million ripoff losses annually. The total yearly take by all trademark infringers is conservatively estimated at $50 million. Companies also spend millions on trademark enforcement programs. Coca-Cola, for example, employs field investigators to guarantee that when a consumer in a restaurant orders a "Coke," he is not served a substitute cola drink. To add bite to their trademark enforcement program, Coke's annual budget recently allowed for 365 prosecutions of "passing off" violations. Trademark modification and modernization programs are another avenue for corporate expenditures. When Standard Oil of New Jersey consolidated its various identities (Esso, Enco, Enjay, Humble) under the Exxon banner, its name change may have cost as much as $100 million (Enis, 1978). Among other considerations, the company was said to be distressed that its Enco mark connoted "stalled car" in Japanese.

Increasing levels of trademark conflict have pressed the courts to develop methods for empirically determining instances of trademark infringement and other trade identity offenses. Similarly, litigants need reliable methods and resources to argue effectively their respective cases. In spite of all this marketplace action, the analytical and evidential tools employed in trademark litigation are poorly developed. Offering possible assistance is an emerging view that the various methodologies of the social sciences have advanced to the point where empirical research can effectively address the validity of assumptions, doctrines, and reasoning of judicial and administrative bodies (Kochan, 1977).

Most scholars acknowledge the Supreme Court decision in *Muller v. Oregon* (1908) as a landmark case in fostering the use of research as legal evidence. In successfully defending an Oregon law establishing a 10-hour workday limit for women, Louis Brandeis's brief contained only two pages of legal citations and more than 100 pages of statistical analysis. As one scholar described Brandeis's efforts,

> That brief represents the classic attempt in the American legal process to harmonize the law with the need for social and legal progress; the technique was to prove a factual connection between the law and the conditions of life which have evoked it, and not through legal syllogisms. (Gerlach, 1972)

At the time of the Muller decision, trade identity conflicts provided an early opportunity to connect the law with the factual "conditions of life." Trademark law was, in fact, an initial marketing-related business area in which applications of behavioral research techniques were considered (Rogers, 1910). As a result of these innovations in trademark law, one might reasonably expect the field today to reflect the current state-of-the-art in behavioral research. Such is not the case. Although there has been some diffusion of behavioral research techniques (particularly survey research methods) into the trademark arena, their use in resolving questions of trademark infringement has been limited in scope and success. While these issues may be particularly interesting to research methodologists, few would argue that procedures for gathering evidence in trademark litigation are merely an academic issue. There are today over 400,000 "active" registered trademarks on the Principal Register of the U.S. Patent and Trademark Office, and in recent years applications for federal registration have increased to an average of 50,000 per annum (Burge, 1980). The crowding of the marketplace with new marks and the competitive forces that encourage the imitation of successful marks place research issues in the center of trademark controversies. In addition, questions of trade identity—or distinctiveness—have grown more complex with the adoption of highly abstract marks. These considerations suggest the need to discuss critically the methods that have evolved under the law for proving trademark infringement and other trade identity issues. Prior to such discussion it will be useful first to review the evolution of trademarks in the marketplace and their protection under the law. Following this will be a discussion of one development that promises to guide trade identity research: the judicial recognition of the psychological nature of trademarks. The results of a pilot study will be reported and, finally, implications for both basic and marketing research will be suggested.

TRADEMARKS AND BRANDS

One authority has concluded that there are three well-received, operational components of a trademark:

1. A trademark must consist of a word, name, symbol, device, or any other kind of designation.

2. It must be adopted and used by a manufacturer or merchant.

3. It must identify his goods and distinguish them from those manufactured or sold by others. (Gilson, 1974, pp. 1-8)

That is, trademarks have identity, persistence, and distinctiveness. They belong to a varied universe of commercial symbols (words, logos, slogans, and other devices). The physical dimension of a trademark may consist of a coined word (Kodak, Ipana, Decca), an ordinary word that has no readily apparent meaning in connection with the product to which it is attached (Arrow and Eagle menswear), a word that suggests the performance of the product (Whirlpool), a coined word suggesting the product function (Kleenex), a foreign word (Lux), a founder's name (Ford), the name of an historically famous person (Lincoln), initials (RCA), numerals (No. 5), a pictorial mark (Elsie the Cow), or a package (the Coca-Cola bottle) (Diamond, 1973, pp. l-2). Trademarks are widely differentiated in form and appearance, and the modern marketer has considerable latitude in selection of a trademark to represent his product in the marketplace.

The universe of commercial trademarks that today distinguish many thousand branded goods and services can be traced historically to marketplace practices that are at least 3,500 years old. The modern usage of trademarks is linked to changing patterns in the production and distribution of manufactured goods during the 19th century. The economic changes resulting from the industrial revolution served physically to separate the consumer from the producer; and the modern internationalization of commercial activities has increased this spread. Trademarks function as cues that bridge this gap, so that the consumer is able to identify the product with its commercial source.

In the United States, the development of national markets encouraged the large-scale manufacturer to devise communication strategies for identifying and distinguishing his products. Following the Civil War national brands began to emerge and supplant the undifferentiated, unbranded, and frequently unpackaged goods that characterized the retail outlets of the period. Accompanying the advent of national brands were large-scale advertising efforts that included the earliest *trade characters* (Sunny Jim, the Campbell Soup kids) and the use of celebrity endorsements (Henry Ward Beecher, Lillian Russell)—all designed to carve out a favorable niche in the consumer's consciousness. The marketplace longevity enjoyed by some of these early national brands suggests the wisdom of the branding strategy. Brands such as Ivory Soap, Eastman Kodak, Campbell's Soups, Quaker Oats, Coca-Cola, Bakers Cocoa, and Steinway piano have maintained strong positions in their respective markets for many decades. Because of its trade identity role, a trademark constitutes an important marketing variable. From a legal perspective, a trademark is a brand or part of a brand that is given protection because it is capable of exclusive appropriation. In everyday discussion and in legal parlance

the terms *brand* and *trademark* tend to be employed interchangeably (Black, 1979; Pattishall & Hilliard, 1974). A trademark is a legal entity that protects the seller's exclusive rights to use the brand name and/or brand mark within a specified market domain.

TRADEMARK DISTINCTIVENESS, GENERICISM, AND INFRINGEMENT

A company with a familiar and well-received trademark has a natural economic interest in guarding it from trespass by competitors and noncompetitors alike. The law has accordingly offered protection to owners of trademarks under the common and statutory law. In general, a trademark is accorded legal protection because of its multiple marketing roles. A trademark:

1. designates the source or origin of a particular product or service

2. denotes a particular standard of quality that is embodied in the product or service

3. identifies a product and distinguishes it from the products or services of others

4. symbolizes the good will of its owner

5. motivates consumers to purchase the trademarked product or service

6. represents a substantial advertising investment and is treated as a species of property

7. protects the public from confusion and deception (Gilson, 1974, pp. 1-14)

To establish and enjoy the rights under federal trademark law, businesses register their marks with the U.S. Patent and Trademark Office. Trade identity *rights,* however, arise not so much from a mark's mere adoption and federal registration as from its bona fide use in commerce (*Hanover Star Milling v. Metcalf,* 1916). Trademark scholar McCarthy (1973) explains that rights are not secured by a race to the Patent and Trademark Office but by a race to the marketplace. The assessment of a particular mark's trade identity rights requires not only a legalistic perspective but a view that embraces a complex matrix of relevant market behavior.

Three aspects of trademark-related phenomena are selected for discussion here: (a) the creation and maintenance of trade identity rights through a mark's acquired distinctiveness, (b) lack of trade identity rights through a mark's loss (or absence) of source-indicating significance (i.e., genericism), and (c) trademark infringement and consumer confusion. These topics are conceptually related, but each constitutes an identifiable body of legal discourse and judicial precedent.

Trademark Distinctiveness

Central to a firm's successful creation and maintenance of trade identity rights is the idea that a trademark's potency depends not only on priority of adoption and use but on its acquired distinctiveness among consumers and throughout the marketplace. There are many legal regulations that govern the technical aspects of a mark's adoption and use. Of special interest here are issues relating to a mark's acquisition of meaning. The degree to which a particular mark may be exclusively appropriated is linked to its interpreted level of distinctiveness. Arbitrary, fanciful terms such as Kodak, Xerox, or Exxon may enjoy broader protection than marks that

rely upon terms taken from the common language. Descriptive, suggestive, and laudatory terms, geographical terms, surnames, and colors constitute "narrow and weak" trademarks because their primary connotation does not identify a specific commercial source. "Secondary meaning" is the legal phrase that refers to a situation where a common term over time acquires a single, source-indicating significance. For example, *Ivory* has acquired a secondary meaning signifying a particular manufacturer's soap, whereas its primary meaning refers to the substance of an elephant's tusk. Similarly, McDonald is a common surname, but it possesses source-indicating significance within the fast food domain.

Because it seems undesirable to allow the withdrawal of common words from the language for exclusive corporate use, the protection afforded marks that rely on everyday terms is narrowly defined: "one who takes a phrase which is the commonplace of self-praise like 'Blue Ribbon' or 'Gold Medal' must be content with that special field which he labels with so undistinctive a name" (*France Milling Co. v. Washburn-Crosby Co.,* 1925).

While law does not preclude exclusive trademark use of common terms, the courts tend to circumscribe the commercial domain within which such a term enjoys trademark protection. The extent to which a trademark acquires source-indicating significance depends on the market interactions of buyers and sellers, the activities of competitors, impinging environmental factors, and the organization's deployment and control of marketing mix variables. A highly distinctive mark becomes a congenial corporate symbol imbued with a "commercial magnetism" that merits protection (*Mishawaka Rubber and Wollen Mfg. Co. v. S. S. Kresge Co.,* 1942).

Generic Terms

Once a firm has acquired a potent trade identity, it may, ironically, need to guard against casual use of its name to identify its product(s). Actor Robert Young's television commercials describe the merits of Sanka *brand* coffee, demonstrating Sanka's concern that its mark not lose its source-indicating significance and, thereby, its exclusive rights to the word *Sanka*.

Trade identity rights may be forfeited through abandonment, assignment without goodwill, licensing in gross, and loss of source-indicating significance. The latter process—that of becoming generic—results when a term's principal meaning to the public is to indicate the product or service itself rather than to imply a unique commercial source (*Feathercombs, Inc., v. Solo Products Corp.,* 1962). U.S. Patent and Trademark Office Commissioner Sidney Diamond (1973) explains,

> Brand names can be oversold. If your product is way ahead of all its competitors, this may be the time to look around for danger signals and take preventative action if necessary. When a product is so successful that the public adopts the brand name as the name of the product itself—as distinguished from one particular manufacturer's version of that product—then the brand name has passed into the language and the manufacturer who originated it no longer has the exclusive right to use it. (pp. 187-188)

Aspirin, cellophane, linoleum, milk of magnesia, and shredded wheat were originally coined as private trademarks but subsequently adjudicated as having lost their source-indicating connotation by becoming common terms. Recently the FTC claimed that Formica's trademark registration should be canceled because the term has become generic. This was the first time the FTC had ever pursued a trademark case on the issue that the mark had become generic. The 1980 FTC Antitrust Improvement Act bars the FTC through 1982 from pursuing action against trademarks on the grounds that the challenged mark has become generic. In another celebrated case, the Court has ruled that *light* by any other name—or spelling—remains a generic word. This ruling affirmed a lower court's decision that *lite* was a generic term used to describe beer's color, flavor, body, or alcoholic content, and it rejected Miller Brewing Company's contention that it had given new meaning to the word light as a name for its less filling, low-calorie beer.

Products may be sold without seeking brand distinction, as commodities, like much produce or like unbranded pharmaceuticals. Here, of special interest is the genericism that represents the anomalous situation wherein a manufacturer suffers a severe loss from its own success in the marketplace. Table 14.1 shows how consumers vary in their interpretation of whether or not a word is a common, generic term or a brand name. These results illustrate some of the hazards and ambiguities. Do they suggest that there is enough strength left in Thermos to warrant its still being a trademark after all; or that Coke, Teflon, and Jell-O are well on the way to becoming generic? King-Seely Thermos Company's current rights with respect to its Thermos mark have been narrowly defined by the courts. Its competitors may refer to their vacuum bottles as *thermos* bottles, but only King-Seely may use the upper case *T* or signify its products as "original."

Marketing communications efforts coupled with vigorous trademark enforcement programs encourage the appropriate public

TABLE 14.1 Consumer Interpretations

Name	Brand Percentage	Common Percentage	Don't Know Percentage
STP	90	5	5
Thermos	51	46	3
Margarine	9	91	1
Teflon	68	31	2
Jell-O	74	25	1
Refrigerator	6	94	—
Aspirin	13	86	1
Coke	76	24	1

SOURCE: *E. I. DuPont & Co. v. Yoshida Int'l*, 393 f. supp. 502, (E.D.N.Y.) (1975).

use of a particular mark. Remedial and/or preventative measures include explanatory footnotes in print advertising ("Orlon" is DuPont's registered trademark for its acrylic fiber), advertising slogans (If it isn't an Eastman, it isn't a Kodak), advertisements devoted specifically to education for proper trademark usage in consumer and trade publications, use of the brand name in association with the name of the general type of product involved (CORICIDEN Cold Relief Tablets), and the application of the brand name to multiple items (Vaseline and Band-Aid products) (Diamond, 1973, p. 190). From the perspective of the originator of the trademark, the judicial history is not encouraging. If a mark seems to have "gone generic," so that its name is widely used as a common noun or verb, the courts tend to view this as evidence of corporate neglect. This problem may prove particularly aggravating for companies that have successful trademark licensing programs. Does *Playboy*, for example, connote a publishing and entertainment enterprise or does it more generally signify a lifestyle? The extent to which *Playboy*'s licensing

program contributes to the latter interpretation tends to dilute its mark's source-indicating significance.

Genericism is one way of looking at the problem of defining the boundaries of a brand as property. In a sense, the boundaries of the "overly successful" brand have become coextensive with the product category, so that consumers no longer discriminate the successful brand from any others. At least, they seem not to do so. The question may be raised as to whether in actuality some subtler discrimination is being made. We will return to this issue.

The hazards of genericism are dramatic in afflicting famous names, but a more common danger is that of infringement. With respect to intellectual property, trademark infringement is analogous to the offense of trespass upon real property. Edward S. Rogers (1926/1974) points out that all trademark infringement cases are in fact cases of unfair competition; "unfair competition is the genus of which trademark infringement is one of the species." The protection of a trademark against infringement is rooted historically in the normative belief that after an individual has created a market through established trademark and "has impregnated the atmosphere of the market with his congenial symbol" (as Justice Frankfurter said), he should be protected from another's use of that mark. Accompanying the right of a trademark owner to control his product's reputation is the right of the public to be free from confusion. Over the years the courts have generally defined trademark infringement as the use by one of a mark that is so similar to the existing mark of another, considering the relationship of the products, that confusion between the two is likely to occur. The central test for infringement remains the likelihood (or the actuality) of confusion.

Examples of trade identity confusion appear in the press regularly. *Chicago Tribune writer* Aaron Gold reported this item in his "Tower Ticker" column of August 23, 1979:

> Many irate concertgoers have been calling Tower Ticker to complain about last weekend's disappointing Chicago Jam I and II (Saturday and Sunday) at Comiskey Park. They seem to be blaming, unfairly, Jam Productions, the Chicago-based concert promotion firm headed by Arny Granat and Jerry Mickelson. Jam had nothing to do with the Comiskey Park concerts. It was a California-based company that also produced California Jam and Canada Jam.

More recently the manager of the $2.85-a-night Palace Hotel in New York's Bowery district complained that he continually receives reservation requests from the corporate bigwigs and jetsetters who have mixed up his establishment with the $120-a-night midtown Palace. Consumer confusion may result in more or less serious damage de-

pending upon the particular situation; and often large financial compensation is sought.

Although "the facts" make every trademark dispute in a way unique, one can nonetheless anticipate the development of relative measures of the likelihood of confusion that would more directly facilitate comparison across cases. Today, quantitative measures of confusion are usually meaningful only within the context of the case in question. To illustrate, survey findings of confusion as high as 49.8% have been held insufficient to signify proof of confusion (*General Motors Co. v. Cadillac Marine and Boat Co.*, 1964); while in another case confusion reportedly affecting only 8% of the sample of purchasers was held to demonstrate the likelihood of confusion in an appreciable number of people (*Grotrain et al. v. Steinway and Sons*, 1973). Such results seem difficult to judge, especially when it is important to recognize that a group of respondents will almost always demonstrate some amount of confusion about even the most distinctive products. As Bowen (1961) has suggested, "Confusion is a relative concept. In crowded fields, i.e., many producers with many related products having many trademarks, a certain amount of confusion is inevitable" (p. 24).

In a 1958 case initiated by 7-Up against an alleged infringer (Fizz-Up), 31.1% of the respondents surveyed seemed to associate these two brands. On the other hand, 15.6% named Coke, Pepsi, Canada Dry, Dr. Pepper, or Hires as the manufacturers of Fizz-Up; and a majority (51.3%) said they did not know who made the product (*Seven-Up Co. v. Green Mill Beverage Co.*, 1961). The Court found these results to be evidence of substantial consumer confusion. These judicial judgment calls will rest on surer footing with better understanding of baseline levels of confusion. Such understanding should lead to more consistent and meaningful examples to the question: how much confusion is enough? Perhaps there should be a conventional "Confusion Discount," to allow for that common (10?) percentage of the population who are confused persons (or at least the 4% in one survey who did not know Harry Truman was president at the time?).

In spite of its central role in testing allegations of trademark infringement, the concept of confusion is today poorly specified under the law. As a result, trademark researchers are without a cohesive framework for observing the behavioral processes that lead to confusion; and they have neither consistent methods for determining its presence nor stable criteria for assessing its likelihood. Aggravating this situation is the court's role in determining the likelihood of confusion. Pattishall and Hilliard (1974) explain that the courts have tended "to reach their conclusions as to the likelihood of confusion, and thus infringement, subjectively and based upon their own reactions as to similarity (between conflicting marks) rather than objectively and based upon evidence" (p. 4).

The proclivity of the courts toward subjective analysis may stem from the tendency to view each trademark conflict as idiosyncratic. This approach ignores the commonalities or general principles that underlie the nature and perception of brands. Investigations of distinctiveness, generic-ness, and infringement require answers to questions about the state of mind of market segments under varying conditions. This necessity points to the employment of the analytical tools of psychology in trade identity litigation. In reviewing 200 years of American trademark law, Beverly Pattishall (1978) concluded that the "recognition of

the psychological nature of trade identity problems and of the reliability of the methods and techniques of that marketing psychological-statistical science for resolving them is indeed one of the notable recent advances of trade identity law."

MARKETING RESEARCH AND THE LAW OF TRADEMARKS

The Psychological Nature of Trademarks

In 1909, psychologist Hugo Munsterberg for the first time called attention to the application of psychology to the problems of trademark law. Several years later one of Munsterberg's colleagues, Edward S. Rogers (1914), voiced the optimism of this era: "The question of what resemblance is enough to deceive is really in my opinion a problem in practical psychology to be solved by modern laboratory methods, by experiment with enough normal people to make the generalization safe."

At about the same time, Richard H. Paynter, Jr., was employed by the Coca-Cola Company to conduct a series of psychological tests related to its litigation against an alleged infringer, Chero-Cola. In 1919, Paynter's results were offered as the first instance of psychological testimony in an actual case of trademark litigation (*The Coca-Cola Company v. Chero-Cola Company*, 1921). They were not, however, admitted by the court as evidence. The psychological nature of trademarks was reviewed in 1936 by Neil Borden, who conducted research in an infringement case by the John B. Stetson Hat Company. Borden observed that for many years judges, lawyers, and psychologists had criticized the methods followed in trademark litigation for determining the likelihood of confusion between conflicting marks. In spite of the developing literature of psychology applied to trademark disputes, the admissibility of behavioral data as legal evidence in courts remained unsettled. Borden (1936) also noted that since the flurry of research conducted some 20 years earlier, he could find "almost no academic studies of special note relating to the psychology of trademark infringement."

The impetus of such research was provided soon thereafter by Supreme Court Justice Frankfurter, who unambiguously argued for the role of psychology in trademark questions: "The protection of trademarks is the law's recognition of the psychological function of symbols. If it is true that we live by symbols, it is no less true that we purchase goods by them" (*Mishawaka Rubber v. S. S. Kresge Co.,* 1942).

Further support for the conceptualization of trademark issues in psychological terms came during the 1950s from U.S. Patent Office Commissioner Daphne Leeds (1956): "In the field of trademark law we are dealing not with tangible things . . . but with psychological reactions and associations. We are not dealing with economics but with applied psychology."

The proponents of behavioral research believed that their methodologies would serve to remedy unscientific approaches heretofore employed in determining trademark infringement. Preeminent among the research techniques adapted for trademark questions are market surveys and "reaction tests."

The Emergence of Survey Research Methods

The appropriateness of survey methods in trademark disputes was suggested by Handler and Pickett (1934) over 40 years ago:

> It may be suggested . . . that the results of the courts would be more certain and predictable if the technique that has been developed in the conduct of market analysis was applied in determining whether two brands conflict. Whether the purchaser is likely to be misled is better ascertained in the marketplace than in the court room.

The major obstacle to the introduction of survey findings as evidence was the allegation that they constitute a form of hearsay. In the Elgin watch case (*Elgin National Watch Co. v. Elgin Clock Co.,* 1928), surveys were offered as evidence but rejected by the court as hearsay. In 1936, surveys were admitted as evidence in the DuPont cellophane case (*DuPont Cellophane Co. v. Waxed Products Co.,* but the outcome did not turn on them. Throughout the thirties and forties, surveys were conducted in trademark cases, but the admissibility of the survey results was unpredictable. It was not until the 1950s that surveys began to enjoy a reasonable probability of being admitted as evidence.

The landmark decision for surveys in trademark litigation was issued in 1956 when the U.S. Patent Office decided a trademark case almost exclusively on the basis of a consumer survey. Pioneering jurist Daphne Leeds explained the rationale of the Patent Office: "The probable reactions and associations in the minds of the purchasers present the real issue in such proceedings as these . . . [a] consumer reaction test, properly authenticated, provides a means of ascertaining what the probable reactions and associations are" (*International Milling Company v. Robin Hood Popcorn Co.,* 1956). By 1961, Bowen observed a trend toward the acceptance of the place of psychology in trademark litigation by noting the increasing number of survey research studies offered and accepted as valid evidence pertinent to pivotal issues. In the marketing literature of this period, Barksdale (1957) and others discussed the growing use of surveys as legal evidence. Today consumer surveys are considered by some to be the "most probative evidence practicable on the frequently complex issues . . . likelihood of confusion" (Gilson, 1974, p. 8-8). Survey methods are now used not only in trademark infringement cases, but in many types of proceedings: antitrust, false and deceptive advertising, unfair business practices, unfair competition cases, design patent infringement, property valuations, and change of venue cases.

The increasing emphasis given survey research methods in trademark infringement conflicts has forced the courts to give close attention to a myriad of issues relating to the validity and reliability of survey results. Documents (and related depositions and testimony) introduced in trademark litigation may include (a) proposals for the survey, (b) pretest reports, (c) specification of the universe used, (d) sampling procedures, (e) level of confidence, (f) sample of questionnaire(s), (g) sample of interviewer instructions, (h) sample of introduction to interviewees, (i) instructions on handling aborted or terminated interviews, (j) where and how the survey was conducted, (k) coding instructions, (l) copy of computer program used or mathematical techniques used to tabulate data, (m) printout of survey results, and so on (Bonynge, 1962; Kunin, 1977). A recent amendment to the Federal Rules of Evidence (Rule 703) has substantially streamlined procedures whereby the courts assess the validity of the research techniques employed.

Advantages/Disadvantages of Survey Methods

The employment of consumer surveys in trademark infringement cases is linked to the courts' growing appreciation of several distinct advantages they offer in gathering evidence relating to the likelihood of confusion. First of all, the scientific sampling procedures developed in survey research will tend to provide better approximations of relevant consumer experiences than previous methods obtained. Prior to the use of surveys, trademark confusion was determined through expert testimony, a parade of witnesses, or the court itself acting in the role of purchaser. These approaches all tended to violate the key sampling principle of representativeness:

> The time when a jury could represent adequately the general knowledge of the community covering all the things that ought to be known in the complex society of today, has long gone by. Nor can the trial judge today where he tries a case without a jury expect to have the knowledge with respect to trademark significance, impressions conveyed by the advertisement, degree of competition, and the like, which must be taken into account in types of competition which are more and more common today. (Pound, 1957, quoted in Gerlach, 1972, p. 3)

A properly conducted survey allows the population of interest in trademark infringement cases to be represented by the respondents selected in the survey sample, although which universe is the correct one remains controversial. A second advantage presented by survey methods lies in their predictive capabilities. Surveys relieve the courts from their previous reliance upon ambiguous and erratic suppositions about how hypothetical consumers might interpret a trademark. Existing methods of survey data analysis permit the translation of actual survey results to probabilistic statements about the likelihood of consumer confusion between conflicting trademarks. As Gilson (1974) explains, "The ultimate inquiry is whether the survey results can reliably be projected to predict the true state of mind of the proper universe of consumers on the issue before the court" (p. 8-96).

Unfortunately, the application of survey methods does not always lead to unambiguous conclusions about consumers' states of mind. Some of the particular liabilities that characterize survey research in trademark litigation appear endemic to this specific methodology, while others may be linked to the relatively poor level of conceptualization in trade identity research. An example of the former is the fact that when large databases (e.g., national probability samples) are required, surveys are extremely expensive. Surveys also require a relatively high degree of technical skill to execute. From a methodological perspective, a serious weakness of survey methods issues from an artificiality that puts a strain on validity. Survey research typically reflects only a surface analysis of a phenomenon under investigation. As Kerlinger (1973) explains,

> Survey information ordinarily does not penetrate very deeply below the surface. The scope of the information sought is usually emphasized at the expense of depth . . . the survey seems best adapted to the extensive rather than intensive research. Other types of research are perhaps better adapted to deeper explorations of relations. (p. 422)

In trademark litigation cases, for example, a survey questionnaire typically asks respondents what comes to mind when shown the name (mark, logo, etc.) of the alleged infringer. Confusion is judged to occur among those who mention the name and/or products of the plaintiff. Whether these people are really confused or not is controversial. If the two marks are similar so that one reminds of the other, does that demonstrate actual confusion or suggest its likelihood? Similarity, reminding, and associating may all be present even though the two marks are known to be distinctly separate brands. The traditional survey, by its detached style of questioning, does not probe much for full association; and responses are simply tabulated across respondents, not related to one another within individuals. Results of the pilot study reported below suggest the practical utility of qualitative research methods that illuminate the logic of individual processes.

A natural and necessary accompaniment of methodological innovation in trade identity research is an information processing perspective that takes into account the multiple levels of symbolic interaction that characterize consumer brand behavior. The outlines of such an orientation are offered in the section that follows.

THE SYMBOLIC ANALYSIS OF TRADEMARKS

In 1961, Bowen recommended (a) the addition of new psychological terms; (b) the development of better indices of confusion, distinctiveness, public acceptance, ease of learning, and recognition and recall; (c) the employment of special techniques of research; and (d) the development of new ideas about trademarks. Today, in spite of the continuing development of the behavioral sciences, and notwithstanding the prodding of trademark scholars and arrests, little seems to have changed in almost 20 years.

Progress at both the methodological and conceptual levels requires that trade identity research directly confront trademarks' symbolic nature. The symbolic dimension of trademarks was forcefully argued by Justice Frankfurter nearly 40 years ago, but trade identity research has tended to focus on the physical attributes and features of brands rather than the subjective experiences that give a mark its meanings to consumers and market segments. It is not enough to know that customers are drawn to various patterns of price and product features. Questions are raised about the meaning of these features. What feelings, beliefs, opinions, and implications are aroused in the customers' minds? The products in the marketplace and their qualities are not merely objects—they are symbolic objects.

As noted by Gardner and Levy (1955) in earlier analysis of the nature of brands and trademarks,

> A *brand name* is more than the label employed to differentiate among the manufacturers of a product. It is a complex symbol that represents a variety of ideas and attributes. It tells the consumer many things not only by the way it sounds (and its literal meaning if it has one) but, more importantly, via the body of associations it has built up and acquired as a public object over a period of time.

The psychological processes that underlie the construction of brand imagery may be ordered along an information processing continuum of sensation-perception-apperception. *Perception* begins at the level of "sheer sensation," where product attributes are physically experienced. This level seems factual and may be scientifically measured; it is easy to focus on the "real" characteristics of external stimuli. Foods have tastes; materials have textures, softness, smoothness, hardness; sounds are soft, loud; objects are varied in appearance, color, shine, and so on. All our sensory equipment may be called on to come to know a particular product or service. We have preferences at this fundamental level. Some people love sweetness, others tartness; some find soft things repulsive; some prefer bold colors or fast beats of sound. At the other end lies *apperception,* where sensations are processed through the perceiver's personal and social experiences, thereby acquiring a variety of individual associations and evaluations. Individual depth interviews elicit such associations and illuminate the character of brand identity in the consumer's mind. They indicate the richness and complexity that surveys avoid and highlight aspects of distinctiveness, generic-ness, and confusion.

Exploratory Study: Products and Brands

In order empirically to investigate these brand identity issues, and to extend their application to the trademark arena, the authors designed a small-sample qualitative pilot study. Twenty-one adult respondents were selected in Dallas and Chicago, and each interviewed for 1 hour. The purpose of the study reported here is threefold. First, the aim was to collect observations that illustrate how consumers construct a psychosociological map of a brand's perceived character. Respondents were asked to mention some of their favorite brands, to select one and tell why they like it, how they became familiar with it, what kind of reputation it has, who the typical users are, and how they visualize the brand. Second, the study sought to learn more about the processes leading to a brand's becoming generic. Interviewees were asked to describe a generic form of their favorite brand and to compare it with other brands. They were also asked to comment on several instances where brands have assumed varying degrees of generic identity. Third, the study aimed to explore the effects of competition on the perceptions of brands, observing how the brands are seen to "divide up" the product domain and how trademark confusion may or may not result. Respondents were asked to report occasions when they bought the "wrong" brand because they mistook it for another. They were also asked how they keep from being confused by the many brands on the market; and their opinions were solicited about several trademark conflicts.

The richness of brand identity. Gaining evidence of the consumer's perception of a specific brand configuration is not easy. A brand is a version of a product. It shares characteristics with the other brands of that product, so that consumers' initial descriptions of brands are often not distinctive.

> It's a light beer . . . it tastes good to me when I come in from work and I've been outside. (Coors)

> It's a well-built car, sturdy and shows good workmanship. (Pontiac)

> I like the cologne for me. And they make a stylish line of clothing. Comfortable, well made, and the fit is superb. (Pierre Cardin)

But further questioning (not usually probed in evidence surveys) may elicit more specificity and visualization.

> It comes in a tall slender can with a lot of silver or chrome color on it. It's a Colorado beer.

> Big Chief Pontiac, that's what I think of and that's what I see. My dad had a Pontiac years ago and it had a picture of Chief Pontiac.

> I see the cologne bottle . . . just the look, that's a hard question to answer . . . of course, the insignia.

In the fullest sense, the extent to which a trademark is distinctively perceived relates to the individual's personal experiences with a brand, product line, or company.

> Back in the 60's my son wanted a tape recorder for Christmas. It was all he wanted. He was just a little kid, and we didn't see any reason to get one that cost much. We considered a Panasonic but a friend said that Sony had a better tone, was easier to work and I got the Sony. We still have it. It has been worked on just one time and performs like it was brand new. I remember at the time I thought it was too fine a product for a little boy, and he'd probably lose it, break it, and I'd have thrown my money away. I was wrong. I also remember my son's words when he saw it under the tree. He said, "Is it really a Sony?" I didn't think he'd even know.

As such associations continue, they show how the identity of the brand radiates into the social environment, through family learning, to broader public definitions.

> I first met Budweiser 10 years ago in Lindsey, Texas. My dad drank it, and so I drank Bud

just because he did. I was in high school and underage to buy beer. So an older friend bought it for us. We'd hide out in the car and send him to get it, then speed off like everybody was watching us.

Levis have the best reputation. Everybody says the same sort of thing . . . and men are as hyped on their Levis as women. In fact, people just call jeans Levis.

From the product attributes in their particular brand configurations, through their public generalization of reputation and segment suitability, each individual arrives at a *core dynamism,* a personal way of relating to a brand (Levy, 1980).

It's my whole wardrobe almost. I wear them all weekend, and put them on when I come in from work. If I want to be dressed up, I wear high heels, a good-looking shirt or sweater, and jewelry and a scarf. If I want to be relaxed and comfortable looking, I wear a loose top and flats. But I always look right, you know. If you have on Levis, you look right, really right.

I feel soft and misty when I wear Alliage. I see myself at my best in looks, and when I look good, I feel radiant and happy. Alliage does that to me. I'm stuck on it, and on Estee Lauder. I only wish she knew how much she does for me.

The particular and the generic. The courts have tended to define what is generic in a unidimensional fashion: A brand term is generally considered generic if its principal meaning to the public is to indicate the product or service itself rather than its source. Following this lead, a researcher seeking to determine the generic-ness of the Xerox mark and employing the custom-

ary survey approach might design a questionnaire that asks: "What do you call a machine that makes photocopies?" A substantial proportion of the survey sample would reply, "Xerox," thereby indicating that Xerox had assumed a measurable level of generic identity in the public mind. Fuller discussion reveals that generic-ness is a more complex phenomenon. The fact is that consumers are readily able to refer to a brand as if it connoted the product or service itself (thus satisfying the traditional definition of generic usage) and in the same breath acknowledge the brand's source-indicating significance.

I work in an office, and we have a 3M. But everyone in the office says "Xerox" when they talk about using the 3M.

I remember when every refrigerator was called a "Frigidaire," we all did that. We'd say, "I'm going to buy a Frigidaire," meaning buy a refrigerator, not the Frigidaire brand.

We always talk about Jell-O, but there's Yummy and Royal—and they would be taking the word from the Jell-O company. Nobody talks about "gelatin salad"—we talk about Jell-O salads, and they can be made with Yummy or Royal or Jell-O.

Jeep is being used in regard to any 4-wheel drive vehicle.

These comments suggest that it is unsafe to conclude that a term has a generic identity just because people use it to refer to a product class, or use it as a common noun or verb as they do with Coke and Kleenex. There is, of course, the hazard that such usage will grow until the time comes when most consumers do not remember that the word used to refer to a brand—as in the cases of aspirin, linoleum, and cellophane. Some significant subgroup in the market may help to defer that time. In defending itself from the FTC, the Formica company noted that it did not sell directly to the consumers who used its name generically but to distributors and dealers who were well aware of its distinctive trade identity.

The recent rise of products displayed and publicized as generic points to another issue. Such products highlight their supposedly anonymous commodity character (although the customers know they are essentially another store brand from Jewel or A&P). They bring to the fore the notion that a generic product is one of lower quality and cost.

> The generic form means there is no brand name. So, I guess the generic form of a Pontiac would be a very plain car, nothing flashy or fancy. Just a plain car with no chrome, no fancy wheels, no vinyl roof tops or glass sunroofs. Just the body and tires. And none of it sounds like much fun.

> Well, I only tried one generic brand. I guess every store has their own generic toilet paper. I guess it would be a little lower in quality. I *know* it is. I tried it at Kohls or Jewel. Generic is definitely cheaper, but that doesn't matter. Generic toilet paper would probably be the same size roll, maybe it would only come in white.

A possible avenue of defense is suggested in trademark litigation where generic-ness is a contended issue. If a brand's image connotes quality and cost dimensions that distinguish it from a generic version of the product, this implies that the trademark in question is not generic. For example, simple linguistic evidence may suggest that *Frigidaire* is a common term meaning re-

frigerator, but the brand's reputation for high quality, durability, and above-average price militates against its becoming truly generic.

There seems a trend against permitting brands to become generic. Modern companies are sensitive to the issue and police it, as already noted. Also, the samples were almost unanimous in resisting the idea that a company that created a well-known name could lose exclusive rights to it.

> I don't know too much about the laws and the rights of the FTC. But that doesn't sound right to me, I don't think the FTC should take a company's name from them.

> No, I don't think the FTC is right. Formica is the name of a company. For all I know it could be the name of a person. I know it's not, but it could be. It seems to me that Formica founded the company and introduced a product that has gone over. It's not their problem. Let the other plastic laminate companies come up with something better.

> What does the FTC think they should do, get a new company name? I don't go along with this.

Confusion is an elusive construct. Miaoulis and D'Amato (1978) recently discussed the difficulty of securing evidence of consumer confusion:

1. Customers who recognize they have been deceived may be reluctant to admit it.

2. Others who technically may have been confused might not come to the plaintiff's attention because they had not acted on their confusion by buying the defendant's product rather than the plaintiff's.

3. Still others may have intended to buy the plaintiff's product, been confused by the trademark similarity, purchased the defendant's product, and while later recognizing the "mistake," been sufficiently satisfied with the defendant's product to disregard the confusion.

In keeping with these points, the respondents interviewed for this study generally had difficulty in recalling instances of consumer confusion, although some were able to recite specific experiences when they selected one brand although another was intended.

> That has happened to me. I didn't realize it until I got home but was too embarrassed to take it back. I used it, it was just a frozen vegetable.

As this comment suggests, consumers may blame themselves for the mistake, not some confusing similarity in brand presentation. There is a segment that inclines toward the *caveat emptor* view, generally, expecting that brands will be similar and that consumers should watch out for themselves and make adequate discriminations.

> I don't know, I'm not a lawyer, but there are so many products on the market there is bound to be more than one of some things using a similar name.

> I don't think there should be a law. They should be intelligent enough to tell the difference.

Others see the need for protecting successful companies from imitators.

> If someone comes out with a similar name I don't think it should be acceptable. They are trying to cash in on the original name and usually at the expense of the original name.

We may be examining states in a typical process whereby brands arise from the commodity realm, achieving some distinction. Being new, the brand might behave with name, advertising, packaging, and so on, like other brands in that area, and thus seem to trespass or not be easily distinguished from an established brand. In time, the new brand becomes more distinctive and is recognized for itself. It might also be that a new brand enters the market and is immediately distinctive—perhaps being an innovator. At this stage, it attracts imitators (or just competitors who seem similar), and confusion is possible. Becoming dominant, a brand may then be so familiar that it again approaches commodity status, its name becoming generic.

RESEARCH AGENDA

The trademark-related phenomena discussed earlier are one aspect of a broader information processing domain: market identity, or image construction. Further investigation here should enhance both the basic theory and management of market imagery and stimulate discussion of critical methodological issues.

Marketing Theory Issues

The research questions outlined below may assist in the construction of a theory of market identity, with examine action of three issues.

The Nature of Cues

There is widespread recognition within the consumer behavior literature that individuals make inferences about products (also services, organizations, etc.) through the use of available cues. Enumeration of cue sources often tends to be ad hoc, with predictable references to product and packaging features, some allusions to environmental and situational factors, less regular citation of friends' opinions and other social variables. The construction of a formal, empirically testable model of market identity requires an enumeration of cue sources that relies upon behavioral concepts as much as obvious product features. Some discussion of the structural nature of products and services addresses this issue by differentiating tangible product components from intangible core and augmented elements (Kotler, 1980), as well as Levy's (1980) distinction between perception and apperception.

Associational Schemata

Research in market imagery tends to assume that consumers rely upon a narrowly circumscribed set of physical cues. This orientation implies a rather direct correspondence between external reality and its subjective interpretation. This view not only ignores the mediating role of motives or traditional sociocultural factors (friends, family, social class peer groups) but fails completely to address both deviant cue agents (enemies, astrologers, gossip columnists) and interpretative networks arising at the level of legends and myths and from culture generally. How individuals seek, select, interpret, and evaluate information has been the focus of much consumer research. Promising research streams hypothesize a reliance upon scripts, schemata,

and prototypes. Further advances have evolved through employment of memorial constructs to represent consumer information processes. While imbued with scientific vigor, these models have placed more emphasis on product perception (narrowly defined) than product meaning (apperception). It seems desirable to avoid an artificial divorce of structural issues from content factors. The trademark arena highlights the utility of a middle range theory that links the two. In recognizing that mere linguistic association is not generally sufficient to demonstrate consumer confusion, the courts imply the existence of a cognitive hierarchy.

Further research should attempt to identify networks of association at various levels of memorial organization: those that are merely linguistic, broadly cultural or group specific, or idiosyncratic; and those that operate at commodity, product line, and brand-specific levels. Are some schemata (e.g., cultural norms and taboos) more stable and/or potent than others? What factors stimulate the salience of particular associational schemata? Basic research is needed to study fully how these processes operate whereby a brand establishes a psychological domain that the law protects like real property.

The Role of Learning

While brand loyalty has been extensively measured and managed, the learning processes through which it evolves have been modeled primarily at the microanalytic level. How consumers learn about various products, favor some over others, and learn to distinguish one from a similar other are central issues in the trademark arena. Several lines of questioning are envisioned:

1. *How do consumers learn to distinguish "nondistinctive" brands?* There may be as many as 100 valid trademark registrations for common terms like *blue-ribbon, zenith, united,* and so on. Eliciting consumer perceptions of such nondistinctive marks may further illuminate the learning processes.

2. *How do consumers distinguish brands (or fail to) in trade identity conflicts?* Using brands in actual or simulated conflict, researchers may learn more about the nature of confusion. Under a simulated conflict scenario the researcher has the ability to manipulate the level of interbrand similarity and, thereby, systematically investigate its effects on consumer perceptions.

3. *How do consumers perceive generic terms?* Some former trademarks have undeniably slipped into the common language (aspirin, cellophane). Others are found in common expression yet retain a distinctive brand identity (Xerox). Further inquiry that focuses explicitly on (a) marks that have gone generic, (b) those that are on the brink, and (c) those that remain highly distinctive should illuminate these subtleties.

MARKETING STRATEGY IMPLICATIONS

Implications for management include the problems of creating a brand identity through awareness of the symbolic nature of a brand and the maintenance of its distinctiveness. The use of qualitative marketing research is emphasized for its value in showing the relation of brand identity to cultural definitions, the learning of the brand's meanings in its social settings, and the core dynamism or subjective interpre-

tation of these meanings by members of market segments. Better understanding of the nature of market identity should broadly facilitate marketing communications efforts. More specifically, within the trademark arena, research efforts may enhance the courts' ability to assess a mark's distinctiveness and predict the likelihood of trade identity confusion.

Methodological Issues

Trade identity research has been advanced in recent years by the various techniques of perceptual mapping and image analysis. Unfortunately these procedures rely upon manipulation of the *presumed* determinants of imaginal perception rather than a convincing explication of the nature and evolution of brand imagery. Trade identity research will benefit from an epistemological orientation that is not merely quantitative but phenomenological, discovery-oriented, process-oriented, and holistic. The combining of qualitative and quantitative methods has been impeded in marketing by the impression that the researcher must choose between the two. Cook and Reichardt (1979) argue that there need be no forced choice between the two paradigms, and the option of combining qualitative and quantitative methods is not only available, but there are strong reasons to recommend it. Further study of market identity issues will benefit not from methodological cloning but from active hybridization.

The many issues touched on above indicate the problems arising from the complicated interweaving of legal and value judgments concerning trade identities and their competitive maneuverings in the marketplace. The judgmental elements will always remain; but basic research in marketing and greater sophistication in applied marketing research would add greatly to the insight and justice the situation requires.

REFERENCES

Barksdale, H. C. (1957). *The use of survey research findings as legal evidence.* Pleasantville, NY: Printers' Ink Books.

Black, H. C. (1979). *Black's law dictionary.* St. Paul, MN: West.

Bonynge, R. (196Thousand Oaks2). Trademark surveys and techniques and their use in litigation. *The Trademark Reporter, 52,* 363-377.

Borden, N. (1936). The determination of confusion in trade-mark conflict cases. *Business Research Studies, 23,* 8.

Bowen, D. C. (1961). Applied psychology and trademarks. *The Trademark Reporter, 51,* 1-26.

Burge, D. A. (1980). *Patent and trademark tactics and practice.* New York: John Wiley.

The Coca-Cola Company v. Chero-Cola Company 273 F. 2d 755 (1921).

Cook, T. D., & Reichardt, C. S. (1979). *Qualitative and quantitative methods in evaluation research.* Beverly Hills, CA: Sage.

Diamond, S. A. (1973). *Trademark problems and how to avoid them.* Chicago: Crain Communications.

DuPont Cellophane Co. v. Waxed Products Co. 85 F. 2d 75 (1936).

Elgin National Watch Co. v. Elgin Clock Co. 26 F. 2d 376 (1928).

Enis, B. M. (1978). Exxon marks the spot. *Journal of Advertising Research, 18,* 6, 7.

Feathercombs, Inc. v. Solo Products Corp. 306 F. 2d (1962).

France Milling Co. v. Washburn-Crosby Co. 7 2d 304 (1925).

Gardner, B. B., & Levy, S. J. (1955, March-April). The product and the brand. *Harvard Business Review,* pp. 33-39.

General Motors Co. v. Cadillac Marine and Boat Co. 226 F. Supp. 716 (1964).

Gerlach, G. (1972). *The consumer's mind: a preliminary inquiry into the emerging problems of consumer evidence and law.* Cambridge, MA: Marketing Science.

Gilson, J. (1974). *Trademark protection and practice.* New York: Matthew Bender.

Grotrian, H. S. Th. Skinweg Nachf v. Steinway and Sons. 365 F. Supp. 707 (1973).

Handler, M., & Pickett, C. (1934). Trademark and trade names. *Columbia Law Review, 30,* 168-201, 750-777.

Hanover Star Milling Co. v. Metcalf, 240 U.S. 403, 412 (1916).

International Milling Co. v. Robin Hood Popcorn Co. 110 U.S.P.Q. 368 (1956).

Kerlinger, F. (1973). *Foundations of behavioral research.* New York: Holt, Rinehart & Winston.

Kochan, T. A. (1977). Legal nonsense, empirical examination, and policy evaluation. Palo Alto, CA.: *Stanford Law Review.*

Kotler, P. (1980). *Principles of marketing.* Englewood Cliffs, NJ: Prentice Hall.

Kunin, L. (1977). The structure and uses of survey evidence in trademark cases. *The Trademark Reporter, 67,* 97-109.

Leeds, D. (1956). Confusion and consumer psychology. *The Trademark Reporter, 46,* 1.

Levy, S. J. (1980). The symbolic analysis of companies, brands and customers. *The twelfth annual Albert Wesley Frey lecture.* Pittsburgh: Graduate School of Business.

McCarthy, T. J. (1973). *Trademarks and unfair competition.* Rochester, NY: Lawyer's Cooperative Publishing Co.

Miaoulis, G., & D'Amato, N. (1978). Consumer confusion and trademark infringement. *Journal of Marketing, 42,* 2, 50.

Mishakawa Rubber and Wollen Mfg. Co. v. S.S. Kresge Co., 316 U.S. 203 (1942).

Muller v. Oregon, 208 U.S. 412 (1908).

Pattishall, B. W. (1978). Two hundred years of American trademark law. *The Trademark Reporter, 68,* 143.

Pattishall, B. W., & Hilliard, D. C. (1974). *Trademarks, trade identity, and unfair trade practices.* New York: Matthew Bender.

Rogers, E. S. (1910, June). The unwary purchaser: A study in the psychology of the trade mark. *Michigan Law Review, 8,* 613-622.

Rogers, E. S. (1914). *Goodwill, trade marks, and unfair trading.* Chicago: A. W. Shea.

Rogers, E. S. (1974). Unpublished lecture notes. In B. W. Pattishall & D. C. Hilliard (1974). *Trademarks, trade identity, and unfair trade practices.* New York: Matthew Bender. (Original work published 1926)

Seven-Up Co. v. Green Mill Beverage Co. 197 F. Supp. 32 (1961).

## Chapter 15

THE TWO TIERS OF MARKETING

Sidney J. Levy

Many authors have stressed the signifi-cance of the role of marketing in the com-ing decade. There seems little doubt that the growth of the global marketplace will continue to enhance the necessity for in-creasing awareness and sophistication on the part of all participants in the world economy. Nevertheless, it seems worth pointing out that as ever, there will be stability as well as change. The passage of a decade will produce little alteration in the circumstances of vast numbers of people. They will continue to strive to sustain their standard of living, in many cases at subsis-tence levels, or at quite modest degrees of comfort. The growth of population in many places continues to outpace the pro-ductivity of the local society; and even as-suming that the globe is capable of provid-ing for its total population in some adequate manner, there is little indication that the world society is going to develop a universally satisfying distribution of goods and services in the near future.

In an ideal world, governments would be benign, the religious would save us, doctors heal us, teachers educate us, and the marketers provision us all. In doing so, product development and distribution would succeed without destroying the rain

This chapter was first published in Lazer, Barbera, MacLachlan, & Smith (Eds.), *Marketing 2000 and Beyond*, 1990, pp. 188-190. Reprinted by permission of the American Marketing Association.

forest or polluting the atmosphere. I believe there will be progress made toward these optimistic goals, that some marketing managers will recognize the need to have larger perspectives, that new products will take advantage of technological innovations to enhance consumption patterns.

At a more mundane level, there will continue to be the proliferation of goods and services, limited only by the ingenuity of marketers to find means of differentiating their offerings and segmenting their customers. The impact of women in the workforce will continue to pervade the marketplace with its changing perceptions of social roles, shifting arrangements, and opportunities for new businesses.

There might be more awareness of two levels or types of marketing challenges, as implied above. The two marketing tiers may be termed *obligatory marketing* and *permissive marketing*. Obligatory marketing refers to the marketing systems that require the involvement of governments, nonprofit organizations, and multinational corporations in their provision of life's fundamentals.

This is the kind of marketing that keeps the great millions of people fed, clothed, and housed in basic, ongoing ways. It is commodity-oriented and economics-oriented, geared to seeing to it that neighborhoods keep going with a viable housing stock, that the stores always have potatoes,

hamburger, milk, and bread—or whatever the local cultural versions are; and that there is fabric for dresses, shirts, and trousers. Keeping this great tonnage moving to enable a basic contentment in all societies is a core task for marketing. Obligatory marketing sees people as large social groups, not only as welfare recipients, but also with essential needs for education, health, and participation in the arts.

Beyond that is the permissive marketing that is more directed by individual choices. It is geared to innovation, variation, and style. It is excited by novelty, changes of a few percentage points in consumption patterns, interesting consumer subgroups, the latest fad. It is important because it enables the expression of individuality, it relates more to the development of the human personality and its psychological aspirations for distinction. Also, out of its inventiveness and elite discoveries come products and services that in time become part of the obligatory system.

The vitality of the marketplace is due to the interplay between the essential and permissive, the core and the periphery. The specific content of change in the next decades will move toward enhancing the great engine of marketing as people of goodwill struggle to take care of the obligatory process, absorbing from the margin the imaginative, quirky elements that make for variety and surprise.

Chapter 16

MARKETING STAGES IN DEVELOPING NATIONS

Sidney J. Levy

As nations develop, the character and emphasis of their marketing activities change in some typical ways. The focus of these activities depends on the resources of the country and its relative involvement in agriculture, industry, and commerce; the result is varied patterns of trade. Seven stages will be discerned here, each with a different emphasis on the nature of its marketing. Given the size and complexity of countries, any progression of stages will not be sharply demarcated in reality, of course; rather, there will be overlapping elements and concurrent phenomena, order reversals, and skipped stages. However, a simple description is a useful heuristic for exploring some of the main marketing configurations and their characteristic dynamisms.

The approach taken here differs from previous descriptions of stages of development. Traditionally, these have been oriented to economic perspectives, with varying degrees of relevance to marketing. As Ronald Savitt says, "The comprehensive studies of

This chapter was first published in *Proceedings,* Third International Conference on Marketing and Development, New Delhi, January 4-7, 1991, pp. 430-434. Reprinted by permission of the International Society for Marketing and Development.

the relationships of marketing and economic development for the most part have been written by historians whose major interests have not always been with the subtleties of marketing" (Savitt, 1988). McCarthy (1988) also notes that economists such as W. W. Rostow (1962) have emphasized production rather than marketing in observing phases of growth.

In contrast, McCarthy focuses more directly on marketing changes; he discusses the marketing-oriented index as a measure of how effectively the firms and middlemen in an area are moving toward their optimum "comparative advantage" position when compared to competing areas. He distinguishes four stages of economies that are:

1. Self-sufficient

2. Surplus-oriented

3. Production-oriented

4. Marketing-oriented

He discusses structural and functional issues but does so somewhat abstractly, without detailing marketing-oriented strategies. This paper focuses on how the nation relates to international trade in its production and marketing of goods, particularly with regard to the use of brands and the perception of them by people in other nations. The situation of South Korea is cited as an example, to illustrate how the overlapping of the seven stages makes for a developmental profile. This illustration is derived from a qualitative study of consumers' perceptions of South Korea following on the heels of the Olympic Games held in Seoul in the late summer of 1988. [Quotations from consumers are offered throughout the analysis.]

SEVEN MARKETING STAGES

A Traditional Peasant Economy

Much has been written about peasant economies that need not be reiterated here. In its classic form the peasant economy is oriented to subsistence. The "peasants" may be hunters, gatherers, fishers, and carvers, and so on, who mainly provide for themselves and their community. If they engage in trade it is limited to local markets or regional exchange; in the extreme instances there may be little perception of the country having imports or exports. On this local basis, marketing is mainly of commodities, and the use of middlemen or commercial branding is rare or absent. Informal or implicit branding arises from the differences in how individuals are perceived for variations in reputation for skill, the quality of their motivation, and results. Some of the character of this marketing stage remains at all subsequent stages and is present in all countries including the most fully developed, where there is still much local trade of goods and services, versions of cottage industries, farmers' markets, and art fairs. In developing countries such as South Korea, localist activity will be particularly notable in rural areas.

Mercantile Resource

At times, countries that are otherwise largely subsistence economies are also part of an international mercantile system and seen primarily as a source of raw materials or staple commodities such as copper, oil, sugar, and so on. In the traditional colonial model, the marketing activity was imposed by the colonizers without local ownership.

In modern versions of this system, where the resources are owned and exploited by the native population, the subsistence forms of marketing decline as domestic wealth (initially dominated by a small elite) makes possible participation in the commercial brand system and movement to later marketing stages.

South Korea now seems economically developed to a marked degree, compared to how it seemed at the time of the Korean war. People recognize that the South Korea of the television show *M.A.S.H.* was not the same country seen on television and read about during the Olympics.

A Source of Cheap Labor and Shoddy Goods

Whether through cottage industry, sweatshop, or more advanced industrialization, a developing country may come to be a source of cheap labor, as to some degree, South Korea is still seen to be in the manufacture of clothing, for example. There are comments about cheap clothing made there that does not wear well; and similar remarks are made about clothes and inexpensive plastic objects from Taiwan and Hong Kong. For many years prior to the Second World War, the United States imported from Japan large quantities of such products that were sold cheaply in "ten cent stores." At this stage, the products are sold anonymously, without brand identity, often in discount stores, giving only the name of the country of origin when the law requires that.

Koreans make a lot of cheap goods, but they are improving now. In the past, when I was in service there, things were pretty shoddy.

A Cheap Source of Goods to Be Labeled Abroad

Rather than selling the goods as brands imported from the developing country, the importers have their own labels placed on them. The quality ranges, depending on the goals of the foreign importers. But some of them will have brand names whose quality image they wish to protect, so there will be designer labels such as Yves St. Laurent as well as discount store labels. Consumers think of South Korea as being sophisticated enough to offer more than cheap and unskilled labor at this point, although they are aware that some of the products are cheaper than those of other countries and that labor costs are somewhat cheaper in South Korea than in Europe or the United States. People are aware that many excellent designer shirts, suits, and other clothing items bear a label saying, as an example, "made for (Designer Name) in Korea." There is the expectation that these things will be well made, but that the designer's firm makes the larger share of the money and takes the credit for the quality.

Reebok tennis shoes are the first thing that come to mind. The tennis shoes are great . . . I know I've seen the "made in Korea" label on many products, but I can't recall which ones.

As the country develops more power in its own image as capable of manufacturing higher quality goods, there is reciprocal enhancement of the image of both the foreign manufacturer and of the country. For instance, one respondent, who has been unfamiliar with Korean products in the past and worries that they might be shoddy, is pleasantly surprised to discover that his GE microwave was made in Korea. That it has the GE label gives him reassurance. That it works well makes him more favorably disposed toward other Korean products.

> I have a GE microwave that says it was made in Korea. It is a quality product, but without GE's brand name, I might not have been as favorably disposed to buy it.

An Exporter of Native Brand Labels of Questionable Quality

Gaining experience in creating branded goods for foreign labels, some companies go on to produce their own brand labels. But the quality may seem uncertain. South Korea produces some labeled products whose quality is doubtful in the eyes of many people. They still see Korea as emerging industrially, but not yet as mature in design, production, and expected quality. This seems particularly true in the area of clothing, soft goods, and cars.

> A car, a radio, a TV, or clothing from Korea? I would expect lower quality than both American or Japanese in each product area, as they are still less industrialized and not as technologically advanced. They make acceptable, but not high quality products, but I cannot think of specific examples by brand. Some of their clothing wears less well.

> In the past, I have purchased some cheap Korean running/sailing shoes, and they have proved to be just that. Cheap and nasty. Didn't wear well. Their cars and electronics are better.

A Source of Good Quality Products and Good Price Value

A major step in development is accomplished when a country comes to be known for exporting products it can label with some degree of pride. When Japan became determined to change its reputation for being a source of cheap, inferior goods, it established a quality control board and undertook earnest efforts to improve its exports. The picture in South Korea is mixed. Products of good quality are made in South Korea now and bear brand labels that are widely recognized as from this source. Hyundai cars are known as Korean products and are praised for good function with reasonable price. There is still a tone of qualification, indicating that a reasonable level of value is present, but one still short of the height of reputation for the products.

> They make Hyundai cars. Having been in one recently, they are really good for what they are meant to be.

Another respondent said, "Probably the Hyundai is the best known product of all." People sometimes know that electronic products are made in South Korea but do not have brand name associations. After watching most of the Olympics and seeing commercials for branded electronic and other products, the viewer could be unaware that the products were made in South Korea, because of the lack of specific identification of the brand with Korea in the commercials. Another respondent, after commenting that many clothes with other names had "made in Korea" labels, suddenly focused in on Hyundai.

> Oh, isn't Hyundai theirs? Quality would be high and about the same as Japanese goods, and better than most American goods.

An automotive writer sums up the situation of low labor costs, improving quality, and good value.

Low labor rates help Hyundai, a South Korean automaker, bring in the Scoupe and its Excel and Sonata sedans at prices below those of competitors. Hyundai doesn't offer the quality of Japanese cars, but its cars are decently assembled, and it's edging closer to the Japanese. The Scoupe's quality is good and is worlds ahead of Hyundai quality of a few years ago. (Dan Jedlicka, *Chicago Sun-Times,* October 20, 1990).

Those who have recently purchased electronics products tend to be more familiar with names such as Samsung or Goldstar as South Korean. Samsung is a familiar brand with known products. They are thought good, but, for those who do not own them, perhaps not quite as high in quality as the Japanese.

Samsung computers are good products, though not quite as high in perceived quality as those from Japan. Hyundai cars seem to be high quality. My friends who own them seem satisfied.

Their products are fine in function, but nothing special, because most of them are knock-offs, imitations.

Recent purchasers of electronic products are more familiar with their origin and more impressed with their quality and good value.

I own a Korean television set, a Samsung. It's a great TV. Very good picture, sophisticated features, and easy to use. The price was very low. I feel I received a great value for my money.

There is also familiarity with Samsung computer monitors.

I bought a Samsung computer screen. It is excellent. Good value and well-designed.

An expectation of increasingly high quality, particularly in regard to electronics and cars, reflects the growing stature of the image of Korean goods, a shifting from one stage to another. When South Korean electronic items are thought of as quality products and well priced, they may still seem more functional than elegant. This reflects a sense of progress in offering distinctive brands, but still with the notion of imitativeness rather than creativity in design.

Gold Star electronics are quality products at a cheap price. Good microwave—I have one . . . Korean products are inexpensive, but not as well designed as the Japanese. They are practical and dependable, but not elegant or sophisticated.

Korean electronic products work very well. They are sturdy and robust, and not quite as high-design as the Japanese or American things, but dependable and less expensive.

There are repeated comments that indicate that consumers think they are smarter shoppers in buying a Korean electronic product which works just well as a more expensive Japanese version, as with this person, with a computer made in Korea, and experience with a Samsung audio system.

They are good in consumer electronics. Samsung and Leading Edge. I have bought a Leading Edge PC for myself and helped a friend pick out a Samsung audio system. Both purchases were finally decided on a cost basis. Lower cost for same performance. They work fine.

Some people think the Japanese may have a slight edge over the Koreans still, but many Americans think that both countries make better electronics products than the United States. The Japanese are still thought more innovative in design and experienced in quality control, but South Korean electronics seem of high quality.

> Korean products may not be as good as the Japanese, but electronics are better than the American. The stuff is probably as well designed as Japanese but might not be put together quite as well, or be quite so innovative. But the quality is pretty solid. They've got something to prove to world markets and so are going to care. Also, Asian discipline counts for something in my book.

The Japanese are sometimes seen as possibly more exacting, because more experienced, in quality and quality control. On the other hand, Korean quality is often thought better than America's particularly due to the perception of decline in American quality.

> The quality would probably be higher than in the U.S., though slightly lower than the Japanese for cars or electronics products. No opinion about clothing.

There is a general recognition of fast growth and development of Korea as an industrial power, with ever-increasing strength in electronics. Frequent comments about Korea as a growing power reflect an awareness of ongoing change and development. This is enhanced by news stories such as that in the *Wall Street Journal* of November 1, 1988, which was headlined, "Korea's Samsung, Emulating Japanese, Seeks Edge Through Merger With Unit." The first paragraph reads, "South Korea's biggest

electronics company will merge with an affiliate today in a marriage that will make it a more formidable player in the world's electronics markets." The author goes on to explain that Samsung Electronics is absorbing Samsung Semiconductor and Telecommunications Co., so that the combined sales for this year, an estimated $5 billion, will include everything from computer chips to televisions. This is described as providing a replay of Japan's technology-export success. Samsung hopes the merger will provide muscle to strike out against the Japanese in markets for more sophisticated technologies. Further, the article spells out the advantages of doing this in some detail and ends by saying that this may be one of the first Korean companies whose shares foreigners can buy directly.

A Source of Distinction, Imagination, and Creativity

A country seems to have reached a high degree of development when it comes to be perceived as a significant source of superior commodities and high quality brands. There may be a dominating role in an industry, such as France in the aluminum industry—although the general public may not be aware of this. There is the kind of general reputation for optical equipment associated with Germany, perfume and wine from France, linen from Ireland, woolens from Scotland, and so on, as shown in many studies of imagery and countries of origin.

Japan has gained eminence in the automotive and electronics industries, perhaps at the heights of the sixth stage in providing outstanding brand names regarded as excellent values. But there is still debate as to whether it has reached the seventh stage of creativity. The *Wall Street Journal* (October

31, 1988) headlined a story on Japan: "Stifled Scholars: Japan's Scientists Find Pure Research Suffers Under Rigid Life Style: They Discover the Job System and Pressures to Conform Prevent Big Discoveries: Ph.D.s Scrubbing Fish Tanks." The article goes on to deal with the fact that "Japan's regimented society may be the secret to industrial triumph. But it seems to spell disaster in the science laboratory."

It says that it is difficult for the Japanese to produce creative basic research because of the inflexibility of their lock-step system. This prompts them to put creative energy and patent applications only into that which they perceive as yielding profits but keeps them dependent on the basic science breakthroughs of the United States and Europe. It describes Japanese scientists who have moved to other countries in order to be free to be creatively productive and quotes Hisashi Shinto, chairman of Nippon Telegraph and Telephone Company, as saying that Japan needs to create more pure science to feed future industries. Nevertheless, the seventh stage is approached as the Japanese communicate more about their culture and its concepts and how these lead to innovations. Mazda car advertising has utilized the harmonious concept of *kansei,* as one example; and a deliberate decision was made by the Nissan company to advertise (not very successfully) the Infiniti car in a manner that referred to its Japanese origin rather than to use the conventional American approach.

In Korea, where it is not a disgrace to change jobs, and the culture does not seem to offer the constricting problems of extreme domination by seniority in its plants or its universities, there is a potential and an opportunity in the situation. There is the possibility of a surge ahead in creativity. Several respondents commented that Korea may yet give Japan a run for its money in the industrial arena if it can fulfill its potential for innovation and development of products.

The foregoing discussion implies that the developmental process is one of increasing two-way interaction across national boundaries. It involves the growth in ability to control quality and to make products of which a country can be proud; and thereby create brands that are respected and admired abroad. It focuses on the importance of gaining a reputation for distinctiveness in one or more areas of expertise, one that seems either to grow naturally out of and to fit the foreign perception of the country's national character or that, on the other hand, causes surprise and amazement at the changes that are producing a fresh and excellent result.

REFERENCES

McCarthy, E. J. (1988). Marketing orientedness and economic development. In T. Nevett & R. A. Fullerton (Eds.), *Historical perspectives in marketing.* Lexington, MA: Lexington Books.

Rostow, W. W. (1962). *The stages of economic growth.* Cambridge, UK: Cambridge University Press.

Savitt, R. (1988). A personal view of historical explanation in marketing and economic development. In T. Nevett & R. A. Fullerton (Eds.), *Historical perspectives in marketing.* Lexington, MA: Lexington Books.

## Chapter 17

DEFENDING THE DOWAGER
Communication Strategies for Declining Main Brands

Dennis W. Rook

Sidney J. Levy

"One of the *worst things* that can happen to a brand is to be flanked by premium brands on one side and by price brands on the other, caught in the middle without a clear or meaningful point of difference to consumers." (Baum, 1990)

Being caught in the middle is particularly aggravating to a brand that once pioneered and captained its product category, and it is precisely the situation in which many main national brands find themselves today. Such brands are often both the first national and largest historical brand in their respective product categories. Many of these have evolved, gradually or more rapidly, into declining marketplace "dowagers" that suffer continuing share erosion from proliferating brand competitors. These losses point to some of the original brand's inherent vulnerabilities. Such declines also reflect the typical dynamics of a product category's life cycle.

As a new product category's sales, profits, and prospects grow, competitive entrants emerge to challenge the pioneer, offering both similar and differentiated features to an expanding market. Even in maturity, a still-growing category may continue to attract new entrants that further chip away at the original brand's position. Whether through market evolution or revolution, this "worst thing" often happens to a once top brand that ends up surrounded by a myriad of "other" brand rivals (McKenna, 1988). Although it may still enjoy substantial sales, share and profit, a dowager brand seems inexorably headed downhill.

This perspective contrasts with recent research aimed at discovering the long-term benefits associated with *brand pioneer* status; for example, enhanced consumer preference (Carpenter & Nakamoto, 1989) and larger market share (Robinson & Fornell, 1985). The latter findings are controversial, and criticism argues that the market share advantages of category pioneers are both exaggerated (Day & Freeman, 1990) and insensitive to the fact that these brands' share losses are the largest (Buzzell & Gale, 1977). There are likely two sides to the story, and characterizing some brands as dowagers highlights both the assets and liabilities of pioneer brands that find themselves in a classic and troublesome competitive situation.

Managers of declining dowager brands necessarily struggle to turn things around, but the task is difficult. Reflecting the frustration of this situation, one brand manager recently pounded a conference table, crying, "How can we stop this erosion of our brand share?" In fact, this erosion probably cannot literally be stopped (Day, 1990, p. 206), but even slowing the *rate* of decline slightly could generate incremental sales and profits. And despite bleak future prospects for some dowager brands, many merit a more vigorous defense than they currently receive. Encouraging this view

are recent marketing successes (e.g., Cadillac) that represent major comebacks in which declining brands rekindled their appeal to both new and lost customers.

In order to focus thinking on the dowager brand's strategic possibilities, the following discussion presents its thinking about dowager brands in three main sections. First, a competitive brand hierarchy is introduced to provide a framework for identifying the structural sources of a dowager's share losses. Second, the discussion critically reviews common managerial prescriptions for managing this "losing" situation and recommends focusing and deploying marketing resources toward discovering and better communicating a dowager brand's benefits and equities to more strategically refined customer targets. Finally, the paper hypothesizes the dissenting rationales of consumers who have moved away from dowager brand usage and offers a generalized approach for developing strategic communication counter-logics and themes for drawing them back.

A COMPETITIVE BRAND HIERARCHY

The general concern with erosion of brand share often implies fragmentation of the market among increasing numbers of brands in the product category, whether they are seen as directly comparable to the original main brand or as proliferated variations. As this fragmentation occurs, with variations in product types and prices, it is inevitable that a brand hierarchy will develop. The hierarchy is multidimensional, so that a high position usually means high price, high quality, high social status, and so on. By putting together such possibilities, a general competitive brand hierarchy may be constructed. The present intention is to examine this hierarchy from the perspective of the beleaguered main brand whose market share is being eroded.

DOWAGER BRANDS

"Dowager" as metaphor. A dowager brand is usually a well-advertised national brand. Often its history goes back in time, and it has been so popular and dominating that its name is almost a generic term for the product. Familiar examples are Band-Aid, Frigidaire, Jell-O, Kleenex, Thermos, Teflon, and Xerox. Consumers often consider these "the original brand" in the product category. Casting about for a designation that would characterize such historical main brands, the term "king of the hill" came to mind, and "grand old lady," but neither seems quite apt. The term "dowager brand" is suggested, and defined accordingly:

> A dowager brand commonly exists in a mature product category and is the brand customers generally perceive to be the category's original main brand. A dowager brand's market position is characterized by historical dominance of its category, followed by share losses to successful brand entrants across various levels of a competitive brand hierarchy.

Two related definitions of the term dowager help explain its relevant brand implications. Historically, the term identified a royal widow in possession of some property or title inherited from a deceased husband; for example, the dowager duchess or empress. This formal designation distinguished the widowed dowager from the wife of the new incumbent of the title.

In everyday usage, its expression refers more broadly to an elderly woman of imposing appearance, stately dignity, dominant personality, and elevated social position, who sets the tone of a social group or community. The dowager metaphor points to various analogies between these *grandes dames* and many of today's declining main brands.

While a dowager brand's advanced age might suggest some degree of infirmity, it also implies maturity and a marketplace history and heritage that newer competitors lack. A reference to property and title further implies that the dowager is still a brand of considerable substance, despite its eroding market share. Brand leadership and even dominance are suggested by the idea that the dowager sets the social tone, and does so with a dominant personality. Despite the inroads made against its position, a dowager brand is likely to enjoy elevated, although perhaps slipping status among its competitors. Finally, although it is still an imposing figure in its brand universe, the dowager is a widow, and the term denotes a sense of loss felt at the turning away by customers and the subsequent decline in social stature and market share.

The dowager's losses. The dowager metaphor personifies a brand, and when viewed as an instance of changing interpersonal relationships between consumers and their brands, the dowager's situation has elements of both crisis and opportunities for renewal (Levy, 1962). The dowager's world is populated with memories of past glories and ambivalence about the future. Broadly conceived, a dowager brand confronts the lifecycle crisis of old age: integrity versus despair (Erikson, 1982). Circumstance varies, and some brands suffer more than others.

Yet, even after considerable share declines, some dowagers brands are still the largest in their respective product categories. One study found that of the top brands in 25 consumer product categories in 1923, 19 were still in first place in 1981 (*Standard and Poor's Industry Surveys,* 1983). By itself, however, this finding tends to mask the share losses experienced by even these enduring top brands. For example, although Campbell's share of the canned soup market remains by far the largest, it dropped 8 points between 1976 and 1986 (70% to 62%). Other dowagers' losses of share have been far more severe, for example, Swanson (frozen dinners), Prell (shampoo), Schlitz (beer), and Ford (cars) (Collier & Horowitz, 1987).

Dowager brands also vary in the recency of their fall from the top. Some venerable brands have lost their number one status in the recent past (Skippy peanut butter in 1984), while other, still-surviving brands fell from the top years ago, for example Ford cars (1920s), and Camel cigarettes (1940s). In addition, the rapidity with which share decline occurs ranges from one managerial planning cycle (e.g., Ashton-Tate's share of spreadsheet software) to centuries, as with Swiss-made watches (Landes, 1984).

Identifying dowager brands. In many product categories, there is a single, undisputed dowager brand (Campbell's soup, Birdseye frozen vegetables). In other cases, it would be misleading to look for a single brand as *the* dowager in its category. Although we have defined a dowager brand as the original main national brand in its category, both managers and consumers may suggest different brands for dowager status. In markets dominated by strong regional brands, consumers might characterize a

major local brand as the dowager. For example, in 1961, now-defunct Lucky Lager was the top beer brand in California (Newman, 1967), so today's older beer drinkers in this region might consider it the dowager beer brand. In addition, consumers' personal brand usage histories foster subjective interpretations of which brand is the dowager. Today's baby boomers, who began brushing their teeth with Crest, would be likely to view this brand, rather than older Colgate, as the dowager toothpaste brand. The possibility of multiple dowager brands existing within a single product category does not dilute the dowager construct but suggests the possibility that several main brands share common histories.

PILOT STUDY

The pilot study reported here sought to explore how consumers identify and think about dowager brands in several household and personal product categories. Seventy-six students in two MBA classes selected 1 among 14 familiar product categories provided in a questionnaire and were then asked to name the "original brand" in their chosen category. Table 17.2 presents illustrative findings for three product categories: shampoo, potato chips, and peanut butter. In shampoo, four different shampoo brands were nominated by 12 respondents as the dowager, suggesting that in a crowded, mature category, the dowager brand's identity may be fuzzy and shared. Similarly, six potato chip brand names were offered as the dowager, reflecting the regional structure of the category. Jay's, Charle's, and Guys brands are likely the choices of potato chip consumers who grew up, respectively, in either metropolitan Chicago, southeast Ohio, or Oklahoma—

TABLE 17.1 Brand Competition Matrix: 16 Potential Dowager Targets

| Brand Hierarchy Level | Dowager Brand User Status | | | |
| | Users | | Nonusers | |
	Exclusive	Dual	Former	Never
Elite brands	NA	2	7	12
Dowager brand	1	NA	NA	NA
Old peer brands	NA	3	8	13
New peer brands	NA	4	9	14
Retailer brands	NA	5	10	15
Generic brands	NA	6	11	16

NOTE: This model is based on the simplifying assumption that both dual and nonusers have a preferred brand in one of the five brand levels against which the dowager competes.

although Lay's is historically the first national brand. Peanut butter's brand population is much smaller, and only Skippy was named as the dowager. A larger sample would likely provide additional candidates such as Jif and Peter Pan.

Whether a single brand, or a set of similar brands, the category dowager faces common threats from similar structural and motivational sources. Despite its shrinking user base, the dowager brand still has a hard core group of loyal users and also gains some share of newcomers to the market. Some customers have tried other brands and eventually returned to the dowager. On the other hand, signs of the dowager's weakness can be observed among those users who are doubtful and considering trying other brands. These movements of consumers toward and away from the dowager brand occur within the context of a competitive brand hierarchy.

BRAND COMPETITION MATRIX

In a mature market, a dowager brand faces varying degrees of competition from as many as five different brand levels: (a) old peer brands, (b) new peer brands, (c) retailer or private label brands, (d) generic brands (in some product categories), and (e) elite brands, as shown in Table 17.1.

Old Peer Brands

Old peer brands are those that have over time competed directly with the dowager. They are regarded as traditional alternatives; for example, such brands as Borden's cheese, Plymouth cars, Heinz soups, and Scott tissue. They might also be seen as dowagers if, in the minds of their managers, they are having share erosion problems. Consumers, too, might consider old peers

TABLE 17.2 Consumer Constructed Competitive Brand Hierarchy

	Product Category		
Level and Feature	Shampoo (N = 12)[a]	Potato Chips (N = 8)	Peanut Butter (N = 4)
Elite Brands (Designer chef specialty)	Aveda Hanza Jhirmack Matrix Nexus Paul Mitchell Pantene Redken Salon Formula Sebastian Vidal Sassoon	Cape Cod Hawaiian Kettle Krunchers O'Grady's Pringles	All Natural Blue Diamond Oz Smucker's
Dowager Brands (Historic main brand)	Breck Flex Johnson's Baby Prell	Charles' Guy's Jay's Lay's Ruffles Wise	Skippy
Old Peers (Other long-term main brands)	Agree Alberto VO 5 Finesse Flex Head/Shoulders Herbal Essence Johnson's Baby Pert Prell Revlon Balsam St. Ives Suave Wella Balsam	Bells Charle's Chips Clover Club Evans' Fritos Herr's Jay's Lay's Ruffles Vitner's	Jif Peter Pan Scudder's
New Peers (New national/ regional brands)	Agree Aussie Shampoo Faberge Finesse Head/Shoulders Helene Curtis Ivory Jhirmack Jherri Redding Pantene Pert Rejoice Salon Selectives Selsun Blue Suave Vidal Sassoon	Cape Cod Eagle Keebler Pringles Ruffles	Goober's Smucker's
Retailer Brands (Store/private label brands)	CUS CVX Jewell Osco Phar-Mor	Jewel Jay's	Grand Union Holsum Jewel Lady Lee
Generic Brands (Bottom-line commodities):	Suave Walgreens	Acme	Peanut Butter White Label

a. (N = refers to the size of the subsample of the total (N = 76) who selected a specific product category.

to be dowager brands; in the shampoo category, the respondents expressed some uncertainty about whether Flex, Johnson's Baby, and Prell are dowager or old peer brands (Table 17.2). From the viewpoint of the dowager brand, old peers seem a lesser brand for having a shorter tenure in the marketplace and for often having a smaller brand share. The usual competitive movement of consumers among the dowager and old peer brands might not seem like an erosion problem, unless an old peer manages to mount an unusual challenge. For example, Schlitz's share of the beer market was eroded not only by Miller's flagship brand (Miller High Life), or even by Schlitz's reputation for poor quality, but by the dramatic market structure changes old peer Miller triggered with its successful introduction of the "light" beer category.

New Peer Brands

These brands are recent entrants in the product category. They are perceived as having substantial national (Pert shampoo, Eagle potato chips, Smucker's peanut butter) or regional (Samuel Adams beer, Holiday Spa health clubs) character. They might be competing directly with the dowager brand, being well advertised and offered at comparable prices. A new peer brand might be a modified version of an old peer; for example, *conditioning* shampoo (Pert), *hard bite* potato chips (Cape Cod, Krunchers), *all-natural* peanut butter. Or an old peer brand in one category—Land O Lakes butter—might be seen as a new peer in the cheese category, with its introduction of packaged cheese slices. New peer brands also likely reflect managers' interests in sustaining a contemporary brand image, as

reflected in the athletic shoe market's current heavy use of national sports heroes.

Successful new peers represent a substantial threat to the dowager brand and cause serious erosion of its brand share. The sheer "newness" of new peer brands tends to reinforce perceptions of the dowager as out-of-date and in decline. When supported by vigorous advertising and promotion, innovative packaging, and special product claims, a new peer brand seems more exciting and inviting than the dowager. Its contemporary glamour may even cause it to be seen as relatively elite. For example, on the basis of its price and distribution, Vidal Sassoon shampoo is a new peer brand, yet its salon positioning and French-sounding name support a more elevated status and imagery.

Retailer/Private Label Brands

The brands at this level are those that seem circumscribed as lesser than national brands. They seem to be locally distributed, not widely advertised, and include private labels that may be regarded by shoppers as store brands. These brands vary among communities; in Chicago, Dominick's Heritage House and Jewel's Hillfarm brand are well-known examples. These are ordinary mass market versions, commonly priced lower than the dowager as well as its old and new peers. They are also likely to be perceived as somewhat lower in quality than the national brands. On the other hand, some private label and retailer brands are expensive and could be classified as elite brands. This depends in part on the status of the retailer, for example, Saks versus Sears store brand apparel. Then again, even a Saks private menswear label is likely to have lower standing among consumers than the elite national brands that Saks offers: Hickey Freeman, Giorgio Armani, Ralph Lauren, and so on.

As a source of erosion in a dowager's brand share, the threat of retailer and private label brands varies across different product categories. Recently, retail grocery store brands (Lady Lee, Heritage House, etc.) were the top selling items in 77 of 476 different categories (*The Washington Post,* July 19, 1989). Not always just me-too entrants, store brands have been product innovators in categories such as ketchup and yogurt (Freedman, 1988). Recession, inflation, improved product quality and packaging, more aggressive promotion, and the decline of generics all fueled both consumers' and retailers' interests in store brands during the 1980s (*Progressive Grocer,* Fall 1989). Retail grocers have invested heavily in their own brands because they offer (a) enhanced profit sources and margins, (b) greater leverage with national brand manufacturers, (c) a means of differentiating themselves from local competitors, and (d) greater control and integration of promotional activities (*Marketing News, January 1987*).

One notable trend is the emergence of *premium* private label grocery store brands. Although largely unadvertised, these brands are supported by high quality packaging and pricing equal to or slightly higher than nationally advertised "name" brands. Without the costs of media advertising, premium private label brands provide a new and enhanced profit source for both their manufacturers and retail networks. This strategy assumes that premium packaging and merchandising will convince consumers that these brands enjoy parity with the national players. A less tenuous factor in the growth of store brands is the state of the economy. A recent Gallup poll found that recession fears caused 20% of the sampled respondents to report that they will buy more store brand products next year (*Wall Street Journal,* December 10, 1990).

Generic Brands

Below the retail and private label brands are the generic brands. They might be classified as a lower level of retail brand, because they vary from store to store and in some product categories do not exist. They are the retailer's bottom line and can be taken as commodities that offer competition to all branded goods. They are generally priced 20% to 40% lower than the national brands. As they expanded in the late 1970s, they gained significant market shares in a variety of product categories: paper goods, plastic kitchen bags, iced tea mix, dishwasher detergent, light bulbs, and others. Sales of generic brands peaked in 1982 (*Business Week,* June 17, 1985), and despite their diminished importance today, they are something of a competitive wild card. In a recession, the financial squeeze on consumers may trigger another resurgence of generic brand popularity, causing further share erosion of not only the dowager, but all national brands.

Elite Brands

Elite brands are located at the opposite end of the competitive brand hierarchy from the generics. Although the dowager may be seen by many as the top brand because it is so well known and still has a large share, those familiar with the range of brands available usually know brands that exist in a more rarified realm. These brands have a small market share, being more exclusive and expensive. They are thought to be "better," of distinctively high quality, and likely to appeal to special segments. They may be so elite as to be virtually unknown to the mass market, like Bookbinder's canned soups or Porthault sheets. They may be specialty brands that are relatively well-known but not widely distributed, like some designer labels in clothing, Matrix shampoo, or Rolls Royce and Lotus cars. They may be quite accessible but not very noticeable compared to bigger brands— for example, Crosse and Blackwell soups or Coleman's Hot English mustard. Elite brands may be old or new and vary in how they contribute to the erosion of the dowager. As these are matters of perception, the managers of a declining elite brand could see it as a dowager; customers and other observers might agree or not.

Elite brands are commonly ignored by dowagers, who do not think of them as threatening competitors. However, some portion of those who shift away from the dowager do go to elite brands, and some newcomers to the market chose the elite from the beginning. These consumers have reasons for not choosing or staying with the dowager, and they are a challenge to the dowager's total market strategy. Although elite brands commonly account for less than 10% of total category sales, a shift of only 1% or 2% toward or away from the dowager represents significant revenue gains or losses. Also, the proliferation of elite brands may signal a general, evolutionary upgrading of the entire category and a permanent increase in the combined share of elite brands. This trend is evident in the shampoo category (Table 17.2).

Elite brands are the sixth and final level of the competitive brand hierarchy. Admittedly, this framework is an oversimplifica-

tion, to suggest a general picture of the competitive environment surrounding dowager brands. The separate conceptual levels in the hierarchy are neither perfectly exclusive, nor do they exhaust all brand possibilities within a product category. Although the hierarchy presented here is based on the combined dimensions of price, quality, and status, other variables may impact the structure of a particular competitive hierarchy.

For example, when prices across all levels of a hierarchy are similar, other differentiating dimensions emerge, such as relative modernity, masculinity, maturity, or technical sophistication. Also, within each level are often finer gradations. The Jewel food store chain offers three separate price/quality brand levels under its store brand umbrella: Mary Dunbar (high), Cherry Valley (medium), and Bluebrook (low). Finally, the data sources used to construct a product category's competitive brand hierarchy are critical. Although it may be hypothesized from manager's general knowledge, it should in practice incorporate both consumers' perceptions as well as historical competitive factors. The limitations of this framework notwithstanding, it offers a general starting point for better understanding a dowager brand's plight, and for improving defensive marketing efforts on the dowager's behalf.

STRATEGIC ALTERNATIVES FOR DOWAGER BRANDS

Regardless of the particular structure of any competitive brand hierarchy, the dowager brand in it commonly confronts a difficult situation. Besieged from above, below, and the side, what can a dowager do to halt its share erosion? Can it make a comeback, or at least slow the rate of its decline? A wide range of strategic alternatives exists, but conventional portfolio analysis is likely to classify many dowager brands as "dogs" and recommend a brand harvesting or divesting strategy. Either withdrawing marketing support or simply putting the brand up for sale may be fiscally attractive over the short-term. Yet, as recent criticism suggests, financially driven strategies may rely on flawed marketing analyses, assumptions, and scenarios (Day, 1990). Divesting decisions may also result from deficiencies in intangible and more elusive resources such as managerial creativity (Sheth, 1985). Regardless of their soundness, neither brand harvesting nor divesting strategies confront the dowager's competitive situation directly. And even where these alternatives are attractive, intraorganizational or external constraints may prevent their pursuit.

MARKETING MIX AND MARKET MODIFICATION ALTERNATIVES

Managers of dowager brands commonly consider two general categories of strategic options for revitalizing their declining brands (Kotler, 1988). One set of alternatives focuses on *marketing mix* modifications that seek to improve the brand's overall quality, features, or style; expand and secure its distribution; optimize its pricing policies; or make its promotional efforts more effective. *Market modification* strategies are more complex but often promise more sustainable competitive benefits. Their strategic thrusts range across new segment/market entry, nonuser conversion, new usage benefits or occasions, increased and more frequent usage, and winning back lost share.

Three currently popular growth strategies are a hybrid of a strong product development emphasis coupled with the objective of reaching new consumer segments. A *brand flanking* strategy strengthens the corporate presence in a category; and it also softens the impact of losses incurred by a declining dowager brand. For example, Proctor & Gamble's Pampers share of disposable diapers sank from 59% in 1980 to 26% in 1988, but its Luvs brand share grew from 11% to 24% during the same period. When a dowager brand is still vigorous and enjoys sufficient consumer and trade goodwill, management often considers either a brand franchise or line extension strategy. In comparison to traditional new product development, *brand franchise extension* has proved to be a relatively low risk-low cost means to move a brand's presence into new and more attractive markets (Tauber, 1981, 1988). A *line extension* strategy keeps the dowager brand closer to home through a product form variation (Joy with lemon) or through a same-brand entry to an immediately adjacent product category (Cheetos popcorn). Many marketing success stories have issued from each of these three brand development alternatives.

Such approaches are more market-driven than portfolio strategies, yet they, too, often fail to deal directly with a declining dowager brand's long-term care. Embedded organizational barriers can discourage more vigorous and immediate efforts on the dowager's behalf. As an "oldtimer" brand, it is easily neglected in the excitement and activities surrounding new product and brand introductions. Something new attracts more managerial attention and aspiration than the old, particularly when the latter is slipping. Still, marketing managers who are vested with dowager responsibilities necessarily seek ways to shore up their brands' positions, and defensive tactics are evident in the marketing mix.

THE PRICE PROMOTION TRAP

As noted earlier, the usual bases for a competitive brand hierarchy are variations in price, perceived quality, and status. Strategic thinking about dowager brands frequently focuses on economic variables, so that pricing issues dominate. The correlation between a brand's price and its ranking is so obvious that it tempts managers to believe that price is all one needs to know. The idea is that lower prices are drawing customers away from the dowager, with the implication that the best defense is to lower prices. This belief has fueled the recent growth in both consumer and trade sales promotions. The tangibility and relative predictability of price-based promotions further enhance their managerial appeal.

The shift toward sales promotion tactics has triggered a "damage-to-brand-equity" tocsin that is intuitively persuasive but still has little scientific support. However, recent studies provide evidence of sales promotion's negative financial consequences. One economic study reports how consumer sales promotions often sacrifice profits in favor of short-term spikes in sales volume (Jones, 1990). Looking at the issue from the trade side, Buzzell, Quelch, and Salmon (1990) assess the large, incremental distribution system costs associated with promotion-driven "forward buying." These conditions are characteristic of what Bonoma (1989) labels *overmarketing* and describes as a competitive situation requiring high "voice" expenditures and constant price promotions in order to "retain anything like a semblance of brand loyalty." Many dowager brands compete in such difficult environments. Here, not only are profit margins sliced, but the brand's marketing dialogue is, in extreme cases, reduced to a quarterly FSI coupon drop.

COMMUNICATING BRAND EQUITY

Obviously, price is an important competitive element, particularly in recessionary times. Yet, despite the tendency for economic pressures to move consumers down the hierarchy, they continue to buy from a mix of levels. Even heavy users of generics or retail brands do not buy them in all available product categories but make exceptions for the dowagers and peers they prefer. Some established brands withstand inroads by cheaper brands, presumably by communicating in some appropriate thematic and stylistic ways. Thus, it is not enough to know that competitors are squeezing the dowager with price appeals, as there remain other bases for brand choices. Perhaps these other bases could be used as avenues for attracting customers back to the dowager, despite the price differentials that supposedly took them away.

This raises questions about what messages the dowager might send through which communication channels. On the surface, dowager brands might not appear to be strong candidates for much advertising support. Their brand awareness is already high, they seem to have little news value, and measuring advertising effectiveness is frustrating. Some dowager communication strategies rely on insistent yet vague "quality" claims that rarely accomplish much. More effective messages need grounding in the dowager's brand equities. A brand's equity is one of its most valuable "invisible assets" (Hiroyuki, 1984), but its intangibility has long frustrated managerial efforts to leverage it (Gardner & Levy, 1959). Brand managers' frequent assignment rotations further discourage cultivation of a long-term, sophisticated sense of the dowager's history, evolution, and meaning (Baum, 1990). Over time, these factors can produce debilitating brand neglect (Aaker, 1990).

One direction for improving dowager managers' understanding of their brands' equities requires investments in in-depth research that delivers more than the brand's statistical placement on a bivariate perceptual map. The dowager's story is more complex, and such simplified solutions offer only a glimpse of the brand's meanings to various customer segments. In addition, such findings often narrowly circumscribe both competitive analyses and strategic alternatives.

As an example of such auto-handicapping, a bright, young peanut butter brand manager recently bemoaned, "I just don't see what we can do with our brand. All the perceptual maps say that Jif *'owns peanutty.'*" Such defeatist thinking unnecessarily circumscribes the rules and dimensions of brand competition. A broader perspective views brand meaning as a core dynamism that emerges from the interplay of related product sensations, perceptions, interpretations, and motivations (Levy, 1986b). Such an analysis interprets a brand's attributes (e.g., peanutty) in the larger context of its benefits, personality, and meanings to various consumer segments (Berry, 1988; Levy, 1959). Taking a more expansive view of marketing situation, the ensuing discussion with the beleaguered brand manager turned up numerous "nutty" alternatives from ideas about crunchiness, Peter Pan, Annette Funicello, "choosier moms," Mr. Peanut, and other aspects of the focal brand's meaning and symbol system.

SOURCES OF SHARE LOSS AND SALES PROSPECTS

In addition to researching a more broadly conceived brand equity, and doing so in-depth, dowager managers can identify their best customer prospects by sharpening their segmentation focus. The dowager's market history implies that it has been tried, rejected, or adopted by a diverse population of consumers. More refined thinking seeks to (a) discover where the dowager's "lost" customers have migrated in the competitive brand matrix and (b) what their dissenting rationales are for leaving the dowager's franchise.

As an initial step toward better understanding the dowager's strategic possibilities, managers need to identify the competitive sources of the dowager brand's share losses, and the specific groups of "lost" consumers that represent the best prospects for returning to the dowager's franchise. This task sounds easier than it actually is. Some managers have insufficient data for drawing definitive conclusions about which competitors are doing the most damage. More commonly, dowager brand managers include in their thinking only the two or three brands that are closest to it in sales volume and market share. This simplifying solution often ignores the overall market direction, especially the proliferation of niche-player "other brands" (McKenna, 1988). The competitive brand hierarchy discussed earlier provides a basis for more dynamic analyses of a dowager brand's problems and possibilities. By crossing consumers' dowager user status with the category's six competitive brand hierarchy levels, 16 separate segments emerge (Table 17.1).

Consumer usage status. The broadest cut divides consumers into dowager user and nonuser group. Despite its share losses, the dowager still enjoys the support of consumers who are exclusive users of it. Where product use makes it feasible, some people have become dual users, or switchers who divide their consumption between the dowager and another or other brands. The nonuser group displays a more definite degree of alienation from the dowager brand. Former users have shifted their allegiance to one or more competitive brands, and no longer buy the dowager. Perhaps the most remote from the dowager are those who come newly to the market and chose a competitor, never having tried the dowager.

Except in rare cases, a dowager is unlikely to stem its eroding brand share by focusing efforts on its exclusive users. Dual users are generally more promising targets. Volume and share gains would build on their current favorable buying patterns and encourage them to make incremental increases in dowager brand purchases. Nonusers are more problematic. Former users, hypothetically, compose a diverse group who have migrated to any number of brand levels in the competitive hierarchy. Considering the dowager's long history in the marketplace, those who have never used it seem particularly remote prospects. Sometimes these consumers have "leapfrogged" it for one reason or other and never used it. For example, many new, young beer drinkers today start out buying light brands, largely bypassing the dowager category of premium beers. On the other hand, such innocence could offer the dowager an opportunity to attract consumers who don't know enough about it to think of it as old.

Brand hierarchy level. The type and characteristics of the brands that surround the dowager add another dimension to the competitive analysis. Considering whether dowager users have migrated toward old peer, new peer, elite, retailer, or generic brands forces a focus on the where and why of the dowager's losses. For example, those currently favoring elite brands may be motivated by status striving and economic improvement, retail and generic users by economic downgrading, and new peer users by lifestyle appeals. Obviously, the specific brand players and overall growth direction of a category up or down the hierarchy produce unique circumstances for any single dowager brand. The purpose here is to provide a framework for investigating the dowager's possibilities. These targeting alternatives may present a frustrating surplus of opportunity, yet by drawing finer distinctions, they should help clarify both the purpose and audience for a dowager's communication strategy. Considering the entire competitive matrix should also assist in answering the question: which consumer target will be most responsive to communications from the dowager brand? In many cases, it is unlikely that managers would focus on only one of these competitive cells. Media efficiency and volume goals often dictate the specification of a broader target.

CONSUMERS' DISSENTING RATIONALES

In seeking to determine the relative values of different advertising strategies for a dowager brand, a diagnosis needs to be made of the reasons consumers have for not using it. The general hypothesis is that for each level in the competitive brand hierarchy, and for each segment of substance at that level, there is a characteristic rationale or set of rationales that justifies *not* using the dowager brand. These justifications are called rationales, although they may not necessarily appear to be rational; but rather they are any explanations or grounds that the consumer may offer. When asked, consumers often phrase their behavior as a positive act, not a dissent, giving as reasons their motives for use of the brand they prefer. But, from the position of the dowager, these reasons can be interpreted as against it, or imply criticism of it, so they are conceptualized here as *dissenting rationales.* An analysis of the meaning of the rationales that are drawing customers away will enable the creation of potential defenses against those rationales.

Such analysis helps further to identify the groups who would be evaluated as potentially susceptible to being drawn back to use the dowager brand, or to use it more frequently instead of alternatives. Some consumers demonstrate this potential by using the dowager brand when it is on sale or couponed, compared to those who resist even then. Thus, meeting the price competition of the other brands is one strategy for wooing dissenters. However, the aim in the present discussion is to address nonprice means of advertising competition.

Consumers' dissenting rationales can be quite idiosyncratic, but they typically focus on one or more of these general factors: (a) their perceptions of the dowager brand's *features* and *performance,* (b) the *benefits* they associate with using or buying it, and (c) interpretations of the brand's overall *image,* including the type of individuals who are imagined to use it. A general, hypothesized universe of dissenting rationales is discussed below, and summarized in Table 17.3.

Dissents: Old Peer Brand Users

Old peer brands are the most comparable to the dowager and compete at the same level. They too go back in time, so the dowager's claim to originality or tradition may seem no greater assurance of know-how, stability, or quality. These consumers are likely to see the dowager as no better than the brand they use. Although their histories may be almost as long as the original brand, old peers are likely to have been introduced with some variation (e.g., packaging, ingredients) that distinguished them from the dowager. This encourages a belief that the dowager brand is *static* in form and design. If an old peer's market share is markedly smaller than the dowager brand's, old peer users may, like elite brand users, view the dowager and its users as commonplace and conformist.

Relative superiority is always likely to be present as a problem—in either direction. However, it is probably a less intense issue here than it is between the dowager and other levels of the hierarchy, especially when prices are essentially the same. Still, perceptions of parity make the dowager's purported benefits questionable to old peer users. There is likely to be an emphasis on subtle but real differences in brand images concerning suitability for kinds of people, instead of higher or lower brand status levels. For example, dowagers Birdseye frozen foods and Gold Medal flour are challenged by losses from consumers who have somehow decided that these brands are "not for me" and migrated toward Green Giant, Pillsbury, or other old peers as better fitting their lifestyles.

Dissents: New Peer Brand Users

Recent entrants in the field draw users who believe the new brand offers something current and different. The dissenting rationales of new peer users are grounded

TABLE 17.3 Consumers' Dissenting Rationales and Dowager Counterlogics

Consumer Target	Strategic Focus	Dissenting Rational	Counterlogic
Elite users	Features/	Inferior	Unusual excellence
	Performance	Mass-produced	High standards (Image only)[a]
	Benefits	Impersonal	Value (Rip-off)
			All-occasion
			Traditional (Narcissistic)
	User image	Lower status	Friendly real people
			(Snobs)
			(Insecure)
Old peer users	Features/performance	No better	Proven superiority
			Standard setter
		Static	Classic (Imitation)
	Benefits	Questionable	Most reliable
	User image	Commonplace	Lifestyle fit
		Conformist	Most popular (Second String)
New peer users	Features/performance	Crude	
		Outdated	Authentic (Gimmicky)
	Benefits	Dull	Reliable (Flashy)
	User Image	Unsophisticated	Everyman (Narrow appeal)
Store label users	Features/performance	No better	Authenticity (Inferior)
			(Imitation)
		Secret producer	Distinctive ("Seconds")
	Benefits	Unnecessary	Subtle merit
			Available
	User Image	Not sensible	Discriminating
			(Undiscriminating)
			Expansive (Retentive)
			(False economy)
Generic label users	Features/performance	No better	Trustworthy (Inferior)
		Secret producer	Distinctive ("Seconds")
	Benefits	Unnecessary	Sensible
		Uneconomic	Minor indulgence
			(Shame/Guilt)
	User image	Irrational	Expansive
			Knowledgeable
			(Undiscriminating)
			(Penurious)

a. Counterlogics in parentheses indicate negative communication alternatives.

in beliefs about their own innovativeness, a fresh technology, or a contemporary awareness they perceive in the new brand. Thus, the dowager brand may seem to be put in the shade, falling behind, and no longer interesting. In comparison to the new features, product forms, and packaging innovations offered by new peers, the dowager is likely to be perceived as relatively crude and outdated. Beyond merely questionable, its benefits seem dull and uninviting. New peer users are prone to see dowager users as comparatively unsophisticated, as not being "with it" by failing to take advantage of the latest, whether in technology, design, or psychology.

Dissents: Store/Private Label Brand Users

Sometimes, customers are indifferent to store and private label brands as brands, buying them at preferred retail outlets for convenience and taking whatever is carried. In some cases, store brands may be more expensive than the dowager and even classified as elite brands; in others, consumers view store brands with uncertainty as to quality. Well-known chain brands have substantial followings. Some customers use them loyally, and many are dual users who use them as well as the dowager brand. Store brand users usually dissent from the dowager on price grounds. They argue that the dowager is no better and not worth the difference in price. They also often believe that the store brand is the same as the dowager, being secretly from the same producer. Osco pharmacies deny their imitations are manufactured by the main brands, but consumers are skeptical.

Store brand users add that one doesn't always need the best of everything, so the dowager brand is "too good" and unnecessary. The lesser product is acceptable because it is not going to be served to company, and the family does not know or care about the difference. If the store brand is used as an ingredient, no one else will know about the substitution anyway. These perceptions encourage store brand users to think of dowager users as being foolish or impractical consumers.

Dissents: Generic Brand Users

The dissenting rationales of generic users are similar to those of store brand users, but they have a flavor of their own. They are prone toward defensiveness about the high visibility of cheap and basic packaging that stigmatizes the customer. On the other hand, users assert that the dowager is no better, or they express surprise that the generic product is as good as it is. This idea further supports the notion that the dowager or another national brand is actually the secret producer of generics. Generic users also emphasize their selectivity by explaining why some generic goods (paper products, peanut butter, applesauce) are particularly acceptable. In other cases, where the generic brand does not meet the dowager's level of quality, generic users argue that such quality is unnecessary in these product categories.

A protective atmosphere is created of there being a rational ingroup that is economically sensible, beating the system, and motivated by getting back to basics, so that the dowager brands are seen as unnecessary frills, as part of the overadvertised, costly way things have gotten unreasonably out of hand. Thus, dowager users can be criticized as being irrational and taken in by the system.

Dissents: Elite Brand Users

Those who use elite brands perceive the dowager from above. They regard their own taste as elevated and their lifestyle as composed of a larger proportion of superior or specialty brands. To these consumers, the dowager seems to have a mass-produced character and is inferior in quality to their specialty designer brands. Also, the dowager's cheaper price is at odds with their more discriminating preferences. If, as often happens, the dowager proudly proclaims itself to be the "Number One" (most popular) brand, this is taken as quantitative evidence of its unsuitability to the elite customer, who seeks greater exclusivity. The elite brand consumer seeks and is willing to pay for more individualized benefits; the dowager's benefits are diffused across the masses and are relatively impersonal. This further encourages elite users to view consumers who favor the dowager brand as lower status.

Elite users who have never used the dowager brand may be the most aloof and indifferent. They have removed it from consideration. Former users of the dowager brand in this segment may have permanently upgraded themselves; their need to display this elite status may be strong, as is their disavowal of connection with the ordinary dowager. Dual users may like to put on airs at times with elite brands.

DIALECTICS OF DEFENSE: STRATEGIC COUNTERLOGICS

This population of hypothesized dissenting rationales highlights the many reasons that consumers have for moving away from the dowager brand; yet, each rationale invites a dialectical counterargument against it. Prior to focusing on specific defensive communication possibilities, it is useful, first, to consider what equities—if any—a brand enjoys from being the category dowager and what defensive resources these provide. Carpenter and Nakamoto (1989) recently found that a category brand pioneer enjoys advantages resulting from its impact on defining consumers' product preference structures. Our pilot study supports and elaborates this finding. The respondents' top-of-mind word and phrase associations to the term *original brand* and their explanations of what it means to say that a brand is "the original" suggest that a mild halo effect surrounds the dowager. Five main

ideas emerged from content analyzing the data. The dowager is seen as (a) an innovator who founded the category, (b) the category product standard setter, (c) a reliable quality guarantor, (d) well-known and popular, and (e) associated with consumers' family biographies.

Exploiting these general perceptions and sentiments might help the dowager, and managers to sometimes launch advertising that explicitly proclaims their brands as the original. However, the mere assertion of original brand status per se has no guaranteed impact on consumers. Also, any dowager's immediate situation requires specific focus on the competitive and consumer dynamics of the brand and its category. At issue here is how to leverage communications that will deflect consumers' dissenting rationales. The argument is that effective advertising can be developed by generating counterlogics and strategic themes. The former term refers to a dialectical argument that addresses a dissenting idea, or related ideas. Strategic themes build on and express one or more counterlogics and reflect the broader thrust of the advertising strategy, the uniqueness of a particular competitive situation, and the intangible added-value brought to the situation by creative personnel.

Themes and counterlogics express degrees of sophistication in coping with dissent. The dowager's claims are constrained by its history and established image. In general, a dowager tends to claim excellent quality; and when threatened, a common reaction is to insist on the claim more intently. It seems reasonable to do this, as it carries conviction, is generally believable, and reinforces the large segment of loyal users. However, as the previous discussion suggests, it is easy for nonusers to dismiss such a customary claim, as they are nonusers in the face of it, and they have found ways to deny its relevance to them. Literal quality claims are also less meaningful to many former users. Either they have been disillusioned and are determined to disagree, or they have lived through that appeal and use a competitor regardless. They can be impervious to the idea. Thus, a conventional literal claim of quality has the primary value of generally maintaining the dowager's brand stature, and perhaps appealing to some newcomers to the market, but it would not seem especially effective in reversing the drain of its brand share. To be effective, a quality appeal—as well as any other plausible dowager counterargument—needs to be disaggregated and customized to take into account the specific sources of resistance to it. The following are hypothesized counterarguments offered to deflect or rebut the dissenting rationales of competitive brand segments. Both positive and negative communication possibilities are suggested. The latter lend themselves to aggressive comparative advertising and are indicated in Table 17.3 by parentheses. Positive counterarguments focus on appealing messages about the dowager's features and performance, its benefits, and those who use it.

Counterlogics: Old Peer Users

Because old peer brands share with the dowager a basic sense of history, as well as comparable quality and price, their users may believe that the dowager brand is no better than their own. However, this does not imply that such beliefs are unalterable. Old peer users might reconsider the dowager if presented with some fresh proof of its superiority, perhaps some unusual excellence resulting from its founding technol-

ogy. As the perceived original brand, the dowager might offer evidence of its status as the category standard setter. Because old peer users are likely to see the dowager as static, this perception might be countered by positioning the dowager as classic. From this perspective, even old peer brands are imitations, or trivial variations on a classic theme.

Emphasis on the dowager's classic style and substance might also counter old peer users' suspicions that its benefits are questionable and foster beliefs that the dowager is the most reliable brand. However, because old peer and dowager brands are not much discriminated by quality or price, they are apt to be used more expressively for psychological reasons. If the dowager seems commonplace, and its users conformist (as Cheer users might see Tide users), lifestyle differences might be involved. If an old peer user feels that the dowager is "not for me," the counterlogic might work toward more distinctiveness, to say that it is indeed "for someone like you." For example, a masculinity theme might be used on behalf of Chevrolet trucks to blunt the appeals of old peer Dodge ("Ram Tough"). Finally, perception of the dowager as commonplace might be countered by positive emphasis on its popularity, or more negatively, on the idea that users of old peers are affiliating with second-string brands.

Counterlogics: New Peer Users

New peers are often similar to the old in challenging the dowager at the same general level of quality and price. They have the added advantage of being new and thus possibly truly innovative. They enjoy the announcement effect and may re-awaken thought about the product area by encouraging trial. Users of new peer brands can feel they are doing something fashionable. They would probably be especially unresponsive to the idea that tradition, stability, and experience should matter to them. The more vulnerable users among this group may have some doubts about the new brand. Although new peer users may perceive it as crude, the dowager is the quintessential brand in the category. By comparison, new peer brands are relatively immature, less authentic, synthetic, and imitative.

Counterlogics might rely on the dowager's assertions of actually being in the current swim, of showing that it is still lively, and keeping up its appeal to modern consumers. As a example of this, Canada Dry and 7-Up have been recently in the curious position of pointing out that they never did contain caffeine, in an effort to be visible among all the new soft drink brands claiming the merits of being caffeine-free. While some new peers offer genuine innovations and benefits, there may be suspicions that many of these are gimmicks. The dowager might suggest that some new peer brands are merely superficial and flashy. Although relatively dull, the dowager is solid and reliable. Against the perception that dowager users are less sophisticated, the dowager might emphasize its universal positioning or even take swipes at the narrower appeal of new brand entrants.

Counterlogics: Retail/Private Label Users

Users of store brands might be wooed with the general idea of improving their consuming status. Perceptions that the dowager is no better might be countered with communications that emphasize the

dowager's *authenticity*, or more negatively, depreciate store brands as *inferior imitations*. Common beliefs that the dowager is the secret producer of store brands might be deflected with communications about the dowager's distinctive qualities and the implication that store brands are manufactured with leftovers or "seconds." The dissenting rationale that the dowager's quality level is unnecessary might be vulnerable to the idea that the dowager has subtle merit; that even as an ingredient, the dowager contributes its advantages. Also, it is generally available, not limited to one retail chain.

There are several possibilities for confronting store brand users' beliefs that those who buy the dowager are not being sensible. One counterargument emphasizes the discriminating nature of dowager users; they can tell the difference, and consumers who can't should know better. A second theme expresses economic expansiveness. Particularly where price differences are not great, advertising could suggest that it's all right to skimp on other products, but not on the dowager, which is worth a small sacrifice. Unwillingness to spend just a little more implies the store brand user is unnecessarily retentive and engaging in false economies.

Counterlogics: Generic Brand Users

It is likely that some generic brand users are firmly convinced of their positions and likely to be unassailable. Some have irrevocably abandoned the dowager, and others are adamant about never using it. Here it is necessary to identify and measure not only specific rationales, but the force of dissent, and to what degree it expresses rejection of the dowager and/or positive affiliation with the generic brands used instead. Several counterarguments against generic users' dissenting rationales are similar to those suggested for store brand users. For example, some consumers are likely to feel uncertain about the objective quality of generic brands, so the "no better" argument might be countered with emphasis on the trustworthiness of the dowager. For example, recent publicity about generics has focused on their adulteration. Some consumers may suspect that generics are really inferior in quality. Also, the "secret producer" belief is probably vulnerable to information about generics being made from main brands' leftovers or seconds.

Facing up to the economies gained in using generic brands, counterlogics might stress the sensible reasons for buying the more expensive dowager—as Stewart's coffee does in emphasizing the greater number of cups gained from its richer product. Coming at this issue from a different direction, the dowager might suggest to generic users the danger of being shamed, of being caught by family or friends using a lesser brand. Or guilt feelings might be stirred; other people may not know the inferior brand is being used, but the user knows. Generic brands are vulnerable to being seen as relatively anonymous. The dowager might attack the generic's lack of identity; the generic seems blank, vague, and implies a lack of taste or discrimination, even penury. Use of the dowager could be suggested as implying either a greater degree of knowledge, or economical self-indulgence that precludes pinching pennies.

Counterlogics: Elite Brand Users

At the elite level, if the dowager is perceived to be inferior, the segment could be surprised by claiming some form of unusual excellence, thus challenging its preconceptions. It might use a claim that denies the mass-produced idea via a distinctive form of production or source of authenticity and uniqueness. "The Real Thing" implies this about Coca-Cola, as does the personalized approach to excellence implied by the use of such prominent company authorities as Lee Iacocca or Bill Marriott. The idea of overly popular appeal might be mitigated by using message sources that represent high standards (fussy customers), high status (a society *grande dame*), or a cultivated palate (Orson Welles, Lynn Redgrave).

Elite brand users might also be vulnerable to negative communications. For example, elites may harbor lingering doubts that they are paying more for a classy image than for actual quality differences. Similarly, because of its lower price in comparison to elite brands, the dowager may claim to be a true value, not a "rip-off." Although elite brand users think of the dowager as providing impersonal usage benefits, a counterclaim could leverage its popularity as evidence of its appropriateness for all occasions ("You'll never go wrong with . . . "), or to position it as traditional. This broad appeal may be used to make the exclusive, personalized benefits elite users seek seem, in comparison, silly or even narcissistic. Finally, counterlogics against elite dissents might be based on user imagery. While elite users are likely to look down on dowager users as downscale, the dowager could communicate its friendliness and its appropriateness for "real people," not snobs or individuals who are so insecure that they need to spend more to affirm their status. Secure elites will not, of course, be moved by these appeals.

STRATEGIC THEMES: DEFENDING AGAINST ELITE BRANDS

One or more of the hypothesized counter-logics may provide valid strategic focus for a dowager brand's marketing communications. Managers will usually want to evaluate the relative appeal of competing alternatives judgmentally or with conventional market research. When a particular counterlogic is chosen, the next critical task involves the executional translation and integration of paper-and-verbal objectives into advertising's multisensory lectures and dramas (Wells, 1988). This is where things can begin to unravel. Cases abound in which advertising's effectiveness has been hampered by collective misunderstanding of what strategic communication directives such as upscale, contemporary, or quality mean. MBAs and MFAs often see things differently. Consumer inputs help bridge this gap. Consumers typically assist front-end strategy development through participation in research of their relevant experiences, attitudes, and evaluations. This information is largely direct, objective, and generally helpful.

Additional information that captures broader, more creative, and more imaginative consumer expressions is particularly relevant to implementing the agency's strategy. Research needs also to probe the relational aspect of consumers' brand lives (Berry, 1988). Various projective techniques can elicit stories, drawings, dreams, and other creative expressions that (a) tap consumers' underlying thoughts and feelings, (b) reveal orientations not ordinarily obtained through direct research, and (c) provide narrative, thematic gestalts that summarize and integrate dynamic elements (Durgee, 1986; Levy, 1986a; Rook, 1988). Such data are often more palatable to creative personnel than statistical surveys, and they also parallel the final creative product in both rhetorical structure and content.

The added value of projective methods to the creative development process is illustrated here in the hypothesized case where a dowager's defensive strategy assumes that former users who now prefer elite brands represent the best sales prospects. Thematic development focuses on one relatively conservative counterargument (value) and one that is more aggressive (snob). These are selected as hypothetical candidates for deflecting elites' beliefs that the dowager is inferior in quality and lower in status.

The respondents in the pilot study were asked to personify two brands in their chosen category: the dowager (original), and a second preferred brand. This required them to characterize each with an imaginary name, nickname, gender, age, marital status, occupation, income level, personality, lifestyle, physical condition, and personal secret. These constructed brand characters are the protagonists in subsequent written narratives. The respondents were asked to imagine that these characters meet at some social occasion and then make up a story about how this came about, what they say to each other, what conflicts occur, and how the story ends.

Thematic Expression of the Value Counterlogic

Earlier discussion criticized overemphasis on price as a means for defending the dowager's declining share. This does not ignore the fact that some competitive situations do support price-oriented thinking. The dowager is in a particularly good position here to target elite consumers who are vulnerable to doubting the value of their more expensive brand preferences. The following story was created by a former user of the dowager moisturizer brand, Vaseline Intensive Care (VIC), who now uses one of the many elite brands available today, Biotherm.

> Liz and Betty meet at a company holiday party. Liz works in the Strategic Management group, and Betty is married to one of Liz's colleagues and teaches pottery at a local museum school. Liz notices how soft and smooth Betty's hands are. Liz asks Betty how she keeps her hands so soft when she works with clay all day. Betty says she uses VIC for her hands and body. Liz says she uses Biotherm . . . Betty has never even heard of this brand. She questions Liz about its price and is shocked to learn that it costs three times as much as VIC! Betty knows how well VIC takes care of her hands and will continue to use it. Liz begins to consider using VIC herself as a result of the softness of Betty's hands, for a third of what she's been paying! (F-29)

This "value" story resonates with contemporary slice-of-life advertising. Although it is narratively quite conventional, it delivers the message and reveals Liz's ambivalence about spending so much and her vulnerability to dowager appeals that offer competitive benefits at a better price.

The invisibility of product usage here would also tend to help win back elite consumers who question the lack of display value. Elite users might even be induced to downshift to the dowager without the added expenses of coupons and/or in-store promotions. Equally important, the narrative data deliver the basic strategy to agency creative personnel in an immediately useful way that encourages alternative story lines

and executions. On the other hand, a value appeal per se ranks low on the criterion of originality and may have little advertising impact (Wells, 1989). A current Suave shampoo commercial, for example, portrays a young woman questioning, "Are you trying to tell me I've been wasting my money on expensive shampoos?" The pervasiveness of value messages today suggests that managers need to exploit this counterlogic with unusual executional creativity or discover more distinctive themes.

Thematic Expression of the Snob Counterlogic

Thematic development of other dowager counterlogics is less straightforward. Advertising based on lifestyle images encourages identification with the sponsoring brand. Among elite brand users, this cultivates a sense of consumer superiority that disparages dowager users as common and less discriminating. This might seem to make the elite target unassailable from this direction; yet aggressive countermeasures might work in some cases. A counterlogic that promotes the dowager's position as the popular, everyman, all-American brand can imply or explicitly disparage the elite brand users as superficial, condescending snobs. The following story was constructed by a dowager brand user (M-26), and it expresses the snob counterlogic through an imaginary meeting of two hot dog brand characters: Oscar Mayer (dowager) and Mr. Vienna (elite).

> Oscar Mayer and Mr. Vienna meet at the refreshment stand during the seventh inning stretch. Oscar is with a group of six friends from work. They all ate before they came to the ballpark, because park hot dogs are too

expensive, and they're saving their money for beer. As he's taking six giant beers from the cashier, someone screams "Home run!," and in the excitement, Oscar swerves around and sloshes beer all over Mr. Vienna and his wife's nice jumpsuit. Mr. Vienna complains to Oscar, "You boor, you spilled beer all over us." Oscar glares at Mr. Vienna and responds, "You'll survive. Go on back to the reserved seats."

This story reveals suspicion that elites brand users are not "regular guys" and can't take a joke (or minor accident). They mix reluctantly and awkwardly with the masses, after which they retreat to their rarified, "reserved" world.

In practice, using negative user imagery is risky and sometimes backfires, seeming mean-spirited and offensive. On the other hand, in comparison to the earlier value story, this dramatic confrontation involves deeper affect and may provide stronger strategic leverage against elite brands and their users. A final sample story further develops the snob counterlogic. Two imaginary mustard brand characters were created by an elite brand user (M-32): Bud French (dowager) and Lance Poupon (elite).

Lance Poupon is having his first date with Erica—a beauty he's had his eye on for some time. Lance picked up Erica in a bowling alley instead of the usual trendy club. Why spend the bucks on an unknown commodity and risk the humiliation of not getting picked to go inside? Erica thinks that bowling would be fun. On the way there, all Lance can do is talk about himself. Career! Money! Career! Career! Therapy! Career! Blah! Blah! Blah! Erica thinks this could be a long night (how many frames are the minimum?), and she checks her watch for the first time as they pull into the parking lot.

Over on lane 6, Bud French scoped Erica and her leather slacks when she lined up at the shoe rental booth. Bud had just finished a big contracting job and was up for some fun tonight! "She looks bored with that yuppie scum," Bud thought at the same time he caught Erica's eye and a demure smile. Bud got patient. He waited until Erica headed for the ladies room, and then pounced her exit. Bud claimed a common friend, and yes, Erica would enjoy meeting over cocktails next week. Bud suggested lowly but with an almost innocent smile, "How about at my cabin in Lake Tahoe?" Erica blushed. Lance Poupon was history. But the bowling was OK. Three strikes for Erica!

This presents a more complex story of the elite-dowager brand dialogue. Rejection of the elite brand is vigorous and deeply rooted. The elite persona is not merely aloof and snobbish, it is a negative icon: "yuppie scum." In comparison to Bud French, Lance Poupon is insecure, narcissistic, dull, and wimpy. This *mano-a-mano* theme is heavy on testosterone issues, and it suggests elite brand image vulnerabilities against which a dowager might direct "regular guy" (or "gal") messages. Humor or fantasy might moderate the negativity of this thematic direction.

DISCUSSION

These illustrative expressions are drawn from a universe of potential strategic advertising themes. Actual marketing practice would employ a more sharply focused research design and sample than this exploratory study used. The point here is to suggest the benefits of gathering more creative, imaginative consumer expressions to bridge the often troublesome gap between brand communication strategy and its implementation. Managers tend to limit their options by involving consumers only in the evaluative phases of strategy development (Zaltman, 1989). Projective research methods provide added value to the strategy development phase; they generate themes that express and narratively summarize alternative strategic logics. Often rhetorically dramatic and fanciful, such exaggerated expressions parallel advertising's amplified communications (Levy, 1978). Also, these consumer-constructed gestalts facilitate the development of a unifying "strategic vision" which, despite its intangibility, is a requisite for sound and sustainable competitive strategy (Day, 1990).

However, methodological finesse is no panacea for the dowager's difficulties, although more creative and in-depth research could only help to improve managers' understanding of their brands' problems and prospects. Yet, the difficulties remain, and their causes endure. This paper began by noting the considerable pessimism that surrounds declining dowager brands. The demoralizing impact of continuing share losses, and the allure of seemingly greener

strategic pastures, often result in dowager brand neglect (Aaker, 1990) or quick-fix tactics such as coupons. Growing evidence about the negative effects of price-based promotions should motivate a more vigorous search for other marketing alternatives.

Some of those close to the problem call for extreme-sounding measures such as brand shock treatment (Baum, 1990). With more detachment, the Marketing Science Institute has recently designated *brand equity* as a capital research topic, which should stimulate programmatic research of it (Leuthesser, 1988). The conceptual framework offered here is designed to encourage more upbeat and focused strategic thinking that directly confronts the dowager brand's situation and seeks to win back dissenting consumers with more effective advertising. At first glance, the numerous communication alternatives hypothesized look like an intimidating abundance of managerial possibility. Yet, by taking the time to consider, develop, and evaluate a larger universe of competitive approaches, dowager brand managers are more likely to end up with the most effective and sustainable communication strategies for defending their beleaguered brands.

APPENDIX

Pilot Study Methodology

The purpose of the study is to ground our theoretical framework in an initial, exploratory study of consumers' ideas about dowager brands, and their perceptions of the competitive brand hierarchies in which dowagers compete.

Sample. A convenience sample of 75 respondents was gathered, composed of

graduate management students at a Midwestern university. International students were not included due to their likely exposure to nontypical brand populations in the product categories studied here. Forty percent of the sample are married, and 60% single; 39% are female and 61% male. The mean age is 27.3 years, and the respondents are higher in income, education, and social status than the average American consumer. Also, their brand usage is skewed toward elite brands. We make use of these non-representative sample characteristics in the paper's final section, which develops strategic counterlogics and themes for defending the dowager against elite brand competitors.

Instrument and data collection. The respondents completed a questionnaire that began by asking them to select from a list of 14 product categories one that they use often and in which they have tried a variety of brands. Seven of the products are in the food category (potato chips, canned soup, mustard, beer, frozen dinners, hot dogs, and peanut butter), and seven are household or personal products (aspirin, shampoo, moisturizer, toothpaste, paper towels, dishwashing soap, and toilet soap). After preliminary questions about their product usage frequency and history, the respondents were asked to name the one brand in the category that is "the original brand." Accompanying this task, they were instructed to identify and assign other brands in the category to one of the other five levels in the competitive hierarchy where they believe each belongs.

After constructing a competitive brand hierarchy, the respondents were asked to explain their choice of one brand as the original. They were also asked what it means in general to say that something is the original brand. Next, a word association technique was used to elicit words and phrases in response to the stimulus phrase: the original brand. The technique generated 213 separate terms or phrases that center around the five main ideas discussed earlier.

Brand character dialogue. The respondents were asked to construct two imaginary brand characters representing (a) the dowager, and (b) one other preferred brand. They were told that the two brand characters meet at a social occasion and engage in dialogue. The respondents were asked to construct a narratively complete story (with a beginning, middle, and end) around this rough outline. The purpose of this exercise is to encourage respondents to express their brand preferences and attitudes in terms of the competitive brands' underlying images and benefits, rather than their attributes and features; and to do so in creative, fanciful ways.

REFERENCES

Aaker, D. A. (1990). What is brand equity? In D. A. Aaker (Ed.), *Managing brand equity* (pp. 1-48). New York: Free Press.

Baum, H. M. (1990, December 10). Shock treatment needed to revive brands in '90s. *Marketing News,* p. 12.

Berry, N. C. (1988, Summer). Revitalizing brands. *Journal of Consumer Marketing, 5,* 15-20.

Bonoma, T. V. (1989, May 8). Overmarketing: Hoist on our own petard. *Marketing News,* p. 8.

Buzzell, R. D., & Gale, B. T. (1977). *The PIMS principles: Linking strategy to performance.* New York: Free Press.

Buzzell, R. D., Quelch, J. A., & Salmon, W. J. (1990, March/April). The costly bargain of trade promotion. *Harvard Business Review,* pp. 141-149.

Carpenter, G. S., & Nakamoto, K. (1989). Consumer preference formation and pioneering advantage. *Journal of Marketing Research, 26,* 285-298.

Collier, P., & Horowitz, D. (1987). *The Fords: An American epic.* New York: Summit Books.

Day, G. S. (1990). *Market driven strategy: Processes for creating value.* New York: Free Press.

Day, G. S., & Freeman, J. (1990). Burnout or fadeout: The risks of early into high technology markets. In L. R. Gomez-Mejia & M. Lawless (Eds.), *High technology management* (pp. 43-65). Greenwich, CT: JAI Press.

Durgee, J. (1986). Point of view: Using creative writing techniques in focus groups. *Journal of Advertising Research,* 57-64.

Erikson, E. H. (1982). *The life cycle completed.* New York: Norton.

Freedman, A. M. (1988, November 15). Supermarkets push private-label lines. *Wall Street Journal,* p. B1.

Gardner, B., & Levy, S. J. (1955). The product and the brand. *Harvard Business Review, 33*(2), 33-39.

Hiroyuki, I. (1984). *Mobilizing invisible assets.* Cambridge, MA: Harvard University Press.

Jones, J. P. (1990, September/October). The double jeopardy of sales promotion. *Harvard Business Review,* pp. 145-152.

Kotler, P. (1988). *Marketing management: Analysis, planning, implementation, and control.* Englewood Cliffs, NJ: Prentice Hall.

Landes, D. S. (1984, January). Time runs out on the Swiss. *Across the Board,* pp. 46-55.

Leuthesser, L. (Ed.). (1988). *Defining, measuring, and managing brand equity: A conference summary* (Report No. 88-104). Cambridge, MA: Marketing Science Institute.

Levy, S. J. (1959, July/August). Symbols for sale. *Harvard Business Review,* pp. 117-124.

Levy, S. J. (1962). Phases in changing interpersonal relations. *Merrill-Palmer Quarterly of Behavior and Development, 8*(2), 121-128.

Levy, S. J. (1978). *Marketplace behavior: Its meaning for management.* Chicago: American Marketing Association.

Levy, S. J. (1986a). Dreams, fairy tales, animals, and cars. *Psychology and Marketing, 2*(2), 67-81.

Levy, S. J. (1986b). Meanings in advertising stimuli. In J. Olson & K. Sentis (Eds.), *Advertising and consumer psychology* (pp. 214-226). New York: Praeger.

McKenna, R. (1988, September/October). Marketing in an age of diversity. *Harvard Business Review, 66,* 88-96.

Newman, J. W. (1967). *Marketing management and information.* Homewood, IL: Richard D. Irwin.

Robinson, W. T., & Fornell, C. (1985, August). Sources of market pioneer advantage in consumer goods industries. *Journal of Marketing Research, 12,* 305-317.

Rook, D. W. (1988). Researching consumer fantasy. In E. C. Hirschman & J. N. Sheth (Eds.), *Research in consumer behavior* (pp. 247-270). Greenwich, CT: JAI Press.

Sheth, J. N. (1985). *Winning back your market.* New York: John Wiley.

Tauber, E. M. (1981). Brand franchise extension: New product benefits from existing brand names. *Business Horizons, 24*(2), 36-41.

Tauber, E. M. (1988, August/September). Brand leverage: Strategy for growth in a cost-control world. *Journal of Advertising Research, 28,* 26-30.

Wells, W. D. (1988). Lectures and dramas. In A. M. Tybout & P. Cafferata (Eds.), *Cognitive and affective responses to advertising* (pp. 13-20). Lexington, MA: Lexington Books.

Wells, W. D. (1989). *Planning for r.o.i: Effective advertising strategy.* Englewood Cliffs, NJ: Prentice Hall.

Zaltman, G. (1989). *The use of developmental and evaluative market research* (Report No. 89-107). Cambridge, MA: Marketing Science Institute.

PART
FOUR

THE SYMBOLIC NATURE OF MARKETING

——— •◆• ———

Dennis Rook: Some managers might be tempted to skip this section on symbols, imagining it as too abstract or remote from their practical interests. This would be incorrect and a missed opportunity, as the articles included here are directly applicable to important contemporary marketing concerns. At the core of Levy's thinking is the observation that consumers buy products and brands not only for so-called functional reasons but for the various *symbolic meanings* that their consumption provides. As a result, it is important and beneficial for marketing managers to understand the symbolic motivations that animate consumers' purchases. Despite the persuasive logic of this premise, the symbolic nature of marketing is often a managerial blind spot, which has pernicious consequences for how managers understand their customers, create offerings for them, allocate marketing mix resources, and design marketing communications.

In 1978, Sid Levy published a textbook, *Marketplace Behavior: Its Meaning for Management.* As a student in his doctoral seminar, I read this book, along with more than a few of the articles in this collection. As I began to form my own opinions about the narrowly circumscribed little studies that seemed to dominate consumer research publications, I found inspiration and direction in Sidney's writings. A particular paragraph in his book still applies to how marketers often limit their thinking about consumers:

> One of the traditionally unfortunate deficiencies of formal marketing lies in its reluctance to deal with the less tangible realms of explanations of human behavior. Given to a narrow sense of realism and practicality and the tenacious grip of the economic mind, marketers tend to resist areas of understanding that have to do with symbols, myths, legends, arbitrary belief, and fantasy.

Arguably, the economic mind's "grip" is still strong. The recent dramatic shift of marketing dollars from advertising to consumer and trade promotions reflects a managerial worldview that depicts consumers as obsessively price-driven and apparently immune to product and brand symbols that reflect their age, sex, social status, maturity, lifestyle, fantasy life, and other consumer characteristics. But the price-driven strategies of the past decade have often produced disastrous consequences. The current revival of brand advertising suggests a returning appreciation of marketing images and symbols and of the role that marketing communications plays in building corporate and brand images.

This section embraces and illuminates the symbolic aspects of marketing. The articles here provide a comprehensive orientation to core concepts of symbolic analysis, and they demonstrate the pragmatic benefits of studying the symbols by which consumers buy. Sid Levy's contributions to this arena are extensive, seminal, and continuing. The lead article in this section, "Symbols for Sale," appeared in the *Harvard Business Review* in the summer of 1959. This is a wonderful and timeless piece; a few dated brand examples notwithstanding, the thinking is entirely fresh. The article translates the abstruse, sometimes murky concepts of (mostly) European symbolists into an equally sophisticated but more accessible language and framework. To paraphrase a recurring theme in Bill Clinton's first campaign, "It's about *meaning*, stupid!" But the obvious is sometimes difficult both to discern and achieve, and "Symbols for Sale," although nearly 40 years old, is an excellent departure point for better understanding of the symbolic aspects of marketing.

Other articles in this section elaborate and extend the seminal thinking of "Symbols for Sale." In 1963, Levy published "Symbolism and Lifestyle," in which he interprets the sum of an individual's consumption of symbolic goods and services as a *lifestyle*. This thinking helps expand conventional analyses that statically link a consumer segment to a focal product or brand's features and benefits, to a much broader perspective that examines the totality of such relationships as an overall lifestyle replete with consumption meanings and motivations. Historically, this article introduced the lifestyle concept to the marketing field some years before the advent of lifestyle psychographics in the 1970s.

Another key element of the symbolic nature of marketing is the concept of imagery, and in "Imagery and Symbolism" (1973), Levy links his seminal work on brand imagery ("The Product and the Brand," 1955) to the various practical concerns that marketing managers have in creating, maintaining, or modifying a brand image over time. The ideas in this article are particularly relevant to the ongoing debate about the relative merits of short-term promotional tactics over longer-term brand image strategies. One constraint to better brand image management is the common but erroneous notion that only certain products are symbolic. In "Symbols, Selves, and Others" (1981), Levy observes that catheters and computers are just as symbolic as cars and cologne, and business-to-business marketers have image management issues similar to those shared by consumer product managers.

As I mentioned in the Introduction to this volume, Sid Levy's work is characterized by its interdisciplinary orientation, and this applies to his thinking about the symbolic aspects of marketing. In "Myth and Meaning in Marketing" (1974), Levy explains the value of anthropological concepts and methods for marketing analyses. With its particular emphasis on symbolic cultural objects and processes, anthropology yields rich insights into the less tangible but significant symbolic realms of consumer experience. Levy's thinking in this article anticipates the emergence of anthropological inquiry in marketing, and the migration of several prominent anthropologists into marketing faculties. In a parallel vein, in "Semiotician *Ordinaire*" (1987), Levy discusses the mutuality of interest between marketing problems and analyses, and those of semioticians. Both involve the formal study of signs and symbols, and recent marketing thought has been enriched by a new reliance on the symbolic theories and methods drawn from semiotics and related fields.

Finally, three articles provide interesting examples of the application of symbolic analysis in different marketing settings. In "Symbols of Substance, Source, and Sorcery" (1960), Levy addresses an audience of creative personnel and discusses how consumers interpret aesthetic symbols involving variation in form, line, movement, and direction. Quite a different setting forms the basis for "The Public Image of Government Agencies" (1963). This is a historically significant work in its application of marketing thought to noncommercial, not-for-profit organizations, showing some of the roots of the thinking that was formulated in the 1969 article, "Broadening the Concept of Marketing." In the context of symbolic analyses, Levy demonstrates that, just like cookies and cereal, government agencies have marketplace images, too. His findings are amusing and provocative, and I invite the reader to consider his conclusion that many people actually want their government to be inefficient and lazy!

A later article, "Meanings in Advertising Stimuli" (1986), is a brilliant essay that shows how Levy's thinking had expanded from the relatively simple, straightforward presentation of "Symbols for Sale" to an elaborate, highly nuanced framework. His discussion of the symbolic meanings of beverages and how to leverage them in a brand's marketing communication strategy is quite a triumph, and it should spark considerable interest among product managers, advertising managers, and scholars alike (as it has already done in some quarters). In their efforts to formulate marketing strategies and plans, marketing managers too often rely on vague stereotyped ideas about quality and value, which almost inevitably blunts the distinctiveness and impact of their consumer communications. The numerous possibilities for symbolic communication presented in this article should make managers' heads spin and help steer them toward more targeted, original, and meaningful marketing messages.

———— •◆• ————

Sidney J. Levy: In 1958 I was working full time at Social Research, Inc., when I received a call from Harper W. Boyd, Jr., then a member of the marketing department at the School of Business of Northwestern University. Anticipating the forthcoming American Marketing Association Summer Educators' Conference, he proposed to moderate a conference about symbolism. The first speaker was to be a poet-sociologist from the University of Chicago who would talk about "symbols by which we live," and I was invited to talk about "symbols by which we buy," with these presentations to be discussed by Henry O. Whiteside, then the director of research at the Chicago office of J. Walter Thompson. I suggested the program be titled "Symbols for Sale." On the occasion, a large audience was gathered, but the poet-sociologist did not appear. I therefore improvised his talk and then gave mine. I then sent the talk on symbols by which we buy to the *Harvard Business Review*, retitled "Symbols for Sale," and it was published the following summer. Harper was impressed by this performance and invited me to join his faculty. I agreed to visit for the year starting in Fall 1961, was then hired as a full professor, and stayed at Northwestern University for 36 years. Maybe life was simpler then.

——— •◆• ———

Chapter 18

SYMBOLS FOR SALE

Sidney J. Levy

The thoughtful businessman is undoubtedly aware of the growing use and influence of social science concepts in the business world. Management gives increasing attention to relations between people, whether among the management group, down the line, between the manufacturer and the retailer, or between the producer and the consumer. There is less preoccupation with the performance of impersonal economic entities.

The modern assumption is that people are faced with alternatives, that they may be motivated in various directions. From this assumption grows the significance of communications and understandings and the concomitant concern with what the people of the world think, with political public opinion, consumer reactions, and so on. Because of this development the science and practice of marketing have been infused with new life.

CHANGING SCENE

We need not belabor the obvious changes in the American scene. They can be readily enumerated. There are more people. These people have more of all kinds of things—

This chapter was first published in the *Harvard Business Review, 37,* July-August 1959, pp. 117-124. Copyright 1959 by President and Fellows of Harvard College. Reprinted by permission of *Harvard Business Review.*

more leisure, more money, more possessions, more pleasures, and more, if not the same, old worries. Sociological and psychological interpretations of the contemporary scene are fashionable now and are, in themselves, a part of the scene—part of the wave of human preoccupation and of self-examination that is growing as we move further and further from grubbing for subsistence.

The less concern there is with the concrete satisfactions of a survival level of existence, the more abstract human responses become. As behavior in the marketplace is increasingly elaborated, it also becomes increasingly symbolic. This idea needs some examination, because it means that sellers of goods are engaged, whether willfully or not, in selling symbols, as well as practical merchandise. It means that marketing managers must attend to more than the relatively superficial facts with which they usually concern themselves when they do not think of their goods as having symbolic significance.

UNECONOMIC MAN

Formerly, when goods tended to mean some essentials of food, clothing, and shelter, practical matters were very important. The consumer was apt to be an "economic man," who was more or less careful of how he distributed his pennies. To do this meant giving closer attention to the concrete value of what he bought, to the durability of the fabric, the quantity of the food, the sturdiness of the building materials.

The philosophy of business was also oriented around these issues, with a few outstanding enterprises intent on creating an individuality of quality and a competitive price. The marketplace was largely occupied

with the things sold and bought. These were often neither packaged nor advertised. Consumers were customers, not audiences.

The modern marketplace, which is exemplified so dramatically in the vast supermarket (food, drug, or furniture store), reminds us daily of the marketing revolution that has come about. There is an astonishing variety of merchandise, all of it displayed in equally astonishing ways. There are frozen foods, precooked foods, plastic containers, and packages with ingenious (often insidious) opening devices.

In this new setting, what kind of man is the consumer? He is hardly an economic man—especially since there is considerable evidence that he does not buy economically. Indeed, he is often vague about the actual price he pays for something; he has few standards for judging the quality of what he buys, and at times winds up not using it anyway!

This is not just a joke. American homes contain many things of unknown price, objects that are bought on time, appliances that would gather dust if not covered, unused basement workshops. Of course, these are extreme examples—they may even be gifts from hostile relatives, who always have furnished homes with undesirable objects. The point is that today, when people shop, they tend to buy lavishly. Consumers still talk about price, quality, and durability, since these are regarded as sensible traditional values. But at the same time, they know that other factors affect them and believe these to be legitimate influences.

NEW WHYS FOR BUYS

This point is worth some emphasis since many people disapprove of the fact that purchases may be made on what they consider to be insubstantial grounds. The fact that people do not buy furniture to last 20 years (sofas average 7 years) may be deplored as a sign of the lightheadedness of our times. On the other hand, such massive, stoutly made furniture may be dismissed from the home at the behest of other values such as comfortable living or changing tastes.

Grandmother cherished her furniture for its sensible, practical value, but today people know that it is hardly the practical considerations which determine their choices between Post's and Kellogg's, Camels and Luckies, Oldsmobiles and Buicks, or Arpege and Chanel No. 5. They know that package color, television commercials, and newspaper and magazine advertisements incline them toward one preference or another. And, what is more, when they cannot really tell the difference among competitive brands of the same product, they do not believe that a manufacturer should necessarily go out of business because he is unable to produce a distinguishable product. They do not even mind if Procter & Gamble Company puts out both Tide and Cheer.

DIVERSITY OF SPENDING

At the heart of all this is the fact that the consumer is not as functionally oriented as he used to be—if he ever really was. Aesthetic preferences have changed somewhat. For example, we no longer go in for stained glass lamps and antimacassars, although the latter were perhaps more attractive than transparent couch covers. Moreover, the diversity of ways in which people can spend their money has had an impact on motivation:

People buy things not only for what they can do, but also for what they mean. At one

level, society has to concern itself with bread for sustenance, and appropriate agencies must see to it that our breads are sufficiently nourishing, enriched, and not poisonously refined. But the consumer is no longer much interested in bread as the staff of life. In the first place, he (or she) is probably on a diet and not eating bread; in the second place, he is apt to be more concerned with whether to buy an exotic twist, to do something "interesting" with a pancake flour, or to pop in a brown-and-serve roll that will come hot to the table to the moderate surprise of the guests.

When people talk about the things they buy and why they buy them, they show a variety of logic. They refer to convenience, inadvertence, family pressures, other social pressures, complex economic reasoning, advertising, and pretty colors. They try to satisfy many aims, feelings, wishes, and circumstances. The pleasure they gain from buying objects is ever more playful. The question is less: Do I need this? More important are the ideas: Do I want it? Do I like it?

LANGUAGE OF SYMBOLS

Answering the questions asked by today's consumer takes the definition of goods into new realms—at least new in the sense that they are now recognized as questions worthy of serious examination. The things people buy are seen to have personal and social meanings in addition to their functions. To ignore or decry the symbolism of consumer goods does not affect the importance of the fact. The only question is whether the goods are to be symbolized thoughtfully or thoughtlessly. Specialists in the study of communications, language formation, and semantics make various distinctions between levels of meaning. It is customary to speak of signs, signals, symbols, gestures, and other more technical terms. Many of the distinctions are arbitrary, expressing the specialists' preference for one or another mode of thinking, and need not concern us here. It will suffice to say that in casual usage symbol is a general term for all instances where experience is mediated rather than direct; where an object, action, word, picture, or complex behavior is understood to mean not only itself but also some other ideas or feelings.

PSYCHOLOGICAL THINGS

From this viewpoint, modern goods are recognized as essentially psychological things which are symbolic of personal attributes and goals and of social patterns and strivings. When going shopping the consumer spends not only money but energy. His attention is stimulated or lies dormant as he moves through the mart. Objects he sees on the shelves are assessed according to standards which he has established for what is important or potentially important to him. For instance,

> A saw may be very useful—and there may be things around the house that need to be sawed, but if he feels that a saw is beneath the way he wants to expend his energy, or allot his attention, he passes it idly by. Perhaps he buys a record instead, or he may choose a HI-FI component; these are objects in an area where he prefers to invest his psychological energies.

In this sense, all commercial objects have a symbolic character, and making a purchase involves an assessment—implicit or explicit—of this symbolism, to decide whether or not it fits. Energy (and money)

will be given when the symbols are appropriate ones and denied or given parsimoniously when they are not. What determines their appropriateness?

IMAGE REINFORCED

A symbol is appropriate (and the product will be used and enjoyed) when it joins with, meshes with, adds to, or reinforces the way the consumer thinks about himself. We are dealing here with a very plain fact of human nature. In the broadest sense, each person aims to enhance his sense of self and behaves in ways that are consistent with his image of the person he is or wants to be. Prescott Lecky (1945) has written an interesting essay on how people behave in consistency with their self-concepts, and many businessmen could doubtless supplement his observations with a number of their own. (N.B. Whenever I re-read this article, this last clause stands out as something added by an HBR editor!)

Because of their symbolic nature, consumer goods can be chosen with less conflict or indecision than would otherwise be the case. Legend has it that Buridan's ass starved to death equidistant between two piles of equally attractive hay; he would not have had the problem if one pile had been a bit more asinine—let us say—than the other. Modern marketing might have helped him. Choices are made more easily—either more routinely or more impulsively, seemingly—because one object is symbolically more harmonious with our goals, feelings, and self-definitions than another. The difference may not be a large one, nor a very important one in the manufacture of the products; but it may be big enough to dictate a constant direction of preference in the indulgence of one's viewpoint. People feel better when bathroom tissue is pastel blue, the car is a large one (at least, until recently), the newspaper is a tabloid size, the trousers have pleats, and so on. It is increasingly fashionable to be a connoisseur or gourmet of some kind—that is, to consume with one or another standard of discrimination.

SHREWD JUDGES

Several years of research into the symbolic nature of products, brands, institutions, and media of communication make it amply clear that consumers are able to gauge grossly and subtly the symbolic language of different objects and then to translate them into meanings for themselves.

Consumers understand that darker colors are symbolic of more "respectable" products; that browns and yellows are manly; that reds are exciting and provocative. The fact that something is "scientific" means it has technical merit, an interest in quality, and (probably) less enjoyment. Theatrical references imply glamor and suspension of staid criteria.

The value of a testimonial may depend largely on whether there is an association (logical or illogical) between the man and the product. For instance, people think it is appropriate for Winston Churchill to endorse cigars, whiskey, and books. But if they are very average consumers, then they are apt to miss (or ignore) the humor of a testimonial for a Springmaid sheet advertisement altogether.

DIMENSIONS OF DISTINCTION

People use symbols to distinguish. As Susanne Langer (1957) says in discussing the process of symbolization in *Philosophy in a New Key,*

The power of understanding symbols, i.e., regarding everything about a sense-datum as irrelevant except a certain *form* that it embodies, is the most characteristic mental trait of mankind. It issues in an unconscious, spontaneous process of *abstraction*, which goes on all the time in the human mind. (p. 72)

More or Less Gender

One of the most basic dimensions of symbolism is gender. Almost all societies make some differential disposition of the sexes—deciding who will do what and which objects will be reserved to men and which to women. Usually it is hard to evade thinking of inanimate things as male or female. Through such personalization, vessels tend to become feminine and motherly if they are big enough. Men fall in love with their ships and cars, giving them women's names.

In America there has been complaint that some of this differentiation is fading; that women are getting more like men, and men are shifting to meet them, in a movement toward homogeneous togetherness. No doubt there is some basis for this concern if we compare ourselves with past civilizations or with hunting and agricultural societies that make sharper distinctions between what is masculine and what is feminine. But the differences still loom large in the marketplace—so large that there are even gradations of characterization. For example, probably all cigarette brands could be placed on a continuum of degrees of gender, as one aspect of their complex symbolic patterning. The same is true for musical compositions and the recorded interpretations of them, of cheeses and the brand versions of each kind.

Sex at Work

Sexual definitions may seem absurd at times and often have only modest influence in one or another choice. But they are at work and form a natural part of, for instance, the housewife's logic and acquired reactions as she makes her selections in the food store and serves her family. She considers what her husband's preferences are, what a growing boy should have, what is just right for a girl's delicate tastes. To take two simple illustrations:

Since smoothness is generally understood to be more feminine, as foods go, it seems fitting that girls should prefer smooth peanut butter and boys the chunky. While the overlap is great, a cultivated society teaches such a discrimination, and children, being attentive to their proper sex roles, learn it early. Indeed, the modern family seems to be greatly concerned with the indoctrination of symbolic appropriateness.

In an interview one six-year-old boy protested that he had never liked peanut butter, but his mother and sister had always insisted that he did, and now he loved it. Apparently a violent bias in favor of peanut butter is suitable to little boys, and may be taken as representing something of the rowdy boyishness of childhood, in contrast to more restrained and orderly foods. Such findings are not idle, since they help explain why "Skippy" is an appropriate name for a peanut butter and why "Peter Pan" was not until he was taken away from Maude Adams and given to Mary Martin and Walt Disney.

Similarly, in a recent study of two cheese advertisements for a certain cheese, one wedge of cheese was shown in a setting of a brown cutting board, dark bread, and a glimpse of a chess game. The cheese wedge was pictured standing erect on its smallest base. Although no people were shown, consumers interpreted the ad as part of a masculine scene, with men playing a game, being served a snack.

The same cheese was also shown in another setting with lighter colors, a suggestion of a floral bowl, and the wedge lying flat on one of its longer sides. This was interpreted by consumers as a feminine scene, probably with ladies lunching in the vicinity. Each ad worked to convey a symbolic impression of the cheese, modifying or enhancing established ideas about the product.

Act Your Symbolical Age

Just as most people usually recognize whether something is addressed to them as a man or as a woman, so are they sensitive to symbols of age. Teenagers are sensitive to communications which imply childishness. If presented with a soft drink layout showing a family going on a picnic, their reaction is apt to be "kid stuff." They are trying to break away from the family bosom. While they might actually enjoy such a picnic, the scene symbolizes restraint and inability to leave in order to be with people of their own age.

Clothing is carefully graded in people's eyes; we normally judge, within a few years' span, whether some garment is fitted to the age of the wearer. Women are particularly astute (and cruel) in such judgments, but men also observe that a pinstriped suit is too mature for one wearer, or that a "collegiate" outfit is too young for a man who should be acting his age.

Class and Caste

Symbols of social participation are among the most dramatic factors in marketing. Like it or not, there are social class groupings formed by the ways people live, the attitudes they have, and the acceptance and exclusiveness of their associations. Most goods say something about the social world of the people who consume them. The things they buy are chosen partly to attest to their social positions. The possession of mink is hardly a matter of winter warmth alone, as all women know who wear mink with slacks while strolling at a beach resort. The social stature of mink, and its downgrading, leads us to marvel that it is now sold at Sears, Roebuck & Co. On the other hand, Sears has upgraded itself and become more middle-class. Shopping at Sears is symbolic of a certain chic among many middle-class people who used to regard it as much more working-class. People now boast that Sears is especially suitable for certain kinds of merchandise, and their candor in saying they shop at Sears is not so much frankness as it is facetiousness—as if to point out an amusing quirk in one's social behavior.

Membership in a social class tends to affect one's general outlook, modes of communication, concreteness of thinking and understanding (Schatzman & Strauss, 1955). Advertising often says different things to people of different social levels. For example, a perfume ad showing an anthropological mask and swirling colors is likely to be incomprehensible to many working-class women, whereas *New Yorker* readers will at least pretend they grasp the symbolism. On the other hand, working-class women will accept a crowded, screaming sale advertisement as meaning urgency and potential interest, while women of higher status will ignore it as signaling inferiority.

Sense and Nonsense

Sometimes advertising symbolism can become confined to a social class subgroup. For example, some upper middle-class people are not sure what is being said in liquor ads featuring groups of sinister men wearing red shoes or handsome males riding sidesaddle. While suspecting the symbolic language may be gibberish, they have some undercurrent of anxiety about not being part of the in-group who use "nonsense syllables" to tell each other about vodka.

DISCRIMINATING PUBLICS

The choice of the appropriate symbols for advertising a product deserves careful consideration. The symbolic messages conveyed in the ad generally correspond to the advertiser's intention—although consumers may discover meanings additional to or even contrary to the intended meaning. A poorly chosen symbol for an advertisement is likely to backfire. For example,

> The headline of an ad claimed that the product was actually worth one cent more than its price in comparison with competing products. Many housewives interpreted this claim as a sign of cheapness; they needed to see only the one cent in the headline to conclude that it was "one of those penny deals." Even to readers who understood literally what was said the effect of talking about merely one cent somehow suggested the idea of cheapening. In other words, while the literal aim had been to refer to the greater worth of the

product, the symbolic means acted to cheapen it.

FINE ARTS AND FINE DISTINCTIONS

Dramas, particularly the theater shows sponsored by General Electric, Kraft Foods, Procter & Gamble, and United States Steel, are interpreted as serious appeals to responsible intellects, the dramatic theater being a symbol of this as opposed to musical and variety shows. Within the dramatic theater finer distinctions are made. For instance, offerings by Ronald Reagan, a sincere, charming man, are considered in keeping with the institutional nature of the General Electric sponsorship (whereas offerings by Red Skelton probably would conflict).

TO EACH HIS OWN CONFORMITY

Some comparatively well-defined modes of living and taste patterns tend to combine individual symbols into large clusters of symbols. The separate symbols add to the definition of the whole and thereby organize purchases along given directions. For example,

The Ivy League cluster of symbols affects the kinds of suits, ties, and, to a lesser degree, the cars and liquors certain people buy.

Being a suburbanite is a broad identification, but it starts one's purchasing ideas moving in certain lines. Name your own suburb, and the ideas leap into sharper focus. Neighbors judge the symbolic significance of how money is spent; they are quick to interpret the appropriateness of your spending pattern for the community.

They decide what kind of people you are by making reasonable or unreasonable deductions from what you consume— books, liquor, power mowers, cars, and the gifts you and your children give at birthday parties.

Some objects we buy symbolize such personal qualities as self-control; others expose our self-indulgence. We reason in these directions about people who drink and smoke, or who do not—and such reasoning will play a role in their choices of doing one or the other. A hard mattress is readily justified on pragmatic grounds of health, sound sleep, and the like, but people recognize the austere self-denial at work that will also strengthen the character. Conversely, soft drinks may quench thirst, but people feel that they are also buying an indulgent moment, a bit of ease, a lowering of adult restraints.

TATTLETALE PATTERNS

It is easy to overlook the variety of meanings conveyed by objects since they range in their conventionality and self-expressiveness. We ordinarily give little thought to interpreting milk at the table, significant as milk may be (unless, perhaps, at a businessmen's lunch). We are observant of dishes, cups, and silverware, however. True, we have to have them, people expect them. But the patterns tell people things about us, and not always the things that we would expect.

Take books: by and large, books are regarded as highly personal purchases. Guests will respect one personally for *Dr. Zhivago* on the coffee table and perhaps raise an eyebrow at *Lolita*. Similarly with magazines: there is a world of symbolic difference between such periodicals as, say, *Look, Popular Science,* and *Harvard Business Review.*

Toward Informality

A whole treatise could be written on another symbolic dimension, that of formality and informality. Many of our decisions to buy take into account the degree of formal or informal character of the object. Housewives constantly gauge the hot dogs that they serve, the gifts that they are giving, and the tablecloth that they plan to use with an eye to how informal the occasion is or should be. The movement toward informality has been a fundamental one in recent years, governing the emphasis on casual clothes, backyard and buffet meals, staying at motels, and bright colors (even for telephones).

Currently there seem to be signs of a reaction to this trend, of a seeking for more graciousness in living. Again, there is interest in the elegance of a black car, a wish for homes with dining rooms, and a desire for greater individual privacy. But the existence of a countertrend does not cancel out the symbolic meaning of casual clothes, buffet meals, and so on; in fact, it may even sharpen awareness of the implications of these products and customs.

SYMBOLIC OBSOLESCENCE

As I have indicated, among all the symbols around us, bidding for our buying attention and energy, there are underlying trends that affect and are affected by the spirit of the times. Every so often there comes along a new symbol, one that makes a leap from the past into the present and that has power because it captures the spirit of the present and makes other ongoing symbols old-fashioned. The recent Pepsi-Cola girl was a symbol of this sort. She had precursors, of course, but she distinctly and prominently

signified a modern phantasm; she established an advertising style somewhat removed from the Clabber girl.

CONCLUSION

I have mentioned just a few of the varieties of symbols encountered in the identification of goods in the marketplace, especially symbols which become part of the individual identities of consumers. The topic is as diverse as our daily lives and behaviors. Generally, people symbolize with relatively little strain; nevertheless, the interactions among symbols which direct consumers' choices are liable to the difficulties of all communications, and consequently warrant study.

This seems obvious if we grant the importance of symbols—but not all businessmen do, of course, and that has accounted for many failures in sales. Greater attention to consumers' modes of thought will give marketing management and research increased vitality and, in turn, add to its own practical and symbolic merits.

Since the concept of brand image was put forth several years ago, the idea has been debased by widespread use of it to refer to any and all aspects of product and brand identification. Now it seems worthwhile to redirect attention to the ways products turn people's thoughts and feelings toward symbolic implications, whether this is intended by the manufacturer or not. If the manufacturer understands that he is selling symbols as well as goods (Gardner & Levy, 1955), he can view his product more completely. He can understand not only how the object he sells satisfies certain practical needs but also how it fits meaningfully into today's culture. Both he and the consumer stand to profit.

REFERENCES

Gardner, B. B., & Levy, S. J. (1955, March/April). The product and the brand. *Harvard Business Review,* p. 33.

Langer, S. (1957). *Philosophy in a new key.* Cambridge, MA: Harvard University Press.

Lecky, P. (1945). *Self-consistency.* New York: Island Press.

Schatzman, L., & Strauss, A. (1955, January). Social class and modes of communication. *American Journal of Sociology,* p. 329.

## Chapter 19

SYMBOLS OF SUBSTANCE, SOURCE, AND SORCERY

Sidney J. Levy

The anthropological background of the study of symbols tends to give them an esoteric sound, especially exemplified in religion and magic, where direct meanings are often obscure and indirect meanings are focused upon and manipulated. Presumably, we understand that the visible and the concrete are being used to represent the invisible and the abstract, in various aspects of a religious or magical ceremony. As time goes by, symbolic behaviors become the things to do, and some of the original indirect meanings become lost—like the various measures taken at weddings to soothe or deceive the demon lover.

The use of symbols is an inherent and natural part of human expression. It serves especially to make possible self-control and detachment. It implies a capacity to hold energy in abeyance, shaped within the vessel of a symbol, rather than to act under the immediate pressure of an impulse. Because people symbolize naturally, all behavior carries a multiplicity of meanings—and all observers react interpretively.

One area has to do with what might be called *symbols of substance*. These are by and large the most readily understood and most readily taken meanings, feelings, and ideas implied by the specific contents of

This chapter first appeared in *Art Direction,* January 1960.

particular shows or the personalities of certain people. One example is the professional salesman or endorser. What these people are like, how they look and behave, the roles they play in relating to other people, develop a set of meanings; their endorsements, implicit or explicit, function as complex symbolic communications. The figures used help people to locate a product rather quickly. A doctor means Science, Health, Authority of the professional; and when the viewer sees a white coat in a commercial he is informed that the product is trying to show a serious attention to technical matters, product quality, and the consumers' well-being. This example also reminds that symbols, like many compulsive rituals, may deteriorate in their vitality. The more current and familiar they become, the less compellingly they convey the original intention. They become debased as skepticism builds up about their symbolic reference until often the opposite enters in. White coats then become (at least to many cynics) an indication of inferiority, of a nonethical product, until some changes, in audiences or meanings, help to refresh the symbol or return it to its initial force. In this respect some symbols are more stable than others.

An interesting dimension in the evaluation of entertainers and professional endorsers has to do with sincerity and morality. These people represent opportunities for vicarious expression of impulses, and they may therefore be more sexual or violent in their behavior than ordinary viewers permit themselves. At the same time, the audience is constantly testing whether the limits of what it can tolerate in its fantasies are being surpassed. This process of "fantasy-testing" may lead to rejection, whether through criticism or through suppression of interest and consequent boredom.

Another area of symbolism is of special interest—that which is expressed primarily through form, line, movement, and direction. This type of symbolism tends to be given less study because its referents are usually very implicit, and viewers' reactions tend to be less articulate about them. Some of these symbols have special value for the nature of the television medium and may be called *symbols of source*.

Four of them are worth noting for the different ways they express the television communication. The first is *approach and retreat*. This refers to the way in which people, titles, miscellaneous objects move from the background into the foreground, usually to announce or present something; and they may leave by retreating into the background. This is a movement that is used frequently, and it usually has a compelling effect. It is meaningful for television since it corresponds to the narrowing three-dimensional shape of the television tube.

More important, it represents the immediacy of the arrival or departure that is going on, a feeling that gives television some of its fascination. It says, "from out here we bring to you," or "we are leaving you," and is therefore peculiarly personal. The "out here" is usually made abstract and mystic, either undefined and empty, or like the sky with its infinity of promise and reward of something offered from above and beyond. Like anything else it can be overdone, poorly or unimaginatively used; stars that come swirling out of the sky are a familiar convention—the movement still says something, but the content is uninspired symbolism.

Probably one of the most effective uses of this type of movement was Jimmy Durante's departure from his old show, as he retreated from spotlight to spotlight, dramatizing strikingly the poignancy of his farewell to the viewer. Frank Sinatra used the same retreat, but its sense of inexplicable loneliness seemed less appropriate than for the clown tragically fading out of sight.

A second type of visual symbol in movement is *rotation*. Television often uses rotating objects. Unlike approach and retreat, rotation does not express the depth of the television medium and its possibilities for relating distant things to the immediate situation. Rotation implies three dimension, but in a narrower way—a well-rounded presence rather than a coming or going. At one level, rotation implies the limitations of television, suggesting that it must go on within the frame of the screen, self-contained, unable to move off in other directions. To some extent, then, it is a confining and frustrating symbol. However, it has some other advantages. Rotation, as a repetitive, endless movement, has a tendency to fix attention and to hold it. Lulling the audience for a moment, perhaps, before the show gets actively under way.

An important meaning of rotation is exhibitionism. The rotating object means that all sides are being shown, that many facets are on display. It is a command to look because something will be shown or revealed. People who rotate imply the same things. A notable example is the way Loretta Young twirls around as she makes her entrance to introduce her show. She is showing off her dress to the ladies who wait for her weekly appearance; she says in a forthright way, "Look at me, all of me," and by implication, all that the play will reveal.

A third type of movement very common in television is *left to right progression* This is less a symbol of source, since it makes no special concession or reference to the nature of television. The movement is quite conventional and not of unusual interest in itself. Basically, it serves a narrative function, holding attention less by dramatic impact of the movement itself, than by anticipation of the sequence to be progressively presented. Therefore, its value derives heavily from how it is employed and whether the content reasonably fits the notion of a narrative. Some fairly clever examples are the title presentation of What's My Line? and the old adventures of the Happy Joe in search of a Lucky Strike.

A fourth symbol of source is *unifying movement,* instances where fragmentation and rebuilding occur, or there is some movement from separateness to unity. This type of movement is a very dynamic one, since it implies conflict and its resolution; it develops toward the satisfaction of a good gestalt; and the audience "roots for" its completion in a participant way. On the GE Theater, the disturbing electrical agitation of the identifying sign before it settles into the stable familiar form sometimes seems almost unbearable in the time it takes to reassure us that General Electric still knows how to tame the wild forces of electricity.

A special case of symbols of source are *symbols of sorcery*. These are any visual activities that seem to be magical rather than following everyday mechanics. Like montages and other techniques, they are not peculiar to television, but they give it a special charm. Sudden shifts of objects in space without intervening movement, the transformation of one object into another, the myriad of gimmicks are normally accepted as part of the valued techniques and potentialities of television. But they still remain astonishing; our thinking is sufficiently primitive or ignorant that magic always lurks as a possibly more interesting explanation—even when we "know" better.

Recently, it was announced that a Church of England commission concluded that human illness caused by demons could be possible. Similarly, the demons of television who can turn a man onto his head, or create a wide array of animated tricks, are a delight because they testify that man's imagination transcends his human condition. The symbols of sorcery are attractive because they do imply power and control of unusual kinds, and for the moment the viewer, seeing them made visible for his benefit, can believe he too shares in this magic. Finally, the use of television magic, of visual symbols that emphasize technique, admits that there is a playing with reality, that the viewer doesn't have to take it too seriously. With his participation, then, he is able to maintain also a sense of detachment and integrity.

## Chapter 20

SYMBOLISM AND LIFE STYLE

Sidney J. Levy

The symbolic nature of consumer objects has received much attention in recent years. At least it has been fashionable to designate various outstanding objects as symbolic, thereby giving lip service to this idea. We comfortably note that language is symbolic, as are visual materials in modern art and television commercials. Having noted this, or used the term to accuse someone of striving for status symbols, the matter is commonly dropped. This usually occurs because it is hard to keep thinking about the symbolic meanings of objects and behavior. To do so requires practice in adopting a view of actions that is sufficiently detached to permit analysis and interpretation and sufficiently empathetic to produce insights. It is usually simpler to deal with the objects and behaviors themselves.[1]

It is easier to take for granted that people do what they do because, being themselves, they must, with no more need for explanation than we normally feel we must offer to explain our own actions. It is easier to explain behavior by categorizing it as the result of the person's being between the ages of 40 and 45, upper middle class, and in the over $15,000 income bracket. If we are daring, we may go so far as to hint that these consumers are sociable or introverted

This chapter was first published in S. Greyser (Ed.), *Proceedings,* American Marketing Association, December 1963, pp. 140-150. Reprinted by permission of the American Marketing Association.

or discriminating in personality. These are all legitimate rubrics and provide convenient and useful ways of dividing up data in order to compare frequency distributions.

But we are challenged to try to analyze *meaning*—and thus become engaged with the study of symbolism and the role of symbols in the daily life of average citizens. Here I must emphasize that in speaking of symbols and symbolizing, I am not referring shyly and euphemistically to the study of phallic objects on cars or to dreams of nudity in the streets—although I would not, of course, exclude such curious phenomena from consideration. As Langer (1951) points out,

> Obvious only in man is the *need of symbolization*. The symbol-making function is one of man's primary activities, like eating, looking, or moving about. It is the fundamental process of his mind, and goes on all the time. Sometimes we are aware of it, sometimes we merely find its results, and realize that certain experiences have passed through our brains and have been digested there. (p. 41)

If this is so, there are several implications. First, as I have mentioned, it is hard to notice people's symbolizing any more than we notice their breathing or blood circulating, unless something goes wrong with these functions. Similarly, we notice symbolizing when it becomes dramatic, blatant, or so alien to our understanding that we are struck by the discrepancy between someone else's meanings and our own. Moreover, since symbolizing is so implicit, asking people about it may elicit no simple answers since the symbolizer may not be self-conscious about what he is doing.

Nevertheless, the pervasive and inescapable nature of symbolizing means that analyzing it is what we are really doing whenever we study human behavior. This then applies to the ordinary actions that constitute consumer behavior as well as the extraordinary. Now, how can we examine symbolizing as a lifestyle force? I would like to start by offering the view that an individual's lifestyle is a large complex symbol in motion. It is composed of subsymbols, it utilizes a characteristic pattern of life space, and it acts systematically to process objects and events in accordance with these values.

A LARGE COMPLEX SYMBOL IN MOTION

Everyone's life has a cycle of some kind. As a total entity moving through time, a person builds a characteristic assertion of who he is and how he regards his own being, and he expresses it in the specific manner of his actions. To realize this is merely to note that people have recognizable personalities that remain familiar to us—they do not appear as strangers each time we meet them. But this also means that there is more to them than that they eat when hungry, sleep when tired, and love when stimulated. They develop the wish to do these things in particular ways regarded as suitable for themselves. And what is thought suitable rests in who they are, how they grew up, their nationality, the groups they participate in or seek, and, ultimately in all of this, the individual person they aim to be.

In a sense, everyone seeks to prove something, and this—or some central set of recurring motifs—is identifiable as the summary fashion of his wrestling with existence. To observe this takes some largeness of view; perhaps it can never be fully observed until a man is dead (as Aristotle pointed out), and then the one person who experienced it all and might know most about it is gone. Still, we do observe other people's lifestyles, even if we capture only fragments and part-motifs.

We can think of people in categorical terms derived from their customary behavior, emotional tone, expressed wishes; by being donors and recipients to their special forms of taking and giving. So the person oriented to display may take attention and admiration from us, the ambitious leader wants us to obey, the careless driver may want to share an accident with us. As they show us themselves, order us about, or collide with us, they bring their lifestyles to our attention. We discover something about the content of their personalities and the special fashion or form they give to it. So perhaps this driver apologizes profusely—as perhaps he always does when he hurts others; this leader keeps insisting it is all for the good of others; and this exhibitionist does it by putting on striking clothes rather than removing them.

As we sense the meaningful currents in people's behavior and emotional expression, we become aware of what they are trying to do and the means they employ. We decide they are generous, moral, corrupt, subtle, bitter, active, sweet; and when we pronounce such as judgments we are usually referring to the ongoing symbolic quality of the person rather than to a specific action. We mean the deeper attributes that go on despite the times he or she is not generous, subtle, or active.

CONTRASTING STYLES OF LIFE

In expressing their values, in describing the kinds of roles they play in life and how they think those roles should be fulfilled, people reveal both real and ideal lifestyles. In one marketing study in Montana, life was described as slow-paced, with the people geared to the rigors and virtues of frontier life where it is cold and demanding; where

the skills and rewards of hunting and fishing loom large; where men are rugged, touched with the nobility of the natural man, and superior to the wan and tender Eastern city man. A man's lifestyle was generally conceived as one of good fellowship, whether with a gun, a rod, or a drink. This may sound like parody; to show the reality of these views, I quote the comments of some of the men describing the people and lifestyle of Montana.

The men here are real good, you can trust them. Most of them are outdoor men; they have to be or else they wouldn't live here. Most of them are honest.

The men here are true Westerners; big, tough, and rugged.

Men are men here, and they are manly. Somewhat more honest and less sharp dealing than in the more civilized parts of the country.

It's wonderful here. It's God's country. I like the frontier atmosphere. Life is casual and leisurely here, no frantic big city pace.

This contrasts with the kinds of lifestyle men in metropolitan environments offer to sum up who they are. Here we find the familiar tunes of urban-suburban people, where men are first husbands and fathers and run to the ragged rather than the rugged.

The men here are very nice, a well-educated group of men who have many outside interests and are very congenial. They're home-loving and conscientious.

Most of my neighbors are young families and pretty well child-oriented. The men are typical suburbanites, very much concerned with crab grass and PTA. They all work hard and bring home briefcases.

To grasp these lifestyles and how they are exemplified in individual lives requires an orientation to configurations, to patterns of ideas, feelings, and actions. We need to sense the man at work, to feel with him the peculiar flavor with which he invests his work or draws from it joy, irritation, monotony, impatience, anticipation, anxiety about today or tomorrow, comfort, competence, pride, a restless urge to succeed visibly, or a restless urge to reach five o'clock. We can think about what kind of motivation is useful in distinguishing the achieving executive from the adequate one, the upward striving white collar worker from the man who just wants to make a living.

To explore this large, complex symbol in motion that is a man's grand lifestyle is to seek to define his self-concept, to describe the central set of beliefs about himself and what he aspires to, that provide consistency (or unpredictability) to what he does. Information about such self-concepts may come from various directions. Two students writing class autobiographies conveyed the contrasting sense of focus each felt about what he sought to achieve in life—one summing up that he wanted to live in accordance with "intelligence, truth, and justice," while the other said his aims boiled down to "thrift, security, and cleanliness." Presumably, the former young man represents a better potential market for books, the latter is possibly more geared to soap.

Such self-definitions can help us perceive the coherence of behavior in housewives who relentlessly pursue antiseptic cleanliness, in children accomplishing characteristically in school, and in doting or dismal fathers. This idea of one's self as "naturally" following its bent, accompanied by the feeling "doesn't everyone?" is the core personal symbol. When we understand this about a person, we can start to trace out the intricate pattern of his actions, to see how it affects the handling of money, choice of clothes, food preferences, interest in shopping, cooking, giving gifts, home work-shopping. We can see how the persisting needs of one woman to bend people to her will can make her a topnotch salesperson, or where the urge to resist in another produces an obdurate purchasing agent.

In anthropological analogue to this thought, Redfield (1955) noted the significance of maize as a vital symbol to the Mayan villagers of Chan Kom in the Yucatan.

> So I began to form another way of conceiving parts as related to one another in a system of activity and thought. This third system is neither chainlike or map-like. It is radial: maize is a center and other things are grouped around it, connected to it in different ways, some by a series of useful activities, some by connections of symbolic significance. The mind goes out from maize to agriculture, from maize to social life, from maize to religion. Maize is always the center of things. (p. 22)

If we can thus think of the lifestyle of a person or a group as having a general symbolic character, one that refers to and expresses a certain central emphasis in motivation and action, we can describe as subsymbols the things—objects, activities—that are used to play out this general symbolic meaning and to embody it. The clotheshorse needs clothes, the bookworm needs books, the cliff-dweller needs cliffs. For example, housing has a meaning that varies with who is to live in it.

Back (1962) noted that in Puerto Rico a public housing project could be regarded as a custodial institution or as a technique for upward mobility, making the most progressive and the most dependent families inclined toward the project. Families falling between these extremes tend to prefer to stay in private housing, even though it may be objectively inferior.

Apartment living versus living in a house provides a contrast in the meanings of subsymbols. Apartment dwellers who are not familially oriented and who use housing that exemplifies the exciting values of urban life, like the freer kind of life it represents:

I like living in apartments. The thing I like best about it is the convenience of having everything taken care of.

Apartment life is very relaxing—no fires to tend to, sidewalks to shovel, and no painting. More time for enjoyment.

Those with a greater yearning to belong and to share in a feeling of some social responsibility see apartments as a stopgap that falls short of true participation in life.

The only advantage to apartment living is that it is a stopgap until you can buy a house.

There is very little opportunity for a sense of community life in an apartment.

MULTIPLE MEANINGS

As these contrasting views of apartment living illustrate, a complication for understanding marketing problems is caused by the multiple meanings of objects and communications. The same person may see several meanings and different people may see different meanings. A picture of a skier shows a man standing on two sticks: This may signify a pleasant sport, a dangerous sport, an expensive pastime, new ways of leisure in America, superior social status at an elegant resort, the competitiveness of

the Olympics, even a cause of perspiration in a deodorant advertisement.

Examples could be multiplied to show how people behave in accordance with their own view of themselves and how they want to do things that fit this view. This extends into interesting realms of action and nonaction. A study of why women do not visit physicians for examination as often as they should to detect cancer showed that one reason was a reluctance to change one's underwear habits—for example, to iron a brassiere in order to seem like the kind of women the doctor is presumably accustomed to examining. It was also clear that some women did not want to explore the possibility of having cancer because they believe it is a venereal disease and would reveal their sexual practices. Such anxieties are similarly related to skin problems among young people, where ideas about self-indulgence, sex, and hostility become interwoven with the sense of self, producing feelings of shame and guilt. For example,

I saw an ad—it was either for pimples or athlete's foot—that was pretty gruesome. It was like some of the awful pictures shown in the windows of the cheap low-class drug stores for skin diseases, and everyone knows what they are trying to show without coming right out and saying: venereal disease.

The utilization of subsymbols affects all customers, not merely buyers of consumer goods looking for status symbols. A study of institutional food buyers showed the pervasive effects of how the buyers defined themselves, their institutions, and their customers, to give their food purchasing its special flavor and meaning. Dietitians and home economists, pursuing their professional roles, tended to emphasize nutritional values and balanced menus; buyers oriented to cooking or the clientele of an establishment devoted to the arts thought in terms of the palate and visual aesthetics; more business-oriented managers made money a foremost consideration in the style of planning they showed. These were occupational lifestyles, each reflecting the typical symbolic configuration that had developed as suitable. The subsymbols of place, titles, preferred suppliers, utensils, foods, all played roles in sustaining the larger significance these people sought to convey.

It is easiest to see objects being employed symbolically where the goal is to display, where visibility is high; and it is in these situations where they probably do reach their fullest flowering and elaboration. In dress, furniture, when "company is coming," and so on, the importance of audiences intensifies the presentation of lifestyle. Nevertheless, one's lifestyle is always going on, even if privately at a different level. It is hard for us to believe that there is ever a time when no one is looking—there is always God. And even if we relax our standards with Him and scratch our behinds, wear our socks a second day, or read faster than comprehension can keep up, our lapses are also part of ourselves. They support the purchase of subsymbolic products that make up the covert lifestyles that let one sneak a secret drink, consume pornography, or watch more television than one likes to admit.

A CHARACTERISTIC PATTERN OF LIFE SPACE

An interesting aspect of symbolism is the significance of life space. As people express their lifestyle, they move through their environment, perceiving it and using it in their own special ways. Probably we can observe a typical continuum ranging from expansive to constricted use of the environment. Higher status people have a larger worldview, they look toward and move toward more distant horizons. They are among that classic 20% of the population who do 80% of the living, using airplanes and long distance telephones in sharply disproportionate degree. Lower status people are apt to use even their own city in narrower fashion, some never going downtown or leaving the home neighborhood. This is not merely a matter of economics, although money (and its relative availability) is a related parameter.

Individuals vary in their yearnings for space, some loving roomy old houses, others preferring restricted, efficient space. Michael Balint (1955) has devoted a book to exploring the psychological consequences of basic interest in things versus basic interest in the spaces between things. He believes that people have fundamental orientations that lead them either to emphasize clinging to objects or to emphasize moving between objects. The latter orientation is characteristic in the thrill-seeking of skiing and roller coasting, whereas clinging to objects turns *ocnophils* (as Balint calls them) toward stability and security. A study of mobile home dwellers highlighted this contrast with cases of women who regretted the fact that their less roots-minded husbands did not provide homes with entrenched foundations and space to accumulate more objects.

Such concerns can be extended into assessments of how people organize objects in the space available. Are they orderly and precise or do they want things to "look lived in?" We may judge people and companies for their lifestyle by how they use space, ranging from Japanese austerity to Victorian clutter, understanding perhaps that a clear desk means efficiency, high status, or a figurehead who lets others do the work. A desk piled high may be interpreted as sloppy or comfortable, the home of a drudge, a procrastinator, or a hard worker. Modern architectural design struggles with whether to "waste space" by leaving open areas or allot everyone a tight cubicle; should an office building be like a hospital or like an atrium, will the public think better of the corporation if the street level is built like an expensive garden plaza instead of having convenient and profitable shops flush to the sidewalk?

PROCESSING OBJECTS AND EVENTS

What are the practical implications of this view of lifestyle that stresses its symbolic character? It emphasizes the fact that buyers see objects and events in the real world as having certain potentialities. These potentialities are scanned, screened, and processed for their symbolic suitability, not only because the products can provide some specific results, but because they become incorporated into the lifestyle of the person. This does not mean all product choices are razor's edge decisions between the real-me and the not-me, with a nod to the fake-me. But still, what do they all add up to?

From a marketing point of view—one that might startle traditional academicians (other than anthropologists, perhaps)—a consumer's personality can be seen as the peculiar total of the products he consumes. Shown a picture of a young man in an advertisement, one female respondent deduced the following:

He's a bachelor, his left hand is showing and it has no ring on it. He lives in one of those modern high-rise apartments and the rooms are brightly colored. He has modern, expensive furniture, but not Danish modern. He buys his clothes at Brooks Brothers. He owns a good hi-fi. He skis. He has a sailboat. He eats Limburger or any other prestige cheese with his beer. He likes and cooks a lot of steak and he would have filet mignons for company. His liquor cabinet has Jack Daniel's bourbon, Beefeater gin, and a good Scotch.

Through his lifestyle does she know him.

If we think of a housewife who uses Crosse and Blackwell soups, subscribes to *Gourmet* magazine, flies live lobster in from Maine to Chicago to serve guests, drives a Renault, and doesn't shave under her arms, we sense a value system engaged in choosing things from the marketplace that add up to a lifestyle quite different from that of the woman who uses Campbell's, reads *Family Circle* for ideas on how to furnish a playroom, makes meat loaf twice a week (stretching it with oatmeal), rides in her husband's Bel Air, and scrubs the kitchen floor three times a week.

By studying these configurations of lifestyle, by observing how people put together those ways of living they think appropriate for a 40-year-old surgeon on the make, a prosperous factory foreman in a working-class suburb, a woman who feels she leads a dog's life and likes to "go out and eat," or "a woman who feels she is not a raving beauty, but is attractive to men," we can find out how they use products most meaningfully for themselves. Close analysis of consumption systems of different kinds of people is revealing, as is accumulating life history information which does not focus so closely on products that it loses the larger ongoing symbolic aims I have been discussing.

CONCLUSION

The descriptions I have made here to capture or convey some of these lifestyle issues seem awkward and inadequate. Much work is needed to study consumer lifestyles, to create a taxonomy of lifestyles that helps us to think more systematically about different kinds of people, to build a theory that illuminates the dynamic process by which people turn their primitive needs into nuanced and elaborated sets of discriminations among the objects in the marketplace. We each know that such a process is true of ourselves, but so often when studied, it seems to fall between the mesh of the research net. It laughs at the grossness of personality inventories or the stodginess of questionnaires that fail to take account of the ludicrous, shy, quicksilver, or perverse elements of lifestyle, the felt absurdity of caring about invisible differences in unessential products.

Earlier work has suggested the importance of symbols in the marketing world, particularly in regard to age, sex, and social class. My present purpose is to reaffirm this importance. It is also to point attention to the fact that marketers do not just sell isolated items that can be interpreted as symbols; rather, they sell pieces of a larger symbol—the consumer's lifestyle. Marketing is then a process of providing customers with parts of a potential mosaic from which they, as artists of their own lifestyles, can pick and choose to develop the composition that for the time may seem the best. The marketer who thinks about his products in this way will seek to understand their potential settings and relationships to other parts of consumer lifestyles, thereby to increase the number of ways he fits meaningfully into them.

NOTE

1. Rioch (1963) has a relevant discussion in distinguishing between two separate problems in communications which face the physician— that of commitment to the patient as a person and that of analyzing the mechanisms involved and their disorders.

REFERENCES

Back, K. W. (1962). *Slums, projects, and people.* Durham, NC: Duke University Press.

Balint, M. (1955). *Thrills and regressions.* Madison, CT: International Universities Press.

Langer, S. (1951). *Philosophy in a new key.* Cambridge, MA: Harvard University Press.

Redfield, R. (1955). *The little community.* Chicago: University of Chicago Press.

Rioch, D. M. (1963). Communication in the laboratory and communication in the clinic. *Psychiatry, 26*(3), 209-221.

## Chapter 21

THE PUBLIC IMAGE OF GOVERNMENT AGENCIES

Sidney J. Levy

Many federal executives are concerned with the public relations of their agencies. They want to do a good job and to have this recognized by the public; but often they find themselves in the position of feeling damned if they do and damned if they don't. Where this is the case it seems as though some sturdy public viewpoints are at work, leading to the thought that it might be useful to study elements in the public image of government agencies, to analyze what complex of goals and feelings characterizes the American attitude.

This paper discusses a small tentative exploration of this problem. The assumption is that beyond the stances of political divisions or formal social philosophies, and putting aside for the moment the peripheral (even if not unimportant) views held by extreme groups in this country, there is a general and typical public outlook that sees American government agencies as having certain purposes, to which they may relate in certain ways.

To formulate a hypothesis on this topic, a small group of people were interviewed

This chapter was first published in *Public Administration Review*, Summer 1963, pp. 25-29. Reprinted by permission of the *Public Administration Review*, American Public Administration.

about their attitudes toward government agencies. They were asked to recall the names of government agencies, to define their purpose, to evaluate the kind of job they do. They discussed specific contacts with government agencies, telling what occurred, how it came about, their treatment and feelings, the outcome, their reactions, and so on. Then they commented more generally on the kinds of people who work in government agencies.

The interviews were focused, open-ended conversations; the people interviewed talked fully and freely. Intensive analysis of this tiny sample is offered in no sense as the results of a formal survey or research, nor as "representing" the conceivable range of experiences and attitudes among American citizens. Rather, the aim was to acquire some expressive data for thinking about the problem, to stimulate ideas and further study of the relationship of the public to government agencies.

THE NATURE
OF PUBLIC IMAGES

It may be useful, first, to comment on the nature of public images. Since 1955, the concept of public images has gained widespread interest. Developed in earlier studies and reported at Social Research, Inc., this concept grew in value to people in advertising, marketing, and management because it provided a coherent, focused way of thinking about products. It put forth the idea that people are governed in their behavior and attitudes toward products by a constellation of pictures and thoughts that sum up for them what the product means to them. Known brands have a kind of identity made up of central conceptions and impressions to which consumers characteristically respond.

Any public object—product, person, institution—has an image for the publics, audiences, or consumers who know of it. Since knowledge always falls short and is always filtered through the capacities and special circumstances of the people who experience an institution, what they know of it is always an abstraction to some degree. But this does not mean that an image is a false, invented projection on a screen (Crispi, 1981), although some images may be less accurate than others. An image is a dynamic relationship between a public and an object, one that takes on persisting qualities through time which determine how the participants in the relationship will behave toward each other. It is a relationship that may not readily change; in some cases it is remarkably stubborn and tenacious. Once people develop a set of ideas and impressions about a product, company, institution, it is part of their characteristic outlook; the more they feel it characteristic of themselves to have the image they do, and the more basic an observation it seems to them to be, the more firmly they will stick to it. They do not yield easily, even, at times, in the face of new or contradictory evidence, because it conserves energy not to change their minds and because they are prone to believe themselves to be correct and right in the first place.

The public image of government agencies is compounded out of many sources. It is influenced by people's conception of American government, by what they seek from it and expect to get from it, by concrete experiences with it and the personnel who represent it. As they discuss these things, people convey a sense of how government agencies loom in their minds, how they want to define and relate to them. The view that comes across is a selective one, with some agencies standing out more than others, with people differing in how strongly or clearly they perceive agencies as impinging on them. And in addition to individual variations due to personal temperament, political philosophy, and so on, there are differential outlooks that grow out of social class position (e.g., higher status people are apt to have broader and more educated knowledge of governmental realities).

IDENTIFYING AGENCIES

In naming government agencies, people show the readiest awareness of two main governmental functions; these are tax collection and law enforcement. The Internal Revenue Service and the FBI stand out in people's minds, followed by Social Security and the Veterans Administration (or Selective Service). That is, after the broad, central perception of government agencies as fiscally demanding and policing, thoughts go in more individualized directions. Older people are quicker to associate to Social Security, younger people (especially males), veterans, and parents of boys are apt to think about the draft or veterans' benefits.

After this most significant quadrant of taxes, police, security, and military, associations spread in miscellaneous directions, tending to be composed of a group of service and regulatory agencies. Prominent among them are the Post Office, Agriculture, the Federal Housing Authority, and the Federal Communications Commission. Then, in the general context of thinking about government agencies, thoughts radiate to the apparently more remote groups that reflect international or foreign emphases: State, Immigration, Defense.

Government agencies loom in a natural progression from those of most immediate concern to the individual, to those that impinge less directly. Views are modified by this perspective. Government agencies tend to mean federal government; and self-interest and experience are important in directing attention. This is not an inflexible process. The FBI is renowned less through personal contact than via publicity, the widespread respect given J. Edgar Hoover, and the personalization he affords his agency over many years. In addition, the FBI seems impressive in its earnest dealing with serious crime, arousing mixed feelings of awe, excitement, and admiration. The broader the individual's horizon, the more likely he is to think of government abstractly and to give more attention to problems of foreign relations. But the average citizen tends not to do this except under pressure of specific crisis.

CONTACTS WITH GOVERNMENT AGENCIES

Contacts with government agencies do not stand out in people's minds. They are inclined to be matter-of-fact about those they have had. Any given contact may have been important or significant to the individual— they do not underestimate the potential or actual influence government actions or decisions can and do have on their lives. Nevertheless, there is a casual tone, as though government agencies are either a minor, integrated part of daily life (such as the Post Office, hardly requiring mention), or they remain mostly in the background to be dealt with as occasional instances arise. The feeling is one of "of course"—it was "natural" to have dealt with the agency in the normal flow of events. For the typical citizen such contacts as they reminisce about usually came to them as requirements, so to speak, including particularly such matters as Social Security numbers, filing of income tax, immigration or customs contact, military experience. In such contacts as these they felt themselves to be ordinary people, fulfilling the law whether they liked it or not, with no undue sense of aggravation. These are essentially routine contacts.

Other contacts have a more individual flavor. They are sought out by the individual to further his own goals. People mention such matters as insurance, counseling for education, requests for information from the Bureau of Standards, from the Government Printing Office. These are essentially voluntary contacts.

The contacts that are apt to be most threatening are those which single people out. The implication of negative personal attention is potentially disrupting and alarming, arousing thoughts of punishment and coercive dealings. Internal Revenue checks, variations in agricultural controls, and security checks have this quality of being essentially arbitrary, involuntary contacts.

REACTIONS TO GOVERNMENT AGENCY CONTACTS AND PERSONNEL

In talking about specific dealings with government personnel about specific matters, people tend to express themselves positively. The personnel handling the situation are regarded as courteous and polite in manner, as showing consideration and reasonable interpersonal attitudes. The matter at hand is described as handled helpfully

and satisfactorily. Delays are not blamed as a problem; the contacts were said to take an appropriate amount of time. Some quotations will convey the complimentary tone of these descriptions.

They were courteous, considerate, and prompt.

I was treated very nice . . . very nice, everybody was most helpful.

Was very fast.

The information was very good and I would have done a hell of a lot of fumbling and wasted a hell of a lot of time tracking it down on my own.

I was treated very well.

She was very soft-spoken and very nice and she explained in detail what we had to do. . . . I was a little bit nervous but they were so very lovely, they are used to nervous people, I guess.

They were satisfied and so was I. It took about an hour, I guess that was all right.

I didn't feel I waited too long, in fact they were faster than I thought.

Of course, not all incidents are favorable ones; as in any volume of human interactions, there are angry, complaining occasions. When such a negative experience has occurred, it stands out in the person's mind as a source of great indignation. An example is a man whose agricultural practices are controlled and whose land is periodically and unpredictably flooded.

You can't raise what you want. . . . I felt hard against them, for putting the limits on us. . . . They built this dam . . . about 6 miles upstream. All we got was indifference to our situation. . . . For example, 2 years ago they threw the gates open during the night and during that time a wreck from the railroad dumped oil into the river. We were irrigating at the time. Being as how it was night we could not see the oil in the river water, the oily water was pumped into the field and the crop totally destroyed . . . it's just that they won't, they just don't care about the farmer and his problems. We could have some warning to move our irrigation machinery up, but we can't get any satisfaction.

This man seems to have some grounds for resentment, since he suffers from a prime form of arbitrary involuntary contact. As might be expected, when he is later asked the more general question, "What kinds of people do you suppose choose to work for government agencies? Why?," he does not evaluate them kindly: "People who don't want to put in an honest day's work or those who can't get an honest job." Elsewhere he elaborates, "There are too many pay-rollers, feather-bedders, political plums handed out, and there's a lot of buck passing."

However, the dominating imagery of other average citizens also derogates government agency personnel. The same individuals who provided the array of complimentary remarks listed earlier when talking about their specific experiences (at times the only contacts they could recall) provide this array of comments to characterize "the kinds of people who choose to work for government agencies."

Only average intelligence

90% Negroes

People who are interested in pensions and security.

They don't want to work too hard.

I think the government employee may not be loaded with initiative.

Conservative people.

Well, I hope they're morally and intellectually honest, but I have my doubts.

They have a tendency to get wrapped up in rules and regulations rather than efficiency.

Further, when asked to say how dealing with a government agency differs from other kinds of business dealings, despite the favorable experiences described, people tend to see the government agency as rigid, complicated, demanding, unknowing, and unconcerned.

Too much red tape, too many departments it must go through, too much time killing, ages pass before anything gets settled. . . . In a private concern they strive to please.

They are stricter, everything must be done properly, they don't stand for mistakes. (Although in her reported experience, she said, "They are very helpful, they realize that there is always room for error in making out the tax.")

One thing that comes to mind is the lack of flexibility.

It's difficult when people do not know what they are doing, this is the trouble with people who get the job with politics. There's always this in government agencies.

Stiff regulations, too much paper work.

When you go to an office on business where you pay for what you want they take care of you.

Along with these remarks on personnel and agencies are attempts to be rational and reasonable, to point out that "well, anybody, really," might work for the government and that how one is treated depends on how one behaves. But, generally, it seems difficult for people to avoid the heavily stereotyped images of government agency people as motivated by laziness, security, and inadequacy, in a setting that is both careless and rigid.

Various explanations might be offered for the tenacity of these views. Some realism may enter in; to the extent that government agencies offer easier havens to people who are discriminated against in private industry, some selection occurs in favor of those seeking this haven. The fact of civil service protections, benefits in "sick leave the government allows," retirement pension, and so on imply an interest in rewards less certain or less distinctly perceived as part of the situation in nongovernment work. Further, despite the growth in fringe and security benefits in private industry, there are the general historic and cultural values placed on the willingness to compete, on the striving for distinctive individual advancement, on the energy and the daring to take a chance, on the autonomy and self-direction of the man in business for himself. These values, not regarded as gen-

erally part of government employment, make "havens" seem too nurturing.

Negroes, because they are strongly protected from prejudice and discrimination—too much so, I think.

THE PURPOSE OF GOVERNMENT AGENCIES

It may be useful to think of this view of government agencies and personnel as reflecting the way the public wants to see them, as growing out of a larger necessity. This larger necessity results from the public's conception of the purposes of government agencies. More literal minded individuals explain these purposes in instrumental terms. They perceive the agency's purpose as one of carrying out its concretely defined functions.

Inspection of meats.

To collect income tax.

Manufacture money and apprehend counterfeiters.

Support of prices on farmers.

Others step up the level of generalization, referring to the more formal regulatory mandate of the agency, where the function implies service to broader governmental goals, or to the impersonal implementation of general responsibilities.

They administer the services.

Supervise.

In a very broad sense, to carry out law enforcement, by that I mean laws made by Congress.

They perform necessary national functions . . . standardization.

The largest reiterated aims refer to service to the public. This fundamental view is repeated in various ways.

For the good of the people.

To aid primarily.

To protect the rights of individuals.

To take care of people.

To take care of things that the individual couldn't take care of by himself.

Service of the taxpayer mostly, well, service of all citizens.

They are supposed to protect you.

That is, the basic wish is to have a benevolent, protective government, one that safeguards persons by rendering routine or "necessary" services without otherwise impinging too strongly. The idea is "When I am not thinking of the government, the government should not be thinking of me." Americans do not want to be singled out by the government (except for meritorious recognition); also, they do not expect to be singled out, nor to have much to do with it other than in the most generalized and matter-of-fact ways.

This feeling of relatively minor active contact with government agencies and its appropriateness as characteristic of American philosophy was reflected in the casual, poised (even if inaccurate) comment of a 45-year-old, college educated, married, upper middle class woman who said, "I have never had personal contact with a government agency."

This attitude is highlighted in comparisons with foreign practices. Even in European democracies there seems to be greater emphasis on registration, on police authority, on face-to-face subservience of the public to bureaucratic officials, on restraint of and governmental knowledge of individual activities and mobility. A French war bride noted, "I thought the ability of calling on the phone was better than having to go there several times for information." And a German visitor remarked, "In Germany the bureaucratic official demands you appear and stand before him, to show he has authority, prestige, and strictness. Here everything is by mail."

THE WISH FOR INEFFICIENCY

In an ideal world a government might be benevolent and efficient. Normally, however, the belief is that efficiency, accuracy, system, and so on come about through severity of discipline, unmerciful application of impersonal principles, and indifference to individual variations and needs. Conversely, we associate indulgence with permissiveness of discipline, adaptation to human pressures, and sloppiness. The hypothesis is suggested that Americans prefer to believe their government agencies are lazy and security seeking, too involved in their own paper work and internal rigidities and carelessness to be authoritarian and punishing to the public. They want to be able to criticize this authority, as soldiers lambaste the food regardless of its quality, to show their security as citizens. It is safer to have a government that is an irritating old uncle who has trouble getting things right, hires too many people for anybody's good, but withal, is a lovable old shoe who means well.

If this interpretation is correct, it suggests that federal agencies cannot easily find generalized approval regardless of the actual merits of their accomplishments, that citizens are made anxious by too much zeal if it smacks of efficiency without heart. Federal executives must reconcile themselves to the negative image that makes people feel safe. Probably the efficiency that will be best received is that which enhances and reassures about bureaucratic intentions by emphasizing service, comfort, courtesy, attention to needs, and patience with the fears of those who would rather not be dealing with the government at all.

REFERENCE

Crispi, L. (1981). Some observations on the concept of image. *Public Opinion Quarterly*, 115-120.

Chapter 22

IMAGERY AND SYMBOLISM

Sidney J. Levy

The concept of *imagery* is an important one in marketing. The term is widely used, both casually and technically, and often in misleading ways. The purpose of this section is to explain what imagery is and how it is conveyed and received. After indicating its meaning, the discussion will take up the role of this concept in marketing planning and communications. How symbolism functions in relation to imagery is then explored, followed by analysis of imagery and symbolism from the viewpoints of participants in the marketing system.

THE MEANING OF IMAGERY

The concept of brand image was introduced in 1955 (Gardner & Levy, 1955) and was widely seized upon (Ogilvy, 1955) because it aptly summed up the idea that consumers buy brands not only for their physical attributes and functions but also because of the meanings connected with the brands. The notion of imagery reminds us that action in the marketplace is based on impressions and interpretations that people derive from their experience of a

This chapter first appeared in Levy, Frerichs, & Gordon (Eds.), *The Dartnell Marketing Manager's Handbook*, 1973, pp. 1136-1145. Reprinted by permission of The Dartnell Corporation.

broader sort than that which narrowly relates to the objects they buy or sell. They cannot learn all the facts available, and they cannot keep in mind all those they do learn. In addition, there are various influences pressing them to have one opinion or another about the product, service, and company at issue.

THE CONTENT OF IMAGES

The image is a result of all these facts and influences, reduced to manageable proportions. Drawn from many sources, the image includes such ideas as these.

1. *Knowledge about technical matters* helps people define a brand. For example, the image of a Hewlett-Packard computer might include the fact that it uses the DOS program, or the image of Jell-O might say it is high in protein.

2. *Awareness of other characteristics* that are somewhat more subjective, that seem like facts, but may or may not be supported by experience, is part of imagery. Here might be included the idea that a certain fabric will launder well, or that a certain movie is very funny.

3. *Beliefs about the value of the object* come to be part of its image. For example, the conviction that a Rolls-Royce is worth the cost, that Budweiser is indeed a premium beer, that Pepsi-Cola has a lot to give—such ideas become bound up in the image of those brands.

4. *Judgments about the suitability of the brand* are influences added to the image. Brands come to acquire a greater sense of appropriateness for some kinds of people than for others. It is part of the image,

then, that one brand is thought to be a cigarette mainly smoked by men, a beverage preferred by teenagers, or a food too spicy for American tastes.

As these points suggest, imagery is a mixture of notions and deductions, based on many things. It is fundamentally subjective, a fact that troubles those who believe marketing decisions should be made only on hard facts and in accordance with their ideas about what is rational or economically sound. The harder fact is, however, that people live by their images, and these are governed by their individual experiences, their values, and how they interpret what comes across to them.

ILLUSIONS AND FACTS

At times, the imagery is indeed largely an illusion—for example, the belief that some product is highly nutritious when it is not, that eating a carrot will contribute significantly to improved vision, that a particular automobile make is near-perfect in quality or that another offers the degree of "functional" transportation believed to be the case. Other images are debatable: Will a sports car enhance one's sexuality and youthfulness? Will flying on a particular airline imply a higher status level or a more attractive lifestyle? No, say some, a deodorant or toothpaste will not make one more alluring to the opposite sex; on the other hand, say others, bad breath and dingy teeth *are* offensive and of no help in social relations, as the advertisements claim.

The idea of imagery is not restricted (as often used) to mean only those aspects of products or communications that are misleading or which try to make things seem more attractive or valuable than they really are. It also refers to any inferences drawn about qualities that seem well-grounded—

for example, the image of diamonds as hard and durable, of prices as rising, of refrigerators as noisy, of candy as sweet, of tires as safer than they used to be, of Mercedes-Benz cars as socially impressive.

LONG-RANGE AND SHORT-RANGE IMAGERY GOALS

There is much discussion among marketers about setting objectives, and planning has first to consider where the enterprise wishes to go. Commonly, however, objectives are thought of in concrete terms relating to sales volume, profit level, or getting customers to be aware of some facts about the product. More recently, marketing managers have been giving attention to what kinds of imagery goals they should have and how to achieve them.

There are many problems involved. Often, managers do not realize how some given action will affect the imagery about their brand or their company, as when an emphasis on stylishness or an upgrading of quality unexpectedly modifies customers' views of a product's value or desirability, or their feelings about a company's suitability to their own habits, tastes, and identities. Managers may not know how to bring about the imagery they want to present, what precise ideas to present, the context in which these are appropriately dealt with, the channels of communication where this might be best accomplished. Their imagery goals may have elements that are in conflict. An example of how inadvertent imagery might come about is the frequent running of sales, whereby the manager is surprised to discover that the product is coming to be regarded as inferior in quality. When a brand creates imagery that boasts of the popularity of the brand, there may be difficulty in trying also to suggest it is an intimate brand. Brands that seem large tend thereby to seem impersonal.

Thus it is that a marketing action (running a sale, designing a package, selecting an advertising theme) is both a short-run effort and an investment in the long-run reputation of the brand. If short-run decisions are made without reference to long-run implications, as is commonly the case under competitive pressures and the varied demands of dealers, advertising agencies, and package designers, the results may be haphazard and confused so that over time the brand image is not well oriented to its market segments, or it turns out to be an image that is different from what the seller would like.

Recently, the growth of sales promotional activities and of the power of large retailers has pressed manufacturers in the direction of offering products that seem more like commodities in the lowered level of brand loyalty shown by customers. Anxiety about this shift has increased the awareness of the importance of brand imagery. Procter and Gamble demonstrates this apprehension in its recent decision to back away from sales promotion in order to re-emphasize the stature of its brands. This re-emphasis on brand imagery is shown in the book on brand equity by David Aaker (1990, 1996), and in the surge of interest in integrated or "total marketing" approaches to creating imagery.

CORPORATE IMAGERY

An important instance of imagery is that which affects the company as a whole. The corporate image refers to the kinds of ideas and impressions people have of the organization in general. Reputation of its specific products and brands will play a role, but other factors are also relevant. Such knowledge, awareness, beliefs, and judgments include the size of the company, its personnel, incidents in its history, its value as a stock, its contribution to the life of the community or the country; and are used in reacting to the company.

The corporate image may be of significance to consumers of the specific products by reassuring them of the responsibility and quality of the manufacturer. It affects the buyers of company shares; it influences the government in its relations with the enterprise; and suppliers to the company will be guided by their image of it. Appreciation of the power of corporate imagery has led many companies to give special thought to communicating with their various publics. Public relations, institutional advertising, community-oriented programs, training programs, corporate literature, the name of the company and its logogram, and marketing activity within the trade are increasingly evaluated for their effects on the corporate image as well as their immediate practical functions.

IMAGERY AND SYMBOLIC COMMUNICATION

An image is an interpretation, a set of inferences and reactions. It is a symbol because it is not the object itself but refers to it and stands for it. In addition to the physical realities of the product, brand, or corporation, the image includes their meanings, that is, the beliefs, attitudes, and feelings that have come to be attached to them.

These meanings are learned or stimulated by the component experiences people have with the product, and these components are particular symbols whose significance is grasped. For example, part of the "real" experience of riding in a convertible is the wind blowing one's hair. This experience becomes symbolic of the convertible, a component with such meanings as freedom, youthfulness, and irresponsibility. As a rider, one feels a release from conventional restraints, and watchers see the riders visibly showing (probably flaunting) their disorderly hair. As a result, Ernest Dichter interpreted that a convertible symbolized a mistress.

Similarly, all other component symbols communicate aspects of the image, acting as messages to the observer. A new package design might be made to serve as a more efficient container than the old one. Symbolically, the new package could also imply a more modern product inside, a company concern with beauty, or an enhanced femininity, depending on the shape, colors, graphics, and illustrations.

SYMBOLS IN ADVERTISING AND PROMOTION

The symbolic actions in marketing are pervasive and inescapable. They are most noticeable and are given most specific attention in advertising and promotion. The structure of a company's office lobby plays a symbolic marketing role, but architects are often either unaware of or indifferent to that fact. However, people in promotional work are apt to be sensitive to the more intangible aspects of their efforts, the possible effects on imagery.

Advertising as an activity is itself symbolic. To advertise is usually understood as a way of being proud and boastful, as something one may do hard or softly. Advertising contrasts with personal selling by usually being some kind of public announcement, a fact that suggests an openness, a prevalence, a quality of being larger than life. It seems democratic, potentially for everyone, and often enjoyable because it is bold, colorful, fantasy-arousing, and exaggerated. On the same grounds, it is adversely criticized because it may symbolize deception, distraction from the true facts, and it seems demanding and intrusive or insufficiently informative.

Whether appreciated or demeaned, advertising is powerful in presenting symbols that help to form people's images. It does this even when the symbolism is resisted. Commercials used to show white doves and white tornadoes in the kitchen, giants' fists in washing machines, white knights transforming laundry, which were frequently criticized as meaningless and insulting to intelligence. At the same time, the symbolic vigor of these messages was pronounced, absorbed attention, aroused astonishment and amusement as well as irritation, and created imagery concerning brand effectiveness. Figures such as Mr. Clean and the women representing Land-O-Lakes or SunMaid products personalize and reassure about their offerings.

SYMBOLIC FORM AND MOVEMENT

Such results come about because people are not merely literal minded, nor do they respond only to the most obvious, explicit statements in advertising. This is evident if one examines the various kinds of advertising symbolism and how they gain their effects.

Viewers of television commercials may come to learn the messages well because they usually have several opportunities. In doing so, they are often especially influenced by such elements of form as animation, music, special word choices, particular forms and shapes, the sequence of events, their pace, and so on. Some of this influence is difficult to describe and to specify, attesting to the subtle symbolic fac-

tors at work. Examples might be the emotional situation aroused when mothers and daughters discuss using sanitary products and the irritation some people feel at the smug tone of the announcer extolling the virtues of Volvo's cars or the nudity shown in Calvin Klein's ads.

The less deliberate or self-conscious reactions to symbolism are also demonstrated by the effects of movement (see also Chapter 19). The kinds of movement used in television commercials are themselves a vocabulary, contributing to imagery in an intricate fashion. Some examples are

1. Rotation, a movement that suggests the confining three dimensional form of the television tube, and a showing off of all sides

2. Approach and retreat, a movement indicating arriving and departing, bringing something to the viewer, or the yearning feeling elicited by a fading away

3. Unifying movement, which occurs when parts are shown that come together to form a whole. The movement is dynamic, leading the audience to want to see the resolution

4. Staccato movement, such as achieved by stop-motion photography. The effect is one of stylization, a quirkiness, a watch-and-wait idea that is sometimes annoying because viewers vary in their rates of ability to integrate such visual material

THE MANAGER'S POINT OF VIEW

The position of the marketing manager trying to promote his brand is not an easy one because the creation of a desired brand image is a complex activity. It draws upon all the symbolic elements discussed briefly above, in a situation that is in constant flux. There is no simple recipe for the symbolic mix that will produce a specific brand image. The problems vary: perhaps the brand is on the rise and needs to be kept aloft, conveying a sense of confidence, of having a sturdy place in the contemporary market, and a suitability for everyday lifestyles. Perhaps the brand is declining. This is an agonizing situation for marketers, since what is wrong is often not apparent, leading to some flailing around and blaming in all directions.

Introducing a new brand is an exciting challenge and opportunity. Customarily, the focus on the product is so great that the manager may neglect the fact that he is engaged in creating a brand image almost from scratch (almost, because he may be constrained by existing imagery about the company and by other products in the line). If he forgets to realize that pricing policy, channels of distribution, media employed, timing, and all the myriad marketing decisions will each be saying something about the brand, defining it and symbolizing it, as well as offering it in practical ways, he may miss the audience.

THE BUYER'S POINT OF VIEW

The world of marketing symbolism and imagery is composed of individual events—products, prices, coupons, advertisements, salespeople, media—and each is handled in some particular way when encountered. Together, these individual events come to form a substantial part of the daily environment. As people move through the day, the multitude of objects and messages that remind them about consuming and buying is almost inescapable and relentless. The

manager's problem is to make himself or herself seen, heard, and noticed among all the communications; the people being marketed to have the problem of sorting out their experience, learning from it, and finding in it the things and the meanings that will satisfy them. They constantly process the symbols they are exposed to, deciding how much attention to give to them, making inferences about the product and the form in which it is presented, and about how well it fits into their goals.

An example of how this goes on in a particular area of marketing is found in consumer incentives. Managers may not realize the extent to which housewives reason and draw imagery from different promotional approaches. When such devices as coupons, contests, premiums, and miscellaneous deals are used, these can be interpreted positively or negatively, not only as means of gaining advantage but for suggesting something about the company or brand. On the positive side, incentives have such meanings as these:

- A large, well-established company
- An aggressive marketer
- A generous, friendly company

On the other hand, negative inferences may be drawn.

- The company is in trouble.
- The product is poor or overstocked.
- It is normally overpriced.

Additionally, each type of incentive has its own symbolic character and appeal. Samples are almost always welcome, seeming truly free and fair. Sweepstakes are fun and get large numbers of entries, but they seem frothy and are usually forgotten quickly and do little to enhance the reputation of the brand. Then again, there are always exceptions when an activity is done well or the source seems especially reliable—for example, the *Reader's Digest*.

Symbolism in Industrial Advertising

Imagery is often thought to be less important in industrial marketing than in consumer marketing. This is a misunderstanding that comes about when the image is taken to refer only to the nonrational mood aspects of communications, which seem more prevalent in consumer marketing. This view overlooks the fact that industrial organizations and their brands also have images, even if the content of those images has to do with reliability, service, delivery dates, and competitive pricing. Imagery is not merely frivolity, as a company can have a stodgy image as well as a stylish or even phony one.

Part of the imagery of industrial communication is a sense of dull technical emphasis, of old-line companies relying on their salespeople, being heavy and serious to the point of depression. Where advertising is used, it tends to be traditional, conventional messages with relatively straightforward reassurances that the company and product can provide the performance the user needs. The product is illustrated, or one of its applications is shown, and a request for inquiries winds it up. The people shown, if any, are often earnest, stiff representatives of the seller or users, or both, in "show and tell" situations.

CHANGING IMAGERY

Some organizations are discontent with this, feeling the result is an imagery that is static, old-fashioned, and false to the energetic character of the company. As newer symbols are used to modify the industrial

and commercial scene, the advertising becomes more "emotional" and colorful, the imagery changes toward greater subtlety. Humor has come to the fore, taking many forms. Verbal and visual puns are common. A bank in New York says to its commercial customers, "The American Capitalist. When his needs are financial, his reactions are Chemical." An ad for Canteen Corporation showed a drinking straw, with the headline, "Are you keeping this management pipeline open?" The sense of good humor starting to pervade industrial advertising may show R&D workers exaggeratedly achieving their marvels. It finds expression in cartoons, whimsy, and many kinds of fantasy. The purpose is to show that the company is not conventional and routine. The use of humor symbolizes that the company has some modern self-awareness, that it is "with it," that it is not just plodding along doing the same dull, unamusing things. An engineer shows his appreciation of more vital industrial advertising:

> The photograph is modern, the catch phrase is up to date, suggests a modern, today, ad approach. This all comes over to the company. . . . I'd expect to see cylinders and fittings—I've seen one that showed all the fittings that were available. I appreciate this. This is an eye-catcher. I like the unusualness of the ad. It's far from the workaday world ads.

IMPLICATIONS

From the point of view developed in this chapter, the main overall task of the marketing manager is to relate all the symbols possible to the general thrust of the company or the product responsibility. He or she can do this by asking and exploring the following questions.

1. *What does he have to sell?* The manager should understand what is sold, in a fundamental way. That is, he or she should learn about the symbolic significance of what is being offered in the marketplace. The meaning of the offering is the central message sent out.

2. *What is the symbolic suitability to the audience?* In studying markets, the manager needs to understand more than the conventional descriptions of market segments. Part of modern study is to learn about the lifestyle of the customers, as the imagery of the brand will be seen through the eyes of people living in diverse ways.

3. *What can the manager say?* All that the manager has to present to current and potential customers constitutes a repertoire of symbols from which he or she can draw in order to put together the image he would like to have. He has to work complexly with what the ideal imagery goals might be; what would be believable given the product, his history, and what the contemporary period allows; and what he or she can control in the face of competition.

4. *How do subsymbols relate to the goal?* If the image the company offers of itself and its brands is a large symbol, the specific actions taken in the marketplace are subsymbols that compose the total. The accumulation of symbolic meanings produces more intense imagery. Each action should be analyzed not only for its immediate value (e.g., reducing inventory, making more people aware of the name), but for what it contributes to the accumulating imagery.

APPENDIX

Additional Reading

Boulding, K. (1968). *The image*. Ann Arbor: University of Michigan Press.

Dolich, I. J. (1969, February). Congruence relationships between self images and product brands. *Journal of Marketing Research, 6,* 80-85.

Dreyfuss, H. (1972). *Symbol sourcebook*. New York: McGraw-Hill.

Goffman, E. (1959). *The presentation of self in everyday life*. New York: Doubleday Anchor.

Levy, S. J. (1971). *Promotional behavior*. Glenview, IL: Scott, Foresman.

Levy, S. J. (1978). *Marketplace behavior—its meaning for management*. New York: AMA/COM.

REFERENCES

Aaker, D. (1990). *Managing brand equity*. New York: Free Press.

Aaker, D. (1996). *Building strong brands*. New York: Free Press.

Gardner, B. B., & Levy, S. J. (1955, March/April). The product and the brand. *Harvard Business Review, 33,* 33-39.

Ogilvy, D. (1955, October 17). The image and the brand. *Advertising Age, 26,* 1.

## Chapter 23

MYTH AND MEANING
IN MARKETING

Sidney J. Levy

The types of explanation (or search) for understanding in marketing are varied. They arise from the necessities of different problems—so that analysis of physical distribution systems is required if goods are to move, study of demand curves helps people think about pricing, and research on color is useful for decisions about package visibility on shelves. Areas of inquiry also depend largely on the taste and characteristic orientation of the marketer and the kind of knowledge that he finds congenial for his approach to problems. The practical, ratio-nalistic approach tends to predominate, with its reliance on the security of quantification of analytic elements. The inferences made tend to stay close to the facts of overt phenomena and measurements that seem related by rather conventional reasoning. Turning to the behavioral sciences has usually entailed a focus on social psychology and psychology, radiating especially in such topics as attitudes, social stratification, and psychographics, where, again, attention goes to scales, classifications, and the linear aggregation of

This chapter was first published in R. C. Curhan (Ed.), *Combined Proceedings, Series 36*, 1974, pp. 555-558. Reprinted by permission of the American Marketing Association.

| 241

discrete items, sophisticated somewhat of late by multivariate analysis.

By comparison, the discipline and traditions of anthropology play a small role in marketing thought (Weiss, 1966). Some lip service may be given (Winick, 1961), but little elaboration, development, or study. When anthropology is thought about, it often does not seem useful. It seems an encompassing view such that its level of generalization is too broad to help with the multitudinous small marketing problems that occur in daily life. Of course, from another perspective, if anthropology is the study of mankind, or nowadays, person-kind, then everything we do and all ways of study are probably parts of anthropology, ways of working closer in on components of the total problem. Thus, like the man who was so pleased to learn he spoke prose, we can be gratified to recognize that in studying marketing, we are already "doing anthropology." However, anthropology also exists as a set of specialties (Tax, 1964). that vary in their interest for marketers.

THE CONCEPT OF CULTURE

Such main marketing texts as Engel, Kollat, and Blackwell (1973) and Howard and Sheth (1969) are typical in giving anthropology its due for one of its central concepts—culture. The concept of culture is useful for several reasons. Not least of these is its potential value for putting to rest (one hopes) the prescription that marketing should concern itself with satisfying *needs*, not with products and advertising that arouse unnecessary *wants*. It may be that scarce resources and an impossibly large population will eventually put everyone at a subsistence level. But even then people in

different areas and of different histories will probably not subsist in the same way. They will insist on having a culture, having wants and trying to satisfy them in their own peculiar ways. Beyond survival, there are only wants—to do it one way or another, whatever it is. A culture is the net result, the aggregation, accumulation, interaction of those ways among any given group of people. When we look back and try to reconstruct the pattern of a past culture from the traces of its passage—its artifacts, its movements, its skeletons, its refuse, and its environment, we call it archaeology. Modern marketing study may be thought of as the archaeology of contemporary life, learning about the meaning of current objects while the users are available to tell us about them. It is still a detective task, the piecing together of a puzzle, but there are a lot more data around.

Anthropologists, like others, must constantly struggle with the problems of levels of generalization. Comparing many societies, one can be oriented toward the largest generalizations—what are the most profound and most general characteristics of mankind? Other workers are more impressed by or more eager to demonstrate human diversity. The only ultimate truth possible is that humans are both deeply the same and obviously different, but both emphases have partisans and are used to advance or to fight ethnocentric biases. The weapons used are as varied as the subspecialties in anthropology: race, linguistics, the size of baboon brains, pottery decorations, and so on. Cross-cultural study is generally intriguing to the layman because it feeds curiosity about exotic ways and it permits members of one culture to feel superior or inferior to another. Just as we say that the bland person has no personality, despite the psychologist's contention that everyone has a personality, so we call one group uncultured, despite its having a culture in scientific terms. These everyday views reflect values being placed on vivacity or sociability in the individual and on some preferred elaboration and cultivation of aesthetic experience in the society.

However judged, among the contents and forms of cultures are the objects and behaviors, the providing and receiving which compose their marketing. Margaret Mead once commented to the effect that 15 minutes in the commercial marketplace of a strange people was enough to tell her what the people were like, implying the intimate relation of the market to the character of the people (and Dr. Mead's perspicacity).

The excerpts from classics may serve to give the flavor of anthropologists approaching the content of marketing. The first is by Franz Boas (1897) on the *Potlatch* of the Kwakiutl Indians.

> Before proceeding any further it will be necessary to describe the method of acquiring rank. This is done by means of the potlatch, or the distribution of property. . . . The underlying principle is that of the interest-bearing investment of property. . . . Possession of wealth is considered honorable. . . . But it is . . . the ability to give great festivals which makes wealth a desirable object . . . rising in the social scale . . . may be done by inviting the rival and his clan or tribe to a festival and giving him a considerable number of blankets. He is compelled to accept these . . . he must repay the gift with 100 per cent interest. . . . The rivalry between chiefs and clans finds its strongest expression in the destruction of property. A chief will burn blankets, a canoe, or break a copper, thus indicating his disregard of the amount of property destroyed

and showing that his mind is stronger, his power greater, than that of his rival.

Similarly, Bronislaw Malinowski (1961) provides an extensive analysis of the *Kula*.

> The Kula is a form of exchange, of extensive, inter-tribal character; it is carried on by communities inhabiting a wide ring of islands, which form a closed circuit. This circuit joins a number of islands to the North and East of the East end of New Guinea. Along this route, articles of two kinds, and these two kinds only, are constantly traveling in opposite directions. In the direction of the hands of a clock, moves constantly one of these kinds—long necklaces of red shell, called *soulava*. In the opposite direction moves the other kind—bracelets of white shell called *mwali*. Each of these articles, as it travels in its own direction on the closed circuit, meets on its way articles of the other class, and is constantly being exchanged for them. Every movement of the Kula articles, every detail of the transactions is fixed and regulated by a set of traditional rules and conventions, and some acts of the Kula are accompanied by an elaborate magical ritual and public ceremonies.

Both Malinowski and Boas go on to discuss at length the systems of exchange they are analyzing, indicating the various rules, regulations, requirements, rewards, and losses that are involved. Cross-cultural study can invigorate observation and sensitivity to one's own society. Students' perceptions of local supermarkets and the citizens shopping there are much refreshed by a reading of Eugene Burdick's description of the Australian aborigine. Further, a largeness of view is required for interpreting general phenomena such as, for instance, the relative failure of the bidet to diffuse into American plumbing despite the common enthusiasm expressed for it by those who know it. Another example of observing general marketing trends in the society is the recent attempt to identify and measure social indicators. Social anthropological study of the American society for marketing insights is a challenge, as much focus on the concept of culture tends to emphasize international marketing and exotic cultural tidbits like the admonition to avoid the number four in Japan because *shi* is also the word for death in Japanese.

CULTURAL SUBGROUPS

Studying the culture of a group is studying the style of life of the people, including, as John Beattie sums up, what actually happens, what people think happens, and what they think ought to happen, their legal and moral values. But anthropologists cannot study all of mankind simultaneously, nor even the total of a given society—could one imagine how to do that? Usually, they are interested in a given group from some particular vantage point, or with regard to their anthropological specialty. Language, economic systems, religious beliefs, family life, and so on become the fulcrum of study or the glasses through which the society or social group is observed. The marketer is especially interested in some of these groups or themes because they clearly fall into his own sphere of problems. Ethnicity and housing, social class and funeral behavior, the culture of the poor, blacks and their rising expectations, changing food habits to improve nutrition, become themes of mutual interest. Such topics and their investigation may lead to a richer understanding of the phenomena and potential course of

actions than the desire to learn about different cultures in order to avoid foolish mistakes like advertising beefburgers in India, using the wrong color for mourning, or not knowing that in England the word *bum* can refer to the behind or arse.

THE STUDY OF MEANING

But the situation is more complex than just having some such superficial ignorance or wrong facts. After all, one never knows all about any group, one's own or anyone else's. A deeper area of interest that is of concern to social and cultural anthropologists has to do with meanings. One of the things that distinguishes many anthropologists is their attention to things that are important to people being studied; they want to learn the *significance* of the cultural events. They thus become involved in analyzing relatively basic themes, searching for the coherence in them. Of special fascination then are such notions as creation, birth, child rearing, kinship, incest, deference and degradation, the role of the gift, the sacred and the profane, the beautiful and the ugly. Commonly, such themes infuse the minutiae of everyday life with implication and basis for marketing action.

One of marketing's traditionally sad lacks lies in its reluctance to deal with the less tangible realms of explanation of human behavior. Given to a narrow realism, practicality, and the tenacious grip of the economic man, marketers ordinarily resist areas of understanding that have to do with symbols, myths, legends, arbitrary belief, and fantasy. Marketing texts gingerly make a few references to symbolism or handle it largely as a technical aspect of communication. Despite the avid involvement of mankind in song, dance, pictures, movies, fairy tales, folk tales, novels, science fiction, and Agatha Christie, less sophisticated marketing studies are likely to restrict themselves to narrow concern with product features and pricing variations. A few patronizing references are made to the absurdity of such "old-fashioned motivational research" ideas as baking a cake being like having a baby, or a convertible car being like a mistress, as if these are the sorts of ideas that do not mean much to people, or which may belong to just odd people—perhaps to savages who know about pregnancy and about intercourse, but not, so to speak, the connection between them.

But everywhere yearnings, aspirations, and interpersonal relations are laden with magical, superstitious, mystical, and religious significance, with private imageries, sentiments, cosmic theories, and ways of relating to nature. Malinowski sees the Kula ring as comparable in meaning to the Crown Jewels of England, to the collecting of sports trophies, with the forces of tradition, of sentiment, of pride that we all somehow experience.

Perhaps the closest marketing comes to an appreciation of these vital forces is in the field of advertising where fantasy, song, and dance are given play, with some awareness of the mythic intrigue these have. The repressive forces of the Federal Trade Commission, obsessed with literalness, will probably not be able to do much to protect us from the strange power of Mrs. Olson, Marlboro Country, and the Real Thing.

But there is some movement on other marketing fronts. At the 1978 annual meeting of the Southern Forest Products Association the conventioneers listened to the presentation of a paper (Levy, 1978) interpreting the meaning of forests and trees. The businessmen tree-cutters were reminded of the forest's connection with the idea of the Great Mother as a place where vegetable life thrives and luxuriates; which represents the unconscious impulses that threaten through demons, enemies, and disease. As in the Dickey story, *Deliverance,* the forest raises the question, can individual men contend with the primitive nature of the wilderness and emerge unscathed from the awful forces of wild waters and uninhibited sexuality? The mystic principles of the tree with its divine animation, its transcendental connection of the three worlds of Hell, Earth, and Heaven, call for awe at its longevity, yearnings to share in its vitality, knowledge, and comfort, and efforts to protect it from the axe and the encroachment of civilization.

Similarly, a meeting in Denver in January 1974 launched a discussion of *The Automobile and the Future of Denver* with a paper on basic meanings of the automobile, touching especially on the historic symbolism of the chariot among other modes of transportation and its role in man's restless quest (Levy, 1974).

So it is, *mutatis mutandis,* that food marketing can never be mainly a matter of taste or education about nutrition—or malnutrition and weight control problems would depend only on supply and information. Clothing is not just a matter of style and drip-dry features—or there would be no cloak of invisibility, need for uniforms, Cinderella's dress, or the fantastic garb of the court of Louis IV.

MEANING AND MARKETING

The point being belabored here is not that belief in fairy godmothers and arboreal demons should be substituted for scientific inquiry. But there are these implications.

Marketing is not only an impersonal economic activity, but in addition to its conventional considerations about exchanges, buying and selling values, income, budget, outlets, and transportation, it is inevitably interwoven with other personal, noneconomic relationships in society.

Marketing meanings are part of the meanings in people's whole life patterns. They reflect, superficially or deeply, enduringly or in passing, the kinds of inner life already mentioned.

A richer appreciation of the significance of marketing will come about if more attention is given to interpretations and relationships at levels not usually studied. As many marketing research questionnaires will testify, a typical arsenal of values is cost, durability, convenience, and delivery date, presumed to be best when low, strong, easy, and fast. Certainly these are common desires, but preoccupation with them leaves problems usually omitted from marketing texts: the desire for transformation and epiphanies, restoration of loss, revenge, or even simpler preferences for satisfaction with expensiveness, fragile things, troublesome dealings, and late arrivals.

The ideal market is like a Heaven— perfect but dull; the real one is the human one on Earth, fraught with emotion, striving, and the symbolic investments that make us care about what and how we market to and from others.

REFERENCES

Boas, F. (1897). *The social organization and the secret societies of the Kwakiutl Indians* (Annual report, 1894-1895). Washington: U.S. National Museum.

Engle, J. F., Kollat, D. T., & Blackwell, R. D. (1973). *Consumer behavior.* New York: Holt, Rinehart & Winston.

Howard, J. A., & Sheth, J. N. (1969). *The theory of buyer behavior.* New York: John Wiley.

Levy, S. J. (1974). *The motor god.* Paper presented at The Automobile and the Future of Denver, Women's College.

Levy, S. J. (1978) Emotional reactions to the cutting of trees. *Marketplace behavior: Its meaning for management* (pp. 46-53). New York: AMA/COM.

Malinowski, B. (1961). *Argonauts of the western Pacific.* New York: Dutton.

Tax, S. (Ed.). (1964). *Horizons of anthropology.* Chicago: Aldine.

Weiss, R. S. (1966). Alternative approaches in the study of complex situations. *Human Organization, 25*(Fall), 198-206.

Winick, C. (1961, July). Anthropology's contributions to marketing. *Journal of Marketing, 25.*

Chapter 24

SYMBOLS, SELVES, AND OTHERS

Sidney J. Levy

As Beth Holman noted in introducing this morning's three papers, they are unusually well-related to the panel topic of consumption symbolism and consumption behavior. Taken together, the presentations explore various perspectives on the symbolic significance of products. Belk, Meyer, and Russell (1981) show that people readily interpret the sizes and styles of houses and cars for inferences about the likely characteristics of owners. Some of these inferences show great consensus, others less so. The results seem to show that there is a broad cultural recognition of the meanings of the sizes and styles, with some variations related to age, social status, and sex. It is perhaps surprising that the consensus is so great, given people's pragmatic knowledge that many circumstances can affect actual ownership.

We might also turn the problem around and wonder what is the logic in the minds of those who do not go along with the majority of the sample. If we assume that they too must be interpreting the symbolism of the different sizes and styles, it would be interesting to know what meanings they are using, and what their characteristics are that incline them to a less conventional inference; or perhaps they are making other conventional inferences.

Perhaps we might group the adults and students who agree and compare them to the adults and students who disagree, to

This chapter was first published in A. Mitchell (Ed.), *Advances in Consumer Research* (Vol. 10, pp. 542-543), Provo, UT: Association for Consumer Research, 1981.

learn more about the decoding process. In a freer style interview, we might explore the associations and thought processes people use—maybe that younger men think a sports car mainly represents youth rather than the success of achieved social status, or that one can be young and successful without being of the higher status that goes with maturity. In any event, the study gives useful support to the fundamental facts of age, sex, and social status as symbolic elements bound up in consensual perceptions of major products and readily decoded as such.

The Scammon, Shaw, and Bamossy (1981) study adds thoughts about another product, the symbolic meaning of flowers, with particular focus on the interpersonal idea of gift giving. By exploring the characteristics of different motives among those who buy flowers, some broad dimensions are suggested about the meanings of flowers and how they may differ in different situations. They are suited to personal use, for gifts on various occasions, and as obligatory gifts for specific situations, and these uses are differentially suited to kinds of consumers, differentiated by age, social class, sex, and other aspects of custom, economics, and so on.

That older women are inclined toward the obligatory event seems consistent with their mature roles as keepers and teachers of proper behavior. They are the mothers who try to socialize the young to say thank you. Also, lower status people are especially obedient to what the rules say is the right thing to give. It might be interesting to select subsamples that more purely represent the three use patterns, to examine them as ideal types. Using people who actually fit all three situations but assigning them to only one, seems to cloud the results. On the other hand, multi-use behavior is probably common, so an approach might be devised that takes account of that reality rather than riding over it.

The complexities of gift giving and the meanings of flowers might both be further explicated by considering personal use as a form of gift giving to the self—"I owe it to myself." I as subject reward me as object. Flowers (or any other product) raise the issue of what is being communicated by the choice of gift. Is it "sheer" obligation? The reward of "pick up" is mentioned; what about some of the ideas and feelings derived from flowers seen as natural, vital, beautiful, sensitive, fragile, elegant, feminine, subtle, luxurious, and so on, in general, as well as the diverse artifactual vocabulary conveyed by roses, orchids, daisies, potted mums, and Japanese Ikebana arrangements? Hirschman (1981) seeks to distinguish technological innovations that arise and diffuse when some physical, technical change meets a need for superior performance from symbolic innovations that arise and diffuse when their social meanings change. As her examples indicate, she seems to refer to a real distinction, it being evident that there are changes in the perceptions of products even though the products do not physically change. However, there are some problems with the terminology she uses and then, as a consequence, with the resulting conceptualization, that are interesting to explore.

By treating *symbolism* and *technology* as dichotomous, in effect Hirschman (1981) denies the symbolic meanings of technological innovations. It is as if to say that symbolic meaning is the same as social meaning (which is true by definition), but that high technology lacks social meaning (which is empirically not true). She qualifies that the dichotomy is for the purpose of describing ideal types and that the two dimensions are continuous and may be interrelated for some product classes. But that does not handle the difficulty which is later compounded by the matrix that shows such categories as high and low symbolism and high and low technology.

There may be some confusion between the popular use and scientific use of these terms. An analogy might be made to the popular and scientific uses of the term *personality*. In everyday life a person may have "a lot of personality" or even "no personality" at all; but to the science of psychology everyone has as much personality as anyone else. Scientifically speaking, all objects have as much symbolism attached to them as people are capable of conceiving—to say something is dull, uninteresting, low in symbolism is to be characterizing its symbolic nature. Therefore, even if we were to grant that there was some objective, nonsymbolic way to determine that there were gradations in height of technology, such a scale could not be inversely related to a similar scale of amounts of symbolism. Objects that are popularly regarded as representing (symbolizing) low technology (e.g., some jewelry, some fertilizers, etc.) might actually be the product of high technology in the eyes of more knowledgeable segments, from whom this view has not yet diffused to other social groups. Similarly, the objects Hirschman (1981) groups as low in symbolism, such as computer systems, lasers, medical equipment, and so on, are in actuality as rich in symbolism as the ideas of the people who know of them. They are not only technological innovations, they are also symbolic innovations and can experience the same kinds of shifts in meaning that are noted for eyeglass frames. For example, the original perception of computers as intimidating business machines is being succeeded by such social meanings as child's play for kids learning in school and playing games with them as they diffuse into the home. To suggest that high technology has low symbolism because it is superior in function is rationalistic and ig-

nores that the lab workers, technicians, and scientists are snobs about their equipment and that even the supposed superiority is a symbolic claim that may yet be shown to be false (e.g., innovative pharmaceuticals with dreadful side effects that turn from miracle drugs into poisonous horrors).

Perhaps all this is to say that from a scientific view there can only be kinds of symbolism, not amounts, except as popularly perceived, and that Hirschman (1981) is pointing to variations in *perceived* levels of symbolism and technology. And, apart from the problems of talking about these matters, her distinction between the changing perceptions of unchanged products that are customer driven and the changing perceptions due to new technologies that are marketer driven remains a useful one.

The discussion of these three papers highlights to me what we might call a serial regress of perceptions, as in a mirror where an observer sees an observer who sees an observer, to infinity. I am made self-conscious in commenting on and trying to sort out my perceptions of these authors' perceptions of their subjects' perceptions; and you will observe mine, perhaps mention them to others, and so on.

The study of consumer behavior often focuses on the self-concept, as a set of perceptions whereby consumers symbolize to themselves who they are. They are able to do this by being self-conscious, being subjects taking themselves as objects. This ability is thought to be derived from early processes, whereby children internalize the attitudes of significant others. Thus, from observing others, we come to observe ourselves, and then by transference continue to relate our self-perceptions to how others will perceive us. We can then have the paradoxical idea of "secret display" whereby even covert consumption is a way of symbolizing to ourselves who we are.

As we go up and back in this process, we tell the others how we perceive ourselves and how we want them to perceive us. We do this by verbalizing it ("I love you"), by acting it out (staying late at the office), and by use of products, services, brands, and so on that are symbolically informative. Because people are complex and layered, their symbolic communications are often not taken at face value. Another way of putting this is to note that any object or action represents many ideas, and any idea is represented by many objects or actions. "I love you" may be deemed insincere, the office devotion taken as a sign of inefficiency, while the ways that insincerity and inefficiency can be manifested are also legion. Cigarettes and guns may be the artifacts of virile males or the superficial signs of underlying impotence, as some exaggerated dresses say sexy or frigid in the same breath. Such complexities lead to the various categorizations of symbols that may need to be taken account of, that were not noticed in this morning's papers; for example, symbols are public, private, formal, informal, conscious, unconscious, and so on.

Another source of richness in the use of products as consumption symbols is the way symbols interact to limit one another or to create new meanings. Giving flowers may say one thing, candy and flowers even more so; and what might have been the effect on

the results if Belk et al. (1981) had combined big cars and small houses or big houses and small cars? The notion of interacting symbols might be extended to encompass the patterning of more complex situations. In this respect we may have much to learn from anthropologists, who routinely examine the symbolic nature of complexes of activities. My awareness in this regard was recently refreshed by a rereading of Clifford Geertz's *The Interpretation of Cultures.*

We academicians observe and think about the relationships among symbols by studying the ways that selves use them and the interpretations made by others who observe the selves. Although we may dignify our observations and thoughts by calling them data and theories, it may be salutary to recognize that we are just more others observing selves; and that data and theories are symbols of our profession. It is necessary to face up to the subjectivity that is involved on all sides. Symbolic analysis is not a manifestation of behaviorism. It frankly requires interpretation. We are studying people's fantasies about personalities, their ages, their sex, and their social status, and in so doing having fantasies of our own. As the three papers presented here this morning demonstrate, it is an intriguing and engaging activity, and I hope we can move it toward increasing richness and sensitivity.

REFERENCES

Belk, R., Mayer, R., & Bahn, K. (1981). The eye of the beholder: Individual differences in perceptions of consumption symbolism. In A. Mitchell (Ed.), *Advances in consumer research* (Vol. 10, pp. 523-530), Provo, UT: Association for Consumer Research.

Hirschman, E. C. (1981). Symbolism and technology as sources for the generation of innovation. In A. Mitchell (Ed.), *Advances in consumer research* (Vol. 10, pp. 542-543), Provo, UT: Association for Consumer Research.

Scammon, D. L., Shaw, R. T., & Bamossy, G. (1981). Is a gift always a gift? In A. Mitchell (Ed.), *Advances in consumer research* (Vol. 10, pp. 542-543), Provo, UT: Association for Consumer Research.

## Chapter 25

MEANINGS IN ADVERTISING STIMULI

Sidney J. Levy

Our immediate purpose in studying advertising and consumer psychology is to satisfy our professional goals of making advertising more effective and to understand people insofar as they are consumers. To achieve these goals, we may give attention to aims of more general character. How people react to advertising is part of everyday communication processes, and to consume is to go about one's everyday business of being a person. Someone is always advertising to us, and we are always consuming something. Broadly speaking, we are not studying doing a particular thing that happens occasionally, such as going to the

doctor or going skiing, although each specific consumption activity is of course part of the total and we usually do focus on those of special interest to us. Nevertheless, we need to embed our inquiries in the larger context that asks what people's aims are and how advertising communications are related to them.

BASIC MOTIVES AND MEANINGS

When consumers encounter advertising, their reaction to it depends on its meaning to them; and its meaning depends on the

This chapter was first published in J. Olson & K. Sentis (Eds.), *Advertising and Consumer Psychology* (Vol. 3, pp. 214-226), 1986. Reprinted by permission of Praeger Publishers, an imprint of Greenwood Publishing Group, Inc., Westport, CT.

characteristics of both the advertising and the people. In his book on *The Birth and Death of Meaning*, Ernest Becker (1962) says,

> "Meaning" refers . . . to the connection of events and objects in an interdependent, self-consistent scheme. . . . Since man is the only time-binding, symbolic animal, he must fabricate meaning in order to build up a dependable and controllable world. . . . Meaning is, then, the joining together of ideas, objects, and people that forms a ground plan of action. (pp. 183-184)

Experience would be merely a chaos of sensations if we did not handle it in ways that make it fit into our developing view of the world. I find Becker's work especially interesting because he emphasizes two thoughts that fit what my experience suggests about the ways people make ideas, objects, and people meaningful to themselves. One emphasis is on how people move from animal behavior to human reactivity, gaining increasing complexity of response up to the capacity for what is called symbolic behavior. As part of this process people become capable of seeing themselves as objects that can be differentiated from lower animals and strive (ambivalently) to distinguish them as human.

Having this capacity for self-awareness has many repercussions. It enables people to conceptualize how they change as they grow, so that stages in the life cycle have different meanings associated with them, as Erik Erikson (1982) has described. The continuity of self awareness is a time-binding phenomenon in which people have memory of the past and the ability to aspire and plan for the future. They are motivated to have consistency in self-perception, so that the content of the life stage is related

to various bases for defining one's identity, such as sexuality, intellectual and emotional characteristics, and physical prowess.

Inevitably, it seems, the necessity for evaluation arises. The awareness of differences with growth and the perception of other people's identities leads to comparisons and judgments about having greater and lesser personal value. These judgments are translated into ideas about prestige and social position: that is, different degrees of virtue, personal and social power, kind of masculinity and femininity, and human refinement.

Becker's second main emphasis is on the way people cope with their anxiety about protecting their self-esteem and constituting themselves as having primary value. Broadly speaking, this means behaving and consuming in ways that suit one's identity and thereby enhance self-esteem. More specifically, it means that consumption is the outcome of how the consumer interprets what is needed to support an identity composed of a particular age-grading, sexuality, and social position, with personality characteristics complexly and subtly derived from the interactions of these basic issues.

From this perspective, we can say that the function of advertising is to symbolize the statuses and aspirations of human identities; and that is how it is interpreted by consumers. We can see this by using examples of how they react to advertisements. Sometimes the reaction is a direct assertion of this point as shown by this bright teenager commenting on milk commercials:

> They should show you a famous ball player through all the life stages; how drinking milk helped him to get where he is today. Start at 7 to 8, show him in the various life stages. These ads don't show me what I want to be.

PRODUCT MEANING

More often, we see less directly how consumers react to advertising as they make inferences about its meaning to them. A primary source of meaning is the product itself. What an ad is about sets up a core that is modified by the other content of the ad and its executional character. Table 25.1 is an example about the beverage industry, which was developed to show how product characteristics and effects are related to the attribution of meaning and inferred suitability for kinds of consumers.

Going from left to right in Table 25.1, this hierarchical structure shows that products are representations, that their forms and features are given meanings. These meanings are ideas about the nature of the product, what it does to and for the users who drink it (who show themselves as users of it, who serve it, and so on). Reading from the bottom, the table sketches in how consumption changes with growing up. In the process, people move from dependence toward autonomy. They gain more self-control and freedom of choice in satisfying appetites. The ability to make subtler discriminations among sensations and tastes, and to tolerate greater intensities, increases, allowing the formation of individual identities. The mature person is free to be self-indulgent or even addictive in self-expression. By becoming acculturated and more refined, learning "unnatural" tastes, people show how far from being animals they are.

There is a parallelism in being young and being lower in social status, at least so that higher status people see lower status people as more gross and less mature than themselves. Lower class-ness also can seem more (traditionally) masculine as drinking milk and beer is associated with males, with imbibing large quantities, and with a boyish liking for sweets and orientation to physical strength. However, in other instances, drinking stronger beverages is seen as more mature, higher status, and also as masculine: strong coffee compared with weaker and more feminine tea.

In tracing how ideas about beverages interact with those about people, the symbolic vocabulary inherent in the structure may be further abstracted. Table 25.2 illustrates that product perceptions are patterns of the meanings derived from consumption effects, preparation processes, colors, quantities, and variety. It says that as consumption effects move from emphasis on nutrition and relatively bland taste to increasing emphasis on intensity of taste and stimulation of "mind altering" sorts, they become perceived as more mature and higher in status. They derive from natural resources and simple processing up through more complex methods of preparation. They move from being light in color through colorfulness to darkness. They go from being consumed in large quantities to smaller units and from homogeneity to heterogeneity in the substances themselves and/or in the variety available for choice.

Parallel to these shifts is movement from perception of virtue to relative vice. The lower levels imply more passivity, then up toward energy and activity and increased sensationalism. Accompanying the evils seen in intoxication, addiction, and other hazards of caffeine and alcohol are ideas of sophistication, potency, vigor, subtlety of discrimination, richness of experience, and depth of thought that surround drinking coffee, wine connoisseurship, and deciding among Grand Marnier, Drambuie, and Kahlua.

The structure suggests boundaries within which products and brands are managed by use of the symbolic vocabulary.

TABLE 25.1 The Synchronic Beverage Structure

Object	Form	Attribute	Meaning	Segment
Alcoholic beverages			Intoxication	Adults
Liqueur	Brandies	Distilled wine	Sipping	Elite
			Intensity	Gourmets
			Discrimination	
Wine	Chateaux labels	Vineyards	Romance	Cosmopolites
		Fermenting	Snobbery	
Whiskey	Scotch	Aging	Sophistication	Upper class
	Bourbon	Grains	Hard drinking	Mature
	Vodka			
	Gin			
Wine	Domestic	Grapes	Low alcohol	Young adults
	Jug			Liberalism
Beer	Foreign	Brewing	Sociability	College men
	Tap	Grains	Democracy	Working class
	Bottle			
	Can			
	Barrel			
Coffee and tea		Caffeine	Pick-up, comfort	Adults
Coffee	Espresso	Brewing	Busyness	Mature adults
	American	Beans	Thought	
			Bitterness	
Tea	Exotic	Leaves	Depth	Old ladies
			Warmth	Ethnics
			Richness	
Soft drinks		Carbonation	Festivity	Adolescents
	Colas	Syrup	Youth	Young adults
		Nuts	Autonomy	Teens
	Fruit sodas	Fruit	Ambivalence	Kids
Fruit drinks		Natural Essence		Healthy people
	Juices	Acidity	Breakfast	Good eaters
		Squeezing	Tartness	Kids
			Virtue	
	Ades	Diluting	Fun	
Soup			Survival	Family
	Vichysoisse	Cooking	Tradition	Ethnics
	Chicken	Meat	Nourishment	Family
	Vegetable		Home	
			Mother	
Milk	Milking		Dependency	Offspring
	Chocolate	Blend	Enhancement	Older kids
	Cow's	Grass	Growth	(Old people)
	Breast	Nature	Mother	Babies
Water	Mineral	Neutral	Thirst	Everyone
	Plain	Clear	Existence	

SOURCE: Compiled by the author.

TABLE 25.2 Symbolic Vocabulary

Preparation	Color	Variety	Quantity	Impact	Meanings	
Complexity	Dark	Heterogeneity	Small units	Intense taste	Discriminating	
						Exclusive
Distillation		of Substance	Sips	Burning	Sophisticated	
Fermenting		or Choice	Jiggers	Dry, sour	Intoxicating	Mature
					Evil	
					Experimental	Classy
Brewing				Bloating	Relaxing	
Steeping	Deep hues			Addicting	Thoughtful	
				Bitter		Adult
Carbonation	Colorful			Burping	Social	
Squeezing				Tart	Autonomous	
					Conventional	
					Playful	
	Light			Sweet		Young
Heating					Nutritious	
Natural elements					Dependent	
Simplicity	Colorless	Homogeneity	Large units	Bland	Virtuous	
					Immature	Universal

TABLE 25.3 The Core Dynamism

Product Feature	Sensation	Perception	Apperception	Motivation	Identity of Segment
External reality	Experiencing product features	Integration of perception	Interpretation of perception	Movement toward or away	Demography

Making milk darker by adding chocolate, for example, raises it in the hierarchy and makes it less immature. Adding alcohol to milk is unacceptable for consumption by children by making the milk too mature. However, adding milk to alcohol to make, say, a Brandy Alexander, moves the alcoholic beverage down the hierarchy toward being less potent, a younger and more feminine drink for adults.

ADVERTISING AND THE CORE DYNAMISM

The assertion of the product with its particular features and how the segments perceive and apperceive it are at the core of the exchange process. The interaction is a dynamic one, changing over time, and involving conflict and mutuality, negotiation, conciliation, and disruption. Thus we may say that the core dynamism describes the specific diagnostic content summarizing who the people in the market segment are and their particular pattern of apperception, motivation, and action toward the product (see Table 25.3).

In learning about the product the customer senses its physical attributes en route to forming perceptions of it. Brands of products contrast with one another along a continuum of degrees of physical difference. In some product areas people have no diffi-

TABLE 25.4 A Thematic Universe

1 How Product Is Made	2 Product Function and Feature	3 Product Benefit	4 Brand Differen- tiation	5 Demography and Sociology	6 Users' Attitude	7 Users' Motive and Its Source
Freeze dried	4 in front, 8 in back	An end to the knocks in your car	No. 1 brand	For executive decisions	More people enjoy V.O.'s taste than any other import	For those who value beauty
Shot from guns	Private tutoring	The aluminum can conserves energy and natural resources	The costliest perfume in the world	Moon watchers Working women		Everyone needs a little comfort
Slow brewed	Soft and supple	Speak Spanish like a diplomat	When E. F. Hutton talks, people listen		You'll be amazed	You're in business to make money
Hand rubbed			Only Pella offers it all			

culty sensing physical differences that actually ("scientifically") exist among brands. In other areas science says there are no differences in the products among its brands, but people believe there are, and in a third case almost everyone believes there are no differences, the brands all being the same commodity. Buyers and sellers are usually interested in finding and creating differences, so there seems less interest in declaring that brands with real differences are the same (although cheap copies and counterfeits try to do this).

In all instances, if there are brands of products, core dynamisms arise based on differential perceptions. That is, images are created that enable customers to make choices among brands, whether or not the brands are physically different. These images are influenced by the associations and evaluations induced by the elements of the marketing mix; and advertising plays its special role in affecting apperceptions. Just

as the product's physical characteristics are interpreted for their symbolic significance, so too are the advertising stimuli. These include all the basic lines, colors, shapes, sounds, smells, and textures that advertising may convey, as well as the more organized experiences in words, sentences, objects, music, and people presented. All these elements are put together in support of advertising themes. The focus of an advertising message is drawn from a universe of such themes.

A THEMATIC UNIVERSE

Table 25.4 illustrates a range of categories of sources for advertising themes with examples casually gleaned from advertisements. Category 1 consists of how the product was made, such as "freeze dried" or "shot from guns." Methods of manufacture, processes, care, technology, historical development, and so on are ways of referring to the origins of the product, thus being product oriented and usually factual in tone. At another level of product orientation, Category 2 refers to facts and ideas about the features of the product, including perhaps how those features work, such as "4 in front, 8 in back" or "private tutoring." Category 3 moves a step away from focusing on the product per se by telling about the benefit to be derived from using the product, whether generally, as in "the aluminum can . . . conserves energy and natural resources," or more specifically, as in "an end to the knocks in your car," or "speak Spanish like a diplomat."

Categories 1, 2, and 3 may be ways of achieving brand differentiation, but Category 4 notes those claims or assertions that focus explicitly on that idea, such as "No. 1 brand" or "the costliest perfume in the world."

Categories 5, 6, and 7 focus more directly on the target markets, their characteristics, their attitudes, and their motives. Category 5 addresses the segmentation by identifying the group at issue, as in "for executive decisions" or "moon watchers." Category 6 is directed toward reports of reactions to the product or brand that have occurred or are promised, as in "more people enjoy V.O.'s taste than any other import." Category 7 aims at more specific identification of the desires that will be gratified by use of the product and brand: "for those who value beauty."

It is evident that these categories are not mutually exclusive and cannot be. All seven categories can be interpreted as ways of achieving brand differentiation and are in the service of that goal. However, Category 4 refers to specific claims of superlativeness or uniqueness. The thematic foci are inter-

mingled, also, for two main reasons. First, advertisements never say or show only one thing, so that regardless of emphasis, other points along the continuum will be included. For example, an ad referring to "the expert's choice" most readily falls into Category 3 because it defines a segment—experts. But the reference to experts also reminds us of the motives that go with the achievement and maintenance of expertise, thereby fitting Category 7, and the reference to choice expresses the attitude of preference attributed to the experts, thus fitting Category 6. In another instance, when Cuisinart says, "our most important products are more enthusiastic cooks," the complexity of this theme can be interpreted in many ways. The reference to "cooks" fits Category 5 by specifying a segment, those who prepare food. (That may seem obvious or natural, but they could have named other segments such as gift givers or busy people or working women, and so on.) They are also claiming superiority for Cuisinart (Category 4) by referring to "our" results. The "enthusiastic" emotion attributed to the group points to the attitude of Category 6. The product benefit (Category 3) is also the gaining of the enthusiastic attitude.

The second reason that makes categorizing themes somewhat difficult is the fact that through various symbolic connections, themes from each point on the thematic continuum imply something about the other points. That is, if a theme refers to the way the product is made, the audience makes inferences from that message. Thus, a theme from Category 1 may be interpreted to mean that the product functions well, that it has quality features, that it is relatively costly, that it is superior to other brands, that it seeks a market of upper-status customers or would appeal to technically minded, masculine segments who are interested in how things are made.

Similarly, if the focal theme stresses that the brand successfully differs from others by selling greater quantity, it implies that the manufacturing is standardized at a reliable level, the product has a mainstream price, and it is used by relatively conforming people.

Such generalized relationships are modified in actual instances by the nature of the product, its number and kind of competition, the ingenuity of the advertising in combining specific points along the continuum, and the style of presentation. The tone of the approach, the use of sex, fear, humor (Sternthal & Craig, 1973, 1974), and the subtleties of art form will carry implications for Points 1 through 7. The appeal of "sheer style" can itself be so great as to seem to make specific product claims irrelevant—as, for example, with the ambiguity of what is actually being said in the surrealistic commercials for Chanel No. 5.

A Study of Thematic Inference

A qualitative study was carried out empirically to explore the way given advertising themes are communicated; that is, the relation between the words used and the interpretations of them by readers. The project was a marketing research study in which six advertising concepts were evaluated. The aim was a general one of gaining insight into how consumers of a food product might respond to the creative possibilities developed by the advertising agency. The six concepts were each printed on a board below a picture of the product package (a well-known processed food). Each concept was embodied in a verbal statement in a paragraph of five to eight lines.

In individual interviews, respondents discussed their use of the product, their brand preferences, and each of the concepts. They talked about their reactions to each concept, how it fit the brand, the meanings and values of the ideas, the kinds of people who might find them appealing; the six concepts were systematically compared for their interest, attention-getting, believability, maturity, modernity, informativeness, and appeals to men and women.

The six concepts had much in common. All praised the product, used some similar language, and generally conveyed the point that this is a high-quality brand. However, it was evident from the discussions that respondents penetrated through the overlapping verbiage in the statements to their main ideas or strategic points. For example, although all were concerned with quality, one of the statements was distinguished by its focus on the central ingredient as of the finest, highest quality. This concept was identified as being the "High Quality" theme. In the other statements the quality idea was handled with different emphases as indicated in Table 25.5. The second concept emphasized quality as of an exclusive order. It mentioned quality ingredients, superior taste and value for extra cost, but respondents' reactions focused especially on the phrase "your most demanding standards." The main theme was identified as "High Standards." The third statement praised the flavor as consistent and the product as guaranteed, thereby reassuring the consumer through use of a "Reliability" theme.

The fourth concept was a statement about the history of the brand. It was described as having a century of experience and expertise and was therefore identified as a theme of "Tradition." A fifth approach cited results of a taste test that proved the client's brand won out over other major

TABLE 25.5 Thematic Inferences

Stimulus	Theme	Meaning	Segment
1. "Finest, freshest . . . highest quality"	High quality	Basic claim Taste appeal Simple direct company pride Innocuous Conventional	For people who want good things For young people, "with it" people For habitually loyal Diffuse segmentation for "everyone" Not for indifferent or opposed
2. "only . . . your most demanding standards . . . always freshest"	High standards	Superlatives, exaggerated Exclusive, snobbish Costly	For fussy people, discriminating Health buffs For high status people Not for poor working class
3. "Consistently . . . guaranteed proof"	Reliability	Company pride Avoid waste	Wise shoppers Brand loyalists Not for impulsive
4. "Heritage dating back . . . century of experience"	Tradition	Merit, to survive Outdated, dull Intellectual	For mature upscale serious people Not for young, "now" hedonistic people
5. "Recent taste test . . . clearly preferred"	Preferred brand	Valid quality Advertising gimmick Conventionality	For committed users For followers, conformers Not for suspicious, individual
6. "made with special . . . technique"	Production method	Technical, informative Basic, complex	Rational, specialized Masculine Not for unintellectual

brands—thus, a "Preferred Brand" theme. The sixth concept statement described a special technique used to make the product, indicating this was a source of its quality, a "Production Methods" theme. Table 25.5 also shows in a summary way how respondents interpreted the themes as they developed further implications about

brand meanings. They interpreted what the company is trying to say or accomplish; they made deductions about what must be true of a company that makes those claims, whether or not those ideas were intended; and they drew inferences about the kinds of people who would or would not find the themes and their meanings appealing.

These interpretations illustrate the process of moving from verbal advertising stimuli to apperceptions of them. They suggest that the commonly measured issues of believability, recall, and persuasion of advertising themes may be less important than—or are importantly related to—meanings and relevance to segments. The respondents' associations are revealing, and have a kind of transparent or plausible logic, once expressed. They also imply that themes are not good or bad per se but are always suitable to some core dynamism, reaffirming the need for clarity of aims. The "Tradition" theme may be termed dull or old fashioned, but it is seen as likely to appeal to serious people who are interested in historical facts, higher status people who value lineage as a source of distinction, and older people who value memories and can identify with having long-established characters.

Sometimes the respondents' interpretations have a certain subtlety, revealing a logic that goes beyond the one ordinarily in the advertiser's mind. The "Preferred Brand" theme claimed that the brand was clearly preferred in a recent taste test. People recognize that the intention of such a claim is to demonstrate that the product must have a valid quality in order to be the chosen one, perhaps with the added idea that just asserting a quality claim would not do, that some skepticism needs to be overcome by proof. For many that is certainly a convincing idea, one they are willing to go along with. Others, however, notice that the claim implies a majority vote, as there is less point to claiming that only some people preferred it (unless a discriminating group was identified, in which case it would become a "High Standards" theme, or perhaps an "Elite" theme). The inference, then, is that the product must be for conventional people who want to conform to common tastes, the sort who do not mind being told by a salesperson that "everybody's wearing it."

This project illustrates how a particular group of creative personnel tried out claims that they believed are competitive in asserting the merits of their brand. The study showed the way consumers interpret the advertising stimuli to have meaning beyond their references to the product.

REFERENCES

Becker, E. (1962). *The birth and death of meaning*. New York: Free Press.

Erikson, E. (1982). *The life cycle completed*. New York: Norton.

Sternthal, B., & Craig, C. S. (1973). Humor in advertising. *Journal of Marketing, 37*, 12-18.

Sternthal, B., & Craig, C. S. (1974). Fear appeals revisited and revised. *Journal of Consumer Research, 1*, 22-34.

## Chapter 26

SEMIOTICIAN ORDINAIRE

Sidney J. Levy

I will start with some personal notes. Many thanks are due to Jean Umiker-Sebeok, who called me last year to suggest that this conference be developed, and who ably undertook to make the many arrangements that turned the plan into reality for our enjoyment today. I had realized only vaguely that a few other marketing people were paying specific attention to semiotics—for example, and notably, Holman's 1981 article on the topic—and I hadn't noticed that many semioticians were interested in marketing. (I also suspect that some of them will not appreciate the interaction that we are cultivating with this program.) Think-

ing about the conference reminds me of the thrust of my own activities in relation to a semiotic approach.

I think back to when the Marketing Department of Kellogg School hired Trudy Kehret-Ward, psycholinguist turned marketing scholar, and to our regret when her career moved her from us to California, taking away the lively exposure to ideas about syntactics and paradigmatics that she provided. I remember my surprise at the growing reception accorded writings of mine that expressed my interest in symbolism in the marketplace: "The Product and the Brand" (Gardner & Levy, 1955), "Sym-

This chapter was first published in J. Umiker-Sebeok (Ed.), *Marketing and Semiotics*, 1987, pp. 13-20. Reprinted by permission of Mouton de Gruyter, a Division of Walter de Gruyter.

bols for Sale" (Levy, 1959), *Living With Television* (Glick & Levy, 1962), "Symbolism and Life Style" (Levy, 1963), and "Interpreting Consumer Mythology" (Levy, 1981), the latter an analysis partly stimulated by my reading of Levi-Strauss. Still, bringing novelty to marketing research is not so difficult, given its youth as a field of study and its relative willingness to draw from other useful disciplines. But I have not claimed identification as a semiotician, and I am not sure whether semioticians are an interest group or that credentials are needed to qualify. If I am a semiotician, I discover that with the surprise of the fellow who was delighted to learn that he spoke prose. Certainly, I am an everyday kind of semiotician, a beginner who confesses that some of the semiotic literature I've recently examined seems so abstract and obscure to me, so humanistically scholarly, as to be quite intimidating. Even such a user-friendly work as *The Name of the Rose* made me regret the lack of Latin in my preparatory education.

Thus, the program we are going to share here makes me eagerly anticipate what I am going to learn from the way people in the marketing field have been making use of semiotic thought, and especially from the way professional semioticians have approached marketing analysis.

If you will indulge the excursus, it might be useful to suggest how my ordinary semiotic interests arose and to relate them to the historic process of marketing study as I encountered it. I first became aware of symbolic meaning, of myth and fantasy, when I was a child and read my way through a substantial portion of that special kind of literature found in the Red, Blue, Green, and Brown books of fairy tales, Greek mythology, Norse mythology, Aesop's fables, the Brothers Grimm, Hans

Christian Andersen, and the *Thousand and One Nights*. In my progress from Mother Goose through Beowulf, I benefitted from these stories in many ways, probably more so than I can describe, reconstruct, or deconstruct here.

My joy in reading was enhanced by a continual sense of wonder and marvel at these stories. They were informative, frightening, and funny; I believed and I disbelieved—almost. I thought that anything is possible, that anything can happen, that human beings are happily and sadly capable of anything, and I have never totally shaken that thought. Apart from the quotidian world of life in a middle-class family and Chicago elementary schools was that strange other world: Once upon a time, long ago and far away, seemed to mean a past world, but happy ever after could still be going on right now somewhere out there. Then it may be that surprises still lurk, that one might wish hard enough or wisely enough, or say the magic word that would be the open sesame to fabulous sights. Did I dream that I would marry a sweet princess, the daughter of an eagle (her maiden name is Adler) or that my younger sister, so earnest a tag-a-long, would one day be wife to an ambassador at the Court of St. James? How is it my son is a Merlin of pure mathematics, that my daughter interprets the law of the realm, projecting from precedent to brief to judgment?

From these tales I derived the conviction that I was very likely a foundling whose true greatness would one day be revealed, freeing me from having to be socialized in ordinary ways. The stories comforted me that the terrible things I feared in my childhood of poverty, parental illness, aggressive peers, and lightning and thunder were like the wolves, monsters, dragons, and wicked people I read about that would be vanquished by heroes, by friendly woodcutters, by the intervention of magical forces. Jack and the Beanstalk, Hansel and Gretel, St. George, and such survivors as Sinbad and Odysseus showed me that I could make it, too.

Most wonderful, perhaps, this literature taught me that it was better to know than not to know, that there was meaning, both obvious and hidden, to be sought, even if it might be dangerous. Out of Pandora's Box came trouble and eventually hope; the locked rooms, the caves, the chests, the bottles: Each had to be opened—perhaps to genie, treasure, or trauma, but opened, nevertheless, because we have to seek and to know. To be free, we must learn the name of Rumpelstiltskin.

Speaking of names, which have always intrigued me, a great moment of revelation came when I realized that my name carries many meanings. Sidney comes from Dionysus, by way of St. Dion and St. Denis; a levy is a tax, a riverbank, a royal reception; and Levites were an ancient sacred caste guarding the temple at Jerusalem. I could enjoy those meanings as substantial and positive, affirming that I was a foundling with royal antecedents. Then I was astounded to realize that Sidney Levy, when spelled backwards, was Yendis Yvel. The hidden meanings there pointed to a yen, a yearning for dis, which is negative, hard, bad; and yvel, or evil. The foundling was a changeling!—a monster had been substituted for the prince. These early discoveries unleashed in me an awareness of the complex levels of meaning. Levy(i) was live but could also be evil and vile; between the good and the bad was perhaps a veil, to save us from being reviled. Everyone has a secret self.

How excited I was at that time to read Hayakawa's (1941) *Language in Action*

and to discover something called General Semantics; it was like a reveille calling to announce that words and things were different. Hayakawa led to that weighty and esoteric tome, *Science and Sanity,* by Count Alfred Korzybski (1933), and his model of the Structural Differential, which hangs in my mind like a sculpture by Miró.

With this background, I was drawn into interdisciplinary study with the Committee on Human Development at the University of Chicago and began my career of investigating the significance to people of companies, products, brands, media, advertisements, persons, and lifestyles. I was increasingly struck by the way motivation interacts with perception—that is, how people's motives lead them to perceive meaning in the objects they encounter and how the meanings of those objects affect their motives. Intrigued by personality study and projective techniques, I studied the Thematic Apperception Technique, learning how to interpret people's storytelling as an avenue to understanding them.

Coming to work in the field of marketing research, I saw how the participants in the marketplace symbolize their lives in the products and brands they consume and also how they tell each other stories in pursuit of their aims. I devoted myself to reading, analyzing, and elucidating those symbols and their patternings.

I was there at the right time in the late 1940s and 1950s. Earlier, intelligence testing had come weightily out of World War I, spurring measurement of human mental levels and abilities and interest in surveying attitudes and opinions. Personality testing burgeoned out of World War II, fostering clinical assessment, intensifying the interest in psychoanalysis and in the use of projective techniques. Anthropological study contributed its ideas about cultural differences and symbolic analysis. The behavioral sciences were thriving, alive with great names, financial support, and excitement about the insight to be gained into human life. In the marketing field, this sense of promise was experienced as various phenomena under the heading of Motivation Research, with the use of depth interviews and projective methods, and narrowly ascribed to the skillful Freudian interpretations provided by Ernest Dichter. The social anthropological approach of W. Lloyd Warner and Burleigh B. Gardner, my mentors at Social Research, Inc., was also acknowledged.

In the 1960s and 1970s, that excitement moderated, as the behavioral sciences and socioeconomic realities did not appear able to provide the Great Society that some had dreamed of. In the face of the recalcitrance of social and psychological problems, the convenience of pharmaceutical intervention, and the facile neurology of right and left brain lateralism, it was replaced with elements of skepticism, disillusionment, and indifference.

Similarly, interest among marketing personnel abated, Motivation Research was said to have died, and attention largely shifted to the systematic measurement that was so readily aided by the rise of the computer. New promise came not from depth psychologies but from cognitive psychology. But Motivation Research never died. It settled down to be carried out by Dichter and several other workers, including my associates at Social Research, Inc., and myself, under the heading of motivational studies, qualitative analyses, and the like. There arose the marketing research vogue of using data conveniently gained from small-group discussions, called focus groups, and the custom of equating this work with qualitative research. Marketing

people need information to nourish their decisions, and focus groups are the fast food of marketing research.

In more recent years, the pendulum has swung again to some degree. Just as people alternate between asceticism and indulgence, liberalism and conservatism, realism and fantasy, they move between the need to find meaning and to measure. The sense of solidity and reassurance found in measurement is eminently satisfying to some people; they agree with the dictum that if something exists, it exists in some quantity and may be measured. But other workers find measurement barren and superficial. They believe that if something exists, it must have a meaning. They want to dig deeper. They relish the constant involvement in the complexities of language, verbal and nonverbal, and believe that we do not understand enough if we do not understand the richness of motivation and perception, and how these interact and influence each other.

We marketing students and semioticians are here to extend our ideas to each other. As a diverse group we have the opportunity for a stimulating and informative exchange. But we come with various preconceptions about marketing and semiotics, and I think there is much room for misunderstanding. Generally, marketing people are pragmatic: They are likely to be receptive to semiotics if it seems to be another useful discipline for analyzing marketing phenomena. But many will be put off, believing that semiotics is mainly a classificatory approach or that it does not seem amenable to measurement or is not useful in making predictions about behavior. There may be negative reactions from those who think semiotics is too "soft," or subjective, merely linguistic, or overly abstract. Probably many will candidly admit that they do not know what semiotics is and will not work to relieve their ignorance.

Among those who are not marketing professionals, we can anticipate many of the usual reactions to marketing. Most people think they know what marketing is. It is also evident that they define it in negative terms. Common tendencies are to equate marketing with bad advertising, pushy salesmen, and shoddy goods; sometimes one or all of these are lumped together to equate marketing with the evils of the capitalist system. While it may seem difficult to refute these notions, given the ease with which bad examples can be found, I would like to suggest a more open-minded perspective.

In my view, a scientific examination of marketing does not rush to judge it (as an idea), or its manifestations in advertising, to be good or bad. Rather, it seeks objectively to define what physical and mental activities constitute marketing, to observe when and how those activities go on, and to elucidate the principles that govern their occurrence. Old-fashioned definitions of marketing said it was synonymous with the activities involved in distributing goods, or with the methods of achieving transfer of their ownership. More recently, marketing was said to be concerned with satisfying wants and needs. These goals or necessities still linger, but a more objective focus has shifted to the core idea of marketing as an exchange process.

A modern, penetrating, sophisticated perception of marketing recognizes that it is an exchange process that goes on everywhere people interact, exchanging goods, services, and/or money. In this view, there are no nonmarket economics, and marketing is not only a capitalistic activity. The content of the marketing mix may differ in the kinds of goods, services, and ideas of-

fered, in the kinds of payments made, in the kinds of communications and distribution channels used. But whether in socialist or capitalist countries, whether in developed or developing countries, marketing exchanges are going on. All of their variations can be studied—and judged according to one's values. But some introspection into the semiotics of one's judgments may be fruitful in distinguishing between the analysis and the opinions of the analyst.

Many marketing people do not want to bother with the controversies that go on among those who theorize about content and methods, philosophies, and ideologies. Because they want to innovate, they mainly seek fresh ideas and new bases for taking action. I have found such individuals encouraging and willing to support marketing research that tries to penetrate the veil that all persons use to bound and protect their inner selves. That means being willing to face up to the challenge of interpreting beyond literal meaning and to acknowledge human motives beyond such conventionally virtuous ones as saving money, being sociable, or seeking durable goods. Recognition of the richness of symbolism accepts the fact of levels in the human personality and may revel in that fact. That view does not revile interpretation or dismiss it out of hand and explicitly respects the necessity of moving from the surface of actions to inferences about invisible elements.

It is not enough to accept the attributes of products as the sources of distinction among them, as conventional marketing analysis is prone to do, resting in such ideas as ingredients, price, size, color, and packaging. The distinctions influencing human action arise from the attributions made by and to persons. Then, one is interested not only in what is signified by the signifier in a general, abstract, or universal sense, but also how it may vary in meaning to different kinds of people. As a psychologist, I have trouble remembering that the word *signifier* refers to the object or its features, thinking instead that the signifier must be the person who has the meaning in mind, that people do the signifying. As students of marketing, we are interested in semiotics for what it can tell us about how people use language, to help us in making progress toward greater comprehension of what people are doing when they communicate. We seek breadth of perspective in learning as well as greater nuance and subtlety. Others may be as shy as I am, a naive, plain semiotician, using language, signs, and symbols in our everyday ways, and in our playful ways, but hoping to become more worldly.

I see our conference as an intellectual voyage; like Sinbad, we may be captivated and we may capsize. But in this venture on the Semiotic Seas, it will be exciting to discuss the role of language in its various verbal, visual, physical, and body manifestations; in its semiotic study; and in its application to marketing. It is especially appropriate that the next speaker is Tom Sebeok, not only because of his eminent position in the field of semiotics, but because if we are to hear the word, it is only fitting that, spelled backward, Tom means just that, *le Mot*.

REFERENCES

Gardner, B. B., & Levy, S. J. (1955, March/April). The product and the brand. *Harvard Business Review,* pp. 33-39.

Glick, I., & Levy, S. J. (1962). *Living with television.* Chicago: Aldine.

Hayakawa, S. I. (1941). *Language in action.* New York: Harcourt Brace.

Holman, R. (1981). Apparel as communication. In E. Hirschman & M. Holbrook (Eds.), *Symbolic consumer behavior* (pp. 7-15). Ann Arbor, MI: Association for Consumer Research.

Korzybski, A. (1933). *Science and sanity.* New York: International Non-Aristotelian Publishing Co.

Levy, S. J. (1959, July/August). Symbols for sale. *Harvard Business Review,* pp. 117-124.

Levy, S. J. (1963, December). Symbolism and life style. *Proceedings,* American Marketing Association Conference, pp. 140-150.

Levy, S. J. (1981). Interpreting consumer mythology: A structural approach to consumer behavior. *Journal of Marketing, 45,* 49-61.

PART
FIVE

CONSUMER ANALYSES
AND OBSERVATIONS

Synchrony and Diachrony in Product Perceptions (*Proceedings,* Association for Consumer Research, 1983)

Consumer Behavior in the United States: The Avid Consumer (Manuscript, 1987)

Effect of Recent Economic Experiences on Consumer Dreams, Goals, and Behavior in the United States (*Journal of Economic Psychology,* 1987)

Giving Voice to the Gift: The Use of Projective Techniques to Recover Lost Meanings (*Journal of Consumer Psychology* 1993)

Cultural Harmonies and Variations (Speech, Fourth International Conference on Marketing and Development, 1993)

———— •◆• ————

Dennis Rook: These 17 articles together constitute an interesting and sophisticated course in consumer behavior, and for readers who have already studied that subject, this material will provide a refresher course and a refreshing perspective. Despite the conventional wisdom that managers benefit from better understanding their customers, and the widely accepted directive to do so, marketing practice sometimes pays mere lip service to these tenets. Marketing plans often crudely characterize targeted consumers with broad demographic parameters (e.g., the omnipresent "housewives 18-49"), with a few pithy references to their lifestyles as "active" or "aspirational." Obviously, consumers' behaviors are more complex and multifaceted, and Sid Levy has spent a lifetime explaining how managers and researchers can achieve richer, deeper, and more useful analyses of their consumers.

At the core of Levy's analyses of consumer behavior is an interdisciplinary orientation. Most contemporary marketing theorists readily acknowledge the interdisciplinary nature of marketing, but marketing studies rarely reflect this fact. While marketing analyses draw from a variety of scholarly behavioral disciplines—most obviously psychology, sociology, economics, and anthropology—the vast majority of research arises within the confines of a single, encapsulated field or subfield (e.g., cognitive psychological experiments). Relatively little research actually reaches across disciplinary boundaries, but it is this integrative quality that distinguishes Sid Levy's writings.

Levy's approach to studying consumers relies on what he calls a polyfocal vision, which he elaborates in the lead article to this section, "Constructing Consumer Behavior: A Grand Template" (1991). In 1991, as president of the Association for Consumer Research, Sid Levy presented the traditional Presidential Address to a crowd of over 600 leading consumer researchers. This paper provides an excellent introduction to the various modes of thinking that consumer researchers use or might consider to expand their perspectives. The other articles included here demonstrate how Levy applies his integrative orientation to studying a wide variety of consumer concerns.

Also, these writings serve as historical evidence of Sid Levy's seminal role in defining the conceptual boundaries of consumer behavior and in introducing behavioral science thinking and methods to the field of consumer research. "The Cake Eaters" (1957) is an early yet timeless analysis of the psychosocial tensions that influence consumers' choices about spending versus saving their money. As the growing American economy increased both consumers' spending power and the number and variety of products vying for attention, these consumption tensions become even more relevant. Levy's "Psychosocial Reactions to the Abundant Society" (1967), his "The Discretionary Society" (1970), and the more recent "Consumer Behavior in the United States: The Avid Consumer" (1987) expand and update his thinking about this core consumer dynamism.

Sid Levy's psychological analyses of consumers draw particularly from his training in psychoanalytic theories, life cycle developmental theories, and theories of personality. His writings have made substantial and original contributions toward the application of these perspectives to consumer analyses. He was, also, a pioneer in studying the profound effects of social stratification on consumption behavior. "Social Class and Consumer Behavior" (1966) is a provocative and often amusing article that illustrates various manifestations of social strata effects, and I hope it encourages some readers to study them more explicitly and vigorously. Levy's longstanding emphasis on marketplace symbols and their cultural meanings laid the groundwork for the emergence of anthropological consumer research in the 1980s. His delightful article, "Emotional Reactions to the Cutting of Trees" (1973), focuses on the powerful cultural symbolism of the tree and provides a refreshing alternative to the contemporary "good-guy/bad-guy" mentality of much discussion about environmental issues in marketing.

Levy's basic thinking extends to particular problems, and several articles illustrate how he analyzes various consumer segments. That central enduring marketing figure of the past 50 years—the American housewife—is analyzed with insight and prescience in "Looking at the Ladies, Lately" (1960). Reflecting the growing interest in marketing from nonprofit organizations (a development which he anticipated in 1958's "Motivation Research" and in 1969's "Broadening the Concept of Marketing"), Levy analyzes the motivations for arts consumption in "Arts Consumers and Aesthetic Attributes" (1980). Several of his pieces reflect his alert, realistic observations of American life: An added example included here is a specific study with Ruby Roy Dholakia on the "Effect of Recent Economic Experiences on Consumer Dreams, Goals, and Behavior in the United States" that appeared in the *Journal of Economic Psychology,* (8, 1987, pp. 429-444).

In his nearly 50 years with Social Research, Inc., initially as a part-time employee, and ultimately as its head, Sidney Levy conducted many hundreds of studies that investigated consumer behavior in numerous product categories. Although we cannot include these proprietary studies here, several articles point to his distinctive, integrative analytic approach to investigating consumers' product category experiences. I collaborated with him on two of these; the first, "Social Division and Aesthetic Specialization: The Middle Class and Musical Events" (1980), examines how consumers experiment with different musical milieu, develop psychosocial preferences, and become fans of a particular type of musical product. In "Psychosocial Themes in Consumer Grooming Rituals" (1983), we demonstrate that beyond conventional concerns about hygiene, consumers' grooming behavior and product purchases are motivated by social, vocational, sexual, and fantasy factors.

Another insightful analysis of consumer behavior in the beverage category appears in "Synchrony and Diachrony in Product Perceptions" (1983). Finally, in his recent "Giving Voice to the Gift: The Use of Projective Techniques to Recover Lost Meanings" (1993), Levy and co-authors Mary Ann McGrath and John Sherry, Jr., creatively explore the complexities of buyer behavior in the billion-dollar domain of gift giving. I hope that the writings in this section show the reader that consumer research is an exciting, complex, and humanistic enterprise and that Sidney Levy helped make it this way.

———— •◆• ————

## Chapter 27

CONSTRUCTING CONSUMER BEHAVIOR
A Grand Template

Sidney J. Levy

This is one of the most exciting times in my life. Some of you may not have realized when I was elected that you were getting the oldest president the Association for Consumer Research (ACR) has ever had. After 30 years at Northwestern University, I have just become a professor *emeritus*. For younger presidents of ACR, election was a fine achievement along the way; for me, it is a kind of culmination or peak of a long career. I submitted my first professional article to the *Journal of Educational Psychology* in 1946; and I recently received an acceptance for the December 1991 issue of the *Journal of Consumer Research*.

It was hard to decide what to talk about today. The good thing was, I had 2 years to think about it since I was elected. The bad thing was, I had to think about it for 2 years. Being a thorough-going obsessive academic, I've had many a sleepless night ruminating about what to say. By now, I

This chapter was first presented as the Presidential Address at the 1991 meeting of the Association for Consumer Research. It was published in B. Sternthal & J. F. Sherry (Eds.), *Advances in Consumer Research* (Vol. 19, pp. 1-6), Provo, UT: Association for Consumer Research.

may actually have forgotten most of my best ideas.

Presidential talks have many possibilities. They are often concerned with urging us toward excellence or creativity. They recall our glorious history and the giants on whose shoulders we stand. They appraise the state of the art, explaining how new methods and new subjects are changing our realms of inquiry. They may look to the future, telling where we are going or where we should be going; Morris Holbrook (1990) recently told us that we should be more lyrical, and last year Elizabeth Hirschman (1991) asked that we be more concerned with contemporary problems such as crime, prostitution, and addiction. When I finally settled to it, I decided that when all was said and done, the only thing I could do was to be myself and to talk about my current preoccupations. What they amount to is a summary of how I think about the study of consumer behavior, in keeping with the integrative thrust in Erik Erikson's (1982) description of the elderly stage of life. I keep thinking about the multiple ways we have of explaining the Consumer Event.

When I started formal study of consumer behavior in 1948, I had certain main interests as a graduate student in an interdisciplinary program. My work for a degree with the Committee on Human Development at the University of Chicago, made possible by the GI Bill, stimulated an enduring concern with the stages of the life cycle. I was absorbed in personality study, especially as expressed in psychoanalytic theories, and as investigated through the use of projective techniques. I also was thoroughly indoctrinated in the importance of stratification as a fact of social life.

These topics intrigued me. I was a set-up for the bold probing of depth psychology because I had always been a shy, introspective boy who read a lot, searching intently to learn about the mysteries of life, especially those related to sex and violence. At the time, I hardly even thought to expect explanations of these mysteries—it was enough to gain an increasingly vivid awareness of the enigmas of human history, the amazing complications of life as conveyed in school, in books, on the radio, and especially in the movies. For a suppressed and repressed boy growing up in a proper household and working class neighborhood, the fear of violence could be mastered somewhat by vicarious experience. There was also the possibility that in these media I might run into some exciting information or depiction of sex, to find out what people really did in private—that is, of course, other people who were beyond the hairy-handed Pee Wee Herman stage, who were more grown-up, more experienced, and more daring than I was. I remember being so irked and frustrated that the best parts of *The Decameron* of Boccaccio were in Latin. The newspapers recently reported a survey of the frequency with which men think about sex: an average of six times an hour. I'll probably use more times than my share during this talk, as I always remember the quotation in a study of sex, contraception, and family planning by Lee Rainwater (1960), from a subject who said, "Before I was married I was scared of sex. I thought it was a crime to do something like that. [Afterwards], I found out that . . . let's put it this way, if God made anything better he kept it to himself" (p. 97).

Depth psychology theories also please me because no matter how challenged or modified by their neo forms, they offer a sense of revelation, of taking us toward a layered understanding of the human psyche, with vigorous positions on what human nature is like, and how behavior arises from the ways our bodies and emerging personalities interact with our families, caretakers, and peers. Depth psychology recognizes issues that should be important in the study of consumer behavior: history, complexity, multi-causation, the symbolic and the evaluative character of experience. The role of motivation becomes salient; we are energetic, impulsive, surging creatures, so we cannot blame everything on external stimuli. And the power of perceived good and evil that we invest in all objects and actions plays its part. If we do not bring such richness to the study of consumer behavior, our constructs are simple, our variables are superficial, and results often just summarize observations or fit our intuition and mere common sense. Then we do not need much expertise. My colleague, Dipak Jain, tells me that in India dream interpreters say that happy dreams are bad omens and unhappy dreams are good portents. I realized that such contradictory complexity is wise and necessary; if only because were it not so, we would take the dreams at face value and would not then need the dream interpreters. In any event, we need subtlety because consumers commonly cannot adequately explain their own behavior, even if Scott Armstrong (1991) provides some evidence that they can predict it better than we can.

The study of social stratification is a way of becoming alert to the inevitability of hierarchy in human affairs. The uneven acquisition and distribution of resources, the different socioeconomic levels in society, make for outstanding variations in consumer behavior, pointing to the dynamic forces of aspiration and competition. As a Depression child, a poor boy in a family that was for a time on relief (as we called welfare then), I learned vividly the realities of some people having more and others having less. W. Lloyd Warner (1949) later taught me that every person occupies a social place that reflects how the community perceives the value of the individual's family status and participation. Circularly, that perception governs how much each of us gets in deference and money and is also based on how that income is translated into symbols of status belonging and expression. A recent survey by NORC showed how the prestige of 740 occupations was ranked by a sample of adults: surgeons, astronauts, lawyers, and college professors were ranked highly, whereas panhandlers and fortune tellers were at the bottom. Such knowledge fed my striving to be socially mobile and to associate with professors— although I confess fortune tellers are still among my best friends, and someone wrote a letter to the editor pointing out that St. Francis of Assisi was a panhandler. I am reminding us of these rudiments of psychology and sociology as a basis for my vision of our common enterprise in carrying out consumer research. I see us all working together in our various ways, seeking to construct and fill out a grand template of what consumer behavior is about. Following in the august steps of the Mendeléeff periodic table, which laid out a pattern of what was known and might be known of the world's chemical elements, of the various visualizations of the atom and the universe, and of the current efforts to map the human genome, I picture in my mind a large configuration that represents an ideal goal of the knowledge toward which we work. This configuration draws upon the many disciplines that contribute to the study of consumers, it respects the numerous methods that are used and encourages the contention of concepts that compete to provide explanations. Thus, this grand consumer research template is integrative and dynamic, organized and full of life.

The grand template stretches over the whole society and its structure, and by extension to other societies, so that we study across cultures to discern their commonalities and differences. Examining consumers in the large social groups that are geographically and culturally dispersed around the world superimposes the template over the globe. It has to address consuming at the level of the great millions of people wishing to be fed, clothed, and housed in basic, ongoing ways. This realm of problems connects us to a commodities-oriented and economics-oriented world in which consumers are at the mercy, often not so tender, of governments, nonprofit organizations, and the multinational corporations that provide or do not provide life's fundamentals of a viable housing stock, sustenance, and some fabric for dresses, shirts, and trousers, to say nothing of essential needs for health, education, and participation in the arts.

We may hope that some day those subsisting hungrily will be elevated to situations in which models of consumer brand choice suited to a prosperous environment will become more relevant to them also, although at even the most basic levels of consumption, one finds subtleties of preference and choice being exercised. The latitudes, longitudes, and isobars of international consumption bring forth issues of cultural diffusion, images of countries of origin, and how consumers will and will not retain their local identities in the face of globalization, the European Community, and the seductive and homogenizing effects of Coca-Cola, McDonald's, Levi's, and Disney parks. There is the need to reconcile and make sense of the admixtures of the old and the new. I recall seeing a timeless looking woman trudging down a street in Bangkok, wearing a coolie hat and traditional shift, bearing on her shoulder a pole with two suspended baskets of fruit. And on her feet were Reebok running shoes.

Thus, considerations of social stratification move us up and down among countries and societies in a Maslovian manner. Maslow is the source of a famous template; I have noticed that his hierarchy of needs is highly favored by students as one of the great explanatory devices of modern social science, and I grew up on it, too. It points to the consumer's need for basic satisfactions of feeding, security, love, and other sorts of intangible, ethereal, and emotional fulfillments, as well.

In forming the Grand Template, ideas about social stratification interact with ideas about the stages of the life cycle. People are born to the socioeconomic status of their families, and they absorb (and react against) the outlook and values provided by that social and interpersonal environment. These basic relations are paradigmatic, dramatized in the various famous Complexes of Oedipus, Electra, Orestes, and Tom Sawyer ("They'll be sorry when I'm dead and gone"). They act as a matrix and initial filter for all social relationships. As people mature in age, they may remain at the same social level or change their position through upward or downward mobility. These two important forms of hierarchy, social status and age, imply increasing superiority with greater levels. Centrally, this increasing superiority refers to having more power, economically and socially. This power is the ability to control and command more resources, ultimately to make more choices, even if the passage of time deletes others. If one remains at the same socioeconomic level, growing up leads to an increase in the resources and power accruing to adults and their increasing capacity to make choices. The nature of the choices—of how to live, what to buy, what to consume—is the outcome of the interaction of social status and age-grading with other main influences. Intertwining with social position and the life cycle are gender and sexuality, group memberships (race, peers, education, occupation, etc.), the nature and events of immediate situations, and the features of products. That is, the person—and as a person, a personality with developed perceptual and motivational propensities—arrives at the Consumer Event, whatever it is, more or less prepared to interpret it and to decide what to do about it.

The definition of the situation at each given moment in time and place is in various ways demanding, permissive, and constraining. It says what one can do, may do, might do, should do, must do, cannot do, and so on, and we professionals work, perhaps even struggle, to analyze scientifically how the consumer's selection among these possibilities is determined by a confluence of circumstances that make the consumer's performance a necessary outcome. If we knew J. Alfred Prufrock well enough, could we predict how he will wear his hair and roll his trousers, or if he would dare to eat a peach?

The choice (the apparent choice?) is the resultant of being that physical person of specific age, sex, social level, trained role, personality facets (self-concepts and attributions) in a mood that is under the influence of the weather, what was previously eaten, being delayed on the expressway, the imminence of a parental visit, the pressure of marketing promotions, and being confronted by products, people, services, and/or ideas of high, medium, or low involvement.

The grand template is a highly ramified nomological network, and everyone who conducts consumer research works at filling in aspects of it, providing content about elements of its structure, its processes, its methods of inquiry, and philosophies about its science and its values. Now, rather than leaving the thought as a blank truistic generalization, I'll indicate some of the content that interests me in the template, ideas about consumers based on my education and the kinds of research in which I have participated.

I see consumers as goal-oriented and seeking, living out their destinies—that is, lifetimes of consuming—that have the potential for infinite variety. I don't know more than anyone else whether it is all random, determined, or allows for free choice. Taken in the aggregate, it may be as stochastic as the dance of subatomic particles seems to be; but we also analyze the Consumer Event as the necessary outcome of its antecedents; and even so, grant each other the dignity of believing we are responsible for our will and decisions. Perhaps consumer behavior, similar to light's being both wave-like and discrete, is both caused and free. Out to consume, people show several principles at work.

A fundamental attribute is memory. Memory refers to our ability to bind time, to be self-conscious, to know ourselves and others over time. Without memory we lose our identity and live sadly only from moment to moment. We older folks joke about it with gallows humor to show that we retain self-awareness—or I would joke about it if I could recall what I just said. Human memory means accumulating and handling knowledge in various characteristic ways. That is why the study of information processing is so important to us. Our research template is possible because we can put our knowledge together in our journals, our classes, and at conferences like this one. Perhaps even more remarkable than memory is our ability to think about the future, to plan, to anticipate, and to imagine the unfolding of possibilities. Beyond memory is the use we make of it to dream about it, to reconstruct the past, to fantasize about the future. Quite wondrous is our need to yield ourselves up to music, pictures, and word play, to keep explaining through history, drama, fiction, biography, songs, movies, opera (both grand and soap), and consumer research, the stories of our lives.

Keeping us powerfully in flux is the fundamental quality of ambivalence. Consumers are ambivalent about the Consumer Event; they are often uncertain, making inferences that vie with each other, as they try to decide in essence who they are and what their decision will signify as to who they are. They must select actions in the template of possible meanings that will assert their position at the intersections of several dimensions. They are quick and relatively thoughtless in their decisions when these positions are well-established. However, more generally, ambivalence leads to some volatility, pendulum swings in consumer attitudes, and movement up and down the template as motivational devotions wax and wane in response to external pressures and opportunities.

Among the forces at work is insatiability. There is an open-endedness to human desires that allows us to keep wanting, that encourages us to innovate and offer endless novelty with the assurance that there will always be those who want this. Thus, out of every node in the consumer template, there grows a proliferation of alternatives, sometimes contrasting dramatically, sometimes extending tiny and, to the jaundiced eye, trivial differences. Yet, we have the capacity to detect them and to find them worthy of making distinctions and preferences. The force of insatiability produces perpetual striving and the extremes of selfishness, greed, and boredom; it maximizes and enlarges the assertion of the individual's power and material substance.

Opposing insatiability is socialization, the pressure upon us to be virtuous, to comply with propriety, to be self-denying and altruistic in the interests of sharing. The goal is to be a good person, giving, nurturant, caring for others, and conserving of resources on behalf of our posterity. Extreme socialization may become rigid obedience, exalting the group requirements and submitting to its norms, consuming according to the prescription of authority; it may become tyranny and pathological consuming. When people go to the extremes of conformity or of egocentricity, they show how utterly vile human beings can be, capable of the most egocentric gratifications in consuming nations, peoples, and even persons—whether in a Hitler Holocaust, a Dahmer dinner, or sexual service on a sleazy city street.

We are all subject to the contention between the issues of individualism and sociality and move between how much we care for ourselves and for others. I spent a year studying in a college social studies course called Freedom and Control, and to this day I still fret about how to resolve for myself the endless dilemmas posed by the conflict between my great American wish to maximize personal freedom—to stubbornly think my deviant thoughts and go my way—and my benevolent desire to live in harmony with my family, friends, and neighbors. Too often I fear I am obedient and conforming, yielding to wear what is in, eating what I am told is good for me, wanting to read the latest highly touted book, and studying how large groups in the public do the same.

I speculate about the sources of these Consumer Events, the ambivalent human nature that motors the template, that makes us think some things are good or bad, desirable or not. I know some of you are familiar with the small piece of the template that I have offered (Levy, 1986) in trying to account for the choices people make among all the beverages available to them. One might suppose that plain milk and water would suffice for us all; and I think they could. But no, we must have them processed, flavored, colored, textured, packaged, and priced to allow us to indicate the character of our distinct and changing social positions, our gender, our stage in the life cycle, our personality strivings, and subtle variations in mood. It is then striking to observe that as people mature from drinking milk as infants and from the healthy soups and juices that good parents provide to loved children, they break free to soft drinks with their festive carbonation, and perhaps to coffee and tea with their bitterness and caffeine. The fullest testament to maturity and freedom to choose among beverages comes with the addition of alcohol. It seems a telling commentary that people apparently aspire to the freedom to drink things that are strong in their effects and usually taste terrible, at least until we force ourselves to get used to them. Beverages are just an example; there seems to be a correlation between being more mature, having higher social status, and doing more or less bad things, because those bad things represent adulthood, independence, the freedom to stimulate one's body and mind and to abandon the innocence and blandness of merely sweet and healthy things and the constraints that

hamper lower status people. These issues relate to the large central problem of good and evil in consumption, about which we are in constant contention, explicitly or implicitly, on a local scale in our small daily choices and on a grand scale in just giving lip service to or really worrying about consuming the resources of Earth.

Aristotle told us that all things come to be by nature or by making, and our competing feelings about nature versus culture have always plagued us. The higher social status represented by beverages that seem hard to take and unnatural to drink reminds that the motivation of people toward higher social status is to gain increasing appreciation of culture and what it creates. That means behaving in unnatural ways by making and acquiring objects, by competing to show one has superior economic power to own and accumulate objects that are rare, individual, costly to make. Thus, as one moves up the template, life becomes more deliberate, the array of choices widens, there is an increasing cachet to being able to make subtle discriminations that are unavailable to lesser mortals.

As I wondered about these matters, I thought that there was also a simple relationship with gender, that being aggressively individualistic and evil was a masculine thing while being well-behaved and compliant was feminine; and I know that much conventional thinking would agree with me because that is one way we have been socialized. Pursuing that line, I thought that the beverage template implied that we are born innocent and virtuous, weak and feminine, and that as we progressed to consume ever stronger liquids, we could eventually become a mature, manly, high-class scotch or brandy drinker, at the pinnacle looking down along a longitude line of the consumption template, on all the lesser lower class, youthful, female weaklings with their watery beer and milky pink ladies.

However, as I sought to generalize these ideas, seeking consistency and parsimony, to fit them to other realms of the grand template, I ran into trouble. Going up the template may indeed provide more variety, and the objects available to higher status people are often costly and rare. Color shifts show also some generality; for example, with clothing as with beverages, immaturity is represented by pure, simple, light pastel colors, youth and young adults by brighter colors, and maturity by depth, richness, and darkness. However, how can we reconcile that with the connection to social status and gender? Traditionally, for instance, dark breads were peasant breads, close to the soil and lacking refinement, so that going up the scale meant gaining access to white bread. To complicate the matter, dark breads lately have become attractive to higher status people.

A similar confusion arises with respect to gender. If going up the template by means of being socialized to free individual choices, to arrive at the sophisticated, high-status, socially powerful male, how can we account for the traditional role of women as socializing the family, seeing to the lifestyle and consumption patterns correct for the position of the family? And how take account of women in newly powerful, high-status roles? My earlier understanding seemed too simple, too parsimonious, too dominated by traditional stereotypes, not fundamental enough in being able to accommodate more varieties of Consumer Events as they arise.

Then a light bulb went on over my head, another one of those illuminations to which I am prone, when something I already know comes flashing back as a fresh insight. I realized that the innocent baby implies the goodness of Rousseau's human beings, uncivilized but noble in a state of nature, being corrupted by the powerful male consumerism and materialism of society and the evil city; and that this was only one theory or philosophy, one thread in reality. Another theory maintains that we are born bad, lustful, gross, egocentric, enslaved by the pleasure principle and that the process of socialization is a benign one in which mothers domesticate and tame the brute, animalistic forces that drive us. Thus, women complicate and modify the beverage template with ideas of refinement, fine glassware, social events, and the notion of becoming more discriminating. They introduce a sense of aesthetics and manners, furnishing the home, the idea of caring for the young and sharing in the community. They foster temperance, compromise, and restraint, and encourage us to obey the social and medically authoritative pressures that tell us to cut out or cut down on sugar, salt, caffeine, alcohol, fat, cholesterol, and nicotine.

I had arrived at a point in this intellectual journey where combining Rousseau and Freud in my fashion told me that men and women were equally important influences in affecting consumers to strive for cultured behavior, with the male principle being bad and the female good. The enjoyment I found in this thought seemed to demonstrate that it must be correct. But I could not stop there. I am an ardent feminist. My mother worked outside the home most of her life; my wife is a wonderfully capable professional woman; and my lawyer daughter has a sharp and realistic legal mind. My women colleagues and students show me their strong intellectual and managerial capacities. I am also realistic about all these women and do not merely romanticize them and their assets. I believe they will be free to be as good and as bad as males. But I don't think being feminist means ignoring gender, sex, and sexuality in their myriad of expressions and effects on consumer behavior, as we cope with working women, dual careers, expensive toys for children of guilty parents, and convenience foods when working becomes more important than eating.

So, pushing on, I was motivated to read and think more about these basic gender roots and roles in my template. I was reminded of the role of great heroes, good loving men, benevolent fathers, of Apollo, symbol of the Sun and the benign, curative traits in men. Conversely, there is the role of Eve as temptress, and Lilith, in some stories said to be Adam's first wife and symbolic of the Terrible Mother; and the many goddesses and witches with great and awful power. One can only conclude that there is ample evidence for the influence of the good father and the bad father, the good mother and the bad mother, and their respective roles in affecting what we find good and bad in our consuming. Marija Gimbutas (1989) on *The Language of the Goddess,* Hans Peter Duerr (1985) on *Dreamtime,* concerning the boundary between wilderness and civilization, where he explains the meaning of witches, and David Parkin's (1986) collection on *The Anthropology of Evil,* help to illuminate for me some of these profound forces. Camille Paglia (1991), in her book, *Sexual Personae: Art and Decadence from Nefertiti to Emily Dickinson,* says men are responsible for that glorious erection called civilization, but in building their towers of transcendence they can never escape the primal pull of the earth mother. That sounds like an anxious situation for men, and they seek security. Paglia's thought brought to mind

a little 4-year-old boy I saw on a sunny day playing naked in the back yard. As he ran about, he clung to his penis. When someone asked him why he did that, he answered, "That's so I won't fall down."

The male and female principles take their different forms, both being inevitably bound together in our resultant mundane consumer actions. Each consumer has an idiosyncratic mix of experiences, prenatally, and from launching at birth, and pursues self-consciousness and identity, carrying these ultimate bisexualities and their mixtures of good and bad, not as a simple ambivalence, but as a fourfold helix. Up the template they intertwine, determining who we are and what we do at moments of decision and consumer action. Each Consumer Event in the template is a summary at a point in time of the particular blend of gender forces, located in a particular cultural setting, expressing our motivations and perceptions directed toward some degrees of individuality and conformity.

The challenge we share is to contribute to the delineation of what I have presumptuously called the grand template in all its breadth and detail, with all our methods, intellectual power, and sympathy. I call it a *template* because that word packs into it so many of the thoughts I have tried to convey here to substantiate the seriousness and profundity of our subject matter. It refers to a *temple,* a sacred place that symbolizes the cosmos and its divisions, to the spiritual and virtuous elements of our aspirations and goals of our consumption of ideas, art, religion. It refers to *temptation,* the need to satisfy our animal selves and uncontrolled impulses. And it means that consumption is *temporary* and needs replenishment. The *plate* tells of our destiny as consumers, what is on our plate as workers in general, and as eaters in particular. The element *late* reminds us of the life cycle, that consuming is finite, that we can consume only so much before we too will be consumed. The *a, t,* and *e* form the word *Ate,* the name of a Greek goddess personifying foolhardy and ruinous impulse, telling us to be self-critical and to moderate our consumption. These letters also spell *ate,* reminding us that we indeed have eaten, and that this luncheon is now finished. I thank you for your kind attention.

REFERENCES

Armstrong, J. S. (1991). Prediction of consumer behavior by experts and novices. *Journal of Consumer Research, 18*(2), 251-256.

Duerr, H. P. (1985). *Dreamtime.* Oxford, UK: Basil Blackwell.

Erikson, E. H. (1982). *The life cycle completed.* New York: Norton.

Gimbutas, M. (1989). *The language of the goddess.* Glenview, IL: Harper & Row.

Hirschman, E. C. (1991). Secular mortality and the dark side of consumer behavior:or how semiotics saved my life. *Advances in Consumer Research, 18,* 1-4.

Holbrook, M. B. (1990). The role of lyricism in research on consumer emotions: Skylark, have you anything to say to me? *Advances in Consumer Research, 17,* 1-18.

Levy, S. J. (1986). Meanings in advertising stimuli. In J. Olson & K. Sentis (Eds.), *Advertising and consumer psychology* (Vol. 3, pp. 214-226). New York: Praeger.

Paglia, C. (1991). *Sexual personae: Art and decadence from Nefertiti to Emily Dickinson.* New York: Vintage.

Parkin, D. (Ed.) (1986). *The anthropology of evil.* Oxford, UK: Basil Blackwell.

Rainwater, L. (1960). *And the poor get children.* Chicago: Quadrangle Books.

Warner, W. L. (1949). *Social class in America.* Chicago: Science Research Associates.

Chapter 28

THE CAKE EATERS

Sidney J. Levy

When I was a youngster there was a phenomenon people talked about that I didn't understand very well. It was called having your cake and eating it, too; and people said it couldn't be done. It seemed reasonable to me that one could not eat his cake and have it too; but I didn't see how the issue arose or what it meant as an aspiration. Since that time, I have spent several years studying the attitudes and behaviors of North American consumers via thousands of interviews gathered at Social Research, Inc., and our affiliate, Canadian Marketing Analysis Limited. I have also learned how to live beyond my income.

With these experiences in mind, I have retitled my remarks. Rather than stick to noting "Changes in People's Living Habits," I would like to offer some speculations on the nature of modern living, focusing on the new consumers, "The Cake Eaters." The modern American cake eater has changed his living habits. He has moved from self-denial as a necessity and a principle, to self-indulgence as a way of life. His ethics now dictate Consumption as a virtue where once they counseled Conservation.

We need not belabor the obvious changes in the American scene. They can be readily enumerated. There are more people, with increases in both the birth rates and longevity. These "more people" have more of all kinds of things—they have more time, more money, more objects,

This chapter was first presented as a speech before the Association of Canadian Advertisers in Toronto, May 1957.

more pleasures, and more worries. We all know these things are going on, that the New Leisure is a problem, that the cost of living and the standard of living have never been higher. Supposedly everyone has moved or is on his way to the suburbs—with some irritable noises from those who are moving back.

As a psychologist, I would like to offer an assessment of the current situation of the Cake Eaters, to examine what they are doing, to conceptualize some of the trends and points of view that are in effect. Sociological and psychological interpretations of the contemporary scene are fashionable now, in themselves a part of the scene, part of a wave of human preoccupation and self-examination that is growing, as we move further and further from grubbing for subsistence.

It should be said that in many basic ways, there is little doubt people have also not changed. When interviewing them about how they live nowadays and how these living patterns compare with those they wanted when they were young, and with those of their parents, they are able to see many differences. But mingled among these differences are still threaded the yearnings for a stable family life, freedom from illness, wishes for the betterment of one's children and for finding a way to happiness in an ever-troubled world. Within this framework, thinking not about the broad picture of goods moving in the market and the dramatic implications of income and sales curves, but thinking about the people in their homes, struggling with raising their children to be clean, obedient, and hopefully affectionate, frozen orange juice and cake mixes don't seem particularly significant.

Nevertheless, there is a redistribution of values going on, a swinging of the several pendulums that direct our social and psychological energies. Through history, we move between emphases on pleasure and austerity, permissiveness and restraint, realities and fantasies; and countries wax and wane as their energies are practical or philosophical, guiding or following. So, too, in the day-to-day living of everyday people there are shifts in emphases on work or pleasure, on getting or spending, on building or laying waste our powers.

For a long time, the American pattern was one of pioneering, of adventure, of self-denial for the fabulous rewards of the long haul, even if these arrived only in an afterlife. Security was less important than severity, and acquiring, husbanding, or developing resources, whether personal or economic, was to the fore. For the average consumer, this meant struggling to make a living, to meet fairly basic needs; necessities took the major share of income, and luxuries were for the rich or the wasteful.

This is changing, and there is a kind of centering movement going on. People don't want to save; they don't want to waste; they want judiciously to consume. They are Cake Eaters because they want to enjoy their substance but not use it up. This is exemplified in many ways, most strikingly by the people who save money in the bank and buy major appliances on credit. It is summed up as a philosophy by the woman who said she wanted to "save a little, spend a little, and enjoy a little."

Presently, American consumers are heavily engaged in living out what might be called a Consumption Fantasy. They want security, possessions, and pleasure, governed by a sense of immediate enjoyment of these goals. Commonly this means, what will it cost per month? One respondent said about friends, "They bought a house out in Harvey for $25 down on GI and $7 toward their own home in payments. What if it is 32 years they have to pay? By laying it out they have their own." Everybody still worries about money—the most frequently named concern in any survey—but they don't worry about it the way they used to. They want to "have their own," and indebtedness is no longer the fearful deterrent it used to be.

The orientation to possessions is very strong. The consumers have their antennae out in a most remarkable fashion. Their faith in the manufacturer is apparently infinite, resting on a firm foundation of research, the spurs of competition, and an implicit acceptance of the fact that our society is now oriented to making new things, better things, miraculous things in a casual way. They know that *new* in an advertisement is not to be despised no matter how overworked, because the world we now live in innovates as easily as invention was once arduous. The pervasive belief is that everything is different nowadays—"all the things they make for babies that they didn't have before" greets all new parents. In addition, the less one has to worry about basic things, the more one worries about peripheral ones. If the object itself can no longer be changed to improve its functioning, its flavor, its nutrition, its ease of handling, or if some new thing cannot be invented that will make the object totally outmoded and inefficient, then we must turn to aesthetics, turn the thing out in several colors, and redesign the package. The consumer is not indifferent because a leisurely people have time for aesthetic discriminations and can elevate their attention above basic product functions. One can develop a more fastidious self-concept if toilet tissue can be chosen for its relevance to the color scheme of the home rather than some more primitive considerations.

The Consumption Fantasy presses hard. Partly it is a fantasy because it cannot be entirely gratified—and even as parents lavish on their children all the things they missed as children, they still fret about whether they are doing the right thing. The Puritan ethic is not totally eclipsed. One woman compared herself with her mother:

> I like to cook like my mother. My husband tells me I am pretty good. I am not as good a trainer of children as my mother was. I think I am too easy-going. I think I was better as a child, too. If Mother told me not to go anywhere, I never argued with her. Times change [Sigh]. Now they dance and everything. Because they have had so many things, they want so many things. They had a lot as a child. I think it is not good sometimes. They got more than they needed. Things come too easy to them. We had to go without. I try to get things for my kids. There are so many more things to want now. Styles change. You got to keep up with the times. Coats become outmoded. They don't want to wear them anymore. They are still good. One of the girls says, "Where did you get that old-style coat?" It belonged to her sister and was new 2 years ago. The idea was, they are sisters, why can't she wear a coat 2 years old?

Her remarks reflect some of the new imperatives that operate to support the Consumption Fantasy. Sets of principles are developing that define the rights of consumers. A few of these can be briefly noted; some are simple, others quite complex.

Convenience is an aim in itself. To say that something is convenient serves to justify it to a fair degree. Lying behind this justification is of course some other logic, being a busy person, generally, being a working woman with no time to cook, being entitled to convenience because one is just as good as anyone else, and so on.

Style is more important than basic function. All automobiles get you there; therefore one may as well choose on the basis of three or more colors. This elaborates. At first, novelty in style tends to be *moderne*; the design seems radical, bright, variegated, regarded as "smart." Then it tends to retrench itself somewhat, to darken without becoming drab, and to elevate itself toward the sleeker, severer modes regarded as "elegant." And all the better for obsolescence if these shifts can be made rapidly.

Other minor rights of consumers could be listed. At the heart of them all is the most fundamental right: *The enjoyment of human life is worth more than the value of toil or of money.* There is a new and growing concern with the human individual. It lies at the heart of the American Dream and is the important idea that tends to become obscured in the surge to accumulate objects. Having wealth and enjoying its fruits liberate energies that tend otherwise to be wrapped up in the bitterness and intensity of the struggle to survive. The fact that these liberated energies create new problems should probably not be blamed on the wealth. The notions that saving oneself justifies the acquisition of appliances, that the person who knocks himself out needlessly is foolish, are finding increasing currency. In an interview with a housewife, she bolsters her intention to insist on doing less work. "I always keep telling my husband that I am worth more than the washing." And in the April 24 issue of the *Chicago Sun-Times,* Ann Landers, who counsels the troubled, admonished a husband as follows: "Confidentially—Old-Fashioned Husband: I have a different name for it, Dad. Your

wife would rather have a washing machine than silver handles on her casket. Stop comparing her with your mother. Welcome to 1957."

But there is much more involved here than the labor-saving of major appliances, even if this is not to be sneezed at. As human energies are freed from work, they need new occupation. Part of the frenzy in the Consumption Fantasy is that it has to take some form, and people want it to have a well-composed form. However, for consumption to have a pleasing and harmonious pattern requires an integrated way of life, a sense of living in a manner that satisfies a personal system of values. In the present period of transition and world revolution, with the new levels of automotive and geographic mobility, with the agonizing struggle to turn the American city into something manageable, it is not easy to find such harmony and satisfaction. Certainly, mass education reaches more and more people, the working classes have surpassing incomes, the persisting vision and reality is of a home of one's own, and the unity of family is grasped for more intently. But still crime and delinquency rise and personal discontents proliferate. The suburban housewife feels isolated and passive, remote from the thrill of the malevolent but fascinating city.

The whole tendency of modern times has been toward liberation, toward liberation of women, of peoples, of children, but the net effect has been a kind of internal and external violence as the liberated don't know yet what to do with themselves. Modern psychology becomes increasingly concerned with the problem of identity. In a rapidly changing world, how can we organize ourselves and our lives in ways that reflect an internal order and discipline, with a knowledge of who and what we are.

We fret and diagnose ourselves with the passwords of psychology, and everybody wants psychotherapy or wishes he could admit he did. A lower middle-class housewife tells the interviewer, "I think I always felt insecure as a child;" the wife of a blue-collar worker says, "My brother had an inferiority complex." In this flux of attitudes, the different social classes seek to stabilize their understandings of the New Psychology. The lower-class mother has now heard about permissiveness and strives for the proper emotional atmosphere in feeding her children. At the same time, upper middle-class people are taking in the newer ideas of setting limits and providing children with the security of structure.

The lower middle-class people, ever in between, mainly feel anxious and hope that nothing will interfere with the home-centered ideal toward which they yearn. Never ones to lag in their attention to a trend, advertising people try harder to understand their audiences via the latest in psychological theories and techniques.

One of the interesting phenomena in the widespread concern with finding identity is the urge to professionalize. Mere work is beneath everyone's dignity, and even to have just an occupation sounds like a roulette ball making its way to a haphazard niche. A profession, however, wraps around the worker a mantle of identity. People with occupations have jobs and they have names, but professionals have positions and titles. Ordinary workers have bosses, but professionals have colleagues, and the higher authority they want to recognize is their own skill. To the original learned professions of theology, law, and medicine, we can now add an ever-growing list of aspirants and *arrivistes*, nursing, engineering, social work, advertising and public relations, to say nothing of—psychology.

Another way in which the current complex problems of achieving identity are manifest is in the criticism of modern conformity. David Riesman mourns the loss of the inner-directed man; William H. Whyte, Jr. is alarmed at the sacrifices of aggressive personal achievement for the sake of group acceptance and harmony. Presumably these are signs of growing social dependency. There is emerging a kind of public rather than private individuality. In the olden days, manners and social prescriptions were relatively tight—the facade was supposed to be a conforming one—with individuality a more or less personal matter. In her study of American national character, Constance Rourke comments that

The mask was a portable heirloom handed down by the pioneer. In a primitive world crowded with pitfalls the unchanging, unaverted countenance had been a safeguard, preventing revelations of surprise, anger, or dismay. The mask had otherwise become habitual among the older Puritans as their more expressive or risible feelings were sunk beneath the surface. Governor Bradford had encouraged its use on a considerable scale, urging certain gay spirits to enjoy themselves in secret, if they must be convivial.

But the modern psyche has been turned inside out. Where formerly there were many makes of cars, most of them black, the individual had a kind of privacy. Now he wants one of the few kinds of cars everyone else has, with a supposed individuality displayed in the color or chrome variations. In this respect, we are like the adolescents who refuse to dress individually for fear of ostracism or ridicule. They all wear dirty saddle shoes, but one is permitted to steal a march by the minor originality of using plaid shoelaces, perhaps.

There are many profound forces at work to produce the current temper and attitude, forces beyond my knowledge or insight. But surely, Cake Eaters don't want to offend anyone or rock the boat, and the Consumption Fantasy thrives on an outwardness of self-expression. Of tremendous influence in the development of the present situation are the mass media. In one sense, it may be said that they have performed a major part in turning our psyches inside out. How people live and how they ought to live has been made a matter of public record to an incredible degree. The mass media have communicated about and surrounded us with vivid new learning. By word and by picture, by splashing before us the golden fantasies of how a more abundant life can be lived, they have defined for millions of people a public conception of how kitchens, living rooms, and backyards ought to be. Along with suburban living where the urban apartment's privacy and anonymity vanish we become self-conscious as in a fish bowl, with mass media color pictures of homes our standard.

The Consumption Fantasy is cumulatively the adman's dream. Like the symbolic murals of man's mastery of the world, showing a dirigible, an ocean liner, a locomotive, and a car; mass media have created a vision of the American home with appliances in every nook, the family together having gracious meals prepared without effort, with a motorboat at the dock, a barbecue pit alongside the now advertised swimming pool for Everyman, and the lurking thought that you too can have a Cessna airplane.

Chapter *29*

LOOKING AT THE LADIES, LATELY

Sidney J. Levy

Much is made today of the idea that women are losing their femininity. A recent survey reported in a Sunday supplement found that one third of the women interviewed and one half of the men felt this way. But dress, outward manner, and various social behaviors are often superficial guides, since their meanings change to fit the times. Not too long ago painted lips and smoking in public bespoke the loose woman. These no longer signify the loose woman, although undoubtedly the ladies have loosened up considerably.

If it is possible for a woman to wear a bullfighter's trousers and still be feminine, what personal qualities constitute femininity? The basic dimension used to identify femininity is that of activity-passivity. Men are supposed to be active and women passive. By definition, then, the modern woman is more masculine, and men anxiously exaggerate the invasions they see. Actually, femininity is not fundamentally a matter of simple passivity, nor the presence or absence of specific kinds of knowledge. Today's active woman may really be increasingly feminine rather than less so.

THE TRUE NATURE OF FEMININITY

This passive ideal of years gone by lingers, but women are leaving it behind. Instead of passivity, true femininity is receptivity.

This chapter first appeared as "Constructing Consumer Behavior" in *Art Direction Magazine*, 1960.

Regardless of her clothes, job, vigor, speech, drinking habits, or initiative in seeking a husband and supporting him through college. This is a modern heroine. A woman's femininity is in her receptivity to people, to experience, to the feelings and needs of her children, husband, and to herself.

Passivity makes a woman an object; receptivity makes her an interpersonal being, finding her fulfillment in self-expression and in how she relates to other people. Passivity implies submission, obedience, duty; receptivity means willingness, invitation, pleasure.

Women differ in their many goals and in how much satisfaction they get from life nowadays. Some of these differences follow social class patterns. Upper middle-class women, wives of professionals and business executives, for example, treasure their individuality and like to aim at expressing their good taste and skill in handling situations with poise. They are the home managers. Lower middle-class women, wives of white-collar workers, are much involved in their children and ambitious for their success. They want to be neat, conscientious, strong, and practical. They are less managers than they are homemakers. Lower-class women, wives of blue-collar workers, often have values similar to middle-class women but are less energetic in pursuing them. They are often "just a housewife." They are particularly anxious to maintain the integrity of their families and less able to do so.

There is one wish that women of all classes have. It lies in the dream of being transformed, of being magically changed into a new person. The reason for this wish may be due to resentment at being the second sex, notorious as having been carved out of an oversupply of ribs, or perhaps because little girls have to wait so

long for evidence of their superiority to men. The cause of the transformation is love, and the consequences are a new status, new interpersonal relations. This wish takes various forms and is familiarly projected in fairy tales and myths.

The lower-class version is the Cinderella story. The girl is a household drudge, a slave to her stepmother and stepsisters. Her transformation is quick and closely linked to fancy transportation, going dancing, and above all, a very beautiful dress. Many studies show that lower-class women are especially interested in dressing up. In one instance, we asked women, "On what occasions do your clothes fit your personality best?" Fifty-eight percent of lower-class women chose "Whenever I look my dressed up best," in comparison with only around 15% for middle-class women.

One lower middle-class version is the story of Snow White. She has a higher status than Cinderella, is exceedingly virtuous, and enjoys keeping house and mothering the childlike dwarfs. Her transformation takes more time than that of Cinderella, who did not have to bother with the middle-class virtues of postponing pleasure. After a suitable wintry sleep being a good girl, Snow White is awakened by a kiss to love and marriage. Similar is Sleeping Beauty, in which the uninvited evil witch symbolizes the middle-class anxiety about not offending one's relatives lest they do you an ill turn.

An upper middle-class version is the story of Pygmalion and Galatea. He sculpts her, and his love brings her to life. This story, and Shaw's adaptation of it, is told from an upper middle-class point of view. The hero is not a mere prince, but a king, which is in keeping with the upper middle-class interest in the special relationship of fathers and their daughters. Also, the girl is transformed gradually, less by magic than by professional skill in bringing out the true character and capacities of the individual. And at the end Eliza is so liberated, she isn't even sure she wants to marry her Pygmalion.

AESTHETIC SOURCES
AND TRENDS

Women are constantly on the alert for sources of information and guidance, looking for cues to orient themselves toward what is currently permissible, especially in the way they fix up themselves and their homes. These sources of transformation range according to their values and access, from the professional to the pedestrian. A designer's wife said,

> A lot of ideas came from more or less trade magazines *Interiors, Arts and Architecture.* We don't have any household magazines around. Then there's this perfectly gorgeous Italian industrial magazine we just drool over. It's called *Industria Italia.* Oh, they have the most fantastic stark contemporary!"

Women who can afford it call in interior decorators, and more women would love to. Interior decorators are one of the guides and go-betweens that many need to help them thread their way through the mazes of self-expression and negotiation. Like realtors and matchmakers, interior decorators advise on what is right, find it, and assume the burden of handling all those other people. Then there are window shopping, store browsing, and store personnel, other people's homes, and the deluge of colorful communications from the mass media, their ads, articles, and illustrations. From all this gathering and gleaning of impressions and ideas, women pick up gratification, information, and confusion. They are confused because it is so hard to tell what is best for themselves. But they also learn and are gratified to be in on all the excitement of changing fashions. It is easiest for them to pick up specific ideas about colors, materials, and styles, hardest to decide how to relate and combine them in a particular setting. New colors, new fabrics, authoritative styles. They are absorbed and work their way into the culture as rapidly as money, wear, and learning curves permit. Homes are changing as people become able to take advantage of teak and marble; of vinyl, cork, or parquet floors; of canvas wall covering, sheer draperies, costly built-ins, pole lamps, carpeted bathrooms, acoustic tile ceilings. Each little American palace becomes increasingly luxurious, with variegated patterns, air-conditioning, brightness, and sensuousness. Probably this sense of indulgence and elaboration will grow, moving us more and more from smartness to elegance.

## Chapter 30

PHASES IN CHANGING INTERPERSONAL RELATIONS

Sidney J. Levy

This paper grew out of a general interest in the nature and conditions of interpersonal relations. In an early study I examined the friendship patterns of a group of children, seeking to observe the ways they relate to one another and some of the psychological facets of their associations (Levy, 1956). Why two people become and remain friends can be explained in many ways and at various levels, all to some degree unsatisfactory. There is always a point beyond which relationships are attributed to mystery, to something fundamentally inexplicable. Certainly, human relations are subtle and complex. Much of the energy that sustains them is derived from unself-conscious

sources. This early study noted some of the psychodynamic processes and characteristics that accompanied specific affiliations, in attempts to explain those affiliations.

One of the problems in the study was how to define a friendship, because children's interactions show varying degrees of stability and external circumstances produce necessary shifts in the structure of the associations. This carried my interest beyond the content of an ongoing relationship to the aspects of change in relationships through time. Recently, this problem was highlighted by an interest in the vicissitudes of the careers of public figures. The question was raised about the possibility of

This chapter was first published in *Merrill-Palmer Quarterly* 8(2), 1962, pp. 121-128.

entertainers renewing their relations with the public once their popularity has declined. This thought inquires, how do renewals of relations come about so that a course of friendship or esteem is revived or given fresh life?

With these various issues in mind, I have prepared a statement to help order the problem by noting significant phases in the course of interpersonal relations and what appear to be characteristic contents. In doing this it seems useful and interesting to compare the growth and development of everyday relationships with those that have been termed parasocial (Horton & Wohl, 1956), occurring between audience members and public personalities. The ebb and flow of human interactions will be noted as stages differing in specific content and duration, with some account of this content and its emotional character.

HARBINGERS

Often there are signs that a relationship is about to be initiated or to become possible. Friends talk up "someone you'd love to know"; matchmakers glow over potential blind dates. In the parasocial world, columnists, advertisements, magazine articles publicize the approach of a new person. Friends ask if you have seen or heard the new comic or actress.

In this way, social appetite is whetted. There is encouragement provided ahead of time by some degree of social approval. Knowing generally that one's circle or members of one's reference group already give a measure of acceptance is apt to stimulate willingness and an element of prior commitment. If it is sufficient, if the harbinger does not arouse resistance by emphasizing unattractive values, the level

of anticipation begins to rise with agreement to participate. This phase allows for testing out in advance whether it seems likely the new person will actually be attractive, by noting who approves and what qualities are being emphasized.

Jokes about matchmakers and about the less desirable features of the blind date reveal some of the agitation felt in this stage as one frets about extending affiliative emotion toward encompassing a new object, as one seeks to defend against the exuberant descriptions being given, as one tries to be realistic about what the new object can provide, and how one's own qualities and behavior will be received.

All these features suggest anticipations are often extreme in self-protective skepticism; in exaggerated fantasies of libidinous pleasure (seduction, a "wowed" audience), sociological rescue from an unhappy role (old maid, bored couple), or in some general self-enhancement (business contact, admiring companion, new listener).

In one or another fashion, there is hope that a measure of primary loneliness will be relieved or that some healing of narcissistic wounds will be fostered—if only so casually phrased as, "Will this be fun for me?" The power of loneliness has in recent years been discussed as a dynamic force with which people must contend or against which they must protect themselves (Fromm-Reichmann, 1959; von Witzleben, 1958; Weigert, 1960).

ENCOUNTER

The initial meeting: The date arrives with his flowers, finally rings the doorbell, a unique crowd gathers, the new couple meet. At this point novelty is usually optimal, with its varied effects. Encounter tests the openness of the individual to new experience. One little boy played energetically and excitedly but individually when a new peer was introduced into his environment. Asked why he didn't play with the new boy, he said, "I will, but I'm not used to him yet."

Encounter is often a troublesome moment. The psyche is jarred by the novel elements; how much to admit and how to evaluate what is presented are in some state of flux. Names just "heard" are promptly forgotten, slips of the tongue are common. In the struggle to focus attention at the appropriate rhythm and level, actors on stage are not clearly understood at the outset; background features and sounds loom prominently, distractingly presenting themselves for judgment. In the poised person, these aspects are mastered quickly or held at bay with tightness of self-control, usually through practiced familiarity with the process of meeting people or through less initial anxiety about the threat of the anticipated encounter.

As the encounter settles into place and focus, there is normally a readjustment from expectations (if there have been harbingers or even only the tentative conclusions preceding a pick-up). While this is going on there is a sense of exploration, even wariness in some people, to check against the prior imagery and fantasies of possibilities. First evaluations are reached: "He really is wonderful," "She's overrated," "I don't know what people see in Newhart," "I think I'm going to enjoy her company," "I think we might make out," and so on.

Some type of association may then begin if enough gratified energy has been aroused. Whether one likes or dislikes the new person or entertainer, there often will be some participation at the initial phase if only due to politeness or deference to the source of introduction, or because of the commotion other people are making about the phenomenon. In the parasocial world it is hard to ignore the entertainer making a splash even if one dislikes him. So just as people do not associate only with those they most adore, part of the audience is apt to be antagonistic, to some degree. Commonly, the more vehemently the newcomer is being accepted and touted, the more vigorously some haters have to join in as audience to observe and feed their resistance. Instances of public figures who arouse this type of mixed audience are Jack Paar and Zsa Zsa Gabor, in comparison to, say, Donna Reed, who probably has few watchers who say they can't stand her.

RECOGNITION

The extent to which the novelty of the new relationship "takes" and moves onto a more stable plane depends on the degree and kind of recognition which occurs. The audience judges in one way or another whether or not "this is something for me." Liking or interest are elicited when the newcomer provides a pertinent gratification in an attention-holding style. If the recognition of such provision is not present sufficiently the novelty may be spurned, having been adequate for a transitory moment, perhaps, for a single viewing, but not meaningful enough for frequent experience. Such might be the case with Chinese music (to Western ears), a wild impulsive character, or other things alien to conventional, moral Americans.

At the extreme, the recognition may be too great. The relevance of the other person for one's own less-accepted motives may be so overwhelming that the experience is either totally unacceptable or cannot bear repetition frequently. This is often true of an insightful play, the sort that lays bare human nastiness well enough to command a wide audience to feel its truth, but who want never to see it again. Some talents have a largeness of insight so narrowly or completely expressed that they can be taken only in infrequent doses. For instance, one might question whether Danny Kaye or Jerry Lewis is not basically too childish for more frequent experiencing by adults.

In the recognition phase, people usually develop a sense of involvement and affirmation. One feels, "I like you," and descriptive terms and feelings often take on superlative and intense qualities—"Wonderful!" "Terrific!" "A lot of fun!" "He's a riot!" "She's just gorgeous!" During this phase the urge to associate is apt to be strong and sustained; engaged lovers are together as much as possible, the singer's records are collected avidly. These features are inflated in this description; at times, the same content is present but controlled and moderated in those whose needs are less intense or who hold back in their interpersonal commitments. This control may be expressed negatively or ambivalently in someone who goes along with the relationship, having further meetings, but adopting the attitude of "I can take him or leave him" or "I don't care much for them, but I'll go."

UNDERSTANDING

From recognition, swept along on the wave of intensity and common, initial overevaluation of the friend, the relationship may develop a sense of intimacy, a feeling of mutuality. With parasocial personalities, the audience imagines there is understanding from the entertainer, which he reveals by his insight, by his capacity to move us, by the attention she gives to things we understand or are pleased to be learning. "How funny, that's just the way it is!" There is familiarity and comfort. The friend may seem "just perfect"; the wish is for him always to "stay as you are." This is the moment of zenith, accompanied by a high sense of idealism and suspension in time, classically underlain with doubts and fears that things can remain this way.

And with good reason, of course, since the tumid situation cannot be sustained. As familiarity grows, the emotional tone usually begins to moderate. The same intensity is not required in order to know the other person, whether biblically or casually. Fewer and fewer unexpected modes of revelation occur. We gain increasing capacity to be detached in viewing the other. More and more of the other one and the nature of experiencing him becomes conscious and available to intellectual examination and potentially to criticism.

Where there is substantial gratification of continuous and basic needs the relationship may settle onto a plateau of overall enjoyment. Within this there will normally be cyclical aspects. The needs that are satisfied by the partner, spouse, friend, or entertainer will rise and fall in degree, possibly finding some climactic pleasure at intervals through some intensification of intercourse, whether social, sexual, or parasocial auditing. In between times there is some relief felt that familiarity now allows a quieter relationship, some resting from the demands of the more intensely romantic period. This customary evolution into a less stringent relationship may be balked for various reasons. Albert E. Scheflen (1960) has discussed the difficulties in "neurotic one-to-one relationships" which lack the flexibility to change.

CRISIS

As the relationship normalizes by becoming fitted into the routines, schedules, and increasingly taken-for-granted coming and going required by other life activities, a continuing reorganization of perceptions is going on. The love object, friend, or entertainer is viewed as part of a context, no longer taking total precedence over other things, but having to compete with them. The energies, which had risen to a peak, subside to some degree and redistribute in more diverse directions. This is inevitable, since an intense focus of energies is maintained by an arduousness the individual cannot afford, the cost of diminished attention to other activities.

In addition, people often become aware that more is being given out than is necessary to obtain the gratification one seeks. Also, the more realistic, colder-eyed view that has been growing begins to balance negatives against positives in the relationship. Is the undeniable benefit which previously loomed so large worth the accompanying shortcomings? Are exhaustingly late dates essential to foster the romance? To the overly striving mate, is a spouse's love enough if his or her social or intellectual skills appear inadequate? Is it worth a whole evening or even a whole hour to get the essence of a particular performer? Is too much devotion, attention, or indulgence required to prevent dissolution of the relationship?

As doubts and competitors arise, the relationship reaches a crisis. With friends or lovers there may be a growth of conflict, recriminations, charges of unfulfillment, of exploitation, of misunderstanding, boredom, and so on. These may lead to disruption. If elements in the situation are not sufficiently intense, or if the amount of disillusion is moderate and available alternatives are weak, the crisis may resolve into armed truce, frustrated restlessness, polite mutuality, a longer cycle of interaction.

NEW RELATIONSHIP

The crisis may occur early or late, it may be brief or prolonged, insidious or candid, covert or explosive. The relationships that survive proceed on new bases. Commonly, some discord is believed to be a usual part of any ordinary relationship. A not-infrequent assumption is that hostile outbursts are essential to the closeness of marital partners, with the conventional understanding that these outbursts should be settled before going to bed, if not by going to bed.

The relationships that are most realistically grounded in the mutual gratification that the friends can get, and in the capacity of the partners to adapt to reasonable degrees of frustration in some aims, will settle into long-term maintenance of a comfortable amount of intimacy and a judicious assertion of separateness or privacy. Long-term, successful marriages and sound, enduring friendships are of this sort.

This is also what goes on with long-lived entertainers. They offer central satisfactions by representing a significant aspect of human life in a vital way. They usually have a distinctive amount of force and self-assertion that command attention and loyalty from the audience. While bland and mild characters can also gain identification and recognition from the audience, their appeal will usually be brief unless accompanied by additional aspects of aggression (Grotjahn, 1957), whether present in the same entertainer (e.g., Chaplin), or in a foil who takes sadistic advantage of the vulnerable one. As such entertainers become familiar and assimilated, the audience diminishes, but it does not abandon them.

RENEWAL

When can the new relationship take on the character of renewal? If the crisis leads to failure, most interpersonal relations do not come back. Full renewal is practically impossible, most people regarding themselves as "sadder-but-wiser" and "good riddance"; paradise once lost is never regained, innocence never re-established. If the relationship cannot be stabilized at a new, readjusted level without exaggerated expectations it will lead to feelings of criticism, boredom, indifference. With parasocial people, one need not argue or pretend interest or say vaguely, "We must get together again sometime soon." Thus, the audience turns away, sometimes gradually, sometimes suddenly, as accumulated subtle indifference finds alternatives. The comeback is not studied much because it is a relative rarity. There are some forms of it that can be identified. A relatively modest form of comeback might be the woman who can be rescued by Ann Landers's advice to make herself more attractive so her philandering husband will stay home. This may occasionally work when the husband, basically, would rather stay home if his wife would just return to this side of aesthetic acceptability.

A form of renewal which occurs among entertainers that is only nominally a comeback is the winning of a new audience through a change in style or a shift in locale. A fading TV comic might be enthusiastically received in night clubs; a declined movie star may find new fame in TV, and so on. The true comeback—the entertainer who is abandoned by his audience and returns to renewed favor with it—tends to

be a theatrical fantasy, more celebrated in scripts than in real life. It is the entertainer's dream, to ward off his fears of oblivion.

Symbolically, it is widely appealing as a theme, because it speaks of renewed potency, of love re-awakened, of never really dying. When it occurs in any form, people can feel gratified. So they thrilled to Joan Crawford revitalized in *Mildred Pierce*; to Gloria Swanson resuscitated in *Sunset Boulevard*; to Frank Sinatra making it as an adult singer and growing in show business as an actor; to Buster Keaton's funny commercials, and so on.

Renewal sometimes comes about because of the persistence of illusions despite disillusions. There are people who divorce and remarry, sometimes several times, before they are convinced that absence does not really make the heart grow fonder, if there is no change in the persons. However, when apart, they forget the disillusion and yearn again for their ideals—especially if a competitor promising more has not appeared. Basically, what is needed here is inner change. If it occurs, perhaps through psychotherapy or some dramatic, revelatory experience, the renewal may be real and enduring. This possibly happened to Red Skelton. The death of his son changed him from a fairly ordinary comedian to a top clown; he gained a tragic depth, moving to a new and very human level of intimacy with his audience and a more mystic sense of his talent.

Renewal of old fixed ties may not occur in dramatic forms; it may go on at comfortable sporadic intervals. Probably Jack Benny, Sophie Tucker, and other show business ancients provide examples of this kind of renewal. In these instances, fixedness and predictability are important elements rather than inner or outer change. The audience is, perhaps, not so great, because it is drawn from the constantly diminishing number who can muster the nostalgia and sense of history to pay comfortable respects to the institution. The problem for such institutions is that they are often granted fairly remote homage, occasional visits to renew the grandeur and marvel; but most of the time life goes on elsewhere.

Theatrical careers, like friendships, are most enduring when stylistic change seems less relevant. That is, the more the entertainer rides on superficial representations, the narrower his audience and the more precarious his hold. His temporary success may be impressive as it rides the crest of some transitory, popular interest, but it often fades quickly and is not renewed unless he can show a larger talent, an unexpected versatility; that is, if he changes himself adequately to tap a deeper motif in society. People in these respects can be compared to children's toys. Some are hula hoops, a get-rich-quick proposition, unpredictably flaring up, then gone; while bicycles and blocks remain to satisfy successive generations of kids.

In conclusion, true renewal is exceedingly rare. It comes about in one form or another when there is a reorganization of perceptions on the part of some member of the relationship, leading to shifts all around. Relationships change in the first place because of many complex reasons: too much of a good thing, maturing tastes, new learning, new mutuality, new inner realities, new outer circumstances. Often friends and parafriends are outgrown, the tinsel turns to tawdry. Entertainers must decide how much they will grow with their audiences, whether to stick with the people who know them best, trying to find what new motivations are appropriate for each 5 years or decade of their careers; or how much they will try for the new audiences coming up.

In daily-life relationships, friends and lovers must similarly, through time, confront these issues. Will they—can they—and their partners relate both deeply and casually enough, with both stability and renewal, to adapt to the demands of a maturing relationship?

REFERENCES

Fromm-Reichmann, F. (1959). Loneliness. *Psychiatry, 22,* 37-43.

Grotjahn, M. (1957). *Beyond laughter.* New York: McGraw-Hill.

Horton, D., & Wohl, R. R. (1956). Mass communication and para-social interaction. *Psychiatry, 19,* 215-229.

Levy, S. J. (1956). *A study in the psychodynamics of interpersonal relations.* Ph.D dissertation, University of Chicago.

Scheflen, A. E. (1960). Regressive one-to-one relationships. *Psychiatric Quarterly, 36,* 692-709.

von Witzleben, H. D. (1958). On loneliness. *Psychiatry, 21,* 37-43.

Weigert, E. (1960). Loneliness and trust—basic factors of human existence. *Psychiatry, 23,* 121-131.

## Chapter 31

SOCIAL CLASS AND CONSUMER BEHAVIOR

Sidney J. Levy

The study of market segmentation is a troublesome one. It raises many questions not easily answered. Numerous studies have sought to determine relationships between particular consumer variables and specific purchasing behavior. All too often these studies are frustrating because they mainly demonstrate that the variables most highly related to the behavior are those that are so close to the behavior as to be redundant in explaining it—or do not explain much at all. Diversity—almost a perversity of diversity—is the easiest generalization to fall back on. When we examine user groups, we find varieties of people, scores, and dimensions; when we examine sociological categories or groups, we find varieties of user behaviors. Either the person high in score on innovation does not show initiative in the area we want to study, or a dramatic example of high status values and philosophy in our sample turns out to be sociologically a lower status consumer. Although these may be exceptional cases, there are surely enough of them to muddy the waters and reduce correlations sharply; and science has the task of explaining exceptional cases in lawful terms, also.

Thus, in trying to classify people as kinds of buyers we encounter the problem of the

---

This chapter was first published in J. Newman (Ed.), *On Knowing the Consumer,* John Wiley, 1966, pp. 146-160.

refusal of so many people to be consistent buyers, or at least consistent in the ways we seek to order their behavior. But all this is to say that the study of market segmentation is certainly in no better condition than much of the behavioral sciences in trying to "explain" any human actions. And indeed the marketers are worse off, because so few people are working to develop the multitudinous series of limited studies designed to test variable against variable which are tirelessly presented in social science journals. Nor are there enough workers governing basic investigations, building the intellectual edifice whose bricks are the little studies. As I understand it, this meeting was designed to serve that function; in a sense to bootstrap ourselves into having some of the kind of knowledge that comes from looking back over one's work and asking what have we found out.

In attempting to do this in the area of social class, I will start by saying, arrogant as the admission of my hope may be, that I did not find a Rosetta Stone of Social Class, or Newtonian Laws of Consumer Action and Reaction. I did not think it would be useful, either, to accumulate findings that show that people of one status or another are more or less apt to buy various classes of products, as facts in and of themselves. We would not be much furthered in our study simply by learning that lower status people buy relatively more hardware store items or Ann Page products, or that higher status people buy relatively more books or Crosse and Blackwell products. There are some such differences; and I would like to point out something of their general character and coherence.

Social class variations are variations in lifestyle. Although social class groups are not sharply distinguished by their behavior in most studies, they do show behaviors that can be viewed as ranging along a continuum or as different patterns using common elements drawn from the core American culture. Differences are often subtle differences so that it is not easy to find truly marked and easily demonstrated contrasts even in such basic aspects as child rearing. This means that to many marketers such differences are not very important or useful, whereas other people do find them helpful in their thinking. Those who do not find these differences useful tend to be impressed by mass society and its increasingly homogeneous aspects, stressing the similarity between a prosperous lower-class and an upper middle-class kitchen, when both are well furnished with modern appliances, often of the same brands. However, even these "same kitchens" may have important differences in them and have been arrived at through rather different marketing processes based on different values, thought processes, and purchasing actions.

Consumer actions are complexly interwoven with attitudes and feelings. The influence of social class on consumers may perhaps be interpreted by putting together a series of ideas which, taken together, show some of this complex; thus we gain by accumulation a sense of the importance of social class as pervasive—even if less meaningful in some areas than in others. Generalizations are offered here that sum up findings from various specific studies carried out at Social Research, Inc. over the past 15 years. The emphasis is on differences, since there is a common tendency to gloss them over.

VALUES

Underlying the many other differences among social classes as consumer groups is the fact of differences in values. Lower status people value education less than middle-class people do. This has repercussions in the market in various ways, since many products are consumed as part of gaining an education, as well as depend on having education. There is a sharper relative emphasis on morality, respectability, doing things right among middle-class people; they believe they can control their destinies and fortunes and achieve success by implementing these values. Lower status people are more apt to seek immediate gratification, to rely on luck, and they are less willing to risk their security. These are well-known sociological findings (Hyman, 1953). They are mentioned here to remind that such broad points of view as these have been repeatedly noted as characteristically varying among social classes. They suggest that social stratification produces different ways of seeing the world—and of consuming, since consuming is ultimately one of the ways in which people implement their values.

One study of femininity (Rainwater, 1962) indicated that the lower-class woman, who feels doomed to the lower end of the economic scale, is not likely to feel proud of what she does. There is little to value because life seems dull and unrewarding.

> I lead a dog's life . . . work . . . I get up in the morning . . . cook all day . . . pick up after four children and a husband . . . sew . . . what would you call that—peaches and cream?

> I consider my life very dull.

> Dull and boring . . . I spend most of my time working and have nothing to show for it.

Those who have achieved more economically show greater content and a more vigorous sense of acquisition; they feel they

have gotten somewhere and do have something to show for it.

> I'm contented . . . more contented than I was 15 or 20 years ago. I collect . . . milk glass and copper things.

> I feel I lead a really happy life, I never had it so good. I collect salt and pepper shakers with a story behind them.

The higher one is in the social scale, the more comprehensive are one's values; there is a greater sense of one's participation in the community, as well as an increase in self-expressive activities. Self-fulfillment is more valued and more pursued as a real possibility.

> I sculpt, sail, and love to dance. I like to read . . . I'm very active from dawn 'til dusk.

INTERPERSONAL ATTITUDES

Another broad factor influencing consumption is the nature of people's interpersonal attitudes. These are, of course, individually ramified in many ways, but some consistencies are visible. Attitudinal differences are seen at the most intimate levels, affecting sexual relations, the use of contraceptives, and conjugal roles. There are consequences in effectiveness of family planning and preferences in family size. For example, lower status people are much less likely to use diaphragms, since their use requires more interpersonal support from the husband than lower class men tend to give their wives (Rainwater, 1964).

More generally, upper middle-class women tend to regard their husbands as companions, to feel like a peer in money matters. They are likely to demand much of themselves for achievement: to be a good wife, mother, an intellectually stimulating being, home economist, child therapist, organization woman, and so on, and also to be a person of composure and competence. As parents, upper middles need their children to be bright, active, strong, lively, and precocious and are given to characterizing their babies as active and alert. They look for products that will add to their success, competence, and proficiency as mothers and fathers.

By comparison, lower middle-class parents are more apt to stress control and conformity, the meeting of values and requirements that relate to cleanliness, politeness, neatness, and order. These parents are most troubled by dirty diapers and the idea of things being messy. Most parents want "good" babies, but lower middles are particularly prone to want them well-behaved, well-scheduled, and manageable.

Working class fathers are relatively distant from their babies.

> I take little care of him, but help when I can. He laughs, and moves around, and seems to know me [at 5 months].

Working class mothers strongly need to enjoy their babies, to get pleasure from them. They will tolerate difficulties with their babies, finding in them self-justification and interpersonal responsiveness. In sum, to simplify, the upper middle wants her child bright and alert, the lower middle wants him properly behaved, and the working class woman wants a gratifying possession ("Babies," 1960).

In terms of more general relationships, lower class women tend to say they dress to please themselves, possibly to excuse their bold dress-up urges; lower middle-class women give some emphasis to other

women and much less to pleasing themselves. Upper middle-class women have a broader sense of display and think of their audiences as spread among themselves, husbands, other women, and men ("Chicago-land Women," 1960).

The narrower interpersonal circles of working class people show themselves in many ways. They make less use of long distance ("A Sociopsychological Study," 1955). They have a tendency to relate socially more to relatives than middle-class people do; in spending vacations, working class people are distinctly more prone to visit relatives, to stay home, or to have the husband go alone, than to follow the middle class custom of going away from home as a family group ("Status of the Working Class," 1961).

SELF-PERCEPTIONS

Consumer behavior may reflect the varied self-perceptions or self-images held by individuals, as such and, to some degree, as they are characteristic of members of social class groups.

These views of oneself provide a source of consumer action, since they are the expressions of needs, of aims, and of the individual's internal logic, all of which find their objects in the marketplace. To the extent that people seek products and services that are congruent with their self-perceptions (as they are and as they would like to be), their self-perceptions are a guide to understanding their marketing behavior. Certainly, individual personality is diverse, more so than the general values held characteristically within a group; relating consumer behavior meaningfully to personality is, therefore, one of marketing research's more challenging tasks. However, that there are some systematic differences among classes is suggested from various directions. For example, in a study of sanitary protection, it was indicated that women of lower social status tend to have more sense of taboo about their bodies and less understanding of them ("Attitudes Toward Feminine Hygiene," 1957). They were prone to think of themselves as having menstrual problems. They were less receptive to the use of tampons, an instance of their lesser receptivity to important changes in behavior, their lesser scientific information, their more traditional ideas and feelings about sexual matters and interpersonal relations, and so on ("Meanings and Motives," 1958).

Compare the ideas and tone of these two women, the first a lower class, ethnic girl.

I am Spanish, you see, and Spanish girls are not made like American girls and are not brought up the same. We would not be able to use anything like that. . . . You see, we are closed up. American girls are opened up at birth, but Spanish girls are not and we are not opened until we are married and then we go to our husbands and he is the one who opens us.

The second is an upper middle-class woman who commented on her use of tampons:

I figured if I could accommodate one thing I could accommodate another.

Higher status people have more pride in their organisms. They think of themselves as fastidious people; upper middle-class women express themselves less urgently when it comes to "needing a deodorant," not believing they smell so bad in the first place. The self-oriented aspects of grooming, of personal pride and self-esteem are prominent in the reactions of higher status women, less to the fore among lower middle status women where general social motives and self-consciousness tend to seem more pressing; lower class women respond more to immediate needs, thinking in terms of tonight's date and special occasions ("Cleanliness, 1955; "Hair Product, 1951; "Toothpaste," 1951).

Definitions of men, what a "real man" should be to fit the goals, norms, and values of his social class reflect many variables, especially those relating to his physical being and his effectiveness in vocational and familial relations. Some relative emphases are discernible among the social classes. Upper middle-class people tolerate a much more "feminine" conception of a real man. They do not think that a real man has to be crudely tough to be effective. They think that being clean, fastidious, and well-groomed is part of being a successful person and demonstrate the kind of narcissism one expects in a higher status person. They think of hygiene, grooming, and dress as especially related to one's career and how it is being lived up to. A higher status man may have distinctive specialized hobbies; some tendency to think of women as pals—and they think he should be a friend; and the idea that masculine know-how finds expression in knowing one's way about the world—in jet planes, restaurants, modern business.

Lower middle-class people think a good man is particularly a good father, a responsible husband, a man who builds a solid home life. He is serious, earnest, somewhat depressed, eager for his children to do well in school so that they might become well-established, and fearful that they might be trespassed against by lower class people. He is the most conventional, generally, in dress, resistant to Ivy League and Continental influences, and hopeful that the double-breasted suit will come back to cover up his bulging middle ("Men's Clothing," 1958).

Working class people think that a real man is a sturdy guy who can make a decent living. Lower class men like to have body know-how, physical adeptness, and manual skills, to understand how things work. They want to get along, to get some fun out of life. They expect to work fairly hard and to relax as hard as they can, because they feel life uses them up faster than it does higher status people ("German men," 1960; "Images of Masculinity," 1961; Levy, 1963; "Marketing to Men, 1963). A study of age grading showed a trend for lower status people to think of themselves as mature and as old at younger ages than do higher status people (Neugarten & Peterson, 1957).

DAILY LIFE

According to differences of occupations and activities (as well as income differences, socially evaluated differences, etc.), the manner in which the whole day is lived includes both subtle and gross differences ("A Day in the Life," 1949; "Life Patterns," 1949) Lower status women are apt to get up earlier in the morning and to feel they can make do with less sleep; in general, working class people are especially faced with the problem of needing to get to bed early and wanting to watch late movies on television ("Attitudes Toward Television, 1964). Middle-class housewives are more likely than lower class women to plan things with some care, to enjoy trying out some new things, to feel a sense of mastery over household chores; lower class women are more prone to agree that "a woman's job is never done."

In general, with increasing status there is more activity outside the home and in the time spent in expressive activities—reading, art, and music, and helping the children do various things. The distribution and use of time shows class trends; for example, the time for the dinner hour varies systematically from class to class. About a fourth of the lower lowers in one sample were likely to be at dinner before 5 o'clock, and very few after 7 o'clock, while more than half the upper middles were still at dinner after 7 o'clock. Also, more time is spent at the meal as status rises. The television set is also much more likely to be on during dinner in lower class homes than in middle-class homes.

These four areas of values, interpersonal relations, self-perceptions, and daily life are broad in character. They reflect the basic facts that groups in our society do different kinds of work, have different types and amounts of financial reward, are evaluated differently along various dimensions of social esteem and importance to the community. As consequences, they think of themselves differently, behave differently, and want differently. In relation to some more specific marketing areas, these differences find further expression.

SHOPPING

Social status appears to affect how people feel about where they should shop. The tendencies here are for lower status people to prefer local, face-to-face places where they feel they will get a friendly reception, easy credit if needed, and so on. As a consequence, the same products (and brands) may be purchased in different channels of distribution by members of different social classes. In the purchase of cosmetics, upper middle-class women are more apt to shop in department stores than are lower status women, who are, in turn, relatively more apt to shop in variety stores. Drug stores seem equally attractive or suitable to all. Studies of department stores also show that among the stores available, there are sharp differences in status reputation and that consumers tend to sort themselves out in terms of where it is appropriate for themselves to shop. This is not a gross either/or phenomenon. Most establishments will have customers of more than one social class. But their loadings will differ, and their purchasing patterns may differ. Upper middles characteristically go to Sears for certain kinds of goods, proportionately different from the array bought by lower status customers; and lower status people often go to Marshall Field's only to buy gifts, or even to acquire a gift wrapping. Food chains are similarly selected as varying in status suitability.

The upper middle-class woman organizes shopping more purposefully and efficiently than women of lower status. She is more knowledgeable about what she wants, where she will go for it, when she will get it; her shopping is both selective and wide-ranging.

I shop in Wanamakers, Lord and Taylor, Bonwit's, and Snellenberg, depending on what I want at the time I'm shopping. I go shopping with a specific thing in mind. I usually group my shopping for the coming season's needs for clothing for myself and the children. I shop for food regularly once a week at Penn Fruit.

Lower middle-class women "work" more at their shopping, showing more anxiety about it, finding nonfood purchases especially demanding and tedious and fraught with uncertainties. Their clothing purchases tend to be more piecemeal than upper middles' are, and there is more orientation to seeking out the best buy for the money.

I'm always buying clothing for the family. I look around and buy the best I can for as little as I can. With supermarkets, I watch for ads on Thursdays. . . . For example, I just bought a blanket and I went to three stores to look. As it happened, we bought at Lits; they had the nicest blanket for the best price.

Lower class women are the most impulsive about shopping, the least organized. They often like to go out just to have a reason to get out of the house.

My shopping is very broad and vague. I don't go anywhere in particular but for food and that I get at Best Market. For clothing, I usually go to one of the department stores or when they have an advertisement to show what is on sale and what is different than the usual run of things. I just shop wherever I find what I want.

The implications of these remarks overlap among women, but the continuum is discernible and finds its most specific expression in the local social orientation of the lower lower class shopper.

Some people like to run around from store to store and buy in them large grocery chains. I sometimes buy can goods there, but the best place, the one I like best, is Greene's (a small grocery store in the block). They'll save things for me and I can always get what I want.

Thus, the goals, methods, and places of shopping form patterns that distinguish members of the different social classes in various ways ("The American Drug Store," 1958; "Credit Buying," 1961; "Hair Products," 1962; "Images of Seven," 1956; "Major Retailers," 1958).

MEDIA

The fact that media are approached and used in contrasting (as well as similar) ways among social class groups is important for marketing understanding. At a rather simple level there are variations; for example, lower status people are less apt to subscribe to newspapers than are middle-class people, and more likely to read and subscribe to *True Story,* for example; they are more likely to enjoy the comics freely, to embrace television, and to watch late movies. Upper middle-class tastes on television are likely to run more actively to current events and drama; moving down the social scale, one finds a relative rise of interest in soap opera, quiz shows, situation comedy, and variety. Middle-class people worry more about the effect of television on their children than do lower class people.

The different meanings of media have been explored in many studies. The media function in varied ways, and each also fits differentially into the lives of the social classes. There are (sometimes sharp) class preferences among the newspapers available in a community, in evaluating magazines, in selecting television shows, in listening to the radio, in how newspapers are read, in receipt and meaning of direct mail; and, in general, in the total volume of materials to which people are exposed and to which they attend in one or another of the media. Higher status people see more magazines, read more of the newspaper, and buy more newspapers. Lower class

people tend to prefer the afternoon paper; middle-class people tend to prefer the morning paper. Studies in the past 3 years of television in 15 major cities show that upper middle-class people consistently prefer the NBC channel, while lower middles prefer the CBS; and these preferences are in keeping with the images of the networks, and the characteristics of the social classes ("Attitudes Toward Television," various years; "The Differing Meanings," 1954; Glick & Levy, 1962; "Magazine Readership," 1962; "The Meaning of Newspapers," 1954; "Newspapers," 1963; "Patterns of Radio," 1962; "The Sunday Comics," 1954).

ADVERTISING

Attitudes toward advertising are diverse and reflect much individual variety. However, the many background factors already noted lead to social class differences in this sphere also. The expressly symbolic nature of advertising is particularly meaningful in aiming it toward the differentiated understandings of members of different groups. Broadly speaking, upper middle-class people are more critical of advertising, suspicious of its emotional appeals, and questioning of its claims. They are trained in pursuing subtle meanings and usually display an attitude of sophisticated superiority to advertising compared to the more straightforward, literal-minded, and pragmatic approach of lower middle and upper lower class people.

This does not mean that upper middle-class people are unresponsive to advertising; although they insist on expressing detachment, they are more strongly appealed to by sheer difference, by approaches that seem somewhat individual in tone, that show some wit, that convey elements of sophistication or stylishness, that seem to appeal to good judgment or discriminating taste, that offer the kinds of objects and symbols that are significant of their status and self-expressive aims. Lower status people are relatively more receptive to advertising that is strongly visual in character, that shows activity, ongoing work and life, impressions of energy, and solutions to practical problems in daily requirements and social relationships ("Attitudes Toward Toilet, 1952; "The General Nature," 1949; "A Study of Thematic," 1961).

Some specific illustrations can be found in women's reactions to promotional advertising, offering coupons and special inducements. Upper lower class women are most receptive when the activity does not seem too difficult. They feel intrigued, economical, shrewd, that they would be fools not to take advantage of many offers that come their way, to cut costs, to get something a little extra.

> I think they are real nice. I like those coupons. I'm not rich enough to throw away 15 cents. I know some people think it is silly to save them, but I don't. Boy, they add up, you know.

Lower middle-class women often feel the same attraction but are more reserved in their reaction, feeling the need to question the utility of offers. They like to feel that they are sensible about their use of offers and promotions, that what they get is important or interesting enough to be worth the effort. They enjoy some sense of complexity, an enrichment of shopping in this kind of participation, but they can also be quite aloof.

> Another one of those. Not very interesting. Too much money to gamble on. If I wanted

one of those I could go out and buy one. This doesn't interest me one little bit, I just wouldn't bother with it.

Upper middle-class women feel the most remote, sensing lower class economic implications and looking down their noses at the quality of premiums, the size of savings, and so on. Their interest vies with their sense of apartness.

> I have never used an offer. I see the coupons in all the papers. They are good for people with large families, they can save a lot if they use the coupons. I find them attractive but I never seem to use them.

> Sometimes they offer knives in a set, Cannon towels, dolls, jewelry, blouses. They might interest some people, not me.

In general, values, level and quality of education, the different social aims, and socioeconomic variations produce such differences in characteristic reactions, although much of this is obscured by the volume of advertising learning that goes on and the protective interpretation that can make the same advertisement mean different things to different people to suit their needs (Levy, 1959, 1960; "The Meaning and Influence," 1960; "A Study of Stamps," 1963).

The kinds of products people want to consume differ, and the reasons for which they consume the same products differ. Going up the social scale, one finds that gum chewing decreases and the reasons given for chewing gum tend to change; more services are used—hotels, motels, airplanes, telephones, dry cleaning, delivery, insurance, investments, and so on; taking of laxatives tends to decline.

There are general differences in whole areas of consumption. The use of food is a good example. Going up the social scale, one finds that food tends to be regarded and used in increasingly symbolic fashion, and going down the scale, one discovers that it is consumed more and more pragmatically. Also, it is apt to be used more self-indulgently at upper middle and lower class levels than at the lower middle, as is also true of drinking. Interest in furniture tends to take different forms. Upper middle-class people prefer to search out furniture that is stylish and in keeping with some specified personal or family aesthetic; lower class people are more apt to emphasize sturdiness, comfort, and maintenance; lower middles have the characteristic "middle" anxiety about doing what is "right," respectable, neat, pretty, and so on ("Chewing Gum," 1961; "Contemporary Patterns," 1961; "The Kroehler Report," 1958; "The Laxative," 1952).

Although the points and summary statements offered above would (when elaborated) have interest in themselves—and did so to various study sponsors in specific instances—they also gain interest for their contribution to a cumulative understanding. They imply a coherence in the marketplace that functions with a consistency that is at least potentially available for continued study. There is suggested a social class structure that may start (or end) with variations in income, but which operates more meaningfully than in terms of amount of money available for spending. However, it has come about that the individual person (or family) exists in and is a manifestation of a milieu that has certain limitations and certain opportunities. The results have recognizable and usually quite logical consequences.

Upper lower class people tend to be defined in their total patterning of personality and ways of living by the fact that society allots them, so to speak, a manual, physical, body-focused assignment. Being the doers, the handlers, they are expected to act or behave overtly, to accomplish in ways that emphasize locomotor activity. In law they are its concrete, physical expression, found driving cars, pounding on doors, laying on sticks and handcuffs. In commerce they sell, serve, retail, handle things, make change, wrap packages. In physical production, they are the mechanics and manipulators, using their hands and muscles with or without skill to produce concrete objects. Such workers, trained to their world, become generally restricted in ego functions. Their orientation is local, concrete, face-to-face, relatively deprived of long range considerations or larger horizons. Immediate gratifications and readiness to express impulses tend to be observed in these people, since they do not usually perceive meaningful incentives to do otherwise.

Lower middle class people characteristically have "the cultural assignment" of applying known principles to defined problems in an accurate manner. Ideally speaking, they are expected to implement laws, regulations, systems, and so on, to be caretakers and intermediary supervisors. As such, in law they deal with its principles as lawyers and clerks; in commerce they may be bookkeepers or accountants, seeing to it that financial methods are systematically and precisely applied. In production, they are supervisors and engineers, again implementing and using known systems and generalizations about physical processes and structures. Such workers, trained to their world, become oriented to a functional and pragmatic view, coupled with anxiety about achieving respectability and success through virtuous performance. This gives them a larger perspective than that found in the lower class, reinforces the importance of education and of deferring gratifications in favor of long-range goals.

Upper middle class people have the cultural assignment of initiating knowledge, establishing policy, exerting judgment, and deciding on the methods and procedures to be used. They embody the intellectual, professional, and managerial point of view. In law they are judges and legislators; in commerce they are managers or controllers, determining the content of the procedures and actions to be carried out by workers of lower status. In a production hierarchy, they may be chiefs, physicists, and scientists. Such workers, trained to their world, emphasize ego processes, an awareness of more distant horizons, large social events, and concern with individuality and achievement. They use more integrated and varied means of satisfying their aims, feeling free to satisfy impulses frowned on by lower middle-class people, and are able to organize their lives from a point of view beyond the power of lower class people.

The differences listed in the earlier series of points that relate more or less closely to marketing have their roots in the differences suggested in these brief descriptions of three main social classes. These differences seem "real" differences, in that they are not simply the result of variations in income but are expressions of the profoundly varied forms of experience that become available to members of each social class. They may be obscured by the commonalities in human aims and in American experience and by the superficial significance of much consumption, but they seem consistent and persistent in governing, where relevant, the consumers' approaches to the market.

REFERENCES

The American drug store: Image, use, and function. (1958). Chicago: Social Research, Inc.

Attitudes toward feminine hygiene. (1957). Chicago: Social Research, Inc.

Attitudes toward television (1964). Chicago: Social Research, Inc.

Attitudes toward television in [various cities]. (Several years). Chicago: Social Research, Inc.

Attitudes toward toilet tissues and their advertising. (1952). Chicago: Social Research, Inc.

Babies and baby care products. (1960). Chicago: Social Research, Inc.

Chewing gum and the consumer. (1961). Chicago: Social Research, Inc.

Chicagoland women and their clothing. (1960). Chicago: Social Research, Inc.

Cleanliness and personal attraction. (1955). Chicago: Social Research, Inc.

Contemporary patterns of food logic and consumption. (1961). Chicago: Social Research, Inc.

Credit buying and its motivations. (1961). Chicago: Social Research, Inc.

A day in the life of Mrs. middle majority. (1949). Chicago: Social Research, Inc.

The differing meanings of women's magazines and television. (1954). Chicago: Social Research, Inc.

The general nature of advertising symbols. (1949). Chicago: Social Research, Inc.

German men. (1960). Chicago: Social Research, Inc.

Glick, I. O., & Levy, S. J. (1962). *Living with television.* Chicago: Aldine.

Hair product preferences. (1951). Chicago: Social Research, Inc.

Hair products and cosmetics. (1962). Chicago: Social Research, Inc.

Hyman, H. H. (1953). The value systems of different classes: A social psychological contribution to the analysis of stratification. In R. Bendix & S. M. Lipset (Eds.), *Class, status, and power* (pp. 426-442). Glencoe, IL: Free Press.

Images of masculinity. (1961). Chicago: Social Research, Inc.

Images of seven Chicago department stores. (1956). Chicago: Social Research, Inc.

The Kroehler report. (1958). Chicago: Social Research, Inc.

The laxative and antacid market. (1952). Chicago: Social Research, Inc.

Levy, S. J. (1959). Symbols for sale. *Harvard Business Review, 57*(4).

Levy, S. J. (1960). Symbols of source, substance, and sorcery. *Art direction magazine.*

Levy, S. J. (1963). *The meanings of work.* Chicago: Center for the Study of Liberal Education for Adults.

Life patterns of Mrs. middle majority. (1949). Chicago: Social Research, Inc.

Magazine readership as related to social, class, age, and sex. (1962). Chicago: Social Research, Inc.

Major retailers in the Philadelphia market. (1958). Chicago: Social Research, Inc.

Marketing to men. (1963). Chicago: Social Research, Inc.

The meaning and influence of promotional advertising. (1960). Chicago: Social Research, Inc.

The meaning of newspapers. (1954). Chicago: Social Research, Inc.

Meanings and motives in the tampon market. (1958). Chicago: Social Research, Inc.

Men's clothing and tailoring. (1958). Chicago: Social Research, Inc.

Neugarten, B., & Peterson, W. (1957). A study of the American age-graded system. *Proceedings, 4th congress of international association of gerontology* (Vol. 3, pp. 497-500).

Newspapers in the social world of Chicagoans. (1963). Chicago: Social Research, Inc.

Patterns of radio listening in the New York metropolitan region. (1962). Chicago: Social Research, Inc.

Rainwater, L. (1962). *Workingman's wife.* New York: McFadden Books.

Rainwater, L. (1964). *Family design: Marital sexuality, family planning and family limitation.* Chicago: Aldine.

A socio-psychological study of telephone users. (1955) Chicago: Social Research, Inc.

Status of the working class in changing American society. (1961). Chicago: Social Research, Inc.

A study of stamps. (1963). Chicago: Social Research, Inc.

A study of thematic coherence in advertising approaches. (1961). Chicago: Social Research, Inc.

The Sunday comics. (1954). Chicago: Social Research, Inc.

Toothpaste: a socio-psychological study. (1951). Chicago: Social Research, Inc.

Chapter 32

PSYCHOSOCIAL REACTIONS TO THE ABUNDANT SOCIETY

Sidney J. Levy

One of the main reactions to the abundant society is to be concerned with it—to reflect on it and to criticize it. Contemporary writings in many fields—economics, sociology, literary criticism, and the popular media—show a steady absorption with issues posed by abundance. Sometimes the issue is material poverty, highlighted by its stark contrast to the prospering millions. Many critics are affronted by affluence and the spiritual poverty they believe it fosters. Other students turn their attention to the processes of change (Warner, 1962), to ana-

lyzing the kind of society they see evolving, the altering institutions, the portents of things to come (dire or marvelous) (Davis, 1967), and how society should seek to direct them (Galbraith, 1967; Meadows, 1967).

In many cases the aim of comment on abundance is to express the writers' values and their perception of what modern life is like. Some point with pride to the remarkable achievements of technology, industry, and commerce and their benefits in health, leisure, and personal expressiveness. Others see sterility, softness, loss of purpose, a

This chapter was first presented as a speech before the Allied Social Sciences Associations meeting, Washington, D.C., December 1967.

kind of creeping doom that is destroying our society in its mindless pursuit of futile values. We are besieged with think pieces that warn of the many problems a prosperous but divided country faces and what must be done before it is too late. Gratefully, most of such articles conclude that it is not yet too late to do something.

As society moves along toward the fulfillment of these dramatic predictions, whether Armageddon or Utopia, one wonders how it is with the people who are the actors, who are living the lives the social philosophers describe. As they move through their daily activities, how do they perceive what their own lives are like; what are their reactions to being producers and consumers in a society of such unparalleled technological accomplishment and material abundance?

The thoughts presented here are findings and interpretations derived primarily from three research projects[1] carried out to study contemporary outlooks of adult Americans (women particularly). The samples were purposive, even though representing a wide spectrum of citizens, and the content of this report should be qualified by awareness of these samples and methods. Between October 1965 and the summer of 1967 more than 1,200 people were interviewed on various subjects. They were drawn from over 20 communities across the country. Of these, about 80% were women; the age range was broad; and social class placement was divided upper middle, 25%; lower middle, 40%; and working class, 35%. The interviews were usually full conversations about such matters as views about modern life, current world conditions, problems and solutions of the day, the nature of family life, the kind of home environment sought, the status and changes in personal, social, and economic conditions, and so on.

Marketing interest is commonly concerned with buyer characteristics or with consumers' attitudes toward specific products. But the studies employed here reflect a larger orientation, the growing tendency for marketers to ask broader questions about the marketplace, to learn about typical viewpoints and social trends that assist them in formulating or modifying policies and general approaches to the public. Thus, the information leads beyond what so many have noted, that affluence leads to increased attention to the characteristics of consumer goods that are nonfunctional.

Reactions to abundance may be described in many ways; they vary in their directness and in the awareness shown by the consumer. This report may perhaps be made more meaningful by illustrating several levels of analysis that give different kinds of findings. Since reactions to abundance must depend on the characteristics of both the consumer and the nature of the surrounding environment, it is necessary to look in both these directions. Further, the dimension of time significantly governs many aspects of consumer reactions. Taking into account these main elements—the consumer, the external environment, and time—five viewpoints will be discussed. These are (a) the modern era, (b) the present year, (c) individual mood or temperament, (d) life stages, and (e) family economic situation and outlook.

THE MODERN ERA

When respondents talk about modern times, what things are like nowadays, they speak from their sense of historical perspective. They make comparisons to other eras and decades, to when they were young. They speculate about what is going on in the world and in America. Their views cover a familiar range of ideas. Essentially, they see a world of rapid change, complexity, and conflict, where science and invention have produced some amazing consequences. These often have a transcendental quality, of having gone beyond the ken or coping of ordinary man in daily life. The great consequences are large metropolitan networks, large governments, businesses, and unions, carrying with them their benefits in prosperity and their side effects in pollution.

As citizens and consumers, people tend to translate these ideas into concrete and immediate terms. The modern era makes available dishwashers, nursery schools, and new foods. It produces a rat race that fosters the sale of alcohol and pills. New social and personal relations are stimulated— early marriages, feelings of insignificance in large work units, sophisticated working women, the intensity of educational demands on young people, the civil rights ferment. The large view makes people feel troubled.

Things are moving too fast. Everything is getting bigger and more complex to solve. Government is trying to lay its hands on all facets of life. Everything is bursting at the seams.

The generations don't understand each other. There is never enough money. There is uncertainty about the future, the possibility of catastrophe, a lack of spiritual and moral security. No leadership, no sense of direction.

It wasn't such a rat race as it is today. If things get any worse, I don't know. The momentum of life today, trying to keep up with the times—no wonder people have to take all

kinds of pills and sedatives to relieve the tensions they're under.

It is like the fall of the Roman Empire. This country is going to end up like Rome.

Traffic congestion, noise, litter, fumes—I've come to accept them. They are serious. If we don't have clean water and clean air, all of us will die. They are serious but I can't change them so I accept them!

Since life is compartmentalized and lived at various levels, what a man thinks he cannot change he accepts. Most people turn from their clucking at the amazing and recalcitrant epoch in which they live and orient themselves to the features of the narrower span of time that is the present.

THE PRESENT

The present is the larger era made manifest in specific current events. It refers to the way things are going right now. To the respondents, it means how the war in Viet Nam is going and whether one's son may be there or have to go; it means the state of the economy in 1967-1968; teacher, gasoline, and bakery strikes; and might the weather be more or less severe than last year. Views on such matters affect public mood and spending. The world may be going to pot or bursting at the seams, but in the meantime what will affect one's own situation in the economic climate? What kinds of plans can be made, given the course of public events that might impinge on one's private life?

There is a mixed sense of unease at this level. People are glad where an advance seems to be made in a tax that did not rise, or in a change in school policy that promises the children educational benefits. Or, not uncommonly, there are people who feel distant or somehow untouched by public events, as if deprived of some potential gains. For example, one person said,

> My folks are on Social Security and I don't think Medicare will help them as you have to be in a hospital and I don't think they are ever going to be in a hospital.

Another shrugged off a question about the President and his programs.

> His programs have no effect at all. I go on living as I did, have my bills to pay and my son to raise. I don't see how they can affect me unless he gives free education.

But wariness and anxious feelings are quite general. Inflationary pressures are complained about with more than usual intensity, fear of the war or despair in the face of it, whether hawk, dove, or uncertain citizen, cast a pall. Problems of the day seem unusually recalcitrant because of intransigence and inadequate or negative leadership.

> Johnson's stand on Viet Nam affects my morale. I feel we are guilty of doing what we accuse certain other countries of doing.

> We must hold the line against the commies somewhere so it might as well be there. My sons will probably be killed, but so will a lot of others.

> I'm worried about the irresponsible Negro leaders. They are the ones who will instigate violence, hatred and lose the sympathy of white people for their cause. The racial problem really worries me.

> The prices will just get higher and higher unless something is done.

These same troublesome events also paradoxically—possibly even shamefully—contribute to the contemporary environment of abundance. The country seems busy and productive, whether the war is viewed as a drain or a spur. There is a sense of building going on, of products flowing forth, of people urgently engaged in pursuing their aims. Within these two large contexts of the era and the present environment variations in response come about for many reasons. Whether the times are exciting or oppressive depends not only on their force but on the individual's resources.

PERSONAL MOOD

In reading interviews as in reading writers of the day, one encounters in each person a characteristic frame of mind. It is one that seems pervasive, to express the person in a recurring way, to be a fundamental that endures through the overtones of temporary fluctuations in feelings. In a study of housewives in which they talked about how their lives have been going, this aspect of general frame of mind was a striking expressive feature. The pace and tempo of the women's rhetoric or semantics showed a rhythm, in modern idiom a typical beat. By observing each woman in this way, she could be classified by her emotional or temperamental rhythm.

The *upbeat women* are hep, "on the ball." They are alert to both traditional and new values, to changing practices and products. They have a sense of rising perspective about their development. They understand the language of the day, they revel in their present abundance, they seek out stimulation and experience. They feel or aspire to be creative and initiating. They feel a sense of resiliency and of vitality, which allows them to take things in stride rather than to set up routines and yield to them. They feel they understand young people and can sympathize with their needs, their revolts, their desires for and against conformity. They want to sustain their youth, to share with young people the willingness to experiment, to try new products, to see another point of view.

> We are emotionally happy. Nothing has happened to me that would be the base of the Great American Novel, but every time I meet a new person, that is an interesting experience. I have become a Girl Scout leader . . . I love to try new foods and do so frequently. . . . Right now decorating is being done in the Mediterranean mood but coming up fast is Colonial American again.

> Things have been good for us. . . . There have been many illnesses, but thankfully we have survived. We moved into a larger house which is more to our liking. . . . I have many new small appliances which I enjoy. . . . Cooking is still a creative art.

The *onbeat women* are conscientious, playful, devoted to maintaining home and family in stable ways. They seek quality and appropriateness, keeping in step, working for lifestyles that are becoming to the husbands' status and the neighborhoods in which they live. Self-control and optimism, support from religion, and constructive thinking orient them toward sensible mastery of their ups and downs.

> Well as could be expected, everything seems to be normal. No sickness or financial worries over the past 3, 4 years. My husband is

an average man, makes an average income. He is in the piano business, he buys and sells. I taught piano until a few years ago, but now I have less time to spend foolishly. . . . This is a troubled world, and there are times when everybody is unhappy. . . . But a woman gets along if she keeps current with the news, politics, wears nice clothing, has a good hair style. It is really Jones' world. Everybody is trying to get ahead.

The *downbeat women* show feelings of disorganization, heavy responsibility, and fatalism. They do not feel able to cope adequately with their destinies, families, husbands. Life seems either troubled or dull to them.

> Let's say fair. We haven't had any real problems. We live here because my husband can drive to work. He feels medium about his job, doesn't mind it, though. What else is there to say? . . . Some days here are just hectic cooking, I just stagger throughout the day. . . . Nothing in particular I like. I would like to get away by myself for a vacation. I lead a dull life, we haven't done much of anything. I guess we have achieved some of our goals, but you are never satisfied.

In addition to the women who are upbeat, onbeat, and downbeat, there are those who are just plain *beat*. They feel that coping is almost beyond them, that demands and circumstances have defeated them or exhausted their resources. Sometimes, one such has to yield, perhaps to a hospital or perhaps to retreat to be near her parents.

> It has been hectic . . . you know, the usual things when you have five children. My husband is a Navy man and isn't home like other fathers. I'm tired and don't like the place that

we live and I am going back home. I want to be near my family and I want my mother now . . . I am never out. I haven't been out now for 6 years. I hardly ever get a chance to go anywhere. I really could go, but I am so tired at the end of the day I don't want to go anywhere. I would like to go on an island by myself and not even talk.

Individual personality thus affects how people can or cannot use abundance. Upbeat and onbeat women are more apt to seek it, use it, master it, and enjoy it; downbeat and beat women, in comparable financial circumstances, feel harassed by plenty and the demands it makes for striving, going out to get it and to make active use of it.

STAGE IN THE LIFE CYCLE

How one relates to abundance is also sharply affected by the life stage of the individual. The capacity for awareness, the level of affluence, the directions and quality of interest in products and services, all undergo great changes with age. This is a truism, but the necessity for analysis remains. The developmental tasks confronting children, adolescents, young, mature, and aging adults have peculiarities that guide what meanings abundance is likely to have for them, since abundance is relative to need. This can be highlighted by dipping into points in the age stream, illustrating some typical outlooks. For example, a 16-year-old indicates the testing out, trying out quality felt about venturing into an increasingly adult world of choices. Things such as food are taken for granted as still provided by parents; others such as clothes must be decided about.

Sixteen is lots of activities, always on the go. You are in the prime of life. It is happy years. You don't have worries other people have, you don't have to worry where your dinner is coming from. It is sometimes hard to make decisions, what to wear, the right thing to wear when you are going someplace. And sometimes you have so many places to go to you don't know where to go. It is hard to decide.

An 18-year-old confronts herself decisively, coming to terms with herself, her career, her financial situation.

I am very sensitive and easily hurt, but I know my friends say how little and cute I am. I now work at two jobs and get the money I need for school and clothes. I will graduate high school, I am not smart enough to go to college. I will get a job in an office.

A sophisticated 20-year-old suggests her enlarged view of the world.

I used to be nervous with men, but now that I work with them, we discuss general things, world situations, work, other people, TV, books, and what movie they have seen lately, sports, and eventually other, on a more personal basis, specific things.

In general, the young people show a reaching out, a sense of their own broadening horizons, a wish to be somewhat more liberated and expressive than their parents; but there seems less intergenerational gap than the publicized rebels suggest. These girls take for granted the numerous products available and expect to make use of the familiar ones.

I'll do the same thing with my kids that my mother does, make them take turns doing housework. In basic things like food I will probably stick to Campbell's, Hunt's, Del Monte, Chicken of the Sea, and Cherry Valley. Mostly in detergents I will stick with Tide and Ajax. Basically you will use what your mother used.

The young wife with a growing family does modify what she learned from her mother, feeling that new ways of child rearing and new household goals teach one how to be modern. Visible in the early years of marriage is an adaptation to new things, a growing and searching, and generally, an orientation to mobility via the many avenues available. Foremost among these is the husband's progress. At this life stage, the mantle of hope is on his shoulders. There are numerous references to going to school to get more credits, room for advancement, a job with a future, diversified opportunities to learn, broaden his knowledge, and give him better prospects.

The dream of a house, or of a new home, or a larger home means improvement of circumstances via change of dwelling and better neighborhood. Others want to fix up their homes to show a degree of advancement. The fantasy of a better future rides high. There is enough youth, enough sense of growth or increasing chances, of getting a greater share in the abundance that the terminology of planning and wishing are continually expressed.

Someday we want a place of our own.

We definitely plan to move in the near future.

Someday I would like to move out to a deluxe apartment.

There are also more personal wishes. The young-maturing housewife dreams of

being rich, staying young, being slim. When she looks beyond feeling preoccupied and absorbed with her children—she makes frequent references to "after my children are in school," "now all I want to do is to raise a family," "after my child is older,"—she thinks about self-expressive activities she might undertake—art, dancing, tennis, writing, volunteer work, and so on.

The more matured families convey a sense of reaching a peak, of settling in with a moderation of the breadth of possibilities. Commonly, the men are working pretty close to their capacity, doing the work they are likely to continue with, with not much more than a few systematic raises to be expected. Ideas of future gains tend to be replaced with acceptance of and hopes within the status quo.

His only prospects would be if he opens his own business which he has no intention of doing.

I doubt that he will go any further in his job than he is now. He makes good money and I have no complaints.

My husband will continue like he has been doing for 20 years until we are on Social Security.

Concern mounts with figuring out how to get through the tighter period when income is settling down, prices keep going up, and the needs of older children for food, clothes, education, weddings, and the like seem to reach a crescendo. One of the meanings of an abundant society is the abundance of things to want in order to participate in it, posing the concomitant problem of sustaining the socially expected level of participation. There is talk about savings, fringe benefits, investments, insurance, as thoughts turn to ways of making it through.

> The stock and pension plan that the company set up helps our future. We have some insurance. We will manage.

> We have savings and then of course there is the insurance program which will go toward the children's education. Clothing for the children is more expensive. They want more at this time and are more influenced by what the others have.

> We save whatever we can spare. We are buying bonds and have a nest egg for the children's education.

The group in their fifties and sixties tend to be in a quieter period when some responsibilities are being reduced, major goals have been met and are being enjoyed, disappointments are solidified into bitterness or resignation, striving is less intense. The man's retirement is a major consideration, with thinking oriented to changes in housing, new lifestyles. The abundant society presses people to remain youthful, to keep up, to be active, independent. Those who manage to do this reasonably well may turn to a new, more convenient home, a new car for travel, new furnishings, new clothes, a kind of carefree blossoming. Income limitations often thwart the aims of older people. Those who feel left out resent the abundant society, seeing those who can make claims on it as grasping and ungrateful.

> No matter where I look for a job I have it thrown in my face that I am too old. . . . I am very lonesome, my life is very lonesome. . . . It is just like being in prison, you can't go out if you have to watch your pennies. It worries me now that the individual is taxed to death.

> . . . Young people ought to be paddled. . . . They are spoiled. It is gimme, gimme all the time. They get what they want and then get into mischief.

FAMILY SITUATION AND OUTLOOK

Putting together the various sources of reactions suggested here produces the complex that is each family's economic situation and outlook. Nor are these matters simply related. It is possible to feel that trends are unhappy in the world but to be optimistic about the material things that will be bought. One person said,

> There has to be an end to the high cost of living. Costs keep rising and I don't think things are going to change. Farmers are going broke. Small stores are being pushed out. I can't feel good about anything.

But later in the interview, the same individual said,

> During the next 6 months or so I will want a new car, a new rug, a new living room suite of furniture. Linoleum for my kitchen, a new lawn mower and new shoes and clothes. I would like a lovely wedding for my daughter. I will probably have enough money to get them.

Throughout the interviews, one sees the intense importance of the interplay between what affluence permits and what abundance provides. There is a general feeling of sharing in or anticipating gaining more of the amplitude of products that make American life full of so many things. This is quite a relative affair. In one notable instance, a lower lower class girl who lives in one of America's worst slums was shown a picture of a barefoot, poorly dressed boy. This was her comment.

> He was very dirty and tacky and he looks like he's hungry. It looks like his family is very poor from the condition of the house. From the looks on the boy's face they're probably out trying to get food or steal food. It looks like a overseas picture. I don't believe nothing like this ever happens in America. If it did, we haven't discovered it because we have too many people on welfare. I think it's something that happens overseas.

In her mind, really poor people must be elsewhere since even welfare is a form of affluence. Among well-established middle- and working-class people the sense of security of income is strong. They recognize that they have useful, rewarded skills, that they have an achieved affluence and a degree of well-being in food, comfort, entertainment, travel, education, that is surpassed historically only by small elites. This does not mean that they feel they have enough, or that if they have enough, that they have all they *want*. The affluence has trouble keeping up with the abundance. The wants keep ascending. Many of them are large and are satisfied by use of credit; the debtor who possesses many products does not feel quite so affluent, despite his abundance.

> You can't hold on to money. It burns a hole in your pocket. He'd have to be a millionaire to afford everything that we want.

It is probably no news that the more people have, the more they want. In some people, this seems intrinsic, merely acquisitive. In others, the growing wants seem more related to wanting to maximize the nature of one's goals, so that they constantly absorb more money as it becomes available. The man who can now afford more insurance for his family feels it reasonable to carry a larger policy, the people who want to travel try to take the longest, most diverse, and in a sense, costliest trips they can squeeze in. Devout homeowners, who include vast numbers of Americans, engage endlessly in pouring money at the walls, basements, appliances, gutters, and sewers of their houses. Each home improvement project may engender another. People who value eating out, night life, living it up, do so in ever more opulent style. Another way of expressing this insatiability is to say that few consumers feel able to satisfy themselves on all fronts. They usually feel that some expenditure is being deferred to permit another; and more discretionary funds would make more experience possible.

As a consequence, while feelings of satiation do at times occur, especially when people become impressed by how much care is required to keep after all their possessions, there is not much guilt, and they generally see no inherent drawbacks to their pursuit of abundance when they are not being asked to philosophize about the subject.

In fact, of course, there are inherent limitations. As noted, there is rarely enough money. And the final two difficulties that hamper the insatiable consumer are time and energy. Even when he has enough money to satisfy innumerable desires, his time to engage in doing so remains limited. He must spend time producing, too, not only shopping and buying. Then, as he gains both money and leisure, he also becomes older and regardless of the proddings of his wife, his energy for vigorous consuming declines and declines. . . . The rest is silence.

NOTE

1. Support and cooperation of Social Research, Inc., the J. Walter Thompson Company, and the Home Furnishings Marketing and Research Council are gratefully acknowledged.

REFERENCES

Davis, F. (1967). Why all of us may be hippies someday. *Trans-action, 5*(2), 10-18.

Galbraith, J. K. (1967). *The new industrial state.* Boston: Houghton Mifflin.

Meadows, P. (1967). Traditional motivations in an age of rapid change. *Business and Society, 8*(1), 19-29.

Warner, W. L. (1962). *The corporation in the emergent American society.* New York: Harper.

## Chapter 33

THE DISCRETIONARY SOCIETY

Sidney J. Levy

It seems presumptuous to attempt another formulation about contemporary American society. The media are flooded with self-examination that agonizes about our problems, such that the more one listens and reads, the more intimidating is the challenge. The pessimists tend to dominate: Certainly, Cassandra is a bolder voice than Pollyanna. Toffler says we suffer from Future Shock, Erlich finds us doomed by the Population Bomb, and journalists keep diagnosing "the distemper of America" (Fairlie, 1969). If the destruction of the waters of the cities, of the planet, cannot be reversed, it no longer matters what kind of society we have, except as we may enjoy watching it perish.

On the other hand, there are voices that say the generation gap is more of an illusion than we may realize; that there could not be so much fuss about dissent if this were not a viable democracy; and that

Regardless of the source of pollution of air, water, or land—smog, noise, garbage, or industrial waste—technological developments and advance in pure science are together probably able to cope with the problem, provided adequate magnitude and scope of research and development are initiated.

This chapter was first presented as a speech at The American Marketing Association Educators Conference in Boston, August 1970.

Ways can be found in principle to do everything that causes pollution . . . speaking technologically only, of course.

The pressures of inflation, recession, awareness of poverty, unemployment, the stock market, and other economic complexities are troublesome and have visible effects on people's attitudes and patterns of money handling. The purchases of cars and durable goods decline, and the latest ideology, consumerism, finds new adherents, both justified and unreasonable. Despite the concern over these matters, buying and selling goes on, and the long-run marketing perspective finds comfort where it can. As a *Citizen Smith* cartoon noted recently, "Outside of Vietnam, air and water pollution, the cost of living, taxes, the general unrest, my job and my situation at home—I can't complain."

We are repeatedly told that the changing marketplace has never been in such flux. An announcement of a typical conference soon to be held points out a long list of products in the leisure industry that offer new opportunities for growth. A report from the Bank of America points out that "the fastest-growing segment of the food industry, convenience stores, [has] increased in number from approximately 500 nationally in 1957 with sales of $75 million, to over 16,500 stores in 1969 with sales of $27 billion" (*Los Angeles Times,* July 14, 1970, Part III, p. 19). Meanwhile, the supermarkets, undeterred by this competition, look ahead to stores that will be "customized," "personalized," and fun for different income levels, different ethnic groups, or perhaps to be even bigger and more automated to increase efficiency (*Los Angeles Times,* May 2, 1970, Part IV, p. 2). This great sense of change is captured in another invitation to a conference to be held next year. It points out that,

The consumer market is experiencing changes of unparalleled dimensions. The many currents of change which have been building since the end of World War II are now beginning to be felt at the marketplace. For example, youngsters born during the birth boom of the early Fifties are now reaching adulthood and the pace of household formation is accelerating. Births, meanwhile, which had been declining since the late Fifties, are turning up again. We are also experiencing many important social changes— more wives are entering the labor force, increasing numbers of persons are acquiring a college education, and the move to the suburbs is likely to accelerate. Most important, perhaps, is the ongoing reshuffle in the nation's income distribution pattern; increasing numbers of the nation's families are moving into the upper earning brackets. (U.S. Department of Commerce, 1970).

Latest census results document the broad changes, telling us that more people now live in the suburbs than in core cities, that since 1960, 16 million people got out of poverty, as defined by the government. Black Americans showed dramatic gains in these 10 years, in the proportions working in professional and technical jobs, and in the proportion earning over $8,000 a year—32% compared to 15%.

With savings at new heights, teenagers accounting for billions of dollars, the Negro market spending more than $30 billion, with some electricians' incomes pushing some physicians' incomes, with disposable personal income rising (even in terms of 1958 dollars) (Krugman, 1968), it is apparent that these growth figures will create and affect new markets. It may be summed up in the statistics which tell us that expenditures in the recreational realm of boating quadrupled from $680 million in 1950 to $2,683 million in 1965, steadily improving to $3,292 million in 1969. Such statistics mean that the concept of consuming is being enlarged, and in more than one way. As society changes, the availability of a widening range of choices alters the substance of consuming: What people buy and how they buy it are revised. At the same time, the concept changes because the kind of thinking about marketing also shifts with new personnel studying it; interdisciplinary approaches are used, and there is pressure to reformulate and reconceptualize the nature of marketing. Often this is a matter of focus or emphasis, whereby categories are changed, not only because the behavior being studied may have changed, but because the scholar's interest moves. An example can be found in Herbert Krugman's article on consumer behavior in the 1968 International Encyclopedia of Social Sciences. He points out that

All of these areas of research involve a move away from descriptive or reportorial research to inquiry guided by the use of theory and undertaken for the purpose of further theory development. This means that the study of the consumer has now finally linked up with the main body of the behavioral sciences. (p. 353)

He goes on to conclude,

As for the consumer himself, we may expect further inroads on his ancient image of himself as a person in want and as one who is preoccupied with the allocation of scarce means to satisfy basic needs. Foote proposes that as the proportion of household expenditures devoted to food continues to fall, (in 20 years it has gone from 30% to 21%) today's somewhat obese consumer may well develop wants that do not require production or consumption, such as stimulating

conversation or the creation of music. The constraint on wants such as these will not be income but learning ability. In short, consumers may yet outgrow consumption. (p. 353)

This comment implies that the study of consumer behavior has been the study of how income was disbursed in the pursuit of food and that consuming is eating. The dictionary tells us this also and adds the ideas of wasting, destroying, using. The economic definition of the consumer further qualifies the contrast with the producer by referring to meeting one's own needs rather than reworking or reselling the goods. The more contemporary, broader understanding of consuming recognizes that it requires the outlay of more than just income (which may remain a scarce resource as long as there is not enough to buy all the things one wants). Other scarce resources include the built-in limits of attention, time, and energy; and if we are to include the kinds of capacities suggested by Krugman's reference to learning ability, there is capacity for enjoyment, visual, auditory, tactile acuity, and so on.

It has never been clear to me why so-called cultural experiences have tended to be excluded from the realm of consumer behavior. Actually, a broadened concept of consuming recognizes that marketing has not just discovered conversation or music. They have been marketplace alternatives since the market began, even if not bestsellers or always available to the mass market. As marketing has pressed on from commodities to products to services and miscellaneous intangibles, it has become increasingly apparent that the consumer is an individual in a position of having to make decisions about allocating his scarce means of all types. He cannot outgrow consumption because in whatever he does, he uses up his experiences and pays some price for them.

In talking about changes in the market-place, there is ample evidence for them, but it is also easy to exaggerate the changes. Entranced with the word *change* and with the word *innovation,* everything begins to look like colored shirts, marijuana, and nudity, with everyone eating only convenience foods, drinking instant coffee, and going to Europe. The problem is to gain perspective and not to overstate the changes that are such highly visible realities. William Wells (1970) points out that the results of a survey of a large sample of people concerning their activities, interests, and opinions showed that these people portray themselves as "happy, home-loving, clean, and square;" and he cautions against confusing the mass of Americans with the swinging young people who are so much in evidence.

Still, this comparison itself, and Wells's reference to the many executives in advertising, marketing, and mass communications who live and work in a metropolitan, cosmopolitan subsociety points to the substantial alternative ways of life that are available in this country. It also means that we need to learn more about the diffusion of ideas and changes so that we can judge when innovators are just doing their own thing, or when their example is a harbinger of a more general modification in the society, and when the young will or will not carry their new attitudes and actions into maturity.

The interwoven influences of changes also need tracing out. The contraceptive pill has led to an enlargement of the average size of brassiere sold—a consequence the clothing industry had probably not anticipated or planned for. Both the hula hoop and the dance, The Twist, increased ortho-

pedic business, detergents brought patients to the dermatologist, and rock to the otologist. The growth in educational level of the population has, in my opinion, permitted more use of humor and subtler wit in advertising than in the past. Also, the so-called square in the middle majority cannot merely ignore actions in the swinging parts of society because they do radiate out to affect him. A fairly dramatic example is the conventional barber, who finds that longer hair is ruining his business. In his resentment, he may refuse to cut long hair when it does show up; and he presses another part of the market by threatening to boycott merchants who employ long-haired clerks, as was recently reported.

The problems of making choices in a complex world with increasing amounts of disposable income can be studied from numerous directions. Much recent and contemporary effort has been going into such studies and into attempts to formulate appropriate theoretical frameworks, more than can be briefly reviewed here. It may be enough to remind us almost randomly of the consumer behavior volumes edited by Lincoln Clark (1958) and by Nelson Foote (1961), an early comprehensive view by Robert Ferber (1962), the Nicosia (1966) model of Consumer Decision Processes, and the broad contribution of Howard and Sheth (1969).

Discretionary may be a poor adjective for describing current society. It implies not only freedom of choice, but also the quality of being prudent. The customary confusion stirred by the distinctions some writers try to define between rational and emotional behavior are thus further complicated by suggesting that the consumer will behave in a cautious or virtuous way, interpreting his goals with reference to what is good for him. In discussing decision making, Ward

Edwards (1968) notes that "there are, of course, a number of well-known counter-examples to the idea that men consistently do what is best for them." But further on he inclines in the other direction:

> What little evidence is available suggests that men do remarkably well at doing what they should, given the information at hand. . . . On the whole, men do well; exactly how well they do, depends in detail on the situation they are in, what's at stake, how much information they have, and so on. (p. 38)

But who determines what is best, or when one does well? These statements highlight the need for the phenomenological viewpoint, examination of how the situation looks from the inside. Many have ably argued for a pluralistic approach, for both internal and external variables. One of the difficulties is that internal approaches are often reduced to relatively formal variables such as psychological traits, which then turn out not to correlate with the marketing behavior being studied.

To understand a discretionary society would seem to require a great deal of empathy, a willingness to attend closely to the subjectivity being expressed verbally and in the behavior. Some of the work that comes nearer to doing this looks at perceived risk, at reactions to information (Cox, 1967), at the way experience and values are defended, reworked, and integrated in the decision making. Work on the subjectivity of consumer experience will probably grow as the myths of the superiority of external, objective, and behavioristic approaches are exposed, and as scientists recognize the importance of the subject matter. Galbraith (1967) has tried to help this along by his overevaluation of television; he is right on when he says:

There is an insistent tendency among solemn social scientists to think of any institution which features rhymed and singing commercials, intense and lachrymose voices urging highly improbable enjoyments, caricatures of the human esophagus in normal or impaired operation, and which hints implausibly at opportunities for antiseptic seduction, as inherently trivial. This is a great mistake. (p. 218)

Listening to consumers talk about their reactions to these "trivial" appeals, their feelings about their resources, and where they can exercise discretion, one observes an interesting spectrum of attitudes and viewpoints. There is a range in awareness of alternatives and options. A consumer's aspirations depend upon his horizons. What does he know about the world, what can he include in his fantasies, what does he think he could realistically yearn for? How much freedom of choice does he subjectively experience? What personal and social constraints does he feel hedging him in? The appraisal of resources goes on constantly, permitting or denying choices—We can afford to go! I'm too tired! I can just fit that in the schedule. Will my vision be good enough ? Will he be able to understand it? And so on.

The process of choice involves working through this awareness, through one sort of deliberation or another, to action. Commitments come into being that are viewed as fixed expenses, one's customary obligations, ordinarily some kinds of necessities and routine activities thought to be basic. Even these are up to one to choose—as one can give up food for alcohol or beachcomb rather than housekeep. Basic necessities may include paying off debts for past frivolities. The discretionary society might better be termed the indiscretionary society, since it is often the freedom to be indiscreet and to indulge one's imprudent choices that makes the freedom seem real.

The process of exercising discretion and indiscretion goes on at several levels. At one level is the choice of products and services in immediate situations. Much more study might be done on the richness of local experience in shopping situations. It has many intriguing aspects. Gerald Bell has pointed to the role of the friend with product-specific confidence that the automobile shopper may lack, a special example of the category that includes realtors, brokers, interior decorators, and matchmakers of all kinds. A husband, wife, and salesman in a men's clothing store form a triad of forces subtly jockeying to affect the result.

Haines (1969) has conveyed some of the expressiveness in consumer behavior with shopping tour protocols. James Carman (1969) shows something of the relationships between careful shopping, attention to special deals, adeptness in timing one's actions, and so on, should a housewife be willing to engage in the strategies he describes. It would also be worthwhile to explore why so many women do not employ these strategies. Kollatt and Willett (1969) discuss the concept of impulse purchasing, criticizing it as too vague, commonly exaggerated, and misleading. The issues they raise highlight the value of examining with more ingenuity what goes on in the supermarket.

Much so-called impulse purchasing can readily be shown not to be unplanned, but impulsive actions do occur in immediate shopping situations. Of interest might be such subjective aspects as the customer's shopping temperament, his susceptibility to point-of-purchase displays and promotional techniques; the function of different moods, the role of haste, and so on. It has

been shown that hunger tends to lead to a fuller cart than shopping after a meal.

Shopping may be carried out temporarily or characteristically with various special feelings: deserving, for example, whereby the shopper feels in need of comfort or that some reward is his due. Gaiety sometimes sweeps over the shopper, often when with others, when the atmosphere takes on a carnival or festive, let's-live-it-up tone. The necessity for maintaining "front" may deter a shopper from buying things he wants because others are, in some sense, watching him and he does not want to contradict his sense of public self. Some shoppers act almost "pseudopodically," wanting to take in all they can, putting out many arms to sweep in a lot, unloading proudly all the substance at the checkout counter.

At another level are prior plans and impulses to act. These relate to making decisions about going out, deciding to decorate a house, buying clothes, and so on. The subjective processes become more involved with accumulating information over time, deliberating, getting advice. The budget and ideas of affording may loom and play a timing role, asking whether to do it now or later. Important also in the timing is the idea of readiness. Some purchases need a ripening, a getting used to the thought enough that one can finally do it. Others have a life cycle readiness about them: Is the woman grown up enough to wear an expensive fur and feel she can carry it off? Is the child ready for a two-wheeler?

Part of timing includes one's reasoning about the order of needs. John McFall (1969) shows how the acquiring of goods follows a priority pattern in which it seems appropriate to buy certain appliances before one buys others. Groups show consistency in this, although obviously not all consumers acquire their household durables in the identical order. Priorities among family members would also be worth examination. How is discretion exercised in determining whose needs and wishes should be met? What are the mechanisms for resolving conflicts and apportioning shares?

Interesting questions about predispositions emerge at the prior level of planning and seeking. Charles Bearchell is investigating home buying; his special interest was aroused by observing that some people looked only at new houses, others looked only at old houses, others looked at both. It is not yet clear what general factors may be at work to produce these differences.

The immediate situation and prior planning levels form the everyday expression of the consumer's lifestyle, a third level of analysis. This is the level of conceptualization that governs and integrates the general character of the earlier levels, to the extent that we are capable of perceiving it. It is often hard to see the larger pattern that is being expressed, how in minor events major themes may be acted out. However, the lifestyle level has its own broad choices, choices that create the fundamental tone, the context, and the most characteristic stamp of the individual and the family: choices of education—how much to strive for, how hard to work at it, where to get it, what kind to pursue; choices of where to live, what community, what kind of housing, what proportion of income to put into housing; whether to stock liquor, books, or both; to travel to posh spots or mass market motels; whether to spend one's time, typically, in listening to music, going out to night clubs, doing things with the children, watching television, being fanatical about a hobby.

Making such characterizations is not novel; it is an old pastime when it comes to studying peoples and societies. About 130 years ago, in *Democracy in America,* DeTocqueville wrote that people with money living in democracies think more of satisfying their slightest needs than seeking extraordinary delights. He says that they indulge a quantity of little wants but do not let themselves give rein to any great disorderly passion, that they are more prone to become enervated than debauched. Whether true then or not, it is apparently not entirely true in our discretionary society. Having money has indeed permitted Americans to indulge a quantity of little wants; and undoubtedly great numbers are more tired than given to sensual excesses. However, that there are disorderly passions seems apparent. Among the many examples all around was an item in Thursday's *Chicago Sun-Times:*

> The Cook County state's attorney's office is investigating a three-day wife-swapping convention that 400 persons attended in Franklin Park. . . . The convention was the First National Swinging (Wife-Swapping) Convention, held in the O'Hare Congress Inn at 3010 Mannheim the weekend of August 14-16.

As lifestyles move in different directions, the choices of ways to live sort out various market segments. As one example, James Bell (1969) reports on mobiles, the people who are geographically mobile. Movers each year account for about 20% of the population; and the sample families averaged one long-distance move every 3 years, a rate nearly five times the national average. They show a variety of interesting marketing characteristics such as spending twice as much money on furniture and appliances per year as nonmobiles with similar incomes.

Another distinctive lifestyle is suggested by the audience for the live professional performing arts in the United States. Baumol and Bowen (1966) studied theatergoers to plays, opera, music, and dance. They find rather modest evidence for the often-claimed "culture boom" and describe the audience as drawn from a very narrow population segment of people who have high education, high income, and are not very young. Working-class people rarely accounted for more than 5% of the audience, and one chamber music concert audience had a median income of $16,000.

Among more ordinary people, who do not move every 3 years or attend chamber music concerts, the sense of discretionary improvement is nevertheless visible. There is the feeling that nowadays people have more things, and they anticipate having more. There is a lively awareness of more places to go and things to do—in fact, L. J. Crampon (undated) forecasts a doubling of annual trips to more than 1 billion by U.S. residents during the next 30 years. The feeling of improvement in material circumstances is commonly expressed:

Things are better. We have more of everything. Twice as much. People can relax, vacation, they have money to spend. We have more conveniences. We don't stick to "do we have to have it?" We like to satisfy our desires.

I think people have it easier today because of higher wages and salaries, more leisure time, more time spent on other things than strictly working for a living, such as vacations, watching television, driving high-power automobiles, have more conveniences. To sum it up, is that people have more material things nowadays.

How much discretion this plenty leaves one is another subjective issue. From the

way many talk it becomes uncertain whether there is any realistic distinction maintained between necessities and luxuries. When asked what percentage of income is estimated to go for essentials, people say things like this:

Too damn much! 75%. The house, all the utilities, furniture, transportation, food, clothing, and education.

I'd say 75%—I'd include rent, utilities, withholding taxes, social security, insurance, food, doctor and dentist bills, clothing, and that's just the bare essentials.

Most of it goes for essentials. The food, the rent, utility bills and medical bills—actually 100% goes for essentials. There is very little left to squander.

When the conversation is pursued further, to what kinds of things are not essential, this latter speaker goes on to say:

I get just a few more clothes than I need. Because I'm a woman and I like pretty clothes. I do go to a lot of baseball games and I splurge on tickets in advance. I'm a baseball nut.

She goes on further to explain another essential purchase, one which caused some debate about affording it:

The humidifier was the last thing we were debating about. It's crazy but every morning we would wake up with a dry nose and throat and a feeling of soreness. So we bought one and we haven't been sick since. It has paid for itself over and over with the reduced doctor bills.

Similarly a working class man tells us:

My whole salary usually goes for essentials, for groceries and other essential necessities. And naturally about 10% for savings which is really important for a man's security. Cigars are not essential, but I like to smoke them. Some liquid beverages. As for activities, going dancing, to parties and theaters with a group of people for an enjoyable evening of fun, are the extras that are important to life.

He explains a recent substantial purchase:

The washing machine. The old one we gave away. We decided—my wife and I—to get a new one. She wanted a portable automatic so it would be easier to wash. The old one and going to the Laundromat could have been used for a while yet. But she wanted an automatic so she wouldn't have to put her hands in water that much. And the time she spent at the Laundromat is used for other duties at home.

Overall, what people want from the discretionary society can be used to categorize them as omnivorous, sufficing, or replete. The Omnivorous Consumer is still working hard at maintaining the acquisitive society, wanting more of all that can be dreamed. Two jobs, another car, more help, latest models are sought; it is easy to solicit from them lists of the things they would like to have, and new goals and experiences keep coming along.

I'd like to make more money and move into a larger home. I'd like to give my family a better environment.

I'd like to have things easier, a maid, a housekeeper, and definitely a new home of our own.

I got a new dishwasher. I balanced the fact of the addition to the value of the house, and the money would be spent anyway, and it is a nice useful luxury.

We went to Washington, New York, because we thought it had something for everyone in the family and got a chance to have this type of education and entertainment. I had never been to New York, so my husband thought it would be a great idea. There was so much to see and learn and, of course, all kinds of plays to see and places to take the kids.

The Sufficing Consumer feels that things are pretty good as they are, that he is rather content and does not wish for much more. Of course, things may not be quite sufficient, and one can add a bit more.

We have an easier way of life, more education, all the modern conveniences. I wouldn't make any major changes—but would like someone to wash my windows, and a few more clothes. Everyone should be able to earn their own way if they can.

The Replete Consumer feels there is so much of everything that some retrenchment would be useful. He is stuffed with material objects and yearns for a return to more basic values and satisfactions, to ways of living that would bring people closer together or to get away from the crowd.

Today there is less family closeness. People are drawn to things outside the home. We don't have the same closeness, living on top of people with friends and family like my parents had.

We just spend too damn much for the house, furniture, transportation, food. I'd like to live out in the sticks, have more land, fewer people around. I would still have lots of friends but see them less often.

And there, these various voices from the discretionary society, we will leave them.

REFERENCES

Baumol, W. J., & Bowen, W. G. (1966). *Performing arts—The economic dilemma.* New York: The Twentieth Century Fund.

Bell, J. E., Jr. (1969). Mobiles—a neglected market segment. *Journal of Marketing, 33,* 37-44.

Carman, J. M. (1969). Some insights into reasonable grocery shopping strategies. *Journal of Marketing, 33,* 72.

Clark, L. H. (Ed.). (1958). *Consumer behavior: Research on consumer reactions.* New York: Harper.

Cox, D. F. (Ed.). (1967). *Risk taking and information handling in consumer behavior.* Boston: Harvard University Press.

Crampon, L. J. (undated). *Travel—the next 30 years.* Cambridge, MA: Arthur D. Little, Inc.

Edwards, W. (1968). Decision making: Psychological aspects. In D. L. Sills (Ed.), *International encyclopedia of the social sciences* (Vol. 4, p. 38).

Fairlie, H. (1969, December 28). *Chicago Sunday Sun-Times,* Part 2, p. 1.

Ferber, R. (1962). Research on household behavior. *American Economic Review, 52,* 19-63.

Foote, N. (Ed.). (1961). *Household decision-making.* New York: New York University Press.

Galbraith, J. K. (1967). *The new industrial state.* New York: Houghton Mifflin.

Haines, G. H., Jr. (1969). *Consumer behavior.* New York: Free Press.

Howard, J. A., & Sheth, J. N. (1969). *The theory of buyer behavior.* New York: John Wiley.

Kollatt, D. T., & Willett, R. P. (1969). Is impulse purchasing really a useful concept for marketing decisions? *Journal of Marketing, 33,* 79-83.

Krugman, H. E. (1968). Consumer behavior. In D. L. Sills (Ed.), *International encyclopedia of social science* (Vol. 3, p. 353).

McFall, J. (1969). Priority patterns and consumer behavior. *Journal of Marketing, 33,* 550-555.

Nicosia, F. M. (1966). *Consumer decision processes.* Englewood Cliffs, NJ: Prentice Hall.

U.S. Department of Commerce. (1970, April). *Survey of current business, 50,* pp. 4, 9.

Wells, W. D. (1970, January/February). It's a Wyeth, not a Warhol, world. *Harvard Business Review,* pp. 26-32.

Chapter 34

EMOTIONAL REACTIONS TO THE CUTTING OF TREES

Sidney J. Levy

The cutting of trees means different things to different people. A spectrum of views will be discussed, to show some major silvicultural orientations and their consequences in people's attitude. Analyzing reactions to the cutting of trees can be done in one way by examining the rhetoric people use in putting forth their view, as well as their formal opinion. Their choice of language, its tone, the kind of words that recur, and the figures of speech used, express their feelings, clothing their ideas with implications and justifications that will make their positions plausible. What-

ever the emotional sources of the positions taken, a thought structure arises, with values being stated and reasoning offered to defend them. Thus, each position has not only its rhetoric, but its logic of appropriate ideas, its claim to certain fact, and recommended action; in the background are deeper seated beliefs and emotions, some of which will be interpreted here.

People who most differ often refuse to debate on the same ground. They confine their attention to the elements that are most meaningful to them. This is apparent in the literature relating to forests and tree cut-

This chapter was first presented as a speech before the Southern Forest Products Association, Atlanta, 1973.

ting. Three main positions are apparent there, with many variations. On the one hand are people who clearly believe that tree cutting is essential, that demand is outstripping supply, and that almost any means are justified to obtain the needed lumber. Their basic view of trees and forests is of economic resources. Concerns are with the number of feet of lumber, the changing distribution system, the various bases for increasing yield and rate of return. A typical article of this type in *Forest Science* ("Which Criterion," 1972) reports a study of two criteria—net present value versus internal rate of return—to determine which is preferable, concluding that in the southern industrial forest, the optimum rotation age is more sensitive to changes in factors such as stumpage rates and annual fixed cost if the rate of return criterion is maximized.

This language, these ideas, are a far cry from those of concern to the environmentalists and conservationists and show no interest in the issues they raise. Moving along the spectrum, there are those who do take notice of the people who object to tree cutting, and speaking as silviculturalists or as industry spokesmen, assert directly opposing views. Fred C. Simmons (1972) is especially vigorous in this direction. He argues that the natural way is bad, that leaving forests alone results in a biological desert. It is better to let in more sunlight than the wilderness permits and better to use the forest for needed wood products. *Commerce Today* ("Woodsman," 1972) fears for the industry with so much competition coming from highways, dams, cities, and suburbs. Even more to show that tree cutting is good, W. B. Hagenstein (1970) says that "clearcutting is silviculturally sound" for one thing because it provides aesthetically pleasing open space in forests.

At the opposite end of the spectrum are those who seem relatively indifferent to the consumers' need for lumber, paper, and wooden products. Partly, they assume the forces that will provide the products are so strong, especially as they are apt to believe that the government either does not know how to control the industry or is on its side. They see several villains: the Executive Office, complex economic dealings that dominate smaller companies, the Forest Service and "narrowly oriented forestry school" graduates who deny that U.S. forests are being abused. Gordon Robinson (1973) discussing "Our Export Forest," maintains that unless exportation of private timber is controlled, enlightened forestry practices stand little chance of implementation. *Business Week* ("Timber Industry's," 1972) examines the struggle and notes the polarity, saying that the industry practice of clear-cutting, regeneration with single species supertrees, and unregulated use of private land fly in the face of conservationist and preservationist interests.

The extremists of these interests reason away from the possibility of "enlightened practices" in forests. They are not merely skeptical of their success, they believe that any interference with the forest is detrimental to it. Michael Thomas (1972) and Clifford E. Ahlgren (1973) perceive the forests' own cyclical destruction and renewal as essential patterns, that serious threats are posed to the sensitive equilibrium established over thousands of years of continuous development.

As might be expected, between the extreme positions has developed a middle ground in which the main issues go on around forest management, ways of resolving the needs to cut the trees and to preserve the forest. Even here, the controversy is still active, with vigorous voices proclaiming the advantages or the hazard of forest management. Robert W. Upton (1972) says "You can't preserve a tree forever, but you can manage a forest." Marlin C. Galbraith (1972) concludes that wood product crops are compatible with other environmental values. Somewhat triumphantly, Charles W. Bingham (1971) relates that thinning, fertilizing, selection, rotation, help to regenerate logged-over land. He says managed forests increase yields per acre, renew oxygen, watershed, harbor wildlife, provide recreation and scenery. Putting his faith in enhancing the environment through science and technology, he finds intensified forest management is the key.

But it is apparent that many cautions are needed. Maki (1972) looks at the pros and cons of clear-cutting and points out that practices should be tailored to fit soil, land form, climate, and species. Similarly, Resler (1972) finds that clear-cutting has benefits for wildlife resources but requires the careful application of scientific knowledge. The benefits of clear-cutting, even-aged management, and prescribed burning do not offset the detrimental aspects for wildlife resources, in the eyes of many, including Pengelly (1972), who writes that the benefits may not be compatible with intensive forest management, especially with scarifying, treeplanting, fencing, and poisoning. The discovery that forests need fires so they may as well be helped to have them with prescribed burning does not reassure people who are skeptical of man's record of controlling his environment.

In an earlier time, cutting trees was an immediate necessity to pioneering, clearing space, and building a home. The imagery of Lincoln the rail-splitter brings to mind no protest from his contemporary tree lovers. The tradition of the lumberjack, of Paul Bunyan, of log-rolling contests, of the excit-ing cry of "Timberrrr" were all-American parts of childhood lore. The connection between the tree cutting and its necessity for shelter, warmth, safety was strong enough, when joined with the magnitude of the forests, to overcome feelings of resistance to tree cutting.

But resistance to tree cutting is not a new phenomenon, as witness the story of George Washington and the cherry tree. George Pope Morris wrote his classic little poem, "Woodman, spare that tree" over a century ago. Now the resistance has grown greatly. Just few weeks ago, this item appeared in the newspaper.

> Vienna (AP)—Which comes first, the animals or the trees? The latter won out in a referendum in which voters decided against plans for a zoology institute to be built in a Vienna park. The construction would have required chopping down about 70 trees.

Despite widespread lethargy in the population, in the face of conservation issues, this incident and the many others in which citizens have chained themselves to trees to thwart the bulldozer point to the potential support that is available to environmentalists and conservationists. As leaders, they can sometimes awaken in others a not very dormant impulse to protect the trees, suggested by the rest of the Morris poem.

> Woodman, spare that tree!
> Touch not a single bough!
> In youth it sheltered me,
> And I'll protect it now.

To understand this desire to protect the tree, analysis will be made in the following directions. First, what are the meanings of trees and forests as interpreted by tradition in folk tale, myths, and religion? Second, what do people say about trees? what are their specific associations? Third, how might these ideas relate to the people who are especially anxious to preserve the wilderness?

Forests have a notable place within the general symbolism of landscape. Cirlot (1962) connects forest symbolism with the idea of the Great Mother: It is a place "where vegetable life thrives and luxuriates. It is free from any control or cultivation, dense and dark, obscuring the sun with its foliage." Thus, it also represents the unconscious impulses that threaten in the shapes of snakes, wolves, and as in Disney, trees that reach out to tear at one racing terrified through the forest. Forests, harboring dangers, demons, enemies, and disease, were among the first places in nature to be dedicated to the cult of the gods. Such a place is also a challenge in man's contest with nature, to his capacity to survive in the face of its worst. As in the Dickey story, *Deliverance,* it raises the question, can individual men contend with the primitive nature of the wilderness and emerge unscathed from the awful forces of wild waters and uninhibited sexuality? The answer may be no, but men still want to go off to the woods where civilization does not make its demands for sobriety, shaving, proper dress and language.

The mythology of the tree is, if anything, even richer than that of the forest, the tree being "one of the most essential of traditional symbols" (Cirlot, 1962, p. 328). The tree has been interpreted as standing for the life of the cosmos—sometimes the idea of life without death, since people often are impressed with the longevity of individual trees as well as the continuity of the family of the tree. The relationship to the tree is a holy one, stretching from the most ancient times when each tree was animated by a divine spirit, to a recent comic strip in which the cartoon character Ziggy plants a tree and proclaims,

> Planting a tree is a sacred trust . . . trees last through the ages . . . empires may crumble, but trees remain . . . a tree is a measure of time. . . . A calendar for the changing seasons. . . . This tiny sapling will grow to become a sanctuary for birds . . . where they can build their nests, and raise their young to grow, and begin the cycle anew.

This scene is in keeping with the old idea that a man has asserted his manhood most fully when he has "built a house, planted a tree, and fathered a son." In relating to the tree, he respects its mystic principles. The tree works in a transcendental way to connect the three worlds of Hell, Earth, and Heaven, via its roots, its trunk, and its aspiring foliage. Numerous trees have been identified as special symbols; the Tree of Knowledge, or of Good and Evil, the Tree of Life, taking form in different societies and cultures, in the Cross of Redemption, in the Nordic mythological cosmic tree, Yggdrasil.

As modern individuals interpret the meanings of trees to themselves, one may wonder whether the ancient ideas still persist. As part of a projective test, a picture of a tree in a landscape was shown to a large sample of people, with the invitation to tell a story about the picture. Some excerpts indicate the kind of tales they told.

> There was something beautiful about that old tree that Gene liked. It had been there as long as he could remember, but it had never ceased to fascinate him.

> Along all rivers and through all valleys, one tree always stands out above the rest. This is

as true in life (humans) as it is with the trees. For example, in a family the father is the "tree."

Here I see a depiction of the timeless fundamental struggle between good and evil. Good is the black shape which looks like a tree. Evil is represented by those white flames licking around the base of the tree, threatening to engulf it . . . the tree of good must be constantly vigilant and aware of those dark and terrible forces that threaten to destroy it.

There's the old tree and there's the house. How I used to love that old tree. How proud I was when I learned to climb it. Funny, it seemed bigger when I was a kid than it does now. I used to feel so warm and secure and satisfied when I touched that tree. . . . You always feel funny going back to something that you once knew well. . . . Wish they hadn't cut off that big branch.

These stories (and many others) suggest that the tree retains important basic meanings. Great yearnings become visible when people talk about the tree. They often reminisce about childhood, they envision escape from stress, finding again the peace and protection of being a child, taken care of by the secure adults, with the tree like a strong, successful father or mother, allowing shade, rest, calm. It seems easy to identify with a tree, to see one's life paralleled in its struggles to survive winds and storms, to bemoan its loss of limb, damaged like oneself. One feels obligated to that great tree, to protect it is to reciprocate the favor, and to be protecting one's own being.

In some people this benevolent attitude toward the goodness of the tree and its identity with the Life Principle takes special hold. They are willing to fight, to protest, to keep the wilderness, to enlist in the cause to maintain the natural character of the environment. Their specific goals vary. Some are ardent about the wilderness, others are more concerned about using resources in a reasonable manner with due thought for their future survival. Others are interested in an equitable use of trees and forests so that they are not consumed for products alone but are also available for other kinds of enjoyment. Those who stress ecological interactions are apt to put forth the value of the watershed, air cooling and cleaning, wildlife protection, and avoiding problems of flooding and erosion. Some emphasize the human comforts, wanting to watch out for tree screens, shelter from climate extremes, cutting noise, and retaining or developing opportunities for recreation. An important persisting devotion is to aesthetics, focusing on the beauty of the landscape, its scenic quality, its sheer excellence as a visual and atmospheric experience.

In a review of studies, Thomas J. Steele (undated) summarizes a pattern of characteristics of wilderness enthusiasts. It shows that wilderness lovers consistently value solitude, independence, and companion groups consisting only of family or very close friends. He pursued the hypothesis thus suggested that people who tended to fit the David Riesman description of highly "inner-directed" people, and those who fit the Karen Horney description of highly "detached" people, would have significantly more favorable attitudes to the concept of wilderness than persons who are either other-directed or compliant. Steele's study supported this hypothesis, indicating that people who lead the way are likely to be rather individualistic and self-sufficient, noncompliant, to rely on their own inner values and standards for guidance in a rapidly changing society.

Examining all the data, two overall sources of devotion to trees seem profound. One is the wish to turn away from the destructive forces of modern industrial society. This affiliation with the grandeur of the past expresses itself in reference to Paradise, the Garden of Eden, in emphasis on the enduring nature of trees, to fears that we will be "devoid of the ancient trees." Continuity with ancestors is implied by use of the word *legacy* and a life pact destroyed by "betrayal" by the U.S. Forest Service. An article by David Holstrom (1972) in the *Christian Science Monitor* urges, "Give a gift of part of the forest in order to save 500,000 years," suggesting something of this participation in the kind of immortality the forest signifies.

The life cycle of the tree, with its vitality and grand growth that are both mysterious and religious, reminds of the sexuality of the tree as a second main source of involvement and inspiration. The tree summarizes in its life cycle and its nature both male and female principles, with its phallic trunk and its maternal foliage. Protests against tree cutting refer to the problems that come about, the loss of seed, the interruption of natural reproductive processes. To cut a forest is to violate it, destroy its virginity; in their biological community, trees come to a climax. These are of course technical terms that do not in themselves imply any peculiar sexuality of aim toward the tree. Still, the way the word *rape* is used, in defense of the forest, and the common attribution to trees of nurturant motives toward the birds nesting in their hair, illustrate the anthropomorphic life people give them. They are like people, but nicer people, and attract the melancholy yearning to be a child again, carefree and protected. The trees' quiet, modest nonanimal sexuality has even been a source of envy to Sir Thomas Browne, who wrote in the 17th century, "I could be content that we might procreate like trees, without conjunction" (*Religio Medici,* pt. ii, #9)

In summary, emotional reactions to tree cutting vary historically, depending on what the people need from them. In early days, their religious meaning was both frightening and awesome, and one could believe trees spoke with the voices of gods. They have humanity attributed to them, it being hard to believe they do not suffer the buffets of the storm and the cut of the axe. They seem giving of life, of shelter, to be grandly sexual and thus capable of our intense identification with them. Areas without them seem exposed and desolate— with no motherly oasis to protect from the harsh blaze of the Sun-father. They can be sacrificed—and presumably willingly die— for the essential housing, fire, and sailing craft of the individual man who builds, plants his seed, and begets his son. But no wonder many feel desperate when it seems we could perhaps destroy them all.

REFERENCES

Ahlgren, C. E. (1973, January). The changing forest: Part I. *American Forests,* p. 40.

Bingham, C. W. (1971, February). Enhancing environment through science and technology. *Journal of Forestry,* pp. 72-76.

Cirlot, J. E. (1962). *A dictionary of symbols*. London: Routledge & Kegan Paul.

Galbraith, M. (1972, Fall). Environmental effects of timber harvest and utilization of logging residues. *Environmental Affairs*, pp. 314-332.

Hagenstein. R. (1970, December). Clear-cutting is silviculturally sound. *Forest Industries*, pp. 26-29.

Holstrom, D. (1972, December). Give a gift of part of the forest in order to save 500,000 years. *Christian Science Monitor*, p. 1.

Maki, T. E. (1972, October). Clear-cutting and soil depletion. *Forest Farmer*, pp. 12-15.

Pengelly, W. L. (1972, November/December). Clear-cutting: Detrimental aspects for wildlife resource. *Journal of Soil and Water Conservation*, pp. 255-259.

Resler, R. A. (1972, November/December). Clear-cutting: Beneficial aspects for wildlife resource. *Journal of Soil and Water Conservation*, pp. 250-255.

Robinson, G. (1973, January). Our export forest. *Sierra Club Bulletin*, pp. 10-17.

Simmons, F. C. (1972, July). Wilderness east?Íno. *American Forests*, p. 3.

Steele, T. J. (undated). *Marketing of the wilderness cause*. Unpublished manuscript.

Thomas, M. (1972, November). Down in the forest. *Geographical Magazine*, p. 135.

Timber industry's struggle for wood. (1972). *Business Week*, 25, 76-72.

Upton, R. W. (1972, July). You can't preserve a tree forever but you can manage a forest. *Pulp and Paper Magazine of Canada*, p. 99.

Which criterion? Effect of choice of the criterion on forest management plans. (1972, December), *Forest Science*, pp. 292-298.

Woodsman, manage that tree. (1972, December). *Commerce, Today*, pp. 11-15.

## Chapter 35

CONSUMER BEHAVIOR IN THE UNITED STATES

Sidney J. Levy

The study of consumer behavior in the United States is extremely vigorous. Pressures on managers to understand the consumer have intensified steadily in recent years and show little sign of lessening. This interest is shown in the numerous marketing research projects that go on continually. It is reflected in the growth of academic researches and courses taught on the subject of consumer behavior. The *Journal of Consumer Research* is a recent development. Meetings and conferences flourish; the specialized trade press and the mass media furnish a flow of news, observations, comments, and analysis of what is happening with the consumer.

As a psychologist, and as one who has been involved in studying behavior in the marketplace for 30 years, I am particularly interested in certain aspects of the situation. These are not the conventional technical parts of marketing concerned with logistics of distribution, the measurements of inventories, sales volumes, return on investments with various pricing policies, and so on. Rather, I am devoted to explor-

This chapter was first presented as a talk before the Nikkei Institute and the Dentsu Advertising Agency in Tokyo, 1977.

ing the subjectivity of the people in the market, trying to understand the kinds of feelings, attitudes, reasoning, goals, and perceptions that make up the people they are and that explain what they are doing. We can raise such questions about the managers, as well.

What motivates managers' attempts to get oriented to the consumer? They have many reasons for wanting to know what is happening. The basic logic can be briefly examined. One central dynamic is provided by competition. It is evident that the fact of competition in itself pushes managers to be alert to the marketplace. Just knowing there are competitors out there making their plans increases the managers' feelings of uncertainty and builds up their thirst for information. Beyond that is the idea that competition provides consumers with alternatives. In olden days when customers walked into the traditional general store, there were commodities in bulk—a sack of coffee beans, a barrel of pickles, a wheel of cheese, and other such goods, with little opportunity for choice. As the goods began to be branded and to arrive with various names and packages, the competition and the alternatives grew. The dramatic variable of choice was highlighted.

One of the important consequences of providing consumers with choices is the anxiety that managers feel about losing customers, should they choose the competitor. If the competition balances out, brand shares might not change much and the situation can be fairly stable and grow with the population; that is a relatively comfortable situation. But what happens when the population growth slows? For example, J. Janvier Wetzel of Broadway Department Stores says, "With population growth down to a trickle compared with its previous level, we're no longer spoiled with

instant success every time we open a new store. Traditional department stores are locked in the biggest competitive battle in their history."

However, there is also another common outcome that continues to concern the managers. As consumers exercise choice, they become practiced in trying things for just awhile. They are tempted by other fresh possibilities they see in the market. If they are interested in cosmetics, they want to search for those that will most enhance their appearance. But perhaps another product or brand will do better, or another, or another. The availability of choices teaches people to be fickle. If other products have merit, as they probably do, why stay with this one?

Of course, fickleness is offset to a degree by people's wishes for the familiar, the habitual, the convenient. It gets tiring to keep chasing after new experiences, as single young swingsters know, and settling to certain products and brands is efficient and comfortable. But still, there remain areas where choice is kept open in one's mind, with a receptivity to the idea of doing things differently. The desire for novelty is kept alive and stimulated by the continuous introduction of new products. The dress has been worn to too many parties and a new one is needed; one wants to try a new restaurant, visit a different country, find out "what's new."

Spurred by competition and by consumer fickleness, the managers strive for advantage by innovating. The marketplace becomes a kind of lottery in which one keeps sending up trial balloons by way of research, test marketing, and new product introductions. In a situation of such ferment, it is not easy to define one's role. Both consumers and managers struggle to determine who they are and who they ought to be. As Mr. Wetzel also said, "We're dancing to the tune of the customer as never before." But what tune does the consumer want to play? That is something customers and managers work out together in the elaborate interplay of the marketplace, as each looks to the other for direction and guidance. People do not want to make their choices haphazardly. Their motives gain in complexity and self-awareness, and the richness of the marketing processes increases. It is a lively time, an intense time, a demanding time for all.

In analyzing the seller-customer interface, we can approach at different levels, and we must do so to appreciate our task. At the broadest level are the cultural trends. In the vast changing scene, how does the manager keep up? He is going to be part of the larger sweep of events, but will he try to sense them in an especially insightful way or will he wait for their impact? Not everyone leads nor wants to. Those who do take advantage of the kinds of resources that venture into the unknown. They traffic with futurologists and brainstormers, they study social trends, they search for imaginative personnel, they immerse themselves in the latest technologies and the latest in art forms. They experiment and they are willing to risk, to tolerate mistakes. Such daring people set styles and fashions. They interact with the consumer in a bold manner, defying his habits, destroying his traditions, thumbing their noses at his conventions. The innovator is likely to orient to those in the population who want such stimulation—to the young, the wealthy, the wild, to the bored and the rebellious, and to those who take the responsibility of leadership in their consumer circles, on whatever basis. Other managers, undoubtedly most of them, are less venturesome. Restrained by industry, organization, finances,

or personality, they wait for the fallout from the creative social forces. That which looks lasting and profitable is adopted. The more alert want to know what is going on; they do some research, keep up on industry developments, and are fairly quick to remodel, redesign, and to benefit from avoiding the mistakes made by the innovators. The rest go along, maintaining traditions until these have passed from the scene, taking the proud or defeated managers with them.

Since presumably few or none of the latter kinds of laggard managers are at issue here, we can turn our thoughts toward the active challenges. There are various perspectives that should concern us. It is most usual to be immersed in one's own industry, its all-familiar content, and the conventional wisdom as to its direction. This seems most practical but can be a misplaced pragmatism. Thoughtful people in a thoughtful organization want to know where the culture at large is going, they want to know how values are changing, and they seek ultimately to determine the impact on themselves.

Let us take up some of these fundamental issues. When life changes in a society, most central will be the impact on the family life, on the parent-child relations, on the interpersonal relations of adults. What is happening here? Very discernible is a drift away from closeness of family and maintenance of ties. This has been a long-term process. With migrations of populations from country to country, from rural areas to the city, and from the city to the suburbs (and perhaps back again), the extended family breaks up, children leave parents physically and emotionally. The notorious gap between the generations grows, mildly or to the point of alienation. There arises the youth culture, with some well-known consequences. Economically, these are not idle results, as witness the sales of jeans, the rock and roll industry, stereo shops, head shops, and other forms of youth retailing, to mention just a few obvious examples. Nor are the results confined to teenagers, but radiate out to other groups in society who adopt modifications of youthful trends.

The loosening of social ties goes in many directions. The divorce rate in the United States reached the 50% mark in 1976, creating more households (to say nothing of many other problems). When one adds the other contributing forces—postponement of marriages, the increased proportion of the aged, and so on—all affecting new living arrangements, it is not surprising that from 1970 to the present, the number of persons living alone has multiplied, the under-35s alone more than doubled. All this despite an uncertain economy and a great lagging in housing starts.

Fortunately, some people are still affiliating, falling in love, and living together—unmarried, married, *menage à trois,* and in communes. Some are traditionally oriented, but others want open relationships. They do not want tense and distant relationships but seek acceptance and self-assertion, respect for their narcissism and privacy.

The elderly are a special case and perhaps in their own way will succeed the shrinking youth population as society's next major demographic problem. Already, their special needs for housing, feeding, and health care are having major repercussions on social security arrangements, the character of communities, and the handling of medical expenditures.

Relevant to the marketer are also the effects on political-social orientations. With so many vibrant changes and such relative egocentricity, the dissatisfactions with established systems is strong. It finds expression in different ways, as contexts differ. In the United States not only is there a vigorous consumerism movement, but also there is a notable movement toward localism and emphasis on local government, with an attendant lethargy (or wait and see attitude) toward national government. The marketing of many products and services makes corresponding adaptations to the flow of resources.

The large movements and re-orientations that are going on are the flux of our times. They find expression in the behavior of customers who are increasingly seeking immediate gratifications. This means an intensification of role-playing and greater freedom and diversity of roles. Clothing is more and more a costume rather than a convention or a uniform, despite the complaints of those who wish there were more guidelines to how to dress. A fresh example was provided in the March 22 edition of the *International Herald-Tribune*:

"ITALY PRESENTS THE 'MUDDLER' LOOK AT AUTUMN READY-TO-WEAR SHOWS"

By Julie Craig

Milan (Reuters)—Italy's ready-to-wear fashion designers have launched a "muddle" look for autumn and winter—a highly individual theme of confusing wear-as-you-like styles. . . . Designers emphasized the look should be one of improvisation—donning individually favorite items without considering the overall result.

Of course, all the diversity and the individualism create new molds of their own. There are new roles but these are still played by many. Individualists are often leaders, and followers need them. Between March 17 and 20, San Francisco housed the

First New Earth Exposition, described as promoting alternative styles of living in a sellout success.

Save water, save electricity; learn a new diet, learn a new discipline; feel good, feel better, feel best; save your soul, save whales, save your feet, and save the world—these and more exhortations were issued by nearly 340 exhibitors and dozens of free lecturers and drew 40,000 persons.

This may sound like a strange and deviant event, but the public utilities in the area thought it important enough to sponsor booths at the exposition. From hippie beginnings come broader currents. The consumerism movement has grown to significant proportions in the United States, enough to give support to a vocal leadership and to produce a steady stream of legislation aimed at consumer protection and advocacy. It may be that the conservation movement, which has already shown some strength in curbing lumbering interests and in other areas, will lead to a major new austerity, especially if President Carter provides enough vigorous push in that direction as he seems to intend. Already noticeable are such activities as wearing sweaters, increasing home insulation, keeping objects longer, repairing them, handing them down, and shopping in garage sales and flea markets, as well as participating in the recycling of paper, glass, aluminum, and so on.

The search for new values and self-concepts has spawned and expanded various industries. Such values as naturalism, personalization, and flexibility are sought. Concrete results appear in the fantastic burgeoning of interest in houseplants, to note one example. Some places are veritable jungles of greenery, and those who fear creeping ivy find it almost impossible to escape. The rental of gorgeous plants to modern offices is a flourishing business, and retail outlets that sell plants are everywhere.

Self-expression runs riot in the avid pursuit of leisure activity. Young moderns come from a generation of parents who worked hard, who were perhaps anxious children of the Great Depression. They were eager to keep the family together. They developed few personal interests beyond their children. When these grew up and away, and the parents were retired, they could do little with themselves but complain about being neglected by their children. The newer generations are not so interested in children and more and more do not intend to have them. They will be equipped to occupy their leisure time in a practiced manner. Among the new roles are found athletic women and aesthetic males. Even sons of tough fathers turn out to be devoted to art, ballet, opera, and a sensitive decor, as well as being able to form a piece of pottery or make a piece of ceramic jewelry for a suburban art fair.

The do-it-yourself movement has become so prominent that a major advertising agency studied its manifestations in auto maintenance, home sewing, and home remodeling on behalf of several clients. From the old carpenter-oriented lumber yards that indulged the occasional citizen seeking a few boards to create a bookcase, there has blossomed the home service center, fully equipped to supply the ambitious do-it-yourselfers, thronging in to shop for their projects—new cabinets, modernized kitchens, added-on rooms, paneling for recreation rooms, and new backyard fences.

Another interesting and challenging phenomenon in the United States might be termed re-ethnification. After a period in which assimilation and Americanization seemed to be producing a relatively homogeneous society in a fairly Anglo-Saxon mold, with second-generation natives properly ashamed of their immigrant parents, the society discovered its pluralism with new interest and pride (despite fresh problems and conflicts over illegal aliens and demands for bilingual education). A cosmopolitanism is invigorated, with enrichment of the language and amplification of the diet. Ethnic restaurants are one of the newest rages. The old ones are still there—the traditional elite eating out in French restaurants, the homey recourse to an Italian pasta or Jewish delicatessen, or the mysterious Chinese excursion. But added to them came the great choices of Greek, Spanish, Indian, Mexican, Mandarin, Szechuan, Vietnamese, Thai, and an intriguing variety of Japanese. No wonder department stores such as Carson, Pirie, Scott and Co. in Chicago regularly schedule promotions centered around imported goods from around the world, and the availability of imports is taken for granted as having popular appeal in innumerable outlets.

With affluence and an overflowing larder, with generous restaurants galore and eating out accounting for almost 50% of the food dollar, with sweets and soft drinks, carbohydrates and calories everywhere, to say nothing of sedentary work and hours in front of television, the Americans feel fat and full and lethargic. But no, that must be solved. One must control weight, be slim, be trim. The battle is on. Physical fitness to save the body's appearance and its health. Walking at least—and jogging and running become a mystical discipline. Exercise equipment for pushing and pulling gains a steady sale. And sports grow and grow. Fishing and golf persist, bowling rises and settles; skiing flares up and millions participate; tennis becomes the latest, with new indoor tennis clubs, and all the players are

smart and snappy in their professional-looking tennis outfits. But now that's not aggressive enough for many, and the latest is racquetball. There you can dress as you will, sweat fiercely, and slam the ball to kill. It is not for the delicate, a far cry from the charms of badminton.

For now, a final, especially important trend, perhaps one that may have more long-run consequences than many others, and which is interwoven with some of the societal changes already discussed. This is the phenomenon of the working woman. The topic is an extended one; some few major aspects will be noted. The economic results are most immediately evident. A working wife adds substantially to family income, making possible a more comfortable lifestyle, putting children through school, buying a home, traveling, enjoying a generally greater degree of self-indulgence. Working women are more clothes-conscious, aware of fashions, and use more cosmetics than women who do not work outside the home. Working women create dual career problems; and they also produce stereotypes about them. These stereotypes are resented, as was pointed out in a recent symposium on "Women and Advertising." "Marketers are missing the point with working-women-oriented advertising," said one working woman. "I don't tend to think of myself in terms of any single consumer description. I function as a working woman, but also as a mother, homemaker, sports enthusiast, as well as an individual."

Similarly, an exploratory study by Susan Douglas (1975) comparing working wives and nonworking wives in both France and the United States had some interesting findings. There was little evidence, for example, to suggest that working wives in either country are heavy users of convenience products and services. Takeout dinners were actually more frequently purchased by nonworking wives in both countries. More generally, the cultural differences that might have been expected were also not very large and did not show deep differences. A main difference was the greater adherence by French women to the ideas that a woman's place is in the home, that politics is a man's affair, and that women with young children should not work.

Otherwise, the author concluded that the main differences between the behaviors of French and American women in regard to shopping may be due to variations in the retail environment, the higher proportion of small retail stores in France, and therefore the delay in the adoption of new products and services. In essence, it is suggested that the retailers may be more powerful in affecting the consumer behavior than are basic cultural differences between the women. The case is of course arguable and will differ in kind and degree from country to country. But it is very suggestive to realize once again the importance of marketing activities by producers and distributors in being aware of what consumers are like, and in studying the trends to assist in determining what they might be like in the future.

REFERENCE

Douglas, S. P. (1975). *Cross cultural comparisons: The myth of the stereotype.* Cambridge, MA: Marketing Science Institute.

## Chapter 36

ARTS CONSUMERS AND AESTHETIC ATTRIBUTES

Sidney J. Levy

> Between the crowd and ourselves no bond exists. Alas for the crowd; alas for us, especially.
> —*Gustav Flaubert*

Where there is no bond between the crowd and the artist, marketing has failed. Such an assertion may arouse feelings of indignation, because the ideas customarily associated with the word *marketing* imply that artists who succeed in marketing their work are corrupt and meretricious. These ideas are based on defining marketing as the willingness to do anything to make a sale. Some people are, of course, willing to do that. However, more fundamentally, marketing is essential to everyone, including all artists. It is not just the promotions used to sell tickets. Marketing points to the fact that almost all artists want an audience, very few being willing to blush unseen and waste their sweetness on the desert air. And, wanting an audience, whatever they do about it is marketing, good or bad.

Marketing refers to the complex of exchanges when the aesthetic product of painting, song, story, and performance is offered to the audience for a price—a price of attention, emotion, and action. In a

This chapter was first published in Mokwa, Dawson, and Prieve (Eds.), *Marketing the Arts*, 1980, pp. 29-46. Reprinted by permission of Praeger Publishers, an imprint of Greenwood Publishing Group, Inc., Westport, CT.

primitive sense, this exchange is enough, the performance in exchange for the astonishment, applause, laughter, pity, and fear. In a complex modern world the audience also has to be informed that the event will occur somewhere; and having many choices of things to laugh at and admire, they may have to be wooed and persuaded to attend. Also, like providers of anything, the artist who does not want to starve in a garret (should a free one be available) needs to be paid, as Mozart's begging letters testify.

Given the above situation, all the conditions for marketing exist—sellers, buyers, products and services, outlets, communications and prices. All that remains is to decide such things as what the offerings will be, where they will be made available, what admission will cost, and what kind and size of audience are desired; then, what means will be used to accomplish these goals. These decisions point to the marketing necessities that face all individuals and organizations, whether artists or others. The objectives of the artist and the arts organization need to be formulated and then means need to be searched out to achieve them. One of the main means that assists in marketing is studying the audience, to understand them better and better. Again, the purpose is not merely to "give them what they want" but to so comprehend their personalities, situations, attitudes, and aspirations that the arts administrator might better see how to forge the bond between them and the aesthetic offering.

Surveys of consumers usually show that Gustav Flaubert was right—only small proportions of the public are active in supporting the arts. Some comfort is taken in the growth of attendance at museums and various kinds of performances. There are notable surges of interest in archaeological artifacts (King Tut and Pompeii), and an occasional retrospective exhibition (for example, Monet, unexpectedly catches on), and some communities develop unusual devotions to orchestra, opera, or dramatic repertory groups. It is interesting to speculate on the causes for such surges and the likelihood of their enduring (Goethe complained of the restlessness of the modern audience). One would like to believe that consumers' appreciation of the arts is a stable outgrowth of affluence, leisure, and education and that, as families cultivate this appreciation in their children, it will take root and continue to develop. Historically, such a pattern is evident, at least as the size of the elite has grown.

But more particular understanding seems to be needed to gain insight into why so many children do not pursue the cultural opportunities afforded them. The dreary finding of the Lincoln Center High School Program and Lincoln Center Elementary Program (*Arts Reporting Service,* April 3, 1972, p. 1), which showed that exposing children to a few live performances had little impact, hints at the magnitude of the problem of cultivating the young audience outside the home. Similarly, the optimistic report published in *Arts and the People* by the National Research Center for the Arts (1973) probably reveals again that adults often give lip service to the value of high culture but fail to attend it seriously.

Explanations do not come easily as the many forces at work in society are complexly interwoven, so that there are regional differences, social class differences, age differences, and various social and psychological bases for diverse aesthetic responses. These can all be studied, broadly and in detail, in attempts to explain the arts consumer's behavior. For example, Smith (1974) offers the hypothesis that decrystalization or decay of social structures is related to an emphasis on deference given to style, such as dandyism in clothing, and the models of taste and demeanor provided by celebrities. In a rapidly changing society, geographic and social mobility make demands on citizens to find cultural entrepreneurs, individuals who offer their images to serve as reference points for orienting modes of expression. In various arenas, these individuals become stars by which cultural voyagers may orient themselves and give legitimacy to the activity. It is hard for the audience to separate out the sheer artistry of Baryshnikov, Sills, Picasso, Solti, or Fellini from the appeal of their personal styles and personal celebrity, if such a separation is conceivable. The tolerance for anonymous art always exists—just as anyone can appreciate the beauty of nature or a strikingly adorned passerby—but the contemporary Western world seems far from appreciating relative impersonality in creativity as found in medieval religious art or the mass-produced look of the recently exhibited modern Chinese peasant art. Modern values highlight individual public figures as stylish creators and want to know about their private lives as well. While this was no doubt true centuries ago for da Vinci and his sodomy suit, and Cellini's escapades, the contemporary mass media and the urge for candor carry celebrityship to new heights, as part of aesthetic appreciation, broadly conceived.

Turning from explanations pitched at this broader cultural level, it is possible to study market segments among consumers of aesthetic experience—to ask what distinguishes significant segments. Findings from such a study will be reported here, with the ultimate goal of suggesting some implications for marketing of the arts. (This chapter builds on an earlier study by Levy & Czepiel, 1974.)

The study examines some of the motives people have for consuming activities commonly regarded as cultural or aesthetic. These are distinguished from work activities by being part of leisure; they are voluntary choice activities that fall on a continuum of social value or prestige at a level regarded as peculiarly meritorious or qualified. They include symphonic music, ballet, modern dance, opera, painting, sculpture, legitimate theater, and so on. The inquiry is exploratory and interpretive in nature. It is not a large sample survey of attendance and audience demographics. Rather, it seeks to learn about peoples feelings, reasoning, and perceptions—to see the place that high and popular arts have in their lives and values and what meaning aesthetic objects and activities have for them. The research consists of the analysis of lengthy conversational interviews with married people (individually, with each spouse) about the kinds of people in the family and their attitudes toward various forms of aesthetic experiences. This method is a holistic one, moving freely among the qualities of the people, their personalities, social positions, and experiences; their attitudes toward aesthetics; and their perceptions of aesthetic attributes. In addition to the freer-style interviews, larger samples were questioned in a more systematic way. These people were tested for scores on a scale measuring Attitude Toward the Aesthetic Value. They were also administered a semantic differential concerning the attributes they wanted for the objects in their lives.

The data are still being analyzed, but some findings can be informally reported here. These will be discussed as follows: Obstacles to aesthetic appreciation and consumption of the arts, avenues to such participation, and preferred factors among aesthetic attributes.

OBSTACLES TO
APPRECIATING THE ARTS

When people are asked why they do not attend cultural events more than they do, or at all, they usually say they would rather do other things, that they do not have enough time, cannot afford it, do not find them interesting or relevant, and so on (Neilsen & McQueen, 1974). These are real obstacles, which mainly suggest that there is insufficient motivation; many who do attend have no more money or time but would rather not do other things and do find the arts interesting and relevant. As people talk more fully about their feelings and opinions, a richer sense of the obstacles emerges, showing that responses reflect the complex social and psychological symbolisms that define the arts.

Elitism seems an ineluctable aspect of the arts. They are deemed to require a refinement or elevation of taste, a capacity to understand and appreciate (appraise, evaluate, enjoy) in a sensitive manner. Those who have these qualities, aspire to them, or are willing to mimic them are proud and feel superior to those who do not. The latter may recognize this situation, as sharply stated by these working-class men:

No art interests me. I bet you are interested in art because you are so reserved and I bet you even went to college, grew up in a better neighborhood. This is a rough neighborhood and I think people who consider art around here would be considered oddball. What I am saying is that you are cultured, I am not. We are from two different worlds.

Those things are too rich for my blood. I don't think it's any fun. I'd be bored. That's for the uppercrust people, the ones that have their noses in the air.

Closely linked to the lower status perception of the arts as overly refined is their relative femininity. Despite the unisex movement, equal rights for women, and the consequent liberation of males to wear longer hair and colorful clothing, there remains the idea that the arts are for women:

I think basically we are a sports-oriented society. We stand in line for baseball and football games but not for theater or concerts. I think for the middle-class society, artistic endeavor has an effeminate connotation.

The actual statistics for games and concerts are probably irrelevant to this opinion. Even a high-status man can entirely disclaim the local aesthetic realm as woman's work:

Our house is very modern. I had nothing to do with it. My wife did it, I just gave her the money.

The arts are intimidating. Because special sensitivity or cultivation is thought to be required, the arts make people uneasy and defensive. Access to the pleasures of sports and entertainment and to understanding of the utilitarian, functional character of non-art seems routinely easy. By comparison, the arts demand mysterious insights and judgments, arrogantly exercised by those who have the nerve to make them. Relatively few people feel competent to cope with art for art's sake. They lack confidence in their own aesthetic reactions, looking dependently to experts or avoiding the problem. When an "artistic temperament" appears, it seems deviant and uncomfortable.

If I wanted to buy art I could do so only if I got an expert. I would be afraid to buy just on the basis of what I liked.

Our Susan is a much more cautious child, more artistically turned, a fine-tuned child. Our Joan is typical, attractive, secure; Joan is a joy.

This uneasiness can extend itself to all the awkward social requirements of dress and behavior in an alien environment. At one end is the rare famous devotee of Chicago Opera House events who turns up in the audience dressed as Giselle or the Black Swan; more common is the woman's thought: "I wouldn't know how to dress or act to go to a theater or concert."

Why do people think artistic personnel have feminine interests and that the arts are the preserve of an elite, and why do they feel intimidated by them? These are not simple or isolated obstacles, they are the consequences of the entire sociopsychological situation that taught them what kinds of people to be. To comprehend the spectrum of outlooks at issue here, it is perhaps usefully shocking to realize how remote is the distance felt by extreme members of the nonaudience for the arts. To lack aesthetic appetite is a form of starvation, afflicting personalities whose lives are generally ungratifying, whose family relationships are generally strained or hateful, or whose emotional tone is desperate, depressed, or deprived. They feel finished (despite, like the following two men, being under 30 years of age), although their lively fluency sometimes hints at their potential vitality and deeper hungers:

What am I? It's hard to describe myself. I am hardly worth describing. I'm a factory worker, married, got three kids. It's the same old grind every day, nothing to look forward to, I work my ass off. I am not getting anywhere in life. Well, I watch baseball, that's about all I like. My wife is stupid, can't even carry out an order or keep the house clean.

She really is a stupid idiot. The kids are always dirty. I don't know anything about my kids, that is my wife's business to watch out for them. I don't want to talk about them. I have never traveled. Theater is trash. Never seen a stage show. Music I can leave alone. I don't read trash like magazines.

I feel inadequate. I have been married 4 years now. I feel so bottled up, I want to get free. Even my wife isn't happy, certainly I'm not, not sure I can survive this marriage. I feel so let down and nobody cares. I want to reach out for some of these art things we've been talking about, but I don't know how. I wish some miracle could happen to make us grow. Jill, my wife, don't have much brains. She drives people away, sits like a log, doesn't do anything. My daughter is sneaky like her mother.

In another instance, a woman is thwarted in her simplest aesthetic yearnings, as both husband and wife attest.

He: I like to sit and relax, get waited on, watch sports on television. I don't care what my home looks like. I want my wife to wait on me hand and foot. No long-haired stuff for me, puts me to sleep. No one plays an instrument, and I have never heard anyone in this house sing.

She: I can't live up to his demands. I am mixed up, upset. If I try to pick out a throw rug, he gets mad. He says I don't have enough horse sense to pick out anything. He tells me how dumb I am. I cut his nails, run his bath, even take his socks off. He wants me to be joyous when I see him at the door. I would like my furnishings improved, buy pretty throw rugs and curtains. I'd like beautiful pictures to hang on the wall, simple furniture, delicate lamps. I'd like a soft look, frilly white curtains.

It is tempting to dismiss such cases as too far from the norm and, perhaps, more the province of psychology and social work than arts administration. But it is also worth noting that such people represent a substantial portion of the population. The *Attitude Toward the Aesthetic Value* scale was administered to a sample of 342 people (of varying social class, age, location in the country, etc.). The instrument calls for agreement or disagreement with statements asserting positive and negative positions about aesthetic activities, their value, support, importance to society, and so on. Despite the general tendency to express virtuous thoughts about such things, about 35% of the sample scored low on the aesthetic value, and only about 40% scored high.

Pathological extremes often reveal dynamics at work in more moderate instances. Here, they suggest that obstacles to aesthetic appreciation are an interaction between the negative self-concepts of people who feel unequipped and hostile and their perception of the arts as hopelessly beyond them. These views are expressed most vehemently by those of lower social class positions. Middle- and upper-class people who have alienated attitudes toward the arts usually express flat disinterest, a lack of experience, or ignorance. They may emphasize the esoteric nature of the arts. And there still are those who regard the arts as immoral in language, exhibitionistic in displays of the body, or reflective of the free behavior of artists:

I rarely buy art work. I don't know enough about it, so I don't enjoy it.

No art museum for me. All you see is a blue border inside a red border, inside a black border, and it sells for $38,000. I just can't see anything there.

I don't know anything about art. The kids have dragged me. I don't understand it.

I'm not really interested in those crazy nuts making fools of themselves. I don't like to see people jumping around or throwing themselves around in dancing.

Higher status people may use subtler ways of disclaiming involvement, perhaps by showing themselves superior to the old-fashioned values represented:

Nowadays I feel the theater is too limiting a medium. My wife has a more traditional view of theater, she still goes. I find theater a bore.

The reality of the obstacles to aesthetic appreciation is great. Some high art simply cannot be understood by that half of the population that has below average intelligence—an intellectual basis for elitism that may never disappear. Various appreciations require more exposure; if cultivation is lacking, it is hard to catch up, to gain that accumulation of subtleties that fills the interstices of experience with richness of reference and association. It is also hard to catch up because it is the nature of certain elites to keep moving toward novel grounds of distinction and rarity, so that by definition the mass is kept at a distance. Also, insofar as some high art is defined by its iconoclasm and criticism of conventions, people who live by those conventions will refuse to attend it. This segmenting process occurs within the high arts realm as well, where avant-garde taste for modern literature, dance, painting, and theater looks down on those who stick with a steady diet of Beethoven, Tchaikovsky, and traditional representational art.

AVENUES TO PARTICIPATION

It seems evident that many people will never be awakened to the pleasures of high culture, their distance and antagonism being so great. But some lower-class and middle-class people do find their way to this enjoyment—the arts may be the province of an elite, but it is not solely an upper-class one. Following are some of the elements that foster consumption of the arts.

The virtuous, uplifting aspects of the arts, their refinement of sensibility and nonmaterialism make them suitable for children. Therefore, the presence of children can bring aesthetics and the arts to the home, beginning with finger-painting and working up.

The children don't watch too much TV. I prefer to get them coloring books, clay, cutout dolls.

I like to buy jewelry for gifts is my point of view. But my son is not very materialistic, he would rather I give him the money to invest in music. We are buying them some art now.

When motivation is not strong, the lack of accessibility makes the situation worse, justifying complaints about time and money as problems. Some decentralization of opportunity helps. The contribution to high culture is often slight, given the theatrical fare at some summer and dinner theaters, serving as a deceptive source of self-congratulation. Bookmobiles carry literature to poor neighborhoods, art fairs are ubiquitous, the suburban theaters remove the excuses for not going downtown—and the atmosphere is elevating.

I have never been to an art gallery. I could never afford an original painting. But I could see something I liked and maybe buy it if I saw it at an art fair.

I had never seen a stage play. We just don't have much interest in stage shows. But 6 months ago we did go to the Drury Lane Theater on 95th Street. We have some friends at our church who arranged this outing so we decided to attend with them.

I saw Pat O'Brien at the local theater near here. We got a free ticket through our organization. I could never go downtown, too far to go and too expensive.

Similarly, recordings and electronic presentations of art (records, Clark's *Civilisation* series, public television's *Great Performances,* etc.) provide enriching experiences and awareness, although not always the willingness to attend live performances:

We used to go, but now see them on TV.

Mobility of various kinds is of special value in fostering knowledge about the arts. In general, the arts are phenomena of the city—and of the great city; it is natural that rural residents show least interest (National Research Center for the Arts, 1973). People who travel to the city and the downtown area are more likely to have exposure and opportunity. Generally, mobility brings with it contacts with new people, new visual environments, and the chance for new enthusiasms and ways of using time. New playmates, new teachers, and new office settings are spurs to new aspirations and kinds of attendance:

A group at the office decided to see *Hello, Dolly,* so we organized to go one evening. First real theater I ever saw.

I have a boss interested in art, I see some in his office. I would like a nice picture someday.

It is a truism that visitors to a city do more museum and theater going than many residents. Many places are filled with tourists. People who never attend theater in Chicago may see several shows in New York or London on a visit, or even go for that purpose. This says that the arts are not part of daily life or are something reserved for vacations, part of escape from the total home environment:

I haven't seen any plays lately. It's the kind of thing we feel we have an obligation to support but can't make time for it. In London we really do a lot. Last time we were there, we saw 14 or 15 plays in a period of a week or 10 days. But that is different.

I travel for the same reason I read, to escape. When I travel I'm interested in the cultural aspects of my destination, museums, galleries, antique stores, plays.

Social mobility is one of the outstanding incentives for involvement with the arts. Taking part in a high status activity confers on the participant a certain cachet (literally stamped on the hand at the Old Town Art Fair in Chicago to indicate a paid admission). It means one has arrived at the higher levels of the cultural life of the community, mingles with the right people, and knows what is going on in the arts world—or in an important segment of it:

We go on Members' Night whenever they have a new exhibit. When we went to the Rauschenberg show, Vincent Price was there.

Through whatever means—status striving, family tradition, tutelage of friends or teachers, the leisure of travel, and so on—the aesthetic motivation takes root in certain personalities. Some experience this as natural for humans or as a growth process; others as an illumination or conversion. Then, looking, studying, buying, attending, and planning become part of one's life:

We are planning on buying more when we see something we both like and can afford. He dreams of owning a Giacometti. I'd be satisfied with a more modest work by Moore or Picasso, or some marvelous ceramics by Edna Arnow.

The full commitment to a way of life that includes the arts is a far cry from the complaints of too little time or money. Examples are these working-class women who do not allow their modest circumstances to deny them:

I saw *King Lear* at Goodman Theater. It made Shakespeare very real to me. I don't think many people realize how exciting it is to see people perform live. . . . When I get a chance to go to art exhibits I enjoy it, I like the exposure. . . . When I go to the Art Museum I like many contemporary artists and I get much pleasure from looking at the old masters. We have one sculptured metal flower. We have one print of a still life by Cezanne. I feel I am growing personally. Now that my children are growing I visit art museums more, I check out everything. I find I especially love sculpture and photography. These are new interests, food for my aesthetic appetites. I love the arts, marvel at artists' creativity and facility. I now use pictures as an integral part of my decorating. I buy what I like.

The attitude of commitment to the arts is most vivid among those of higher status. Aesthetic interest seems pervasive, shared in the family, and finds expression in numerous directions; it is varied, subtle, inquiring, subjective, direct and hedonic. It may be both traditional and trendy:

> Happiness comes in finding what makes you feel good. My wife is a good woman, bright, perceptive. She reads everything, does needlepoint. In art sometimes we have quite different tastes. She plays the trombone. We go to the movies and enjoy them. Even a film like *The Wild Bunch* has a macabre sort of beauty. My home is full of things I love either aesthetically or sentimentally. Bentwood rockers, an oriental rug, art work by Strobel, Dahlstrom, King, a Tiffany lamp, a four-poster bed. I like variety. In my room I use an American flag graphic paper, in my bathroom St. Laurent towels and shower curtain. We like to go to museums, one man shows.

> We want to create a continual stretch atmosphere in our home, pushing farther toward goals beyond our reach in terms of books, literature, social activities, and relationships. We go to art fairs, we love to take rides to antique shows, and to explore.

> My baby is extremely musical and he sings whole songs or he goes and brings the guitar for us to play. We like movies, have seen several done beautifully. Financially, we manage the money for those shows we want to see, and I am usually dying to see them. We collect antiques and objects of fine art. When we were first married we had more paintings than furniture. We like painting, sculpture, ceramics. A home isn't a home without books and musical instruments. We

> can always find some extra money to buy a painting that appeals to us. We put some money in a painting fund weekly for a long time. We never pass up something we really like even if we can't afford it. Aside from being an exceptionally good husband and father, my husband complements my personality because he is even, I am not. He is gentle, artistic, creative. He can sit at home and make wire sculptures for hours.

This qualitative analysis sketches in motives and feeling tones along a continuum of arts consumption, reflecting low, moderate, and high aesthetic attitudes. It highlights the complex of cultural-social-psychological situations characterizing varying degrees and styles of affiliation with the arts.

AESTHETIC ATTRIBUTES

Another way of approaching people's perceptions consisted of execution of semantic differential scales. Respondents were asked to judge the idea "The Objects in My Life Should Be . . . " as shown in the Appendix. The purpose was to observe the choices made between each pair of words describing basic qualities of experience or aesthetic attributes. These terms are taken as building blocks that make up larger concepts. In choosing between them, respondents may show underlying consistencies through the clustering of their choices. This clustering was observed by means of factor analysis and will be summarily reported here.

The words that tend to go together are inferred to have some common element in people's minds, one that guides the preferences they are expressing. The specific aesthetic attributes may thus be taken to represent more fundamental aesthetic dimensions. Factoring gives only the relative strength of the clusters. The fundamental aesthetic dimensions that the clusters represent are matters for speculation and interpretation, and anyone may play. Six main factors are described here, the first three being the most clear:

Factor I: bold, exciting, thrilling, crowded, active (retiring, peaceful, soothing, alone, leisurely)

Factor II: familiar, real, symmetrical, matching (strange, fanciful, asymmetrical, contrasting)

Factor III: hard, sturdy, practical, technical, powerful, profitable (soft, delicate, decorative, emotional, graceful, social)

Factor IV: stage plays, curved, painting, (movies, angular, photograph)

Factor V: sophisticated, outstanding, luxurious (sentimental, customary, comfortable)

Factor VI: dramas, serious, dramatic, alone (musicals, funny, pretty, crowded)

Some factors seem more evident than others, being mainly a matter of redundancy in the list of words. In the other instances, the words seem to be different facets of a broader principle. Factor I stands out because of its focus on vigor. It might be called the activity or excitement factor. It suggests that people in general want stimulation, feelings of liveliness; activity, movement, and excitement are important. The majority tended to select all five stimulation words, and almost three fourths of the sample chose *bold* and *active*. This factor

was especially pronounced among younger people; men went for *thrilling* and *crowded* somewhat more than women did, and the factor was more important to middle-class people than to lower-class people.

Factor II is the realism factor, and it reflects the fundamentally conservative or conventional orientation of the population away from the unusual. Eighty-six percent (greatest consensus shown) chose *real* and 79 percent, *familiar*; there was some greater tolerance for *contrasting*. The realism factor is greatest among the lower class, but interest in the *strange* and the *fanciful* is not great, even among upper middle-class people. More young people can accept the strange.

Factor III suggests a conventional sex-typing sex identity dimension, with traditional masculine elements opposed to traditional feminine elements. As a result choices are more evenly divided in the sample, despite some general tendency toward preferring the *sturdy* and *practical*. Sex differences are most pronounced here, with choices by males and females going in the expected directions, modified somewhat by greater interest in feminine attributes among the upper middle class compared to the lower class.

Factor IV is less clear in its significance. There is a strong general preference for the *curved* rather than the *angular*. And it is something suited to the three-dimensional rounded character of theater or the flowing character of painting, versus the film. The results reflect the greater choices of the movies by men, lower-class people, and young people, and the greater acceptance of the legitimate theater by higher-status people, women, and mature people. Perhaps this factor refers to the Arts, per se, and their open-life human quality, compared with the stiffer, impersonal, canned character of photography.

TABLE 36.1 Factor Analysis of Aesthetic Attributes

Factor I: excitement		Factor IV: the arts	
Bold/retiring	.633	Stage plays/movies	.684
Exciting/peaceful	.613	Curved/angular	.343
Thrilling/soothing	.597	Painting/photograph	.455
Crowded/alone	.450		
Active/leisurely	.359	Factor V: social status	
		Sophisticated/sentimental	.613
Factor II: realism		Outstanding/customary	.381
Familiar/strange	.644	Luxurious/comfortable	.333
Real/fanciful	.585		
Symmetrical/asymmetrical	.584	Factor VI: seriousness	
Matching/contrasting	.509	Dramas/musicals	.442
		Serious/funny	.378
Factor III: sex identity		Dramatic/pretty	.376
Hard/soft	.449	Alone/crowded	.353
Sturdy/delicate	.542		
Practical/decorative	.445		
Technical/emotional	.447		
Powerful/graceful	.548		
Profitable/social	.486		

Factor V seems to be oriented toward social status. Most people (82%) claim to prefer *comfortable* to *luxurious,* perhaps being sensible about it; generally, they would like things to be *outstanding.* The main differences are between the higher and lower social classes, the latter being especially oriented toward the *sentimental* and the *customary.*

Factor VI seems to be a heavy-versus-frivolous or seriousness factor. It carries with it a tone of introspection and withdrawal, against the light-hearted crowd at the musical comedy. Choices tend to be divided, despite the usual appeal of the easy and popular. Women and young people are more inclined to prefer the *funny,* the *pretty,* the *crowded, musicals,* and the *soft.* Men, older, and upper-status people incline in the opposite direction. Perhaps it is a maturity factor. The six factors are summed up in Table 36.1.

These results are a kind of oversimplification, and they repeat that commonly observed motives and behaviors toward the arts are derived from the factors here identified as excitement, realism, sex identity, the arts, social status, and seriousness. But they remind one that preferences for aesthetic attributes are blended to express the self-definitions and aspirations of the audience. The factors imply that there are powerful consistencies at work, dictating the felt appropriateness of given forms of experience for major segments of the population who act out these feelings.

MARKETING OF THE ARTS

Modern thought regards marketing as a process of exchange between individuals and groups, each of whom wants something and offers something. The study of marketing is the study of the participants and their aims and conditions of exchange and the complexity of events, situations, locales, and relationships arising from the mutual attempts to accomplish their purposes. The present material has examined some aspects of this exchange by focusing on the consumers and how they perceive the arts, rather generally conceived, and on the nature of their aesthetic aspirations.

This information does not in itself tell artists and art administrators what to do to market the arts. That, fundamentally, rests in their objectives and the means they are willing to undertake. Marketing the arts does not necessarily mean increasing the size of the audience, but it may. It does not mean persuading people to spend more money for the arts, but it may. It does not mean using advertising or hiring marketing personnel, but it may. It does not mean changing the offerings to cater to the masses, though it may.

Marketing management seeks to implement the goals of the organization (and the individual) through helping to define and clarify those goals and by taking actions that will successfully contribute to the required exchange relationships. What might

the above findings imply for making such plans and efforts? A few general suggestions are offered.

1. Some problems of personnel and management attitude may require attention. Museum administrators have been found to vary significantly in their orientations toward the institutional mission. The client, inner, and professional orientations were identified and shown to be in conflict at times. For example, highly client-oriented administrators wanted a large future attendance increase, regarded the museum's services as particularly valuable to visitors' lives, attributed to visitors a high capability in judging the quality of the museum services they receive, and favored intimate staff-customer interaction in preference to detached dealings. The highly inner-oriented administrator did not think the museum's clients were especially capable of differentiating degrees of quality in museum services to them (Thrasher, 1973).

2. It is likely that the audience for the high arts will continue to remain quite limited. Substantial portions of the population do not believe these are necessary to their lives and will resist all blandishments and opportunities. Many objections made by consumers are rationalizations of lack of interest, so extreme efforts by arts administrators, except for the most missionary, are probably not warranted.

3. Enlarging the audience for the arts requires taking account of the perceptions of the potential audience. The rates of nonparticipation are so high that it might be supposed that almost any reasonable effort could bring in some of those who express willingness. In the New York State study,

Arts and the People, nonattendance within the past 12 months (prior to the study in 1973) was as follows:

	Percentage not attending
Ballet or modern dance	83
Concert or opera	65
Theater performance	58
Science museum	44
History museum, site	43
Art museum	41

Nonparticipants harbor many inhibiting images of the arts as relatively austere and effete, effeminate, esoteric, inaccessible, too demanding of study and concentration, arrogant, and so on. Coping with these attitudes is not easy, but progress is made when experience shows the contrary or reorients the negative value. To bring about the experience, marketing usually recommends incentives, free samples, easy trial, and starting with examples that most contradict the opposed imagery. Personalities help in this endeavor—men who are masculine, such as Edward Villella and opera singers who are not foreign divas, such as Leontyne Price. English translations help, as in the television broadcast of Verdi's *Otello* or the use of supertitles.

The growth of informality is an asset to the more common consumption of the arts. Assuming that high culture needs special dress or manner is an obstacle, analogous to the ceremonial approach to wine drinking. Then, again, one might believe that something important in the total aesthetic experience is lost when certain standards or protocols are compromised or that the high culture has descended from the lofty level that was part of its ambiance and charm.

4. However, municipal park concerts, free street theater, and barefoot beach walk art exhibits point to segmentation among arts consumers and do not prevent elite groups from dressing for first nights. Taking account of market segmentation, addressing it, and increasing it are important ways of marketing to the diversity of the population. This is not a new idea, as witness the levels of donor, patron, sustaining member, contributing member, and the like at some museums. But, many arts institutions have little information and rather vague ideas about the segments they serve and could serve. Categorizing segments and defining them by demographic characteristics, interests, needs, and levels point to different sets of actions that might be taken (Ryans & Weinberg, 1978).

An important segment to search out are the people who truly feel frustrated yearnings, whose deeper hungers for aesthetic gratification are in need of feeding, but who are thwarted by circumstances, ignorance, location, family, or money. These include women still locked at home, young people with promising sensibilities, and upwardly mobile people who would like to find their way to elite experiences.

5. There is too little study of the obstacles to learning and enjoyment as these appear to the consumer—not of the usual litany of time, money, and distance but of the closer-in deterrents. Despite Ticketron (or including it), there are common problems with box offices and getting tickets; there are erratic and often peculiar refreshment arrangements, a paucity of knowledgeable or helpful personnel, and a dearth of information. Most museums display and explain in the archaic and restrained fashion that encourages fast walking through

static rooms with suspicious or indifferent guards and no place to sit.

6. If the plain fact is that most people want stimulation and excitement, they do not usually see it in the arts but go, rather, to sports, picture shows, and so on. This may not be the fault of the arts themselves, as their fans do find them stimulating. What makes enjoyment possible at the high level is the enthusiast's ability to echo to the fabulous perfection of Bach, grasp the architecture and flow of Schubert's A-Major Quintet, or recognize the daring of Rodin's Balzac, the point to Mondrian, or the organic insight of the Pilobolus dance group.

Hopefully, that will come eventually. In childhood there is fantasy and constant newness, supplanted by the safety of realism and familiarity, to be overcome by creativity and imagination. Indirection is needed as well as appeals to lesser motives, status striving, the excitement of glamorous people, the value of a good investment in a work of art or the bargain in a membership, the promise of a richer life for one's children, the social pressure of everyone doing it, and the changing roles in sex identities of young moderns. Like the churches and the charitable fund-raising organizations, the arts institutions need sisterhoods, young couples clubs, Saturday night mixers, golden age festivals, and kiddie kontests. Sometimes there are spiritual results, too.

7. The arts administrators are trying collectively to change the society. They face a great deal of competition and must promote their products and services in the marketplace of aesthetics. Like all organizations they must study audience needs in order to interact in a desirable way with that audience. Then they can survive and grow. With enough government money and leadership, anything can happen. In the meantime it will be one person at a time, one family at a time, one community at a time, lured by bargains, social competition, carnivals, charismatic figures, and changing images, through activity and excitement, to the sublime.

APPENDIX

Semantic Differential

Circle: O — when you feel *very* much this way
o — when you feel *rather* much this way
x — when you feel *slightly* this way

The objects in my life should be . . .

comfortable	O	o	x	x	o	O	luxurious
leisurely	O	o	x	x	o	O	active
customary	O	o	x	x	o	O	outstanding
decorative	O	o	x	x	o	O	practical
stage plays	O	o	x	x	o	O	movies
curved	O	o	x	x	o	O	angular
crowded	O	o	x	x	o	O	alone
serious	O	o	x	x	o	O	funny
smooth	O	o	x	x	o	O	textured
real	O	o	x	x	o	O	fanciful
dramatic	O	o	x	x	o	O	pretty
plain	O	o	x	x	o	O	ornate
exciting	O	o	x	x	o	O	peaceful
technical	O	o	x	x	o	O	emotional
graceful	O	o	x	x	o	O	powerful
dramas	O	o	x	x	o	O	musicals
social	O	o	x	x	o	O	profitable
sturdy	O	o	x	x	o	O	delicate
photograph	O	o	x	x	o	O	painting
sophisticated	O	o	x	x	o	O	sentimental
traditional	O	o	x	x	o	O	futuristic
bold	O	o	x	x	o	O	retiring
symmetrical	O	o	x	x	o	O	asymmetrical
familiar	O	o	x	x	o	O	strange
hard	O	o	x	x	o	O	soft
seen	O	o	x	x	o	O	heard
matching	O	o	x	x	o	O	contrasting
words	O	o	x	x	o	O	pictures
thrilling	O	o	x	x	o	O	soothing

REFERENCES

Levy, S. J., & Czepiel, A. (1974). Marketing and aesthetics. *Proceedings, American Marketing Association,* pp. 386-391.

National Research Center for the Arts. (1973). *Arts and the people.* New York: Publishing Center for Cultural Resources.

Neilsen, R. P., & McQueen, C. (1974). Performing arts consumer behavior: An exploratory study. *Proceedings, American Marketing Association,* pp. 392-395.

Ryans, A. B., & Weinberg, C. B. (1978, September). Consumer dynamics in nonprofit organizations. *The Journal of Consumer Research,* pp. 89-95.

Smith, T. S. (1974, October). Aestheticism and social structure: Style and social network in the dandy life. *American Sociological Review,* pp. 725-743.

Thrasher, S. D. (1973). *The marketing concept in museums: A study of administrative orientations in cultural institutions.* Ph.D. dissertation, Northwestern University, Evanston, IL.

## Chapter 37

SOCIAL DIVISION AND AESTHETIC SPECIALIZATION
The Middle Class and Musical Events

Sidney J. Levy

John A. Czepiel

Dennis W. Rook

It is easy to notice that the audience for high culture in the United States has grown greatly in recent years. In the 15 years since the establishment of the National Foundation on the Arts and Humanities, hundreds of millions of dollars have been pumped into the arts industry to support its growth. With the encouragement of concerts in the park, numerous local theaters, movies about ballet dancers, television broadcasts of operas, symphonies, dance groups, and plays, it has become possible to say that more Americans are attending opera than the games of the National Football League. It seems that the opera audience grew from 1,700,000 in 1963-1964 to 9,760,000 in 1977-1978 (Lipman, 1979).

These results are pleasing to those who believe that the market for the arts may be and should be constantly extended. Other people are more skeptical. First, it may be said that the figures are quite misleading if

This chapter first appeared in E. Hirschman & M. B. Holbrook (Eds.), *Symbolic Consumer Behavior* (pp. 38-45), 1980, Provo, UT: Association for Consumer Research.

they are taken to imply that high culture has displaced sports in the affections of the general public. Second, the emphasis on quantity is regarded by some to have adverse artistic consequences. An eloquent spokesman for this viewpoint is Samuel Lipman (1979). He refers to the use of "techniques of direct-mail advertising, so noxious when they are used to sell a commercial product . . . being brought to bear on the consumer. . . . What kind of audience can be found through this undignified, vulgar, and half-crazed search?" (p. 59). The issues he raises—the "millions without intellectual training, background, or even any clear idea of what they are being either forced or gulled into attending," and the interferences with artistic integrity that come from trying to please and retain a mass audience—may certainly be debated. But they reinforce the issue of elitism, with aesthetic appreciation of high culture as something that distinguishes the qualified audience from the vulgar one, many of whose members are, in Lipman's words, "for all artistic purposes, dead."

Such broad characterizations of market segments tend to lack content. It would seem useful to focus more closely on what the nature of the arts product is for those who seek high culture and how it varies among segments. In an earlier paper (Levy, 1980), some report was made of attitudes toward high cultural experiences, and aesthetic factors were identified. These factors (aesthetic attributes labeled Excitement, Realism, Sex-Identity, the Arts, Social Status, Seriousness) differed in their appeal to audience segments by age, sex, social class. Different parts of the population have different motives in their seeking for aesthetic satisfactions: for example, upper middle-class people were much more likely to say they prefer something dramatic over

something pretty, while lower middle-class and upper lower-class people tended to choose the pretty. From the previous work, and from participant observation in the cultural scene, the following assumptions and reasoning are set out as a basis for the present project.

The cultural elite is the small minority of the population that is relatively devoted to such arts as opera, ballet, symphony, chamber music, classical literature, legitimate theater, and the fine plastic arts. The adherents are primarily traditionalist (especially with regard to music) but include a subgroup that is receptive to modern and avant-garde productions. The high culture elite is mainly a portion of the higher status people in the society—upper middle-class professionals and managers, especially—but also draws from the middle majority (lower middle class and upper lower class), especially the upwardly mobile youth with college education. The elevated socioeconomic characteristics of the elite audience may have been modified since they were described in the 1966 econometric study, Performing Arts—The Economic Dilemma (Baumol & Bowen, 1966), but probably not very much. A recent study by the League of New York Theaters and Producers indicates that 41% of the audience for the Broadway legitimate theater has household income over $25,000 a year, and 31% has incomes between $15,000 and $25,000.

In general, the high arts product is what the elite (including the artists, critics, and consumers) define it to be. They argue about criteria, specific content, relative merits of performers and works, but there tends to be a consensus that the arts product is creative, distinctive, serious, worthwhile, somehow humanly elevated and penetrating in its insight or impact—and perhaps ultimately indescribable, ineffable, beyond words. The society tends to agree to all this in a broad fashion, but the matter is also controversial, interwoven with contending values and preferences. Some people below the elite give it assent and admiration from the outside, accepting their own inability to share the proper cognitive and emotional responses, but granting the existence of high art, occasionally buying it to show their good intentions. Others disparage the elite and its interests, regarding them as frauds who pretend to find meaning and merit in obscure language, absurd daubings, and boring music.

The large social divisions set off high culture from popular culture, with considerable fuzziness created by subtle gradations in the two realms (including the fact that "elitism" does not always operate: some culture the elite regards as high has been popular (Macdonald, 1961). Also, there is probably a general factor of interest in cultural experiences that cuts across social class boundaries; and those who appreciate high culture may also enjoy popular culture. More germane to interest in marketing segmentation are the differential preferences within the elite, who sort themselves out as having specialized tastes. Some like opera but not ballet, some go only to the symphony or to hear chamber music. Some concentrate on collecting modern art.

musical performances, evaluating various kinds of musical events for whether or not they wanted to attend them. The events included offerings from opera, symphony, musical comedy, pop musicians, "show lounge" entertainers, and rock performers. Respondents were asked to discuss their reasons for choosing the events they said they preferred, how at-home listening compared with live attendance, how they came "to like this kind of musical performance," how their interest was fostered and developed. They then discussed in a detailed manner their most recent attendance at a live musical performance. They talked about how they learned about the event and obtained tickets, their participation in activities prior to the performance and after arrival at the performance site. They commented about experiences during the performance, described the audience members and their behavior, and summed up the meaningfulness of the event. In the following analysis, reactions to attending high cultural events (opera and symphony) will be compared with going to musicals and rock concerts, to highlight the segmentation aspects, as well as commonalities in consumer behavior. The results will be summed up and interpreted in four main sections: (a) shopping for events, (b) at the event, (c) learning one's preferences, and (d) characterizing the musical arts product.

METHOD

These aesthetic specializations were explored with a sample of 25 middle-class people (12 men, 13 women; 14 under 30 years of age, 11 over 30; 8 under $20,000 per year, 9 between $20,000 and $39,000, 8 over $40,000). They were interviewed about their preferences and attendance at live

SHOPPING FOR EVENTS

Attitudes toward going grow out of wanting to attend live events and reflect both basic interest in the general type of event and specific knowledge and curiosity about the particular show. Respondents were repeat customers who defined themselves as people who attend the kind of performance being discussed. Especially important to them is the motivation to experience a live show. The sense of immediacy is compelling; there is the feeling of being "present at the creation" that is lacking with recorded or broadcast performances. Listening at home has its own assets, but mainly as an acceptable substitute for, or complement to, the real thing. Being at the theater enlarges the event and the self, it is exciting, absorbing—interacting with the performers, one becomes part of the performance, as if in a Berkeleyesque sense one divinely conjures it up by being there to see and hear it. As with all real (sporting, entertainment) events, there is the risk and tension of newly unfolding events, the spontaneity of mistakes, the reassurance of professionalism.

> Because there is electricity when the soloist sings—the experience of *creating* the song then and there . . . it's more of an experience when you *participate* in it.

> It's more of an intimate experience, sharing it with audience and with performers.

> I like the excitement of live contact and the atmosphere of audience response.

> You are able to react with all your senses and absorb so much more of the performance; you're close to it, it's real, you can spend time examining all the aspects of the production.

These ideas are common to theatergoers regardless of the level of culture involved. The live event seems like a focusing glass in generating a lot of energy, compared to listening at home where the passive listening stance and ready distractibility scatter energy.

> You can actually feel the *power* of the group.

> The sound is special, especially in Wagner—maybe it's the *energy*, with a recording I never just sit and listen at home, usually knit, do things.

> At home I get too easily distracted. At the concert hall your attention is held. . . . I like the sense of *grandness* you find in the theater.

With live performance so clearly superior, it may be wondered why there is not more attendance. The present data do not throw much light on that, being focused on attenders and their attending. But there are some hints. The usual objections to the time and money required are raised. Several went because they used twofers, were given tickets, were invited, or were otherwise strongly motivated to overcome problems of scheduling, buying tickets, babysitters, transportation, adverse weather, parking, and so on.

It also seems evident that a main obstacle to more frequent attendance at live musical performance is its very special character—that which makes it so desirable to begin with.

> I like getting dressed up for a high art form—it's a certain amount of respect for the artist. . . . I'll listen to records because sometimes I don't have time or money to go to the opera.

A live performance is a rich diet, it is not part of everyday life; and particularly so in the case of high cultural events. The ticket outlay, the dress-up, the exalted nature of the occasion including the strong demand for homage to the great performers, all require an emotional charging up that seems sensibly to occur at relatively infrequent intervals. This is true at all levels of the cultural hierarchy, so that records, FM, and TV may be acceptable most of the time, with a rush for tickets when a great event occurs and sells out in a couple of hours, whether it features Horowitz or The Who. All this raises the interesting general question of how much energy consumers are willing to put forth to attend musical performances. Typical attendees of rock concerts, for example, may spend several hours waiting in line to purchase tickets, an hour or more in transit to the concert, 3 or 4 hours at the concert site, and 2 or 3 hours exiting the event and returning home. In contrast, a season ticket holder for a symphony orchestra or opera expends on the average much less time shopping for and consuming the arts product. Then again, some go to London or Bayreuth for the season.

Respondents were asked about the circumstances leading to their most recent attendance, how they learned about the event, got tickets, and so on. These are people who keep up with what is on the market of musical performances. They hear about them on the radio; see articles and advertisements in the newspaper, in mail pieces, on bus cards; they read critics' reviews and hear word-of-mouth communications. Getting tickets for rock concerts and musicals is more spontaneous than getting them for symphony and opera. The latter events have a season and a series and rely heavily on subscriptions. The burdensome aspect of going compared to the pleasure of being there is highlighted by the way subscribers talk about needing this commitment.

> I buy annual seats to "force" myself to go—that way I am committed in advance, have prearranged dates.

> We've gotten into the routine of subscription series—when you're busy that's the way to do it.

> I would have liked to be a subscriber, but couldn't afford it, and since nonsubscribers get poor seats I wasn't tempted to go too often.

The ardent goer does not always complain about making the arrangements.

> It's not burdensome to make arrangements; I'm glad for the opportunity to go and hear music.

> As for plans, arrangements, etc., half the fun of the (rock) show is the anticipation, the making of traveling plans with companions, and obtaining various stimulants.

Another interesting aspect of the shopping situation is the role of personal influence. As mentioned, word of mouth is especially important as a way in which members of the various segments share and reinforce their mutual interests, air their opinions, instruct on what's in and what's out, and authenticate themselves as valid members of the group who love that kind of music. The two-step flow of communication process is generally notable in this market. Because people so commonly attend musical events in groups, someone may act as the "sparkplug." The sparkplug takes the initiative in selecting the event, recruiting partners, and obtaining tickets, or these duties may be delegated.

> A friend had tickets.

> We represent a foundation, where the president of the foundation invited us.

> I called friends to see if they wanted to go; several didn't want to go due to having heard bad things about the show, or had seen it.

> I was asked to go out on a date and the guy got the tickets. I don't think I've ever gone out and gotten tickets myself.

One of my friends did most of the work coordinating the people going, ticket money, and so on.

Lots of times we use theater for entertaining, we take people or are invited.

Frequently, also, it happens that tickets are sold or given away among friends or acquaintances. In the world of high culture recitals and concert series, there often seems to be available a greater supply of tickets than people are willing or able to use, after all.

This was last minute plans, I took the tickets from someone else. I was given these tickets by someone who knows about my interest. I took a friend.

I called to see who could use a ticket, I just didn't—oh, it's hard to go to an opera every week.

Attending musical performances is part of leisure and recreational life. There are various references to "after work" and weekends. The plan to attend becomes a marked point on the calendar, and the date is looked toward with curiosity, anticipation, and excitement. Ticket holders want to see and hear for themselves, to judge if the Chicago Symphony is greater than the Berlin, if *Evita* is as good as the London reviews or as awful as the Los Angeles reviews, to get to the show before Lansbury leaves *Sweeney Todd* or before Lucy Arnaz leaves *They're Playing Our Song,* and so on. A degree of advance preparation may take place—listening to relevant records, getting critics' views ("I have Friday night tickets to the Philharmonic and have the luxury of reading about the opening"), reading the libretto, discussing the program with oth-

ers, and so on. Some attenders are especially motivated by the urge to have close contact with the performers. In high status circles this may take the form of stage parties for opera stars and among the rock crowd the "groupie" phenomenon is well known.

THE EVENING ARRIVES

The evening of the event, the "consumption system" gets under way. The main stages involve food and drink, transportation, social and psychological characteristics of the convening, the performance, and its aftermath. All these aspects may be either elaborate or casual. Elaborate preparation highlights the social aspects of attending musical performances. In some cases, high status is stressed, with champagne dinners and formal dress or elaborate summer versions on the Ravinia Park lawn. "Going out" may include dinner and the show or something after the show; or it may be just trying to get there on time, with problems of sitters, traveling, parking, bad weather, sometimes trying to get last minute tickets.

The social aspects of attending are evident with most people but are given different kinds of emphasis in the interviews. Those who are interested in the high cultural events of opera, symphony, or recital tend to see the social situation somewhat abstractly, as a formal necessity that the performance have an audience to interact with, as an occasion for various kinds of "proper" social behavior. There is a noticeable kind of self-consciousness about one's exaltation, spiritual elevation, and civility in being part of the well-behaved group.

Had drinks and buffet before the recital. Didn't know anyone but the host and hostess at first. I thought this was a very civilized, unusual experience I was about to participate in.

Everyone stands around the lobby and talks, sees other friends, it's a big social, it's buzzing . . . the social element disappears once you get to your seat.

Audiences are very important, but need to be educated.

Respondents who spoke about attending musicals were in some respects the most casual about preparations and arrivals, especially in New York. Attending was likely to be part of a date, to involve hitting box offices to see about getting in, taking tourist friends, going right from work, and so on.

Two couples went, no pre- or post-theater activity. Ran over from work, just sort of hoped that it was good.

Had friends in from out of town—just went around box office to see who had tickets. Usually recommend a musical if they're seeing just one when in town.

He asked me what 1 wanted to do and I said, *Annie*. Worked all day, went to theater.

The immediate social excitement of going out to an event was most explicitly vigorous among young rock concert goers. They emphasized the specific interpersonal aspects of dating, grouping, of getting together for social interaction around and at the musical event, including sharing alcohol and other drugs, and the expectation— even the fear—of lively crowd behavior. The intensity is pronounced.

We drove all over the area picking up the people in my van, then partied all the way to

Providence, Rhode Island, where the concert was.

I felt an overriding desire to see the band— mailed for tickets, and while waiting for the show the drummer died, so I was disappointed. I couldn't wait for the show, it was the event of the year. I went with old, good friends, all really into it, four close friends. We went to dinner before and bought T-shirts before the performance.

I was looking forward to the concert very much due to my fondness for her music and also due to the fact that I had a hot date for the show. Before the show we partied at a friend's house who lived near the club, partaking mostly of beer and scotch, marijuana, and due to my temporary possession of a couple hundred dollars, cocaine.

I was looking forward to seeing a good concert and plenty of good-looking ladies.

It was kind of spooky. I never like the idea of being around all those people at one time. I felt kind of stiff, but loosened up once the music started.

Rock concert goers seem to worry more about whether the performers will show up; whether their seats will be taken, with some resulting hassle; the pushing of the crowd being dangerous; and, as one respondent said, "with me possessing enough stimulants for a felony conviction didn't help."

During the performance many respondents, regardless of type of musical event, tend to describe a kind of communion with the performance, a kind of deep, essential yielding of the self to the experience.

(*Don Pasquale* at the Metropolitan) During the performance, I have no sense of myself,

I feel at one with the music, the conducting, a feeling of "at onement."

(Patti Smith) During the performance, due to the intensity of Patti Smith, I found myself connecting mentally with her, and I let myself go.

(*The King and I*) The whole thing is upbeat, just keeps flowing. You can lose yourself in musicals compared to psychological dramas.

(Bob Marley and the Wailers) I was feeling especially good. Very at peace, but charged up. Very uplifted.

Those who prefer rock concerts tend to experience the involvement as a kind of catharsis, as total unification of the performers and the audience, with a vivid sense of participation.

You interact with others as though you've known them all your life.

The strong music soon had everyone up and dancing and shouting.

Everyone was swept up in the music.

We were all taken up in the spirit of the event.

Everyone in the show almost acts as one.

Those who prefer high cultural events do not expect such a group phenomenon to be so noticeable. They may emphasize their own individual emotional reactions.

I ended up crying and enjoyed it thoroughly.

I can be completely mesmerized.

And they often specifically discriminate themselves from the rest of the audience. Regardless of their inner emotions, they expect to be rather self-controlled.

I was not so aware of the audience. They reacted to the opera with mild enthusiasm and responsiveness. They came to hear the music, people don't go to the opera unless they like music.

In most cases, a process of evaluation also is operating; audience members have to decide whether the performance is good or not. They distinguish between the best part and the worst and how this performance compares with others. Attenders at all kinds of events exercise these kinds of judgments and easily distinguish between the most and the least compelling parts of the performance, according to their standards.

The most exciting part was the second half of the show which went from medium intensity to an almost orgasmic climax in the encores. By far the dullest part was the 45-minute wait in our seats for the show to begin, and the back-up band, who were depressingly bad.

It was exciting to see a young woman play the violin very expertly. I wished her well. She played with more gusto than talent.

I hated it—weak, half-assed music, tired jokes, was disappointed, bored, and angry that the show was so successful. The piano song was the most exciting. For once, there was a surprise and cleverness in the show.

It was *Tosca*. I was watching for the differences between City and the Met.

The first piece was not complicated enough musically.

The London Symphony wasn't too good, but I was surprised and pleased by Davis's performance.

Bad playing in general—attacks are off, horns are breaking, audience talking, tempo bad—wanting to leave before completion.

The behavior of the audience gets a lot of attention: their clothes, talking, movements, age, sex, race; their applause, coughing, closeness of attention, and so on, all are noteworthy and are used as bases for judging where the respondent stands relative to the rest. Each kind of event is regarded as having a typical audience, and respondents are often sensitive to the symbolic appeals that select audience segments. The rock audience is described in the interviews as young, 65% males, and might be "mostly college types," or "about 75% black because it was *Earth Wind and Fire.*" There are various uniforms, with jeans almost everywhere and mixed degrees of dress-up or costumes.

Jeans, leather, T-shirts, boots and sneakers were *de rigueur.* I wore my ripped jeans, T-shirt, and black skinny tie punk uniform.

Dressed to kill, all jazzy, lots of blacks, few whites. I was like them all dressed up, all fancy dress, unreal for me, big heels, shawl/poncho kind of thing.

The audience at musicals is described in more middling terms, a sort of mixed bag of all sorts of people, reflecting the wide "class-less" appeal of musicals. Middle-class respondents tend to feel superior to the average audience, thinking themselves more knowledgeable and being regretful that the audience has deteriorated.

The audience loved it. They seemed to be touristy, out-of-town . . . my tastes are more developed and cultivated, I'm probably better educated than most of them.

I feel I'm smarter than the rest of the audience, but similar in mutual enjoyment of musicals.

More and more I'm disappointed, they're just sitting there in jeans.

Nice cross-section of middle-class Angelenos. Dress varied from neat matrons in cocktail dresses to hip—much better judgment and taste.

The audience for high culture also shows variety in dress and knowledgeability, especially as some events attract younger segments who approach more casually. The presence of in-group members adds a special fillip to high cultural events, whether music students, a connection to the composer, or a select group of some sort. Europeans lend a special ambiance and luster, as does the presence of patrician money, jewels, furs, providing an imprimatur that helps to locate the event.

Interesting mixture of Europeans, stuffed shirts—on the whole a fairly stiff crowd of wealthy types. . . . Someone kissed the mother of the performer. I looked at ourselves as sort of peeking through a curtain at a rarefied environment.

Older, definitely, upscale, evening clothes, lots of minks, very classy. One thing I don't like is the chi-chi element—women who are there strictly for social reasons—Great Gatsby-like.

There were variations—minks and diamonds and ski clothes.

The audience came to see a Menotti opera, probably most of them were subscribers, young opera enthusiasts, similar to me. I was different, being there from having friends who were close to the composer and having been in works by Menotti.

The behavior of the audience is commonly said to be usual, or what is expected from the occasion. The higher the status of the culture, the event, and the audience, the more restrained the audience is apt to be. With status and maturity, people are expected to sit quietly, to know when to applaud and when not. They are not supposed to disturb each other with whispering, rattling papers, or coughing, and often show their fussiness with annoyed expressions and reprimands when these behaviors do occur. The contrast with the rock scene is marked, given the shouting, dancing, jumping, wandering about, cheering, smoking, drinking, and eating that go on there. American audiences (unlike Bayreuth) for high culture are supposed to be polite and well-behaved. Even disapproval is not expected to be vigorously shown.

Sit quietly, expected behavior, applaud when it is over.

You get reprimanded if you say one or two phrases even during the overture.

At Bayreuth there are contests between the proponents and opponents, who will boo and yell bravo for a half hour or so after the performance.

Can you imagine an American audience rioting over Stravinsky?

LEARNING ONE'S PREFERENCES

Respondents usually explain their musical preferences as having been learned in childhood or young adulthood. Both high culture and musicals are especially talked about as part of early family life. Often, musical parents, music lessons, and participating in shows are mentioned. Not infrequently, the child was "dragged along" until the finer things of life somehow took hold. These interviews do not illuminate the reasons why opera and symphony devotees continued to accept and attend these art forms, compared with others who did not. It is probably significant that middle-class rock music fans almost never attribute their learning about rock to their parents; on the contrary, rock is recognized as an anti-parent choice.

It was also very much of a status thing in my social circle to be hip on the latest groups, and more importantly, to be "into" the higher status groups, that is, the more radical ones who parents disliked the most, the flashiest.

The implication is that childhood high culture consumers tend to conform to parental standards; then again, some enjoy both high culture and rock, while others rebel and prefer rock but later return to the parental model. It is evident that the process of learning preferences is a complex one that may go on through life, and more study is needed of the social and psychological factors affecting it.

My parents used to take me—*Annie Get Your Gun, Oklahoma, South Pacific*. It was fun, an outing. Especially living in Brooklyn and going into the city.

Mom always liked opera and dragged me against my will. I ended up crying at the performance and enjoying it thoroughly. I was not brought up going to things like *Musica Sacra*. I was influenced by my wife with a strong musical background. I went to Bach's B Minor Mass with her before we were married.

After initial exposure, the development of interest in musical performance takes many forms. Records, newspaper reviews, magazine stories, and attendance all play a part in the process. While generally a social process, it sometimes is pursued individually, with active and inactive periods, fits, starts, and hiatuses.

I bought records of musicals for a while, a kind of hobby in high school.

Ran out to buy albums, I would attend concerts when I heard of them—but I would have had to have heard a song of theirs on the radio and liked it.

I try to dig up every review I can find because I don't know as much as most opera goers.

After my first symphony (performance) I kept pursuing it by attending and listening to classical radio. I read about it.

This activity sometimes became a solitary pleasure in addition to its social character.

I usually went alone—actively pursued it, exposed myself to different kinds of music. I went to opera to try it, but I don't like it now.

I did everything on my own, I didn't do any formal study. I have no in-depth knowledge but just being in a concert hall is a great pleasure.

I went to live performances at clubs like Café Society up in Harlem. I didn't buy many records. Frequently went alone.

For many, records, reviews, and attendance are not sufficient. Music increasingly becomes something that is to be mastered and created at first hand. The consumer becomes the performer. Passive consumption is not enough for those who demand greater depth of knowledge, understanding, and experience. They "consume" printed music and instruments.

I began taking singing lessons at night. Then at about 20, I began singing professionally, for weddings, and so on.

Learned to play show music on the piano, studied it in school and college. Both parents promoted interest, were supportive and encouraging. No friends were involved.

In high school bought show records, did musicals in high school and summer camp.

THE MUSICAL ARTS PRODUCT

The large general purpose is to explore the consumption of aesthetic experiences and to increase understanding of the arts product. The topic is a grand one and has not been neglected by artists, philosophers, critics, art historians, psychologists, and others. The views are also diverse, with such intimidating predecessors as Aristotle on the nature of tragedy, Tolstoy explicating "What is Art?," Dewey on *Art As Experience,* Sir Joshua Reynolds's Royal Academy lectures on the nature of masterpieces, Tom Wolfe on *The Painted Word,* and Igor

Stravinsky's witty essays, to mention but a few.

The task is made harder by definitional disputes and hairsplitting and the different issues posed by capital "Art," art objects, art forms, and what distinguishes the high from the low. A broad perspective is helpful. In his rich and absorbing analysis of the Balinese cockfight, Clifford Geertz (1973) says that it is like any art form in the way it renders ordinary experience comprehensible by highlighting a particular view of the essential nature of themes important in the society. At one point he says,

> An image, fiction, a model, a metaphor, the cockfight is a means of expression; its function is neither to assuage social passions nor to heighten them (though, in its playing-with-fire way it does a bit of both), but, in a medium of feathers, blood, crowds, and money, to display them.

Something of the same might be said of the rock concert, as the British beat poet Michael Horowitz did recently, in commenting on the way punk rock abstracts the rage of desperate youngsters. In the present instance, the more modest aim is particularly to notice some of the ways middle-class consumers regard and gravitate toward the musical experiences they prefer. They were not asked to define the musical arts products. But from their discussions of their experiences, and their explanations of what these mean to them, some inferences may be made about the molar character of the product.

In fact, such an endeavor is not universally encouraged; some chafe at the very idea of viewing aesthetic artifacts as marketplace products. Such a metaphor is, however, essential if we are to think about the providing and acquiring of these experiences. For such purposes the musical arts product can be assigned to the economy's service sector; yet this economic classification should not mask the fact that some musical arts products are distinctively uneconomic and the bond between performer and audience is usually secondarily commercial. The fiscal structure and the participants' pecuniary motives may vary from one musical form to the next, but musical arts products are characterized by varied distribution systems that involve in the aggregate millions of sellers and buyers—performing artists, skilled craftsmen, designers, technicians, agents, lawyers, entrepreneurs, financiers, students, teachers, parents, fans, hangers on, subscribers, and so on. Few would argue that no exchanges are transacted here, no services "delivered." Whether for profit or not, art products are undeniably amenable to the stratagems of market research. Acknowledgment of marketing's emerging role in arts management should include a note of caution against premature statistical analysis of narrowly conceived audience attributes. Rather, emphasis should be directed toward explicating the central behavioral dimensions that characterize performing arts consumption.

The preference within marketing for the usual variables of price, quality, and convenience is ultimately an inadequate perspective from which to examine the symbolically laden musical arts products. Through examining consumers' views, the issues they raise can be given greater centrality.

First, it may be noted that whatever the musical arts product may be—Helen Gardner (1936) says the essence of art is mysterious, intangible, indefinable—the high culture consumers tend to look upon it as experience necessary to their ways of life.

It's extremely important, part of what keeps me going, keeps me happy; I wouldn't survive without it. Music can get into my soul, is a highly emotional experience.

I need music in my life, it's an integral part.

It does the soul good. It's important that I have the opportunity to do this, even if we don't go that often.

Very important because it gives me pleasure, and I find it spiritually renewing.

Part of the significance of the high arts product, and its strength, seems to derive from this union of pleasure and virtue, the absorbing of a beauty that is also spiritually beneficial. In rather striking contrast, consumers of lower musical art forms tend to deny the necessary character of their affiliation.

Hey, this is no religious experience. It's just nice to see a live show once in a while for a nice night out.

They're not as important now because I do not have that much time or money to check out good concerts. . . . It doesn't affect me that much, except that I'll be singing a particular song for a while.

I really enjoy them and think about going to them (musicals) a lot, but there's a lot more things that take precedence.

Perhaps a larger sample or a sample of lower status devotees would bring out more intense expressions of need.

The high arts product has about it a quality of endurance, in itself and in its effects. The contrast with the ephemeral character of popular art is mentioned re-

peatedly. Low art is said to be more sheerly sensational, assaulting the senses.

When I come home I'm so wound up in a wonderful way. It's a lasting experience for me, not like going to a musical comedy, which is forgettable.

The experience of the show (*Evita*) is not really significant—it is an escapist moment. I don't feel very strongly.

We heard Jonathan Schwartz at Michael's Pub. It was distraction, excitement. . . . I feel elation when it's over, for a short time. I'm very spoiled, I dismiss pleasures readily.

The idea that mass culture is ephemeral recurs. Rick Kogan in the *Chicago Sun-Times* recently commented on this.

Sensations come and go frequently in the rock 'n roll business. Today's star is tomorrow's nobody, today's catchiest tune is tomorrow's forgotten melody, today's rabid fans are tomorrow's missing persons. Most rock is not lasting. Tasteless and pure ephemeral vogue. None of these people will be remembered in a few years.

The relativity of some of these views is also apparent as this same last respondent seeks to justify his own superior preference for a popular singer by remarking, "What I prefer is tasteful and apparently of lasting value. Fifty years from now they'll still be playing Mel Torme." Perhaps low art facilitates only an existential catharsis. But then again, perhaps to deny the intensity of the role of low art in the lives of its fans and its lasting effects on their emotions or personalities is part of the snobbism that often accompanies elitist attitudes.

The "directional" character of musical experiences is of interest. All of these experiences may give one a greater sense of oneself or a removal from oneself. High culture is seen to *elevate* the listener to spiritual realms; middle culture entertains, distracts, and *diverts;* and in the minds of some, low culture (e.g., punk rock) *degrades* the participants (some of whom use the expression "to get down"). Good music soothes the savage breast, while bad arouses it; status differences in art indicate the ways people use it to assert their degrees of refinement as human beings, distancing from their animal nature.

Among the various issues that occur in the recounting and evaluating of the arts product may be distinguished those relating to (a) the work of art itself, (b) the performing artists, and (c) the musical performance. In actuality, of course, these elements occur as an integrated experience, and greatness is achieved when they are all optimal. But they can be evaluated separately, and they may be conceived as having differential importance for different levels of arts products. The high cultural partisan tends to give the strongest appreciation to the work of art itself. The music itself is the fundamental creation, even if it is sometimes hard to separate it from its composer and the performances that embody it. The purist may try to be rid of the reliance on the artist, as in these remarks recently in the *Chicago Tribune,* by Gerald M. Stein, protesting the cult of Sir Georg Solti.

> I am rather unhappy at the news of Solti's intention to continue leading our band. But then, I usually go to concerts to hear music, not performers. And I'm afraid those of us who do so make up a minority of the Chicago Symphony's audience. . . . Those of us who feel this way realize Solti's rightfully praised

skills as an interpreter of a limited repertoire do not compensate for his inadequacies as the arbiter of musical taste in our community. . . . Let us hope the audience has not been persuaded to value Solti more than it values music itself. If it has, the worst possible outcome is *already* at hand.

Respondents often emphasize their relationship to the material.

> If I go to Puccini, I know I'm going to cry. If I'm going to hear Wagner, I'm so moved that I'm lost.

> I love German opera because it has some transcendent meaning.

Audiences for popular culture performances, of course, make distinctions between different performers' versions of the same material and have preferred materials, also. But they seem likely to respond more directly and aggressively to the particular performer and experience of performance.

> Best thing that can happen is that everyone attending the performance and also the musicians playing the music can almost meld into one.

> Everyone enjoys the music without distraction.

> They really get into their performance, the second performance is better because they're warmed up. They make you feel the music.

> Linda (Ronstadt) drives me wild.

At all levels the performing artists are appreciated because they bring the music to life, and because they vary in artistry among them and from one performance to another. Mr. Stein might get rid of Solti, but presumably he still needs the orchestra. The different artists and their performances are also essential to the critical faculty, enabling exploration of nuances in execution and interpretation and the display of one's aesthetic sensitivity and judgment. A not so subtle aspect of the arts situation is where it goes on. Becker (1974) has recently described a work of art as a social network of collective cooperation. The collection of organizations and persons linked together for the production and distribution of a musical arts product speaks symbolically about the nature of the product and prescribes conventions that delineate the domain of the arts product and guide performing arts consumer etiquette.

There has been some discussion in the service marketing literature that it is difficult to conceptualize or even describe a service sector product independently of its system of distribution. Performing arts products exemplify this concept. The often simultaneous and inseparable nature of service production, distribution, and consumption fosters an interaction between product and retail image. For example, the splendor of the Chicago Opera House symbolically distinguishes its musical products from the rock extravaganzas housed in the utilitarian amphitheater or stadium, the more sophisticated productions at the Park West in Lincoln Park, or the disreputable-seeming musical products offered in the proliferating New Wave outlets. From the perspective of market segmentation, this variance in distribution systems informs one not only of the existence of different types of musical arts products; it depicts a market "atmosphere" that varies from one product to the next; and it throws light upon the cast of characters who populate an art world and even suggests their motivations for participating.

From a marketing point of view, the arts product as a saleable entity comes into being particularly with the performance. While the musical arts product may be intangible, if one excludes the T-shirt and orange drinks sold in the lobby, it is produced and consumed live at a particular time and a retail place and becomes tangible in the persons of the performers, their instruments, costumes, and actions, all of which are sensorially "consumed" through visual, auditory, and vibratory means. The experience may be a service, and sometimes ineffable, but the consumers are not insensate. And it is ultimately their expression and categorization of these experiences that determines the segmentation of the performing arts audience.

CONCLUSION

This paper has described some elements evident in the behavior of consumers of musical events. The behavior is seen as a component in the larger pattern of arts consumption. The present part of the pattern is one in which social status is expressed by attendance at events that are symbolically hierarchical, with accompanying attitudes of deference and disdain toward the different musical levels.

> Opera is not unhealthy, blasting loud, it's based on literature, has some substance to it . . . it is more highly developed.

> I don't consider rock music to be music.

By concentrating on preferences among middle-class consumers, only a portion of the status hierarchy is examined. Some interclass comparisons can be made as both lower middle-class and upper middle-class people are included. The consumers of opera, symphony, and chamber music tend to be more mature and established members of the upper middle class. By staying within the middle class it is possible to observe specialization of preferences and recognize that age makes an important difference, given the devotion to rock by young middle-class consumers; and the general affection for musicals.

The analysis proceeds mainly at a low level of abstraction, partly because some of this description is a useful groundwork,

and sketching it may help to foster discussion and theorizing. Probably an obstacle to objective analysis is the strongly evaluative views that pervade attitudes toward the arts. It is illuminating that some of the emotional responsiveness to various art forms is talked about in similar terms, so that in certain respects popular culture seems to elicit semantics comparable to that of high culture. At the same time, the differences are also present and generally acknowledged, especially the importance attributed to peer dynamics among popular musical areas and the more private, intellectualized, and virtuous complexities attributed to high culture.

REFERENCES

Baumol, W. J., & Bowen, W. G. (1966). *Performing arts—The economic dilemma*. New York: The Twentieth Century Fund.

Becker, H. S. (1974). Art as collective action. *American Sociological Review, 39*(6), 767-776.

Gardner, H. (1936). *Art through the ages*. New York: HBJ College and School Division.

Geertz, C. (1973). *The interpretation of cultures*. New York: Basic Books.

Levy, S. J. (1980). Arts consumers and aesthetic attributes. In M. P. Mokwa & A. Prieve (Eds.), *Marketing the arts*. New York: Praeger.

Lipman, S. (1979, January). Funding the piper. *Commentary, 67*, pp. 54-60.

Macdonald, D. (1961). *Masscult and midcult*. New York: Partisan Review.

## Chapter 38

PSYCHOSOCIAL THEMES IN CONSUMER GROOMING RITUALS

Dennis W. Rook
Sidney J. Levy

Advancement of symbolic analyses in consumer research has proceeded less rapidly than progress in such areas as behavioral measurement and quantitative data analysis. A major factor discouraging the symbolic interpretation of products, brands, and companies is the widespread reluctance to deal with the less tangible realms of explanation of human behavior (Levy, 1978). Such inhibition has tended toward narrowly conceived, static, and ultimately unrealistic portrayals of human behavior and motivation. Recent work exploring the deep structure of consumer myth systems serves to guide interpretation of the various symbolic logics that underlie product and brand usage behavior (Levy, 1981). The present study investigates the relationship between consumer myths (as evidenced in fantasy expressions) and their enactment in everyday ritual behavior.

Although ritual phenomena pervade daily living, behavioral scientists (cultural anthropologists excepted) have tended largely to neglect the dynamics of ritual systems. Some relegate ritual to the domain

This chapter was first published in R. P. Bagozzi & A. M. Trybout (Eds.), *Advances in Consumer Research*, 1983, (Vol. 10, pp. 329-333), Provo, UT: Association for Consumer Research.

of primitive savages, while others perceive ritual activities solely in the context of religious dogma and practice. Recent discussion more thoughtfully considers ritual as a critical social mechanism in industrial nations (Bocock, 1974; Douglas, 1978). Ritual behavior includes the often elaborate public occasions that mark significant civic, seasonal, aesthetic, or religious events (Turner, 1967). The familiar *rites de passage* belong to this type of ritual expression (Gennep, 1908). Also included are midrange rituals that accompany the celebration of special family occasions, or even more common household "events" (Bossard & Boll, 1950). At the other end of this conceptual continuum are the everyday behavior ritualizations that may be either personal and private (prayer, grooming) or more interactional and public (the weekly visit to the beauty shop). Many daily grooming practices are often treated as habits—a redundancy for repetitive behavior—rather than as motivated. Erik Erikson (1980) provides a useful theoretical framework for observing and interpreting this everyday ritualization of behavior.

The context chosen for this research is the arena of consumer grooming rituals. The term *grooming* refers to diverse procedures applied to the body: cleansing, anointing, cutting and scraping, marking, shaping, coloring, and scenting (Vlahos, 1979). An individual's grooming ritual is conceived as consisting of a complex behavior helix relating to his or her (a) personal hygiene, (b) attractiveness of appearance, (c) social role preparation, and (d) acceptability. Grooming behaviors thus extend from basic biological into sociological and even cosmological territories. Grooming practices are part of our "body language," and as such provide a rich context for symbolic interpretation. The products dealt with such as cologne, facial makeup, hair dryers, tub and shower, and so on are among those readily recognized as subject to cultural variation and less dominated by easy rationalization in practical and economic terms.

The research instrument employed in this study is a modification of the Thematic Apperception Test (Morgan & Murray, 1935). This projective tool offers much to the behavioral researcher, especially in areas thought to involve substantial potential for defensive reactance. Although cited as the most widely used projective technique in marketing research (Kassarjian, 1974), its scholarly neglect represents a significant lacuna in consumer analysis.

GTAT STIMULI AND ADMINISTRATION

Any picture can elicit stories and provide material for analysis about the respondent. But study of a given realm such as grooming is facilitated by using pictures showing related behaviors. From a pool of over 100 candidates, six pictures were selected through pretesting and judgment and subsequently used as a Grooming Thematic Apperception Test (GTAT) stimuli. Their selection was based on several evaluative criteria suggested by Henry (1956), Murstein (1963), and others. Each author has a preferred list, but they agree generally on the importance of five basic criteria for selecting and/or constructing thematic pictures.

First, it is useful if a picture has relevant *latent stimulus meaning*. In GTAT Figure 38.1, for example, a woman is shown wearing hair curlers and applying some lotion or makeup. Research interest was

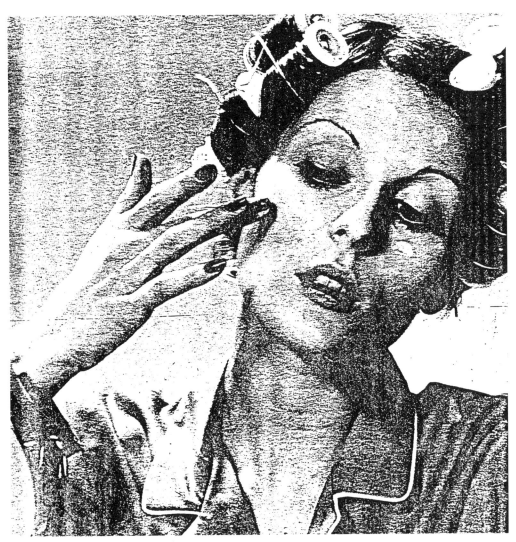

Figure 38.1. Woman in hair curlers

focused not so much on facts about hair curlers and skin care per se but on the fantasy material that surrounds such behavior. The six pictures selected raise various emotional issues stemming from one's grooming experiences and motives.

Second, pictures should depict various interpersonal relations such as those involving basic family dyads. One GTAT picture does this explicitly (Figure 38.2). The

others show individuals alone to fit the common grooming situations. Since such personal grooming is interpersonally motivated, it was assumed that this dimension would also be tapped without direct depiction.

Third, the pictures should represent varying degrees of objective reality, from clear-cut representations to more ambiguous, illogical, or nonobjective arrangements. The research interest here is not in individ-

Figure 38.2. Interpersonal situation

ual, clinical assessment, but rather in the discovery of modal grooming themes. Imposition of fewer degrees of freedom is justified by this relatively narrow purpose, orienting the results toward relatively conventional and socially characteristic results. Even so, there was sufficient variation in respondents' stories about the same pictures to suggest the individuals' projective mechanisms were not unduly inhibited.

Fourth, the pictures should be sufficiently intense in quality to intrigue the subjects and to demand that they propose some sort of solution to it. Although grooming procedures are part of most people's everyday routine, their centrality to self-image, sex role, interpersonal, and vocational issues guarantees some baseline psychic involvement. Fifth, the pictures se-

lected and the situations portrayed should be appropriate to the culture of the group being studied. Subjects were drawn from a broad population of young American adults from diverse social strata. The six GTAT pictures included representations of individuals in a working-class environment (Figure 38.2) and in an upper-status motif (Figure 38.3).

The other pictures cannot be so easily ranked. The six GTAT stimuli included pictures of: (a) a young to middle-aged woman in curlers doing makeup, (b) a couple sitting in a living room, (c) a young man applying after shave or cologne, (d) a woman sitting in a bath tub, (e) a young man blow-drying his hair, and (f) a person taking a shower. (The latter three pictures are not reproduced here.)

Figure 38.3. Young man grooming

SAMPLE

Forty-five young adults (23 females, 22 males) participated in the study. Respondents were elected in college classrooms and in other field settings. The average age of female respondents is 21.5 years (range 19-27) and for males 22.5 years (range 19-28). In addition respondents were selected in roughly equal proportion from (a) working class, (b) lower middle, and (c) upper status (upper middles and uppers combined) populations. Social status was measured objectively using Warner's *Index of Status Characteristics* (ISC) instrument in combination with respondents' level of education and parental occupation information. Assignment to so-cial division relied on holistic interpretation of the data rather than a single score.

RESULTS

Respondents took from 35 to 60 minutes to complete their GTAT stories. A substantial majority constructed full-size stories averaging 175 to 250 words each—thereby satisfying the widely used 200-word criterion for respondent involvement. The types of stories constructed ranged from socially conventional plots to unusual, highly fantastic themes. Although respondents are usually asked to construct imaginative and dramatically complete stories, they often do not do so. Here, the extensiveness of fantasy elaboration, and the amount of expressive energy were impressive. Young adults apparently need little stimulation to involve themselves in such realms of experience. Quite a few stories were also notably sad in tone—a finding consistent with the characteristic tenor of results that rely upon TAT-type instruments but also compatible with the problems on people's minds.

CONCEPTUAL FRAMEWORK FOR DATA ANALYSIS

William E. Henry (1956) provides a comprehensive framework for interpreting data gathered through TAT procedures. Of the many areas of mental life potentially illuminated through TAT administration, there are four focal points of this analysis of grooming fantasies: (a) basic emotional attitude, (b) sexual adjustment (feelings of adequacy and anxiety, and role perception), (c) acceptance or rejection of impulse life, and (d) approach to interpersonal relations. The expressive content of these stories is viewed as representing projections of individual needs and motives interacting with forces from the social environment; stories about "others'" grooming rituals reveal one's own conscious and unconscious needs and attitudes, and the unconscious impulses involved. Psychosocial conflicts relating to personal appearance and self-presentation issues should also emerge in respondent's dramatic constructions.

Erik Erikson's (1980) work is relied on for interpretation of respondents' stories. In *Toys and Reason*, Erikson extends his dynamic theory of psychosocial development to the arena of behavior ritualization.

The elements of ritualized adult interplay are explained as originating in the conflicts, or crises, associated with the five developmental stages preceding adulthood. The relative success (or failure) an individual experiences at each stage impacts the thematic content of adult ritualization, and more generally, personality. In pure form, the healthy individual's expression would emphasize interpersonal trust, autonomy, initiative, industry, and clear personal identity; while the seriously disturbed personality would exhibit distrust, shame, guilt and inferiority, and a diffused identity. The discussion that follows describes and interprets the thematic content of young adults' grooming fantasies. Table 38.1 suggests the relation of Freud's psychosexual developmental stages in the formation of personality to Erikson's psychosocial stages with the accompanying psychological and characterological elements in behavior ritualization.

The analysis sees the contribution of these levels to the young adults working on the sixth and seventh levels above them of intimacy and generativity.

NUMINOUS ELEMENTS

The numinous elements in adult ritualization originate in the infant-oral stage of development. Whether an individual is basically a trusting or a mistrustful personality is significantly influenced by life's experiences during this period. More than simple attitude clusters, the numinous elements that rise here are so basic as to possess mystico-spiritual qualities. In the context of personal grooming rituals, numinous themes describe the "before and after" magic that transforms the individual into a

TABLE 38.1 Stages in Personality Development

Freud Psychosexual Stages	Erikson Psychosocial Stages	Ritual Behavior Elements
Genital	Identity versus identity diffusion	Ideological
Latent	Industry versus inferiority	Performing
Phallic	Initiative versus guilt	Dramatic
Anal	Autonomy versus shame	Judicious
Oral	Trust versus mistrust	Numinous

new man or a new woman. Grooming routines are often seen as involving dramatic personality reversals—for example, from the tired and withdrawn me to the energetic and outgoing me. Underlying such expressions are sentiments describing the "wondrous" and "miraculous" results of various grooming procedures. Individuals who might otherwise disparage supposed romantic or age-retardant product claims appear quite able to suspend their disbelief and fantasize about magical lotions, elixirs, and other forms of social war paint. Respondents' stories commonly cite the captivating qualities attributed to grooming products and procedures, as well as the physical magic they provide.

> Betty has an important interview with a large corporation. She has gotten up early to prepare and make sure she looks her best. She is using a special face cream that will make her look years younger. (LM-F-21)

> With a little bit of cover-up the blemishes are just barely noticeable, and her self-confidence is restored to what it was before the zits popped up. Her date is wonderful, and he asks her out for next Wednesday—after con-

fessing that she is one of the most beautiful girls he's ever seen. (UM-F-21)

Such stories take on a fairy tale quality corresponding to the before-and-after approaches that pervade the promotion of grooming and cosmetic products—and such classical transformations as Cinderella and the frog into a Prince.

Another numinous theme emphasizes the healing qualities associated with grooming routines. Grooming activities are widely described as occurring in silent places of contemplation and restoration. Lower-status respondents tend to stress the relief of physical discomfort ("my aching body"), while upscale individuals stressed grooming's private, meditative aspects. Showering and particularly bathing are valued as inviolable personal space and as providing opportunities for retreat from the world. The healing dimension of grooming fantasies often involves preparation for quiet evenings at home, and for rest and sleep—but it may also facilitate transitions from work to play.

> I have to get another job—my body is killing me. And this hot bath feels so good. (UL-M-24)

Poor Katie—she's had one hell of a day. Now she's relaxing and contemplates in the midst of the luxury of having a moment to herself—and she thinks of the day's events as the night quickly approaches. (LM-F-23)

"I love taking baths," thought Belinda, "just turn on the hot water, lock the door, sit back, relax, and let my thoughts just glide away. Oh, let's see, I think I'll go on a safari today—just me and Jabar." (UM-F-21)

Whether for physical rejuvenation or for psychic adventuring, such fantasies are more elaborately constructed among females than males. Responses to stimulus No. 4 (woman bathing) illustrates this idea. Men tended to see the individual depicted as a pathetic beast of burden soaking her tired bones, while women were generally more sympathetic to her, were more likely to stress the enjoyment of a private moment.

A third numinous element, common to both sexes and across social divisions, depicts grouping's relationship to getting lucky, particularly in interpersonal relationships. Quite a few stories are sad in tone, telling of past disappointments and cautious anticipation of meeting someone "new." The plot is often accompanied by the hope that one will finally get lucky, that good fortune is overdue, especially to have sexual success. Viewed from this perspective, grooming rituals operate mantra-like to anchor positive energies and give the individual a better chance with a new person. Typical subject responses exemplify the various logics that link grooming procedures to helping luck along a bit.

He's wanted to go out with this girl all semester and now he's got his chance. He doesn't want to blow it, so he's going to make

sure his hair is a perfect as John Travolta's. (UM-F-21)

Joe has to look good wherever he goes—he works out a lot on his body and gets ecstatic pleasure out of blow-drying his hair. . . . Will he get lucky tonight? Joe thinks so. (UM-M-25)

This young man is getting ready for a big date, maybe the Prom. He is using an after-shave to appear more grown up than he is. Undoubtedly he will get lucky once the girl smells his aftershave. (LM-M-26)

Reflecting a basic, mistrustful orientation, a small but distinctive minority of stories describe the hopeless individual for whom luck has run out. The main characters are drug-addicted or alcoholic, abandoned, and suicidal individuals. Grooming issues were generally buried as hopeless beneath such plentiful misery.

JUDICIOUS ELEMENTS

This second behavioral element in Erikson's (1980) ritualization framework originates in conflicts surrounding the individuals' learning of basic rights and wrongs—the cornerstone for which, in Freudian thought, is the child's toilet-training experience. Successful resolution of this developmental crisis fosters self-perceptions of rightfulness and autonomy, while relative failure induces a sense of wrongfulness and shame. Grooming behavior—not surprisingly—very much involves issues of right and wrong.

An earlier study by Levy (1961) reveals how women (men were not sampled) from diverse social strata and of various ages tended generally and readily to use graphically presented grooming cues as evidence revealing another's personality, vocation, family life, and sexual conduct, deduced from such signs as skirt lengths, amount of lipstick, elaboration of hairdo, and so on. Forceful judgments about the appropriateness, normality, and even morality of any given look often accompany these interpretations. Based upon the results of the present study, men are also able to so classify and evaluate others, and to use the grooming vocabulary.

Grooming is, first of all, sanctioned behavior. In spite of the casualness and humor respondents see in the grooming domain, there is widespread recognition of prescribed norms for personal appearance and of (sometimes severe) sanctions that ensue when the rules are violated. Grooming is seen as directing outcomes in both the vocational and romantic arenas, and it is used to assign individuals niches in the social hierarchy. Not surprisingly, the young adults sampled in this study place much emphasis on the use of grooming routines to judge maturity, capability, and romantic availability. There is also some reaction against perceived pressures to fit the mold. For example, the young executive is described as really being very superficial, the career woman lonely, and the young Romeo a bubble brain. This ambivalence is expressed in the idea that although grooming is a social necessity, too much emphasis on appearance connotes frivolity, not a thoughtful person.

> This man was runner-up in the Mr. Young Stud contest. He won the talent section of the competition with the performance you see above—successfully blow-drying his hair in 7 min. 15 sec. But he got edged out in the shorts modeling segment by the man who was eventually crowned Mr. Young Stud. (UM-M-25)

DRAMATIC ELEMENTS

The third dimension in Erikson's (1980) ontogeny of ritualization framework originates in the dynamics of learning to initiate playful activities in childhood. Successful task resolution encourages the development of an independent and initiating personality, while sufficient unresolved conflict fosters a guilty, delinquent orientation. This is a period of the elaboration of narcissism, dramatizing the self and displaying the body. It may foster the search for sensual experience. Several common themes illustrate how respondents in this study deal with these issues in the context of their grooming fantasies. Much emphasis is placed on the notion of the big event. Although grooming is an everyday activity, considerable importance is assigned to extraordinary situations. Stories describe individuals' preparations for a critical job interview, for a special date, for a television appearance, for a concert performance, or for a marriage proposal.

> She is very pensive as she shaves her legs. Tonight her boyfriend has something important to ask her. She wonders if he will pop the question or just ask for another tiny loan until payday. (UM-M-27)

> This gentleman seems to be preparing himself for a fun night out on the town. He seems a bit too happy for it to be a mere night out with the boys. So I would say it would be in the company of some lovely lady. (UL-M-27)

Needing some justification for considerable allocation of time, effort, and money to grooming procedures, individuals construct extraordinary payoffs for their investments. Much emphasis is placed on achieving the perfect look such occasions are commonly thought to demand. More than self-gratifying narcissism, such behavior announces that the individual who lavishes such loving attention on him/herself also has the desire for response from other people. The prevalence of the big event theme also highlights the anxieties that surround the search for a vocation and a mate, as one story poignantly illustrates.

> Tonight I have tickets for the new musical *They're Playing Our Song* at the Drury Lane Theater. and I'm taking a new girl I met at the office. She's beautiful and really has potential. I'm putting my best foot forward donning my new suit and my Pierre Cardin aftershave. Although I love the single life, it can be lonely, so I want this to be a good night. Who knows, I might find a companion out of this. (LM-F-23)

Grooming is valued as a mechanism for bridging the gap between individual anxieties about various interpersonal interactions and the social contingencies that require them. Grooming procedure are viewed as *cranking up* energy to overcome reluctance and hesitation. Like a tribal war chant, some stories resonate with the themes of off-to-social-battle. Self-congratulatory and confidence-building sentiments charge the atmosphere.

> That shower felt so good and I'll wear the best cologne I've got. Well, I look great. . . . sharp. She's ready for me, well here I go. (UL-F-24)

> Oh! I'm so cool in the morning. They call me smooth and cool. Because I come to work looking so nice. Well, I need a shave and a shower so I can keep on looking cool and smooth. (LM-M-19)

These internally generated exhortations parallel a third element of dramatic elaboration: the call to action. Beyond the rudimentary whipping up of social energy, grooming rituals inform about motives. Overwhelmingly, young adult fantasies about grooming products and practices are filled with the urges to get ready and to join in.

> Marilyn hurriedly rolls her hair and applies gobs of makeup between swigs of warm beer. Barney arrives and they're off for a night of action. (UM-F-20)

Evoking the lyrics of many Bruce Springsteen songs, respondents' stories are filled with characters running off into the night with hot chicks and cool studs, going in fast cars to action-filled arenas of intoxicating romance and adventure. Social status appears to exert powerful influences over the dramatic elaboration of these ideas. Lower status romantic fantasies are characteristically similar to the *Cinderella* story. The drudgery and suffering of real world life is relieved by the intervention of an adoring Prince Charming. In contrast, upscale fantasies parallel the *Snow White* storyline, which emphasizes independence and achievement, gaining control and power. The action components in individual stories reflect these thematic differences. Lower status stories are more likely to emphasize discos and dances as destinations, while upscale fantasies tend to involve exotic real world destinations (safaris, prisons) or metaphysical territories (LSD trips). Several stories told by upper-status females involved degrading interactions with working-class punk types. While the appeal of libidinal action pervades the grooming fantasies of young adults generally, the ritual behaviors of different social classes will most likely be connected to quite different personal myths.

A final dramatic element suggests a difficult resolution of the play-age childhood period. These delinquent fantasies involved rebellious individuals who refuse to "give in" and modify personal appearances even to get a job. Stories include hostile parents, rejecting employers, and unempathetic peers. Grooming issues here symbolize the conflict and guilt involved in the refusal to conform.

FORMAL ISSUES

With school age comes the crisis of performance. Positive resolution encourages an industrious orientation and feelings of success, while unresolved conflicts foster a sense of inferiority. The formal elements of grooming rituals emerge vividly in the stories collected for this study. Performance standards are on the minds of many young adults. Much emphasis surrounds having one's hair, or face "just so," or perfect. One reaction to this pressure is the theme of *never enough time*. Stories involve characters who rush to get ready, running late, and who are often interrupted in the midst of their grooming routines by the door bell or the telephone. While this may correspond to actual events (people are busy and do run late), there is also the element of passive rebellion against society's performance standards. This theme was more notable among women than men, and more unenthusiastic stories are told by them

about getting up 2 hours early to achieve the look.

Many stories place value on having the right stuff. When confident in one's sexuality these individuals are portrayed as investing their grooming rituals with enthusiastic self-assurance. As the beginning to a busy day, such an individual's grooming routine sets the tone for industrious achievement. The young adults sampled here demonstrated some ambivalence about the value of high standards. Several stories told of meticulous grooming preparations that led to ultimate disappointment: The girl likes scruffy not clean-shaven guys, the new guy is really a drip, he/she doesn't get the job after all. Overall, such stories combine release of anxiety and feelings of resentment toward society's grooming standards. There is an element of intimidation in these perfect images. One young man illustrates his ambivalence.

> Another morning. I'm 3 years out of a good Eastern school, and one and a half into a great marriage. My job is a real challenge. I think I can really go somewhere with it. Everything seems to be working out. It better. (UM-M-23)

Reflecting less successful resolution of the crisis in performance standards are the themes suggesting inferiority feelings. Many stories described the behavior of a klutz, or loser, who can't seem to do anything right. Anxieties differ significantly by sex. Women exhibit the strongest feelings about the physical effects of aging and about finding mates. Men are more preoccupied with anxieties about their relative size and potency. The phallic symbolism in stimulus No. 2 (blow dryer) appears to have agitated quite a few male respondents. Responses describe the young man in the picture as sexually confused, as wanting to have sex with the blow dryer, as an insecure and undersized "zero" compensating with a large electrical appliance.

IDEOLOGICAL ELEMENTS

With adolescence comes the famous identity crisis. Previous unresolved conflicts, converging with the biosocial conflicts of approaching adulthood, create existential pressures. Individuals respond by mentally creating ideal types who represent an appealing adulthood. Because maturity is still in the future. these images may be abstract or cartoonlike: Superman, Daisy Mae. When these ideal types correspond to iconic public individuals, the response can be intense and enduring: Elvis and Marilyn are examples.

In the search for role models, themes cluster around common ideas about who has the right stuff. The male athlete is a popular standard bearer for lower-status individuals. He is a virtuous and easy-going individual who grooms himself to keep clean and fresh. He has a conventional interest in pretty girls and puts considerable emphasis on colognes when grooming for romantic interactions. His darker side is loutish and sadistic and of below-average intelligence. A lower-status female counterpart is the media girl.

> Here I am getting ready for the 6:00 news and I only have 10 minutes to get ready. If this dressing room wasn't so small I could have been done. Oh, no! Good evening, this is the 6:00 o'clock news and my name is Rita Carson. (UL-F-24)

The appeal of the media girl seems to be in her glamorous but nonintimidating role. She is a news reader, not a journalist, and her profession is used to justify massive narcissism. Her unattractive features include vanity and insincerity.

Lower-middle class ideals focus on someone who is one-of-the-guys. He may seek out involvement in the romantic arena, but his center of gravity is still his high school or college buddies even after marriage. He, too, may be an athlete, but his sport is Zaxxon or Tron rather than varsity. He uses deodorant. He may not use cologne generally, but when he does it supports his desire to be a lady killer. He can be either suave or crude, but he is a classic single out on the town hunting for sexual triumphs.

> "Where to tonight?" that's what Vance is asking himself. He could cruise Faces or maybe Mother or maybe all the Rush Street bars between Oak and Division. The new cologne he just bought should knock the ladles out. Well, not out but if he's lucky it'll knock 'em down. Once they're down Vance can knock them out on his own. Knock them out and knock them up. Who's going to be the lucky lady tonight, Vance? (LM-M-26)

Among men, the lady killer is often one of the guys with a lot of luck. For women, he may be an older man, or a working-class individual. His grooming product usage is above average, but not by a great teal. Among lower-middle class females the working woman may be married, is practical, and spends a lot of time on her appearance. She works hard in a man's world with varying amount of gratification. Upscale individuals idealize the junior executive who dresses well and make decisions and is very serious about his—or her—career. This person is more likely to be single than married. He/she spends a fair amount of time on personal grooming. Men are likely to use body talc, cologne, a blow dryer, even a facial bronzer. Under certain circumstances such behavior might be interpreted as effeminate, but here it is justified by everyone's general agreement on how important personal appearance is in the business world, relying on the same logic as the media girl.

Grooming appears equally capable of facilitating the assumption of either forbidden or virtuous social roles. Individuals who fail sufficiently to resolve the adolescent identity crisis experience, in Erikson's (1980) words, role diffusion. This element was evident in the numerous story themes that describe an individual "blown away" by circumstance, devoured, or vanishing into nonexistence.

Yes, Tony Baretta fought off the Mighty Mite for nearly 10 minutes. His arm bulging, the "Mite" consumed him. (LM-M-23)

As she bathes she notices more and more bubbles. She assumes it is normal because this new bubble bath is supposed to give you more bubbles than you can imagine. Finally there are so many bubbles that she panics and commits suicide. (UM-M-21)

As he raised his Mighty Mite portable hair dryer with the 10 different speeds on the handle he accidentally pushed the drying speed to 10 and was so blown away that it blew him right out of his apartment's bathroom window. (UM-M-21)

These themes evidence the use of humor and fantasy to express anxiety about the

pressures of growing up at such high speed. Other instances of severe struggle with role diffusion include fantasies of negative and secret identities. Among male respondents, there is the threat that too much grooming will be interpreted as effeminate. Some respondents described the young man depicted in stimulus No. 2 (blow dryer) as homosexual or transsexual.

This is a photograph of Joe Hill. Most weekends and many week nights too, Joe transforms himself into Josephina. He tries not to do too many drugs because it's tough on his complexion, but he's drinking his white wine—hoping to calm his tension about the Grace Jones concert tonight. Tomorrow will find Joe in his apartment, naked and alone, with no idea of what happened after 3 a.m. (UM-F-21)

This secret identity scenario typically involves a story's main character adopting a radically different, and usually secret, name and persona. With a new, secret identity the path is cleared for participation in socially forbidden behavior, without sullying one's real, virtuous self. For example, the interpersonally awkward Skinner acts out his aggressive sexual fantasies when he becomes "Ricky"; or the housewife dons a wig to facilitate her entree into adultery. Secret identities are adopted not only to pursue taboo behaviors but to cope with more conventional anxieties and disappointments.

Slim Joe, the dud of your high school, can only be tough once a day, and that's when he is by himself in the bathroom. There Joe becomes "Mighty Mite." (UM-F-19)

Candy is a contented housewife living a nice upper-middle class life. Although her mornings are hectic around the house, the afternoons are all to herself. Candy enjoys dressing up and playing Model when no one else is home. (LM-M-21)

CONCLUSION

The fascination with magical effects, the various struggles to cope with social norms, and the dramatic elaborations that characterize respondents' grooming fantasies point to complex motives and—pervasive ambivalence. It seems evident that projective methods of research can provide useful access to fantasy life, bringing to our attention the less tangible realms of experience.

A question naturally arises about the relationship between one's fantasy and "real" lives. Research currently in progress will address this issue further by relating individuals' responses on the projective instrument developed for this study to their performance on other instruments and questions related to product and brand use. So far these various grooming tales show that the consumption of bathroom furnishings, hair dryers, soaps, makeup, shampoos, colognes, shavers, underwear, and so on, affords complex ways of expressing ones' sexual and social striving. The products are not merely aids to cleanliness and sensory pleasure; they are means of coping systematically with the demands for growing up in particular ways in American society.

REFERENCES

Bocock, R. (1974). *Ritual in industrial societies*. London: George Allen & Unwin.

Bossard, J. N. S., & Boll, E. S. (1950). *Ritual in family living*. Philadelphia: University of Pennsylvania Press.

Boyd, H. W., Jr., & Levy, S. J. (1963, November/December). New dimensions in consumer analysis. *Harvard Business Review*, pp. 129-140.

Douglas, M. (1978). *The world of goods: Toward an anthropology of consumption*. London: Allen Lane.

Erikson, E. (1980). *Toys and reason*. New York: Norton.

Gennep, A. van (1908). *The rites of passage* (M. B. Vlzedom & G. L. Coffee, Trans.). London: Routledge & Kegan Paul.

Henry, W. E. (1956). *The analysis of fantasy*. New York: John Wiley.

Kassarjian, H. (1974). Projective methods. In R. Ferber (Ed.), *Handbook of marketing research*. New York: McGraw-Hill.

Levy, S. J. (1961). *How American women see feminine types*. Chicago: Social Research, Inc. (for the Public Relations Board, Inc.)

Levy, S. J. (1978). *Marketplace behavior—Its meaning for management*. Chicago: AMA/COM.

Levy, S. J. (1981). Interpreting consumer mythology: A structural approach to consumer behavior. *Journal of Marketing, 45*(Spring).

Morgan, C. D., & Murray, H. A. (1935). A method for investigating phantasies: The thematic apperception test. *Archives of Neurological Psychiatry, 35*.

Murray, H. A. (1943). *Thematic apperception test manual*. Cambridge, MA: Harvard University Press.

Murray, H. A. (1965). Uses of the thematic apperception test manual. In B. I. Murstein (Ed.), *Handbook of projective methods*. New York: Basic Books.

Murstein, B. I. (1963). *Theory and research in projective techniques*. New York: John Wiley.

Turner, V. (1967). *The ritual process*. Chicago: Aldine.

Vlahos, O. (1979). *Body, the ultimate symbol*. New York: J. B. Lippincott.

## Chapter 39

SYNCHRONY AND DIACHRONY IN PRODUCT PERCEPTIONS

Sidney J. Levy

There is a stream of marketing theory that draws upon such fields as symbolic inter-action (Blumer, 1969) and semiotics, the study of signs and symbols (Eco, 1979). These disciplines have contributed to mar-keting thought since at least the 1940s and '50s, when their concepts were used and disseminated by the followers of theorists such as Charles Peirce (Cohen, 1923), Alfred Korzybski (1933), George Herbert Mead (1934), and W. Lloyd Warner (1959). This application was reflected in work by Erving Goffman (1959), Lee Rainwater (Rainwater, Coleman, & Handel, 1959),

Sidney J. Levy (Gardner & Levy, 1955), and other colleagues. More recent workers in this realm include Russell W. Belk (1979), Elizabeth C. Hirschman (1981), Morris B. Holbrook (1981), Rebecca H. Holman (1981), Trudy Kehret-Ward (Kehret-Ward, Johnson, & Louie, 1985), Dennis W. Rook (1984), and Michael R. Solomon (1983).

The thrust of this work is toward ana-lyzing the meanings of objects and experi-ences. It focuses on the marketing exchange process as an exchange of symbols in which consumers use product and brand images to express their self-images (Levy, 1959). In

This chapter was first published in *Proceedings,* American Marketing Association, 1983 (revised). Reprinted with permission of the American Marketing Association.

the present paper, these images are taken to be the result of differentiations in meaning attributed to products, along various structural continua and hierarchies. As Douglas and Isherwood (1979) have said, goods

> are arranged in vistas and hierarchies that can give play to the full range of discrimination of which the human mind is capable.... Consumption uses goods to make firm and visible a particular set of judgments in the fluid processes of classifying persons and events. (pp. 66-67)

The customary level of analysis has been molar, using products as the symbolic objects, and examining their connection with various consumer ideas and characteristics. For example, Belk, Mayer, and Bahn (1981) ask what qualities do people attribute to the owners when shown pictures of large or small houses and cars; and report the connections made between size of product and ideas about age, social status, and other attributes. The relation of gender concepts to sex-typing in product images is discussed by Allison, Golden, Mullet, and Coogan (1980). In varying degree, also, attempts are made to study where meanings come from; that is, what assumptions, logics, and basic concepts are being drawn upon by customers or managers in making their inferences. The main links have been between the kinds of consumers and their images of the products and brands (Gardner & Levy, 1955). Less attention in basic research has gone to explaining the component elements that act as determinants in forming images, although Christian Pinson (1981) has surveyed the cues consumers use in their perceptions. Much recent work explores the psychological processes used in making categories. Also, practitioners such as designers often show awareness of the implications of color and form (Hillmer, 1984).

This paper is an extension of earlier work (Levy, 1981) that pointed to the way consumers structure fundamental generalizations about food, making symbolic distinctions among them to express identities by gender, maturity, social status, and concomitant psychological qualities. It explores how product attributes are categorized in the inferences consumers draw from them and theorizes about the underlying logic that determines how these attributes are found suited to respective market segments (Bourdieu, 1984).

The ideas designated as synchronic make up the structure of meanings, or sign system, that is operative in a given time. They are the particular set of paradigmatic distinctions that prevail and govern at that time. Diachrony refers to the variation in those ideas over time, with changes in the combinations and intensities of symbolic elements. As Dennis Porter (1984) has summarized, the dichotomy between synchrony and diachrony is that between structure and event. The product context used here to sketch the theory in its application to marketing analysis and management is that of beverages, with soft drinks as a specific category. First, the general synchronic structure is described. Second, this structure is elaborated to specify how particular beverages fit into it. Third, an empirical study is reported that applies a synchronic and diachronic approach to the beverage brands of 7-Up and Coca-Cola.

THE SYNCHRONIC BEVERAGE STRUCTURE

The Synchronic Beverage Structure (SBS) is a hypothesis that asserts the contemporary structural relationships between five hierarchies of symbolic attributes and three hierarchies of symbolic inference or meaning. The SBS says that (a) the preparation of the product, (b) its color, (c) its relative variety and (d) quantity, and (e) its physical impact are major sources of meaning; that they are interpreted for (f) their psychosocial qualities, and thus for their suitability to (g) degrees of maturity and (h) social status. The SBS is represented in summary form in Table 39.2. Reading the chart from left to right, this structure says that the products are representations, that their forms and attributes embody ideas that are either imposed on them or inferred from them (as may be debated by behaviorists and vitalists) by consumers. Horizontally, these ideas indicate the nature of the product, what it does physically and subjectively to and for the users who drink it (who show themselves as users of it, who serve it, etc.), and what kinds of people are therefore perceived as suited to it.

Reading up from the bottom, the figure sketches in how consumption changes for different levels of the life cycle. The products at the lower end derive directly from natural sources and simple processing up through more complex methods of preparation. They move from being light in color through colorfulness to darkness. They go from being consumed in larger quantities to smaller units; and from homogeneity to relative heterogeneity in the substances themselves and/or in the variety available for choice. Parallel to these shifts is movement from perception of virtue to relative vice. The lower levels imply more passivity, then up toward energy and activity and increased sensationalism. Accompanying the evils seen in intoxication, addiction, and other hazards of caffeine and alcohol are ideas of sophistication, potency, vigor, subtlety of discrimination, richness of experience, and depth of thought that surround drinking coffee, being a wine connoisseur, and deciding among liqueurs such as Grand Marnier, Drambuie, and Kahlua.

As consumption effects move from emphasis on nutrition and bland, sweet tastes to increasing emphasis on intensity of taste, body impact, and stimulation of "mind altering" sorts, they become perceived as more mature and higher in status. In the process, people move from dependency to greater autonomy. They gain more self-control and freedom of choice in satisfying their appetites. Their ability to make subtle discriminations among sensations and tastes and to tolerate greater intensities increases, allowing the formation of more individual identities. The mature person is free to be self-indulgent or even addictive, as forms of self-expression.

By becoming socialized and more refined, learning to tolerate and enjoy "unnatural" tastes and making finer distinctions, people show how far from being animals they are. Mary Douglas (1984) points to this psychosocial capacity for human complexity as a basic proposition: "It starts from the assumption that unlike livestock, humans make some choices that are not governed by physiological processes. They choose what to eat, when and how often, in what order, and with whom" (p. 3).

There is a parallelism in being young, animal-like, and being lower in social status, at least so that adults see children, and higher-status people see lower-status people, as more gross in their food consumption and less mature than themselves.

The synchronic structure indicates that products within bands are categorized hierarchically and that category bands are also categorized hierarchically. The information that is used in making inferences from the hierarchy says, summarily, that complexity of preparation, darkness of color, heterogeneity of choice, small units of consumption, and intensity of physical impact are

TABLE 39.1 The Synchronic Beverage Structure

Object	Form	Attribute	Meaning	Segment
Alcoholic beverages			Intoxication	Adults
Liqueur	Brandies	Distilled wine	Sipping	Elite
			Intensity	Gourmets
			Discrimination	
Wine	Chateaux labels	Vineyards	Romance	Cosmopolites
		Fermenting	Snobbery	
Whiskey	Scotch	Aging	Sophistication	Upper class
	Bourbon	Grains	Hard drinking	Mature
	Vodka			
	Gin			
Wine	Domestic	Grapes	Low alcohol	Young adults
	Jug		Liberalism	
Beer	Foreign	Brewing	Sociability	College men
	Tap	Grains	Democracy	Working class
	Bottle			
	Can			
	Barrel			
Coffee and tea		Caffeine	Pick-up, comfort	Adults
Coffee	Espresso	Brewing	Busyness	Mature adults
	American	Beans	Thought	
			Bitterness	
Tea	Exotic	Leaves	Depth	Old ladies
			Warmth	Ethnics
			Richness	
Soft drinks		Carbonation	Festivity	Adolescents
	Colas	Syrup	Youth	Young adults
		Nuts	Autonomy	Teens
	Fruit sodas	Fruit	Ambivalence	Kids
Fruit drinks		Natural Essence		Healthy people
	Juices	Acidity	Breakfast	Good eaters
		Squeezing	Tartness	
			Virtue	
	Ades	Diluting	Fun	
Soup			Survival	Family
	Vichysoisse	Cooking	Tradition	Ethnics
	Chicken	Meat	Nourishment	Family
	Vegetable		Home	
			Mother	
Milk	Milking		Dependency	Offspring
	Chocolate	Blend	Enhancement	Older kids
	Cow's	Grass	Growth	(Old people)
	Breast	Nature	Mother	Babies
Water	Mineral	Neutral	Thirst	Everyone
	Plain	Clear	Existence	

SOURCE: Compiled by the author.

accompanied by attributions of discriminating taste and sophistication. The general wisdom supports these ideas with the logic that says more elaborate preparation is costly and shows the greater social power of the recipient to command the greater effort; that darkness is richer, stronger, more mysterious; that having greater choice is costly, requires knowledge and the ability to distinguish; that small amounts are more intense, precious, and exclusive; and that being able to sustain marked physical impact shows strength or freedom from conventional restraints: all these qualities imply a consumer who has the requisite experience and socioeconomic power to rise higher in the structure compared to those who are still too young or socially benighted.

The values related to gender are more complexly intertwined than the association of age grading and social status, especially given the changes going on in sex roles and the perceptions of them. Traditionally, women have occupied an inferior position, with femininity accorded a lower power status than masculinity. Women were also regarded as immature, being smaller, weaker, more emotional, and being kept more circumscribed in experience. At the same time, women are thought to have more delicate sensitivities and to be responsible for the expression of the family's taste and refinement. Thus, they are paradoxically the keepers of the family's social status and in this sense represent a civilized and elevated humanity. Social status is a broad idea, as it derives simultaneously from its roots in occupation and social power, where it favors the man's role; and from its symbolic expression in social activities and the character of the household, where it favors the woman's traditional role.

The concepts shown in Table 39.2 form a structural template of the abstractions that consumers draw upon in forming their perceptions of specific products and brands. The latter are objects that exist temporally, changing diachronically in accordance with the degree to which they meet the contemporary needs. To illustrate this thought, the beverage structure is developed in more specific terms, as shown in Table 39.1 and described in this section.

The hierarchies and continua discussed here are offered in a frankly speculative and hypothetical manner. The goal is to lay out an overall perspective, one that may suggest possibilities for more research, even if particular points may not accord with the experience of individual readers. The structure of ideas is based on how main beverages are perceived and used in American life, but the aim is to see broad dimensions at work. Other societies may share these basic perceptions, even if not everyday usage. For example, despite the complexities due to cultural variations in the consumption of milk, as shown by Farb and Armelagos (1980, pp. 186-189), who note that many peoples avoid the use of milk entirely after weaning, nowhere do people reserve milk for adults and raise children on beer.

THE FUNDAMENTAL BEVERAGES: WATER, MILK, AND SOUP

In some original sense, beverages serve two main purposes: slaking thirst and providing nutrition. They are required for maintaining the fluid environment of the body and assisting in its nourishment for growth and energy. Water is the most basic liquid, in itself and as the main component of other beverages; it relieves thirst and is the vehicle for other nutritive substances. Water is a universal good; its natural, elemental character (earth, air, fire, and water) makes it a standard for comparison with other

TABLE 39.2 Symbolic Vocabulary

Preparation	Color	Variety	Quantity	Impact	Meanings	
Complexity	Dark	Heterogeneity	Small units	Intense taste	Discriminating	Exclusive
Distillation		of substance	Sips	Burning	Sophisticated	
Fermenting		or Choice	Jiggers	Dry, sour	Intoxicating	Mature
				Evil		
				Experimental	Classy	
Brewing				Bloating	Relaxing	
Steeping	Deep hues			Addicting	Thoughtful	
				Bitter		Adult
Carbonation	Colorful			Burping	Social	
Squeezing				Tart	Autonomous	
					Conventional	
				Playful		
	Light			Sweet		Young
Heating					Nutritious	
Natural ele-ments					Dependent	
Simplicity	Colorless	Homogeneity	Large units	Bland	Virtuous	
					Immature	Universal

beverages that are evaluated by how close they come to its innocuousness, whether they are exalted as pure and virtuous or put down for being insipid or dilute.

Water is clear, harmless, and comparatively tasteless. It is undifferentiated and homogeneous, free or inexpensive, and widely available (putting aside for the moment the case of costlier bottled waters). Because of these characteristics it is casually consumed, suited to be drunk frequently and in ample quantity. It is not thought to represent the taste or preference of particular segments, by age, sex, or social position, although special devotion to drinking water speaks of virtuous aims, an exaggerated search for fundamental natural means to health.

Milk is also perceived as a fundamental drink. It is less elemental than water (water, water, everywhere), but it is a natural prod-uct created by the body—like blood, sweat, and tears. Aspects that consumers use to interpret milk are its source, color, texture, contents, and effects. Its whiteness suggests purity, its thickness and sweetness make it seem rich. It contains especially butterfat, protein, and calcium, so that it is a substantial food. Despite the variations available, it is perceived as generally homogeneous and undifferentiated, so that consumers do not feel strongly about exercising discrimination among brands of milk.

For a young person, milk has the benefit of becoming an important part of the bones, teeth, muscles, and other tissues. That fact also means milk gets less desirable to consumers as they mature and do not need it to become part of the body, so that the nourishment becomes too fattening and too threatening of kidney stones and other calcium deposits. Being fattening and associated with maternal provision and childhood dependency, it becomes particularly unattractive to adolescent girls. As physically active and eternal "boys," males are more likely to continue to find milk appealing; but less so with higher social status and greater sophistication. The low position of milk in the beverage structure may be modified some by the recent concern about osteoporosis, but the synchronic elements that define milk are likely to thwart the arduous efforts of the dairy councils or of government leaders seeking to substitute it for wine among French adults, as noted by Roland Barthes (1972).

> [Milk] is now the true anti-wine: and not only because of M. Mendes-France's popularizing efforts . . . but also because in the basic morphology of substances milk is the opposite of fire by all the denseness of its molecules, by the creamy, and therefore soothing, nature of its spreading. . . . Moreover, its purity, associated with the innocence of the child, is. . . . calm, white, lucid, the equal of reality. (p. 60)

Soup is a more culturally developed and elaborated version of water or milk. It is thirst-quenching, filling, more varied in texture. Soup comes in quantity—big pots, mass bedrock feeding as in soup kitchens, it is easy to consume and suited to people who are weak, immature, sick, and poor. Soup is a presexual, primordial life-giving stuff implying universality, tradition, maternal love, survival, dependency. It may be visually colorful, perhaps differentiated in appearance from surface to depths, as well as in substances, with interesting solid particles. It is a step up from milk in its differentiation, but prior to more demanding sensory experiences. It has the variety available to span a spectrum to more stimulating

and exotic versions, so that there are types suited by their special associations (in ingredients, ethnicity) to higher status and more mature people when eating out or having elegant meals (e.g., vichysoisse, gazpacho).

In sum, the fundamental beverages are universal, chemically neutral, come in quantity, and are related to being healthy. They are suited to the young and as general concepts tend to be sweet and bland, lacking in sophistication. They are valued as virtuous, but not high as symbols of social status. These generalities apply especially to water and milk, with soup acting as a bridge to more mature experiences.

BEVERAGES OF CHILDHOOD

To satisfy the variety seeking that accompanies growth, fruit drinks come more to the fore. Juices diluted with water make for cheap, sweet, flavored quantity. Taken as juices, the amounts tend to be smaller, more precious, and more stimulating to the palate. Greater tartness and intensity become tolerable; flavor preferences among orange, grape, and Hawaiian Punch show the process of personality individuation going on. The pastel-colored products seem innocuous and healthy, and well related to fruits and their vitamins as natural and fitting for kids, but less infantile or sheerly virtuous than milk because of their high sugar content or greater acidity. Ades are more clearly youthful, but juice can be drunk by virtuous adults without detracting from their maturity or higher status, especially if it is fresh and expensive.

THE MILD EVIL OF SOFT DRINKS

Soft drinks cross a dividing line toward self-expression and worldliness. They are widely consumed away from home. They are not thought to be "good for you" and are thought to be drunk more for pleasurable thirst-quenching and energetic stimulation than for any nutritive benefits. The sugar or sweet taste remains a youthful and lower-status quality, but the two main elements of carbonation and caffeine are exciting aspects that distinguish soft drinks. The carbonation gives a "spritzy," tickling, burping, festive experience, and the various other ingredients—acids, natural and artificial flavors, caffeine, cola, syrups, artificial sweeteners—suggest a somewhat mysterious concoction. What substances they come from—nuts, leaves, caramel—may be unclear or even generally unknown, as with root beer.

Soft drinks are thus suited to the adolescent temper, particularly, satisfying drives toward self-indulgence, independence of parental restraint, conformity to peer group, and addictive experience at a mild level. If these motives are extreme, the youngsters press on to include alcohol.

In the range of soft drinks, the more wholesome-seeming are the light, bright, fruit-flavored (with orange less mature than the more austere lemon-lime). The concerns about diet, sugar, and caffeine produce more nuances and opportunities for making discriminations in adult and self-controlled directions.

terness of these brews make them widely exalted as rich adult tastes, something that is "bad for you," that could not and should not be coped with by children.

Coffee and tea come from beans and leaves and go through more complex processes of preparation than squeezing fruit. Like soft drinks, they are more cultural objects, less natural than water, milk, and juice, thus more sophisticated and subject to judgment. The coffee- and tea-drinking experiences imply a mature capacity to make discriminations and to have individual taste preferences among the many varieties available. Maxwell House recently aired an advertising campaign featuring coffee as the beverage consumed when you're not a kid anymore. The character of coffee and of experiencing it are vividly described by Leah Wallach (1984) in her essay, "A Confirmed Coffee Addict Spills the Beans."

At the "lower end" of the coffee and tea band in the beverage structure is iced tea, sweet, diluted, prepared and served in volume, soothing and refreshing, suited to many people. At the high end are the extreme versions—very floral and fragrant teas and the intense espresso or Turkish coffees in their tiny sipping servings. Between tea and coffee, tea has been traditionally defined as the more delicate beverage, comforting to the sick and suited to elderly females.

THE ADULT CHARACTER OF COFFEE AND TEA

The focus on caffeine in soft drinks is a recent issue, but its stimulating presence in coffee and tea has long been a main part of their definition, even before the substance was specifically identified. In addition, the warmth, the darkness, and the relative bit-

THE ANALOGOUS HIERARCHY OF ALCOHOLIC BEVERAGES

The degrees of effect on the taste buds and on the body increase in going from the blandness of milk to the tartness of fruit juice, to the stimulation of carbonation and caffeine, to the dramatic impact of alcohol. In general, the greater the stimulation, the greater the evil, the more daring the consumption, the more sophisticated the drinker (with due qualification for the illness also attributed to the excessive drinker). Thus, consumption of alcoholic beverages is perceived as an adult activity, engaged in by sophisticated (urbane, worldly, complex, etc.) people in mature social settings such as bars, cocktail parties, and before dinner.

The spectrum of alcoholic beverages forms a hierarchy that is analogous to that among the nonalcoholic drinks. In a sense, beer is the milk of alcohols. It is not highly differentiated as a substance from one beer to another; although some basis for adult connoisseurship occurs, it is not status-giving in the larger society. Beer is often consumed in large quantities, it is thought to be less intoxicating than other alcohols, and it is regarded as fattening. It is readily associated with urine, with gross habits and physical reactions, and suited to young adults, college boys, immature drinkers of alcohol, and lower-class males. Among higher-status drinkers, beer is a way of relaxing, letting down standards, being informal, showing democratic camaraderie.

Wine offers some competition to beer for the favor of young drinkers and for being swilled by lower-class winos. It is lower in the hierarchy when it comes in jugs, is identified merely as red or white, is sweet rather than dry, and is used casually as a mealtime beverage. (Champagne may be the adolescent ginger ale of wines, festive with carbonation.) The rich coloration and the individuality related to the mysteries and lore of vines, soil, vintage years, and fermentation, and the subtleties available for sipping and endless taste discriminations, place wine in an elite tradition and elevate the user. It is linked to religious symbolism, a kinship to blood, and a level of civilization in living that makes it an especially romantic drink for high-class courtship.

To illustrate this point, respondents in milk and wine marketing research studies were asked to fantasy a dream about the beverage. The milk fantasies were typically of being regressively immersed in oceanic quantities of milk, whereas the wine fantasies tended to be about drinking wine as a prelude to seductions and other sexual encounters (also see Chapter 52).

A range of choices and degrees of conformity and distinction are provided by gin, vodka, rum, bourbon, and scotch, and so on and their various brands and prices. Gin and tonic is a popular summer drink (the iced tea of alcohols?). It—and other spirits—are perhaps perceived as less manly and statusy than scotch. The acme of alcoholic beverages may be the brandies and liqueurs. They are so rich in concentration, intensity of flavor, and price that ordinary drinkers cannot bear them. They are consumed in elegant sips on those distinguished occasions when the appreciative drinkers feel themselves to be at the height of refined living.

CHANGING PRODUCT PERCEPTIONS

The bands in the structure of beverage categories indicate boundaries within which products and brands may change over time with shifts in the consumers' perspectives. The basic logic of color, ingredients, and impact on the body may be relatively enduring (dark is strong and alcohol is intoxicating), but specific products and brands will be affected also by new information, so that the weight of preferences in the market may change. Sex roles, nutritional studies, health communications, advertising emphasis, and so on create reorganizations in consumers' interpretations of how they want to behave.

These shifts reflect changing values, such as the contemporary preoccupation with physical fitness among many groups in the population. They also reflect the ways managers use the symbolic vocabulary of beverage characteristics (see Table 39.2). By altering the intensities, combinations, or interactions of contributing variables, marketing managers can create new entities or modify the position of a product or brand, moving it up or down the hierarchy in implied maturity, prestigiousness, virtue, and gender suitability.

Water added to anything moves it down in maturity and status; and it is moved upward by modifying its pristine character, as with carbonation or French labels. When milk is made darker by adding chocolate, it is raised in the hierarchy, making it seem less immature. An adult who prefers plain milk might not make this distinction, but people generally do; and seen developmentally from the bottom, infants are almost never fed milk with chocolate in it, whereas older children and adults more often have it that way. The same phenomenon is observed in the candy product hierarchy, where adding milk to chocolate lowers it in maturity compared to darker, bitterer chocolate. Similarly, a tiny amount of wine in water or milk might be given to a child as an amusing introduction to alcohol, but, generally, adding alcohol to milk would be unacceptable for consumption by children, making the milk too mature. However, adding milk to alcohol to make, say, a Brandy Alexander, moves the alcoholic beverage down the hierarchy toward being less potent, a younger and more feminine drink for adults. An experiment comparing the social position of Virgin Marys when described as vodka plus tomato juice or as tomato juice plus vodka, showed that vodka with tomato juice in it has higher status than tomato juice with vodka in it,

even when the proportions are the same (Levy & Sternthal, 1986).

Apparent contradictions need resolution. For instance, vodka looks like water, seeming weaker in color than beer or coffee. But because it is known to be a strong alcoholic beverage, it has some of the mysterious paradox of an oxymoron: the product's kick is concealed, making its potency surprising, adding some charm to its appeal. The fact that it is alcoholic is more important than that it is colorless, but the lack of color also affects its meaning. Its Russian origin adds much to its complex meaning; just as the French origin of Perrier adds élan to that water.

A STUDY OF STABILITY AND CHANGE IN PERCEPTIONS OF SOFT DRINKS

The relative positions outlined in the basic beverage structure were examined in closer detail to see how products and brands compete within a category. A study was designed to measure perceptual relationships between two soft drink brands, Coca-Cola and 7-Up. Ideas about relationships between these two beverages were suggested by an early marketing research study (Levy, 1960), and that study was partially replicated in order to observe in what ways perceptions of these two brands had remained the same and/or changed.

1960 and 1983 Synchronic Views of 7-Up and Coca-Cola

Judgments and Factors

The specific method used was a series of bipolar adjectival scales, shown in Table 39.3, on which respondents made ratings of beverage concepts, named as Soft

Drink to represent the product area, and two brands, 7-Up and Coca-Cola.

In the 1960 study, the purpose was to develop evaluations of the strength of these product concepts as part of a systematic analysis that could be repeated at intervals, titled, *Brand Image Concepts Evaluation Program* (BICEP). The three concepts were rated by a sample of 160 housewives, each of whom judged two concepts, rotated in order of presentation. The sample included middle- and lower-class women, with and without children, from various parts of the country. Usable forms totaled 282, distributed as Soft Drink ($N = 91$), 7-Up ($N = 94$), and Coca-Cola ($N = 97$). In 1983, the same universe of housewives was tapped, with Ns of 97 to 100 rating the three beverage ideas. The purpose was a partial replication that was not aimed at measuring specific trends. The full 1960 raw data are long gone, so that comparisons are made between the 1983 data and the results that do remain from 1960. The comparisons were made in three main ways.

1. Deviations from the midpoint on the bipolar ratings

2. Factor analyses of the two sets of results

3. Correlations of the beverage idea ratings with those for a set of abstract concepts

Deviations From the Midpoint

1. The SBS is addressed to a relatively fundamental structuring of product perceptions. Thus, it was expected that all the soft drink ideas would be rated positively in the direction of such "virtuous" attributes as Good, Clean, Safe, Pretty, and so on, rather than Bad, Dirty, Dangerous, Ugly. This was true in both 1960 and 1983.

2. The general character of the specific concepts also remained relatively constant. That is, despite the large sums of money spent on promotions in the intervening years (e.g., when Philip Morris acquired 7-Up, it announced that $40 million would be spent to make it the No. 1 soft drink), it was expected that the relative positions of Soft Drink, Coca-Cola, and 7-Up in 1983 would be unchanged from those in 1960. That is, 7-Up would be more highly rated on virtuous terms than Soft Drink, and Coca-Cola less so. It would be expected that 7-Up would be more virtuous than Coca-Cola because it seems based simply on citrus fruits and is colorless. It is, thus, thin, watery, innocent of harmful ingredients. Coca-Cola is derived from a complex (even secret) recipe using exotic coca leaves and cola nuts with properties that seem richer, heavier, and more stimulating. Therefore, it would seem stronger, riskier to drink, and more exciting than 7-Up.

The three beverage ideas do deviate significantly from the midpoint toward an array of positive terms. They are all seen to be lively, good, clean, full, wet, and so on, as would be expected of soft drinks. At the same time, there are consistent differences between 7-Up and Coca-Cola. They are apart on many of the word pairs, with 7-Up seen significantly more as Thin, Steady, Soft, Safe, Good, and Clean; and Coca-Cola significantly more as Fat, Full, Strong, Wet, Exciting, and Fast.

Factor Analyses of the Two Sets of Results

3. When the 1960 ratings were factor analyzed, the results showed the usual main factors of Evaluation, Potency, and Activity, with 7-Up higher on Evaluation and Activ-

ity and Coca-Cola on Potency. In keeping with point 2, above, it was expected that in 1983 Coca-Cola would remain the more potent brand and 7-Up be judged the more virtuous brand. The role of Activity was less clear, as New-Old was important in that factor and distinguished 7-Up as newer than Coca-Cola, which was less likely to be the case after 23 years when neither familiar name would seem new. In 1983, when 7-Up and Coca-Cola are compared on these factors, 7-Up is scored higher than Coca-Cola on Evaluation ($t = 3.34$, $p < .001$), Coca-Cola is more Potent ($t = 1.49$, $p < .065$), and Coca-Cola is more Active ($t = 1.65$, $p < .05$). These results reinforce the idea of Coca-Cola as less "good for you" but as more vital.

Abstract Concepts and Soft Drink Brands

4. The bipolar adjectival approach implies that complex concepts are built up out of simple basic perceptions of physical reality. If so, the profiles formed by these scales should be similar for related ideas and show this by being positively correlated. To test this logic, 17 abstract concepts were judged by samples of subjects other than those who judged the soft drinks, but using the same list of word pairs. The abstract concepts were Anxious, Childlike, Enjoyable, Emotional, Feminine, Immature, Lower Class, Masculine, Mature, Personal, Popular, Radical, Self-punishing, Shy, Sociable, Suburban, and Urban. The Semantic Differential profiles for these concepts were then correlated with those for 7-Up and Coca-Cola. This novel procedure circumvents asking people directly to rate the soft drinks on such ideas as these 17 concepts. Rather, it asks the question: "How does what people have in mind when

they think of the idea 7-Up compare with what they have in mind when they think of the ideas Urban, Popular, Immature, Sociable, and so on?" It is not a way of measuring how popular 7-Up is, but of seeing whether the idea Popular and the idea 7-Up have similar semantic building blocks as measured by the Semantic Differential (see Table 39.3 for an example).

Drawing upon the implications of the SBS and the 1960 BICEP study, it was expected that (a) both 7-Up and Coca-Cola S.D. profiles would correlate most positively with the concept profiles that closely reflect general soft drink ideas: for example, Enjoyable, Popular, and Sociable; (b) both 7-Up and Coca-Cola profiles would correlate least positively (or negatively) with concept profiles that represent negative ideas such as Lower-Class, Anxious, Self-punishing, Immature; (c) where there were differences among the three concepts, 7-Up would correlate more highly than Coca-Cola with gentler, less powerful concepts such as Feminine, Suburban, and Shy; and (d) Coca-Cola would correlate more highly (or less negatively) than 7-Up with stronger, more troublesome, and sophisticated concepts, such as Urban, Radical, Self-Punishing, and so on.

The highest positive relationships include the expected agreeable concepts of Enjoyable, Popular, and Sociable, with no difference between 7-Up and Coca-Cola. The two brands also have high semantic relationships with the concepts Masculine, Childlike, Mature, Feminine, Personal, Suburban, and Emotional. Lower positive (or negative) relationships are indicated with the concepts Lower-Class, Immature, Urban, Anxious, Radical, Self-Punishing, and Shy, these ideas apparently being less in character with the perceived nature of soft drinks. At the same time, these are the concepts that distinguish the

TABLE 39.3 A Semantic Differential

Now, we'd like you to judge _____ on each word pair below. First, decide which side (word) is most appropriate. Second, HOW MUCH or TO WHAT DEGREE you feel this way. There are no right answers. Your own opinion is what matters. Even where you don't have a strong opinion, BE SURE TO MARK A CHOICE. Otherwise your opinion can't be counted.

Circle: O — when you feel *very* much this way

o — when you feel *rather* much this way

• — when you feel *slightly* this way

tight	O	o	•	•	o	O	loose
lively	O	o	•	•	o	O	quiet
safe	O	o	•	•	o	O	dangerous
ugly	O	o	•	•	o	O	pretty
bouncy	O	o	•	•	o	O	smooth
weak	O	o	•	•	o	O	strong
stiff	O	o	•	•	o	O	limp
old	O	o	•	•	o	O	new
thin	O	o	•	•	o	O	fat
thrilling	O	o	•	•	o	O	soothing
dry	O	o	•	•	o	O	wet
clean	O	o	•	•	o	O	dirty
loud	O	o	•	•	o	O	soft
empty	O	o	•	•	o	O	full
steady	O	o	•	•	o	O	change
dull	O	o	•	•	o	O	sharp
deep	O	o	•	•	o	O	shallow
relaxed	O	o	•	•	o	O	tense
good	O	o	•	•	o	O	bad
slow	O	o	•	•	o	O	fast
little	O	o	•	•	o	O	big
exciting	O	o	•	•	o	O	calming

most between 7-Up and Coca-Cola, consistently placing Coca-Cola on the more negative side.

There are interesting subtleties suggested in the results. They imply that people can see soft drinks as both mature and childlike, so that both adults and children can drink them; but the negative correlation with the concept Immature means adults are not stigmatized by drinking them, merely having fun and being lively and youthful. Also, even though 7-Up is a less active and less powerful (and more feminine) concept than Coca-Cola, its thin, less sweet character and use as a mixer with alcoholic cocktails make it more mature than Coca-Cola, equally suited to males and less lower-class consumers.

A Comparison With 1960 Results

The similar study carried out in 1960 made it possible to observe aspects of the soft drink brands that have changed in consumers' eyes. Comparisons at the three levels of analysis—word pairs, factors, and concept correlations—are summed up.

1. The same basic character of soft drinks is apparent in both 1960 and 1983: The three beverage concepts deviate significantly from the midpoint toward *lively, clean, good, relaxed, full, pretty, safe, wet, bouncy, strong,* and *sharp.* A rise in rank order for the words *thrilling, exciting, fast, strong,* and *bouncy* may reflect the fact that the soft drink domain has increased its appeal to people. Its consumption has grown, as coffee has declined (overall, despite Starbucks) and there has been a great deal of competitive and upbeat advertising for soft drinks. It is reasonable that the

category would be perceived as more vigorous and stimulating.

2. The spread between 7-Up and Coca-Cola is comparable in both years on such word pairs as *thin-fat, soft-loud, good-bad, clean-dirty.* A marked decline in difference between the brands on *new-old* reflects the general familiarity of both brands and an increased awareness of 7-Up; also, the brands switched sides on the pair *slow-fast,* enhancing the relative vitality of Coca-Cola, despite 7-Up's higher level of carbonation.

3. The word pairs are somewhat differently clustered into factors for the samples in the two years, so that direct comparison is not warranted; but inspection of the clusters suggests that 7-Up remains higher than Coca-Cola on Evaluation, and Coca-Cola remains higher on Potency and Activity.

4. The correlations with abstract concepts show some stable patterns and some changes. The basic relationships seem to be unchanged. The correlations with Enjoyable, Sociable, and Popular, and the negative relationship with Lower Class, are about the same in 1960 and 1983.

This consistency seems remarkable and is a reassuring illustration of this method, as it confirms what we know, that the soft drink ideas are enjoyable, sociable, popular, and not lower class. But because it shows it indirectly, revealing that these three beverage ideas and these four abstract concepts share a common underlying semantic, it supports the validity of the technique.

Also, in 1960, Coke was more highly correlated than 7-Up with the concepts Urban, Radical, Self-Punishing, Anxious, and Emotional, and 7-Up was more akin to

Shy, Suburban, and Feminine. These results imply that Coca-Cola was, and remains, the more psychologically complex entity, gratifying in its more intense or dramatic sense of self-expression.

5. Some interesting changes also occurred. 7-Up apparently increased its sense of suitability for grown-ups, moving from a nonsignificant correlation with Immature in 1960 ($r = .05$) to a markedly negative one in 1983 ($r = -.46$). 7-Up increased its correlation with Mature (from $r = .49$ to $r = .69$, while Coca-Cola decreased from $r = .70$ to $r = .54$). The implied gender differences were greater in 1960, when Coca-Cola was more markedly masculine and less feminine than 7-Up. 7-Up has become more acceptable to males while remaining a more feminine object than Coca-Cola.

DISCUSSION

These results point to both synchronic and diachronic elements in the perceptions of soft drinks and of the example brands. The passage of 23 years did not much af-fect the basic perception of soft drinks. They remain fun drinks, above the health-giving ones and below the more thoroughly adult, intense, and alcoholic ones. What has changed is the growing view of soft drinks as less immature in narrow suitability to children. An increased preoccupation with health has fostered the interest in diet drinks and in products without caffeine.

One effect has been to make 7-Up a more adult brand and less narrowly feminine. Nevertheless, despite the changes in the population, and in 7-Up's increased maturity, it has not increased in general consumption. Many millions of dollars have been spent to bring about a changed view of 7-Up, such as the "Wet and Wild," "UnCola," and "America is Turning 7-Up" campaigns, and of late, its emphasis on being caffeine-free. It has had some ups and downs, but its brand share remains around 5% to 7%. The perception of 7-Up relative to Coca-Cola remains more Shy and Sub-urban, still less acceptable to the audience that values the greater power of Coca-Cola, whose dark mystery gives Coke the edge in being less soft, safe, good, clean, and in other ways more desirably daring and exciting.

REFERENCES

Allison, N. K., Golden, L. L., Mullet, G. M., & Coogan, D. (1980). *Advances in consumer research* (Vol. 7, pp. 604-609). Provo, UT: Association for Consumer Research.

Barthes, R. (1972). *Mythologies*. New York: Hill & Wang.

Belk, R. W. (1979). Gift-giving behavior. In J. N. Sheth (Ed.), *Research in marketing* (Vol. 2, pp. 95-126). Greenwich, CT: JAI Press.

Belk, R. W., Mayer, R., & Bahn, K. (1981). The eye of the beholder: Individual differences in perceptions of consumption symbolism. In *Advances in consumer research* (Vol. 9, pp. 523-530). Provo, UT: Association for Consumer Research.

Blumer, H. (1969). *Symbolic interaction: Perspective and method*. Englewood Cliffs, NJ: Prentice Hall.

Bourdieu, P. (1984). *Distinction: A social critique of the judgment of taste.* Cambridge, MA: Harvard University Press.

Cohen, M. R.(1923). *Chance, love, and logic.* New York: Harcourt Brace.

Douglas, M. (1984). *Food in the social order: Studies of food and festivities in three American communities.* New York: Russell Sage Foundation.

Douglas, M., & Isherwood, B. (1979). *The world of goods.* New York: Basic Books.

Eco, U. (1979). *A theory of semiotics.* Bloomington: Indiana University Press.

Farb, P., & Armelagos, G. (1980). *Consuming passions.* Boston: Houghton, Mifflin.

Gardner, B. B., & Levy, S. J. (1955, March/April). The product and the brand. *Harvard Business Review,* pp. 33-39.

Goffman, E. (1959). *The presentation of self in everyday life.* New York: Anchor.

Hillmer, D. (1984). *Design power.* Omaha, NE: Hillmer Graphics.

Hirschman, E. C. (1981). Symbolism and technology as sources for the generation of innovations. In *Advances in consumer research* (Vol. 9, pp. 537-541). Provo, UT: Association for Consumer Research.

Holbrook, M. B. (1981). Some further dimensions of psycholinguistics, imagery, and consumer response. In *Advances in consumer research* (Vol. 9, pp. 112-117). Provo, UT: Association for Consumer Research.

Holman, R. (1981). Apparel as communication. In E. Hirschman & M. B. Holbrook (Eds.), *Symbolic consumer behavior* (pp. 7-15). Ann Arbor, MI: Association for Consumer Research.

Kehret-Ward, T., Johnson, M. W., & Louie, T. A. (1985). Improving recall by manipulating the syntax of consumption rituals. *Advances in consumer research* (Vol. 12, pp. 319-324).

Provo, UT: Association for Consumer Research.

Korzybski, A. (1933). *Science and sanity.* New York: International Non-Aristotelian Publishing Co.

Levy, S. J. (1959, July/August). Symbols for sale. *Harvard Business Review,* pp. 117-124.

Levy, S. J. (1960). *Brand image concepts evaluation program.* Chicago: Social Research, Inc.

Levy, S. J. (1981). Interpreting consumer mythology: A structural approach to consumer behavior. *Journal of Marketing, 45,* 49-61.

Levy, S. J., & Sternthal, B. (1986). *The hierarchical organization of category objects in memory.* Unpublished manuscript.

Mead, G. H. (1934). *Mind, self, and society.* Chicago: University of Chicago Press.

Pinson, C. (1981). *Consumer inferential judgments about products.* Ph.D. dissertation, Northwestern University, Evanston, IL.

Porter, D. (1984). Anthropological tales: Unprofessional thoughts on the Mead/Freeman controversy. In N. F. Cantor (Ed.), *Notebooks in cultural analysis.* Durham, NC: Duke University Press.

Rainwater, L., Coleman, R. P., & Handel, G. (1959). *Workingman's wife.* New York: Oceana.

Rook, D. W. (1984). Ritual behavior and consumer symbolism. *Advances in consumer research* (Vol. 11, pp. 279-284). Provo, UT: Association for Consumer Research.

Solomon, M. R. (1983). The role of products as social stimuli: A symbolic interactionism perspective. *Journal of Consumer Research, 10,* 319-329.

Wallach, L. (1984, September). A confirmed coffee addict spills the beans. *Metropolitan Home,* pp. 91B-91D.

Warner, W. L. (1959). *The living and the dead.* New Haven, CT: Yale University Press.

Chapter 40

CONSUMER BEHAVIOR IN THE UNITED STATES
The Avid Consumer

Sidney J. Levy

Ten years ago, I visited Tokyo and spoke about Consumer Behavior in the United States (see Chapter 35). Thus, I can compare the present situation with the trends that were going on at that time. Some general issues that I noted at that time are not only the same but have intensified. For example, the pressures on managers to understand the consumer were seen then to be growing increasingly urgent. This was seen as generally due to the increasing force of competition and the resulting fragmentation of the marketplace. Those pressures are now stronger than ever and do not show any signs of lessening. However,

some of the causes and the results have shifted and may be worth examining at the current time. The important influences affecting consumer behavior at present will be discussed as: (a) technological, (b) economic, (c) sociocultural, and (d) psychological.

THE DESIRE FOR TECHNOLOGICAL INNOVATION

Americans are as enthusiastic and receptive as ever about inventions, new equipment, devices, gadgets, and improvements. They

---

This chapter is based on notes for a talk given in Tokyo, 1987.

show this in their acquisition of electronics, and desire to upgrade their possessions. The microwave oven and the VCR are more and more taken for granted as objects for the home, along with large screens, compact disk players. Consumers used to be wary of the computer, but now they are intrigued by it and are using it increasingly for everyday purposes. There is growth in electronic games and in the many add-ons available: modems, hard disks, accelerators. People are waiting for high-definition television and starting to look forward to the great benefits that may come with superconductivity.

ECONOMIC CHANGE

American consumers are experiencing a general material prosperity. The average household income is close to $30,000; the average U.S. worker earns about $310 per week. Although people complain as ever about the cost of things, their purchasing power is extremely high, and they spend and charge at a vigorous pace. Compared with previous years, the relative cost of such things as kitchen appliances, men's clothing, beer, a gallon of paint, and chicken have markedly declined. The strongest obstacles are found in the health, education, housing, and automotive areas, where costs are felt to be comparatively high. But, nevertheless, in these areas consumption remains substantial and active.

SOCIOCULTURAL PHENOMENA

Changes in demographics lead to shifts in emphasis in consumer behavior. These changes come about in a variety of ways. In 1977, I noted the long-term reduction in

the birth rate, the sharp rise in the divorce rate, the increased longevity and growing proportion of the elderly and aged, the postponement of marriage, all contributing to the great number of persons living alone.

But now various forces are modifying some of these trends. The fear of AIDS has led to the tightening and greater stability of some social ties. For that and other reasons, the divorce rate appears to have peaked and shows signs of declining; working women are more eager to have children; single households are growing more slowly as many young people stay home or return home. The role of immigration and ethnicity is increasing in its impact.

CONSUMER PSYCHOLOGY AND BEHAVIOR

There is a general sense of intensity about consumption nowadays that reflects a prosperous but anxious society. The preoccupation with shopping has become noticeable, with people engaging in going shopping not only to purchase for their needs and wants but also as a kind of leisure time activity. In some instances, it seems to fulfill a psychological urgency toward acquiring and maintaining a constant flow of goods and services. The richness of objects and experiences necessary to be a modern consumer keeps one perpetually chasing after things, constantly having to go to the store, to buy things, to make things, to fix up things, to replace things, to see things, to try new things, in an endless process of developing and replenishing the wardrobe, enhancing the decor of the dwelling, finding gifts, and so on.

The searching for personal and social satisfactions finds special emphasis in various directions. One example is the wish for excitement, visible in the stimulation in motor sports, sky diving, and other various ways of experiencing adventure and thrills, if only in the vicarious enjoyment of movies.

Another dimension lies in the marked spread of interest in the arts, theater, and museums. Community theaters are proliferating and thriving, attendance at exhibitions is large, and the purchase of art objects has reached amazing heights. Consumers also spend their time and energy in other ways that reflect concern with the adverse consequences of this eagerness to consume. They watch television and read about the loss of the world's forests, they worry about the rising cost of electricity and what to do with nuclear waste and the great tide of garbage that is fouling the planet. They are frustrated in knowing what to do about these problems, so they wish they had better political leaders; they send money to an organization concerned with environmental problems, and then they go shopping.

## Chapter 41

EFFECT OF RECENT ECONOMIC EXPERIENCES ON CONSUMER DREAMS, GOALS, AND BEHAVIOR IN THE UNITED STATES

Ruby Roy Dholakia

Sidney J. Levy

Consumer outlook brightens in mid-1983 after a long, low slump . . . and can be expected to lead to favorable consumer spending in late 1983 and early 1984.

—*ISR Newsletter,* Autumn 1983, p. 5

The baby boomers are going home again, returning to traditional patterns of American suburban home ownership and away from condominiums.

—*Providence Evening Bulletin,* April 11, 1984, p. C-6

Consumers cool to new products—data comparing new-product introductions show trial and repeat purchase to be lower for post-1982 introductions than pre-1982 products.

—*Marketing News,* January 3, 1986, p. 1

This chapter was first published in the *Journal of Economic Psychology,* 1987, *8,* 429-444. Reprinted by permission.

Reports such as these in the technical, popular, and trade press indicate several shifts taking place in consumer purchases of various goods and services. To a considerable extent, the quantitative changes in consumer expenditures are predictable from measures of consumer confidence which are monitored regularly (Curtin, 1982; Katona, 1974; Linden, 1982). In addition, there is some research evidence to indicate that more fundamental shifts are taking place in consumer values and expectations (Elgin & Mitchell, 1977; Mitchell, 1980; Rogers & Leonard-Barton, 1979; Steinberg, 1983) that are leading to more drastic alterations in varied aspects of consumer goods, services, and processes (Shama, 1981).

The confidence measures are particularly dynamic and sensitive to the economic environment. In the past 20 years, the Index of Consumer Sentiment as measured by the Institute for Social Research had fluctuated considerably and generally has moved lower from the high of 101 reached in 1969 ("Consumer Outlook," 1983, p. 5). Van Raaij and Gianotten (1982) have distinguished between two components of the consumer confidence measure and found both components to have declined in The Netherlands after 1949. The value shifts, however, represent more fundamental changes and should be indicative of more stable and enduring consumer behavior. Frequently these two forces point toward opposing trends: for example, a shift back toward the conventional, single-home, suburban dwelling while the values appear to indicate a preference for more nontraditional housing ("Baby Boom Adults," 1984, p. C-6). The question raised, therefore, is: how profound are the value shifts? It has fueled concern among marketers who attempt to decipher whether recent purchases represent a basic shift in consumer values or only adaptive responses to high fuel and other prices. Housing analysts, for example, had predicted from 1979 and 1981 surveys that "condominiums were going to be the wave of the future" ("Baby Boom Adults," 1984; Goetze, 1983), yet recent behaviors indicate a return to traditional mechanisms.

AN EMPIRICAL INVESTIGATION

In this paper we report an empirical investigation of the effect of subjective economic experience on consumer goals, expectations, and behavior in the United States. The focus is on core consumer goals and behavior rather than specific product-related goals and behavior. Consumer orientations are conceptualized to be strategic or tactical. Strategic orientations reflect fundamental consumer goals and values which are shaped over a long period of time. Tactical orientations reflect specific buying and consuming modus operandi. It is our hypothesis that economic experiences influence consumers only at a tactical level but not in their strategic orientations to consumption. In other words, strategic orientations will resist the influence of recent economic changes while tactical orientations will be modified as consumers adapt to the same economic changes.

What do we know about consumer values? Katona (1975) has argued that consumers hold on to middle-class values longer than objective reality might seem to require; and that consumers change their level of aspiration more easily upward than downward. Wells (1970) and Levy (1970) have put forward similar arguments in favor of stable rather than dramatically changing consumer values. Cross-cultural comparisons indicate American consumers to be particularly optimistic. While expectation of future progress is partly shaped by past progress, optimistic expectations in the U.S. have exceeded the index of past improvements (Katona, Strümpel, & Zahn, 1971, pp. 49-50). These appear to indicate:

1. Basic consumer goals and values form over a long historical process (Hondrich, 1983) and are fundamental to the consumption process of a society. In the U.S., past achievements have supported and created a legacy of rising expectations and pro-consumption values. It is unlikely that these basic values will be downscaled due to the negative effects of recent economic activity (Katona, 1974; Levy, 1970; Wells, 1970).

2. The economic environment does affect buying tactics and short-range orientations. When the economic environment is negative, tactics and short-range orientations undergo essentially forced adjustments; this allows flexibility in matching specific consumer characteristics such as income changes with basic goals and values such as ownership of durables (Caplovitz, 1963; Kasulis, Lusch, & Stafford, 1979; McFall, 1969).

Methodology

A structured mail questionnaire was used as the instrument for a national mail sample. A random selection procedure was employed to select respondents from telephone listings of cities and towns in 13 states. The states represented different economic conditions of prosperity and economic activity.

The mail questionnaire was sent to 638 respondents in mid-March 1983 followed by a postcard reminder. A second questionnaire was mailed 4 weeks after the first questionnaire. Five hundred and thirty-nine respondents were reached by the mailing procedure, and replies were obtained from 226, for an overall response rate of 35% or an effective response rate of 42%.

Findings

Sample Characteristics

Representativeness. The demographic profile of the survey respondents represents a wide spectrum of the American consuming public. A comparison of the sample characteristics with the 1980-1981 profile of the U.S. population reveals sample comparability with respect to marital status, household size, and home ownership (see Table 41.1). However, the survey respondents are older than the national distribution of population, with the 18 to 24 age group being particularly underrepresented. Similarly, the educational and income achievements of the sample are also higher; college graduates are disproportionately represented in the sample while the lowest income groups are underrepresented.

Nonrepresentation of the sample with respect to age and education poses a less severe constraint on the survey findings than the income characteristic since income is a household characteristic. The survey sampled only one member of each household, and the self-selected respondent is likely to be different in terms of education and age than another member of the household. For instance, the median number of school years completed for adults aged 25 and over was 12.5 years in 1980; however, it was 12.9 years for adults aged 25-29 years (*Statistical Abstract*, 1986, p. 133).

TABLE 41.1 Sample Representativeness: Comparison of National Population and Sample Characteristics

Characteristic	National Population [a]	Sample	χ^2	df
Housing				
Owner occupied	68.6%	73.6%	2.5	1
Renter	31.4	26.4		
Age				
18-24 years	18.2%[b]	7.2%	18.7*	2
25-64 years	66.0	74.3		
65 or more	15.8	18.5		
Marital status				
Single	12.9%[c]	14.0%	1	2
Married	62.9	60.2		
Widowed, divorced, or separated	24.2	25.8		
Education				
Less than high school degree	33.6%[d]	10.8%	108.7*	3
High school degree	34.4	26.7		
Some college	15.7	28.5		
College degree or more	16.3	33.9		
Household income				
Less than $5,000	10.5%	4.1%	26.4*	5
$5,000-$9,999	14.9	7.8		
$10,000-$14,999	14.4	15.2		
$15,000-$19,999	12.3	14.7		
$20,000-$49,999	40.7	52.6		
More than $50,000	7.2	5.5		
Household size				
1 person	23.0%	22.1%	3.1	3
2 persons	31.3	34.2		
3 persons	17.7	20.3		
4 or more persons	28.0	23.4		

a. Source, Statistical Abstract 1982-83. U.S. Department of Commerce, Bureau of Census.
b. Percentage of population aged 18 or more.
c. Percentage of householders.
d. Percentage of population aged 25 or more.
*$p < 0.05$.

However, household income seems to indicate sampled respondents to be drawn from a somewhat higher socioeconomic range than the national population. These characteristics have been taken into account in the analysis of survey responses.

Nonresponse bias. About 15.5% of the original sample could not be contacted due to lack of a forwardable address. The potential bias created by this nonresponse has been estimated from the questionnaires of the early and late respondents. This is one way of estimating the bias due to nonre-sponse (Donald, 1960; Newman, 1962). The two subsamples are found comparable in all respects except their level of education. Due to the comparability of the two subsamples, further analyses have been performed on pooled responses.

Impact of Economic Environment

Given the experience of high inflation, unemployment, and interest rates at the time of the survey, one would expect the economic environment to have a negative impact on the consuming public. This is borne out by the survey responses. One might casually expect the lower socio-economic strata of the population to be affected more by these environmental threats; however, the survey responses appear to suggest that it is the middle socio-economic groups who more strongly feel the threats of the environment as barriers to their aspirations and achievements. This seems in keeping with the classical anxiety of the middle class concerning its upwardly mobile aspirations.

Recent economic experiences. The recent years of inflation, unemployment, and re-source shortages have affected the per-ceived subjective reality of most consumers and the majority perceive the experience in a negative light. In response to the question, "how has the recent economic situation affected you," only 21.3% of the respondents indicated a strongly or somewhat positive experience while another 21.6% perceived neither a positive or negative experience. Fifty-seven percent, however, indicated a strongly or somewhat negative experience. Katona (1951, 1975) has been the leading advocate in using consumer expectations and attitudes to predict economic behavior.

These subjective responses were used to categorize the survey respondents into three experience groups—positive, neutral, and negative (Table 41.2).

Characteristics of the three experience groups. Comparison of socioeconomic characteristics indicates significant differences among the three experience groups with respect to education, income, and occupation (Table 41.2). Despite the sampling of respondents from relatively higher socio-economic groups, respondents experiencing negative effects of the economic environment appear to be disproportionately drawn from higher education, income, and occupation categories.

A discriminant analysis using the SAS canonical discriminant procedure identified education and similarity of current home with the ideal home to be the 2 most important individual characteristics from a set of 15 characteristics (Table 41.3). Income and occupation did not contribute to the differences in the groups when all the individual difference variables were taken into consideration. The mean scores of these two distinguishing characteristics indicate that the negatively impacted group is more educated and perceive their current home to be more dissimilar from their most desirable home.

As reported by Shama (1981), the impact of stagflation appears to be particularly a middle-class phenomenon, their status being most vulnerable to threat.

Effect of recent economic experiences on consumer goals and expectations

Since past experiences affect future sentiments and expectations, it is likely that the largely negative impact perceived by the survey respondents would affect their

TABLE 41.2 Socioeconomic Profile of Economic Experience Groups

| | | Economic Experience Group | | | | | | | |
| | Positive | | Neutral | | Negative | | | | |
Characteristic	N	%	N	%	N	%	χ^2	df	p
Group membership		21		22		57			
Age[a]									
Less than 25	7	16	14	28	18	15	4.5	2	> 0.10
More than 25	38	84	36	72	103	85			
Marital status									
Never married	4	9	6	13	21	17	5.74	4	> 0.2
Married	29	63	33	72	68	55			
Divorced, widowed, or separated	13	28	7	15	35	28			
Household size									
1 person	13	28	11	23	23	18	3.94	4	> 0.40
2-3 persons	20	43	24	51	74	60			
More than 3 persons	13	28	12	26	27	22			
Education[a]									
Less than high school degree	37	57	15	32	21	20	95.4	4	< 0.001
High school degree	18	28	18	38	38	36			
More than high school	10	15	14	30	45	43			
Income[a]									
Less than $15,000	28	56	14	31	44	36	16.46	2	< 0.001
More than $15,000	22	44	31	69	78	64			
Occupation									
Blue collar	25	54	15	32	34	28	14.27	6	< 0.03
Clerical/sales	3	7	8	17	2	20			
Technical	2	4	3	6	15	12			
Managerial/professional	16	35	21	45	50	40			

a. Adjusted for sample non-representation.

goals, expectations, feelings, and behavior. We have hypothesized the effect of recent economic experiences to manifest itself at a tactical rather than a strategic level of consumer behavior. We expect, therefore, to see comparable responses for general goal and expectation statements but differences in responses to tactical feeling and behavioral statements.

General goals. The survey respondents were given a statement on The American Dream:

TABLE 41.3 Discriminant Analysis of Three Economic Experience Groups

(a) Variable selection.

Number of variables entered: 15
Number of variables selected: 2

			Selection criteria	
Variable	F	p(F)	Wilks Lambda	p(λ)
Education	5.95	0.003	0.94	0.003
Similarity of current home with most desirable home	4.58	0.01	0.90	0.0004

(b) Canonical coefficients (standardized).

	CAN 1	CAN 2
Education	0.88	−0.54
Similarity	0.58	0.83

"To be able to own your home, nicely furnished and two cars. It means to be able to travel and to be member of local clubs." The overall mean score of 2.42 on a 1 to 5 scale indicates that the survey respondents agreed with the statement of The American Dream; however, the degree of agreement was not extremely strong. Agreement scores reveal no significant differences in the participation of the three economic experience groups ($F = 1.1$, df 2/223, ns). The negatively impacted groups agree with the statement of The American Dream as much as the positively impacted group. In terms of broad consumption aspirations, therefore, recent economic experiences do not appear to have a major impact in differentiating the three groups of survey respondents.

Consumer's life goals. The respondents were given a list of eight life goals (comfortable life, sense of accomplishment, family security, happiness, freedom, pleasure, self-respect, and social recognition) from Rokeach's (1968) list of terminal values in order to assess the importance of each of these goals. The goals were individually rated on a 5-point scale in terms of importance, and the factor analysis of the importance ratings yielded two basic goals—seeking of pleasure and seeking of social recognition (Table 41.4).

Two scales were developed with the items loading high on the pleasure factor and the items loading high on the social recognition factor. When the importance scores of these two factors are analyzed, we find no significant difference among the three economic experience groups. Seeking of pleasure and social recognition appear to be of comparable importance ($F < 1$, $df = 2/223$, ns).

Consumer's mobility goals and expectations. In addition, the respondents assessed the importance of place, job, and social

TABLE 41.4 Factor Analysis of Consumer Goals

	Factor loadings	
	F1	F2
Pleasure	0.83	
Happiness	0.79	
Freedom	0.66	
Self-respect	0.66	
Comfortable life	0.49	
Social recognition		0.57
Sense of accomplishment		0.87
Family security		0.69
Variance explained	25.6%	18.5%
Factor label	Seeking of pleasure	Seeking of social recognition

class mobility. Using a 5-point scale, the respondents indicated the importance of each of the three categories of mobility. The responses indicate that the three economic experience groups assigned similar importance scores to place ($F = 1.1$, $df = 2/223$, ns), job ($F = 1.5$, $df = 2/223$, ns), and social class ($F < 1$, $df = 2/223$, ns) mobility.

The respondents also assessed their past experiences and their future expectations. Specifically they were asked: "Looking at your own life, how difficult was it for you to move from—one place to another? one job to another? one social class to another?" to assess past experiences. Similarly they were asked: "Looking at the future, how difficult do you think it will become to move from—one place to another? one job to another? one social class to another?" to determine future expectations. Despite finding some restrictions on their past place mobility by the negative economic groups ($F = 3.5$, $df = 2/223$,

$p < 0.03$), the experience does not appear to affect expectations of future mobility. All three groups are comparable with respect to their past experiences, except past place mobility, and future expectations.

The analysis of consumer goals and expectations indicates that recent economic experiences have not affected the American consumers even though they perceive differences in recent economic experiences. Despite a decade of slow growth, the changes in the economic environment are still not strong enough to affect the basic optimism and buoyant aspirations of the typical American consumer. In terms of broad consumption aspirations and goals, the American consumer remains upbeat and optimistic.

Consumer feelings and behavior. While it has been hypothesized and established that American consumers share similar goals and expectations, there are differences in the way individual consumers execute their

TABLE 41.5 Effect of Economic Experience on Tactical Behavior

Dependent Variable	Economic Experience Groups		
	(1) Positive	(2) Neutral	(3) Negative
Comparison shopping[b]	2.05[a]	2.17	1.70
	(0.172)	(0.164)	(0.098)
	$F = 3.71$, $df = 2/207$, $p < 0.03$		
Bargain hunting[c]	4.04	3.28	3.69
	(0.211)	(0.20)	(0.12)
	$F = 3.36$, $df = 2/207$, $p < 0.04$		
Energy consciousness[d]	2.08	1.81	1.77
	(0.167)	(0.159)	(0.095)
	$F = 1.24$, $df = 2/207$, ns		
Feelings of economic difficulty[e]	2.63	2.99	2.23
	(0.19)	(0.181)	(0.108)
	$F = 6.95$, $df = 2/207$, $p < 0.001$		
Feelings of self-control and confidence[f]	3.50	4.04	3.66
	(0.212)	(0.202)	(0.120)
	$F = 1.90$, $df = 2/207$, $p = 0.15$		

a. Mean scores (sd) on a 1-5 scale where 1 = *strongly agree* and 5 = *strongly disagree.*
b. Statements: I am more of a comparison shopper; I repair durable goods rather than replace them.
c. Statements: I drive more to get better buys; I buy more on credit.
d. Statements: I am more energy conscious; I look for energy saving devices.
e. Statements: It is harder to make ends meet. It is harder to make financial plans.
f. Statements: I have little influence over what happens to my life; I cannot improve my economic position.

behavior in order to achieve the similar set of goals. These differences are considered to be tactical rather than strategic, and it is hypothesized that recent economic experiences will affect tactical consumer behavior and feelings about the behaviors.

In this study we find significant differences in the ways consumers go about achieving their consumer goals. In terms of exerting greater effort at purchasing and consuming goods, we find the negatively impacted groups engaging in greater com-parison shopping and in repairing rather than replacing durables. The negative and neutral impact groups also drive more to get bargains and buy on credit (Table 41.5). Although there is little difference in the energy consciousness of the three groups, all of them appear to have become more energy conscious.

The overall impact of the economic situation has also influenced consumer feelings. The three groups are significantly different with respect to subjective feelings of economic difficulty and hardship (Table 41.5). The feelings of hardship and difficulty are not translated, however, into feelings of despair and lack of confidence.

DISCUSSION

In discussing the American way of life, Stein and Hill (1977) find "what is American is not the product but the process of movement and advancement, individually and collectively." This psychology of optimism and dynamism has become a particular characteristic of American life where future expectations have outstripped past achievements (Katona et al., 1971).

In this survey of the effect of recent economic experiences, we find consumer aspirations and expectations to be similarly buoyant and upbeat. Basic consumer dreams and expectations remain unaffected despite the negative economic experiences of the majority of the survey respondents. Owning a nicely furnished home and two cars, travel, and club membership appear to be still the dream of the majority of consumers. The optimism is evident from responses to survey questions regarding future expectations of place, job, and social class mobility as well as the importance of pleasure, social achievement, and mobility as goals in life. Feelings of restrictions of place mobility in the past do not necessarily translate into lower expectations of future mobility. Feelings of hardship and economic difficulty do not translate into feelings of despair and alienation. These findings parallel those from other studies. In 1967, Levy summarized this phenomenon when he found consumers compartmentalizing and living their lives at several levels so that "it is possible to feel unhappy about the world but be optimistic about material things" (p. 12).

The socioeconomic characteristics of the three economic experience groups indicate that it is the middle class who most feel the negative impact of the economic environment. Minarik (1979) and Shama (1980) have both argued for the same result but for different reasons. Minarik has emphasized the impact of inflation on real income while Shama has stressed the problems of achieving high middle-class aspirations in a dwindling environment. Furthermore, the impact of the economic experience groups on tactical behaviors and consumer feelings indicate that it is the middle class who are engaging in comparison shopping and bargain hunting. Van Raaij and Eilander (1983) found similar results when they hypothesized that higher social classes will engage in a diversity of economizing tactics. This survey generates data which seem to indicate that higher social classes engage in the economizing tactics because they perceive the environmental impact to be more negative, *not* less negative as Van Raaij and Eilander (1983) suggest.

It is apparent from the survey responses that the people feel recent negative experiences to be temporary setbacks. The buoyant consumer aspirations are supported by a history of steady economic progress in the past, particularly during the decades of the fifties and sixties. Even though economic growth in recent years has been small, this has not yet affected consumer dreams and expectations. As Wilson (1980) notes, "the middle class dream cannot be easily cast aside for it is embedded in the image we have of ourselves as human beings" (p. 143). Current consumer adaptations, therefore, appear to be at the tactical rather than at a strategic level as consumers modify the way they purchase a product or service through greater comparison shopping and no-name brand purchasing (Mitchell, 1973; Shama, 1981). Van Raaij and Eilander (1983) have similarly argued for a hierarchical order in economizing tactics with the more difficult lifestyle changes being undertaken last.

Easing of inflation and interest rates and the falling oil prices are bound to facilitate the continuation of consumption-oriented values. There are problems, however. Despite the pervasive optimism and buoyant expectations there are several threats to current consumption goals and orientations. First, the economic environment itself appears to be squeezing the middle income groups the most, leading to a greater polarization of income distribution (Steinberg, 1983; Wilson, 1980). Under these conditions, tactical changes might not continue to serve as sufficient responses to the environmental threats. Second, there are political pressures to shift allocation of resources away from consumption into capital investment and savings (Peterson, 1982). These pressures imply a higher cost of achieving the middle-class dream of home ownership and other major consumer durables. Unless aspirations are changed substantially, the reality may be a shocking one for many (Sheppard, 1982).

These changes have several implications for the study of consumer behavior. Surveys of consumer confidence are likely to emphasize the transitory changes and fail to recognize the basic stability in consumer goals and aspirations. Similarly, studies of consumer values have to identify individual and environmental variables that deter-

mine fundamental changes and those that are transitory. Also, theories of consumer behavior which have developed in a period of rising affluence may not be appropriate for insights into consumer processes under conditions of diminishing choice. Alternative theories of consumer behavior need to be developed for these situations, such as a theory of compensatory consumption (Gronmo, 1984). Finally, comparative studies need to be conducted to identify how long- and short-term consumption orientations are evolving and adapting to changing environmental conditions in different socioeconomic contexts. These appear to be major challenges for consumer research in the changing environment.

CONCLUSION

The survey of the effect of recent economic experiences on consumer dreams, goals, and behavior in the United States reveals stability in basic consumption orientations that have developed over a long period of time. It is easy to overlook this stability when temporary changes in the environment affect patterns of purchasing behavior. However, it is important to determine when changes in the purchasing patterns reflect value shifts that represent significant departures from the dominant consumption orientations. This is yet to be accomplished.

REFERENCES

Baby-boom adults buy older homes. (1984, April 11). *Providence Evening Bulletin*, p. C-6.

Caplovitz, D. (1963). *The poor pay more*. New York: Free Press.

Consumer outlook brightens in mid-1983 after a long low slump. (1983). In *ISR Newsletter* (p. 5). Ann Arbor: Institute for Social Research, The University of Michigan.

Curtin, R. T. (1982). Indicators of consumer behavior: The University of Michigan surveys of consumers. *Public Opinion Quarterly 46*, 340-352.

Donald, M. N. (1960). Implications of non-response for the interpretation of mail questionnaire data. *Public Opinion Quarterly, 24*, 99-114.

Elgin, D., & Mitchell, A. (1977). Voluntary simplicity. *The Co-Evolution Quarterly, 3*, 4-18.

Goetze, R. (1983). *Rescuing the American dream: Public policies and the crisis in housing.* New York: Holmes & Meier.

Gronmo, S. (1984, February). *Compensatory consumer behavior: Theoretical perspectives, empirical examples, and methodological challenges.* Paper presented at Winter Educator's Conference, American Marketing Association, Ft. Lauderdale, FL.

Hondrich, K. O. (1983). How do needs change? In L. Uusitalo (Ed.), *Consumer behavior and environmental quality* (pp. 56-73). Hampshire: Gower.

Kasulis, J. J., Lusch, R. F., & Stafford, E. F., Jr. (1979). Consumer acquisition patterns for durable goods. *Journal of Consumer Research, 6*, 47-57.

Katona, G. (1951). *Psychological analysis of economic behavior.* New York: McGraw-Hill.

Katona, G. (1974). Psychology and consumer economics. *Journal of Consumer Research, 1*, 1-8.

Katona, G. (1975). *Psychological economics.* New York: Elsevier.

Katona, G., Strümpel, B., & Zahn, E. (1971). *Aspirations and affluence: Comparative studies in the U.S. and Western Europe.* New York: McGraw-Hill.

Levy, S. J. (1967). *Psychosocial reactions to the abundant society.* Paper presented at the Allied Social Sciences Association Meeting, Washington, DC.

Levy, S. J. (1970). *The discretionary society.* Paper presented at Educators Conference, American Marketing Association, Boston, MA.

Linden, F. (1982). The consumer as forecaster. *Public Opinion Quarterly, 46*, 353-360.

McFall, J. (1969). Priority patterns and consumer behavior. *Journal of Marketing, 33*, 50-55.

Minarik, J. J. (1979). Who wins, who loses from inflation? *Challenge, 22*, 26-31.

Mitchell, A. (1980). *Changing values and lifestyles.* Menlo Park, CA: SRI International.

Mitchell, G. (1973). *Strategies, perceptions, and expectations regarding price changes and real income in a time of inflation: An exploratory study among Las Cruces, New Mexico, households.* Unpublished paper, Center for Business Services, New Mexico State University.

Newman, S. W. (1962). Differences between early and late respondents to a mailed survey. *Journal of Advertising Research, 2*, 37-39.

Peterson, P. G. (1982, February 7). Consumption by the middle class is killing tomorrow's prosperity. *The Providence Sunday Journal,* p. B-1.

Rogers, E. M., & Leonard-Barton, D. (1979). *Voluntary simplicity in California: Precursor or fad?* Paper presented at the annual meeting of the American Association for the Advancement of Science, San Francisco, CA.

Rokeach, M. (1968). *Beliefs, attitudes, and values.* San Francisco, CA: Jossey-Bass.

Shama, A. (1980). *Marketing in a slow growth economy: The impact of stagflation on consumer psychology.* New York: Praeger.

Shama, A. (1981). Coping with stagflation: Voluntary simplicity. *Journal of Marketing 45*, 120-134.

Sheppard, N., Jr. (1982, April 25). Unemployed professionals find their belief in the American dream fading. *The New York Times,* p. 40.

Stein, H. F., & Hill, R. F. (1977). *The ethnic imperative.* University Park: Penn State University Press.

Steinberg, B. (1983, November 28). The mass market is splitting up. *Fortune,* pp. 76-82.

Van Raaij, W. F., & Eilander, G. (1983). Consumer economizing tactics for ten product categories. In R. P. Bagozzi & A. M. Tybout (Eds.), *Advances in consumer research* (Vol. 10, pp. 169-174). Provo, UT: Association for Consumer Research.

Van Raaij, W. F., & Gianotten, H. J. (1982, August/September). Consumer confidence, expenditure, and curtailment. *Proceedings XXXV ESOMAR Congress, Vienna.*

Wells, W. D. (1970). It's a Wyeth, not a Warhol world. *Harvard Business Review, 48,* 26-32.

Wilson, J. O. (1980). *After affluence: Economics to meet human needs.* San Francisco, CA: Harper & Row.

## Chapter 42

GIVING VOICE TO THE GIFT
The Use of Projective Techniques to Recover Lost Meanings

Mary Ann McGrath

John F. Sherry

Sidney J. Levy

The field of consumer-object relations has recently emerged as a significant area of inquiry. Renewed attention has been devoted to understanding the meanings of gift giving as a result of this emergence. In this study, we employ projective techniques to uncover meanings that are less accessible by more direct measures. We analyze these meanings and demonstrate the utility of projective techniques as a complement to other methods of investigation.

The metamorphosis and growth of ethnography as an accepted method of consumer inquiry has brought both excitement and skepticism to the discipline. Participant observation, which views researcher-as-instrument and eschews detached lurking in research settings, encourages diversity in data collection and analysis techniques. In-depth interviews with key informants are often combined with observations to access the emic perspective of consumers.

This chapter was first published in *Journal of Consumer Psychology*, 2, 1993, pp. 171-191. Reprinted by permission of Lawrence Erlbaum Associates, Inc.

The emic perspective is the native viewpoint of the informant; its counterpart, the analyst's interpretation, is the etic perspective. Several articles have demonstrated the kinds of results that these techniques offer (Belk, Wallendorf, & Sherry, 1989; Sherry, 1990; Sherry & McGrath, 1989).

In the pages that follow, we seek to demonstrate that the careful use of projective techniques, applied in conjunction with ethnographic methods, can illuminate aspects of consumer experience that are difficult to study. In the context of studying the sensitive topic of gift exchanges, we turned to projective methods. Our desire to extend our inquiry beyond the boundaries of both the gift shop and social politesse led us to these methods. We suggest that when used carefully and in conjunction with other methods, projective techniques can yield rich, enlightening, and novel research insights.

The investigation on which this article is based was designed to generate meaning and develop theory, not to test them or measure their distribution. Because the contribution of this study lies in its qualitative richness rather than in statistical power, we have not tried to provide any illusory sense of precision through quantification. We have tried to reveal the range and variation of interpretations among a particular population and suggest the significance of those findings for the phenomenon of gift giving at large. What is at issue at this stage of exploration is not how many people responded in a particular way, but the very fact that there is a range of hitherto undocumented response to a phenomenon that might eventually be calibrated, once its significance is more precisely understood. Thus, we have employed in the following account the existential-phenomenological mode of hermeneutic

analysis of recent popularity in consumer research, rather than conventionally positivistic content analysis.

A THEORETICAL FRAMEWORK FOR PROJECTIVE METHODS

Rook (1988) asserted that protective techniques represent a combination of psychoanalytic theory, clinical social psychology, and cultural anthropology. The development and use of the techniques have a long and illustrious history in psychology (Anastasi, 1988; Kassarjian, 1974; Murray, 1943, 1946). Perhaps the best-known and most extensive use of the adapted Thematic Apperception Test (TAT) is the work of McClelland and his associates (McClelland, 1985; McClelland, Atkenson, Clark, & Lowell, 1953/1976), who studied the need to achieve as a motive for behavior.

Projection is generally understood to mean attributing to others characteristics individuals cannot or will not see in themselves. The theory put forth by Freud is distinguished today as classical projection (Rabin, 1968) and is considered to be one of the defense mechanisms used by the ego to avoid anxiety (Frey-Rohn, 1969/1974). Later, Jung incorporated the Freudian defense mechanism into his theory of personality but claimed that these defense mechanisms are not developed as a means of defining the ego but rather are manifestations of patterns that are already present in the unconscious (Jung, 1954/1977).

A modified, broadened, and more applicable version of classical projection is referred to as *attributive projection*. Freud (1911) initially related projection to psychosis but later assessed that it was implicit to the human personality. He wrote that

It has a regular share assigned to it in our attitude to the external world. For when we refer to the causes of certain sensations to the external world, instead of looking for them (as we do in the case of others) inside ourselves, this normal proceeding, too, deserves to be called projection. (p. 452)

This more generalized assessment, although not altogether divorced from the original, elevates projection from the level of mere defense mechanism to one of pervasive psychodynamic process that encompasses a host of mental operations not routinely subjected to conscious evaluation. Thus Levy (1985) employed projective techniques to elicit a range of responses, both positive and negative, and conscious as well as unconscious, to elicit projection of varying degrees of visibility from varying levels of personality.

The history and utility of projective techniques in consumer research has been well documented (Sherry, McGrath, & Levy, 1992, in press). Levy (1985) and Rook (1984, 1985, 1988) strongly encouraged consumer researchers to adopt these techniques, especially to explore the neglected topic of consumer fantasy. The use of relatively unstructured tasks to encourage consumers to project characteristic modes of response without regard for impression management is undergoing something of a renascence (McGrath, in press; Mick, DeMoss, & Faber, 1992). The covert material that these techniques are especially appropriate for unearthing promises to aid researchers in rethinking some of their fundamental assumptions about behavioral phenomena. When regarded as "headband procedures" (Anastasi, 1988, p. 622) for increasing our analytic reach into issues concerning either individuals or populations (Paul, 1989)— whether those issues are personality traits or situational influences— the techniques are useful complements to the consumer research tool kit. This article focuses on the use of projection to animate an object and contrasts these animated projections with direct responses to inquiries on the same topic.

PROJECTIVE ANIMATION

The concept of animation is rooted in a variety of traditions. Poetry, religion, science, and often advertising challenge the imagination to envision real or imagined life and spirit in material forms of reality. Nida and Smalley (1959) summarized three distinct conceptualizations of animation. The hyperphysical form contends that objects have a conscious, separable spirit. The immortal soul, which is the focus of many religions, and the belief in ghosts or spirits of the dead are examples of this first format. In a second notion, objects are conscious, or semiconscious, but their consciousness is not a separate entity. The belief that HAL, the homicidal computer in the film *2001: A Space Odyssey* (Kubrick, 1968) is "alive" or the idea that a piece of technology, such as an overhead projector, may choose to undermine a presentation or the acceptance of raisins that sing, dance, and play musical instruments are all examples of this second idea. A third type of animation conceptualizes that objects are not conscious but that they are possessed by a separable essence, usually a soul or spirit. A person possessed by a demon, a haunted house (or a haunted overhead projector), coffee with the spirit of Mrs. Olsen, or whiskey holding the spirit of Jack Daniels exemplify this notion. These last two conceptualizations have been of particular interest to marketers. Gardner and

Levy (1955) recognized these aspects of animation early on and set an agenda for understanding and revitalizing the phenomenon of the "brand" that researchers and practitioners are just now rediscovering.

It was Boas (1940) who first explained animation as projective; he interpreted its existence as a person's recognition of power in self and in others. This conceptualization is similar to Freudian attributive projection. It refers to the process of "ascribing one's own motivations, feelings, and behavior to other persons" (Rabin, 1968, p. 10). Nida and Smalley (1959) noted that people project and animate objects with spirits like themselves, apparently knowing the difference between people and spirits, but behaving as if such differences are superficial. Freud applied the conceptualization to interpersonal relationships rather than to person-object relationships, but in each case the result is both a defense mechanism available to avoid potentially painful experiences and a vehicle of mastery for exerting some measure of control in a phenomenal universe (Frey-Rohn 1969/194). Piaget (1937/1954) argued that a discriminating animism is a characteristic stage in the development of a child's concept of the world.

THE APPLICATION OF PROJECTIVE ANIMATION TO GIFT EXCHANGE

This study is an extension of an ethnographic investigation of activities in two midwestern American gift stores (McGrath, 1989; Sherry & McGrath, 1989). In the ethnographic study, we established a degree of intimacy with members of these two populations. In certain areas of investigation, however, we found that participant observation and in-depth interviewing pro-duced limited responses. When we specifically attempted to detail the transformation of an object into a gift and how persons bond with gift-objects, we found that informants were often either unable or unwilling to verbalize their feelings and experiences. Beyond issues of deficiency and resistance, a truly skillful interviewer is needed to facilitate the processing of such a demanding task. We surmised that projective methods might help to tap these less readily elicited insights. The ethnography had hinted at the significance of the gift, but what consumers understood to be the essence of the gift remained elusive during our initial field study. We then looked to projective animation to bring the gift to life in our follow-up study. We stood by to listen as respondents animated the gift, as if allowing it to speak for itself.

Through projective animation, our goal was to elicit understanding of what has been called the *interiority* of the artifact (Scarry, 1985). Interiority has to do with the quickening of matter, that is, the investing of objects by people with metaphysical properties. This concept is being refined by researchers at the crossroads of semiotics and ethnography. It is shaped by the tradition of motivation research (Dichter, 1975; Murray, 1943) and is evolving into a subgenre of consumer research. Concerned with object relations, literally—the psychosociality of objects—we term it *materiality,* to contrast the condition with the negative connotations of materialism, and to avoid some of the less helpful ontological connotations of interiority. The goal of projective animation is to reveal this materiality. Through the use of projective stimuli, we aspired to topologies and appraise how consumers animate and singularize objects to the status of gifts (Belk et al., 1989). As in other marketing and consumer studies, we use projectives not as psychometric tests but to focus generally on aggregate themes and thereby seek to minimize methodological concerns of traditional clinicians (Rook, 1988). Again, because our subject is gift giving in a holiday context, both characterological and situational aspects of projective elicitation are intriguing.

Our approach was to begin with the ethnographic finding that gift-objects were imbued with a specialness that respondents found difficult to articulate. We wanted to enlarge and deepen this significant emergent interpretive theme with a combination of projective animation and direct questioning. The findings from projection and questioning are presented separately to illustrate their utility, differences, and complementarity.

METHOD

The study described here extends our previous ethnography (McGrath, 1989; Sherry & McGrath, 1989) and documents part of a program of research that resulted from it. The ethnographic study suggested a number of issues relating to gift exchanges that required further clarification through an alternative methodology. Six themes emerged that were addressed in our larger study. These are specifically related to the ineffability of the gift, interiority and animation associated with the gift, negativity and ambivalence associated with gift exchanges, issues related to gift returns and disposition, gifts given to the self, and gender and age differences in gift giving and gift shopping. This article focuses on the first two of these six themes. Elsewhere, we have detailed findings and interpretations related to returns and negativity and ambivalence (Sherry et al., 1992, in press).

The Respondents

The respondents in this study comprise a population of 83 female shoppers whose names and addresses were chosen randomly from the mailing lists of two Midwestern gift stores that were the focus of our original study (McGrath, 1989; Sherry & McGrath, 1989). The mean age of the sample was 49, and the majority of the women (58%) were married. All but one were high school graduates, 69% were college graduates, and 41% indicated some postgraduate education. The median income of the respondents fell into our redefined $50,000 to $74,999 category, and 23% admitted to having incomes above $100,000 annually. Thus the demographics of this group position them as upper-middle class. This ranking is reinforced both by their preferences for the focal stores and their suburban locale.

Each respondent completed a self-paced, written projective survey instrument and returned it to us in a postage-paid envelope. The study was conducted during November and December and was purposely timed to coincide with the Hanukkah-Christmas gift exchange season. Respondents who elected to participate offered detailed, thoughtful, and articulate responses.

Instrument Design

Our instrument was a written, self-administered questionnaire consisting of the following sections: (a) a series of sentence stems requiring completion; (b) a set of direct, open-ended questions on gifts and stores; (c) a modified thematic apperception task, which we abbreviated as "tat" to distinguish it from Murray's original; (d) a dream fantasy; and (e) a number of demographic questions. Each instrument contained a total of 31 sentence stems that

TABLE 42.1 Stem Codes

Elicited Theme	Sentence Stem
Ineffability	Gift giving . . .
	The gift I hated to give away . . .
	The gifts I still treasure . . .
	Searching for exactly the right gift . . .
	After the holidays a gift I have given . . .
Interiority/animation	A perfect gift . . .
	No gift ever . . .
	When people say, "It's the thought that counts," . . .
	What a gift really means . . .
	If gifts could talk . . .
Negativity/ambivalence	The wrong gift . . .
	The problem with gifts . . .
	Last minute shopping . . .
	To owe someone a gift . . .
	Most gift stores don't . . .
Returns	People who return gifts . . .
	When someone returns a gift from me . . .
	Returning a gift for something you want . . .
	A gift I would never return . . .
Gifts to self	If I give a gift to myself . . .
	I hesitate to give myself . . .
	When people hint for gifts . . .
	I give myself a gift . . .
	I reward myself when gift shopping . . .
Gender/age	The older I get, giving . . .
	When men shop for presents . . .
	Women never give . . .
	Men always give . . .
	When I was younger, giving . . .
	When women shop for presents . . .

explored each of the six themes. These are specified in Table 42.1.

The six topics were also probed through the pictorial tats. Each questionnaire contained three pictures about which the respondent was to construct a story. In all, 15 different pictures were culled from a collection of over 100. Pictures were selected based on the criteria suggested by Rook (1984, pp. 117-119; 1988, p. 261), that is, latent stimulus meaning, depiction of various interpersonal relations, varying degrees of objective reality, sufficient intensity, and cultural propriety. The inclusion of three different pictures in each questionnaire resulted in five different versions of the instrument. Two of the pictures related to ineffability and interiority are included in this article as Figures 42.1 and 42.2, respectively. Each respondent told a story about 3 of 15 different pictures used in the study. The pictures were rotated among respondents to balance order effects and minimize fatigue. All projective items were pretested for comprehensibility and evocativeness.

The directiveness of our projective probing varied across items, but our goal was to give respondents permission to impose their own dramatic structures on the responses. We sought to obtain a range of responses across the parameters of interest. Forced choice demographic questions were the most constraining. Sentence stems enforced concision and demanded only a punchline or similarly pithy closure. The tats gave respondents more freedom to elaborate, within the framework of a narrative structure, on whatever the picture elicited in them. The dream fantasies posed a framing topic but left the content and genre of the response entirely to the respondent's imagination. As Levy (1985) noted, all stimuli are occasions for projection.

We varied our stimuli to encourage a variety of responses to a common set of concerns. In that way, we were able to capture range, as well as to triangulate across techniques (whether ethnographic or projective) and analysts.

INTERPRETATION

As documented in our other accounts (Sherry et al., 1992, in press), individual analysts "proposed, elaborated, defended, and negotiated interpretations" (Sherry et al., 1992, p. 48) and brought a variety of perspectives to the analysis. This is a nuanced version of the "close reading" content-analytic procedure advocated by semiotical oriented consumer researchers (Sherry & Camargo, 1987; Stern, 1989) and a variation of the "hermeneutic circle" procedure espoused by phenomenologically oriented consumer researchers (Thompson, 1991; Thompson, Locander, & Pollio, 1989).

The hermeneutic circle in which our interpretation was forged—the same process which gave rise to our instrument—bears some description. Although each of the authors shares a common research focus in consumer behavior, each is formally trained in a different discipline. Marketing, anthropology, and psychology oriented the investigation. A range of clinical experience is brought to this interdisciplinary effort as well. Further, the bi-gender nature of the research team provided some balance and synergy to the process of interpretation. The researchers analyzed the data individually; met to discuss, defend, and discard their individual analyses; and negotiated an interpretation of the data in light of each others' understandings. As the literature suggests, such hermeneutics resembles a hybrid between Delphi technique and interrater reliability measure. Context categories were neither predetermined prior to analysis nor established merely by preliminary consensus. Rather, interpretations emerged in discussion of each others' analyses. We tried less to reduce diversity in interpretation than to stimulate the additional intraceptive intuition necessary to help our orientations converge.

RESULTS

In this study, we attempted to have respondents articulate what makes an item appropriate for a gift and what imbues an object with "giftness." This was explored through three distinct lines of questioning. In the first instance respondents were asked directly "What makes a gift different from just any item you might get in a store?" In addition, two techniques for projective animation were employed—incomplete sentences and storytelling. The result is a proliferation of qualitative data. The detailed findings are grouped by stimulus type, and the summary integrates the three overlapping sets of findings.

Direct Questioning

When asked directly about the distinction between a gift and a commodity, respondents gave fairly direct, though often superficial, answers. Perhaps the question seemed too obvious, making in-depth answers difficult to elicit. On the whole, responses to direct questioning tended to be brief, neutral, or slightly positive in their evaluation of the gift-exchange process and at a low level of abstraction. The brevity and inarticulation of these written responses paralleled the unclear, tongue-tied reactions we encountered in our ethnographic interviews on the same topic.

Several respondents emphasized the specific roles of the giver and of the recipient. Typical donor-related responses were "gifts are given!," "the intent of the giver," and "someone bought it with you in mind." A gift "can be any item—the intention of the donor is key to the 'giftiness' of it." The receiver is also pivotal in the process, as indicated by the following verbatim responses:

When you give a gift, you are trying to please. The only thing you get out of it is the pleasure of the recipient.

The gift will bring pleasure to the person receiving. Every item in a store can be a gift to someone. The secret is the way the gift is presented to the receiver.

Some specific distinctions were made as to how gifts can differ from items chosen for one's self:

Gifts tend to be less practical and often times something you would not buy for yourself. . . . A really good gift reminds me of the person that bought it and thus has more special significance than something I buy for myself.

The gifts I try to buy are usually those things that the receiver wouldn't buy for himself, but that he really needs, or would delight in having. If I know a person wants a particular item, I'm happy to buy it.

Sometimes it is useful, but a lot of times it is frivolous.

A gift should be something no one needs, but it gives pleasure. A gift should have a playful element to it, even if it is very useful.

A few respondents criticized the implication in the wording of our question that gifts are to be found in a store. The importance of individualization and personalization emerged when respondents commented that the best gifts are handmade or homemade.

I like to give a gift that is handmade. I'm lucky because I'm very creative that way, so this is easy for me to do. I like to receive a handmade gift. I would never give that away even if I'm not 'crazy' about it. When the person who gave it to me comes to my home, I put it out or use it to please the giver.

Another type of gift is one that a person has made, be it sewing or even a school shop project like a magazine holder or spice rack.

The following is one of the lengthier and more complex answers obtained through direct questioning. Although the response is relatively brief, it differs from most explanations in that it incorporates several specific factors and criteria for assessing "giftworthiness."

A gift should be a happy, thoughtful process. When the giver is happy about the gift, that makes it a special gift. A gift should come from the heart. A gift from someone who can't afford much can be any little inexpensive gift. A gift should always show some thought behind it. Or it should be what someone really wants or asked for.

Projective Responses

The following typify the responses achieved through the use of projective animation and tend to be more complex, abstract, and indirect than those just presented. In addition, the written projective responses tend to be quite imaginative and creative. The storytelling methodology elicited lengthier responses than those acquired through direct questioning. In addition, both projective formats revealed socially unacceptable and unconventional responses.

Sentence Completions: The Gift Speaks Directly

This section details the findings of the sentence completion exercises specifically designed to animate the gift. The sentence stems used are underscored. The data were reduced in a number of ways. Sometimes

responses could be ordered along a continuum in which dimensions were specified by emic content. For example, responses might range from positive to negative, difficult to easy, or cognitive to sensory. Sometimes emic terms clustered around particular concepts or categories, such as homemade, effortful, or authentic. Analysts looked for a way to characterize the range of respondents' meanings, while attending to emergent patterns. Thus, although it is interesting to learn, for example, that gifts must embody labor to authenticate their value, the nature of that labor is often suggested in the emic terms themselves. In the following paragraphs, we sample the range of some of our responses, and propose an emic analysis.

We begin with our desire to understand, from an emic perspective, just what a gift is, because informants were fairly imprecise in their responses to some of our awkwardly direct questions. Responses to the ineffability theme reveal an ambivalence toward gifts and giving. Respondents complete the stem *gift-giving* along a continuum bounded by strikingly opposed visceral or sensual descriptions: *revolting* and *a turn-on.* Between these poles, the process ranges from negatively charged meaning clusters (irritating, obligatory, mundane, effortful) to positively charged ones (spontaneous, rewarding, fun, pleasurable). Gift giving is a highly cathected activity.

The search process is also described in vivid, psychosomatic detail, with respondents stressing the downside of the experience. *Searching for exactly the right gift* is described in terms of *sickness* and *pain*; it is *frustrating* and *stressful* as well. Respondents are enervated by search, finding it *exhausting, tiresome, tedious, time wasting, time consuming,* and *hard.* Some find it alternately meaningless and view search as *fruitless, futile, nonsense. At its least offen-*

sive, search is merely necessary. Respondents may view search as *terrific* in a polyvocal sense: It inspires both terror and wonder. When search is valued, it is a *challenge,* a *thrill,* or an *art.* It may be merely *enjoyable,* actually *fun,* or ultimately *fulfilling.*

Few respondents had difficulty recalling *the gifts I hated to give away.* Gifts that are *unappreciated* or *obligated,* ones the giver would not buy himself or herself or ones he or she needed, and miscellaneous specific items constitute negatively charged regrets. Givers lamented parting with presents they themselves *wanted* or *loved.* Some respondents hate to give *any* or all gifts, whereas others have *almost asked to have back* gifts once given. In some cases, the gift is *duplicated* or *kept,* becoming in effect a gift to the self.

The gifts I still treasure can be characterized in terms of source, sentiment, and substance. In increasing order of importance, gifts are valued from friends, loved ones, and family. Prized are those from parents and siblings, and most esteemed are those from children. Gifts that encode love, effort, and singularity are especially cherished. If the gift serves a mnemonic function, if it is handmade, or if it is unexpected, it is valued above others.

Respondents' perceptions of the disposition of gifts were tapped through the completion of the stem *after the holidays a gift I have given.* In best-case scenarios, the gift is *kept, displayed,* and *enjoyed.* Occasionally, the gift *keeps on giving* to the recipient, and in some cases, the respondent reports that such an experience *gives to me.* A gift may literally be *consumed* on receipt and thereby give transient or ephemeral pleasure. In worst-case scenarios, a gift *loses its flavor,* gets *put away* or *forgotten.* The gift may come to *represent a bill* and may be discovered to be *half price*

after it is given. Worse still, a gift may be *returned* or *exchanged.*

What, then, are the ineffable qualities of gift giving? There is a somatized tension regarding the nature of the gift and the ritual of search that threatens to provoke more anxiety than elation among our respondents. Effort must be invested that may never be repaid or that may be spurned entirely. The gift may be extremely difficult to give, whether due to the relationship the donor has forged with the recipient or with the gift object itself. The gift becomes a palimpsest of sorts, once given. Its meaning can be expunged and reconfigured, if not negated entirely. Even the most treasured gift our respondents might collectively envision—a surprise present handmade by children and invested with personal significance—is alternately reflective of the issues of asymmetry and altruism hedging most gift relationships. It is literally priceless. The purity of this perfect gift resides at least in part in the rarity of its occurrence.

Responses reflecting the interiority and animation themes are similarly ambivalent. Our respondents envision a *perfect gift* in terms of inspiration, investment, and impact. The gift must be *wanted* and *needed*; it should also be *deserved.* It must be *appreciated* as well. Such a gift *touches both* the donor and recipient, and it is *fun* to give. A perfect gift requires considerable investment. It must be *carefully* and *thoughtfully* chosen by the donor. It is *hard to achieve* and *difficult to find.* Some respondents view this gift as their *ultimate goal,* whereas others believe there is *no such thing.* If it is eventually secured, the gift may be a *godsend.* The impact of the gift on the recipient is critical. An *unexpected* or *surprise* gift is best. The gift is *not simply materialistic,* and the donor may feel it is *too extravagant* for himself or herself. For some, the gift should *fulfill a wish.* It shows the donor that *I am known,* because the gift encodes *a portion of thyself* within it.

That gift giving is motivated by agonism as well as altruism is recognized by our respondents. Some believe *no gift ever* can be *too grand,* whereas others assert that no gift ever is *really a gift. Ideally, no gift didn't give pleasure, harms, lets you down, is unappreciated,* or is *meaningless.* Practically, no gift *should be rejected* or go *unacknowledged.* Realistically, no gift *completely satisfied* or *completely represents feelings.* Some respondents admit that no gift ever *pleased me tremendously, matches the anticipation, is as good as either the getting or unwrapping or giving,* or even *is enough.* Respondents note, somewhat more cynically, that no gift ever *was uncomplicated* or *went without an underlying statement.*

Respondents assume a defensive posture when interpreting what is meant when people say, "It's the thought that counts." Recourse to this adage is tantamount to *lying,* or at best mouthing something that is *not true.* It is spoken in the service of reducing *guilt* or of rationalizing a *bad gift.* Some respondents regard the speaker as *being philosophical* or feel the words are *true.* Respondents do not appear to regard gift giving as merely the discharging of an obligation. The quality and quantity of thought invested in the gift is crucial: It should not be *fleeting.*

The tension between the labor value or sacrificial ethic and the affective load borne by the gift is pronounced among respondents. For some, *what a gift really means* resides in how much *expense, imagination, taste, talent,* or *time* is invested in the effort. Others believe such meaning is *not always apparent.* Others still view the gift as a repository for this meaning: It is a *token of remembrance* which may encode *caring,*

sharing, thoughtfulness, private sentiments, pleasing, and *love.*

An especially instructive set of responses was elicited by speculating *if gifts could talk.* Gifts assume four postures in respondents' characterizations, which are summarized in Figure 42.1. Some gifts are humble, and beg "Don't return me," "Please like me," and "Don't leave me in a corner." Others are haughty and say and act differently. "Hah! We have the upper hand. Admit it!" They "swell with pride" and tell people to "choose more carefully." Some even "laugh at people." Still other gifts are helpful, because they "guide purchase" and "convey caring." These kinds of gifts would make us "more appreciative," and some would even disclose the time budgets on which they were purchased. Finally, one group of gifts seems clearly hateful. These gifts would "start a fight" or "cry." They are "scary," contain "nasty surprises," and prompt "broken friendship." Respondents feel we're "lucky they don't [speak]," because "We'd be appalled and embarrassed." Some of these gifts would "mutter, 'money, money, money.'"

The projective sentence completion exercise indicates that the interiority of the gift is multifaceted. Its meaning is susceptible to misreading, but meaning must always take precedence over appearance. The gift must be earned both by the donor and by the recipient. It must be more than bought; it must be built or birthed. The gift must be invested with effort yet represent the immaterial self of the giver, whose essence must paradoxically be inferred from the gift. It must be a surprise even when expected. It must confound obligation. It encodes opportunity and danger and invites the recipient to pluck the strings attached. It ingratiates and insults, hurts and heals. It speaks out of both sides of its mouth.

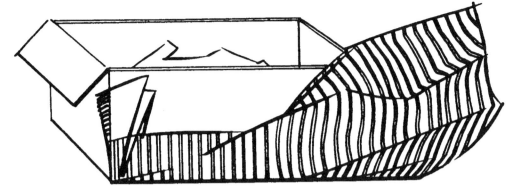

Figure 42.1. Opened gift box

Projective Stories: The Gift Materializes

The following are several stories that animate the gift and reveal its pivotal role in relationships. Figures 42.1 and 42.2 are reasonable facsimiles of visual stimuli that produced these responses.

The figures and texts have been chosen to illustrate the interiority or inexplicability of the gift. For expository convenience, we first present the story (or set of stories) and follow it with our interpretation of its meaning.

Figure 42.1 Stories

I looked at the box lying on the floor, tossed aside after the contents had been lovingly removed. In my hands I held a small terra cotta cottage, unadorned, open at the back to allow for a small candle to shine through its open windows. To those around, it appeared to be a lovely gift, something everyone who knew me would understand my delight with it. But as my fingers clasped the cool clay house, I knew that only one person truly understood the significance of the gift. Only the woman sitting on the floor close to

the warmth of the fire looked at me with loving question her eyes shining in the firelight. I answered her unspoken query with smiling assurance. The gift was a risk, a reaching out toward a new relationship, a symbolic gesture, taken from a story I had written about a journey. The path of the journey was blocked with obstacles which this woman had helped me overcome. But somewhere in the depth of struggle, our paths had separated. I had needed to build my own house, and the study ended when I greeted the woman as she came to my house as friend and colleague. And now she was truly "at my house," reaching out with friendship with her gift of the lovely terra cotta cottage. I set the cabin on the mantle, lit the votive candle inside, and smiled with a deep secret happiness. Leaning over, I picked up the empty box, carefully folded the tissue within, and replaced the cover. As I set it out of the way, the woman smiled too, and I know that this gift was precious indeed!

There were two items on my Christmas "wish list," one large and one small. Either one would have strained our meager resources. As a starry-eyed newlywed, I assumed love would conquer all—even financial limitations. On Christmas morning,

Figure 42.2. A gift machine

I scanned the gifts under the tree, looking for an unusually large or small box. To my delight I saw a large one that couldn't be anything but the elegant roasting pan I wanted so badly. My husband seemed as anxious as I to have the package opened first. Disappointment crept up on me as I tore open the box and found it stuffed with crumpled paper. I was close to tears before I found the one crumpled paper that contained a tiny box. Love did conquer all. The ring I had wished for was in the tiny box.

Interpretation: Telepathic bonding. In these stories prompted by the simple picture of an opened package, several ideas about the bond between the giver and the receiver emerge. The receiver assumes that the giver has access to her "wish list" to discern among objects that will delight or disappoint. The recipient articulates a shared meaning in the chosen object that is intense, complex, and impactful upon the relationship between donor and recipient. The gift assumes the joint role as touchstone to the past and as beacon to the future of the relationship. McCracken (1989) found similar meanings attached to objects on fireplace mantels. In addition, these stories capture an anxiety about the process that is not articulated elsewhere. The recipient is hopeful that the symbolic communication and telepathy will work, but she approaches the exchange with shaky confidence. The relief and joy that accompany the aftermath of a successful exchange allow for the construction of an elaborate post hoc explanation that transforms the fitting into the flawless.

Figure 42.2 Stories

The pretty young woman, fresh out of modeling school, is given her first assignment. She approaches the job with great enthusiasm. But what is this? A whole new way to shop sounds OK, but by computer? Don't they know she's unmechanical? She tries, but her bright smile fades when she just can't get the thing to work. Frantically, she calls the service number but they say no one can come until Friday and this is Sunday. Desperate, she tries again to make the machine work. Then totally frustrated and angry, she kicks the machine and immediately it begins to operate. But it won't stop and now she is inundated with gifts to such an extent that she piles some on top of the machine. She manages one more smile and then, the alarm goes off, she opens her eyes and decides maybe being a secretary isn't so bad after all.

Ellen spotted this new machine in the subway. At first it seemed the answer to her dreams—easy gift giving that handled everything in 5 minutes. But the actual choices were disappointing, somewhat limited, and overpriced. After browsing through the selections, she felt guilty about her waste and vowed to spend more time on her siblings' gifts.

Interpretation: Deus ex machina. The heroine of the first narrative embodies a vocational struggle between the forces of beauty and utility that seems to reflect the tension between the symbolic value and exchange value of the gift. Mechanical giving sounds good in theory, but it is inherently suspect. The machine must be forced to give (machine abuse touches an appropriately neoluddite chord in gift culture), then literally swamps the donor with gifts. The mechanical process buries, rather than liberates, the donor. The machine's revenge is over giving; it honors the letter but not the spirit of the custom. As in most of our narratives, the hypocrisy is observed but then rationalized or papered over with facework. The second story recognizes the growing conflict between time pressure and kinship obligations in contemporary society. Once again, a labor value theory of gift giving is espoused. If effort is spared, the donor must suffer guilt. Effortless gifts are contradictions, intrinsically unrewarding. In the story, guilt prompts a social resolution and a return to tradition. Search and shopping must be appropriate to the occasion they serve.

CONCLUSION

The research process which we began in earlier work (Sherry & McGrath, 1989) investigated the dynamics of consumer-object relations at an ethnographic level. We recognize that the study of the nature of the bond between consumers and objects is still unfinished. This article has explored one more avenue into this topic by examining the gift exchange both directly, through observation and questioning, and indirectly, through projective animation.

The progression of our efforts has run roughly as follows. The results of direct question-based inquiries initially compelled us into the field setting of retail sites to explore the impact of context on gift-giving behaviors. Participant observation gave us insight into issues that are typically unreported by consumers and allowed us to pose questions directly to consumers in a fashion that less phenomenologically driven investigators might not envision. Directive and nondirective interviewing proved both productive and frustrating. The more deeply we delved into apparent meanings, the more we discovered the need for greater subtlety in eliciting meanings otherwise lost to researchers and informants alike. Our need to sanction the kind of creative introspection that would allow already articulate informants to elaborate and disclose further their insight into problematic issues led to our employment of projective techniques. We centered these techniques around focal concerns and structured the tasks from fairly directive to fairly nondirective, in order to elicit as broad and deep a range of insights into phenomena as the patience of our respondents would permit.

An observation on the efficacy of techniques is warranted, at both macro and micro levels of study design. Our tenure in the field setting, our acuity as observers, and our skill and sensitivity as interviewers each acted as a constraint in the original

ethnographic study (Sherry et al., 1992, in press), and inspired our subsequent use of projective techniques. Further, the greater utility of projectives in tapping subtle or repressed motives could conceivably be an order effect, because any inquiry beyond our initial questions could prompt more elaborate introspection. Although we rotated items in our instrument to diminish order effects internally, the mere fact of our earlier ethnographic presence could have encouraged some respondents to think more richly. Given the negotiated nature of an ethnographic interview and the obtrusive nature of participant observation, order effects are both inevitable and desirable. Our goal was to provide informants and respondents with enough opportunities (and tools) to overcome any frustrations they might experience in describing to us conditions they felt to be significant. Indirection proves quite useful in this regard because it moved respondents beyond conversational norms and underdetermined rejoinders. Projectives provided one more persuasive argument to consumers that their thoughts and motives were genuinely opaque to researchers (and perhaps to themselves) until revealed in their responses.

The several methodologies used revealed distinctly different views of the gift. Direct questioning most often characterized the gift and the exchange in its ideal form. Respondents related how the act of giving should be: selfless, magnanimous, and heartfelt. The reception of the gift should be pleasurable and surprising, yet the object should be something desired by its receiver. Projective animation revealed the gift in the harsh light of reality. Its presentation and reception are tinged with anxiety, cynicism, hostility, anger, and power. These are aspects more comfortably hidden behind the mask of impression management. Consider, for example, the disposition fantasy reported by one of our respondents:

> It's the day after, and there sits a lovely, expensive gift from my daughter-in-law who I know hates me. She did the obligatory thing but it feels empty. I don't want to keep it and pray for charity to flood my brain so I can offer sincere thanks. My daughter-in-law would then become warm and loving and we'd be a family again. But I've done that. She only gloats over her own good taste. Sooo, do I break it? Give it back to her at the next occasion? Return it? Bury it? Contribute it to her garage sale next spring? No, next time she's here—While she is watching—I have an accident and feel guilty ever after.

Fantasy is culturally patterned, subjectively compelling and behaviorally impactful; it may be revelatory of social problems as well (Caughey, 1984). Fantasy that is repressed or suppressed because of its inherently threatening nature may well be unavailable to directive elicitation. Projectives provide access by backgrounding the question frame. In this verbatim, kinship relations are characterized, object relations are illuminated, and consumer behaviors are integrated by such dynamically opposed principles as hatred and love, nobility and baseness, altruism and agonism, solidarity and optimism, and joy and guilt. Disposition options range from killing, through burying, to resurrection (via lateral cycling). It is to the nature and significance of such ambivalent forces that we believe future research attention must be turned.

Our projective study points us in several new research directions. Clearly, it is time to return to the field. The responses and our interpretations can now be recontextu-alized, by reseating them in the retail settings that initially gave rise to them. These materials can be used to begin the process of autodriving (Heisley & Levy, 1991; Rook, 1989) on-site, which will initiate another round of inquiry into the nature of ambivalence attached to gift giving. Such hermeneutic alternation between methods and between stakeholders should deepen and balance our understanding of gift giving. It may even suggest further methodological refinements—experiments seem indicated—in the investigation. Tandem, real-time studies are also warranted by our results. For example, the emerging interest in the phenomena of gifts to the self might usefully be mobilized by a multimethod study that employed participant observation, interview, projective tasks, survey, and experiment as part of the original design. Our groundedness in the sites and rapport with informants makes such an ambitious undertaking feasible. Finally, the issue of consumer-object relations, which has long been the unexamined ritual substratum of marketing and consumer behavior, has been elevated to a focal concern. It is approachable by a range of methods, once its salience is made apparent to researchers. Gifts constitute a rich example of the "stuff" that people use to produce consumption. The approach we have advocated in this article needs to be extended to the world of goods beyond gifts—items both remarkable and mundane—to unlock more of the principles by which people make themselves. It is the combination of methodologies that presents a wide range of responses and weaves a composite image of gift exchange that is multifaceted, richly complex, and painfully paradoxical. It allows us to recover those meanings that might otherwise be lost to consumer research.

REFERENCES

Anastasi, A. (1988). *Psychological testing.* New York: Macmillan.

Belk, R., Wallendorf, M., & Sherry J. F., Jr. (1989). The sacred and profane in consumer behavior: Theodicy on the odyssey. *Journal of Consumer Research, 16,* 1-38.

Boas, F. (1940). *Race, language, and culture.* New York: Free Press.

Caughey, J. (1984). *Imagining social worlds: A cultural approach.* Lincoln: University of Nebraska Press.

Dichter, E. (1975). *Packaging the sixth sense: A guide to identifying consumer motivation.* Boston: Cahners Books.

Freud, S. (1911). *Totem and taboo.* New York: Moffatt, Yard.

Frey-Rohn, L. (1974). *From Freud to Jung: A comparative study of the psychology of the unconscious.* New York: Putnam. (Original work published 1969)

Gardner, B. B., & Levy, S. (1955). The product and the brand. *Harvard Business Review, 33,* 33-39.

Heisley, D., & Levy S. (1991). Autodriving: A photoelicitation technique. *Journal of Consumer Research, 18,* 257-272.

Jung, C. (1977). *The collected works of C. G. Jung* (R. F. Hall, Trans.). Princeton, NJ: Princeton University Press. (Original work published 1954)

Kassarjian, H. (1974). Projective methods. In R. Ferber (Ed.), *Handbook of marketing research* (pp. 85-100). New York: McGraw-Hill.

Kubrick, S. (Producer and Director). (1968). *2001: A space odyssey* [Film]. Los Angeles: MGM.

Levy, S. J. (1985). Dreams, fairy tales, animals, and cars. *Psychology and Marketing, 2*(2), 67-81.

McClelland, D. (1985). *Human motivation.* Glenview, IL: Scott Foresman.

McClelland, D., Atkinson, J., Clark, R., & Lowell, E. (1976) *The achievement motive.* New York: Irvington. (Original work published 1953)

McCracken, G. (1989). Homeyness: A cultural account of one constellation of consumer goods and meanings. In E. Hirschman (Ed.), *Interpretive consumer research* (pp. 168-183). Provo, UT: Association for Consumer Research.

McGrath, M. A. (1989). An ethnography of a gift store: Wrappings, trappings, and rapture. *Journal of Retailing,* pp. 421-449.

McGrath, M. A. (in press). Gender differences in gift exchanges: New directions from projections. *Psychology and Marketing.*

Mick, D., DeMoss, M., & Faber, R. (1992). A projective study of motivations and meanings of self-gifts: Implications for retail management. *Journal of Retailing, 68,* 122-144.

Murray, H. (1943). *Thematic apperception test manual.* Cambridge, MA: Harvard University Press.

Murray, H. (1946). *The TAT technique in the study of culture-personality relations.* Provincetown, MA: Journal Press.

Nida, G. A., & Smalley, W. A. (1959). *Introducing animism.* New York: Friendship Press.

Paul, R. (1989). Psychoanalytic anthropology. *Annual Review of Anthropology, 18,* 177-202.

Piaget, J. (1954). *The construction of reality in the child* (M. Cook, Trans.). New York: Basic Books. (Original work published 1937)

Rabin, A. I. (1968). *Projective techniques in personality assessment.* New York: Springer.

Rook, D. (1984). *Consumer products as ritual artifacts.* Doctoral dissertation, Northwestern University. *Dissertation Abstracts International, 44,* 3148.

Rook, D. (1985). The ritual dimension of consumer behavior. *Journal of Consumer Research, 12,* 251-264.

Rook, D. (1988). Researching consumer fantasy. In E. Hirschman (Ed.), *Research in consumer behavior* (Vol. 3, pp. 247-270). Greenwich, CT: JAI Press.

Rook, D. (1989). I was observed (in absentia) and autodriven by the consumer behavior odyssey. In R. Belk (Ed.), *Highways and buyways: Naturalistic research from the consumer behavior odyssey* (pp. 48-58). Provo, UT: Association for Consumer Research.

Scarry, E. (1985). *The body in pain.* New York: Oxford University Press.

Sherry, J. F., Jr. (1990). A sociocultural analysis of a midwestern American flea market. *Journal of Consumer Research, 17,* 13-30.

Sherry, J. F., Jr., & Camargo, E. (1987). "May your life be marvelous": English language labeling and the semiotics of Japanese promotion. *Journal of Consumer Research, 14,* 174-188.

Sherry, J. F., Jr., & McGrath, M. A. (1989). Unpacking the holiday presence: A comparative ethnography of two gift stores. In E. Hirschman (Ed.), *Interpretive consumer research* (pp. 148-167). Provo, UT: Association for Consumer Research.

Sherry, J. F., Jr., McGrath, M. A., & Levy, S. J. (1992). The disposition of the gift and many unhappy returns. *Journal of Retailing, 68,* 40-65.

Sherry, J. F., Jr., McGrath, M. A., & Levy, S. J. (in press). The dark side of the gift. *Journal of Business Research.*

Stern, B. (1989). Literary explication: A methodology for consumer research. In E. Hirschman (Ed.), *Interpretive consumer research* (pp. 48-59). Provo, UT: Association for Consumer Research.

Thompson, C. (1991). The lived meaning of free choice: An existential-phenomenological description of everyday consumer experiences. *Journal of Consumer Research, 17,* 346-360.

Thompson, C., Locander, W., & Pollio, H. (1989). Putting consumer experience back into consumer research: The philosophy and method of existential phenomenology. *Journal of Consumer Research, 16,* 133-146.

Chapter 43

CULTURAL HARMONIES AND VARIATIONS

Sidney J. Levy

We can look at development and marketing from many perspectives. At the Third International Conference on Marketing and Development 2 years ago, I suggested a longitudinal view, relating development to the various stages that societies go through as they change the character of their marketing activity.

SEVEN MARKETING STAGES

1. A traditional peasant economy

2. A mercantile resource

3. A source of cheap labor and shoddy goods

4. A cheap source of goods to be labeled abroad

5. An exporter of native brand labels of questionable quality

6. A source of good quality labels and good price value

7. A source of labels of quality, imagination, and creativity

I reminded the audience of these seven stages of movement from traditional subsistence peasant economies to the sophisticated innovations, technologies, and cosmopolitan interactions among the groups we identify as highly developed. That per-

This chapter was first published in *Proceedings,* Fourth International Conference on Marketing and Development, San Jose, Costa Rica, 1993. Reprinted by permission of the Network for Marketing and Development, University of Rhode Island.

spective may help us see where we are and where we might be going. It indicates that modernization of agriculture and industry, and increasing relations with out-groups, with the creation of distinctive marketing entities (i.e., countries as sources of goods and experiences, companies, brand names), tend to have some similar general consequences. When the results are increased diffusion and greater wealth, as successful development implies, the standard of living rises, birth rates fall, geographic and social mobility increases, and there is growing pressure toward cultural homogenization. These are the outcomes of ever freer trade and the revolution in communications made possible by marketing advances via television, computers, satellites, and other media.

Nevertheless, as we look across the globe, with its variations in peoples, environments, resources, and histories, it is evident that these results do not come about in an even manner. On the one hand, we can search for harmonies, to show that despite the diversity of cultures, there is a common humanity, with everywhere basic interests in family life, religion, music, dancing, art, and the need to make a living. That there are these fundamental commonalities fosters optimism about our shared values and goals, and the possibilities of a global marketing system.

At the same time, cultural variations persist, with their entrenched ethnicities and nationalisms. These variations produce divergent philosophies and aims and are themselves useful sources of marketing dynamics. They come about from having different locations, histories, languages, and stages of development. The result is different raw materials and competencies, products and brands, and other reasons for comparative advantages and disadvantages. These diversities foster beneficial trade in goods and services and the vast tourist in-

dustry as curious people go to look at foreign garb and monuments, and to loll on remote beaches.

Unfortunately, cultural differences do not stop with the encouragement of benign trade and the stimulation of sightseeing travel. When carried to extremes, they also create divisive group identities, with their power struggles, corruption, and violence. These desires to protect entrenched interests in resources, land, customs, religions, languages, and so on are readily stirred by fanatical or cynical leadership.

We need variation. A single homogenous world culture—as T. S. Eliot noted, a time when everyone is tea-colored—would probably be a dull place. Marketing thrives on variation: on competition, innovation, segmentation, on differences that are interesting but are also tolerated, compromised, negotiated, and based on a striving for mutual understanding.

I will note some studies related to the international scene, that I have worked on with former and current students at Northwestern University. Mary Lee Stansifer studied the issue of standardization of marketing efforts. She gathered data in Costa Rica, Mexico, and the United States, exploring the role of similarities and differences in relation to innovation characteristics and the indications for standardization strategies versus adaptation strategies.

She used the Rokeach Value Survey, measuring Terminal Values, or goals, and Instrumental Values, or personal attributes. Americans give more emphasis to social relationships and fun, Costa Ricans and Mexicans emphasize spiritual, aesthetic, and inward values, for example, Inner Harmony. She shows that the three societies are similar on products that are practical, functional, such as batteries, soup, jeans, and soft drinks, and perceived similarly, are good for standardization. Also, products that have a well-known identification with the home country may come as is, so to speak, such as jeans and Coca-Cola.

Objects or services that seem to require more adaptation are viewed differently in the three countries, if personal or expected to reflect local culture, as with products such as deodorant, toothpaste, and pain relievers.

Eduardo Camargo compared Brazil, Japan, and the United States for their values and strategies relating to ingratiating behaviors—that is, their attitudes toward different kinds of tangible incentives used to encourage buyers to do business with sellers. On Rokeach Terminal Values, he also found that the United States differs from Brazil in greater emphasis in Brazil on Wisdom, Inner Harmony, and greater emphasis in the United States on Accomplishment, Comfortable Life, Family Security, and Exciting Life. In both Stansifer and Camargo, Ambitious is more notable for the United States than for any of the other countries, Japan, Brazil, Costa Rica, and Mexico. Perhaps most notable is the lower ranking given to the Terminal Value of a Sense of Accomplishment.

All the societies in Stansifer and Camargo strongly claim the importance of being Honest and Responsible. But Camargo also finds some variations in how people in his three countries perceive ingratiating behaviors as being ethically acceptable, although the broad nature of the evaluations is the same for the three. That is, there are subtle differences in how lunch, tickets, trips, large cash sums are judged, even though they are rank-ordered similarly. The Japanese tend to find all gifting more ethically acceptable than the U.S. and Brazil samples. The Brazilians distinguish less among the gifts, bunching them in the mid-range, while the Ameri-

cans take the most spread-out view, being more black and white about incentives, more inclined to moralize puritanically, or to be lax at the acceptable end. The Japanese have the most organized ideas about gifting, with precise and refined understandings and prescriptions for handling obligations, the occasions for gifts, their character and wrapping. Camargo describes the many conceptual requirements of the Japanese system for following the rules, compared to Brazilian life where there is a strong orientation to beating the system, and to the American style of pragmatic problem solving.

Ramya Neelamegham is examining Mexico, Japan, and the United States for the way their consumption baskets, that is, the typical sets of goods and services they consume, relate to their people's levels of life satisfaction. She explores the relativity of the relationship between consumption and life satisfaction, given the influence of cultural values such as abstinence, levels of deprivation, social comparisons, and aspiration levels.

Seong Yeon Park is interested in how Americans and Koreans compare and contrast in their gift exchange motivations and behavior, in general, and with particular reference to the workplace. She examines the role of the Confucian ethic compared to the American individualism in affecting gifting behavior. Especially notable are the obligation to give gifts up the line, which tends not to be expected or is even frowned upon in American organizations, and the intense motivational power of the concept of *face*.

Such inquiries contribute to the understanding needed to carry out the common calls we hear for global and local thinking and action, in the perpetual struggle to balance conflicts and harmonies.

PART
SIX

QUALITATIVE
METHODS OF
MARKETING STUDY

——— •◆• ———

Dennis Rook: In "Stalking the Amphisbaena" Sid Levy jokes about observing a revival of qualitative marketing research, at various intervals, over the past 50 years. I suppose this could be characterized as somewhat wishful thinking, yet historical evidence supports Levy's observations. As the basic concept of marketing broadened in the 1960s and 1970s (see Part II), so did its underlying theories and research methods. At almost any subsequent point in time, it is possible to observe marketing dialogue about new ideas and research protocols borrowed, progressively, from clinical psychology, sociology, cultural anthropology, semiotics, and rhetoric. As each of these disciplines offered distinctive, qualitative research tools, their introduction into the marketing arena attracted a spurt of interest and excitement. Thus, the "revival" of qualitative research in marketing occurred gradually, but with periodic spikes of growth.

This gradual diffusion notwithstanding, two key historical periods stand out and merit some attention. In both of these, Sidney Levy played a key role. The first period is now widely labeled as the Motivation Research era, which began after the Second World War. Its name reflects management's then-new focus on the motivational aspects of consumers' buying behavior. Levy chronicles this era in a 1958 article, "Motivation Research," which details both the thinking that gave rise to it and the kinds of qualitative research that hundreds of businesses came to use to better understand their consumers. In the 1950s and 1960s, this type of research was so pervasive that some social alarmists decried its use (e.g., Vance Packard's *Hidden Persuaders*). Levy reflects on these ethical and related issues in a more recent piece, "Marketing Research as A Dialogue" (1988), which is included in this section (Chapter 53).

One important aspect of this period was the degree to which managerial and academic thinking and research practices were relatively in sync, and mutually informed each other. Articles reporting qualitative studies appeared in journals targeted to both audiences, and various books chronicled the burgeoning qualitative research armament and its marketing applications. Sid Levy's writings and activities during this period illustrate a harmony between marketing theory and practice that is generally lacking today. The hundreds of commercial studies he engineered at Social Research, Inc., in Chicago, contributed to his seminal theorizing about brands, images, and marketing symbols. His writings on these topics were published in the era's leading business journal, the *Harvard Business Review*. (See "The Product and the Brand," Chapter 13, and "Symbols for Sale," Chapter 18). Interestingly, compared to the contemporary obsession with technical procedures, methodological issues raised fewer hackles back then. Although critics attacked motivational research for both specific flaws ("too Freudian") and more vague "excesses," it was largely absorbed into the marketing mainstream as necessary and beneficial to strategic and tactical concerns.

At the same time, however, qualitative research was beginning to disappear rapidly from marketing's academic literature. This was clearly the case when I began the doctoral program in marketing at Northwestern University. Sid Levy was the Ph.D. coordinator in the marketing department. I had taken his Consumer Behavior seminar during my first year and began to think about continuing to study with him. At some point during my second year, Sidney invited me to analyze data that he had obtained to evaluate corporate candidates for executive placement and promotion. The methodology involved is described in an article in this section, "Thematic Assessment of Executives" (Chapter 46). Rather than gathering dry, fixed-format questionnaire items, the research instrument asked respondents to construct stories for a set of pictures. These narratives reveal candidates' ideas about work, professional ambition, authority, and interpersonal relationships. I took a stab at interpreting these variables from the stories of several respondents, prepared a written analysis, and turned it in to Sidney. He appeared pleased with my work and asked if I would like to do some more analyses. Like my first experiences with chocolate, massage, and sex, I was hooked, and I decided to place qualitative research methods at the center of my doctoral studies.

When I informed my classmates of this decision, most were mortified, almost as if I was about to violate a taboo. When I told one fellow student that I had registered for a course in ethnomethodology from distinguished sociologist Howard Becker, he blurted out, "You can't do that!" Reactions were more emotional than rational; and the few counterarguments that attempted to dissuade me (e.g., "you'll never get published") were intellectually uncompelling. These ideas actually deepened my resolve, but they also gradually faded as I began to collaborate regularly with Sidney and to publish qualitative studies of trademarks and brands, arts consumers, and consumer rituals. Still, the larger environment seemed unreasonably hostile about qualitative research. More eminent marketing figures suggested pursuing qualitative research *after* "paying your dues" in the statistical trenches; others simply dismissed qualitative research as prescientific; and a few big shots communicated the bizarre idea that "no one except Sid Levy" can do it right.

However, at roughly the same time that I was brooding about these issues, a revolution of sorts was brewing in various academic locations throughout the United States and Europe. Dissatisfied with existing theory and methods, a critical number of bright and professionally prominent consumer researchers, most of them professors of marketing, began working with qualitative methods in the early-to-mid 1980s. Their numbers steadily increased, and their research made its way into scholarly publications. The ensuing paradigm shift marks the second revival of interest in qualitative marketing research and triggered its reappearance in the academic literature. Sidney Levy played a distinctive role here, too, although quite a different one from what we described in the Motivation Research era.

In some ways, nothing changed. Sidney continued to publish theoretical and empirical articles about old and new concerns. But the field's response to his work had evolved dramatically. The new generation of qualitative researchers looked on Sidney as a model, a source of inspiration, and for many, a hero. On numerous occasions I have heard him described as a "guru," and occasionally as a "deity," which Sidney finds embarrassing, I think, and which I find dumb, because this implies some arbitrary mystery, religiosity, and strangeness. As I anticipate the reader of this volume will conclude, Sid Levy has no secret mantras; his ideas are straightforward and in print.

During this period in the 1980s, Levy's work was recognized in various ways. He was named American Marketing Association/Irwin Distinguished Educator for 1988, and he was selected as a Fellow in the Association of Consumer Research. Fellow designation here is quite rare and undiluted. A publication included in this section, "Interpreting Consumer Mythology: A Structural Approach to Consumer Behavior," won the best theory article in the *Journal of Marketing* for 1981, an award Levy first won in 1970. He was elected as President of the Association of Consumer Research for 1991. These accolades were doubly gratifying because they served not only to recognize the work of a distinguished, seminal scholar, they symbolically "opened the door" for others with aspirations to master recently taboo qualitative research methods.

However, the historical neglect of qualitative methods by academics was not without its consequences. Academics, after all, write textbooks. Marketing research textbooks have largely been written by statistically oriented professors, and their coverage of qualitative research is extremely thin and often inaccurate. Because managers learn marketing research from these texts, their sophistication about qualitative methods is often low. As a result, business uses of qualitative methods have atrophied into an extraordinary reliance on focus groups. The articles in this section offer an antidote for this drought. They also chronicle Sid Levy's extensive involvement with in-depth interviews, projective techniques, and other qualitative methods as vehicles for conceptualizing and investigating consumer behavior.

The lead article in this section, "Qualitative Research" (Chapter 44) provides an excellent, retrospective overview of both the history and logic of various qualitative methods. Some of this material is extended in "Motivation Research" (Chapter 45), written at the height of this historical era. "Musings of a Researcher: The Human Side of Interviewing" (Chapter 49) is a charming and amusing piece that brings the reader into the world of the "ladies" who actually execute managers' qualitative research designs in the field. Today's marketing managers would benefit from reading this and, as a result, might place fewer preposterous and unproductive demands on research respondents and field personnel.

Some of the articles in this section are more explicitly methodological in orientation. Two articles focus on the distinctive qualities and benefits of projective research methods: "Thematic Assessment of Executives" (1963), and

"Dreams, Fairy Tales, Animals, and Cars" (1985). The latter is broader in scope and provides both theoretical and operational guidance for using various projective techniques. Focus groups receive Levy's attention in "Focus Groups: Mixed Blessing" (1973). His often humorous treatment captures the feeling of real focus group research and pokes at the question raised frequently today, why we so eagerly spend over half a billion dollars annually on such murky and strangely social research activities. An alternative, individual depth interviewing, provides the foundation for Levy's theorizing in the previously mentioned, award-winning publication, "Interpreting Consumer Mythology" (1981).

Several of Levy's articles anticipated and laid groundwork for the migration of anthropological thinking into marketing. Historically, "Myth and Meaning in Marketing" (1974) was an invitation to consider the role of anthropological thought and methods; while "Hunger and Work in a Civilized Tribe" (1978) elaborated further the role of cultural studies in consumer research. An earlier publication, "New Dimensions in Consumer Analysis" (1963) was classically ahead of its time in anticipating the kind of important but excruciating detail that consumer ethnographers value. In 1981, "Interpreting Consumer Mythology: A Structural Approach to Consumer Behavior" showed how one might apply an anthropologist's thinking to some modern eating habits. The study reported as "Autodriving: A Photoelicitation Technique" (1991) grew from Deborah Heisley's collaboration with Sid Levy (her dissertation adviser). It builds on her course work with Howard Becker and his interest in photography as a method of research. The article's interdisciplinary and qualitative character is a fitting closing to this volume, especially as it harks back in that respect to Sidney's two pieces presented at the beginning.

——— •◆• ———

Chapter 44

QUALITATIVE RESEARCH

Sidney J. Levy

Qualitative research has been important in marketing research for over 50 years, but it is still unevenly known and understood. *Qualitative research* is a general term that needs discussion because it is not used consistently. In the marketing trade press, qualitative research is sometimes used to refer only to "focused group interviewing." John Lofland (1971) uses a broader definition, referring to "field" or "qualitative" research and indicates that its two basic techniques are intensive interviewing and participant observation; but he does not exclude other techniques. The term qualitative naturally implies nonquantitative, as if enumeration and calculation were ex-cluded, but despite this name and occasional controversy about the matter, qualitative research is not opposed to quantitative research and is not conducted without regard to quantities.

In the chapter on the design of the study called *Boys in White,* Howard S. Becker and his associates (Becker, Geer, Hughes, & Strauss, 1961) contrast their qualitative methods with conventional techniques of analysis that depend on data gathered in a standardized way for systematic comparison and statistical tests.

Since our data do not permit the use of these techniques we have necessarily turned to what

This chapter was first published in Levy, Frerichs, & Gordon (Eds.), *The Dartnell Marketing Manager's Handbook,* 1994, pp. 270-286. Reprinted by permission of The Dartnell Corporation.

is ordinarily vaguely referred to as "qualitative analysis." Qualitative analyses of field data are not new in social science; indeed, many classics of social research have been based on such analyses. But the methods of arriving at conclusions have not been systematized, and such research has often been charged with being based on insight and intuition and thus not communicable or capable of replication. (Becker et al., 1961, p. 30)

The report of their study attempts to show by its explicit and careful presentation that qualitative analysis can be made communicable and replicable. Although Becker et al. (1961) includes various charts and 45 tables, it is mainly a verbal presentation that integrates observations and interview data, citing fieldnotes, verbatim quotations, and input from various personnel (observers, faculty, students, etc.). The analysis, results, findings, conclusions, implications, and recommendations are interwoven to create a complex interpretation of the situation being studied.

COMPARING APPROACHES

It is evident that there are many approaches to gaining information and understanding. Quantitative and qualitative approaches will here be regarded as supplementary or complementary at times, overlapping or redundant at times, mutually exclusive or contradictory at times. That is, the kinds of learning each provides may be different but fit together so that using both approaches would give a fuller or more rounded outcome; or the two sets of data may seem to explain each other. They may appear to be two different but compatible views of the phenomena. The findings may be basically the same, providing verification or re-

inforcement or merely a superfluity of information. The findings may differ in ways that seem incompatible, leading to the belief that (charitably) both are correct "at different levels" or that one of them is invalid. Which method is valid in such cases is often difficult to judge; people are likely to argue for their preferred answer or their preferred methods, and the usual conviction carried by numbers—even those that are inaccurate—commonly takes precedence.

A way of coming closer to the present goal of understanding the qualitative approach is not to engage in such antagonism as suggested above, but, for clarity's sake, to define the basic character of the two approaches and to compare and contrast them. This contrast has been well accomplished by Robert S. Weiss (1966) in an article titled, "Alternative Approaches in the Study of Complex Situations." He distinguishes there between the *analytic* and *holistic* (or qualitative) approaches, making these main points:

1. *There are two quite different approaches to the task of making a complex situation understandable*: one that can be characterized as analytic, and one that can be characterized as holistic. In research designs, the analytic aim leads naturally to the survey; the holistic aim, to case studies, small sample studies, or, if the situation permits, to a field experiment.

2. *In the analytic approach* investigators are prepared to see a complex situation as a tangle of related elements. They take as their task the isolating of elements from each other, or, perhaps, the identification of a small number of linked relationships. This approach requires the identification of the important elements of the complex situation and, almost invariably, some attempt

at quantitative measurement leading to a statement of their interrelations. For example, it having been decided that convenience is an important element in the decision to open an account at a bank, the survey may show how that variable is related to the place of residence of respondents. The two elements, convenience and place of residence, were identified prior to the survey.

3. *In the holistic approach* investigators see a complex situation as containing within itself, perhaps hidden from casual view, a system of interrelated elements constituting its underlying structure, in terms of which the phenomena of the situation are to be understood. They are concerned with identifying the nature of the system rather than with focusing on particular independent-dependent variable relations. The chief interest might be phrased as "Taking it all together, how does the whole thing work?"

Rather than relating convenience to place of residence, the problem might be, what is the pattern of money management in the family that leads to various forms of savings placement?

4. *Neither of these two approaches is preliminary to the other.* It is sometimes argued that the holistic approach is essentially exploratory, hypothesis-generating, and therefore preliminary to the more definitive, hypothesis-testing, analytic approach. In practice, either approach may support the other; identified regularities may help to clarify the whole system, or examining the system may help reveal some regularity.

5. *The careful study of a single case is the most promising strategy* for understanding how elements are organized in

at least one instance, even though the problem of generalization remains. The holistically oriented investigator finds in such close study a density of empirical detail (sometimes called a "thick description") that makes the approach ideal for the development and testing of complex models of the organization of the case elements.

6. *There are several grounds for generalizing from a case study.* If the values of essential elements of the system are given, then the system as a whole must result; the particular case serves partly as an argument for the theory and partly as an illustration of its application. The generalization is to a theoretical level rather than to a descriptive level; and there is no suggestion regarding the frequency with which the organization occurs. That is, the single case follows the laws that have produced the organization of the system. If a survey had come before, the frequency of the cases may already be known.

7. *Small sample studies are natural extensions of the case study approach.* They usually lead to groupings of cases that display similar organization and to the development of typologies. Summaries of such findings are generalizations concerning the consistent organization to be found within a series of real instances, where the consistency is believed to be not simply fortuitous but rather a reflection of the basic structure and dynamics of these instances.

Another way of comparing research approaches and their value for providing different kinds of information is suggested by Morris Zelditch, Jr. (1962) He notes the interaction of three types of information with three types of methods. The three types of information are:

TABLE 44.1 Methods of Obtaining Information

Information Type	Enumeration and Sample	Participant Observation	Interviewing Informants
Frequency distribution	Prototype and best form	Usually inadequate and inefficient	Often but not per se inadequate; if adequate it is efficient
Incidents, histories	Not adequate by itself; not efficient	Prototype and best form	Adequate with precautions, and efficient
Institutionalized norms and statuses	Adequate but inefficient	Adequate but inefficient except for unverbalized norms	Most efficient and hence best form

Type I: Incidents and histories. An incident might be a log of events during a given period—a description of a shopping trip, preparation of a meal—including the complex of ideas and explanations that went on. And a history is a sequence of incidents. Both incidents and histories are configurations of several properties of the object or event being studied.

Type II: Distributions and frequencies. These report observations that are identical, such as the number of people who own a given product, who have seen a given advertisement, and so on.

Type III: Generally known rules and statuses. This kind of information tells what the customs of the group are, the rules of behavior governing who does what, the expected procedures, the norms to which people are supposed to conform.

Three broad classes of methods are (a) participant observation, (b) informant interviewing, and (c) enumeration and samples. The criteria for judging the value of the procedures are defined as *informational adequacy* (accuracy, completeness of data) and *efficiency* (cost of added information). Table 44.1 sums up an evaluation of the three methods, in terms of these criteria, indicating how well they provide the three types of information.

Qualitative research is located to the right in the figure, being oriented to learning about incidents and histories and the norms and statuses they embody. In marketing, the interview is a central method, and some participant observation is used. Not included here are projective techniques and other psychological methods, although depending on their form and handling, they can be used for each of the types of information.

THE PHENOMENOLOGICAL PERSPECTIVE

In the process being presented here, the basic intention of qualitative research is to understand the behavior at issue as incidents, histories, norms, and statuses, putting to the side distributions and frequencies, except as they are included in the configuration of properties. In order to reach that understanding, it is regarded as imperative to interpret the data gathered.

The qualitative researcher interprets what the people in the sample are like, their outlooks, their feelings, the dynamic interplay of their feelings and ideas, their attitudes and opinions, and their resulting actions. Doing so requires a theory or a theoretical orientation that guides the researcher. The conduct of surveys tends to be predicated on a theory that accepts the reported data largely at face value. The data may be taken as an estimate rather than literally, and cautions are offered about sources of error. But practically speaking, most marketing research survey reports give tables of percentages with little or no qualification, and the figures are usually dealt with as matters of plain fact, even if at times puzzling. The research report may sum up the numbers that stand out as large or small, thereby interpreting that they are important. Beyond that, interpretation of the results is often left to the receiver of the report.

Qualitative analysis usually emphasizes a phenomenological perspective. That is, a basic theoretical assumption is made that human behavior is the result of people's perceptions of themselves and their environment. Most qualitative analysis is thus an interpretation of how the people being studied interpret the objects, communications, and other people that are involved in the topic being researched. The main features of qualitative research with regard to marketing are these:

1. The marketing problems studied are, in some sense, general ones, broad questions, or patterns of behavior in the marketplace rather than specific details and variables.

2. When specific details and variables are focused on, the main aim is still to understand how they fit together to make sense of the whole situation.

3. The researcher inevitably has hypotheses in mind to guide the study, but may not specify them or their importance. He expects to "discover" what variables are important rather than to go in thinking he knows them.

Lofland (1971) points to the central nature of this issue, in observing that qualitative study of people is a process of discovery.

> It is of necessity a process of learning what is happening. Since a major part of what is happening is provided by people in their own terms, one must find out about those terms rather than impose upon them a preconceived or outsider's scheme of what they are about. It is the observer's task to find out what is fundamental or central to the people or world under observation. (p. 4)

4. The study is thus likely to be intensive rather than extensive, to learn "in depth" about what people do, what they think and feel, and why, rather than or in addition to how many do it.

5. The basic tasks, then, are those of interpreting, integrating, and synthesizing, rather than measuring, although measurements may be used as inputs. Qualitative study is a way of thinking, not merely the absence of measurement.

6. Relatively small samples—sometimes even single cases—are used in qualitative research because the usual assumptions governing statistical surveys are not required.

Some thinkers believe that qualitative research is not part of the scientific method; it is accused of relying on subjective interpretation and may not use precise measurement. This view is not a reasonable one. The words and events being interpreted are data in the real world and, handled in organized ways, can lead to the discovery of what are regarded to be fresh facts and fresh knowledge. If such scientific requirements as publicity, disinterest or objectivity, and critical consensus are aimed for, the use of qualitative research is an important part of scientific method in gathering and analyzing empirical information about people.

Qualitative research may be used at various levels of inquiry or for various purposes. When research is termed basic or universalistic and is aimed at larger generalizations about human behavior, the qualitative approach can play an important scientific role. It is also useful in studying specific or particularistic problems that are more limited in their situations or purposes; thus, it cuts across the procedural problems that distinguish the two directions of generalizations.

Because qualitative marketing research deals with people, and because it tries to understand them in their personalities, incidents, and histories, it is an intriguing research approach. Also, because it looks for internal relationships and candidly relies on interpretation of what often seems to be a welter of kinds of data (rather than avoiding these problems through the use of statistical units), it is a controversial method. For the same reasons, it lacks familiar formal algorithms and therefore seems a difficult method. As with other work, the difficulty is reduced by careful study and practice to further the explicit-

ness and realism that will promote the state of the art. The following brief history of qualitative research in marketing may serve as a step in the direction of this understanding.

A BRIEF HISTORY

Gathering intelligence about the marketplace on an informal basis has gone on as long as there have been marketplaces. Marketing research can include any forms of acquiring, recording, and analyzing market information, and there have always been explorers, scouts, runners, agents, representatives, salesmen, spies, tax gatherers, census takers, and other government functionaries with vital statistics, and so on, to provide word of the status of the market; in this light, even Joseph's interpretation of the Pharaoh's dream led to a form of marketing planning for the storage and distribution of grain.

More recently, Donald M. Hobart (1950) tells how modern marketing research began at the Curtis Publishing Company.

There was a time when marketing research did not exist. About the year 1910 an idea was born. It was one of those ideas, simple in themselves, which are destined to move men along new paths of endeavor. The father of this idea was Mr. Stanley Latshaw, at that time the advertising representative in Boston for The Curtis Publishing Company. . . . He was not satisfied with the way in which he and his salesmen sold advertising space. Neither they nor their customers knew much about markets and the wants and habits of consumers and dealers. . . . But such information did not exist. That fact is difficult of realization by the modern business man with a wealth of facts and figures to guide him. How was it to be obtained? Mr. Latshaw devised a plan, and not too easily, sold it to Mr. Curtis. The plan to implement the original idea was as simple as the idea itself. The plan was to hire a competent man, turn him loose with a roving commission, and then see what happened. The man whom Mr. Latshaw hired for this untried work was the late Charles Coolidge Parlin, a schoolmaster from a small city in Wisconsin. (pp. 3-4)

THE GROWTH OF SURVEYING

This marketing research activity was part of the general rise of social surveys in the United States. Following the tradition of the first U.S. Census in 1790, and spurred by the English work of Charles Booth in 1886, many large-scale projects were carried out (Parten, 1950; Young, 1939). By the 1920s, community studies were flourishing, with growing demand for sociological measurements. Similarly, the growth of psychological testing, stimulated by the use of intelligence measurement in World War I, added to the general interest in gathering data about members of the public. Concern with public opinion and the factors impinging on it led to studies of the mass media, notably radio, then later other broadcast and print media. Awareness of the role of public opinion grew with studies of the nature of the public in the writings of Walter Lippmann in the 1920s; studies of newspapers and their readers especially emphasized political implications. In the 1930s, psychologists (notably Gordon W. Allport and Hadley Cantril) examined the role and impact of radio. The 1940s and 1950s were a kind of golden age of com-

munications study as psychologists, sociologists, political scientists, historians, and journalists (and many others, especially under the leadership of Samuel A. Stouffer, Robert K. Merton, Paul F. Lazarsfeld, and Bernard Berelson) delved into the various media.

The role of communications in influencing voter behavior, the effects of propaganda, and public opinion polling were all part of the climate that fostered marketing research into buyer behavior. For example, in 1926 General Foods Corporation established a panel of homemakers that acted as a consumer jury for testing new products; in 1932 the Psychological Corporation set up what was probably the oldest continuous poll of buying behavior.

A great deal of this survey work was aimed at measuring the characteristics of audiences, their awareness of information, their ownership of goods, their purchasing actions, their voting intentions, and their listening and readership habits. Much emphasis was placed on learning what people did and the statistical differences among them in terms of age, sex, education, income, occupation, marital status, and so forth. The goal of understanding behavior was central, of course, but it took a lot of time, energy, and ingenuity to find out what the actions were, per se, as an important first step. By comparing the characteristics of groups that did different things, some understanding was gained. It is meaningful to know that the average age of the user group is higher than that of the nonusers, that the heavy users are in the lower-income brackets, and that the election victory is due especially to the votes of a certain ethnic group. The reasons why these relationships existed were not much studied, but the findings could be speculated about and taken to affirm or question previously held hypotheses.

THE RISE OF
QUALITATIVE ANALYSIS

During this period of growth in polling and surveying, research was directed at the dimensions of the market. The idea was to learn especially about the size of the market, its major divisions, its distribution in space, and to obtain estimates of the demographic characteristics that sensibly related to the buying and selling actions at issue. In the 1930s, hints began to appear in the marketing literature that some people were dissatisfied with those research aims. The information being gained seemed too descriptive and mechanical, insufficiently explanatory. The psychological profession was flourishing in its own movement from a measurement phase to an interpretive phase. Personality analyses and the use of projective techniques came to the fore, expressing a clinical attitude in addition to the traditional laboratory focus. Instead of IQ measurement, as in World War I, qualitative personality assessment was given main emphasis by the Office of Strategic Services (OSS), precursor to the CIA.

Similar interests arose in the marketing research field, partly through its own evolution and partly through diffusion from the behavioral sciences. Psychological theories, insights, and methods began to enrich marketing thinking in general as well as its research. In 1935, Paul Lazarsfeld wrote "The Art of Asking Why in Marketing Research." It was a landmark article that may fairly entitle him to credit as one of the fathers of the application of behavioral science methods and thinking to modern marketing research. (In Chapter 50, I will suggest that the sire was Malinowski; no doubt there were several fathers.) Consumer goods companies pioneered, using outside research organizations and consultants, including academicians interested in applying behavioral science ideas to business problems. In 1939, Ernest Dichter carried out qualitative analyses of Ivory soap and Plymouth cars.

Having some traditional receptivity to psychology, advertising agencies were aware of the explorations that were going on in the communications field (Poffenberger, 1925; Strong, 1913). They played an important role in the growing competition among brands and were increasingly aware of the resulting segmentation in the marketplace. In trying to account for the segmentation, demographic information was not always sufficient or satisfying. Sometimes, for example, there were no significant differences between two user groups in their age, sex, and income distributions, so those characteristics did not appear to account for their different marketing behaviors. Often, too, the reasons users gave for their different brand preferences did not discriminate among the brands, a fact referred to as the long recognized problem that there are discrepancies between what people say they do or think or like and what they actually do, think, or like. The reasons people give may not be all the reason, and they may not understand their own behavior well enough to explain it.

The study of consumers was intensified in several directions after World War II. The needs of the time and the growth of social science technology found expression in the work of many pioneers. Building on the interests of W. Lloyd Warner (social stratification and symbol systems), Burleigh B. Gardner (human organization), and William E. Henry (analysis of fantasy),

Social Research, Inc., was established in 1946. Ernest Dichter gained increased prominence as a psychological consultant with insightful and provocative analyses of consumer behavior. The same year, the Survey Research Center embarked on annual *Surveys of Consumer Finances,* providing data for the economic psychological analyses of George Katona and his associates. Companies increasingly commissioned more and more qualitative kinds of marketing research projects.

The results of the early work on social-psychological aspects of consumer behavior gradually worked their way into the academic literature; initially, reports of commercial studies were more likely to be found in various trade publications such as *Advertising Age, Tide, Printers' Ink,* and *Advertising & Selling.* In 1947, the *Harvard Business Review* published Ernest Dichter's "Psychology in Marketing Research," asserting and illustrating the importance of distinguishing between the usual "rationalized" explanations for actions and customers' deeper, unconscious reasons. Such admonition reflected the attempts in the late 1940s to get past the "lists of motives" that had previously made up much of the psychological approach to explaining customer behavior (Copeland, 1924; Duncan, 1940; Kornhauser, 1923; McGregor, 1940).

INDIRECTNESS AND DEPTH

The idea that direct answers to direct questions give results that are misleading, incomplete, inaccurate, or superficial naturally turned thoughts toward indirect methods of eliciting information. The use of projective techniques, which were flourishing in psychology, seemed promising. They were used richly in the work of Social

Research, Inc., with adaptations of the Thematic Apperception Technique, incomplete sentences, word associations, and other methods. For example, *Tide,* a news magazine of advertising, marketing, and public relations, reported on Social Research's work in analyzing the symbolic meanings of greeting cards and of soap operas, using methods adapted from the disciplines of social anthropology and psychology (*Tide,* October 17, 1947, December 5, 1947). The kind of indirectly derived insight that a projective approach might yield was dramatized for the marketing profession by a single simple experiment reported by Mason Haire in 1950. He showed samples of women a brief shopping list and asked for a description of the woman who had prepared the list. The list was varied by including or omitting a brand of instant coffee. The respondents who saw instant coffee on the list projected their ideas about instant coffee by tending to describe the buyer as less oriented to home and family, compared to the descriptions given by those who saw the list without instant coffee (Haire, 1950).

Because the usual structured questionnaire was often found to be insufficiently informative, research workers found it useful to develop more conversational interviews. Sometimes these interviews were carried out by psychiatric or psychological personnel and were compared to the free association sessions connected with psychoanalytic therapy. Because of this, such interviews came to be called *depth interviews.* Also, in the late 1940s and after, the work of Carl R. Rogers gained prominence for the nondirective interview. Despite theoretical differences between these approaches, both rely on the subject introspecting and talking freely so that thoughts and feelings are explored and brought forth more fully. It is further believed that mental content will then emerge that is less superficial, less guarded, and that reveals more of the person's actual state of affairs.

MOTIVATION RESEARCH

The wave of interest in marketing research using behavioral science methods and principles that began to grow around 1940 seemed widespread by the mid 1950s. The work that was most intriguing tried to link marketplace behavior with personality traits, to explore consumer motivations, and to analyze perceptions of products and brands. *The Chicago Tribune's* Pierre Martineau commissioned a series of basic product studies (beer, cigarettes, soaps and detergents, and automobiles), which he subsequently publicized via numerous industry presentations. (A personal aside: In these presentations Martineau was often challenged by surveyors because the sample sizes—e.g., 300 respondents—seemed small to them; and he asked how to defend himself. I told him that we were exploring motivations, not measuring frequency distributions of known variables; he said, "Then let's call it Motivation Research;" and so it was.) As the subject became popular within industry, the literature on the topic grew. Numerous articles discussed motivation research; and books by Martineau (1957), Joseph W. Newman (1957), George Horsley Smith (1954), Harry Henry (1958), and Vance Packard (1957) variously presented concepts, methods, applications, defenses, and criticisms.

At times, hostility to the new methods and practitioners was intense. Motivation researchers were accused of offering false panaceas—or conversely, dangerously ef-

fective insights. Allegedly, they used inadequate or improper techniques and samples, were arrogant and ignorant of business. They used language the critics said was obscure jargon; they came up with ideas that were condemned as irrelevant or impractical—or just silly. The vice of subjectivity, with its supposed lack of validity and reliability of findings, was especially emphasized. The sound of battle can be heard in some titles of articles of the period.

"Politz Tags Motivation Research 'Fake,' 'Hah!' Hahs Dichter Group," *Advertising Age,* September 19, 1955, p. 3.

"Battle of Embittered Ph.D.s," *Advertising Age,* 1955, September 19.

"Research Rivals Trade Blows," *Business Week,* 1955, October 29.

"Is Motivation Research Really an Instrument of the Devil?" William D. Wells, 1956.

The trade press publicized amusing interpretations from Ernest Dichter, such as a convertible car represents a mistress, teenagers use soap to wash off sexual guilt, and baking a cake is analogous to delivering a child. Some thought these were large doses of Freud & Co., although the insight about cakes seemed less ludicrous when The Pillsbury Company translated it into the successful jingle, "Nothin' says lovin' like somethin' from the oven."

By 1958, the pros and cons had been pretty thoroughly reviewed and exhausted. A good compendium of these views was compiled by Robert Ferber and Hugh G. Wales (1958) in *Motivation and Market Behavior.* Although there was no clear consensus as to what constituted motivation research, Newman (1957) provided a comprehensive view. Using a case approach he shows the breadth of understanding that was sought in so-called motivational studies. Other writers focused on specific techniques, giving the impression that motivation research was synonymous with certain psychological methods. James Vicary specialized in the use of word associations; others used systematic personality tests to correlate personality variables with marketing behavior. Franklin Evans tested whether Ford and Chevrolet owners had different personality patterns on the Edwards Personality Inventory. J. Walter Thompson advertising company used this same test to measure personality variables among members of its consumer panel, to determine, for example, whether scores on the Innovativeness variable correlated with consumers' innovative behavior in the supermarket. Kassarjian has thoroughly reviewed the results of personality studies (Kassarjian & Sheffet, 1975).

Much motivation research was in actuality a full expression of qualitative research, and at times it was called that, to avoid some of the confusion about it or to compound it. The latter name was aimed at showing that all the methods of the behavioral sciences—not just the survey and attendant statistical techniques—could be used to illuminate a problem.

During the decade of the 1960s, the interest in motivation research subsided. It became fashionable to think of such research as having been a fad of the 1950s. That was true to some degree, as the experimenting with projective techniques declined, and the full scale use of formal personality instruments was largely abandoned. The criticisms of motivation research— despite being in many instances defensive and unreasonable—took their toll. Also, the surge of behavioral science personnel who had moved into the market-

ing research field did not continue to grow at the same rate. Two sets of pioneers had been especially important in fostering the initial wave of motivation-qualitative work. Such figures as Ernest Dichter, Burleigh B. Gardner, Steuart Henderson Britt, Harriett Bruce Moore, Dietrich Leonhard, Hal Kassarjian, Louis Cheskin, Herta Herzog, Virginia Miles, William D. Wells, and several others were not succeeded by comparably significant workers.

The second group who played a special role were the daring business people who had the curiosity and imagination to support innovative research projects, who were willing to learn about methods that were unconventional and seemed quantitatively insecure. These included George Reeves and Sandy Gunn of J. Walter Thompson, Henry O. Whiteside of Gardner Advertising and later J. Walter Thompson, Hugh McMillan and Jack Bowen of Campbell-Ewald, Leo Burnett of Leo Burnett Advertising. Pierre D. Martineau of *The Chicago Tribune,* Gerhardt Kleining of Reemstma in Germany, Dudley Ruch of Pillsbury, John Catlin of Kimberly-Clark, Robert Gwynn and Dan Bash of Sunbeam Corporation, George Stewart of Swift and Company, Beland Honderich of the *Toronto Star,* and many more. In many organizations, such individuals were not present, and their numbers did not easily multiply.

In addition to the slow growth of knowledgeable and interested personnel, qualitative research moved out of the limelight. It was absorbed into the more routine activities of some research departments and companies, as each of these came to claim to "do it" too. Burgeoning interest in the use of computers and cognitive processes put it in the shade. And it tended to be assimilated into the general field of consumer behavior, which had by then crystallized into the main form in which marketing teachers and practitioners thought about the application of behavioral science concepts to marketing. About a dozen years of related work culminated in the substantial integrations by Engel, Kollat, and Blackwell in 1968 with their text, *Consumer Behavior*, and by Howard and Sheth in 1969 with *The Theory of Buyer Behavior*.

On the practitioner side, the 1970s saw the rise of the marketing research method called the focus group. The method was not new, having a history in the study of group dynamics (Lewin, 1948), small groups (Bales, 1950), and convenient survey methods (Parten, 1950). Social Research pioneered also in the late 1940s. The shift from the open-ended but focused individual interview to using a similar procedure with groups was discussed by Merton, Fiske, and Kendall in 1956. It shortly found its way into the marketing literature with such articles as "Group Interviews Reveal Consumer Buying Behavior" by Munn and Opdyke in the *Journal of Retailing* (1961), an article by A. E. Goldman in the *Journal of Marketing* called "The Group Depth Interview" (1962), and a story in *Printers' Ink*, "Market Testing by Group Interview (1962). By the 1970s, use of the focus group had swept through the business community. It had become the preferred and

prevalent method for doing qualitative research. In many organizations it was (and is) considered synonymous with qualitative research and was the only method used to get qualitative information. Over the years there was toying with the use of participant observation and attempts at creating ethnographies and thick descriptions. The latter methods have rich potential, and in the 1980s this anthropological influence became more substantial, if still short of flourishing.

In the early 1990s the situation of qualitative research in marketing may be summed up as follows. Applied and scholarly work continue to interweave. In applied work, the focus group method is entrenched and in widespread use, for various reasons and with various difficulties. Other methods are used unevenly and sporadically, or not at all. The use of one-on-one interviews is increasing again because of the fullness and richness of the information that can be obtained. Here and there one or another projective technique is applied: for example, matching pictures of people with brands of beer drinkers, getting people to tell stories to pictures and to relate various kinds of fantasies, and so on (Levy, 1985). Ethnographic approaches—participant observation, detailed descriptions—have been found useful.

REFERENCES

Bales, R. F. (1950). *Interaction process analysis.* Cambridge, MA: Addison-Wesley

Becker, H. S., Geer, B., Hughes, E. C., & Strauss, A. L. (1961). *Boys in white.* Chicago: University of Chicago Press.

Copeland, M. T. (1924). *Principles of merchandising.* Chicago: A. W. Shaw.

Dichter, E. (1947, Summer). Psychology in marketing research. *Harvard Business Review, 25,* 432-443.

Duncan, D. J. (1940). What motivates business buyers? *Harvard Business Review, 18.*

Ferber, R., & Wales, H. G. (1958). *Motivation and market behavior.* Burr Ridge, IL: Irwin.

Haire, M. (1950). Projective techniques in marketing research. *Journal of Marketing, 14,* 649-656.

Henry, H. (1958). *Motivation research.* London: Crosby Lockwood & Son.

Hobart, D. M. (Ed.). (1950). *Marketing research practice.* New York: The Ronald Press.

Kassarjian, H., & Sheffet, M. J. (1975). Personality and consumer behavior: One more time. In E. Mazze (Ed.), *Combined proceedings* (pp. 197-201). Chicago: American Marketing Association.

Kornhauser, A. W. (1923). The motives-in-industry problem. *Annals of the American Academy of Political and Social Science,* pp. 105-116.

Lazarsfeld, P. (1935, Summer). The art of asking why in market research. *The National Marketing Review, 1,* 26-38.

Lofland, J. (1971). *Analyzing social settings.* Belmont, CA: Wadsworth.

Levy, S. J. (1985, Summer). Dreams, fairy tales, animals, and cars. *Psychology and Marketing.*

Lewin, K. (1948). *Resolving social conflicts.* New York: Harper.

McGregor, D. (1940, Autumn). Motives as a tool of market research. *Harvard Business Review, 19,* 42-51.

Martineau, P. D. (1957). *Motivation in advertising.* New York: McGraw-Hill.

Newman, J. W. (1957). *Motivation research and marketing management.* Cambridge, MA: Harvard University Press.

Packard, V. (1957). *The hidden persuaders.* New York: Pocket Books.

Parten, M. (1950). *Surveys, polls, and samples: Practical procedures.* New York: Harper Bros.

Poffenberger, A. T. 1925). *Psychology in advertising,* Chicago: A. W. Shaw.

Smith, G. H. (1954). *Motivation in advertising and marketing.* New York: McGraw-Hill.

Strong, E. K., Jr. (1913). Psychological methods as applied to advertising. *Journal of Educational Psychology, 4,* 393.

Weiss, R. S. (1966). Alternative approaches in the study of complex situations. *Human Organization, 25*(3) 198-206.

Wells, W. D. (1956, October). Is motivation research really an instrument of the devil? *Journal of Marketing, 21,* 196-198.

Young, P. V. (1939). *Scientific social surveys and research.* Englewood Cliffs, NJ: Prentice Hall.

Zelditch, M., Jr. (1962). Some methodological problems of field studies. *American Journal of Sociology, 67,* 566-567.

Chapter 45

MOTIVATION RESEARCH

Sidney J. Levy

In the past 10 years (c. 1948-1958) a particular way of studying the human factors important in consumption has gained widespread attention and interest among businessmen and market researchers in the United States. This way of studying the consumer has generally come to be called *motivation research;* it is both a method and a symbol of something new in consumer study, and it is the subject of much controversy.

Motivation research can best be defined as research applying the knowledge, theories, and techniques of the behavioral sciences to the study of the behavior of consumers and of publics. As such, it is one branch of applied social psychology, similar in a way to the study of human relations in industrial and other organizations, or to the various action researches concerned with problems of racial integration, discrimination, or juvenile delinquency. As with any applied research in the social, biological, and physical sciences, motivation research draws heavily on the more academic disciplines, both in personnel concerned and in the ways it approaches particular problems.

The behavioral sciences center in psychology, sociology, and anthropology. Motivation research intimately involves these

This chapter was first published in Specht Brager (Ed.), *Community Organizing* (2nd ed., pp. 125-129). Copyright © 1987 Columbia University Press. Reprinted with permission of the publisher.

disciplines as well as some particular sub-fields, such as psychoanalysis, semantics, anthropological behavior, and the study of cultural patterns involved. These sciences provide a rich understanding of human behavior in areas to which consumer behavior is obviously tied.

The behavioral sciences, whose province is the study of man—the way he behaves and why—are relatively young. The last 60 years or so encompass tremendous progress in our understanding of the individual and his personal responses (psychology), the influence of man's social environment on his behavior (the province of sociology), and the ways societies and cultures organize group life and maintain continuity through time (anthropology). Thus, although the behavioral sciences do not show the same formally developed and tested precision as, for example, chemistry, much is nevertheless known about human behavior, and the knowledge is available for application over a wide range of problems.

Motivation research, as a branch of applied psychology having to do with consumer and public behavior, is the newest applied field However, the points of view, the methods, and the techniques have been used before and, often, were perfected in other areas of applied research. The study of human-behavior-at-work is the most obvious parallel since it also involves problems important to business.

Beginning in the 1920s, many studies have applied principles of the behavioral sciences to such problems as those of people working together in groups, the motivation of workers and executives, and communication between various levels in work organizations. As a matter of fact, several organizations in the motivation research field also study aspects of human relations in industry, since the required background knowledge is similar and overlapping in both areas.

Perhaps the most important development in applied behavioral sciences was the impetus given during the Second World War. Clinical psychology, the study of processes in abnormal behavior, and ways of testing for them, mushroomed because of the medical-psychological problems of the armed forces and of veterans after the war.

There were a host of other problems, too, that social scientists were called on to study during the war—problems having to do with the characteristics of the enemy, ways of better understanding and predicting the enemy, problems of morale and persuasion at home, and the like. Social scientists were called on to study and help train government people in the ways of technically equipped, culturally unknown enemies, such as the Japanese, and comparably alien allies, such as the people in the Malay Peninsula, Burma, and the Philippines. Heretofore esoteric scientists moved out of the academic world of theory or pure research to tackle the great pressing human problems of carrying on a war in unfamiliar areas and among people with whom they had had relatively little experience. A great deal of work and a great deal of study, in both personnel and enemy psychology, went on under the auspices of the Office of Strategic Services, and many prior techniques for personality measurement and assessment of cultural material were developed and tested there.

Internally, the social sciences became involved in assessing the influence of information and propaganda both within the armed services and among the civilian population. One of the first efforts in motivational analysis of advertising and its effectiveness was conducted by Robert Merton in connection with the war bond drives. Another project for cooperating social scientists, including anthropologists, sociologists, and psychologists, was that of discovering effective ways to persuade housewives to use less attractive but nourishing foods and to encourage them to serve balanced meals in spite of wartime disruptions in food habits. After the war, the armed forces used a number of social scientists, particularly in Germany, to investigate and advise on problems connected with denazification and other public opinion problems in Germany.

These various experiences during the war gave impetus to the development of motivation research in two ways. First, behavioral scientists learned that they do have something practical to contribute to problems which involve understanding normal people going about normal activities, including consuming. Second, many businessmen while serving their government in wartime had acquired some understanding of these behavioral sciences and gained confidence that such disciplines could help with consumer problems. With this came greater familiarity with the social sciences and a decline in the feelings of strangeness and distance often associated with any unknown area of knowledge.

At present, then, motivation research is widely used by business in the United States to provide knowledge about the consumer. It is difficult, however, to assess the extent of motivational research as we have defined it here. Research is often called motivational simply if someone asks respondents why they do this or that, without any utilization of the background knowledge we have discussed. Nevertheless, we do know that well over 1,000 truly motivational studies have been carried out by the few research organizations specializing in this work and by the motivational research departments of a few advertising agencies.

There are probably not many major product areas that have not been subjected to fairly extensive motivational research by more than one practitioner. Automobiles have been thoroughly studied, and the three leading automobile manufacturers in the United States have used motivation research fairly extensively. This is also true in the appliance and food products fields. Particular problem products, like instant coffee and cake mixes, have been studied over and over and over again.

During the 10 years of the technique's greatest development, several problem areas have been marked out as appropriate to motivational research inquiry:

1. Studies of the social and psychological factors influencing the consumption of products and brands

2. Studies of the sociological and psychological characteristics of the consumers of various products and brands

3. Studies of the rational and emotional content of print and broadcast advertising, and ways in which such advertising can be made more effective

4. Studies of people at various levels in the industrial distribution system, such as retailers, purchasing agents, and wholesalers, to discover attitudes and motivations involved in their business decisions and ways of most effectively appealing to them

5. Studies of the social and psychological characteristics of the audiences of particular mass media, the most effective ways to approach them, and the meanings and functions those media have for the audiences

6. Studies of media directed toward helping editors and producers improve the editorial content of magazines,

newspapers, radio and television programs, popular records, and movies.

7. Studies of the public images of corporations, the factors influencing positive and negative attitudes toward corporations, as a guide to public relations work

8. Studies of government institutions and recruiting programs for the armed forces, oriented toward improving the public image of the institution and making it more attractive to potential recruits

9. Studies of the public conception of various retail stores and ways in which interest in a store can be heightened and its advertising improved

Most of the motivation research work done is in connection with the first three points: consumers' attitudes, feelings, and motives in relation to products and brands and the advertising for these. However, an increasing amount of work is being done in connection with media, as advertisers and agencies become concerned with the more intangible sociopsychological characteristics and values of the mass media they use; and as publishers and producers become concerned with attracting a wide market for their media and satisfying that market's media needs more fully.

Noncommercial organizations, both governmental and private, also become concerned with their market, whether that market be patients for physicians and dentists (so that professional organizations sponsor research), or financial contributors (in which case a charitable body may commission a study), or citizens or volunteers or voters (in which case the government or political parties may be interested in research).

## Chapter 46

THEMATIC ASSESSMENT OF EXECUTIVES

Sidney J. Levy

The assessment of personnel is a topic that recurrently arouses mixed and troubled feelings. At intervals, criticism flares up in protest against psychological testing. The criticisms take various forms but tend to boil down to charges of such things as invasion of privacy, unethical activity, injustice to individuals, inadequate instruments or absurd items, impersonal harshness, or statistical cold-bloodedness. Many writers clearly have a narrow idea of the nature of psychological testing. One of their basic sets of assumptions seems to be that all psychological testing is blindly normative and that its customary effect is to discard men of great potential contribution because they answer ridiculous questions in nonconforming ways.

The purpose of this paper is not to answer these charges or attempt directly to argue them. Rather, it seems useful to provide some greater content to the discussion of psychological testing by describing some aspects of how it has been done by one organization. This may only feed the flames; but it may also provide substance for those who would like data for thinking about the problem.

There are many ways of assessing men, most of them more or less imperfect since human behavior is complex and variable enough to make both the assessor and the assessed inevitably fall short. This does not keep people from seeking to improve their predictions when decisions are to be made. Much as the critics may resent it, personnel do not in some ineffable, self-manifesting fashion find their own ways into optimally fitting jobs (especially if there is one job for more than one applicant) either as new applicants or candidates for promotion. Someone has to use his best knowledge of the man to decide about him. It is also true that many people who have such decisions to make feel that they want help in making them and that through the customary processes of division of labor and specialization of knowledge, there may be those who can assist.

TEST PROTOCOLS

Since 1948 our staff has handled projective test protocols of some thousands of subjects. As test analyst, supervisor, and company administrator, I have worked on a large portion of these materials and have concrete knowledge of how we test, how we analyze and report the results, and how our clients use the reports. My plan is to tell something about our tests, our procedures, our client relations, and to offer a few thoughts about executives as they have appeared to us.

The main work of our company is business research (products, consumers, institutions, communications), with an emphasis on qualitative analyses of data. These analyses draw freely on a variety of disciplines, since our staff includes people trained in anthropology, sociology, social

psychology, and psychology and people from the University of Chicago's Committee on Human Development. Thus, our inquiries examine data for their reflections of cultural processes; social structure, function, and influences; symbolic meaning; individual dynamics; and developmental patterns.

Testing of executives (and other people in companies) is one activity embedded in this social science matrix. Historically, it grows out of early activity in organizational consulting, with executive testing used as one of the techniques of evaluating a company's higher echelons and diagnosing its human problems. In recent years our testing has been more purely a part of the personnel function, emphasizing selection and evaluation for shifts in internal organization.

THE BASIC INSTRUMENT

The basic instrument used in our work is a variation on the *Thematic Apperception Test*. This instrument is an example of a projective technique. Such techniques are based on the logic that people's behavior is invariably meaningful and expressive of their personalities. Thus, given a standard but relatively ambiguous task, such as telling a story about a picture, what a person does reflects how he structures and interprets life situations and reacts to them. Projective techniques came into prominence as testing devices during World War II, and with the growth of clinical psychology, became an important part of the armamentarium of psychological tools. These techniques are also widely used in nonclinical settings as part of many kinds of social science research.

The modification we use consists of a series of 10 pictures developed and chosen by William E. Henry and Harriett Bruce Moore. These pictures are combined in a bound booklet with a request for a drawing of a person, a series of incomplete sentences, and a fact form. The folio is entitled *Executive Personality Evaluation, The Henry-Moore Test of Thematic Production* and contains instructions for complete self-administration. It is almost invariably filled out by the individual taking the test; only occasionally are the stories dictated.

Usually, each test is independently analyzed by two people, with one responsible for drafting a report and the other acting as checker and editor. Most difficult protocols, all protocols being more or less difficult, will be jointly discussed, or additional staff members are asked for their judgments.

Our reports are discursive, written along an accustomed outline which covers such topics as Placement Pattern, Mental Organization or Intellectual Characteristics, Personal or Individual Characteristics, and Interpersonal or Working Relationships. The report attempts to describe how the individual functions:

- The kinds of work areas he prefers or toward which his skills are oriented
- The levels of ability he brings to bear
- The kinds of problems he handles most effectively; those he ignores, slights, or distorts
- The quality and handling of his energy
- His idiosyncratic hierarchy and constellation of motivations
- His attitudes toward authority
- Typical dealings with peers
- His orientation to those of lesser status

The process of interpretation we use follows particularly the thinking described by William Henry (1956). The materials are gone over once rapidly to provide a general impression, an overall judgment of the individual's performance. Then follows a sequence analysis and an integration of the results into a summary report. This approach is essentially a qualitative, subjective one. It means sailing in the heavy Seas of Inference where complex psychological and social crosscurrents can easily engulf the unwary. Some sources of security are derived from principles and knowledge in the literature, from the rich content of dynamic analytic psychology, from the provocative perspective of symbolic interaction which orients us to the meanings in even conventional behavior, and from the stream of studies of projective techniques.

PRACTICE MAKES PERFECT

In addition, of course, practice reduces imperfection; as in any art or skill that seems intuitive, free style, or impressionistic, many guides are developed and used. Usually, an unspoken body of more or less systematic generalizations is derived from the expressive reactions and responses to a standard stimulus. By now we have gained a full sense of the issues presented by each of the pictures in our test. Each picture may be defined as implicitly asking a large, manifold question, to which the story is a complicated answer. The broadest parts of the question are, "Who are you, what are you like? Show something of yourself by the way you write about this picture."

The working hypothesis is that the act or event of a response is a highly condensed funneling into a few words of a distillation of the man's being, his history, his current nature, and his aspirations. In a sense, from his first word, he begins to write his autobiography. This does not mean that his whole history and being can be read there totally, easily, or accurately, due to the barriers created by the fact of condensation as well as other mechanisms of presentation but that it is potentially there for examination. More realistically, particular personality elements, facets, trends, qualities can be discerned, how much and how well varying with the observer. Thus, any story expresses something of the essential person, his situational mood, his characteristic affect, his customary coping techniques, his self-regard, social outlook, and so on. The assumption is that his performance style must bear meaningful relationships to his lifestyle.

Determining these relationships is made easier by knowing the typical range of responses to the projective stimuli as these vary among individuals and among groups. Each sentence stem, each picture, offers a focal issue. We are aware that sentence completions to the stem, "It's embarrassing . . . " have three modal responses: to forget a name or face, to be caught without money, and to discover one's fly is open. It is amazing how often "the most disgusting thing . . . " is a drunken woman.

LATENT ISSUE

Similarly, we have learned that the issue latent in our first picture (which shows a man seated at a drawing board) is that of work. In a complex, variegated way it inquires, "How do you feel about yourself as a worker, what is your sense of task, career, vocation, dedication, concentration? What kinds of ego mastery do you bring to bear in applying yourself to work; what level of aspiration do you show; and so on?" Because the man is shown seated, there are implicit questions relating to passivity to which subjects respond with acceptance or some kind of restlessness.

This issue is more sharply and directly posed later by a picture of a silhouetted figure leaning idly in an impressionistic doorway. Here reactions range from strong denial of passive aims (conventionally expressed in stories of men who are eager to return to work), through acceptance of a reasonable degree of relaxation (in stories of men on vacation or taking it easy at home), to an extreme group who interpret the figure to be an Oriental prostitute awaiting customers.

There are many problems in analyzing these materials. Normative ideas are most useful in assessing groups and in locating a man rather generally. Engineers are apt to describe and reason from specific pictorial elements and structures; salesmen are likely to describe events in people-oriented stories; financial workers tend to be very factual and tightly organized; and so on. However, when the goal is to evaluate a particular individual, many qualifications must enter in to modify the gross generalizations. The most crucial problem is how to put together the piecemeal insights derived from the parts of a man's performance into a holistic judgment of his capacity and effective functioning. Oriental prostitutes have been perceived by able heads of companies and by alcoholic failures on the sales force; what this fact implies has to be subtly integrated into the implications of less exotic erotic apperceptions.

QUALITY IS A QUESTION

I have observed that test analysts are usually able more quickly to note a man's characteristics than to judge his quality. It is easier to be impressed by a striking response, an amusing symbolic reference, than to think what it may mean for the man's problem-solving ability. Test interpreters with clinical experience seem to find it easier to diagnose the presence of anxieties, family conflicts, bizarre content, sexual deviation, and hostile attitudes than to integrate the presence of such processes in a nonclinical subject into a picture of his typical work behavior. This is not to disparage the clinician but to indicate the difficulty of describing "normal" individuals in vocational action, where large numbers have clearly failed to resolve the Oedipal situation, with diverse but not always incapacitating effects on their ability to earn a living.

With due regard to the presence of interesting negative clinical content and how it affects a man's work behavior (since of course it does), evaluating executives turns one's attention especially to judging positive resources in the personality. Often this seems best accomplished by giving due credit for formal characteristics. Does he do the task; is it sufficiently organized to be clearly followed; is it terse, overelaborated, or adapted to the space provided; does he finish? Is he concrete in seeing problems, very literal or practical; does he use abstractions and generalizations to further specific conclusions, does he present them in platitudinous, windbag fashion?

Similarly, on the more personal side, there is much tolerance in the average work environment for individual aberrations as long as they are kept reasonably private. To summarize this a bit cynically: superiors want their subordinates to get things done; work associates want an adequate degree of self-control and apparent amiability from their peers; and subordinates want bosses to maintain a fair distance.

BASIC AIM

A basic aim governing the preparation of reports is that earnest attempts will be made to describe the man's personality and likely job performance in an apt way, so that a responsible person reading the report would be helped in making a decision about the man's placement. Our reports try to avoid usurping this decision. We do not want to say that a man should or should not be hired as a sales manager or as a controller but that he would perform in the role in the described fashion. The logic is: Everyone has to earn a living; this man works best at certain kinds of problems, in such-and-such situations, typically with this-or-that attitude toward superiors, associates, and subordinates. He has various vocational assets and limitations. The same report might mean "OK, that's fine" to one potential employer, "he'll do," to another, and "he's not the kind of guy we're looking for" to a third. In this sense, while the report may in practice serve clearly to qualify or disqualify a man, our goal is to emphasize the report as an aid to judgment, partly because we don't want the irresponsibility of a choice we do not have to live with; partly because we never can know enough about someone else's job situation; and partly because, as with some other man's wife, we'll never understand why he likes her regardless of our opinions.

It may be asked, why do clients want these reports, what advantage do they see in descriptions derived from projective techniques? We are still at times astonished to be asked to test a man who has been with a company for several years. He is being considered for promotion, but his superiors are uncertain or are arguing about whether he can undertake greater responsibilities. Others are more acutely uncertain when considering new personnel, feeling that interviews are too precarious to be used alone for important employment decisions. Usually, the man's technical qualifications are known; the anxiety is about the kind of man he is, how he deals with people, and what he is likely to do in the higher reaches of decision making where intangible factors and imagination may be most useful. This leads them to cast about either for some aid in reassuring themselves that they are getting a man who is likely to do well on the job, or at least to reduce the odds that they will make a serious mistake. One man told a prospect he was asking to take the test:

> Frankly, I do not understand such tests, but the results have, in the past, been helpful to us as one more avenue through which we may become better acquainted with a prospective associate.

It may be useful here to indicate more of the thoughts and reactions of people who have made use of this kind of testing. Before becoming a client of ours, one large company asked a business consultant to determine what would be a feasible testing procedure for them. The consultant experimented by administering a battery of paper-and-pencil tests to a group of men in the corporation. These included the Ohio State University Psychological Test, the Miller Analogies Test, the Thurstone Temperament Schedule, and Kuder Preference Record-Personal.

INDEPENDENT ASSESSMENTS

In addition, we were asked to make independent assessments with the projective test folio I have described to you. One

hundred and twenty-five men were tested. The consultant's report gave examples that compared individual profiles and analyses based on the several tests. He concluded as follows:

> The profiles were studied carefully and an interpretation was made by studying the high and low scores. It can be seen that this interpretation has required a good deal of reading between the lines. . . . The interpretations based on the Henry-Moore Test of Thematic Production are much richer and deeper than those based on the profiles. . . . From the SRI report we have a much better understanding of the profile results . . . we would strongly recommend continuing the testing program with Social Research, Inc. Furthermore we would recommend that the paper-and-pencil portion of the test battery be eliminated with the exception of the OSU. The SRI does a far more effective job of measuring executive potential.

This is an abbreviated history of how we acquired one of our major clients. In preparing this paper it occurred to me that it would be interesting to pursue the experience of this particular client company. I asked the director of personnel three questions. Because his answers seem a fair summary of the reactions we have encountered over the years with our clients, I would like to quote his comments.

> How do you use the projective personality tests?
>
> These are used principally in evaluating candidates for management assignments either through internal promotions or transfers or from outside recruiting. To the greatest extent possible we attempt to form our own judgments about the person first and subsequently look to the psycho-

logical evaluation for confirmation or challenge. This process is probably followed fairly consistently by our personnel people, less so by line executives who make the decision about the appointment. Another use made of the test when taken by present employees is that of self-reflection; in other words, to stimulate insight about themselves.

What changes have occurred in your expectations and use of the report?

Since 1956, when we first began using these evaluations, we have made no significant change. Our executives continue to be impressed with the sharp, usable picture the evaluations provide. In my personal opinion the report has proven very useful to all of us involved in the selection procedure, personnel and line management as well, in providing an organized appropriate format to put our thoughts about a person into focus. Since very few of us have any psychological theoretical training, the format of the evaluation is most helpful.

What are the pros and cons in using the reports?

Pros: The evaluations provide a penetrating, quick, comprehensive psychological view of a person being seriously considered for an important assignment. This is all the more important when a stranger is under consideration. Not having a staff psychologist, the evaluations are uniquely helpful. Another pro has already been described: that of training our own management, including personnel people, especially in identifying the psychological characteristics of managers.

A good share, probably over half of the employees, who have taken this test, have been stimulated to think in a more organized, penetrating way about themselves. How much good this has done is, of course, impossible to describe.

Cons: Perhaps the greatest difficulty we have experienced is in making too superficial an interpretation of the test result against the demands of the assignment and the milieu in which the individual will operate. This point is demonstrated every time we have had occasion to release or demote someone. Subsequently, when reviewing the evaluation made at an earlier date, the causes of the difficulty are almost invariably contained within the report; but we have not read them to be the warning signals which they subsequently prove to be. I am inclined to think this is more a deficiency in our skill in relating the report and other data to the prospective situation than in the content of the report, although I would enjoy discussing this point with you.

As this suggests, problems of communication are ever present. Without resorting to unmistakable and overstated colloquialisms or final remarks that flatly praise or condemn a man, a judicious report can sound obvious, obscure, contradictory, or inconclusive. We have encountered all these criticisms. It is not always easy to tell how much the criticisms are justified or how much they are a form of resistance to dealing with this kind of information. People who buy tests as well as people who buy research often ward off the results by claiming "I already knew that," "I don't understand it," "It's wrong," or "So what?" Resistance or reality, some clients disappear on such grounds. Others work to understand the reports, ask questions, and figure out some meaningful relation between the written document and the man they are thinking about.

EXECUTIVE PERSONALITIES

I will close with a few comments on executive personalities. The plural is necessary since it is apparent that effective executives come in a great variety of forms. While there is some truth in the notion of the interchangeable man who can run anything regardless of industry as long as he knows how to work through people, most real executives are experienced and suited for particular kinds of work where their personalities find congenial expression. This is often reflected in the way companies and industries attract people with typical personality syndromes. One large milk company draws men with distinctly nurturant trends. Executives we have tested in the clothing industry stand out in my mind for their emotionality and somewhat heavy moral sense. Research and personnel people appear prone to detachment and often an obsessive tendency to neutralize problems rather than to see their action consequences. Successful men in a given field often seem to be those who add a dimension in their personalities that oppose or temper the trends characteristic for their occupations, being research people who can select and make concrete recommendations, engineers who are sympathetic to human strivings, financial experts who can synthesize as well as analyze, salesmen who are not too intent on gaining human response, and, I hope, psychologists who do not feel they know everything about people.

Which last point reminds me, the use of projective tests raises questions in the area of integrity: how to guard one's own and that of the other people involved. Many paper-and-pencil tests carry the implication of greater voluntary self-examination and control, giving the feeling that people have some freedom in rating themselves on the items, thereby presenting themselves as they wish to appear. They are often more anxious about a test in which they fear anything they say may somehow be used against them. One young man, in discussing a test report which questioned his work habits, commented, "That's true, but I wish my boss wasn't being told about it." In each report, test analysts must decide how much and how little may be said about a man, and how phrased, to serve the client company and to protect the individual in accordance with high professional and ethical standards.

It seems reasonable to believe that business will continue to use many ways of assessing personnel. For some purposes a rapidly reached score on a paper-and-pencil test or battery may serve to reduce the hazards to company and applicant of hiring first-come first-served or choosing on the basis of the hirer's on-the-spot reactions (which some critics like, as poor as it may often be). In other cases, projective techniques will remain valuable, being one of the few approaches available to assess intangible and subtle aspects of personality and thereby to amplify the chances of making a more informed decision in a difficult area of judgment.

REFERENCE

Henry, W. E. (1956). *The analysis of fantasy.* New York: John Wiley.

Chapter 47

NEW DIMENSION IN CONSUMER ANALYSIS

Harper W. Boyd, Jr.
Sidney J. Levy

In recent years there has been an outpouring of management literature dealing with a subject which has become known as *the marketing concept*. This line of thinking has been well summarized by Peter F. Drucker (1954):

> If we want to know what a business is we have to start with its purpose. And its purpose must lie outside of the business itself. In fact, it must lie in society, since a business enterprise is an organ of society. There is only one valid definition of business purpose: to create a customer. (p. 37)

A logical starting point, under this approach, is to concentrate on the functions that the product serves in satisfying a customer's needs instead of becoming preoccupied with the physical aspects of the product itself. Phrased in terms of functions, companies sell such things as transportation, nutrition, energy, comfort, self-expression, escape, intellectual development, and conformity; rather than cars, bread, oil, pillows, pens, novels, textbooks, and uniforms.

Certainly, this is a good start. By taking such a conceptual approach, many compa-

AUTHORS' NOTE: We wish to acknowledge the helpful insights contributed by Professor Edward C. Bursk.

This chapter was first published in the *Harvard Business Review*, November-December, 1963, pp. 129-140. Copyright 1963 by President and Fellows of Harvard College. Reprinted by permission of *Harvard Business Review*.

nies have sharpened their marketing effort by (a) researching and analyzing why customers (or potential customers) buy (or don't buy) particular kinds of products or services and (b) surveying and identifying particular groups of customers (or potential customers) who differ from one another in why they buy (or don't buy) the products. The same companies have also used the marketing concept to instill more sense of direction in the nonmarketing functions of the business and to unify their overall organizational effort.

FOR FULL EFFECTIVENESS

But general adoption of a customer orientation is not enough. Such an approach can still fall short of full effectiveness. The trouble is that it does not ensure that customers' needs and wants will be understood and spelled out in the comprehensive, meaningful detail that they could and should be.

It is the purpose of this article to point out the value of thinking and making decisions in terms of consumption systems. This, we will show, is an effective way to avoid use of generalizations or unrelated specifics and of achieving more innovation, greater market penetration, and more coordinated planning of the total marketing (and corporate) effort.

By the term *consumption system* we mean the way a purchaser of a product performs the total task of whatever it is that he or she is trying to accomplish when using the product—not baking a cake, but preparing a meal; not installing a transmission, but building an automobile.

There are at least three layers of increasingly greater depth in the analysis of customers for full marketing effectiveness:

1. *Looking beyond purchase behavior to use behavior.* Whatever reasons people have for buying (or not buying) a particular product are clearly rooted in how they use that product; and how well it serves the use to which they put it becomes particularly important at times of repurchase. Here focusing on the consumption system, though this is broader than the use of the particular product, does ensure that the use behavior of the consumer will not be overlooked since it has to be included as part of the consumption system.

2. *Deliberately studying the total consumption system for the sake of additional insights.* The use behavior for a particular product is bound to be affected not only by the problem to be solved or the task to be performed by the use of that product but also by the related products and related use behaviors that make up the total consumption system in which it plays a part; and these effects are subject to marketing applications.

3. *Analyzing the consumption system in the further detail of the many interrelated subsystems resulting from different kinds of people making different use of the same product or the same use of different products.* Here we can combine market segmentation with consumer motivation for maximum effectiveness. Because these different subsystems reflect the different goals that people have in using products to solve their problems or perform their tasks, it is possible to pinpoint marketing action to each individual subsystem and/or to reassemble such individual marketing actions into a coordinated master strategy.

Let us now look at these three layers of successively greater depth in more detail. As we shall see, many marketers already look at use behavior, and a number study the consumption system (sometimes without labeling it as such, sometimes in the narrower version of behavior patterns); but there are very few, if any, who carry their analysis to the ultimate step of interrelated subsystems.

USE BEHAVIOR

Many companies are sophisticated enough to realize that purchases are made not for the sake of the product but of the product's functions—that is, what the product will do in satisfying needs and wants. But unless they actually think in terms of *how* the consumer is using the product, they may slip into the error of taking product-oriented action. And one way of making use orientation inescapable is to think in terms of the consumption system in which the product plays a part.

Thus, a manufacturer of wristwatches will recognize that he is serving people's needs to know what time it is. Yet he might still concentrate on making his watch simply a better timekeeper for the money and pay major attention to the accuracy and dependability that lead people to buy or not buy his particular brand or model.

But the customers' need for such features depends, in turn, on the use to which they put watches in actual practice. First of all, what is the problem to be solved or the task to be performed: the scheduling of events, the organization of individual effort, the synchronization of related activities, the meeting of social obligations, or what? Second, what other products or services do people use to solve their time problem (e.g., clocks, bells, telephones, other people's actions or statements); and what are the circumstances (light, physical position, degree of hurry, presence of others,

nearness of clocks, and so on)? It could turn out, for example, that for most people it is more important to be able to read the time quickly and clearly than to have it actually measured to the precise second. In any event, understanding the use behaviors of watch wearers forces attention on the product features and selling appeals that will lead to more effective marketing.

TOTAL SYSTEM

However, if marketers only look at the use behavior for their particular product or service and do not go on to wring the full meaning out of the way that product fits into the total consumption system representing the wider problem or task which it is being used to solve or perform, they still may miss valuable leads to marketing action.

Consider the housewife. She uses many different systems as she goes about her household tasks—cleaning house, preparing food, laundering clothes, caring for the baby, getting ready to go out, and the like. Here the housewife, like other consumers, functions much as do other economic entities. She buys, transports, and changes raw materials into finished products in a sequence of events that is more or less efficient, more or less satisfying. Thus, a manufacturer who wants the housewife's "business" has to produce and sell a product which will, in meaningful ways, "plug into" the systems relevant to her. He has to have a practical understanding of what she is doing—the various products she uses, the different actions she takes—the total system in question.

Example. Here is a general description of the steps involved in laundering clothes. In studying this system, the reader should keep in mind that only a bare skeleton is being presented; for the system to be truly meaningful much more would have to be known about housewives' feelings, thoughts, and attitudes about what they are doing. (Some speculative marketing implications are added in parentheses simply to illustrate the kinds of possibilities.) The week's accumulation of laundry is sorted into piles. The housewife classifies the clothes to be processed, either by observation or by some predetermined set of "rules." Thus,

- Men's white shirts may be handled routinely, but an unusually soiled pair of trousers may require a decision to be made. The housewife may use such standards as appearance, soiling, wrinkling, odor, length of wearing, and type of cloth as bases for her decisions.

- Perhaps the man's shirts will be delivered to a Chinese laundry some distance away. (Here a special service is being used. Why is this service so unique? On the other hand, how much of a nuisance is it? Might the Chinese laundry begin pickup and delivery? Couldn't the large commercial laundries duplicate this type of laundering?)

- The sorting continues. (How distasteful is sorting to the housewife? Perhaps a powder to reduce odor and mildew in the laundry hamper would be useful. Or perhaps a method of precleaning clothes so that soaking is eliminated would be welcome. Could some kind of sorting rack attachment to an appliance facilitate the process?)

- White goods form one pile—sheets, pillowcases, towels, underwear, and so on. This requires hot water and bleach. Especially dirty spots may need individual attention with a brush. (Perhaps a tube of aerosol spray of a special cleaning substance could take care of these.)

- Another pile includes the colorful items—blouses, linen napkins, girls' frocks. These may or may not need hot water. They may possibly need a bit of mending. (Maybe a little laundry sewing kit would be handy for this.)

- Still another pile needs very special handling. Perhaps it includes socks, delicate undergarments, synthetics, woolens, to be subdivided into those needing cold water, warm water, hand washing, and so on. (Possibly the sink that has been designed out of laundry rooms still has its place after all.)

- Some things are to be dry cleaned—sent out or taken to a coin-operated machine. (When will home dry-cleaning machines be available? And will there be a market for them?)

Doing the laundry. The products that will be used must be at hand—often a messy array of boxes, bottles (glass and plastic), spray cans, and jars. Like an alchemist the woman will juggle an assortment that may include more than one brand of detergent, bluing, starch, bleach, water softener, fabric softener, spot remover, soap, and hand lotion! (Conceivably, there is room for an integrated line of laundry products with compatible ingredients and matched containers to help organize the array of cleaning staples.) Let's see how the system continues and note what other questions arise:

- Piles of clothes are put into the washing machine. Since the piles are of different volume and weight, there are problems in loading. Overloading is not uncommon; underloading is a wasteful irritation. (This problem has been solved by new models that adapt to smaller loads, but are there other refinements still possible?)

- There are different kinds of washing machines. The consumer has to judge which is best for her and then live with it. "I'd like one that does everything automatic, but my service man says those give more trouble, and that I'm better off with my simpler machine," is a statement commonly heard among housewives. (Clearly, reliability is still an area with marketing potential.)

- Nearby is the box of detergent. The giant box is a real chore to handle and to lug from the supermarket. (Volume delivery would seem a good solution; and perhaps home delivery of barrel-size containers would offer possibilities. Also, since laundries are such wet places, why don't they do something about the boxes that collapse? Plastic containers or plastic-bottom boxes would alleviate this problem.)

- Frequently the detergent is added to the wash by pouring from the box "about one cup." There is a general problem of imprecision; women are likely to overdo. (Perhaps the directions should be more explicit, or there should be warning lights or bells; and perhaps the detergent manufacturer could include measuring cups or one-cup automatic dispenser chutes.)

- What to do about bleach is a question that needs to be resolved. It is strong and threatening, but routinely useful; powder is safer, but possibly less effective. Bleach may be hard on clothes. It is disheartening to have clothes get frayed and threadbare. On the other hand, they will wear out and it is exciting to contemplate the possibility of a new garment. (The rapidity with which new types of bleaches enter the market indicates that there remains an unsatisfied need here.)

- Washing chores vary with the kind of machines women have—whether a washer-dryer, or separate appliances. As the process goes on, the clothes are spread around in different states of handling—dirty, wet, dry, ironed, waiting ironing from last time, poorly done pieces that need redoing, things that need touching up. (Laundries and utility rooms are not always well planned, even in new homes. There is still a market for intelligent architectural attention to working space and its organization. On the other hand, may there not also be a certain amount of pleasure in being ankle deep in clothes that are gradually working their way to cleanliness?)

- Dealing with lint is a problem. Lint removers (Scotch tape, sticky drums, and the like) for dry clothes, and lint removers in appliances are helpful, but still a bother. Washer and dryer lint traps are commonly neglected and may lead to mechanical problems. Many housewives end up washing dark things by hand to avoid lint. (Surely improvements are possible here.)

The housewife continues with the laundry task, perhaps also attending to children, preparation of meals, alert to clicks, buzzers, bells, agitator rhythm, and so on. Strangely enough, doing the home laundry is more complicated and more time-consuming than it used to be, owing to the proliferation of fabrics, machines, and washing ingredients. All the way through the system, many products are being used—softened water, implements, appliances, cleansers, aids—some casually, some with irritation, some with pleasure. Too much detergent may produce too many suds; too much softener makes the clothes feel too smooth (even "slimy"); too much bleach is a hazard; the iron may scorch; a pipe leaks; buttons pop off; the dryer burns too hot—but the result may be, to the housewife, a fragrant, warm, fluffy pile of gratified accomplishment.

This analysis of the home laundry system is meant only to be suggestive; a properly done, more intensive, detailed analysis would be voluminous. But, hopefully, even this overly general analysis does indicate how knowledge of the total system, more fully and carefully dissected, can alert the manufacturer to certain facts:

- The housewife is acting in an orderly or purposeful way, in the terms in which she defines her problems and tasks.
- There are a series of interrelated steps which require consumer decision making based on knowledge, expectations, and standards (as well as on ignorance, surprise, and uncertainty).
- Any laundry product is used with other products with which it must be compatible.

Questions arise from this type of analysis that point the way to new products or to a clearer understanding of consumer motivations by which old products can be marketed more effectively.

INTERRELATED SUBSYSTEMS

Many companies have gone quite far in another direction: identifying consumer groups, usually called market segments,

that have different characteristics which (a) make them particularly good prospects for different varieties of product or service and (b) make special product designs or marketing efforts directed at them enough more effective to more than repay the added cost of the specialization. But note how much more effective such segmentation can be if, again, it is tied not only into consumer characteristics (like income, geographic location, or education) but also into the different consumer goals that distinguish various consumption systems and subsystems.

Not only is every product (or service) part of some total consumption system, but also there are usually several distinct and definable subsystems in operation, because:

1. *Most problems can be solved with several different products,* and most tasks can be performed in several different ways. Think of the various activity patterns which are in operation merely in the process of washing men's shirts—by hand or machine at home, commercial laundry, the Laundromat, Chinese laundry, bachelor service, and so on.

2. *Different people have different goals in solving a problem or performing a task.* Thus,

- Our wristwatch manufacturer can focus on occupational use railroad engineers, executives, secretaries, night watchmen, and so on (with a different subsystem for each, if he finds it worthwhile to go that far). Or he can focus on social use, in which case he may find problems and opportunities among people who are obsessive about being on time (which suggests automatic timing devices) versus people who use time maturely as a way of relating to other people in a socially synchronized way (and just how they do it may give him clues to watches for children, cocktail wear, and jewelry adornment).

- Similarly, a manufacturer of a fabric softener will develop one kind of orientation if his interest is in consumption systems which relate to fabric protection. Longevity, resistance to weather and insects, odor, and hygiene—these will be the basic functions he will focus on. But if his interest primarily relates to fabric beautification, then softness, wrinkle resistance, color enhancement, and so on will be the functions of interest to him.

- A company in the petroleum industry will follow quite different courses depending on whether it sees itself as fitting into a system which provides power, automotive service, transportation facilitation, or, as some companies are tending, as part of a system involving a conveniently located channel of distribution for a variety of products.

3. *People have different goals for different parts of a total consumption system.* For example, a home gardener may want to cut his grass as painlessly and quickly as possible, but he may enjoy lavishing great care on his rose bushes.

Example. Now, see what happens when we combine all of these differences—people, products, and goals—into a network of subsystems. For this purpose let us develop our gardening example in detail.

Suppose there are three major types of gardeners: (a) owners of small properties, casual about gardening; (b) owners of small properties, careful about gardening; and (c) owners of large properties, casual about gardening. In real life, the lines would not be drawn so sharply, there would be much overlap, and there would be other types of gardeners; but let us assume that for practical purposes they comprise most of the market.

Further, let us take three kinds of gardening products—lawn mowers, sprinklers, and chemical sprays—and see how they fit into the three separate systems of the three major types of gardeners. Actually, the three consumer groups differ among themselves in the goals that they have for each of the products. Even more significantly, within each consumer group the gardeners have different goals for the three different products, springing from the different ways they use the products in their total gardening consumption systems. Thus, there is a constellation of goals in each case (in real life there would of course be as many more sets of goals as there would be different products or different uses involved).

Consider, first, the three different gardening systems for the three different types of gardeners (identified by the relative size of their property and their general attitude) as far as their lawns and roses are concerned:

- The small, casual gardener drags out the lawn mower when the grass begins to look untidy (to his wife, most likely), gets the job over with as quickly and easily as he can. But he loves and enjoys his roses, in part because they do not seem to call for the same effort, in part because they are more rewarding. So on other, more numerous occasions, he tends his roses, pruning them a little, raking around them a little; and if the bugs are eating the leaves, he will eagerly buy some chemical preparation and spray them, with much concern that he has the right brand. On still other occasions, when the grass looks dry (to his wife) or the roses look thirsty (to him), he'll do some watering, letting the spray cover grass and bushes alike.

- The small, careful gardener, however, will treat both his lawn and his roses with great care, on a planned schedule, with different amounts of care and different kinds of treatment for each. He is particular about having his grass just the right height—not letting it get so high it looks shaggy or cutting it so low it burns—but also varying it according to the season and weather. He applies his insecticide and does his watering before it is needed, being sure the spray doesn't wash the chemical off the roses, never watering the lawn in the heat of the sun, and doing a lot of deep soaking around the roots of the rose bushes. Note that he needs a watering device which will not just take care of the lawn but will be right, in a quite different application, also for the roses; that he will buy different kinds of chemicals, whose properties he knows from reading a horticultural magazine; and that it is more important for his lawn mower to have adjustable blades than to be easy and simple to use.

- As for the large, casual gardener, every Saturday morning (if he plays golf in the afternoon) or every Saturday afternoon (if he plays golf in the morning), he gets out his power mower and begins to enjoy the spectacle of himself riding up and down on his flashy steed. From time to time he dismounts, for a quick drink or to

get the watering started where he has just mowed, or both. Finally, he gives the roses a quick going over, not noticing the destructive work of the bugs unless it gets so bad that it mars the appearance of the total landscape—and then, if it does, he sends out impatiently, and with some annoyance, for something—anything—with which to spray them. He really enjoys the mowing, because it shows him off, but the roses are only a necessary background, and the watering is a nuisance.

Next, note that each of the three gardener types has a different set of goals for each of the three different products, depending on how he uses them; and even though all are gardeners, interested in lawns and roses, their use behavior for just this much of their total gardening add up to three times three, or nine, subsystems.

Now consider, more fully, some of the marketing implications of looking at gardening as a consumption system made up of consumption subsystems:

1. *Mention has already been made of the implications for product design* in the case of one product—lawn sprinklers. In the same way—but with different results, because the subsystems of consumption are different for the other two products—the insecticide manufacturer and the lawn mower manufacturer can design their products to fit the needs of the three major types of gardeners. There are also implications if any one of these manufacturers is thinking of diversifying into other products. If an insecticide manufacturer with a strong following in the small casual group wants to capitalize on this fact in the mower market, then he must have an economy-model mower to go with his high-quality spray.

2. *In the matter of distribution channels,* the same insecticide manufacturer faces a dilemma. His lawn mowers may sell through hardware stores and discount houses, but the same people who buy mowers there will go to a garden center for their rose bush sprays (for the sake of professional advice). His alternative, then, might be to expand his line of sprays and attract the small, careful group B, thus capitalizing on his position in that type of outlet. On the other hand, the manufacturer of lawn mowers bought principally by the small casual group could easily diversify into sprinklers, since they would be bought by the same people at the same kind of outlet.

3. *As for advertising,* there would be the same crisscross (in some cases, reinforcing, in other cases, conflicting) of quality and complexity versus economy and convenience. Involved would be not only the kinds of appeals to be used, but also the media to convey them, the amount of money to be spent, and even the timing. Manufacturers of lawn mowers and sprinklers for groups A and C would spend less on national advertising, more on cooperative advertising (with dealers) or promotion of sales in local newspapers. Manufacturers of insecticides would stress chemical quality, early in or ahead of the season, in horticultural journals, in order to reach group B; and do dealer promotion with garden centers during the season, for group A. And so on.

4. *In pricing, too,* the problems and opportunities for the nine subsystems would differ because of the different uses (and attendant goals) of the three market segments for the three products. The insecticide manufacturer can charge a high price for his product sold through garden centers to groups A and B, but he had better have a cheap product (under another brand

name, perhaps) for sale through hardware stores to group C. And the lawn mower manufacturer who observes many group A gardeners paying a high price for insecticides dare not conclude that these same gardeners will also pay a high price for his mowers.

The important point is that many of these insights would not result from generalizations either about market segments or product use, generalizations which would hide the sharp differences that become apparent from looking at the total consumption system and the nine subsystems corresponding to the three different products and the three different types of gardeners.

If one thinks of the consumer as operating a manufacturing process by which some end product emerges, it is easy to see that a variety of systems and subsystems would be in operation at any one time and that they would have some degree of relationship. While we have no desire to complicate the system concept further by introducing the notion of still wider systems, it is important for any seller to go far enough in his thinking to relate one consumption system to any wider systems which exist and which have an important effect on the operation of the system in which he has an immediate interest. For example, a marketer would be ill-advised to define a consumption system for a gardening product without recognizing that this system is related to and dependent on a wider system of acts and ideas pertaining to the whole changing pattern of leisure time in this country.

INDUSTRIAL PRODUCTS

Systems for industrial products are in some ways easier to specify if only because they are more precise and logical in their operation. It can be well argued that anyone producing an industrial good should develop a system which starts with the consumer and moves all the way back to the production of the goods that, in turn, produce the goods (and so on) which are consumed by the consumer. The producer of industrial goods or supplies can typically be more successful if he helps his potential customers "create a customer." To do this requires that he understand the (relative) totality of the system even if, at best, he learns this primarily from research done by customers.

At the very minimum, a seller of an industrial product should concern himself with "where" his product fits into the manufacturing process of his potential customers. It must be compatible with prior parts of the process as well as with subsequent steps. Any change in any part of the process is likely to have an effect on all other parts—a fact that the manufacturer selling into the system must keep in mind. He can better protect against obsolescence, as well as do a better job of selling, if he knows his constraints; that is, if he understands the needs of the system.

Take, for example, the manufacturer of plastic materials designed to be used in the packaging of food: This manufacturer would—or should—be concerned with a protection system which would solve such problems as spoilage, prevention of color fading, shrinkage, product visibility, and ease of storage and shipment. To market his product effectively, he would have to know and understand the various production systems currently in use by manufacturers of different food products: for example, fresh fruit and vegetables, smoked meats, poultry, fish and seafood, and cheese. In addition he would have to know the distribution systems in use, including physical handling, shipment, storage, shelf life, ex-

posure to store traffic, markups, and amount of handling. Further, he would be interested in the consumer system that the product is a part of, including place of storage, product life span in terms of replacement rate, and need for resealing.

As an actual case in point, the Cryovac Division of W. R. Grace & Company developed a vacuum-sealing process which in actuality was a major component of the total production, distribution, and consumer systems for meat, poultry, cheese, and fish. Since the Cryovac process necessitated the use of manual or automatic machines, company salesmen had to perform such activities as helping train labor, helping in the promotion of Cryovac-wrapped products to the trade, and helping to show how to install a product line using the Cryovac process.

Agricultural machinery also illustrates the value of the system concept, although there is little to suggest that most such manufacturers have applied themselves diligently to learning about the various farm systems in effect. With the growth in the number of large farms, we find many analogies between farming and manufacturing. More and more machinery is being required to displace high-cost labor. Yet it is doubtful if many manufacturers consider the farm as a systematic production unit and have studied the nature of the job to be done (for instance, on a time and motion basis) to determine the most efficient "factory layout" and machinery required.

On the other hand, farm machines have been developed which represent integral systems unto themselves. Some of these machines might have been developed earlier if manufacturers had analyzed the total process. Take, for example, the harvesting of corn: Until recently the corn combine piece of machinery was limited to harvesting shelled corn in either a moist or dry state. Corn cobs were left in the field. Such a machine, of course, represented a radical improvement over earlier machines, since it picked and shelled, whereas previously, different machines were required. Now corn can be picked, shelled, and mixed or combined in the form of whole shelled corn with broken cobs by a single machine. In fact, some machinery manufacturers sell in terms of "systems" which require the use of two or more pieces of machinery to do a total job. Thus, in corn harvesting, one can by the addition of a dryer, a wagon dump, a chuck (storage) wagon, and escalators (for moving corn into the bins) complete the entire process with one basic machine.

In the past few years, the agricultural industry has experienced substantial unrest caused by the innovative tactics of smaller firms versus the giants who have continued largely to sell machinery on a dollar-per-pound-of-iron basis. Much of this new machinery gives evidence that the inventors understand, at least pragmatically, the nature and functioning of the system approach. Thus, for example, a new ingenious mechanized potato harvester has been developed that permits a crew of 8 to do the work of 30 diggers.

MARKETING DECISIONS

The analysis of consumption systems should be helpful to the management of a firm in many ways. It can serve to identify more precisely the company's corporate objectives, construct a plan of action, organize to carry out the plan (including finance, R&D, and production as well as marketing), and set up a control-reappraisal system. Here, however, we will discuss the relation of consumption systems to marketing strategy and gather together a few of

the more important implications to show how this focus on consumption systems helps to enrich and coordinate various planning and decision-making areas in marketing.

Product and Product Line

When the manufacturer knows and keeps current the details of the consumption systems pertinent to his products, then he is in a better position to assess opportunities (perhaps he can meet housewife standards with a new or modified product) as well as threats (for example, the development of new washing machines which clean by vibration). We can also assume that a knowledge of the more important systems will help him to innovate, or at least provide him with a better understanding of the chances to innovate. The part his product plays in the total system, when made reasonably explicit, should enable him to gain a better understanding of his role in the consumer's life. Further, he has a point of reference from which to judge how the passage of time and the actions of his competitors may be changing the system. Consequently, he will be better able to spot new opportunities as they arise.

More often than not, innovations are actually little more than a rearrangement or collapsing of the parts of a given system. This rearrangement usually represents an easier, or less costly, or more attractive, or more efficient way of solving the basic need. In most cases, the rearrangement of steps involves combining and shortening. Most consumer goods innovations have, in recent years, been of this type. Many new products have been created when several "specialized" products have been combined into one. Thus:

- A classic example is in the home laundry field where detergents, bluing, and softeners have been combined.
- Combination has been accomplished with a number of food products such as ready-to-eat cereals with sugar added, lemon-flavored sugar lumps for tea, frozen vegetables with butter sauce, cake mixes which include eggs, and, of course, precooked meals.
- In the world of machines for use in the home, the electric refrigerator with automatic defrosting, the gas or electric stove with its automatic timer, the radios and hi-fi sets which turn themselves off, the TV sets with their armchair controls, and the garage doors that open on signal, all are examples of admirable ingenuity that did not require tapping novel scientific principles.
- The car has been the locale of many innovations, all involving a shortening of steps—automatic transmissions, longer greasing intervals, more miles to an oil change, push-button window washers, to note a few.
- The innovations in cameras have centered recently around doing away with the light meter, the range finder, and even the developer as separate parts of the system.

If a manufacturer knows where his product fits into the steps in a system, he can better estimate the possibility of effecting innovation. This is accomplished by an examination of the steps prior to and subsequent to the point at which the product in question enters the system. He can frequently estimate the vulnerability of his current product by evaluating the other products which enter the system before and after his own product or are used in direct conjunction with it. Innovation by reaching back or by reaching forward in the system is, as has been stressed earlier, a common fact of life.

Research and development personnel need such a precise frame of reference within which to work. Knowledge of the steps in the individual consumption systems as well as the variety of alternative systems employed should provide them with the challenge, as well as the operational objectives, they so badly need. Assessing what they can do, both with current technology and with the future technological changes, can help them provide the company with a higher return on R&D investments.

It is important, also, not to let one's thinking become too behavioristic. Just analyzing the mechanical steps in a system may not in itself generate useful ideas. In analyzing any consumption system, the engineer should think about the "problem" that users may feel at any given point. People are not always looking for efficiency, economy, and the like, as most impersonal analyses tend to assume. They may want distraction, aesthetics, individual expressiveness, pretentiousness, speed, and quiet.

Advertising Strategy

Advertising effectiveness obviously depends on the availability of a considerable amount of detailed information which will permit the determination of the role to be played by advertising, the advertising objectives, the proper choice of advertising copy, the coordination of advertising with other sales promotion activities, and the preparation of the advertising budget. Since consumers typically think in terms of product functions subjectively, and concern themselves with the ways in which products fit into their activities, it would seem that the systems approach would prove extremely helpful in advertising—if only because it presents a unified picture of the process by which a given task is accomplished, including the rationale, standards, and emotions involved. At the least such a wholeness would help the advertiser see his product in relation to the total operation, to see its relative importance to other products used in the system, to understand more fully what its real contribution is to the user, and to learn more about why it is used.

Knowing the point of entry of the product into the consumption pattern makes the appropriate appeals more apparent. It poses this question: What is the unique role the product plays in bridging the gap between prior and subsequent steps? Sometimes after analysis of the true action system, rather than the presumed, an advertiser may call for changes in his appeals that go counter to the overly generalized beliefs about consumer behavior that are accepted in his industry. Here are two examples:

1. The decision to sell fresh chilled orange juice as a "refreshing drink always available from your refrigerator" is a case in point. But an analysis of the consumption system for fresh squeezed juice shows obstacles to this idea. Housewives typically serve juice in small glasses and have not prepared it in quantities to be stored. They regard it as precious. Also it is acid in content, they believe; too much is not healthy. And if it stands, its value declines. In the light of this analysis, what should the advertiser do to modify the situation?

2. Aiming Gleem toothpaste at "people who can't brush after every meal" represents an interesting recognition and ex-

ploration of an actual system with which many people feel uncomfortable because it is not the sanctioned system. The TV situations showing why a busy life precludes brushing after every meal are ones with which the housewife can readily identify. Here the advertiser is adapting to reality.

Pricing Policy

As part of solving his price problems, the manufacturer explores the preferences and educability of his consumers. An analysis of the consumer systems employing his products will be extremely helpful. If, for example, a "new" product has little effect on the totality of the way consumption is currently organized in terms of time, general cost, and final satisfaction in the goal, there is little reason to believe that it will command a premium price. All too often the manufacturer exaggerates the importance of his new item, failing to realize that it is but a very small part of a ramified pattern.

Conversely, he may underestimate the importance of a small item which actually may have much to offer in a lengthy or relatively unpleasant system. Here is an interesting illustration:

A manufacturer of point-of-sale displays used at trade shows and conventions designed a prefabricated unit consisting of a number of panels that could be locked together with fiber plugs. The appearance of this prefab unit was equal to that of the highest priced wooden displays and could be set up by two men in less than one hour.

Rather than take essentially a cost approach to the problem of what initial price to charge for such a new unit, this manufacturer would have been well advised to study the consumption system for all such units and determine what effect the prefab unit would have on the total system. The costs and time involved in the selling process, the shipping costs (from one show to another), the deterioration owing to improper handling during shipment, the assembly time at the convention site, the dismantling time, the frequency and extent of refurbishing—all these and other components should be analyzed before an attempt is made to arrive at a "best" market price.

Pricing may also be related to the expected life span of a product. Instead of waiting to see how long an object lasts in wear, manufacturers should maintain an up-to-date, ongoing knowledge of how well and how long the product keeps functioning in the system. A far more realistic pricing strategy will be the result.

Personal selling

The salesman's role or mission is changing in many firms—especially those selling technical products to industry. More and more, he is looked upon as a communication link between the seller and the marketplace. Increasingly, he is the "feedback" agent as to what the market wants and needs, as well as being the vertical thrust agent who sells the product. It is obvious that to execute these roles with efficiency requires an understanding on his part of the systematic process facilitated by his product. For example:

A salesman selling building materials must be able to demonstrate to architects, contractors, and engineers that his product is not only compatible with other products in the system, but that it is not at odds with the human factors which may be involved, for instance, existing skills of labor.

House-to-house and route salesmen should be aware of the characteristic ongoing patterns of living they are attempting to break into. A route man is asking an established system to alter and make a position for him in the stream of events. Thus,

A study for the Jewel Tea Company by Social Research, Inc., found that a large number of "customers wanted a route man who was friendly, congenial but 'not too nice,' submissive, and conforming to requests and routines. He should be sensitive to the amount of socializing desired by the customer, allow her to set the pace, and then follow it quickly and willingly. He should follow a regular schedule of visits."

CONCLUSION

An analysis of consumption systems should provide manufacturers with data which are useful in many marketing decision areas. Such analyses give a perspective of the process by which consumers satisfy their basic wants and needs; they make available a framework within which the company can exercise its imagination in product innovation, in advertising strategy development, in pricing policy, and in sales activities.

But systems can only be understood if they are seen as a series of interlocking steps. This coherent, connected view avoids the distortion resulting from studying bits and pieces of market information which are the usual fare of the marketer. In particular, the systems approach should facilitate innovation, since most "new" products are new only in the sense that they are a combination of products used in two or more steps in a system.

Today's rapidly increasing expenditures for R&D require that the efforts of creative personnel be directed toward obtainable and meaningful innovations. These can best be achieved through an understanding of consumer systems relevant to their companies' products. Such an approach should be welcomed by technical personnel once they are trained to think along such lines.

REFERENCE

Drucker, P. F. (1954). *The practice of management.* New York: Harper.

Chapter 48

FOCUS GROUPS
Mixed Blessing

Sidney J. Levy

The focus group interview is a very fashionable method of gathering marketing research information. This vogue has grown rapidly in recent years. It is so popular that in many minds it is synonymous with qualitative research and is commonly the only qualitative method used. The basic idea of the focus group is a simple one. A group of people is brought together to discuss some certain topics, commonly for 1 to 2 hours. The interviewer—leader, moderator—raises various issues, focusing the discussion on matters of interest to the researcher (and the client) in accordance with an outline or general guide.

GATHERING THE GROUP

In convening a focus group, it is necessary to think about how many people should be present, who they should be, how they are chosen and recruited, and where the meeting should be held.

The optimal size of a focus group is usually taken to be about 8 people. Actual group sizes range down from 15 people. Generally speaking, 4, 5, or 6 are too few people: The conversation may seem somewhat concentrated, too easily turning on the willingness of one or two to do most of the talking.

This chapter was first presented as a talk before the Bank Marketing Association Conference, 1973.

The participants are more likely to feel exposed, on the spot, excessively pressed to participate whether ready or not. The discussion is especially vulnerable to the personalities and biases of the few individuals present and therefore may be too narrow in consideration of the topic. Nevertheless, on the logic that it is wasteful to have groups with people who don't get the chance to talk much, some (Super) groups are deliberately set up to include only three people (a triad), or even two, selected for being known as willing and voluble and therefore good informants.

At the larger end, 10 or 12 people tend to be too many. As the group grows in size, opportunities for each person to talk decline, people have to wait more for their turns and are frustrated by more views that they have less chance to respond to. They are also more widely dispersed in the room or around the table. The tendency for the group to fragment becomes great, and, as a result, the problems of controlling the conversation are magnified. There are likely to be distractions, frequent murmuring, dissipation of remarks in side conversations, sly antagonisms. The moderator is pressed toward the role of disciplinarian and classroom behavior, cautioning the group to be quiet, asking for a show of hands, questioning individuals in turn to be sure everyone gets a vote. These problems grow without necessarily enlarging the pool of information or range of themes that emerge.

The exact number of people that will attend is often unpredictable. Twelve are invited in hopes that eight will come, but all twelve may come. Ten are invited and only six show up. In more than one instance, no one has arrived.

The composition of the group is based on the research problem. Sometimes a varied group is wanted, for the interplay of diverse views on a topic that all can discuss. For example, a group with both men and women, young and mature, can talk about the new bank automatic tellers in a lively, interactive way. However, sharp diversity or division in the group is hazardous. Consider housewives and career women in one group, discussing cooking for the family; or a mixture of slim, young upper-status North Shore matrons and a few stout ethnic mamas talking about budgeting; or a few technical minded plant engineers meeting with a few lawyers on the subject of personal financial planning. Perhaps the results are potentially intriguing—but they are more likely to be a fiasco as the participants struggle to find some common ground or fight battles of age, sex, and class differences.

Usually, the group is selected to be a relatively homogeneous one, brought together because of some unifying element out of which the discussion can grow: dog owners, people without checking accounts, people unfamiliar with a new appliance, mothers of infants, and so on. Excessively narrow homogeneity is also a problem, as the more precise the quota or rare the type sought, the harder it is to set up the group.

Groups are gathered in a variety of ways. Sometimes telephone screening is used. Field workers may just inquire around for people who fit the quota; frequently, potential respondents are solicited in central locations (malls) where focus groups facilities are located. A list of people may be provided by the client. Field organizations have usually accumulated files of respondents with known characteristics that can be drawn upon. To avoid failures, some researchers carry out a secret search for verbal people. The problem of no-shows is handled by desperate last-minute calling around, by overrecruiting, and sometimes by having reliable contingency friends in the wings.

The location of focus group interviews can be almost anywhere convenient. In earlier days they were often held in such settings as a moderator's home, a respondent's home, an advertising agency conference room, the client's office. Hotels, motels, meeting rooms at churches, fraternal organizations, and "Ys" have been used. Marketing research organizations or units in advertising agencies nowadays usually have special facilities, or access to behavioral science laboratories, where viewing through a one-way mirror can go on, as well as audio-and/or videotaping. Many places can accommodate a relative crowd of watchers who want to observe; sometimes there are as many as two or three times the number of people being watched! Ordinarily, it is useful to have a kitchen area adjacent, whether for products that are being tested, or to be able to serve coffee, lunch, dinner, to the group. A main general need is finding a locale that is quiet enough to permit a good taping of the sessions. It is easy to forget that street noises, children playing, nearby typewriters, may not hurt the discussion but can hamper the recording.

CONDUCTING THE GROUP

It is apparent that there is no one best way to conduct a focus interview. The people who conduct them are often interviewers who have learned how to do it from their experience, not from any literature on successful discussion techniques.

First comes the introduction of the topic. A most fruitful approach is to have a somewhat chatty beginning by the moderator.

Too fast a start does not let the group settle down a bit, relax, get oriented, begin to pay attention. To accomplish a comfortable start, it may seem better if the moderator does not have a canned opening but explains the subject of the meeting in his words. Then again, a formal statement can set a useful tone of serious, work-orientedness about the matter at hand. Clients and researchers are often anxious about the opening and often try to overcontrol the moderator. They should realize that good discussions are not dictated or forced, and a relaxed, good-natured atmosphere is most conducive to self-expression.

To avoid preoccupation with guessing the "true" purpose of the meeting, as much candor as is feasible should be used in telling the subject matter to be discussed. However, only general terms are necessary, as telling specifically *why* the information is being sought usually distracts the respondents, leading them to short-cut the conversation by focusing too much on being helpful and trying to tell the client what to do about his problem. Of course, they will try to do that anyway, whenever they think they know what the problem is.

A good moderator stays on top of the discussion, striking a balance between friendly permissiveness and the directness needed to keep the discussion focused and moving along. The moderator has to be willing to retire and allow participants to talk to each other, moving in and out as the relevance of the conversation requires. Relevance is not always easy to judge on the spot as a speaker works around his point, so patience is required. But the time constraint is sharp, especially as there is a tendency to overload the discussion with too many topics "as long as we've got the group."

Fear of losing rapport commonly makes moderators overindulgent, leading to repetition of ideas, whereas most groups respond well to lively leadership that keeps the talking vigorous by intervening when needed. Mere technique is insufficient: Interest in the topic and alert listening by the moderator are the important means, not artificial animation.

The emotionality of groups is a curious feature. Some are determined and sturdy; a buoyant conversation will go on as if it hardly matters what the moderator does. Some groups are delicate and fragile, needing wooing and encouragement. In other instances, the chemistry is awful, a creeping lethargy takes hold, the liveliest response is apathy, and the situation may be hopeless. Sometimes it can be rescued by "blasting," that is, raising the most dramatic or controversial aspect; by shifting gears and calling for a break; or by confronting the problem by exploring why the group seems to be uninterested. Not infrequently groups are overstimulated, so giddy with the novelty, the attention, the rewards, the social situation, their self-consciousness, or the absurdity of discussing some unlikely topic for 2 hours that a contagious hilarity takes hold, with exaggerated comments and hysterical laughter. These reactions need interfering with, perhaps by shifting attention to something about the physical arrangements, the taping, a comment about getting "back to work," or again, examining the reaction itself, asking why the topic seems so funny.

After concluding the session, it may be useful to keep the tape recorder running as the group breaks up. In this postsession freedom, respondents often make relevant or insightful remarks about what has transpired.

The moderator is like a conductor, orchestrating an improvisation. The task calls for adeptness and awareness of what is going on, what people are doing and feeling. It means giving everyone a chance without taking dull roll calls. Tact is needed to hold down the rusher who wants to say everything about the topic all at once. The good moderator is prepared for this, ready to extract from the overflow one of the issues for discussion, while deferring the others. A major challenge is control of the dominating person, whether an eager, a know-it-all, or a garrulous one lacking terminal facilities, without withering his or her cooperation. It is too easy to shut people up, so that they withdraw and refuse to contribute further. The moderator has to respect the participants' sensibilities and know when she can get away with a blunt, good-natured "Will you please shut up?" or "Let's hold it down," or "Not everybody at once." Special skill is needed to make judicious interruptions, responding to speakers while also cutting them off, so that they feel their point has been made and the floor can be yielded to others.

Questions often arise about matters other than the behavior of the moderator. For example, what is the effect of tape recording? Usually people take recording in stride. It is common, familiar, and lends gratifying importance to the activity. The tape recorder serves as a kind of assistant to the moderator, as it can be appealed to in calls for order, the need to have people keep just one conversation going. In general, it is best to deal matter-of-factly with taping, not to make an issue of it, nor to play back people's voices in hope of reassuring them, as they find themselves unnatural. Videotaping is less usual and an elaborate idea; it arouses more self-consciousness and anxiety about one's appearance, uncertainty that one has come to the meeting properly dressed or with hair done right, suggesting more exposure, less anonymity. It is also flattering to be "on television," although the moderator may have to be prepared to explain what will be done with the videotape if people worry about where they will later be viewed.

The role of client participation also raises questions, as it can be a troublesome issue. It is a topic that needs a good understanding before the meeting. If client personnel attend, the simplest way is for them to be unseen and unheard in another room, and that is commonly the case. Often, these viewers send in notes with their thoughts and follow-up questions; or transmit these to an earphone worn by the moderator. It is customary to tell the respondents that there are observers; usually this fact recedes into the background unless something happens to remind.

JUSTIFYING THE APPROACH

Group interviewing came about as an evolution of the interest in qualitative behavioral research. As individual respondents were rescued from being merely ciphers and tabular inputs, their patterns of views, attitudes, and feelings became important to the search for psychological insight. The depth interview depends not on having a systematic interrogation but on giving the respondent a chance to talk freely. It was a reasonable extension to conceive of interviewing several respondents at once. The practical necessity for doing this arose when seeking reactions to television commercials or to new products too cumbersome to carry around from door to door. In such instances, the value of a small manageable audience was evident, especially if an illuminating conversation were held in addition to polling members of the audience. In short order, other benefits, both real and imagined, fueled the surge of interest in focus group interviews. Four central ideas are especially powerful.

It is a common fallacy that group interviewing is economical. The economy idea has a face plausibility, given the ratio of respondents to interviewers; it is as if several interviews are being accomplished in the same time it would take to do only one or two. In fact, however, for several reasons the cost of a group is likely to be greater than that of interviewing all members individually. The respondents are usually paid more to cooperate, with rates ranging easily up to $50 or more, depending on how precious or hard to get they are. The expense to recruit respondents may be $50 a person. The respondents will be fed, the facility needs to be rented, taping is extra, and so on. Experienced moderators (not the research analyst) can cost hundreds of dollars; and they need helpers to serve as receptionists, baby sitters, kitchen workers, and so on at various rates per hour. The more popular focus grouping becomes, the more these costs rise. Commonly, the analysis and report writing are prepared by another research worker. When professional analytic time for report preparation is added, a report on a group of 8 to 10 respondents could easily run $10,000—all depending on who is doing it for whom, and how much it can be marked up for that client, with some significant savings for running more than one group.

The credibility of a group discussion is almost magically reassuring. A group of people chatting seems more natural than an individual being interviewed. It is easy to imagine that the participants are more likely to come out with what is truly on their minds. The interaction is viewed as multiplicative, making each respondent a richer source of information than he or she would be alone. Also, greater confidence in the results obviates doing more research. Groups are cheap if they are substituted for a large-scale survey. It has been observed that results of a group discussion will be accepted and acted upon with important decisions by people who would never be content with a research report based on the responses of the same number of people individually interviewed. The issue is not quantity of data, as eight people talking for an hour each provide more data than eight people talking to one another for 2 hours, but the supposed greater validity that has been gained.

Clients like to participate in groups. A most distinctive advantage of focus groups is the chance for clients—marketing managers, advertising agency creative personnel, R&D engineers—to join and, at times, to bypass the research personnel by directly seeing and hearing respondents conveniently gathered together where they can be observed. In this way, they feel they are getting quick results, the participation, stimulation, and sense of conviction gained from perceiving the live expression of opinions. They enjoy not having to rely on the intervening analysis of a research report. Often, getting to attend focus groups in various cities is a kind of boondoggle; more than one focus group was held in a city because of its great restaurants.

Focus groups are quick. When managers commit to research, often after long delays, they want the results quickly. Focus groups can often be scheduled soon and be done in short order. In addition, having watched a group, the viewers are often confirmed in their prior judgments, or think they have gained the insight they sought, and feel no need for further analysis or report, gaining economy in cost as well as time.

These three features—economy, faith in the group, and client participation—have led to groups being widely used (and misused) as the method of choice. Focus groups are best used when indicated by the results to be gained from their special nature.

A basic value of the focus group is the opportunity for multiple interactions. A good interview makes use of that fact to learn about the social dynamics and immediate interpersonal features of the topic at issue. That might include how people talk about it in conversation, their vocabulary, phrases, inflections, and so on, as these are informally stimulated. An interviewer can do this in a personal interview, and does, but in a group another respondent may seem to offer more realistic or more casual cues and modes of expression. Also, a provocative member of the group is not accused of the sin of "leading the respondent," as an interviewer might be. As part of the interaction, respondents may be moved to challenge and defend their views with relative spontaneity. The researchers can observe how controversy comes up and how it is resolved.

Each group meeting usually develops a characteristic social tone concerning the subject being discussed, illuminating its significance as a social topic. It is useful to observe whether people can exchange views easily and fluently or whether the subject is socially awkward. Is it exciting, interesting, sobering, readily made absurd, does anger build? Or perhaps uncertainty, wariness, tentativeness seem to dominate.

A focus group discussion is especially useful for gaining a quick overview of main themes, points, issues, variables, and so on that are to be structured into a questionnaire or other subsequent study design.

A focus group is especially valuable for discussion of trends that are social, economic, and style-oriented. As the individuals will usually represent different points of view and points on the trend continuum, their interaction can highlight the interplay of these points. This will be more obvious with a heterogeneous group, and perhaps an interesting, subtler matter with a supposedly homogeneous group.

Given different knowledge about a subject among the members of the group, they will learn from one another, showing something of how information and attitudes are absorbed or resisted.

The social facilitation of a focus group can be useful when the participants' awareness of common ideas, problems, and emotions stimulates a freer expression than might otherwise happen. This suggests that a focus group is potentially a therapeutic experience, making it necessary to interpret the results with some care, as the marketer's interest might not find the same reactions out in the market under more ordinary circumstances.

There are other cautions that should be offered, as argument against the use of focus groups, especially when they are substituted for using any other research approaches. In their current popularity, they are overused, as some market researchers are inclined to use them for almost every project, with inadequate attention or weight given to their limitations or shortcomings.

DRAWBACKS

A true focus group session does not consist of several people being interviewed individually but concurrently. A major obstacle to achieving a fruitful conversation is the "surveyor's urge" to get a vote from everyone, or to inquire about consensus: "Do you all agree, then?" Meetings are often wasted by being run in that manner, not with a conversation going on among the members, but with each one being asked in turn to voice a response to a specific question. Some of that may be necessary and helpful, but when a good discussion gets going, which is the goal, it is a mistake to expect an intensive exploration of each person's pattern of background, experience, outlook, attitudes, choices, and so on. Such patterns are visible in pieces but cannot be pursued as they would be in an individual depth interview.

Each group has a certain composition and a life of its own that has to be allowed to function if it is to achieve its best results. Given this fact, problems can also arise that can interfere with getting the information one is seeking despite the skill and competence of the moderator. As noted, there are usually more dominant members, and others who refuse to be drawn out in public. Whether opinionated, knowledgeable, or merely gabby, the more vocal people are useful, often providing just what the discussion needs. Then again, they have been known to kill it. The others in the group may be so intimidated, angered, overwhelmed, or persuaded, that despite the leader's best efforts, they will not speak up.

There is only so much time available for the meeting. The whole group is thus at the mercy of the latecomers and the slow talkers. Highly idiosyncratic behaviors or ideas are sometimes expressed that take up a disproportionate amount of time and are not useful to the general discussion.

Regardless of focusing and skillful management, systematic coverage of the topics at issue may not be possible. Focus group interviews often have much repetition, get hung up on certain issues, and may not permit a balanced analysis. It is thus sometimes hard to say what kind of cross-section of information is represented by the content of one or two group sessions.

Analysis of the discussion is hindered by problems in identifying who said what, or in relating later comments to earlier comments by the same person. A researcher listening to an audiotaped discussion usually loses a great deal of material due to mutterings, noise, simultaneous talking, changing of tapes, to say nothing of those gruesome occasions when there turns out to be nothing at all on the tape or its backup.

Focus groups seem able to discuss just about anything, including men's underwear, feminine hygiene, and personal finances. Nevertheless, many people are inhibited by the public nature of the group, and it often seems the harder way to explore private topics. Also, on any topic, pressure to talk, on the one hand, and to give others the floor as well, may interfere with getting into various kinds of details that need a more relaxed and reflective atmosphere. To the extent that the asset of a focus group is its heightened social immediacy, it should not be used when the social aspect is undesirable. Social competition, exhibitionism, problems in self-esteem, veneer, histrionics, negativism, compliance, and so on, can unduly complicate the analysis by the distortions they introduce.

The foregoing drawbacks and analogous problems may afflict any research method. But the risk in focus interviewing is relatively great, as so many eggs are being put in one basket. Just as any one individual interview can be a poor one, a relative failure, so can a group discussion. Quality variation is less important within 100 interviews, but it is a truly dismal experience when perhaps only one or two groups have been scheduled, and when many watchers are involved, including an eager and then disappointed or angry client. Forewarning of this possibility is useful, to foster realism by anticipating that the group may not work out very well, but the loss remains.

It is evident that the focus group interview is a complex technique with many pros and cons, more so than its widespread use might suggest. Like most tools, it can be used casually or more rigorously. This discussion is designed to air some of the relevant issues, so that practitioners and managers can assess the potential value to them of this particular research method.

Chapter 49

MUSINGS OF A RESEARCHER
The Human Side of Interviewing

Sidney J. Levy

The growth in volume of marketing research puts strain on the interviewing resources of the country. Recruiting, training, controlling, and evaluating interviewers are tasks that make special demands on those who handle fieldwork. The researcher-interviewer interface is one that has not been much explored, and my purpose is to express informally some ideas stimulated by the problems of understanding the human situation in the field.

As a start, my thoughts turn in a reminiscent direction, wandering back to the early days of working on qualitative research at Social Research, Inc. Thinking idly about interviewing and interviewers, I remember Mrs. Burlun. Mrs. Burlun was a squat, cheery woman of about 60. Her daughter started interviewing for us, and then along came Mrs. Burlun. Mrs. Burlun did not know that we did "motivation research"; it wasn't called that then. She didn't fret about whether asking people questions was immoral, unethical, or intrusive. Normally, she did not even understand me when I would explain a project to the interviewers. Afterward, her daughter would explain more clearly what I wanted. But Mrs. Burlun had hold of certain basic ideas very well. She met her quotas, usually on time; she asked the questions as they were written and wrote down the answers as they were given, briefly or fully and with characteristic idiomatic expressions. There was

This chapter was first presented as a talk before the Marketing Research Association in Chicago, 1975.

never any worry as to whether Mrs. Burlun asked all the questions or interviewed the people she had said she did. *Validation* was no problem with Mrs. Burlun because she wanted to do what was right.

After Mrs. Burlun I remember Mrs. Smith. A quick, vigorous woman, she said she liked interviewing because she came from the Western mountains and wanted outdoor air. When Mrs. Smith interviewed a housewife, she went after her like a terrier, exploring remarkably a richness of personal anecdotes. Rarely was there a remark that might arouse an unanswered speculation in the mind of a frustrated research analyst, since the remark would also arouse questions in Mrs. Smith's mind and she pursued them inquisitively. We felt we knew Mrs. Smith's respondents like intimates and relatives; and they may well have found the experience therapeutic. Mrs. Smith didn't need to be told to *Probe,* because she wanted to know, too.

A third great lady of the interviewing trade was Madge Miller. She was a big round woman and candid about it; and a very moral person—maybe not the best one to send out on a liquor study. She baffled me because when she came into the office I had the impression she never stopped talking, making me wonder how her informants ever got a word in edgewise. Nevertheless, her interviews were voluminous records of detailed discussions of the research topics. Somehow, she rarely found respondents who had very little to say because her desire to tell us what they had said was so great that most of her interviews were like herself, plump with words. There was no need to tell Madge Miller to *Report Verbatim*; she knew no other way. We should honor the memory of Madge Miller.

I think about these women and the many other interviewers I have known over the years. Their handwriting ranges from crys-

tal clear to interviews that go unread and wasted—and bless those who type. Interviewers come in every conceivable size, shape, hairdo, and education. It is apparent that there is no one kind of good interviewer. Of course, one may set up optimally desirable qualifications. The field director I rely on the most, Leone Phillips, recently listed the following qualifications for an interviewer:

> She should be healthy, active, energetic, intelligent, have a sense of humor, be tactful, persistent, adaptable, tolerant, interested in people, with a sense of responsibility, careful attention to details, and so on. She should be 25 to 55 years, have 20 hours available including A.M., P.M., and weekends, have High School or better, a car, legible handwriting, stenographic skills, membership in organizations. She should be willing to work on demand for a relatively low hourly rate.

Frankly, I have met such a woman (age 23) only once in my life, and I married her. (N.B.: 46 years ago. SJL) In addition to marveling at the diversity of interviewers, I also think about the goals of marketing research organizations. These include serving clients and associates by gathering information and processing it either into tables or verbal conclusions. The wish and hope are to do these things competently, efficiently, accurately, and economically, as well as imaginatively and insightfully. The trouble is that involved in the enterprises are two groups known as interviewers and researchers. A great deal of energy goes into the relationship between researchers and interviewers, and often there is much tension in this relationship. As we all recognize, dimly or sharply, this tension comes about because researchers are very eager to impress upon interviewers that they should be honest, careful, precise, closely attentive to instructions and the wording of questions; while interviewers are very eager to impress upon researchers that interviewing is in general impossible, that the questions are poorly worded, and that any new techniques included are an insult to human intelligence. The researcher is restlessly anxious because "God knows what is going on out in the Field"; while the interviewer is inclined to agree with Nancy Cooley that complex questionnaires developed by brilliant analysts without actual interviewing experience are the biggest problems in market research interviewing today. The interviewer doubts that such long lists of repetitive items are really essential; while the researcher thinks "I've got troubles of my own explaining to the client why the study is going to be late, why one city looks as though the interviewers must have tipped the respondents to the sponsor's brand name—and why are so many respondents always being interrupted by babies and telephone calls?"

In short, the interviewer wonders why researchers must be so demanding and unreasonable; and the researcher wonders why this array of individuals, with all their individuality, has to intervene themselves between those lovely respondents and the research report. My favorite field director recently commented, "I am continuously amazed at the little awareness and tolerance research people have for the problems interviewers face in the field."

I mention these issues without offering any solution, since I don't think the situation is going to change readily. I think interviewers must reconcile themselves to the facts that the demands are going to become greater and that they are just going to become more skillful. That is, I believe they are going to continue to develop as they have in the past. Years ago, we decided to show people pictures during the inter-

view and have them tell stories. Back came the interviewers, agonizing about how it couldn't be done. Back came the sterile, uncooperative little stories told to the pictures. But the second time and the third time the stories got better and better, fuller, and more individually expressive. The interviewers found more people willing to tell the tale. Then we tried incomplete sentences, and went through the phase when hardly anyone would behave as though it was a sensible task. Nowadays, thousands of interviews are rapidly and (almost) casually gathered with such picture stories and rounded off sentences.

We have gone through the same thing with devices called Comparimeters, Q-Sorts, Semantic Differentials, and numerous other approaches, all testifying to the fact that interviewers have unusual capacity to grow, given the appropriate stimulation. I doubt that much can be done to adapt the researchers, although I do counsel them to try to understand what can and cannot be accomplished in the Field. Still, knowing how well interviewers can rise to a challenge, it would be a pity to underestimate them. This brief look at the individuality of a few interviewers and this mention of the complex but inevitable tensions in the researcher-interviewer relationship suggest something of the psychological background to the interviewing situation. Clearly, it is a very human situation, fraught with some sense of struggle to accomplish the ever-pressing deadlines, to think on your feet, to be systematic without being barren.

Turning from this background to the interviewing situation itself raises some interesting questions. Why is interviewing so hard? Perhaps we might take a deeper look at the psychology of interviewing, to try to discern what lies at the heart of what goes on in the interviewing situation.

Interviewing is a special kind of social situation. It usually seems apparent to non-interviewers that it is hard to do, while they simultaneously exaggerate the pleasure they suppose must be in it. Clients are often surprised that people even allow themselves to be interviewed. They are astonished at how long an interview can be and that people will cooperate without being paid to respond (N.B. The good old days!). Also, many who try interviewing are unable to do it. They cannot make a contact; or having made one, they cannot gain cooperation; or they are unable to sustain an interviewing conversation.

The reasons why interviewing is hard for any given person are varied. Energy may be lacking, or verbal fluency, or the capacity to talk and write simultaneously. Some people find it difficult to keep in mind what they are being told. Individual reasons for failure are as miscellaneous as people and their abilities or disabilities.

Beyond such reasons are larger meanings that make the interviewing situation potentially (and actually) difficult. An interview is a human encounter, burdened by several facts. One fact is that the people are usually strangers to each other—or should be. The encounter of strangers is generally a troublesome one. To be approached by a stranger makes one wary. We wonder, what do you want of me? There is a fearfulness about being interrupted in the pursuit of one's own activities. This atmosphere is well-expressed in the first stanza of "The Rime of the Ancient Mariner."

"It is an ancient Mariner, and he stoppeth one of three (the other two did not fit his sample?). "By thy long gray beard and glittering eye, Now wherefore stopp'st thou me?"

The psyche is jarred by the novel elements; many hasty decisions have to be made. How much of the new stimulations can be taken in, how should the other person be judged to decide whether to continue further? People may look poised, but inside they are full of wonderment, questioning, trying to learn quickly, to figure out what is going on—all is in flux. The quota calls for a young mother, and can that be a lamp in the living room, and must the dog bark so, and we're doing a study, does she look like she's turning away, who's that coming down the stairs, oh, I almost dropped my clipboard; while on the other side is a disrupted quiet moment at the ironing board, or I was upstairs doing my hair and I thought it was Thelma, do you smell something burning, Oops, you've let the cat get out. Who me, you want to interview me, how silly, I don't know anything!

Names just heard may be promptly forgotten—"who'd you say you represent?" Slips of the tongue are common, demonstrating the confusion and lessening of self-control at the moment. One interviewer on a study of Kotex introduced herself as "Mrs. Jones of Sicial Resooch, doing a study of Katz."

Even after things settle down and the people in the situation are able to focus their attention at the appropriate rhythm and level, putting distractions enough aside, many problems remain. Why is there the oft-mentioned problem of rapport? Being questioned seems to be intrinsically a negative affair. It means one is expected to be in a compliant, obedient frame of mind. Traditionally, the words and situations associated with questioning have negative implications. An interview is a form of interrogation, possibly a cross-examination. Carried far enough it is an Inquisition. The situation harks back to childhood, to giving an accounting for oneself to Authority, of defending oneself against accusations of wrongdoing.

In the interview situation this parental authority often becomes the mysterious They and Them. The interviewer may say apologetically. "They want to know the silly question" and implies *They* will punish me if I don t get an answer. And the respondent can shift hostility away by asserting, "You can tell *Them* for me that the product or the advertising or the questionnaire is no good."

Tucked away here is the fear of saying the wrong thing or of not knowing the right answer. One of the earliest versions of the dangers of being questioned comes down to us from many centuries ago—about 400 B.C. A Field Supervisor named the Goddess Hera sent an interviewer named the Sphinx to the city of Thebes. This interviewer is described as a monster with the face of a maiden and the body of a winged lion. "What is the creature which is two-footed, three-footed, and four-footed; and weakest when it has most feet?" Every failure to find the answer cost the Thebans a life. Finally, the best respondent turned out to be a wandering stranger named Oedipus. He answered the question with the word *Man*. This got rid of the Sphinx, and as a premium Oedipus was awarded the throne of Thebes.

This story may exaggerate the hazards of interviewing, but it symbolizes the fact that it has always been regarded as dangerous to expose oneself to inquisitive strangers; and it helps us understand why even some modern citizens may refuse to do so.

It is fortunate for us all that these negative features of interviewing—the fear of trespassing on someone's privacy, the resentment at having one's secrets or one's ignorance exposed—are more than offset by those factors that answer the question, Why is interviewing easy?

The first plain fact is that most people are willing to be interviewed, regardless of anything. Being interviewed does at least four important things for a person. For one, it relieves loneliness and boredom. It does this in the casual sense for someone alone at home or stuck all day with the conversation of a 4-year-old. And it relieves loneliness in the deeper sense for all people with the basic urge for contact with others. Therefore, it is no wonder that the wariness on the doorstep turns to cordiality at the kitchen table, that "I'm busy with the laundry and have only a few minutes" turns into "have another cup of coffee" an hour later.

Another motive that facilitates interviewing is the urge to confess. Most people carry a sufficient load of guilt about a variety of large and small acts and wishes in their lives that they are glad to have someone—especially a stranger—who will listen and allow some relief of their feelings. The extreme examples of people who confess to murders they didn't commit make us cautious about the overly cooperative respondent who will confess to anything to feel a sense of justification in how she treats her husband or serves broccoli souffle or uses substitutes for coffee, orange juice, or butter.

The quest for any kind of knowledge can be a challenging enterprise, containing in it the seeds of revelation of the mysteries of life. We are all detectives at heart. Participating in a research implies sharing in this search for knowledge; it means being a witness giving evidence to prove one thing or another, contributing one part to the puzzle, what do people think, why do they behave one way or another? Sometimes respondents want to know how other people have answered the questions, and they take satisfaction in the part they have played.

In all these instances, whether seeking contact, expiation, or knowledge, there is a larger aim at work: the wish to demonstrate or to affirm one's worth as a person. When the interviewer arrives and says in effect, I need you, your views are important to me, tell me more, your opinion is sought by vast sponsoring institutions, the respondent feels a sense of enlargement. Here is testimony from the outside world that one is a chosen person singled out by fate from the multitudinous anonymity of modern life. The respondent feels wooed and inwardly preens with pleasure even while making complaining noises. Rapport comes about and blossoms when for a time, in its own peculiar way, the interview means that one has worth. When we see at times the ardor of the response, the way the respondent may cling to the interviewer reluctant to end the interaction, clearly for the moment it is a situation of love.

This brings me full circle because I am reminded again of our friends, Mesdames Burlun, Smith, and Miller. I think each in her way was an excellent interviewer because she did value her respondents and was able to communicate to them that they—with us—are involved in an intriguing kind of work, one that thinks people and knowledge of their states of mind are central to carrying on the work of our world.

## Chapter 50

HUNGER AND WORK IN A CIVILIZED TRIBE

Or, the Anthropology of Market Transaction

Sidney J. Levy

Does the field of marketing need anthropology, as it so evidently needs and employs mathematics, psychology, and economics? Implicitly, there can be no doubt of it—although explicit interest has been less noticeable. In 1961 Winick discussed this topic in the *Journal of Marketing*. He noted that anthropologists and marketers have been slow in finding common ground. His summary of what anthropology is about and how it might be used is excellent in laying a groundwork and a plea for greater communication between the fields of anthropology and marketing. He shrewdly observes that marketing researchers may do more anthropological research on modern culture than anthropologists do (Winick, 1961).

Some of the same broad ground was gone over by Glock and Nicosia (1964) a few years later, in an article reflecting (though not mentioning) the overlap of anthropology and sociology. Somewhat curiously, although writing in the *Journal of Marketing*, they appear to be exhorting sociologists to interest themselves in the marketing field and to blame them for re-

This chapter was first published in *American Behavioral Scientist*, 21(4), 557-570. Copyright © 1978 by Sage Publications, Inc.

linquishing the study of consumption behavior to economists (Glock & Nicosia, 1964, pp. 51-54).

Since that time, not much communication has occurred, but there has been some uneven growth in applied studies by marketing researchers and minor discussion in the literature. The easiest access to anthropology seems to be through the concept of culture. Most recent marketing textbooks salute anthropology with the idea of culture, usually with some brief lip service. Gist (1974), in one recent example, does so narrowly by selecting one of the most limited definitions of culture, "enlightenment and excellence of taste acquired by intellectual and aesthetic training" (p. 18), which is not the technical and more inclusive concept (despite variations) used by most anthropologists. Other culture-conscious teachers admonish marketers to avoid making mistakes by using the wrong words or offending local customs. Among the best summary perspectives on the topic of culture in the marketing literature are Wadia's (1967) article, "The Concept of Culture in the Analysis of Consumers" and Sturdivant's (1973) chapter in *Consumer Behavior: Theoretical Sources*.

The dichotomy between marketing practitioners and marketing educators is important here. If interested in inquiry, the practical manager calls upon marketing theory as it applies to the content and methods of marketing research. The theory usually remains implicit, the research being addressed to learning facts about the market that will enable marketers to make specific decisions. Academicians may not have the same goals as marketers. It is a misnomer to refer to scholars and educators as marketers (except insofar as they sell their services), and elsewhere (Chapter 9) it has been suggested they be termed mar-

cologists (Levy, 1976) to indicate their research orientation to the field. Aspiring to a scientific approach, their need for theory development is great and seeks to rise above the sheer data-gathering emphasis in most marketing research.

Studies at the marketing research level are primarily descriptive and are similar to early ethnographic reports that noted the interesting behaviors of exotic societies. When done by scholars, such marketing studies turn up at intervals in the *Journal of Marketing* telling about the current state of the marketing system in Egypt, Poland, Australia, or the Soviet Union. In other numerous instances, marketing research studies are commercial projects that attempt to characterize consumer user groups, usually in rather narrow statistical terms, or that summarize the product-use behaviors and attitudes of most immediate interest to the marketing managers. These studies usually do not find their way into the marketing literature, providing little basis for the growth of general knowledge or theory. The kind of understanding sought in most marketing research studies is so circumscribed that few approach the richness and sophistication of ethnographic and ecological data shown, for example, in the work reported in *Environment and Cultural Behavior*, edited by Vayda (1969). There are many reasons for this, including the specificity of the problem formulation in business situations, the common limitations placed on funds and personnel, the lack of an anthropological orientation, and the tendency to take the familiar cultural context largely for granted rather than as an object of study.

There seems less excuse for academic and professional research workers to neglect the possibilities for conceptual enrichment in behavioral studies that might be gained from a more anthropological perspective, and the situation is changing, as will be noted along the way. In the following discussion, a brief overview of some main conceptual issues in anthropological theory will be taken up as a vehicle for observing how these ideas are represented in marketing activity and thinking; and to suggest where developing the relationships further might be of benefit. The sequence roughly observes the conventions of anthropological chronology, thereby illustrating some parallelism in the development of ideas in both fields.

The history of anthropological thought shows the processes typical of many disciplines: the founding thinkers and their germinal ideas, a succession of concepts as new workers enter the field, the splitting and cycling of specialization (due to the growth of ideas and personnel, the need to concentrate efficiently, and controversy), and synthesis as larger insights are developed.

Anthropology focused early on the idea of evolution in which progress is an important value, as human beings are judged to move from primitivity to civilization. The study of family relations became integral to such analysis, with the Western European monogamous and patrilineal kinship system taken to represent the most civilized culmination, in keeping with a supposedly upward evolution of society.

Such invidious comparisons subsided (they certainly did not disappear) as anthropologists moved toward a more objective analysis of individual histories of societies, with some attention to the diffusion of invention from one group to another. Scientific method and subtler theories of the nature of society grew, especially with the work of Boas (1896). Kroeber (1915) stressed the superorganic view of society in which the personal or individual was only

illustrative of the larger ideas. The search for overarching ideas, such as values, continues in modern study.

The concept of culture was modified from its equation with civilization and societal superiority to that of cultures, each being studied with "an increasing realization of the connections between the various habits and habit products shared by members of the same community" (Oliver, 1964, p. 8). Observing these connections and shared habits turned attention to the meanings of cultures, and in cultures, and how these meanings came about. Sapir and Whorf (1941, pp. 75-93) studied the relationship between cultural categories and language. Benedict's popular books, *Patterns of Culture* (1934) and *The Chrysanthemum and the Sword* (1946) dramatized the idea that cultures are like personalities on a larger scale. She tried to understand individual behavior as "caused" by cultural patterns, to bring out the consistencies of thought and action.

Linton's (1936) development of the concepts of status and role gave fresh impetus to thinking about how the individual relates to the culture. He pointed to the meanings of the individual's position and the actions by which he expressed them. This work is reflected in the contemporary use of the concept of social stratification. Many marketing research studies examine the social positions of the members of the sample and attempt to relate the marketing behavior of the respondents to their socioeconomic status. Some of the richness of attention to market segmentation was perhaps foreshadowed by Linton's categories—universals, specialities, alternatives, and individual peculiarities that come about through variations in the degree and nature of sharing of cultural content.

The complexities of anthropological thought multiplied considerably with the American work of Linton and, in Europe, the contributions of Durkheim, Mauss, Malinowski, and Radcliffe-Brown. Generally speaking, they (and others) brought to bear theoretical positions that highlighted the barrenness of vast undigested accumulations of ethnographic data. The earlier radical empiricism was disparaged for suffering from the lack of adequate organizing theories. Durkheim (1938, 1964) focused on understanding the collective nature of society, how its structure, norms, and other social facts function as the social group is maintained or changed. Radcliffe-Brown (1952) stressed the social structure as the most fundamental part of social anthropology. He saw society as a social system whose general forms could be abstracted from observing the concrete relations among individuals. His concern was not with them as individuals, but as persons who are complexes of their social relationships.

Malinowski (1939) disputed Radcliffe-Brown's interpretation of functionalism, being more concerned with the biological and psychological foundations of individual need satisfaction. Given this emphasis, and his analysis of the Trobriand Island exchange system called the *Kula* (1961), Malinowski might well be regarded as a founding father of the behavioral science approach to marketing. He sees seven basic needs from which secondary social needs are derived: nutrition, reproduction, bodily comforts, safety, relaxation, movement, and growth.

In examining the collective social life, Mauss (1954) elaborated the significance of reciprocity. The phenomenon of gift giving was analyzed for the light it cast on the nature or social solidarity, on the importance of exchange prior to the modern economic market. He points to the triple obligation to give, to receive, and to repay.

> In the systems of the past we do not find simple exchange of goods, wealth, and produce through markets established among individuals. For it is groups, and not individuals, which carry on exchange, make contracts, and are bound by obligations; the persons represented in the contracts are moral persons—clan, tribes, and families; the groups, or the chiefs as intermediaries for the groups, confront and oppose each other. Further, what they exchange is not exclusively goods and wealth, real and personal property, and things of economic value. They exchange rather courtesies, entertainments, ritual, military assistance, women, children, dances, and feasts; and fairs in which the market is but one element and the circulation of wealth but one part of a wide and enduring contract. (p. 3)

Malinowski refers to the semicommercial and the semiceremonial aspects of the Kula exchange system; and Mauss emphasizes the premarket and nonmarket aspects of giving and receiving. They were more interested in the social and noncommercial significance of the exchange and perhaps impressed with the unusual or exotic interweaving of motives. In modern marketing study, it is possible to see that all "ordinary" transactions are similarly invested with significance, that a woman's bridge luncheon, a family dinner, the arrival of the new car, and so forth are as meaningful and as expressive of numerous social contracts, cultural values, and so on as the Kula and the potlatch of the Kwakiutl. Most of such transactions still await, however, their Malinowskis, Mausses, and Boases of marketing to elucidate them. But the neglect is not total.

Traditionally, functionalism has been taken to be purposeful and constructive in its results—just as many marketing thinkers tend to assume that marketing exchange moves toward equity and mutual satisfaction. So the functionalist inquired: how well did the activity, the relationship, function to promote some socially desirable goal or harmony, mutuality, equity? Some workers have been interested in the role of conflict, an issue that has grown of late. Epstein (1967) criticized economists for tending "to neglect the interactions and conflicts between the market and other social institutions" (p. 229). Marketing study can be less faulted on this ground. Much attention has been given of late to conflict in the channels of distribution (Stern & El-Ansary, 1977, Chapter 7); to conflict problems arising from consumerist criticisms of television, advertising, product defects; the activities of the Federal Trade Commission and other regulatory agencies, and so on. Levy and Zaltman (1975) have written about the various levels of marketplace conflict, subjective, transactional, competitive, commercial, and social. An interesting example in another direction is found in the article by Bloom (1977) on advertising in the professions.

The early evolutionary perspective subsided but never died, and in the past 30 years or so, it has returned with special impetus from the work of Steward (1955) and White (1959). Its modern version is inspired by growing knowledge in paleoanthropological studies and theories about changing levels of organization and shifts from unspecialized cultures to more differentiated ones. White sees cultural evolution as an increase in energy harnessed per capita per year, or as the improvement in technological efficiency. Sahlins (1960) wants the efficiency to be accompanied by

higher levels of organization, and he offers the distinction between specific evolution of cultures in their variations and the general evolution of life forms.

The concept of evolution, whether in its early Spencerian character or the recent formulations of Sahlins, may direct attention to the cross-cultural study of contemporary marketplaces. A search for hypotheses and criteria might test how the marketing system, globally conceived, is moving through a general evolutionary process, especially insofar as trade increases among the West, Japan, Iron Curtain countries, China, Third World blocs, and so on, so that there is a movement toward an increasingly integrated world marketplace of ever higher levels of organization or efficiency in energy utilization. Cross-cultural study might also compare specific evolutionary patterns in given societies, using such criteria as efficiency, organizational complexity, technological elaboration, and so on.

The market may need its own criteria for evaluating progress, such as indicators of need satisfaction and perhaps a concept of retrogression as marketing complexity leads to trade-offs in use of time, retreat from participation, and the inclinations to discard, replace, or not use products because of the difficulties in getting them repaired. Most marketing textbook discussions tend overeagerly to justify the role of marketing and its costs, when a comparative point of view will show the basic necessity of marketing in some form or other, while varying in its dynamism and evolutionary character.

In any event, the evolutionary perspective requires a greater sense of history than has been visible in marketing study and among the people engaged in marketing. Typically, they tend to focus on the recent past, the present, and the near future. This characteristic orientation implies a belief in the nature of marketing as essentially non-scientific, an ever-emerging, freshly formed problem whose past is probably not lawful or relevant. At some level, this may be true, but it does not accord with the stability, even the rigidity, of some market institutions and of various kinds of public response; or the contingent character of the typical broad pattern of stages in marketing development.

The early days of marketing study were parallel to the particularistic, ethnographic approach in anthropology. Specific commodities were studied, each in turn, for the facts of their existence and handling. In the study of markets, their components, their census and actuarial details, then and now, a wealth of data are available for the testing of hypotheses of broader sorts. In an attempt to transcend the marketer's customary (and understandable) preoccupation with market segments and their variations within the society, Firat (1977) seeks to analyze a consumption pattern that was dominant regardless of socioeconomic strata, subcultures, peer groups, and other reference groups. Wharton (1978) is engaged in an unusual study that also goes in this direction. By comparing large amounts of census-type data from various communities where television was introduced at different times, she is attempting to measure its impact on other forms of consumption.

The concepts of structure and function, broadly speaking, have been applied to the study of marketing and tend to be basic to its orientation. The marketing system has a structure, given the institutions that comprise it and the form of their interconnections. This is especially noticeable in the distribution system where the channel structure has been well described (Stern &

El-Ansary, 1977, Chapter 7). Despite his own valuable work in this area, Stern believes that the field has been generally neglected and is in need of more theoretical development. The market structure has been described in various other respects, as attention is given to the ways numerous organizations, associations, household and family relationships, as well as social strata, interact to accomplish marketing purposes.

The conflict mentioned earlier between Radcliffe-Brown and Malinowski highlights the classical and persisting difference between thinkers who do not accept a psychology of individual subjectivity as relevant to understanding either society or people and those who find such a psychology imperative. Marketing scholars show this customary division, also. They tend to be primarily behaviorists whose work is confined to impersonal data, structural variables, and analysis of phenomena as they are understood by the observer (etic approach) rather than analysis of the phenomena as they are perceived by the actors or cultural participants (emic approach). This dichotomy seems profound, like that between Platonists and Aristoteleans, between Aristoteleans and Galileians (Lewin, 1931, pp. 141-177), or between conservatives and liberals. As Langness (1977) says, "There are those who still argue that technoenvironmental factors are basic, causal, and relatively unaffected by human thought or belief. . . . [But the new view] also insists on recognizing the input of the creature itself" (p. 146).

In the realm of marketing behavior, there is interest in the subjectivity involved in marketplace action and consumption and its interpretation. But most work still remains at the rather surface level of measuring attitudes and simple cognitions, or accepting interviewee self-reports at face value—since how else can they be tabulated? Interpretations tend to be confined to the interfaces of the variables, and especially (and practically) focusing on those that are controllable by the marketing manager. It is often frustrating, however, to observe how little insight is gained this way, how little guidance for future decisions, especially as changes occur in the environment due to actions by competitors, the government, or other social forces not being taken into account.

Opposed to those anthropologists who follow White in his naming of the technological system as having the primary role, with their relative indifference to the individual's mental content, are the workers who place human symbolizing at the center of anthropological inquiry. Scholars who theorize in this direction believe that culture is fundamentally a system of symbols and that it is essential to study people's conscious and unconscious ideas (Geertz, 1973). Individuals may be important to the analysis, with the goal of studying their relation to society; or the symbols may be studied as supra-individual concepts.

Outstanding among the symbolically oriented anthropologists is Levi-Strauss, whose work is controversial and often found difficult. He (Levi-Strauss, 1966) is interested in the universality of basic human mental processes and their varied manifestations. His structural analyses of myths search for the underlying regularities in the way humans think. He (Levi-Strauss, 1958) is less interested in what a given myth means to the society where it occurs but looks for variants of the myth from more than one society in order to analyze its deeper structure, that is, the model of reality that is being represented by the combinations or relations of elements and by groups of elements.

Somewhat more directly connected with the concerns of marketing people are the symbolic issues addressed in the analyses of economic anthropology, especially in the emphasis found there on the nature of exchange. Firth (1967) quotes Sahlins, "A material transaction is usually a momentary episode in a continuous social relation. The social relation exerts governance: The flow of goods is constrained by, is part of, status etiquette" (p. 3).

As this quotation indicates, economic exchange and social exchange are not different exchanges but are different perspectives on the same phenomenon; all exchanges can be interpreted as both economic and social. Marketing has always taken transactions as nuclear events, but often in a rather casual manner rather than as a focus for analysis. Defining marketing as an exchange rather than as "the movement of goods," or the "transfer of ownership," is a recent style (Bagozzi, 1975, pp. 32-39) and leads both to a convergence with the study of social exchange in sociology or social anthropology and to some controversy as to which exchanges are marketing exchanges and which are not. Firth (1973) first says there is a marked disjunction between the market operations of buying and selling and those of gift-giving; but then goes on,

"Yet as anthropologists and sociologists have realized since the work of Thurnwald, Malinowski, and Mauss about fifty years ago, the opposition between these two spheres of transaction is by no means so clear-cut."

He points to the social aspects of commercial transactions and to the elements of calculation, reciprocity, and profit in other spheres of exchange. He is basically affirming what in the marketing field has come to be referred to as the "broadening" concept of marketing, which avers that no matter what other significance exchanges may have for sociologists, political scientists, anthropologists, marriage counselors, and so on, they are all marketing exchanges as well. If so, marketing analysis has to give increasing attention to the "etiquette" Sahlins referred to, to understand the marketing that goes on when what is exchanged is not only money for products but the intangibles of their social meaning, the exchange of the meanings of the objects in the fantasy, mythic, and symbolic life of the exchangers (Levy, 1974, pp. 555-558). The analysis of symbolism in the marketing realm is likely to grow slowly, at least in America where the "hard-headed" positivist approach is so prevalent, and given the automatic avoidant reaction of many to the notion of symbolism as tainted with supposed Freudian pansexuality or Jungian mysticism. The preference for a functional viewpoint has been apparent, as Alderson (1957) has discussed. It fits the sense of face plausibility and close logical connections typically sought in marketing research. Endless marketing studies use the readily derived seller variables of convenience, delivery, price, taste, or the analogous buyer attributes of use, nonuse, or more personal qualities such as sociability, venturesomeness, and so forth. These variables are rarely pursued in depth, as the more urgent goal is commonly to measure the variables in relation to one another or to the demography of market segments.

Richards' (1948) classic *Hunger and Work in a Savage Tribe* illustrates the functional method in the full fashion it may be pursued, as applied to nutrition among the Southern Bantu of Africa. To accomplish the analogous task in modern America is hard to conceive although partial attempts are made. Study of hunger and work in a "civilized tribe" is rather assiduously addressed by the major food companies and related media. They examine current attitudes toward food, the widespread preoccupation with weight control and the relation of diet to health and disease, and the use of food to communicate complexities of social status and interaction. For example, *Better Homes and Gardens* has sponsored research on changes in these outlooks (Social Research, Inc., 1972); many such investigations have been carried out by General Foods, Kraft, and so on, usually, of course without being published. Such projects vary considerably in their depth and theoretical sophistication, some being excellent in their probing attempts to gain insight, while others are primarily rather simple surveys on some items of interest.

Two interesting cultural changes can be observed given such studies. One is this growing awareness in marketing of its cultural context, a recognition that knowledge of the large matrix is needed. Another is the change in general cultural content that is being explored. Profound alterations are occurring in the self-concepts of Americans, with perhaps the outburst of pride in the bicentennial events a paradoxical celebration of the end of a traditional concept of American life, an end in transition for some time. Partly involved is a general shift in the concept of man, in the ancient struggle to relate his body and its persistent mysteries to his environment and to his awareness of himself and other people.

Other aspects arise from the national history. The simple opposition of materialism to spirituality no longer suffices, as the spiritual feather their nests and the materialists search for a meaningful relationship. Manifestations of challenge in the situation include the changing role of women, which daily gains in its intensity and impact on the marketplace. The melting pot boils with renewed vigor, as the re-ethnification of America continues, resigned to bilingualism, and rejoicing in the cosmopolitan restaurants. The special needs of the elderly are having major repercussions on social security arrangements, the character of communities, and the handling of medical expenditures.

The preoccupation of Americans with the body with regard to its health, its exercise, its sexuality, and its feeding seems to be moving to a crescendo, a symphonious interaction of governmental regulation, research, extensive reporting by the media, and the new narcissism. Another curious unifying force is the widespread awareness of the celebrity. Public figures apparently have no privacy any longer and are hardly protected by any moral or ethical inhibitions; usually a sympathetic curiosity prevails, justifying a steady exposure of the personal, marital, economic, sexual, political, and medical experiences of narrowly to widely famous people. Politicians and entertainers always were fair game, but new heights are reached when Elizabeth Taylor's latest husband runs for the Senate, Dr. Salk marries Picasso's former mistress, Mrs Carter has a D and C, and Mick Jagger says he did not have an affair with Mrs. Trudeau.

Cultural patterns and their changes are important to marketers, given their impact and claims (Yankelovitch, Skelly, & White, Inc., 1977). A notable example of this interest appears in the July 1977 issue of the *Journal of Marketing* where nine articles accumulate to a broad anthropological (or gynecocentric?) picture of various features of the changing status and activities of women (Scott, 1976). Many marketers neglect such work because they find it difficult to reason or to make inferences about its import for marketing actions. Marketing teachers and students study the larger

and changing scene and its relationships to marketplace actions (Levy, 1968, pp. 17-23; Vinson et al., 1977, pp. 44-50), and more of this might be done with a particular eye for a theory of action implications. As Lehman (1977) observes, "the proper directions for product design, advertising strategy and public relations activities can be mapped out only when research is seen in the total marketing context."

To sum up, an anthropological approach implies the attempt to grasp the society as a whole, to examine the culture in some grand sense, and to study specific cultures. The culture and the cultures may be studied for their evolving character, for cross-cultural comparisons, to learn about the diffusion of influence, about structures and functions. The search for knowledge goes on at many levels, from the descriptive to the dynamic, from the behavioristic to the symbolic. Summary implications for marketing thinking include the following:

1. *A sense of breadth in thinking about the market* so that its large-scale structure is defined and explored and the complexities of its sets of relationships are revealed. This might refresh speculations about how society (and societies) carries out the marketing function, as marketing thinkers see this, as distinct from economists or political scientists.

2. *A richer sense of historic process* than seems generally taught is needed, so that marketing people can appreciate the context of their field and the more encompassing necessities they express by their own actions; and also then a greater awareness of future possibilities.

3. *More functional analyses are likely to come about* that go beyond the generous

flow of correlational and discriminant analyses to qualitative explication of the meanings of products and services.

4. *Interpretation of the meanings of products and services,* not in themselves alone, but in their social symbolic role, as means of exchanging communications and furthering social processes, will lead to a fuller understanding of why marketing managers do what they do and why customers buy and consume as they do.

5. *These goals may require "deeper" analyses,* approaches that draw upon levels of meaning that seek to relate surface phenomena to the shadow life, as in the shadow market of secret consumption, or

in the stealing and cheating that rise and fall with the virtuous marketplace. Also, the conventional market's myths require delineation for many purposes, not least to enable our society to develop policies with cognizance of these myths. For example, Morgan (1971, pp. 13-16) discusses a myth of psychopharmcology that supports the proliferation of drugs, myth here being "the description of a phenomenon with the language and concepts of another phenomenon (or set of phenomena) to promote an intervention or maneuver that the culture finds useful." Examination of our myths of everyday life may help us to observe as scientists of marketing what is being done with the marketing system.

REFERENCES

Alderson, W. (1957). *Marketing behavior and executive action: A functionalist approach to marketing theory.* Homewood, IL: Irwin.

Bagozzi, R. P. (1975, October). Marketing as exchange. *Journal of Marketing, 39,* 32-39.

Benedict, R. (1934). *Patterns of culture.* Boston: Houghton Mifflin.

Benedict, R. (1946). *The chrysanthemum and the sword.* Boston: Houghton Mifflin.

Bloom, P. N. (1977, July). Advertising in the professions: The critical issues. *Journal of Marketing,* pp. 103-110.

Boas, F. (1896, December). The limitations of the comparative method or anthropology. *Science,* p. 4.

Durkheim, E. (1938). *Rules of sociological method.* Chicago: University of Chicago Press.

Durkheim, E. (1964). *The division of labor in society.* New York: Free Press.

Epstein, S. (1967). Productive efficiency and customary systems of rewards in rural South India. In R. Firth (Ed.), *Themes in economic anthropology.* London: Tavistock.

Firat, A. F. (1977). *The social construction of consumption patterns.* Ph.D. dissertation, Northwestern University, Evanston, IL.

Firth, R. (1967). *Themes in economic anthropology.* London: Tavistock.

Firth, R. (1973). *Symbols public and private.* London: George Allen & Unwin.

Geertz, C. (1973). *The interpretation of cultures.* New York: Basic Books.

Gist, R. R. (1974). *Marketing and society.* Hinsdale, IL: Dryden Press.

Glock, C. Y., & Nicosia, F. M. (1964, July). Uses of sociology in studying consumption behavior. *Journal of Marketing,* pp. 51-54.

Kroeber, A. (1915). Eighteen professions. *American Anthropologist, 17,* 2.

Langness, L. L. (1977). *The study of culture.* San Francisco: Chandler Sharp.

Lehman, C. C. (1977). Ambiguities of "actionable" research. *Journal of Marketing, 41*(4), 21-23.

Levi-Strauss, C. (1958). *Structural anthropology.* New York: Doubleday.

Levi-Strauss, C. (1966). *The savage mind.* Chicago: University of Chicago Press.

Levy, S. J. (1968). Making the changing scene. *Proceedings,* College Teachers of Textiles and Clothing, pp. 17-23.

Levy, S. J. (1974). Myth and meaning in marketing. *Combined proceedings,* American Marketing Association, pp. 555-558.

Levy, S. J. (1976). Marcology 101 or the domain of marketing. *Proceedings,* American Marketing Association.

Levy, S. J., & Zaltman, G. (1975). *Marketing, society, and conflict.* Englewood Cliffs, NJ: Prentice Hall.

Lewin, K. (1931). The conflict between Aristotelian and Galileian modes of thought in contemporary psychology. *Journal of Genetic Psychology, 5,* 141-177.

Linton, R. (1936). *The study of man.* New York: Appleton-Century-Crofts.

Malinowski, B. (1939). The group and the individual in functional analysis. *American Journal of Sociology, 44.*

Malinowski, B. (1961). *Argonauts of the western Pacific.* New York: Dutton.

Mauss, M. (1954). *The gift.* New York: Free Press.

Morgan, J. P. (1971, November). Psychopharmacology: Metaphor to myth. *Relevant Scientist, 1,* 13-16.

Oliver, D. L. (1964). *Invitations to anthropology.* Garden City, NY: Natural History Press.

Radcliffe-Brown, A. R. (1952). *Structure and function in primitive society.* New York: Free Press.

Richards, A. (1948). *Hunger and work in a savage tribe.* Glencoe, IL: Free Press.

Sahlins, M. D. (1960). *Evolution and culture.* Ann Arbor: University of Michigan Press.

Scott, R. (1976). *The female consumer.* New York: John Wiley.

Social Research, Inc. (1972). *The changing perception of food in modern life.* Des Moines, IA: Meredith.

Stern, L. W., & El-Ansary, A. I. (1977). *Marketing channels.* Englewood Cliffs, NJ: Prentice Hall.

Steward, J. (1955). *Theory of culture change.* Urbana: University of Illinois Press.

Sturdivant, F. D. (1973). Subculture theory: Poverty, minorities, and marketing. In S. Ward & T. S. Robertson (Eds.), *Consumer behavior: Theoretical sources.* Englewood Cliffs, NJ: Prentice Hall.

Vayda, A. P. (Ed.). (1969). *Environment and cultural behavior.* Garden City, NY: Natural History Press.

Vinson, D. E., et al. (1977, April). The role of personal values in marketing and consumer behavior. *Journal of Marketing, 41,* 44-50.

Wadia, M. S. (1967, December). The concept of culture in the analysis of consumers. *Proceedings,* American Marketing Association.

Wharton, J. D. (1978). *A study of the effects of the introduction of television on consumer purchase behavior using an interrupted time-series quasi-experimental design with switching replications.* Ph.D. dissertation, Northwestern University, Evanston, IL.

White, L. A. (1959). *The science of culture.* New York: Farrar, Strauss & Giroux.

Whorf, B. L. (1941). The relation of habitual thought and behavior to language. In L. Spier (Ed.), *Language, culture, and personality: Essays in memory of Edward Sapir* (pp. 75-93). Menasha, WI: Sapir Memorial Publication.

Winick, C. (1961, July). Anthropology's contribution to marketing. *Journal of Marketing, 25,* 53-60.

Yankelovich, Skelly, & White, Inc. (1977). *Raising children in a changing society.* Minneapolis, MN: General Mills.

## Chapter 51

INTERPRETING CONSUMER MYTHOLOGY
A Structural Approach to Consumer Behavior

Sidney J. Levy

Qualitative research in current marketing study usually involves focus group interviews, sometimes depth interviews, and projective techniques (Bellenger, Bernhardt, & Goldstucker, 1976). There is a resurgence of interest in the analysis of expressive verbal materials elicited by such data-gathering methods, but little contemporary marketing literature exists about such analysis. The goal of this paper is to explore and illustrate the idea that verbal materials elicited from people in the marketplace are a form of storytelling that can be analyzed as projective. The responses of a consumer telling about the purchase and use of products may be approached from varied viewpoints. Here, the remarks (the protocol) are taken as a literary production we might interpret in ways comparable to those of clinical psychologists, social anthropologists, and literary critics. A recent view of anthropological concepts (Levy, 1978) especially stimulated the attempt to use the Levi-Strauss structuralist approach by likening consumers' household anecdotes to the myths that he has mined so richly.

This chapter was first published in *Journal of Marketing, 45,* Summer 1981, pp. 49-61. Reprinted by permission of the American Marketing Association.

In open-ended interviewing about the consumption of products, respondents are often asked to describe the product features the family members prefer, to characterize family consumption patterns, to tell about recent instances of using the product, and to explain how and why given products are used. The results of such interviews are commonly reported in a somewhat literal manner, in tabulations of use frequencies, in lists of features cited, in verbal summaries that most people said this or that, or even in lists of verbatim comments without additional comments by the researchers. Ordinarily, the goals are to learn facts of usage and reasons given for and against the product.

Such handling of the data often seems barren and frustrating because it is not sufficiently penetrating, does not tell enough about the meaning of the product in relation to the lives of the users and its place among other products. The approach suggested here is to avoid accepting the responses as if they are scientific observations to be tabulated as measures. Rather, the assumption is that the products are used symbolically and that the telling about their uses is a way of symbolizing the life and nature of the family; thus it requires a theory of interpretation that determines how the data are to be related and understood. Sanche de Gramont (1970) illustrates the point:

I like to imagine these Three Wise Men of the Occident bent in contemplation over a South American Indian myth about a boy who steals a pet pig from his father and roasts it in the forest. Freud would conclude that the boy is symbolically killing his father because he desires his mother. Marx would say that this youthful member of the proletariat is seizing control of the methods of produc-

tion in the class struggle against the landed gentry. Levi-Strauss would find that, in cooking the pig, the primitive Indian boy had achieved the passage from nature to culture and shown that his thought processes are no different from Einstein's. (p. 7)

A conventional marketing approach would probably accept the boy's explanation at face value and conclude that he was hungry, that the pig was convenient, cheap, and tasted good.

The question is raised: If consumer responses are stories (or parts thereof) that tell about the family, how shall the stories be interpreted? Some guidance may come from observing how various kinds of stories are studied, as their analysts search for meanings in such as fairy tales, plays, novels, psychological test responses, and myths, en route to studying consumer research protocols.

In reading fairy tales, as a first example, the reader (consumer) reacts directly with ideas and feelings. Bruno Bettelheim (1977) explains in detail the sources of the consumer satisfaction, showing how fairy tales enrich psychological development and assist in solving fundamental human problems. He points out the message the fairy tales get across to the child in manifold form:

that a struggle against severe difficulties in life is unavoidable, is an intrinsic part of human existence—that if one does not shy away, but steadfastly meets unexpected and often unjust hardships, one masters all obstacles and at the end emerges victorious. (p. 8)

As people mature, the literature of plays and novels remains endlessly absorbing, as is the storytelling on radio, in the movies, and on television. The audience is insatiably curious to know what the characters did, what happened next, and how did it come out? Underlying is the belief that the fictions are significantly related to real events, that experiencing the simulated version in this vicarious way is intellectually and emotionally beneficial and/or destructive.

By extension, the lives of authors are of interest to their readers. Even people who have not read the writer's work can enjoy reading about the writer as a person (to have more knowledge, to feel like an insider, to reduce the stature of great figures, to be reassured or titillated by their humanity, their ordinariness, or their bizarre genius). Other analysts want to find clues to illuminate the writings, to understand better the meaning of *Finnegans Wake* or *Alice in Wonderland*. And others want to explore the nature and processes of creativity as they go on in creators or as they are manifest in their productions.

Thus, the search for meanings expressed in a story goes on at various levels:

1. The experiencing and direct interpretation by the reader is fundamental.

2. That experience is abstracted, generalized, and explained by a scholar for the insight it provides into human nature.

3. The work (product) is interpreted for the means by which it achieves its effects.

4. The teller of the story is studied as a unique source of inspiration or an example of a type. Where the authorship is anonymous, as in folktales, myths, and many fairy tales, or has its roots recognized in ancient chronicles, the source may be interpreted as part of some national or ethnic character.

5. The author is studied to develop and illuminate the meaning of the work.

6. Relationships between the author and the work are studied and interpreted as examples of general processes of expression, whether the focus is on how the author's personality is visible in the writing or on the means by which self-expression was concealed or transformed.

In the same ways, a protocol in which a consumer tells the story of how the product is consumed can be examined for how the consumer interprets the consumption experience, what it tells about people in general, to see how the product features are related to consumption, to learn what the protocol says about the segment it represents, to observe how the individual consumer's character, personality, and lifestyle help explain the nature of the product, and what the instance explains about the general nature of that kind of consuming.

Having suggested the problem in a general way, this paper will examine the nature of interpretation of self-expression, lay groundwork for application to the study of consumer behavior, and give an example of such application.

MODES OF ANALYSIS

There is intuitive recognition that authors of stories must express their personalities in the story. Projective techniques as research and clinical tools explore the ways people transform and externalize their experience in some narrative form, as a general phenomenon and specifically in response to given materials, in accordance with David Rapaport's (1942) formulation of the projective hypothesis, as follows.

All behavioral manifestations of the human being, including the least and the most significant, are revealing and expressive of his personality, by which we mean that individual principle of which he is the carrier. This formulation of the projective hypothesis implies a specific definition of the term "behavior," which includes all of the following aspects: (a) behavior historically viewed in the life-history, (b) behavior statically viewed as reflected in the environment with which the subject surrounds himself, as the furniture of his house, the clothes he wears, etc.; (c) expressive movements; (d) internal behavior, including percepts, fantasies, thoughts. (p. 213)

Characteristically, interpretation of projective techniques follows two paths. In the first, specific components of the story (test protocol) are tabulated and used systematically to evaluate either an individual's responses or the empirical validity of generalizations about groups. An example of this approach is the case of the Rorschach: Certain perceptions of the inkblots are so common they are designated as popular responses. One element of an individual's adjustment is then derived from the number of popular responses he/she gives, as norms suggest it is too many or too few. However, counting popular responses or the length of stories to establish norms for population groups in a purely empirical manner is relatively superficial, compared, say, to having a theory about conformity, rigidity, deviance, and the meanings of the specific perceptions. In the second, qualitative analysis accepts introspection as data and looks for subjective meanings, thus facing the necessity for interpretation. It is phenomenological and interested in symbolic interactionism, trying to see what lies behind or is meant by the manifest behavior. This viewpoint considers social events to be unlike events in the natural sciences. The social events are selected and attended

to because of their significance to the people involved and thus are psychological events in social contexts.

By the logic of the projective hypothesis and the definition of human events as symbolic, interpretation becomes a process of searching for meaning, that is, finding out how mental phenomena—such inner representations of experiences as ideas, imagery, and consumption fantasies as forms of storytelling to the self—are related to interactions with other people and the physical world.

Leslie Stephen wrote that people's doctrines do not become operative in behavior until they have generated an imaginative symbolism. We make distinctions among these imaginative symbolisms by classifying types of narratives. One kind of tale commonly told within a social group is the myth. Formal interpretation of myths is concerned with classifying and explaining grand myths—those tales of the gods, beasts, and heroes that are about the creation of the world, human birth and death, taking form as accounts of floods, supernatural creatures, matings of gods and mortals, heroic family romances, saviors and seers, and cataclysmic physical events. The aim is to demonstrate the similarities and differences among cultures of their grand myths, the sources of the myths, and to explicate the realities to which the mythological symbols referred (Frazer, 1927).

In recent years, the study of myths was much invigorated by the work of Claude Levi-Strauss. He notes reasons why distinctions are made between tales and myths but does not regard them as fundamental. He calls tales miniature myths and sees them all as susceptible to the same type of analysis. This analysis involves certain main features at the heart of Levi-Strauss's contribution.

1. The purpose of myth is to provide a logical model capable of overcoming contradictions or paradoxes in natural and social experience.

2. Interpretation of myths seeks their essential structural characteristics (in contrast to a functional analysis that links the myth to the social situation that is its local context).

3. The structural analysis reveals universal human cognitive processes. These mental operations consist of creating patterns rooted in the perceptions of opposites, manipulating binary relations, and developing mediating terms and triads in various sequences and aggregations.

4. A holistic attitude is required, the analysis being addressed to the clustering and interdependency of elements.

The fundamental character of a myth points to its universal mode of thought, the way it transcends local culture. As Levi-Strauss (1963) says, "its substance does not lie in its style, its original music, or its syntax, but in the story which it tells" (p. 210). When one takes the many versions of the myth (for example, the stories of Oedipus, including the Homeric, Sophoclean, and Freudian), a structural analysis takes account of all the variants, to arrive at the structural law of the myth. That is, what is it really about? The analysis reaches the conclusion that the myth struggles with the contradiction between the idea that human beings originate autochthonously and the idea that they are born of the union of man and woman—out of one or out of two.

Stories are analyzed by breaking them down into gross constituent units Levi-Strauss calls mythemes. The mythemes re-

sult from a play of binary or ternary oppositions. For example, in a tale a king is not only a king and a shepherdess a shepherdess, but these words and what they signify become tangible means of constructing an intelligible system formed by the oppositions: male/female (with regard to nature) and high/low (with regard to culture), as well as the possible permutations among the six terms. In this way, Levi-Strauss discerns a universal metalanguage, recognizing, as Miriam Rodin says, the way in which underlying relational principles order cognition across several domains.

Edmund Leach (1974, p. 76) offers broad structural schema in Figure 51.1, summarizing the relative positions of men, animals, and deities in Greek mythology in a matrix formed by the oppositions above/below, this world/other world, and culture/nature. The analysis will be extended in this paper by amplifying the left side of this structure, elaborating Men in Cities as men, women, and children in high and low social statuses.

If we take the idea that myths are ways of organizing perceptions of realities, of indirectly expressing paradoxical human concerns, they have consumer relevance because these realities and concerns affect people's daily lives. The issues of male/female, nature/culture, and high/low, for example, are not reserved to storytelling occasions about kings and shepherdesses but are also being acted out in everyday behavior. Some marketing study approaches the same generalized, universal level as the grand myths. In his dissertation on *The Social Construction of Consumption Patterns,* Firat (1978) wrestles with the paradox of poor and disadvantaged consumers establishing irrational consumption patterns in cars and expensive foods. He seeks to show how society induces patterns that express such fundamental structural antinomies in consumption as

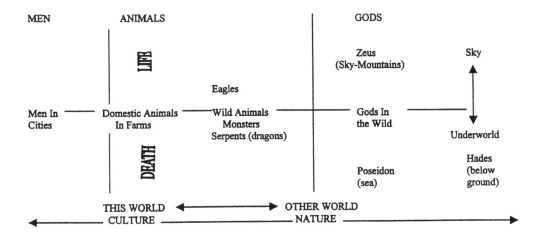

Figure 51.1. Structural relations in Greek mythology

duces patterns that express such fundamental structural antinomies in consumption as individual/collective, private/public, and passive/active. At this level of analysis, individual choice behavior is almost irrelevant, being interpreted as a manifestation of conformity to the culture's dominant consumption pattern. In another universal vein, the work of Daniel B. Williams (1976) examines individual consumer purchasing behavior, interpreting the decision-making process to a highly generalized level. In analyzing the problem spaces or mediums for problem solving used by the individual purchase problem solver, Williams identifies such space attributes as within the organism/ outside the organism, fast/slow, high/low, and phenomenal/transphenomenal.

The idea of taking the consumer protocol as a kind of story to be interpreted draws from various traditions. Robert P. Abelson (1976), for instance, discusses the concept of cognitive script, defining script as "a coherent sequence of events expected by the individual, involving him either as a participant or as an observer" (p. 33). Scripts are formed by the linking of chains of vignettes, the latter being "the raw constituents of remembered episodes in the individual's experience." He insists on this holism and criticizes the "elementaristic, stilted, and static" positions common among cognitive and social psychologists and stresses the way vignettes are "coherently linked." Vignettes in the consumer's script correspond to the mythemes Levi-Strauss observes in myths, where he similarly insists on the necessity for analysis of clusters or bundles of mythemes. As with scripts, myths may be dealt with particularistically as factual descriptions of recalled events, as traditional marketing research questionnaires typically do; or as revealing basic universal human structures, as Levi-Strauss seeks to do. In between, we may seek to interpret sufficiently to get below the surface and concretely enough to apply the ideas to consumer events.

THE PRESENT STUDY

To gather scripts, vignettes, or mythemes as an illustrative instance for this paper, a sample of six consumers was interviewed at length about the various family members, their individual characteristics, and especially their attitudes and behavior in relation to food. The respondents are married middle-class housewives with young children living at home. Each was asked to talk about her husband and children and how they like and dislike their foods prepared. The women were particularly asked to relate family stories, those little tales or bits of family lore that are repeated to family and friends as ways of typifying the family members. These interviews were interpreted using a background of hundreds of depth interviews from marketing studies of many food products. It should be understood that numbers are not relevant here. The purpose is to illustrate the use of a qualitative, structuralistic approach, not to sample for representativeness, to measure distributions, nor to compute the significance of differences.

The tales that were gathered are taken as susceptible to interpretation at the various levels and in the various modes noted earlier: as descriptions of consumer experiences, as projections of the housewife storyteller, as revealing the family members, as symbolizing the abstracted functions serving the participants and the social unit, and as mundane, secular, little myths that organize consumer reality in accordance with underlying logical structures. Levi-Strauss (1969) points to three levels at which versions of myths may be situated: myths of origin and emergence, myths of migrations, and village tales in which "the great logical or cosmological logical contrasts have been toned down to the scale of social relations" (p. 333). The little myths of the family are a fourth level of toning down. Little myths are generalizations about the family and its members, told in the form of anecdotes that use selected facts drawn from the fund of past experiences.

The analysis proceeded by close reading of verbatim transcriptions of the interviews. Observing how respondents project their perceptions of themselves and their families, their language, assumptions, emotional tone, logic, and choice of incidents, the following issues were interpreted.

1. Purposes served by the telling of little myths

2. Values preferences portrayed

3. Theories used in accounting for the behavior of family members

4. Structural relationships of characteristics and categories that are used

PURPOSES

The stories serve an interwoven set of purposes. Like grand myths, they refer to origins of the group and explain how ancestors came together and what life was like in those days. Typically, there is a Paradise Lost aura to the stories—"What fun we used to have going to the lake."

> I remember we used to all get together, and my uncle had a truck with just wooden sides on it and we would go up and picnic, the whole family, aunts, uncles, cousins, and everyone would ride on the back of the truck. There was always somebody there for you. We would go up to lakes and swim, we would have a picnic out at the lake. It was just nice because everybody went; it was something that everybody joined in on.

The stories act as retrospective affirmations of ties and conflicts when relatives reminisce and to induct new group members by marriage, birth, and friendship into family traditions by transmitting a fund of important values, ideas, and characteristics. They instruct in the lifestyle of the lineage, the kind of housing, clothing, transportation, recreation, and food it was and is customary to consume.

The stories illustrate specific relationships and personalities. Often, there is a self-justifying quality: The story proves that the people really are (or were) like that.

> I had a car when I was 16; I got it as a graduation present, and my sisters and I and my cousins—my one cousin, we're all very close—we were out. I don't know, I think we went to McDonalds, or whatever, and we were supposed to be home by 9 o'clock, and we didn't get in until 9:30, and, sure enough, we came to the door and my mom says, "Where have you been?" and I just said, "Oh, ask Jean," who was my cousin, who was behind me. And my mom says something about "this time you're really going to get it," and out shot a hand, and I ducked and Jean ducked, and my baby sister got it. And that— wasn't that it was that hard, but it was harder than a love tap. Sure enough, Jean and I were always the ones that were ducking, and my sister was always the one who was getting it. That's typical.

Abstracted from the flow of childhood events, this little myth becomes paradigmatic and polished. Some of the details are offered as less important. Maybe it was not McDonald's, although saying that it was indicates the innocence of the occasion. The "sure enoughs," the "always," and "that's typical" highlight the mythic character of the story, the way it verifies and generalizes

the teller's virtue and cleverness, the sibling rivalry, the mother's role, and so on.

VALUES AND PREFERENCES

In selecting stories to tell, the respondents project their concern with certain values. Middle-class women highlight middle-class values deemed important for transmission through the generations. As telling stories is a method of maintaining family traditions, it is not surprising that the importance of family unity is repeatedly asserted as such a value. One's childhood was part of a close family or regretfully was not; the mother now strives to have a close family or regrets that maturation and modern lifestyles are destroying that closeness. Closeness is evidenced in doing things together, sharing enjoyable experiences such as family picnics, sports outings, travel, hobbies, meals, household projects, in living nearby, in helping one another, showing concern about the children's companions, and occasionally in some special intimacy of emotional communication or understanding.

The dimension of conformity to or deviation from manly norms comes up in relation to food. The traditional husband is a "meat and potatoes man."

> His favorite meal is pot roast with potatoes and carrots and onions in a big pot.

> He likes roast and gravy. That would be his most special meal. Roast and potatoes, and a vegetable, and lots of bread and butter.

> He's kind of a meat and potatoes man.

This pattern reflects the central American diet; therefore, it seems proper and hardly requires explanation. It often goes

TABLE 51.1 Consumer Explanations

Behavior	Explanation
Chicken liver, calves liver, I don't even prepare.	I think the whole world hates liver.
I used to make tongue quite a bit.	My older son said, "How can you eat tongue with your tongue?" So that was the last time we had tongue.
I learned to modify the wine and butter: I cook very simply now.	My husband got terrible chest pains.
Polish sauerkraut. He hates it.	He says the whole house stinks for weeks after you make it . . . He takes after my father. They both have a queasy stomach and they hate smells.
All of a sudden I find myself taking a piece of cake or something, if it's yummy looking.	I don't even like it, but I've got this idea that it's going to help me bowling. It sounds silly, but that's the truth.
I'm the only one that likes eggplant.	You kind of have to develop a taste for it. I like all those weird vegetables.
They like everything.	Probably because I don't give them a choice. Even when they were little kids, I started getting them into all sorts of different vegetables because I like vegetables.
My daughter would not eat meat at all.	A neighbor is a vegetarian, and the woman would tell her they kill that poor little animal, how can you eat their meat?

on in the context of "he eats everything" except perhaps the conventional hatreds (liver) or less usual foods, such as artichokes.

As a cultural subgroup each family also has its local values. It is easy to gather an array of summaries of family tastes. Women generalize that "they" all love chicken, they're not crazy about fish, we don't eat any raw vegetables, they all like it rare, they like casseroles. Such remarks are usually not literally true (as fuller discussion reveals) but are imaginative generalizations (not imaginary) that symbolize the kind of family being described as stubborn eaters, narrow eaters, easy to feed, and so on, and show what kind of woman the homemaker is to cope with such a family.

CONSUMERS' THEORIES

The above kinds of behavior may seem conventional but are often left unexplained because they are so taken for granted or seem so easily accounted for as a common learning. But husbands who are not meat and potatoes men require explanation; when a family member departs from the norm of eating what the mother regards as an ordinary diet, a problem is posed. The ideas put forth by the women to explain food handling and preferences or aversions take many forms, as shown by examples in Table 51.1. Some stories are mystery stories; the behavior seems baffling, arbitrary, inexplicable.

The two kids split an egg, the older one takes the yellow and the younger one takes the white. I haven't the faintest idea why they feel that way, I really don't. For instance, he won't eat the potatoes and gravy if it runs into the meat. I don't know why. He has this huge plate, and he separates it all on the edges, nothing in the middle.

A framework that operates in the thinking of the respondents has such elements as these:

1. *The process of acquiring and inculcating tastes in the service of health beliefs and propriety is a conflict-filled one.* Cooks are motivated to get the family to eat what is served by various moral imperatives, such as that's what people like us eat, the food comprises a healthy diet, and providing it and eating it are ways of showing love (and other emotions). Although there is more pleasure and satisfaction involved than in the cleaning part of housekeeping, families do not harmoniously eat everything but refuse, resist, or disparage, as well as praise.

2. *There is a natural hierarchy of desirable to offensive attributes of foods.* Any extreme may be troublesome, such as in foods that are too fatty, greasy, spicy, rich, and so on. The extremes (e.g. salty, slimy) may be enjoyed (caviar, anchovies, oysters) but go on at the periphery of what is ordinarily healthy or suited to usual tastes. Some foods are thought likely to affect anyone with their typical actions of producing burping or wind (radishes, cucumber, beans, onions), looseness (spinach, prunes), or hardness (rice). Sweet foods seem naturally easy to like.

3. *Individuals vary in being physiologically vulnerable, perhaps prone to weight gain or peculiarly sensitive to certain substances.* Illness, skin eruptions, respiratory distress, and so on may be explained as simply idiosyncratic reactions or as allergies rooted in either psychological or social factors, or in just that kind of body. Taste preferences are explained at all levels—as due to some sheer physiology of the taste buds, as inherited in the genes, as socialized by ethnic context and by family practices, and as due to novel patterns of individual experiences, beliefs, and habituations.

STRUCTURAL RELATIONS

Food preparation, service, manners, and consumption are all used in symbolic ways. As Levi-Strauss (1978) notes in *The Origin of Table Manners,* "Thus we can hope to discover how, in any particular society, cooking is a language through which that society unconsciously reveals its structure" (p. 495). The participants communicate through their food behaviors, using the underlying structure both consciously and unconsciously.

The American situation is difficult to interpret in a clear-cut way because the available vocabulary is so large. The food products and artifacts come from the whole globe and reflect a mixing of traditions from many societies. The possibilities for different patterns become useful in expressing cultural pride, intergenerational and assimilational conflicts, and individual peculiarities. New little myths about microwave ovens, kiwi fruit, alfalfa sprouts, and pouch cooking need to be gathered to learn the fundamental meanings they will have in the American cuisine. However, the present interviews, interpreted against a background of numerous studies of food products and attitudes, suggest how individual and familial variations draw upon the general vocabulary.

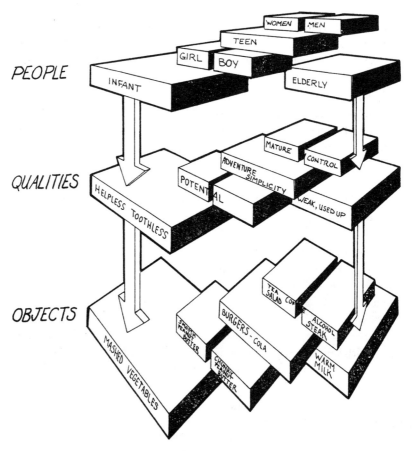

Figure 51.2. Age and sex differentiations in foods and their meanings

Sex and age grading. The roles of sex and age grading are pronounced in distinguishing between the varied suitabilities of foods and methods of preparation. We can distinguish between babies and teenagers, boys and girls, and also observe some of the dimensions at work that affect different food suitabilities. Babies need milk and soft, mushy, undifferentiated foods. Ideas of nurturance, comfort, and easily digested nutrition go in this direction, so that similar foods are regarded as suited to the elderly and the sick. The organisms are weak and should not have strong stimulation in spiciness nor in being too hot or cold. Boys are stereotypically expected to prefer chunky peanut butter, girls the smooth, and gradu-

ally, the preference for homogenous dishes yields to mixtures and combinations. With some maturity the hamburger comes into its own as a youth food, especially appealing to teenagers. A lamb chop or salad is perhaps just right for a woman and a roast or steak for a man. Figure 51.2 illustrates some typical relationships of age, sex, foods, and their attributes.

Social status. Along with age and sex dimensions with their varying degrees of strength and weakness, social class distinctions are pervasive. These are interwoven; thus, there is a tendency to equate higher social position with strength, maturity, and food professionalism and lower status pref-

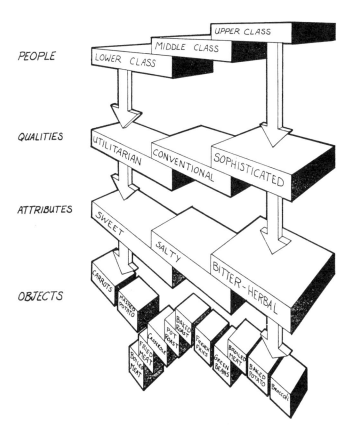

Figure 51.3. The social status structure of food symbolism

erences with softness, greasiness, and sweetness. Going up the scale, conventionality of preparation yields increasingly to elaboration of methods, greater use of herbs and spices, and usage of unusual foods and ingredients. These qualities are not reserved to the upper classes, of course, but form part of the aspirations of lower-status groups as well and are emulated on special occasions. The ability to cook with appropriate sophistication and skill may be achieved through special study or left in the hands of professional chefs, and enjoyed while eating out. Figure 51.3 indicates a status hierarchy and some of its attributes.

Eating out(side). The in-or-out locus is a structural element that speaks of conven-

tionality and festivity, family unity and separation (Figure 51.4). The conventional core is the meal at home, maternal, comfortable, familiar, dependent, and routine. To eat away from home carries more exciting meanings. Outdoor, backyard, park, beach, imply freedom from conventions, return to nature, primitive methods of cooking and eating (with fingers), no manners, and lively physical and social activity.

Going out to eat at another home implies some formality, dress-up, a step up in the elaboration of preparation or distinctiveness of the dishes. The idea of going out to eat at a restaurant interacts with the meanings of the various types of establishments to fit the sex and age grading and family status dimensions. The choices

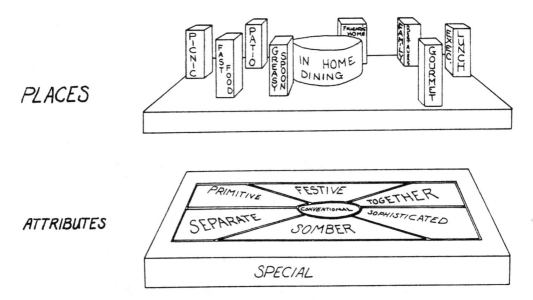

Figure 51.4. Eating at home and eating out

range from lower-class greasy spoons and forthright EATS cafes, through miscellaneous youthful fast food and family-style restaurants, to elegant, cosmopolitan dining rooms. Moving the family unit from the home to the restaurant tends to express a festive attitude and the relaxation of parental responsibility; this attitude becomes even more pronounced for children and adds elements of separation and liberation when they go to fast food restaurants on their own. Lower-class cafes and fancy restaurants are adult in meaning, places for adults at work away from home (truck stops, executive business lunches). At the heights, haute cuisine with its subtle sauces and other exotic efforts, symbolizes an elite use of leisure, an extreme degree of refinement of the palate, and attendant sybaritic sensibilities. People eat dishes they never have at home and go beyond ordinary meats to expensive cuts and seafood.

Beyond the cooked. Cooking is aimed at numerous objectives—making substances more chewable, more digestible, safer, warm and comforting, and more interesting to the taste. It is a process of culture, as opposed to the natural, and its degrees of status tend to be equated with distancing from the primitive and animal eating of raw food. As indicated above, these degrees of status are expressed in complexity, subtlety, particular foods, methods of preparation, and settings. Basic qualities range from an infantile, homogeneous, mushy, boiled grossness to a highly differentiated awareness of textures, ingredients, seasonings, and nuances of preparation.

Little myths are dynamic and change as new experiences become available. Recently added in the raw-to-cooked dimension is a new myth of high-status consumption that might be termed transcendental or self-conscious rawness. Like a kind of conspicuous underconsumption or like the French court dressing as Watteau shepherds and shepherdesses, one finds elegantly dressed partygoers eating various raw vegetables with their fingers (crudités) and exclaiming over their daring in eating raw hamburger (steak tartare) or raw fish (sushi). With a heightened physicality (exercising, jogging), the sophisticated return to nature goes with natural rather than processed cheeses, live bacterial processes in yogurt, yeasts, and yerba, peasant grains and dark breads. It is a retreat from over-refinement, a cycling down to rescue the effete body and restore its sexual vigor, mingled with the elite cosmopolitanism of imported dishes.

In much of this consumer behavior there is no contradiction; rather, the social group prescribes roles and their accompanying symbols; and consumers participate by adopting the roles and symbols suited to their identities. However, animating the process are the deeper contradictions and conflicts that question whether the physical differences attributed to age and sex differences are properly fitted to the culinary and dietary differences. That is, are we preparing and eating the right things? Women should be good cooks by their maternal nature; but the highest art and science of cookery paradoxically tend to be attributed to male chefs (*pace,* Julia Child). Is hierarchy real? Are the foods, dishes, methods, and deferential service sufficient in their symbolism to reassure the elite that it is truly elevated? Does eating and thinking make it so?

Perhaps even more fundamental to the little myths, given the insistent refinements of gustatory perception and the aesthetic superiorities with which mothers and elites seek to socialize the young and those of lower status, is the struggle with the basic question: Am I an animal or am I a person? How do we reconcile the animal nature of the eaters with the human culture of the cooks, the intractable fact of the body with the refinements of civilization?

MARKETING IMPLICATIONS

This article has been an exploration and stops with some concluding comments. It has demonstrated a qualitative approach to the study of consumer behavior, as follows: We can enrich our understanding of consumer behavior by taking consumer protocols as stories that use a sociocultural vocabulary. The analysis blends functional-symbolic-structural logics to observe that a dietary behavior is probably not well understood in isolation or by focusing narrowly on product attributes in the way that much marketing research does. Soler (1979) reminds us of this.

> It must be placed into the context of the signs in the same area of life; together they constitute a system; and this system in turn must be seen in relation to the other systems in other areas, for the interaction of all these systems constitute the sociocultural system of a people. (p. 25)

Consumer behavior in the food area uses fundamental generalizations about the meanings of products in a broadly conventional way, within which dynamic processes of individuation and differentiation go on. The little myths show how the basic vocabulary of cooking and eating is used to express identities by males and females, the young and the mature, and people in low-, middle-, and high-status positions. General modeling by age, sex, and social status is a familiar one to marketers; here the analysis observes how specific symbolic distinctions are being made among specific foods, ways of preparing them, and in some of the ideas they represent, such as family unity/dispersion, naivete/sophistication, routine/festivity, sickness/health, grossness/subtlety, conformity/deviation, sacred/profane, and so on.

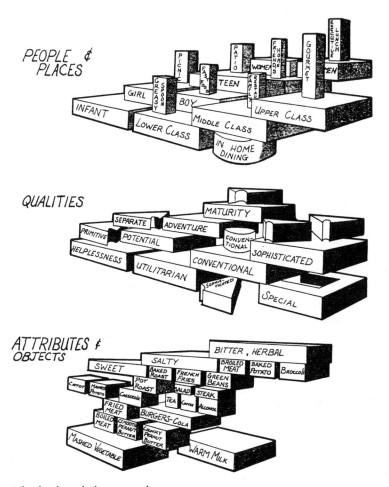

Figure 51.5. The food mythology complex

Figure 51.5 sums up the complex structure of the food mythology. It is drawn to resemble a three-dimensional urban scene, suggesting the cultural sophistication operating to organize biological statuses, sex roles, age gradings, and social positions in terms of both psychological dimensions and food attributes such as taste, texture, appearance, and method of preparation. The marketer works within this complex, using the symbolic vocabulary to define and position the product.

The broad brushstrokes indicated above may encourage further study of how families develop their particular little myths; how common cultural little myths change over time; how facts of behavior are modified in the telling; what the facts or the modified telling are being used to say; how marketers participate in creating the symbolic vocabulary; and how they may use the consumers' mythology on behalf of their specific products and brands in their continuing dialog with consumers.

REFERENCES

Abelson, R. P. (1976). Script processing in attitude formation and decision making. In J. Carroll & J. Payne (Eds.), *Cognition and social behavior.* Hillsdale, NJ: Lawrence Erlbaum.

Bellenger, D., Bernhardt, K. L., & Goldstucker, J. L. (1976). *Qualitative research in marketing.* Chicago: American Marketing Association.

Bettelheim, B. (1977). *The uses of enchantment.* New York: Vintage.

de Gramont, S. (1970). There are no superior societies. In E. N. Hayes & T. Hayes (Eds.), *Claude Levi-Strauss, The anthropologist as hero* (pp. 3-21). Cambridge: MIT Press.

Firat, A. F. (1978). *Social construction of consumption patterns.* Ph.D. dissertation, Northwestern University, Evanston, IL.

Frazer, J. G. (1927). *The golden bough: A study in magic and religion.* New York: Macmillan.

Leach, E. (1974). *Claude Levi-Strauss.* New York: Viking.

Levi-Strauss, C. (1963). *Structural anthropology* (Vol. 1). New York: Basic Books.

Levi-Strauss, C. (1969). *The raw and the cooked.* New York: Harper & Row.

Levi-Strauss, C. (1978). *The origins of table manners.* New York: Harper & Row.

Levy, S. J. (1978, March/April). Hunger and work in a civilized tribe. *American Behavioral Scientist, 21,* 557-570.

Rapaport, D. (1942). Principles underlying projective techniques. *Character and Personality, 10*(3), 213-219.

Soler, J. (1979, June 14). The dietary prohibitions of the Hebrews. *New York Review of Books, 27,* 24-25.

Stephen, L. (1968). *English men of letters.* London: AMS Press.

Williams, D. B. (1976). *An information processing theory of individual purchasing behavior.* Ph.D. dissertation, Northwestern University, Evanston, IL.

## Chapter 52

DREAMS, FAIRY TALES, ANIMALS, AND CARS

Sidney J. Levy

Projective research methods are not new to marketing research. In the late 1940s to 1950s, in the heyday of what was called Motivation Research, several techniques were used to explore marketing topics. Researchers experimented with various derivations from the Thematic Apperception Technique, as well as incomplete sentences, word associations, drawings, fantasy tasks of different kinds, and even such an obscure device as the Szondi Test. George Horsley Smith described the adaptation of these clinical methods in his 1954 book on motivation research in marketing and advertising, and Joseph Newman's 1957 volume on motivation research and marketing management illustrates some cases with examples. Robert Ferber and Hugh G. Wales discuss projective techniques at length in their 1958 book on motivation and market behavior.

Among those references and the otherwise voluminous literature that is available about projective techniques can probably be found much of what is needed for actually using them. Nevertheless, their use in marketing studies has diminished rather than grown, since the '50s. Few people are

This chapter was first published in *Psychology and Marketing*, 2(2), 67-81. Copyright © 1985. Reprinted by permission of John Wiley & Sons, Inc.

skilled and confident enough to make easy and fluent use of projectives. Those who are interested may feel frustrated in the face of the general low level of acceptance. However, the signs of growth of qualitative research studies that go beyond focus grouping to intensive exploration of individual consumers suggest that there is more willingness to confront the interpretive challenge posed in analyzing projectives. This paper is oriented toward encouraging that willingness.

David Rapaport (1942) stated the projective hypothesis as indicating that "all behavioral manifestations of the human being, including the least and the most significant, are revealing and expressive of his personality, by which we mean that individual principle of which he is the carrier." Thus, any question (or stimulus) proposed to a respondent in research that elicits behavior is fundamentally a projective technique. However, what can be learned about the respondent will be affected by many circumstances. Respondents are not merely being expressive, they are expressive in relation to the nature of the stimulus and how they receive it.

1. *The more specific the question, the narrower the range of information given by the respondent.* When the stimulus is more open and responses are freer, the information provided tends to be greater. Because structured questionnaires restrict responses (yes or no or one of a few multiple choices) and do not allow much individuality of expression, they are not thought of as projective. Actually, in order to answer even yes or no, the person has to draw on his individual experience and project it; but the response does not give much insight into that individuality. At the other extreme are questions that encourage fantasies or that present respondents with great ambi-

guity which requires them to reveal their associations and their ways of organizing experience, thus making the projective aspect most apparent. In between is a spectrum of possible approaches with greater or lesser opportunity for eliciting projection.

2. *The stimuli may be aimed to elicit responses at different levels of personality.* Some address the more superficial, outward, or conventional kinds of behavior. The goal may be to observe the conforming aspects of the respondents, the way in which ordinary reactions are given to common social ideas. In other instances, respondents may be stirred by material for which conventional guidelines are less readily available. Then the underlying resources of the person are brought into play.

3. *The direction of research interest may be aimed especially at learning about the respondents' psychosocial characteristics*; or it may be aimed especially at learning about the respondents' perceptions of the marketing object and behavior that is of concern. When focusing on the respondents per se, materials might be used that do not refer to the product at all.

4. *The research goals of diversity, depth, and direction thus guide the selection of stimuli in terms of their form and content.* When the research subjects have made their responses, the data can be handled in several different ways. A relatively simple method is to use content analysis, classifying the responses into a distribution of categories whose frequencies are then reported. This procedure comes closest to that used in traditional marketing research where interview data are taken as given and organized into tables. In essence, such methods accept the responses as facts and present them in summary or aggregated

form. Commonly, the research report offers no interpretation of the data or notes how the findings compare with prior results or magnitudes that had been expected.

The distinguishing essence of the procedure in using projective techniques as such is an emphasis on interpretation. That is, rather than (or in addition to) telling what the data are, greater stress is given to what the analyst thinks they imply. In doing this, the analyst proceeds on the assumption that the responses are better understood taken in relation to each other, and that inferences may be made about them at levels other than face value. That is, the projective functions as a way of asking indirect questions. In the extreme case, the interpretations might be offered without citing the data at all. Several examples will illustrate these different ways of using projective procedures.

ANIMALS, CARS, AND PEOPLE

In some instances, when discussing competitive brands, respondents have difficulty in directly articulating the different images they have of them. They can be helped to express their impressions by being asked to relate the brand to other kinds of objects. Often used are stimuli such as cars, animals, and human stereotypes to assist in bringing out the respondents' associative processes. They are asked such questions as these:

1. If Brand A were a car, what would it be?

2. Why might it be that car?

3. If it were an animal, which one might it be?

4. Looking at these people, which ones do you think would be most likely to use the following brands?

5. Tell me the two people most likely to use that brand.

6. Why is this person most likely to use that brand?

Observing the clusters of choices made is itself helpful in analysis; but the explanations people give for their choices are important for understanding what aspects of the cars, animals, and people they see as relevant. Of course, asking about the kinds of people who use the product or brand is just a step away from asking respondents directly about the reasons for their own use. But it is often more informative because users commonly explain their own use by referring to not-very-differentiating product virtues and hesitate to see it as expressing something characteristic of the kinds of persons they are. In addition, the choices of types of people form a pattern, showing some of the variation in psychosocial meanings of the product and its brands, with further distinctions between users and nonusers.

Two brands were compared for choices made among cars, animals, and people. Users of Brand A associated their brand distinctively with cars that are either prestigious and expensive or somewhat rugged, showing two main dimensions in their view: Mercedes-Benz, Corvette, Rolls Royce, Porsche, Maserati, Jaguar or Jeep, Blazer, and various pickups. Nonusers of Brand A represented it also with rugged cars but otherwise as more out of the mainstream than classy. The cars named for B, its main competitor, were predominantly standard and work cars, with few high-class cars and little difference among users and nonusers. That is, from these data alone it could be inferred that Brand B is a mainstream brand with widespread suitability, whereas Brand A is attributed to specialized segments.

Figure 52.1. Types of people

The animal choices reinforced these impressions. Brand A animals were strong and proud (lions, tigers), heavy (elephant, rhino), and offbeat (koala, zebra), whereas Brand B associations were dominated by horses and other more ordinary domestic animals.

These brands were seen as especially used by males, and the animals named suggests that. However, when the respondents made choices of people for the two brands from the array shown in Figure 52.1, a richer picture emerged. The special segments seen in Table 52.1 as fitted to Brand A are almost exclusively male, whereas Brand B's appeal is able to include women and a definitely younger audience.

The sensitivity of the method is shown by comparing animal choices made in an-other study of an exclusively female brand, which was seen as appealing to two main sources of motivation—those related to beauty, grace, and sinuosity (snake, python, leopard, swan, panther, Persian cat) and those related to affiliative needs for cuddling and protection (kitten, poodle, Pekingese, puppy, teddy bear, little bird).

DREAMS

As another form of fantasy, dreams may give access to the character of the person and to the character of the product. In one study, consumers were asked to use a new product for several days, during which time they maintained a diary giving various facts about their experience with the product.

TABLE 52.1 Choices of Kinds of People

		Brand A (N = 120)	Brand B (N = 120)
# 1	Ordinary man	18	6
# 2	Mustached man	48	41
# 3	Young girl	1	24
# 4	Young businessman	8	18
# 5	Businesswoman	2	11
# 6	Older businessman	26	10
# 7	Hard-hat	72	39
# 8	Party girl	6	12
# 9	College student	14	32
#10	Housewife	2	2
		200%	200%

They were also asked to report on any dreams they could recall during this trial period. Some of the dreams seemed to refer to the symbolic significance of the product. In a more direct approach to the use of this fantasy method, respondents have been asked during an interview about a product to "imagine the you are having a dream" about that product. "Tell me what might happen in that dream—describe the situation, what is involved, what happens, and how it turns out."

People readily provide these "day-dreams," and such little fantasy vignettes are useful for eliciting a rather free projection of implications about the meaning of the product. For instance, in a study of attitudes toward milk, this method produced stories along the following lines.

Having a bath in milk. Throwing buckets of milk all over people. Raining milk, everything covered in white. I'd probably be in the bath with a lot of people, having orgies.

I'd probably overdose on it. I'd be swimming in it or going down a river on a raft or water ski in it. Be in a Jacuzzi of milk where someone was pouring in cornflakes and strawberries.

I might go swimming in it. I like to swim. I'd meet a pretty girl and land on a cookie island.

It appears that the task frees people in several ways. They are often humorous, taking the request for a dream as a kind of joke. They exaggerate and think of self-indulgence in both milk and sex. The impression of a general tendency was reinforced by a study of chocolate in which there were similar fantasies of wallowing in great quantities of chocolate. But more differentiation was shown when a sample of wine drinkers were asked for a dream about wine. The same good-natured responsiveness appeared, as well as the same visions of sexual success. But the idea of wine is more mature than that of milk or chocolate. There were fewer expressions of regressive immersion in wine or ideas of sheer quantity. Rather, the fantasies were of sophisticated people, elegant settings, and romantic seductions where the wine acts as the cue and catalyst.

> A very attractive woman is sitting at her vanity table, putting on her makeup. She hears the doorbell ring. She squirts some perfume on her neck and goes to the door. She opens it slowly and there stands Mr. Gorgeous, holding a bottle of wine, sparkling from the light of the candle. She takes him by the hand to the bedroom. That's the end.

> It would be a sexy dream. I would be drinking wine out of a beautiful stemmed glass in a man's apartment, a magnificent apartment, a penthouse overlooking the East River. We are drinking this delicious white wine, probably a Pouilly Fuisse. Whatever I hoped to come true really does come true. I'm not going to be explicit at this moment. You use your imagination for the end of my dream.

> At a picnic lunch, with a girl, near a lake under shady trees. We polish off a couple of fifths of wine, fall in love, make love, and become real close real fast. We vow to stay in love and plan to meet like this once a week, which we do and cement our relationship. It leads to our living together to see if we want to spend the rest of our lives together.

PICTORIAL SYMBOLS

Showing pictures of human stereotypes helps respondents to sum up their thoughts as they think about the ways the people might symbolize or fit the character of the product or brand. Another means of accomplishing this kind of analysis through the use of visual symbols is to use not only sketches of people but of other stock signs. This method is a simple pictorial analog to using a list of descriptive words. It permits a change of pace and variety in the interview and some openness for respondents.

Figure 52.2 is a set that has been used as a convenient device to elicit projections to various objects. In a study of perceptions of major hotel chains, respondents were shown the set of visual symbols and given these instructions.

> I'd like you to play an association game—Here are some pictures. For each hotel that I name, please pick two of the pictures that come closest to fitting how you feel about that hotel—Why did you select that sketch for that hotel?

Their choices of symbols gives a quick summary of meanings associated with them. The top-ranked hotel in the group studied was associated with Trees-Sun-Globe-Diamond-Lady as being expensive and luxurious; and the other highly regarded chains similarly had Diamond and Lady chosen. All but the top hotel had Meeting chosen. The Sun went with resort and vacation ideas, the Beef with good food. A big pragmatic chain would be mainly Meeting-Beef-Globe. If it is a fun place for a meeting, it might be Beef-Meeting-Circus-Sun. While a conventional questionnaire may show little distinction among descriptions of major hotel chains, the pictorial choices and their explanations allow for subtler reactions.

STORYTELLING TO PICTURES

Whether asking about the product (or brand), or seeking to learn about the respondents, the use of stories has particular

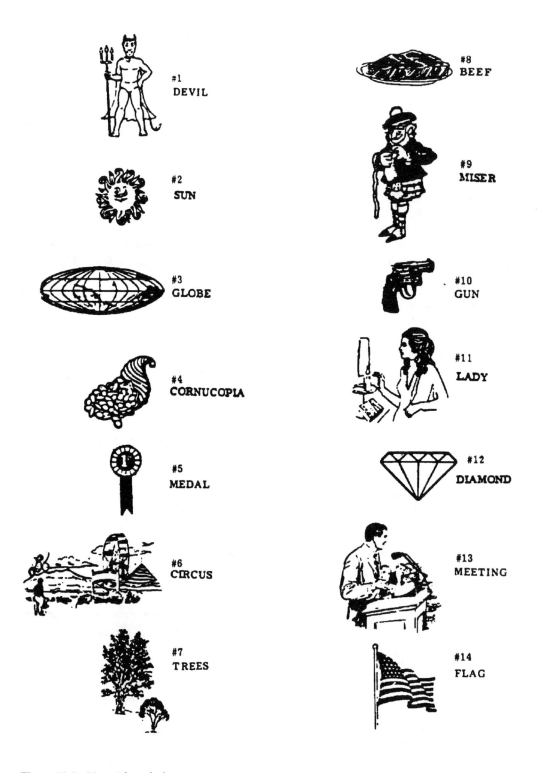

Figure 52.2. Pictorial symbols

Figure 52.3. Two women shopping

merit in providing richness of data for interpretation. Often, stories are solicited by showing pictures. The pictures may be oriented around the product, as in Figure 52.3, where two women are shown in a supermarket. The drawing is crude and vague, so that realistic clues do not dominate reactions (and to demonstrate that sophisticated drawing skills are not needed to prepare the stimuli). The respondents were told that one woman is purchasing a dry soup mix. They were asked which she might be and for a story to be told about

her. Then the other woman is said never to have tried a dry soup mix, and the respondent tells what she is like and what she is told by the first purchaser. Without asking more specifically than that, the stories become vehicles for the respondents' use to express (a) how they feel other people might think about them for using this product, (b) their attitudes toward the family and feeding them this product, (c) their ideas and reasons for and against using the product. Projected into the stories were four main use profiles or types.

Figure 52.4. Two boys buying hot dogs

1. *The creative woman*: The dry soup user is the good cook, what you call a creative cook, and she creates miracles with these package soups. By adding to hamburger you can create meat loaf that is extraordinary. The other one just doesn't know the magic some dry soups can create in your cooking.

2. *The practical, modern woman*: This one is a young mother with small children who likes the convenience of dry soup to make easy meals. It's easier to store than cans because she can buy more of it and it offers a greater variety of flavors. . . . She is younger, more apt to try new products, and experiment.

3. *The lazy or indifferent woman*: The one on the outside is looking at dry soups be-

cause they are easy to reach, easier to carry home from the store than canned. She feels they are easier to fix. She is lazy and bored and takes the easy way out when she is cooking. She likes to shop and get away from the kids. She has five or six that get on her nerves. She is just going to get envelopes and fix a big batch for them.

4. *The underprivileged woman*: She has to buy it because she has a very large family and these are more economical, the dried are lower in price, 3 to 4 cents a serving. The dry soup buyer says the dry is just as good in taste and nutritional value.

In another instance, two boys are shown (Figure 52.4) and said to be thinking about buying hot dogs. One is said to buy the brand his mother asked him to get. The other little boy is said to buy the brand he

Figure 52.5. Tell a story

wanted. Respondents told stories about the boys, who would buy what his mother requested and why, which would buy another brand, and so on. The brands discussed are thus shown to have levels of virtue and appeal to the youngsters; with choices related to the ways the boys are dressed and their attitudes toward hot dogs, mothers, money, and so on. The obedient boy is middle class and buys a conventional national brand; the other indulges himself, buys a more frivolous-seeming brand, and pockets the change.

The research purpose may not inquire into brand perception but can be one of learning about psychological characteristics of the respondents. A brief variation of the classical Thematic Apperception Technique can serve this purpose. Figure 52.5 has been used, the respondents being asked to tell a story about what they see in the picture, what is going on, what led up to it, and how it will come out. The stories told by users of one brand tended to be relatively calm, peaceful tales accepting of the figure as relaxed, contemplative, idle, and so on. These tales suggest a market segment that is relatively conventional, able to relax, and accepting of the moment; ideas that were meaningfully related to the image of the brand.

Someone leaning on a fencepost looking out toward the mountains. After dinner just watching the sunset, just thinking about the beauty of his surroundings.

Man being very introspective, thinking about someone in his past. Good thoughts, peaceful thoughts. Some random occurrence, just walking along the beach, very romantic. I don't think there's an ending, it's just a passive moment.

The users of the main competitive brand had more troubled aspects to their stories. More negative emotions and adverse events were described. They appeared to be people who saw more complexity in life and sought to come through difficulties toward resolution. Their outlook was compatible with a brand that represented a stronger sense of striving and achievement.

It's a male leaning against a post. He's young, confused, and depressed; maybe contemplating something. His posture tells me he's thinking about something serious. He's thinking about a woman, thinking about his relationship. He's going to come out OK.

It's a man in a real reflective mood. He's leaning against the frame of his childhood home that's burned down, but he still has memories. He thinks about the good and bad times.

The person is depressed and standing in a doorway. Somebody has just left him, an argument. Hopefully, she'll come back and say I'm sorry, I didn't mean it.

FAIRY TALES

In a study of women's attitudes toward kinds of femininity, understanding was sought of women's self-concepts, aspirations, relationships, and so on. As part of the interview, to assist in observing some of their values along these lines, respondents were presented with the following plot summaries of four stories from fairy tale and operatic literature. They were asked to

tell which of these stories is most appealing. Why do they like it the best? How is it different from the other stories? What is the best part of the story? What do they think this story shows about people that is important? They were also asked which of the stories is least appealing. Why do they like it least? What is the worst part of it? What can people learn from this story?

Presented Plot Summaries

Cinderella. Cinderella has a mean stepmother and stepsisters. She does the dirty housework. She wants to go to a ball, too. Her fairy godmother magically gives her a ball gown, glass slippers, and a coach. She is the belle of the ball, and the prince falls in love with her. At midnight, she leaves, losing one of her slippers. The prince finds the slipper, looks for her, and finds a girl whom the slipper fits, and it is Cinderella. They wed and live happily ever after.

Brunnhilde. Brunnhilde, the Valkyrie, disobeys her father, the god Wotan, so she is put into a magic sleep within a circle of fire. Siegfried, the hero, rescues her and they get married, but Siegfried is deceived into betraying Brunnhilde, so she plots against him. He is killed, and Brunnhilde rides her horse into the flames of the funeral pyre.

My Fair Lady. Eliza Doolittle is a poor flower girl found on the street by Professor Higgins. Her lower-class speech and appearance are handicaps. She learns from the professor how to talk and look like a lady. She then wants to be independent.

Snow White. Snow White's stepmother is a wicked queen, who is jealous of Snow White's beauty and goodness. She plots to kill Snow White so she can be the most beautiful in her magic mirror. Snow White is spared by the huntsman and goes to keep house for the seven dwarfs. The Queen finds out and gives Snow White a poisoned apple. Snow White lies unconscious until awakened by the prince's kiss. They wed and live happily after.

The selection of stories was based on a progression in the fantasies the tales represent. Cinderella is the bedrock romantic tale, so to speak, in which the most magical transformation from rags to riches occurs. The Cinderella tale is ever captivating for this gratifying solution to all of life's problems. It is the most popular tale among the respondents, because going dancing in a ballgown is such a pleasant idea and because Cinderella is tenacious in her dreams, and they come true.

> I can relate to it. I was the oldest in my family and I had to do all the housework. Of course, I didn't have such a happy ending. The story has a little of a magical background. If you wait long enough, your dreams will come true.

The Snow White story is a more middle-class tale of a passive virtuous girl, envied for her beauty, manipulated by others; but a good mothering person to the dwarfs. She is awakened to adult sexuality by the prince's kiss and has the classical happy ending. Modern women tend to look for more self-assertion in their role models; but they also appreciate the complexity and darker touches of the story.

> There's jealousy and love. There are different kinds of people. The best part is when the huntsman gets the heart of a deer and puts it in a box and says it's Snow White's. It's different from the other stories because

there's a little touch of horror in it. It teaches a moral lesson about vanity.

My Fair Lady also has the charm of transformation, but a more mature appeal due to its realistic tone. Eliza overcomes her handicaps through education and effort, not magic.

> She started with nothing and turns out to be a lady. There's no prince to ride off into the sunset with. I like the part about her being a lady. People are what they make of themselves.

> She wants to be independent. The others have women who are sad and begging. It tells of independence, and women like that idea.

Brunnhilde's story is the least appealing because of its many negative elements. Women are especially pained by the implication that other people are not to be trusted, even when they are beloved. On the other hand, the story is exciting and points to the realities of life not being lived happily ever after.

> It's exciting. The fire, the rescuing, and the killing. It doesn't end happily like the other stories, but it still tells a good tale.

> I like Brunnhilde because it's so sad and romantic. I think it shows love is all-consuming. I like the end best, and it's different because it doesn't have a happy ending.

WORD ASSOCIATIONS

The use of word association has a long history. In a casual sense, all questioning is a form of word association. Often, it is apparent that asked a full question, respondents answer as if they heard one main word in the sentence that triggers their response in a "klang!" way; rather than considering the idea more deliberately. Thus, a list of words or phrases, called a word association, may well serve the same purpose of eliciting the respondents' main ideas in a truncated fashion; and perhaps be quite efficient. For example, in a study of women's attitudes toward soaps and detergents, each respondent was instructed to say the first thing she thought of on hearing a series of words read one at a time. Here are the responses of two women of similar age and family status.

Stimulus	Mrs. M	Mrs. C
washday	everyday	ironing
fresh	and sweet	clean
pure	air	clean
scrub	don't; Ray(husband)	does clean
filth	this neighborhood	dirt
bubbles	bath	soap and water
family	squabbles	children
towels	dirty	wash

The sets of responses are quite different, suggesting how the women differ in personality, and in their attitudes toward housekeeping and its problems. Mrs. M.'s associations suggest that she is more resigned to dirt, seeing it as somewhat inevitable, with little implication that she can or wants to do much about it. It is her husband who does the hard cleaning. Nor does she get pleasure from her family. Her most positive associations are sensuous, self-oriented ones. Mrs. C sees dirt, too, but is energetic, factual-minded, and less emotional. She is ready actively to combat dirt; and her weapons are soap and water. Of course, one would not want to be restricted

to inferences from such a limited amount of information, but the example illustrates the potential richness of even just 10, 12 words from each person.

SUMMARY

The various examples of projective methods were presented to illustrate these main ideas:

1. *Projective techniques are a varied and flexible means of eliciting information.* Examples in addition to those noted above are: (a) incomplete sentences: "This meeting is . . . " "If I were to use a projective method . . . ", and so on; (b) People have been asked to draw pictures. "Draw a picture of a person with a cigarette." (c) In a study of air freight, respondents were asked to describe the personalities of Mr. Emery Air Freight and Mr. Federal Express. In the milk study: "If you were to imagine a Mr. Milk or Mrs. Milk, what would such a person be like? Describe how he or she would look. What sort of personality he or she would have." (d) Sometimes respondents are asked to name public figures, past or present, who would use various brands, and why; in other instances, they are asked to match specific public figures with the brands.

The design of methods seems mainly limited by the researcher's inventiveness.

2. *If we demystify these methods, they can be seen merely as various ways of asking questions about products and about people.* Their use recognizes that there is no single right way to ask a question and that some questions might as well be fun, perplexing, challenging, at times even absurd. In some cases, the method may be no better than a

direct question, in which case it might be used for the sake of variety, a change of pace, sustaining interest among respondents. In some cases, projectives do not seem useful; as is true of many direct questions. But often, the projectives make it possible for people to express themselves more fully, subtly, perhaps even to represent themselves more fairly. When that happens, the methods do achieve a greater validity than methods whose reliability seems more comforting to researchers.

3. *The necessity for intelligent interpretation of projective data raises questions about reliability, given the varied skills among research analysts.* However, competence in doing any research is a challenge to us all. Projectives do require the "nerve of interpretation," but the reliability will increase with our willingness to try and to keep trying until we share the methods as familiar tools among the rest in our research quiver.

REFERENCES

Ferber, R., & Wales, H. G. (1958). *Motivation and market behavior.* Homewood, IL: Irwin.

Newman, J. W. (1957). *Motivation research and marketing management.* Cambridge, MA: Harvard University Press.

Rapaport, D. (1942). Principles underlying projective techniques. *Character and Personality, 10*(3), 213.

Smith, G. H. (1954). *Motivation research in advertising and marketing.* New York: McGraw-Hill.

Chapter 53

MARKETING RESEARCH AS A DIALOGUE

Sidney J. Levy

As a teacher and marketing researcher, I encounter a wide variety of people in the marketplace—students, marketing practitioners, other executive and professional personnel, and consumers, in both business and nonbusiness settings. The issues and problems that relate to the interest of the consumer as they interact with the interests of those who offer their goods and services are many. It is my theme that the marketplace is a dialogue, both harmonious and contentious. The conflicts between marketing research and the consumer interest arise

from differences in goals, the discrepancy between ideals and practice, and the conflicts among basic values.

CROSS-PURPOSES IN THE DIALOGUE

Marketing research is carried out by great numbers of people whose aims and ethical concerns range considerably. In general, they are supposed to be guided by the purposes and codes of ethics provided by

This chapter was first published in E. S. Maynes (Ed.), *The Frontier of Research in the Consumer Interest* (pp. 653-658), 1988. Reprinted by permission of the American Council on Consumer Interests.

such groups as the American Marketing Association and the Marketing Research Association.

All these virtuous directives take for granted that marketers have the right to conduct marketing research in the first place. Further, it is a fundamental tenet that marketing research is essential to serving the consumer's interest. As Kotler (1984) states it, "companies can serve their markets well only by researching their needs and wants, their locations, their buying practices, and so on" (p. 64).

The guidelines of the American Marketing Association call for the betterment of society, presenting goods, services, and concepts honestly and clearly; supporting free consumer choice, and accountability. The Marketing Research Association specifies numerous though different goals: objectivity, accuracy, protecting anonymity and confidentiality, promoting trust among the public, avoiding misrepresentation, and so on.

From such statements we might suppose that there would be no difficulties with the consumer interest, as everyone presumably has it in mind. But that would be naive. There is no single view of the consumer interest nor is there a single path to the betterment of society. It is more realistic to recognize that there are diverse interests. The market may be viewed as a place where people communicate by language and action to arrive at mutually satisfactory consummations. But it may also be viewed as an arena where they contentiously express their individual and group aims even when these are not satisfying to others.

Marketing research is one part of this communication process, a dialogue that may be both harmonious and contentious. Such a dialogue cannot entirely produce accord because the objectives of the participants are not the same and because there is

no final resolution to the differences that arise about specific methods and how they relate to people's objectives and to their underlying values.

Much marketing research is harmonious with a general concept of the consumer interest, gathering either innocuous information or data that clearly serves consumer goals. Marketing researchers often share the same goals as consumers, clearly seeking information that will benefit consumers. Examples of market research that serves both consumers and market researchers would be efforts to learn what product improvements are desired, what new products are sought, what information consumers want, how well they interpret the language being addressed to them.

Then again, marketers may have other goals in mind of which consumers would not approve, such as learning how to increase consumption of a product widely regarded as "bad," or testing advertising appeals that would reduce store inventories even though stockpiling at home might not help the consumer, or learning about "unconstructive" consumer motives in order to exploit them.

IDEALS VERSUS PRACTICE

It is possible to feel virtuous about one's aims as a market researcher and to desire the best for consumers without adhering to the standards of the AMA and the MRA. For example, many researchers have no qualms about "borrowing" the names of survey respondents to generate lists of potential customers. Why should one suffer pangs of conscience, if one believes the product is a good one that will benefit the people on the list?

Researchers differ as to what kind of respondent briefing should be done.

Should respondents be told who is sponsoring the research study? It seems only right to do that; speaking personally, I would like to know. But knowledge of sponsor's identity may interfere with people's spontaneity or objectivity. Worse, it might jeopardize their willingness to respond. On the other hand, do they not have to be interviewed in order "to be heard"? Presumably not, since the right to be heard certainly includes the right not to be heard. Against this is the requirement of some democracies that citizens must vote!

Should market researchers seek to elicit information only when respondents are clearly aware of the information they are providing? Sometimes the understanding sought in research might best be gained indirectly, under conditions where the respondent is providing information without being aware of it. This is often the purpose of unobtrusive measures, participant observation, and projective techniques. Here the respondents or consumers may not realize that their behavior is being watched; they will not know how their projective responses or behavior will be interpreted.

The idea of interpretation is itself a thorny one. Some people object to methods that could reveal information that respondents themselves would prefer to deny or to be concealed. A counterargument is that interpretation is applied to most human communication; even the information that the respondent gives knowingly is subject to interpretation. Is it much different to interpret information obtained without the respondent's direct knowledge and consent? Further, some argue that structured questions and rating scales, brief check-off questionnaires, or the chance to make a few remarks in a focus group interview do not represent genuine two-way dialogues. To be ethical, Ted Karger (1986) argues that

researchers can best serve the public, their organizations, and their own professional development by understanding consumers fully: "Then, much more often, they would probe deeply into the hearts, minds, and behaviors of the people—would employ comprehensive personal dialogues to serve as penetrating diagnostic interviews—so that the vox populi becomes vividly clear" (p. 2). Karger's argument thus justifies the use of indirect means, lacking respondent consent, as a means of fully understanding the consumers and thus responding to them.

In some fields, standards for research with human subjects require that subjects be debriefed or provided with information about the results of the study. Sometimes, some kind of debriefing may occur in marketing research. Usually, however, respondents are dismissed with thanks. Often their participation is induced by a monetary incentive that heightens cooperation and reduces criticism. Paying people to be interviewed could be taken as a way of corrupting them, perhaps interfering with their desire to avoid the interview. Then again, such payment may be taken as a sign of the urgency of the desire to elicit the consumer's voice, of the importance of the research to its sponsor.

THE CONFLICT OF VALUES

Underlying these and other troubling matters in the conduct of marketing research are fundamental conflicts of values. Marketing research is a quest for information and understanding. It takes advantage of an implied freedom of inquiry. Whether this freedom should extend to commercial inquiry probably depends upon whether one believes that commercial speech is protected. For example, Laczniak and Michie (1979) approve of government's constraints on business practices and express anxiety about the use of "marketing" methods to disseminate concepts they term "ethically charged" and "controversial" because "when someone 'markets' an idea, the first amendment limits the level of restraint that is possible" (p. 225).

Advertising Age, conversely, worries that William Rehnquist's nomination as Chief Justice may represent the end of an era for advertisers who welcomed the expanded First Amendment protection in Supreme Court decisions of the 1970s and '80s.

Should marketing research help consumers achieve greater freedom of choice? Should they be asked what they want? Marketing research is often used to study the needs and wants of marketing segments with an eye to providing them with new products. There are several sources of controversy here. Many critics believe that it is fine to *satisfy needs,* but that marketing research is often in the position of *creating wants.* It is not clear why the creation of wants is per se a bad thing, although it is easy to cite horrendous or seemingly indefensible examples. Others argue that the task of defining needs versus wants is a semantic hornet's nest, something not worth the pain. Still others feel that once we progress beyond primitive man's cave, club, fire, and mate, all other products and services represent wants that were created— by some force in our society.

Some assert that it is not in the consumer interest to widen the boundaries of choice, as this is economically inefficient and wasteful of resources. In their view marketing research should be used to learn what the boundaries of choice should be. Inquiring into consumer choice implies an encouragement of private spending and inter-

feres with the more publicly useful ways money might be spent, as J. K. Galbraith has so often reminded us. This implies that consumers may not know their own interests, at least not in the aggregate, and therefore should not be asked what they want. Instead they should be given what is good for them. Of course, then it might be useful to do marketing research with those who have (or take?) the responsibility of determining what is good for the consumer; as well as with those who are having the alleged good done to them.

The many issues that put the desirability of marketing research into question could be taken as a basis for drastic inhibition of marketing research. In my view these problems should not prevent the conduct of inquiries by marketing managers. They should be free to carry out marketing research without revealing their identity and entire aims as long as their business is arguably legitimate and their purposes no more harmful than the society is willing to tolerate at that time.

As a teacher of students studying for a master's degree in management, I seek to make them aware of these issues and to encourage them to work out their own positions (with which I often disagree). As a research supplier, I reserve the right to work for clients whose goals I support and to avoid those whose values I reject. In undertaking market research, I consider myself free to ask consumers any questions that seem appropriate to the problem and that fit my values concerning courtesy, respect for the dignity of respondents and for their right to respond as they wish. The interpretation of their responses to questionnaires or other instruments is my responsibility. I seek to understand and convey their "true" feelings or views as accurately as possible.

As a consumer and potential respondent, I support the right of organizations to conduct marketing research even though I find some of it annoying. I consider myself free to refuse to fill out questionnaires I receive in the mail, to do them hastily or partially, to avoid interviewers or to talk freely, to guard my responses as my personality dictates, perhaps even to tell whatever lies I can tolerate in myself when I answer questions, to put my answers in the best light I can, and in general to protect my interests as I see them. I expect the respondents in my researches to do the same.

REFERENCES

Karger, T. (1986, July 4). Your opinion counts—only if researchers really listen. *Marketing News*, p. 2.

Kotler, P. (1984). *Marketing management: Analysis, planning, and control.* Englewood Cliffs, NJ: Prentice Hall.

Laczniak, G. R., & Michie, D. A. (1979). The social disorder of the broadened concept of marketing. *Journal of Academy of Marketing Science, 7*(3), 214-232.

## Chapter 54

AUTODRIVING
A Photoelicitation Technique

Deborah D. Heisley
Sidney J. Levy

Oh, wad some power the giftie gie us
to see ourselves as others see us!
It wad frae monie a blunder free us,
an' foolish notion.
— Robert Burns, 1786

This article presents a literature review that explains the antecedents and values of visual research. Then it illustrates the use of photographs and audio recordings of informants to enrich interviews. The term *auto-* *driving* indicates that the interview is "driven" by informants who are seeing and hearing their own behavior. Autodriving addresses the obtrusiveness and reactivity inherent in consumer behavior research by

This chapter was first published in the *Journal of Consumer Research, 18*(3), December 1991, pp. 257-272. © 1996 by the Journal of Consumer Research, Inc. All rights reserved. Reprinted by permission of the *Journal of Consumer Research* and the University of Chicago Press.

explicitly encouraging consumers to comment on their consumption behavior as the photographs and recordings represent it. Thus, the research aims for a negotiated interpretation of consumption events. The results suggest that photographs offer exciting challenges to informants by encouraging their need to explain themselves.

Photographs and recordings show people to themselves. People become markedly self-conscious and seek to explain and justify themselves. We discuss a research method that is designed to enhance informant involvement and to elicit enriched qualitative information concerning events as informants perceive them.

In this study, we used photographs of informants going about their evening meals as stimuli for projective interviewing. Then we used an audio recording of the initial interview as the stimulus for another iteration of projective interviewing. This technique is termed autodriving, using the combining form meaning self, *auto-*, to indicate that the informant's response is driven by stimuli drawn directly from his or her own life.

Autodriving gives the informant increased voice and authority in interpreting consumption events (Sherry, 1988). Autodriving can be useful to consumer researchers for the way it enriches the body of qualitative data to provide a "perspective of action" (Gould, Walker, Crane, & Lidz, 1974; Snow & Anderson, 1987; Wallendorf & Arnould, 1991). *Perspective of action* describes informants' efforts to "make the system meaningful to an outsider" (Gould et al., 1974, p. xxv). In addition, autodriving helps the informants "manufacture distance" (McCracken, 1988) from their own common perspective of their everyday lives. Through autodriving, the informants can "see familiar data in unfamiliar ways" (McCracken, 1988, p. 24).

The autodriving method is based on projective and visual research methods. Projective techniques have been used in consumer research for some time (Ferber & Wales, 1958; Newman, 1957; Smith, 1954), and there exists a substantial body of literature in consumer research and psychology on how to construct and administer projective devices and interpret the results (Levy, 1985). This article will focus on the use of photography as a projective stimulus.

HISTORY OF VISUAL RESEARCH

In 1839, Louis Jacques Mande Daguerre and William Henry Fox Talbot announced their separate discoveries of how to make a photographic image. Since we recently celebrated over 150 years of photography (see "150 Years," 1989, and National Gallery of Art and The Art Institute of Chicago, 1989), it seems appropriate to survey its use in the social sciences and consumer behavior. This review summarizes how photography moved from illustration and documentation to serving as research data in the behavioral disciplines.

Several classic studies form the foundation of visual sociology. *Street Life in London* (Smith & Thompson, 1877/1969) and *How the Other Half Lives* (Riis, 1890/1957) show urban life in the late 19th century. Lewis Hine's photographs of immigrants arriving at Ellis Island are a symbol for our nation. From about 1896 to 1916, the *American Journal of Sociology* routinely included photographs that dramatized the need for social reform.

The "muckraking" nature of early visual studies subsequently led sociologists to shy away from the method as unscientific (Becker, 1975; Harper, 1988; Stasz, 1979).

Also, the ideographic and ethnographic nature of the visual data was challenging, and some researchers found it hopelessly unsystematic. Methods with a quantitative emphasis came to dominate the social sciences; sociology struggled to be viewed as a science, and visual research methods were largely abandoned.

In anthropology, Franz Boas was one of the first to use photographic methods. In 1894 he directed a professional photographer in the visual documentation of the Kwakiutl village, Fort Rupert. Boas also used photographs of masks and rituals to interview informants and to study dance and movement. In the early 1900s, making still photos was standard procedure for anthropologists in the field, but the photos were used mostly to illustrate the text, not as stimuli for gathering further data. Gregory Bateson and Margaret Mead (1942) established new standards for visual research with *Balinese Character: A Photographic Analysis,* a book based on fieldwork that they did from 1936 to 1939. In this classic of visual research neither the text nor the photographs stand alone; the pictures are studied for what they say, providing a richer understanding of the culture.

Motion filming progressed less rapidly than did still photography due to the cumbersome nature of the equipment that it required. In 1898, Alfred Cort Haddon conducted the first filming in the field at Torres Straits. Robert Flaherty's (1921) seminal *Nanook of the North* was an early ethnographic documentary. Flaherty originated the "participant camera"; he lived with his Eskimo informants for 8 years and involved them closely in making the film. They viewed rushes of the film, and their comments were actively considered (Chiozzi, 1989; Rotha & Wright, 1980).

During the 1930s, the entertainment motion picture industry displaced ethnographic films as a popular culture product, leading to the demise of most ethnographic filming. Although Mead and Bateson's "Character Formation" series in Bali was filmed during the 1930s, it was not released for 20 years. However, documentary still photography and photojournalism abounded. *Life* magazine was first published in 1936, and *Look* was published in 1937. The huge, celebrated Farm Security Administration (FSA) project was launched by the U.S. government to document midland post-Depression rural America. Dorothea Lange's *Migrant Mother,* Walker Evans's view of Pittsburgh, and Arthur Rothstein's *Dust Bowl in Oklahoma* are examples of the national treasures that this project produced. Simultaneously, several acclaimed photographers explored and developed the photos. Projects that emerged from this group include *Harlem Document* (1937-1940), *Portrait of a Tenement* (1936), and *Dead End: The Bowery* (1937) (Chiarenza, 1982).

After the war, lightweight cameras and synchronized sound revolutionized filmmaking. Luc de Heusch and Jean Rouch furthered the 1960s boom in ethnographic filmmaking that became known as the French Movement. Rouch and Edgar Morin (1961), a sociologist, collaborated on *Chronicle of a Summer,* a cinéma vérité film about Parisians' thoughts in 1960. The film shows the informants being interviewed and then their responses after viewing their own interviews. Finally, an article reports on interviews with the informants after the film was released (Morin & Rouch, 1962/1985). With this version of autodriving, Rouch and Morin made a landmark contribution to the cinéma vérité style of film and set a standard for ethnographic visual research.

The early 1970s brought two more notable films. *An American Family* is a cinéma vérité film about a middle-class family living in Santa Barbara. Gilbert Craig and his film crew followed the Loud family for 7 months, a time period spanning Mr. and Mrs. Loud's decision to divorce, the son's revealing his homosexuality, and the daughter's romance with one of the camera crew. Although the family was highly involved with making the film, after the film's release Mrs. Loud turned vehemently against the project. Seeing herself and her family as others saw them sparked her reaction, which also led to a national debate about film ethics.

Still photography in sociology was reinvigorated in the 1970s with the help of Howard Becker's (1974, 1975, 1978a, 1978b) photographic analyses of society, and during the seventies and eighties visual sociology grew as a scientific method (Becker, 1981; Harper 1982, 1987b; Wagner, 1979b). The first International Conference on Visual Sociology was held in 1983. *The Visual Sociology Review,* published by the International Visual Sociology Association, premiered in 1986.

Along the way, anthropologists continued to use photography, perhaps because of the general interest in seeing exotic cultures. However, there was significant discouragement from the positivist community about the extent to which the photographs could be treated as data (Collier, 1987). Visual anthropology, beyond merely illustrating cultures, experienced real growth in the 1970s. *Studies in Visual Communication* was published from 1974 until 1985. Another quality journal, *Visual Anthropology,* premiered in 1987, and many anthropologists now enjoy membership in the Society for Visual Anthropology.

John and Malcolm Collier's (1986) classic *Visual Anthropology: Photography as a Research Method* is required reading for serious students of photography. The Colliers (1986) are credited with developing photoelicitation as a research method:

> Photographs are charged with psychological and highly emotional elements and symbols. In a depth study of culture it is often this very characteristic that allows people to express their ethos while reading the photographs. Ultimately, the only way we can use the full record of the camera is through the projective interpretation by the native. (p. 108)

Worth and Adair (1972) took photoelicitation a step further by having their Navajo informants make the photographs.

In psychology, photoelicitation was neglected. While depth interviews were a psychological tradition, they were wedded to the word, with some use of abstract visual stimuli (i.e., Rorschach ink blots and thematic apperception test drawings). In the late 1970s, psychotherapy using photography became a discipline with a growing body of literature (Fryrear & Krause, 1983); phototherapists formed the International Phototherapy Association and published the journal, *Phototherapy.*

In sum, photography has evolved as follows. In early stages people marveled at capturing an image. Then pictures were used to report or illustrate, for archival purposes, in family albums, documentaries, histories, and as evidence. Finally, photographs became works of art, a status that is still debated, with relatively recent acceptance by some museums and galleries. In behavioral science, pictures are now used for psychotherapy, and, as will be discussed below, they are also used as research data and as stimuli for gathering further data.

VISUAL RESEARCH TODAY

Today visual researchers employ photography as a scientific research method. They have shown that prints, film, and video can be used effectively (a) to create cultural inventories, (b) as projective stimuli, that is, in photoelicitation, and (c) to examine social artifacts.

Cultural Inventories

Photographic collections are made to "inventory" people, objects, and events. "Visual anthropology and the camera's eye can extend and refine scientific description by including detail and nuance presently lacking from the written field records of sociology and anthropology" (Collier, 1979b, p. 271).

Collier (1979a) suggests macroanalysis, microanalysis, and microimage analysis for the interpretation of photographic cultural inventories. A macroanalysis is an open-inquiry approach to studying the prints, films, and videos "in order to respond to their holistic content" (p. 164). The product of this method is a phenomenological and narrative presentation commonly seen in ethnographic videos and films (Aron, 1979; Ewen, 1979; Harper, 1987a; Lokuta & Cohen, 1983; Lyon, 1969).[1]

Microanalytic approaches decompose photographs into inventories of items that are categorized according to their cultural or theoretical significance. Microanalysis is readily accepted by traditional scientific researchers because they see the camera as an objective recorder producing valid and reliable data (even though there is always

the potential for selection bias): Another photographer at the same location at the same time, with the same lighting, focal length, film speed, and so on, could reproduce essentially the same data. Studies of static objects and spatial arrangements (houses, buildings, fields, streets, and irrigation systems) often depend on this approach (Harper, 1987a). Of course when photographs include people in action who are engaging in complex activities, the pictures are more evidently the result of the interaction between the specific photographer and the subjects. Issues of simple reliability are replaced by more sophisticated analytical ideas to cope with the changing reality (Collier, 1987; Ewen, 1979; Lincoln & Guba, 1985; Skinningsrud, 1987).

The microimage approach involves applying proxemics, kinesics, and choreometrics to the study of photographic images. Proxemics is the measurement of spatial relationships. Kinesics is the study of body language. Choreometrics addresses movement through time. These techniques were developed by Hall (1974) Birdwhistell (1969), and Lomax (described in Collier, 1979b), respectively. Film and video are typically superior for microimage analysis (Collier & Collier 1986), but they are not essential. Family therapists Woychik and Brickell (1983) have their clients pose for group portraits throughout therapy and use kinesic and proxemic techniques to examine progress: "Each family has its own concept of how to pose for a family portrait, and the position within the viewfinder that the individuals take can clearly indicate internal family dynamics" (p. 317). Anthropologist Peter Woolfson (1988) applies proxemics and kinesics to films of physician-patient interaction to investigate the role that nonverbal communication plays in establishing rapport.

Projective Photoelicitation Techniques

In the 1950s, during the height of interest in motivation research, projective techniques were frequently used in consumer behavior research. Levy (1963a 1963b, 1980, 1981, 1985) continued to use projective techniques for his investigations of consumption behavior and the meanings of goods during what was otherwise a period of relative dearth for published projective work. Increased use of projective methods in consumer behavior research (Levy, 1981, 1985; Rook, 198b, 1988) has accompanied the recent growth of qualitative methods in consumer behavior (Belk, Wallendorf, & Sherry, 1989; Holbrook, 1988; Hudson & Ocean, 1988; Rook, 1988; Sherry, 1989).

Projective techniques are based on the logic that a person's behavior is invariably meaningful and expressive of personality and cultural values. "Thus, given a standard but relatively ambiguous task such as telling a story about a picture what a person does reflects how he structures and interprets life situations and reacts to them" (Levy, 1963b, p. 4). Researchers typically use a standardized picture stimulus to elicit stories across a sample of informants. Such picture stimuli range from extremely ambiguous Rorschach tests to more or less ambiguous drawings, to more or less ambiguous photographs. Collier and Collier (1986, p. 125) organize these projective tools according to the level of expected response. Their organization corresponds to Levy's (1985, p. 68) observation that "the more specific the question, the narrower the range of information given by the respondent."

Verbal responses elicited from people in the marketplace are a form of storytelling that can be analyzed projectively (Levy, 1981). Photographs can also elicit stories, and photoelicitation techniques can be useful in any phase of the research process. For certain exploratory purposes investigators are often uncertain about what questions they need to ask. To a certain degree, autodriving allows informants to interview themselves, to provide a perspective of action (Gould et al., 1974), and to raise issues that are significant to them. Photoelicitation may also provide a check on the validity of the researchers' findings (Becker, 1975, p. 27; Lincoln & Guba, 1985). Suchar (1988) stresses the increased validity that photoelicitation adds to a cultural inventory approach. Collier (1979b) also documents the effectiveness of photographs as projective interviewing stimuli:

Photographs as probes in interviewing ask their own questions which often yield unpredictable answers. The imagery dredges the consciousness (and subconsciousness) of the informant, and in an exploratory fashion reveals significance triggered by the photographic subject matter. The content of the imagery which photographically is an outside view is used projectively with the informant to give us an inside view of our research territory. (p. 274)

Caldarola (1988) sees photoelicitation as a central methodological technique in a collaborative mode of visual research:

The interviewing in particular became an exceptional source of rapport and a method of eliciting detailed information about economic transactions, technical skills, and social variables. More importantly, the interviews encouraged the informants' active participation in the research program by demystifying the photographic research process. (p. 440)

Visual anthropologists successfully use photographs as projective devices in their studies of cultures (Gates, 1976; Norman, 1984). Collier (1979b) used photoelicitation techniques in a study of French farmers' migration to English mill towns in the Maritime Provinces of Canada (Cornell University, 1953, reported in Hughes, 1960). From this study he concluded:

> Beyond the cultural inventory, the photograph as a probe and stimulus to interviewing has proven to be consistently invaluable. In tests carried out for Cornell University we compared the value of interviewing with and without photographs and discovered that the picture interviewer could continue his interrogations indefinitely, as long as he continued to bring in fresh photographs. In contrast the exclusively verbal interviews became unproductive far more quickly. In terms of subsequent content analysis, picture interviews were flooded with encyclopedic community information, whereas in the exclusively verbal interview, communication difficulties and memory blocks inhibited the flow of information. (p. 281)

Visual sociologists have successfully used photoelicitation techniques in their studies of group behavior (Harper, 1984; McMahan, 1978; Stokrocki, 1984). Rosalyn Banish (1976), in her seminal photoelicitation work comparing London and Chicago homes, asked an informant (male, stockbroker) whether a portrait she had taken of his family in their drawing room would give "strangers the right idea." Her photoelicitation technique combined with an effective question helped the respondent manufacture distance from his everyday behavior (McCracken, 1988) and observe that "people would get the completely wrong idea, but it's the one that we try desperately to give [laughter]" (p. 88).

Psychologists also use photoelicitation techniques. Akeret (1973), Entin (1979, 1982), Wessels (1985), and many others (Fryrear & Krause, 1983) used family photographs for projective purposes in therapy.

Social Artifacts

Analysts examine prints, films, and videos made by members of a group for indications of what the group values (Belk et al., 1989; Conger, 1982; Musello, 1979; Norman, 1984). The assumption is that people project personality and cultural norms into their photography, much as they do into their stories about pictures.

> Imagery may be studied as data *of* culture when it is examined as the product of particular groups within defined socio-cultural contexts. The task in regard to such "native artifacts" is to decipher recurrent themes, motifs, and formal patterns; to understand those values and rules which may shape their production, use, and interpretation; and to examine what function they serve within the culture of their producers. (Musello, 1988, p. 475)

Entin (1982) and Wessels (1985) use archival family albums in family therapy, reflecting the concept that "what is chosen to be photographed, recorded, and documented for the family album reflects the ideals, traditions, and values of the family" (Entin, 1982, p. 209).

In many cases, the social artifact approach is combined with the cultural inventory or photoelicitation approach. Cultural inventory methods of macroanalysis, microanalysis, and microimage analysis may be applied to photographic artifacts to interpret their meanings. For example, Entin

(1982) and Wessels (1985) use macroanalytic, microanalytic (e.g., who is and who is not in the pictures), kinesic, and proxemic techniques in their analyses of archival family album data during family therapy. Also, it is most useful to interview relevant informants projectively with photographic archival data to get the inside view or perspective of action that Collier (1979b) and Gould et al. (1974) mention. Entin (1982) and Wessels (1985) projectively interviewed their informants using archival photographic data as stimuli.

VISUAL RESEARCH IN CONSUMER BEHAVIOR

At the 1985 Association for Consumer Research Conference, a special session on visual research in consumer behavior provided an introduction to the use of still and video photography as a research method. The session included three presentations. Wallendorf and Westbrook (1985) examined the meanings people attach to clothing by applying macroanalytic and microanalytic approaches to photographs of people with a garment that they felt "inclined to discard" and one that they would "never abandon." Rook (1985a) presented home movies collected from students to illustrate ritual product usage and symbolism. Heisley and Levy presented the autodriving technique discussed in this article. Later, Holbrook applied macroanalytic, microanalytic, and autodriving techniques to photographs of his jazz (1987) and art (1988) collections to analyze his own consumer behavior. Wallendorf and Arnould (1988) proxemically analyzed photographs of consumers with their "favorite things."

Visual research has primarily gained momentum in naturalistic consumer behavior research. Hirschman (1988) used a macroanalytic technique in her study of upper class WASPs. The Consumer Behavior Odyssey (Belk, 1991) participants employed photography and videotaping extensively in their cross-country exploration of American consumption, inventoried the contents of these visual documents, and used them for autodriving purposes. Their archive includes 4,000 still photographs and slides and 137 videotapes lasting 1,518 minutes each (Belk, Sherry, & Wallendorf, 1988; Belk et al., 1989). The Odyssey participants even produced a video documenting the project, the method, and some of its major findings (Wallendorf & Belk, 1987). A recent study of Thanksgiving used 2,500 photographs for macroanalysis, microanalysis, microimage analysis, and a form of unguided autodriving (Arnould & Wallendorf, 1989; Wallendorf & Arnould, 1991). An ethnographic study of a farmers' market included making over 1,300 pictures that were analyzed with macroanalytic, microanalytic, and proxemic methods (Heisley, McGrath, & Sherry, 1987, 1991). In her study of health beliefs and rituals in a Hispanic community, Anderson (1991) used the projective device, pioneered by Worth and Adair (1972), of having the informants make photographs. She then conducted cultural inventories on the photographs. Now she is returning to the field and autodriving the informants. Durgee, Holbrook, and Wallendorf (1991) applied a cultural inventory approach to photographs of upper middle-class homes to analyze taste in house and interior design. Other fieldwork to date that has used photographs primarily for illustrative purposes includes O'Guinn's "Touching Greatness" project (O'Guinn 1987, 1991; O'Guinn & Belk, 1989) and ethnographies of a flea market (Sherry, 1988), a Hispanic community (Peñaloza, 1990), and a homeless community (Hill & Stamey, 1990).

In summary, visual sociology and anthropology have laid the foundation for visual research in the behavioral sciences, and consumer behavior researchers have begun to employ it. The following study offers further insight into the usefulness and relevance of autodriving for consumer behavior research.

RESEARCH PROBLEM

The research problem was a methodological one. Our aim was to investigate the photoelicitation technique called autodriving (a term first used many years ago in an article in *Psychiatry*) using visual and audio recordings of informants as projective devices for interviewing. We used a multiple iteration approach to autodriving. First, photos were taken of a family's dinner preparation and consumption. Then the informants were interviewed using the photographs as interview stimuli. At the third session, informants were shown the photos again, accompanied with an audio recording of the first interview, and asked to comment on these records. Our interest was in exploring how the iterative autodriving process would work as a projective technique and in improving it for future use.

METHOD

Context of the Study

We chose the context of family meals as an interesting area of study. Meal behavior is a universal phenomenon that differs across cultures and subcultures (e.g., social classes and ethnic groups) and stages in the family life cycle. This area is significant because of the practical importance of food consumption and family life in society, as well as for its symbolic richness (Douglas & Isherwood, 1979; Farb & Armelagos, 1980; Levy, 1981; Minsky, 1983).

> In all societies, both simple and complex, eating is the primary way of initiating and maintaining human relationships. . . . Cultural traits, social institutions, national histories, and individual attitudes cannot be entirely understood without an understanding also of how these have meshed with our varied and peculiar modes of eating. (Farb & Armelagos, 1980, p. 4)

Informants

Three families were photographed as they prepared and ate an evening meal. The families were middle-class residents of the same suburban neighborhood, in early phases of the family life cycle. The first couple, Jane and Paul Borge (names disguised), owned a single-family home. They were both 36 years old and had two children, ages 4 (Leon) and 8 (Sarah). Paul was a film producer, and Jane was a housewife. The second couple, Laurie and Arnold Cagan, owned a three-story home and rented out the ground-level apartment. Laurie was 30 years old and a computer programmer. Arnold was 32 years old and a writer in the public relations field. Laurie and Arnold's son, Joshua, was under the age of 1. The third couple, R. B. and Dawn Mars, had been married less than a year and had no children. Dawn was 27 and R. B. was 31; both were industrial salespeople. The Marses rented the upper story of a single-family home that had been converted into two single-story apartments.

Making the Photographs

Heisley enlisted the families' help for a documentary photography project. The families understood that she would photograph the preparation and consumption of their evening meal. They were acquainted with her, but they did not know her well. On an evening designated by each particular family, Heisley arrived before the preparation of the meal. Using a 35-millimeter camera, a normal 50-millimeter lens, and a flash, she exposed 172, 103, and 125 frames of the three families, respectively. No audio recordings were made at this stage.

Many frames were taken to achieve a high level of coverage. The photographs were not taken to investigate specific a priori hypotheses that could drive a highly articulated shooting script (although the method could also allow that; see Wagner 1979a). Rather, a general interest in the relationships of family members as expressed in mealtime activities drove the photography.

After developing the photographs, questions of editing and cropping arise. Editing generally refers to the process of selecting negatives to print. Contact sheets are made by placing all the negative strips for a roll of film in a transparent 8 by 10-inch sleeve and developing a picture from it. One 8 by 10-inch contact sheet has the information from an entire roll on it; each picture on the contact sheet is the size of a 35-millimeter negative. Contact sheets are the raw data. As a photographic project develops, the analysts may return to the contact sheets to code them and to select prints for further analysis as findings emerge.

In selecting the photographs to print, we took several issues into account. First, we chose a series that, in our opinion, represented the flow of events that took place that night. Second, the technical quality of the photographs had to be good enough to be used effectively in projective interviewing. Heisley is an amateur photographer (as many researchers are), so the quality of the image used for projective interviewing was sometimes an issue. Finally, in the printing of the selected images, no cropping (changing the initial framing of the event) was done. It seems wise to avoid cropping in the initial phases of the research because insights are developing and the researcher is not yet sure what may be important. Also, because all the photographs were shot with the same standard lens, full-frame printing allows the comparison of photographs and provides more information about the distance of the photographer from the informants (Heisley et al., 1991). However, as the project becomes more focused, cropping the photographs to emphasize particular points of interest might be useful, just as quotations are excerpted from verbal data.

Macroanalysis of Photographs

From the initial film exposures of the families, we developed images for use in projective interviewing. We showed these photographs, displayed in chronological sequence, to a sociology class studying documentary photography, and the group discussed them. This staffing was useful in employing the macroanalytic, holistic approach recommended by Collier and Collier (1986) and H. S. Becker (personal communication). The staffing provided information about which images stimulate curiosity, which images might need further clarification, which images might be relatively distinctive to that family, and what meaning or information the photograph might hold.

Autodriving the Informants

The next step was an autodriving phase. We interviewed the informants about the dinner using a set of photographs as the initial stimuli. We chose the set to represent the main events of the evening and to include all those present, both alone and together. As an aid to the informants' reconstructing the evening's events, we arranged the photographs chronologically. They could have been grouped differently (e.g., all mother-daughter, father-son, mother-son, and father-daughter photos could have been grouped together to focus on differences in family role expectations by gender). Such groupings are ways of raising implicit issues for the autodriver.

This first autodriving interview was audio-recorded. In the second iteration of autodriving, done at a later date, we asked the informants to go through the photographs again while listening to the recording of their first interview. The informant and the interviewer stopped the tape to make a comment or to ask a question. This second iteration was also audiotaped.

The first interview was with Jane Borge and lasted about 50 minutes. The length of Jane's responses decreased after about the 12th picture (there were 17). We did not inform her at that time that we intended to do a second, audio iteration of autodriving. The second iteration was cut short at the 12th picture because Jane became tired and impatient by the 9th picture, and she was ready to stop by the 12th picture. We decided to use fewer (14) photographs to interview Laurie Cagan and to inform her of our intent to conduct a second iteration.

Laurie did not go into as much depth with the initial "photos only" iteration of autodriving as Jane had, but her second "photograph and audiotape" autodriving seemed more fruitful than Jane's. The audio recorder was cumbersome for autodriving. It required a high level of motivation to interrupt the recording to make a comment, and it was difficult for us to know when to stop the audiotape for the informant.

Finally, with R. B. and Dawn Mars, we reduced the number of photographs to 10, and we eliminated the second iteration of autodriving. Nevertheless, these interviews were more productive, perhaps because of the changes in format, and possibly because the interviewer was gaining more facility in interviewing with these materials.

In summary, we made several changes as we explored and refined the autodriving technique. First, we reduced the number of photographs used because productivity fell off sharply with later ones. Second, the first informant, Jane, did two iterations of autodriving (visual and audio), but we did not inform her of our intent to do the audio iteration. The second informant, Laurie, did both iterations of autodriving (photos and then audio) and knew that we intended to do the second iteration. Finally, the third and fourth informants, R. B. and Dawn Mars, only did autodriving with the photographs. These last two interviews were the most successful.

RESULTS

The interviews were transcribed, and, in conjunction with the pictures, the results illustrate the elicitation of issues in three areas: (a) product associations, (b) role re-

Figure 54.1. Borge family eats dinner

lations, and (c) reactivity. The ethno-graphic present tense is used in the description of the results.

Product-Related Associations

When asked to "tell me whatever you think about when you look at [these photographs]," informants are prompted by the photographs to notice furnishings and utensils that are present. Because their confrontation with the photograph manufactures distance from their everyday reality (McCracken, 1988), they feel the need to explain those objects; often they note whether the products that they use are distinctive in some ways. For example, Jane Borge's response to a picture of her family eating the meal (Figure 54.1) provides

naturalistic expressive content about fondue sets as wedding gifts:

This is a fun meal. I enjoy fondue . . . shortly after we were married it was kind of an "in" thing to have. . . . It was a common wedding gift at that time. . . . I'd fix chocolate fondue or meat fondue with oil. And then it sort of sat, because while the kitchen was being worked on we used a small upstairs kitchen. . . . When we moved into this kitchen, I was reminded of it when there was a football party and I thought it was a good winter recipe. We enjoyed it, it was real good.

Later quotations also show how mentions of other utensils, chairs, clothing, foods, and cleansing products are spontaneously introduced as informants seek to account, or provide a perspective of action, for the scene being observed. The informants project the way in which products are socially embedded (a common gift, an "in" thing), and syntactically fitting (a winter recipe). Later examples (handling a TV remote control, kitchen cleansers, dinner rolls, produce, etc.) show the projection of deeper motivations and how products are used to act out the complexities of interpersonal relations. Thus, autodriving elicits associations between products and consumption from the consumer's point of view. These stories can then be analyzed for what they project about how household objects are perceived, organized, valued, and handled (Levy, 1981).

Variations in Role Behavior

Preparing and eating a meal creates an arena in which the family acts out role relationships and issues of power and conflict associated with those roles. We discerned three patterns of roles in these households.

The ambivalent wife and mother. Jane is a full-time housewife and is in charge of preparing meals. Her 8-year-old daughter, Sarah, is not fond of helping in the kitchen, and Jane talks about not forcing her. She is uncomfortable in her role as the socializing mother and does not want to force her daughter into the traditional housewife role that she chose for herself. She works patiently with her 4-year-old son as he learns to do various tasks. This tempers her classification as a traditionalist who would feel the need to train her children in roles appropriate for their gender.

Survey or straight personal interviews might be able to elicit a description of the roles that family members play in meal

preparation. But when the photographs ask the questions, nuances of the family's interactions surface. Jane's response to a particular photograph (Figure 54.2) is an example: after noting that her daughter had been unwillingly stemming the spinach, she is stirred to discuss her own ambivalent feelings toward her role:

> I was Betty Crocker Homemaker of Tomorrow in high school, embarrassingly so. I think I'm a good cook and I enjoy it. . . . Sometimes I don't want to do it, but most of the time I do enjoy it. . . . I didn't like that image of myself. . . . Sometimes I wish I wasn't so domestic. But it's my nature and I'm real happy doing it. . . . Every so often I sort of wonder if it would have suited me, I know it wouldn't have, but I sort of wish I had had the personality where I could have stayed with my career and not chosen to stay home with the kids although I wouldn't have been happy doing that.[2]

The good father. A microanalysis of the photographs indicates that Arnold's primary role during meal preparation is to interact with his child. He arrives home from work, greets Laurie and Joshua, and plays with Joshua while Laurie completes and serves the meal. Autodriving confirms this behavior as role playing that she appreciates. While viewing a photograph (Figure 54.3), Laurie explained,

> So, Dad comes home from work. This is really classic, even now. It seems that Joshua will often be in his high chair when he walks in. And they have an exchange, and usually Joshua will go upstairs with Arnold, I don't know if he did this night or not. That's a nice picture. I like that. You know, they have a little exchange there, and Joshua will sometimes go upstairs while Arnold changes from

Figure 54.2. Sarah Borge stems spinach

Figure 54.3. Arnold Cagan greets son Joshua

his work clothes. Which is nice for me, 'cause then it gives me a chance to try to actually finish the meal up.

The dominant husband. The newly married Marses talk about sharing the tasks surrounding their meal, and the pictures show their togetherness. But autodriving makes it clear that R. B. dominates how things should be done, particularly given his strong concern with eating healthily.

If Dawn said "let's eat fried this, or let's eat greasy that," I'd say I'm not eating it and I'm not letting you eat it either 'cause I love you and I don't want to have you fill your veins full of that junk and you'd end up having a bypass. . . . We gave up the dairy and that was my influence because of my dad and his bypass. . . . We [were] reading these articles on osteoporosis and so we got a little concerned, so we incorporated the dairy back in. . . . That's our glass pot . . . certain pots are not healthy . . . aluminum is supposed to be a cause of Alzheimer. . . . The paranoia came from my grandmother and her Alzheimer's disease. . . . I'm very well aware of these things—I think from my running and knowing how different foods affect my performance, seeing my dad with a bypass, being in the medical sales profession and going to hospitals and seeing people who are messed up a lot of it may, in fact, be related to diet.

Power Relations

The autodriving technique provides informants with enough distance to observe the structure of power surrounding their mealtime activities. A striking example occurs in the Mars family, when R. B. comes to recognize his assertions of power. R. B. and Dawn ate dinner (sandwich, soup, and yogurt) sitting on a couch with R. B. sitting on the end. While looking through the photographs (Figure 54.4), he notes their positions:

With the couch, it's funny, it reminds me of Archie Bunker who always had his chair. It's funny how Dawn and I have picked our spots on the couch. I always sit here and Dawn always sits there. We've picked our spots and sometimes in the morning I'll switch it around and *I'll* sit here and Dawn will sit there and she won't say anything to me but I'm very aware that I'm switching on purpose, just so Dawn can sit there so I don't have the Archie Bunker seat. Not that that's a position of power, but I like it because it lets me have the remote [television control; laughter]. I guess it's a position of power because it lets me have the remote [laughter]. Don't tell Dawn.

The photoelicitation enables R. B. to project his ambivalence about his desire to dominate his wife on the one hand and to have her be an equal on the other.

Conflict

When shown a picture of Leon covering his mouth at the dinner table (Figure 54.5), Jane's comments relate to the problem of table manners, and people's influencing other people's eating.

He's holding his mouth and he doesn't want something. . . . I think I do remember that [my brother-in-law] was trying to get him to eat that night, I think some trick that Leon wouldn't buy. . . . My brother-in-law and Paul were talking about this meal they had with my mother-in-law, who was upset because my brother-in-law broke a roll in half

Figure 54.4. R.B. and Dawn Mars eat dinner

Figure 54.5. Leon Borge politely covers mouth

and buttered it and ate the roll, rather than breaking it, each piece, each bite-size piece and buttering it. And he was saying how some of her rules are not practical. She's real fussy. When she visited us—that was last October—she did think Sarah had very good manners, so she was pleased with that. I certainly don't go overboard on it. Actually, Paul is more like his mother; he insists on good manners more than I do.

The autodriving illuminates the way in which "small" consumer behaviors about eating rolls and butter are ways of acting out family relationships—here, conflicts and mixed feelings about pleasing a fussy mother-in-law. Similarly, there is a notable amount of discussion by R. B. and Dawn Mars regarding conflict around meals that characterizes the intensity of adjustment at the beginning of their marriage. It ranges across how to grow sprouts, the reason not to use Comet cleanser, and how to wash broccoli.

> He has a different method. I used to do them in the dark, but he does them in the light. . . . You soak them overnight in a jar, and then you drain them. What R. B. does is lay them in the sun on their side. . . . You have to rinse them and let them dry out. With the moisture and the heat, they sprout. I've done it where you keep them in the dark those first few days, kind of incubating them. You rinse them and they're moist and they're dark and they're warm, and after a couple of days, once they're big, then you take them out and let them get green. But R. B. just grows them all along without really covering them. They do OK too. . . . I think I'm more easygoing than R. B. is. He's got particular ways of doing certain things. And sometimes *I'll* say, "I'm doing things this way, because that's the way I want to do it." And that has been a

certain adjustment. And he'll say, "Oh, you're right, you don't have to do it my way." And I say "good." Sometimes I have thought "this is crazy," you do find yourself doing things . . . if it's something that really doesn't matter that much to me—a good example is Comet, if you breathe that in, that's terrible for you—I never thought about it. R. B. will only buy that Softscrub stuff because it's already in the liquid and you don't breathe it. Yet at the same time, I *like* Comet! It does a better job. But I would never go out and buy it now. So it's one of those kind of things that you give in to the other person. . . . Like, the way you wash the broccoli. . . . R. B. has a very strategic way of washing the broccoli, and it's not the same way I do it. So, when I do it and he's watching me, inside he's thinking "why don't you do it my way?" and vice versa. I think overall R. B. is more meticulous and more careful about things in general like that, because that's just the way he is. So maybe what might seem careless to him is just my way. What does it matter what way I wash the broccoli?—it's still clean. But no, you have to dunk it in and out of the water 15 times and shake it in the air [laughter]. . . . No, I'm exaggerating here. Overall, he's all right [laughter]. Oh, I'm getting divorced tomorrow. Just don't tell him what I said [in mock concern].

The few excerpts cited here illustrate how readily the photoelicitation method brings out some of the family dynamics, the consumers' fretting about when to take a stand about products and their handling, when to yield, the struggle of newlyweds to accommodate each other. Dawn's description of how she grows the bean sprouts may be interpreted as a projection of her more nurturing, maternal approach: she wants to incubate them, letting them grow big in a warm, dark place.

REACTIVITY AND OBTRUSIVENESS

Hirschman (1986, p. 242) warns against using audio and video recording tools because (a) they are obtrusive, (b) they call "undue" attention to the presence of the researcher, (c) they can alter behavior, and (d) there is an ethical issue if recordings are secretly made. However, researchers who use audio or video recording believe that (a) important patterns of behavior survive obtrusiveness, (b) a skillful worker will use the recording process to establish rapport between the researcher and the informants, and (c) if the nature of the research calls for precise on-site recording, then some version of audio, visual, or written recording must be used. Audio and visual recordings are not inherently more obtrusive than note taking; moreover, they are more exact and may be less threatening. Further research may examine the comparative effects of particular kinds of stimuli in facilitating or interfering with results.

The least amount of reactivity to visual recording occurs when participants are absorbed in an important activity (Becker, 1975, p. 28). De Heusch (1962/1988) differentiates three types of sociality for which reactivity is minimal: ritual or ceremonial sociality, intensive sociality, and technical sociality. Family meal behavior involves elements of all three types of sociality. There is a strong ritual element in preparing, serving, and consuming the family meal; the preparation usually requires concentration; and there are technical or practiced movements that are performed to complete the task. The audio and visual documentation stage becomes more useful and less intrusive as informants increasingly engage in these socialites. When informants are allowed to conduct their activities without

constant interaction with the observer, informants are freer to act as they normally do. Later, through autodriving, informants can be asked the questions that a participant observer would normally interrupt to ask. The informant and the researcher can then examine the visual record to explore the process together, taking time with each aspect of the event, to arrive at a negotiated interpretation of it.

There is also less deviation from routine activity if (a) the photographer is relaxed and natural, (b) the informants are frequently photographed, and (c) the informants are accustomed to being observed while performing their activities. The implication is that photographic observation of informants on multiple occasions (as is common in good ethnographic research) enables the photographer to capture a realistic picture of normal activity. (Or perhaps posing will become part of the norm, as it is in modern weddings.)

In the setting used for this research, if subjects behave as if a dinner guest were present, one might expect the most natural behavior to occur among families who frequently entertain dinner guests. If a special guest is observing, they follow some ideal notion of a meal, or perhaps a more festive one. Analysis of the photographs, followed by the autodriving technique, distinguishes behaviors that the informants associate with daily mealtime activity from ones they associate with an ideal meal. Upon viewing the photographs, informants talk about the ways that they change their behavior and how it might be different without a visitor.

The Borge family. The group that staffed the photographs of the Borge family (macroanalysis) observed that the people seemed comfortable and natural. Jane Borge mentions that, because of being observed, she served the meal later than usual, and there-

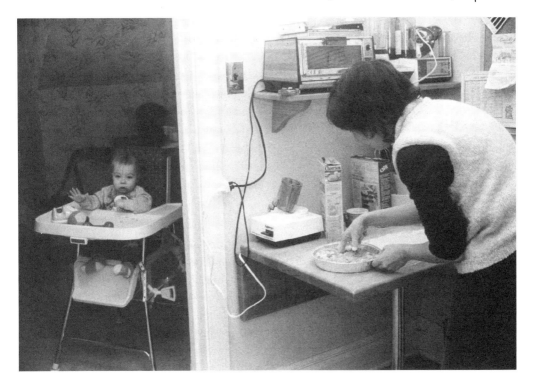

Figure 54.6. Laurie Cagan fixes dinner

fore the children were tired. Other than that, however, despite the fact that her two brothers-in-law and the photographer were there, she notes the "typical" character of the evening: People often photograph her family (as her husband is a film producer); they often entertain dinner guests; her out-of-state brothers-in-law are living with them for a while as they complete a job; people often live with them temporarily; the fondue is left over from a dinner she prepared earlier in the week, and so on. In sum, it appears that deviation from the family's routine meal behavior is not a marked factor.

The Cagan family. Macroanalysis of the photographs indicated that Laurie's son tends to watch the photographer. This behavior frees Laurie to more closely approximate her ideal meal and prompts her

to discuss the seeming (exaggerated?) frequency with which things are more hectic. Looking at a picture of Joshua calmly sitting in the high chair while she was preparing the meal (Figure 54.6), she remarks,

> That's funny. Things ran pretty smoothly I'd say. . . . I think he was pretty well-behaved and he was probably intrigued by you being there, too. . . . Of course, the nights when it's not good, you seem like you have a million of them, I don't know if you ever really do though, I mean it's just, you kind of remember that evening when I held Josh as I tried to roll out a pie crust or whatever. [Laughter.] Kind of your joints remember it, your back remembers it.

During the second iteration of autodriving Laurie Cagan responds,

Well, I guess I'm sounding coherent [laughter]. Seems odd to me listening to yourself talk. One thing, I thought about this when we were looking through the last pictures I was thinking too that I can't say that I was totally unaffected by the fact you were coming over in that I definitely don't think I could have had someone coming over taking pictures if I had decided to make something from scratch that evening. I just wanted to say that. But, I would also say that this probably is kind of the way I do make meals ideally.

She is self-conscious, but judicious, in her evaluation.

The Mars family. Dawn Mars, in the newly married family, comments on a dichotomization of meals into rushed and not rushed and notes the cleanliness of the apartment.

This is a very organized picture. Everything looks pretty much in its place—gives me a good feeling. That's not how it usually looks! Usually things just get too out of hand. We'll be good for a couple of days, then everything gets disastrous. . . . It's like, we don't let anybody in. Barricade the door!

Dawn is interpreting the difference between the "front" and the "back" of social situations à la Erving Goffman (1959). R. B. Mars also explains their reactivity when looking at a photograph of him and his wife preparing dinner:

We're doing our own thing. I think if you weren't there we probably would be talking between ourselves and sharing the day's activities or intimate thoughts or Dawn would be telling me maybe about some challenge she had at work or I would maybe be giving some advice on how to handle this turkey or that turkey. So we'd be talking amongst ourselves. I think we're a little self-conscious 'cause you were taking the pictures.

DISCUSSION

On the technical side, it is evident that there is much room for experimentation with materials, understandings, and time in using photoelicitation techniques. Autodriving is an approach that can be adapted to the responsiveness of informants and various applications of interest to the researcher. We offer three suggestions for using the autodriving approach.

1. *Limit the photos per session to a pretested number that is productive.* Collier's finding that an interviewer could "continue his interrogation indefinitely" with photographic stimuli referred to successive interviews. Collier and his team also experienced wear-out in single interviews (Collier & Collier, 1986, Chapter 8).

2. *Use easily manipulable, discrete units of media for the autodriving stimuli.* Still photos are handy for the approach. Also, if informants' comments were put into discrete units of written transcripts, autodriving might be facilitated. Audio recordings (and probably video recordings) can make autodriving cumbersome, but these techniques seem worth more study.

3. *If the intention is to do multiple autodriving iterations, there is a trade-off between informing and not informing respondents up front.* The knowledge that informants will have to go through the materials again may modify their first response or result in the loss of a subject, but it builds goodwill and increases the probability of having a successful iteration.

Autodriving's ability to elicit meaningful insights has been illustrated with four informants from three middle-class suburban families in reference to their consumption of evening meals. The autodriving method highlights the informants' views of ordinary realities. As they observe the moments fixed in time by the photographs, informants distinguish among elements of the typical, the unusual, and the ideal. Autodriving thus helps in recognizing and addressing the effects that the researcher introduces, in contrast to the common approach that either assumes the researcher does not influence the informants or ignores that influence.

In addition to the exciting nature of the stimuli, photographs inevitably present an oversimplification of the family's life. Unlike the usual interview, photographs challenge the respondent. A photograph motivates people to provide a perspective of action, to explain what lies behind the pictures, and to relate how the frozen moment relates to the reality as they see it. Informants feel compelled to fill in the details to guard the family against misperception. Autodriving provides a type of member check to increase the credibility of the researcher's interpretation. Thus, autodriving is a positive step toward achieving the negotiated understanding that contemporary social research emphasizes as desirable (Lincoln & Guba, 1985; Sherry, 1988).

Autodriving is a projective technique that asks more specific questions than classic projective stimuli such as Rorschach tests, thematic apperception tests, and defined line drawings do. It is useful to consumer researchers because the photographs are made in the researcher's context of interest. Auto-

driving relieves the stress that results from informants' being only the subjects of the interview; instead, they become observers as well and join in interpreting the photographs with the researcher (Collier & Collier, 1986).

The autodriving technique allows the researcher to learn about the nature of informants' reactivity to his or her presence and observation of the meal. The reactive tendency is toward the informant's ideal notion of a meal. Autodriving elicits associations that focus on products and consumption from the informant's point of view. Autodriving leads informants into expressing and analyzing the nuances of their family roles. This procedure manufactures the distance (McCracken, 1988) that enables informants to discover and express the power and conflict relationships that are implicit in their everyday realities.

The informants in this research express themselves in their mealtime behavior and then "correct" their versions of this behavior by reacting to the pictures; thus, they become projective interpreters of their own actions. The researcher then interprets further. Autodriving makes it possible for people to communicate about themselves more fully and more subtly and, perhaps, to represent themselves more fairly. Interpretations of mealtime events were negotiated by the researcher and the informant; such an approach can enhance the validity of consumer research.

NOTES

1. A good method for a project is to maintain an area in which photographs are constantly on display. Project participants can arrange the photos according to the various themes they identify, and this encourages speculation on meaningful organizations.

2. Jane eventually acted on this ambivalence when her children got older and began attending school. She and her husband now own and operate a successful film production company.

REFERENCES

Akeret, R. U. (1973). *Photoanalysis: How to interpret the hidden psychological meaning of personal and public photographs.* New York: Wyden.

Anderson, L. (1991). *Native image-making: Health beliefs through the eyes of informant camerapersons.* American Marketing Association's Winter Marketing Educators' Conference, Orlando, FL.

Arnould, E. J., & Wallendorf, W. (1989). *Thanksgiving day feasts: A pictorial analysis of consumption.* Association for Consumer Research Annual Conference, New Orleans.

Aron, B. (1979). A disappearing community. In J. Wagner (Ed.), *Images of information* (pp. 59-68). Beverly Hills, CA: Sage.

Banish, R. (1976). *City families: Chicago and London.* New York: Pantheon.

Bateson, G., & Mead, M. (1942). *Balinese character: A photographic analysis.* (Special Publications of the New York Academy of Sciences, Vol. 2, W. G. Valentine, Ed.). New York: New York Academy of Sciences.

Becker, H. S. (1974, May/June). Blessing the fishing fleet in San Francisco. *Society, 11,* 83-85.

Becker, H. S. (1975, May-June). Photography and sociology. *Afterimage, 3,* 22-32.

Becker, H. S. (1978a, February). Do photographs tell the truth? *Afterimage, 5,* 9-13.

Becker, H. S. (1978b, January/February). Rock medicine. *Society, 15,* 76-79.

Becker, H. S. (Ed.) (1981). *Exploring society photographically.* Chicago: Mary and Leigh Block Gallery.

Belk, R. W. (Ed.). (1991). *Highways and buyways: Naturalistic research from the consumer behavior odyssey.* Provo, UT: Association for Consumer Research.

Belk, R. W., Sherry, J. F., Jr., & Wallendorf, M. (1988, March). A naturalistic inquiry into buyer and seller behavior at a swap meet. *Journal of Consumer Research,* 14, 449-470.

Belk, R. W., Wallendorf, M., & Sherry, J. F., Jr. (1989, June). The sacred and the profane in consumer behavior: Theodicy on the odyssey. *Journal of Consumer Research,* 16, 1-38.

Birdwhistell, R. L. (1969). Still photographs: Interviewing and filming. In *Kinesics and context.* New York: Ballantine.

Caldarola, V. J. (1988). Imaging process as ethnographic inquiry. *Visual Anthropology, 1*(4), 433-451.

Chiarenza, C. (1982). In A. Siskind, *Pleasures and terrors.* Boston: Little, Brown.

Chiozzi, P. (1989). Reflections on ethnographic film with a general bibliography. *Visual Anthropology, 2*(1), 1-84.

Collier, J. (1979a). Evaluating visual data. In J. Wagner (Ed.), *Images of information* (pp. 161-169). Beverly Hills, CA: Sage.

Collier, J. (1979b). Visual anthropology. In J. Wagner (Ed.), *Images of information* (pp. 271-282). Beverly Hills, CA: Sage.

Collier, J. (1987). Visual anthropology's contribution to the field of anthropology. *Visual Anthropology, 1*(1), 37-46.

Collier, J., & Collier, M. (1986). *Visual anthropology.* Albuquerque: University of New Mexico Press.

Conger, A. (1982, Autumn). Some observations about contemporary Cuban photography: The union of Cuban writers and artists (UNEAC). *Studies in Visual Communication,* 8, 62-80.

de Heusch, L. (1988). The cinema and social science: A survey of ethnographic and sociological films. *Visual Anthropology, 1*(2), 99-156. (Original work published 1962)

Douglas, M., & Isherwood, B. (1979). *The world of goods: Towards an anthropology of consumption.* New York: Norton.

Durgee, J. F., Holbrook, M. B., & Wallendorf, M. (1991). *Systematic recording: Using visual research methods to record and analyze upper middle class women's taste in house and interior design.* Paper presented at the American Marketing Association's Winter Marketing Educators' Conference, Orlando, FL.

Entin, A. D. (1979). Reflection of families. *Photo Therapy Quarterly, 2*(2), 19-21.

Entin, A. D. (1982). Family icons: Photographs in family psychotherapy. In L. E. Abt & I. R. Stuart (Eds.), *The newer therapies* (pp. 207-227). New York: Van Nostrand Reinhold.

Ewen, P. (1979). The beauty ritual. In J. Wagner (Ed.), *Images of information* (pp. 43-57). Beverly Hills, CA: Sage.

Farb, P., & Armelagos, G. (1980). *Consuming passions.* Boston: Houghton Mifflin.

Ferber, R., & Wales, H. G. (1958). *Motivation and market behavior.* Homewood, IL: Irwin.

Flaherty, R. (1921). *Nanook of the north.* Chicago: International Historic Films, 16 mm, 57 ml.

Fryrear, J. L., & Krause, D. A. (1983). Phototherapy introduction and overview. In D. A. Krause & J. L. Fryrear (Eds.), *Phototherapy in mental health* (pp. 3-23). Springfield, IL: Charles C Thomas.

Gates, M. (1976). Measuring peasant attitudes to modernization: A projective method. *Current Anthropology, 17*(4), 641-665.

Goffman, E. (1959). *The presentation of self in everyday life.* Garden City, NY: Doubleday Anchor.

Gould, L. C., Walker, A. L., Crane, L. E., & Lidz, C. W. (1974). *Connections: Notes from the heroin world.* New Haven, CT: Yale University Press.

Hall, E. T. (1974). *Handbook for proxemic research.* Washington, DC: Society for the Anthropology of Visual Communication.

Harper, D. (1982). *Good company: A tramp life.* Chicago: University of Chicago Press.

Harper, D. (1984). Meaning and work: A study in photo elicitation. *International Journal of Visual Sociology, 2*(1), 20-43.

Harper, D. (1987a). The visual ethnographic narrative. *Visual Anthropology, 1*(1), 1-19.

Harper, D. (1987b). *Working knowledge: Skill and community in a small shop.* Chicago: University of Chicago Press.

Harper, D. (1988). Visual sociology: Expanding visual sociological vision. *American Sociologist, 19*(Spring), 55-70.

Heisley, D. D., McGrath, M. A., & Sherry, J. F., Jr. (1987). *The farmers' market: An analysis of an alternative marketing system.* Paper presented at the American Marketing Association Winter Marketing Educators' Conference, San Antonio.

Heisley, D. D., McGrath, M. A., & Sherry, J. F., Jr. (1991). "To everything there is a season": A photoessay of a farmers' market. *Journal of American Culture, 14*(Winter), 53-79. Reprinted in R. W. Belk (Ed.), *Highways and buyways: Naturalistic research from the consumer behavior odyssey* (pp. 141-166), Provo, UT: Association for Consumer Research, 1991.

Hill, R. P., & Stamey, M. (1990, December). The homeless in America: An examination of possessions and consumption behaviors. *Journal of Consumer Research, 17*, 303-321.

Hirschman, E. C. (1986, August). Humanistic inquiry in marketing research: Philosophy, method, and criteria. *Journal of Marketing Research, 23*, 237-249.

Hirschman, E. C. (1988). Upper class Wasps as consumers: A humanist inquiry. In E. C. Hirschman & J. N. Sheth (Eds.), *Research in consumer behavior* (Vol. 3, pp. 115-147). Greenwich, CT: JAI Press.

Holbrook, M. B. (1987). An audiovisual inventory of some fanatic consumer behavior: The saint tour of a jazz collector's home. In M. Wallendorf & P. Anderson (Eds.), *Advances in consumer research* (Vol. 14, pp. 144-149).

Provo, UT: Association for Consumer Research.

Holbrook, M. B. (1988). Steps toward a psychoanalytic interpretation of consumption: A meta-meta-meta analysis of some issues raised by the consumer behavior odyssey. In M. J. Houston (Ed.), *Advances in consumer research* (Vol. 15, pp. 537-542). Provo, UT: Association for Consumer Research.

Hudson, L. A., & Ocean, J. L. (1988, March). Alternative ways of seeking knowledge in consumer research. *Journal of Consumer Research, 14*, 508-521.

Hughes, C. C. (1960). *People of cove and woodlot: Communities from the viewpoint of social psychiatry.* New York: Basic.

Levy, S. J. (1963a). Symbolism and lifestyle. In *Toward scientific method: Proceedings of the winter conference of the American Marketing Association* (pp. 140-150). Chicago: American Marketing Association.

Levy, S. J. (1963b, Summer). Thematic assessment of executives. *California Management Review, 5* (Summer), 38.

Levy, S. J. (1980). Arts consumers and aesthetic attributes. In M. P. Mokwa & A. Prieve (Eds.), *Marketing the arts* (pp. 29-46). New York: Praeger.

Levy, S. J. (1981, Summer). Interpreting consumer mythology: A structural approach to consumer behavior. *Journal of Marketing, 45*, 49-63.

Levy, S. J. (1985, Summer). Dreams, fairy tales, animals, and cars. *Psychology and Marketing, 2*, 67-81.

Lincoln, Y. S., & Guba, E. G. (1985). *Naturalistic inquiry.* Beverly Hills, CA: Sage.

Lokuta, D. P. (photographs), & Cohen, D. S. (text). (1983, Winter). Ukrainian-Americans: An ethnic portrait. *Studies in Visual Communication, 9*, 36-52.

Lyon, D. (1969). *The bikeriders.* New York: MacMillan.

McCracken, G. (1988). *The long interview.* Newbury Park, CA: Sage.

McMahan, R. L. (1978). *Visual sociology: A study of the western coal miner.* Unpublished dissertation, Department of Sociology, University of Colorado, Boulder.

Minsky, R. M. (1983). Perspectives in the study of food habits. In M. O. Jones, B. Giuliano, & R. Drell (Eds.), *Foodways and eating habits: Directions for research.* Los Angeles: California Folklore Society.

Morin, E., & Rouch, J. (1985, Winter). The point of view of the characters. *Studies in Visual Communications, 11*, 71-78. (Original work published 1962)

Musello, C. (1979). Family photography. In J. Wagner (Ed.), *Images of information* (pp. 101-118). Beverly Hills, CA: Sage.

Musello, C. (1988). The family album (a review of the film by Berliner, A.), *Visual Anthropology, 1*(4), 475-478.

National Gallery of Art and The Art Institute of Chicago. (1989). *On the art of fixing a shadow: One hundred and fifty years of photography.* Boston: Bulfinch/Little Brown.

Newman, J. W. (1957). *Motivation research and marketing management.* Boston: Harvard University Press.

Norman, W. R., Jr. (1984). *An examination of centenary united Methodist church using the photograph as artifact.* Unpublished dissertation, Department of Anthropology, Ohio State University, Columbus.

O'Guinn, T. C. (1987). *The marketing and consumption of religion: Hearts, minds, and money.* Paper presented at the American Marketing Association Winter Marketing Educators' Conference, San Antonio.

O'Guinn, T. C. (1991). Touching greatness: The central Midwest Barry Manilow fan club. In R. W. Belk (Ed.), *Highways and buyways: Naturalistic research from the consumer behavior odyssey* (pp. 102-111). Provo, UT: Association for Consumer Research.

O'Guinn, T. C., & Belk, R. W. (1989, September). Heaven on earth: Consumption at Heritage Village, USA. *Journal of Consumer Research, 16,* 227-238.

Peñaloza, L. (1990), *Atravesando fronteras/border crossings: An ethnographic exploration of the consumer acculturation of Mexican immigrants.* Unpublished dissertation, Department of Marketing, University of California, Irvine.

Riis, J. A. (1957). *How the other half lives: Studies among the tenements of New York.* New York: Hill & Wang. (Original work published 1890)

Rook, D. W. (1985a). *Consumers' video archives and household rituals.* Paper presented at the Association for Consumer Research Conference, Las Vegas, NV.

Rook, D. W. (1985b, December). The ritual dimension of consumer behavior. *Journal of Consumer Research, 12,* 251-264.

Rook, D. W. (1988). Researching consumer fantasy. In E. Hirschman & J. N. Sheth (Eds.), *Research in consumer behavior* (Vol. 3, pp. 247-270), Greenwich, CT: JAI Press.

Rotha, P., & Wright, B. (1980, Summer). Nanook of the north. *Studies in Visual Communications, 6,* 33-60.

Rouch, J., & Morin, E. (1961). *Chronicle of a summer.* New York: Corinth Films, 16 mm, 90 ml. (transcript by S. Feld & A. Ewing [1985]. *Studies in Visual Communication, 11*[Winter], 38-70).

Sherry, J. F., Jr. (1988). *A sociocultural analysis of the flea market.* Working paper, Kellogg Graduate School of Management, Northwestern University, Evanston, IL.

Sherry, J. F., Jr. (1989). Postmodern alternatives: The interpretive turn in consumer research. In H. H. Kassarjian & T. S. Robertson (Eds.), *Handbook of consumer behavior* (pp. 548-591). Englewood Cliffs, NJ: Prentice Hall.

Skinningsrud, T. (1987). Anthropological films and the myth of scientific truths. *Visual Anthropology, 1*(1), 47-70.

Smith, A. (text), & Thompson, J. (photographs). (1969). *Street life in London.* New York: Blom. (Original work published 1877)

Smith, G. H. (1954). *Motivation research in advertising and marketing.* New York: McGraw-Hill.

Snow, D. A., & Anderson, L. (1987, May). Identity work among the homeless: The verbal construction and avowal of personal identities. *American Journal of Sociology, 92,* 1336-1371.

Stasz, C. (1979). The early history of visual sociology. In J. Wagner (Ed.), *Images of information* (pp. 119-136). Beverly Hills, CA: Sage.

Stokrocki, M. (1984). The significance of touching in an art awareness experience: A photographic analysis, elicitation, and interpretation. *International Journal of Visual Sociology, 2,* 44-58.

Suchar, C. S. (1988, Fall). Photographing the changing material culture of a gentrified community. *Visual Sociology Review, 3,* 17-21.

150 years of photojournalism. (1989). *Time,* Special Collector's Edition, Fall.

Wagner, J. (Ed.) (1979b). *Images of information.* Beverly Hills, CA: Sage.

Wagner, J. (1979a). Avoiding error. In J. Wagner (Ed.), *Images of information* (pp. 147-160). Beverly Hills, CA: Sage.

Wallendorf, M., & Arnould, E. J. (1988, March). "My favorite things": A cross-cultural inquiry into object attachment, possessiveness, and social linkage. *Journal of Consumer Research, 14,* 531-547.

Wallendorf, M., & Arnould, E. J. (1991, June). "We gather together": Consumption rituals of Thanksgiving Day. *Journal of Consumer Research, 18,* 13-31.

Wallendorf, M., & Belk, R. W. (1987). *Deep meaning in possessions: Qualitative research from the consumer behavior odyssey* (video-tape). Cambridge, MA: Marketing Science Institute.

Wallendorf, M., & Westbrook, R. A. (1985). *Emotions and clothing disposition.* Paper presented at the Association for Consumer Research Conference, Las Vegas, NV.

Wessels, D. T., Jr. (1985, Winter). Using family photographs in the treatment of eating disorders. *Psychotherapy in Private Practice, 3,* 95-105.

Woolfson, P. (1988). Non-verbal interaction of Anglo-Canadian, Jewish-Canadian, and French-Canadian Physicians with their young, middle-aged, and elderly patients. *Visual Anthropology, 1*(4), 401-414.

Worth, S., & Adair, J. (1972). *Through Navajo eyes: An exploration in film communication and anthropology.* Bloomington: Indiana University Press.

Woychik, J. P., & Brickell, C. (1983). The instant camera as a therapy tool. *Social Work, 28*(4), 316-318.

INDEX

ABOUT THE AUTHOR AND EDITOR

Dennis Rook is Professor of Clinical Marketing at the University of Southern California in Los Angeles. He received his Ph.D. in marketing in 1983 from Northwestern University's Kellogg Graduate School of Management, where he specialized in studying consumer behavior using qualitative research methods. He then joined the marketing faculty of the University of Southern California. In 1987, he left the academic environment for the Strategic Planning Department of DDB Needham Worldwide Advertising in Chicago. Subsequently, he served as director of qualitative research services at Conway/Milliken & Associates, a Chicago marketing research and consulting company.

He rejoined the USC marketing faculty in 1991. His published research has investigated consumer impulse buying, "solo" consumption behavior, and consumers' buying rituals and fantasies. These and other studies have appeared in the *Journal of Consumer Research, Advances in Consumer Research, Symbolic Consumer Behavior,* and *Research in Consumer Behavior.* In 1985, his dissertation research was honored by the Association for Consumer Research, and in 1988, he was appointed to the Editorial Board of the *Journal of Consumer Research.* His current research focuses on the theory, design, and conduct of focus groups.

He has served as a research and marketing consultant for companies in the consumer packaged goods, financial services, communications, and entertainment industries. The bulk of his consulting research involves the use of customized qualitative research tools to develop new product opportunities, identify brands' equities, discover consumer motivations, and develop brand positioning possibilities.

Sidney J. Levy is the Coca-Cola Professor of Marketing and Head of the Department of Marketing, College of Business and Public Administration, University of Arizona, as of September 1997. He is a psychologist, having earned his Ph.D. from the Committee on Human Development, University of Chicago. He is a licensed psychologist in the State of Illinois and a member of the American Marketing Association. He joined the faculty of the School of Business, Northwestern University in 1961 and taught there for 36 years. In 1982, he was honored as a Fellow by the Association for Consumer Research and named a life member. In 1988, he was named AMA/Irwin Distinguished Marketing Educator. In 1997, HEC-University of Montreal named him a Living Legend of Marketing. He was elected president of the Association for Consumer Research for 1991. He was chairman of the Kellogg School marketing department from 1980 to 1992.

His central interest is in studying human behavior in everyday life activities, exploring interpersonal relations, work activities, consumer behavior, communications, and public response. His research examines social memberships, cultural influences, symbolic interaction, and complex motivation in personality. Discussion of these explorations with their theoretical and practical consequences have appeared in the *Harvard Business Review, California Management Review, Public Administration Review, Merrill-Palmer Quarterly, Business Horizons, Journal of Marketing, Journal of Consumer Research, Journal of Retailing, Journal of Business Research,* and *Personnel Journal.*

His articles have been widely anthologized; those of special interest to marketers include "The Product and the Brand," "Symbols for Sale," "Social Class and Life Style," and "Broadening the Concept of Marketing." For the latter, he and Philip Kotler received the Alpha Kappa Sigma award for best article in the *Journal of Marketing.* "Interpreting Consumer Mythology" received the Maynard Award for the best theoretical article in the *Journal of Marketing* in 1981. He wrote *Living With Television* (1962), *Promotion: A Behavioral View* (1967), *Promotional Behavior* (1971), *Marketing, Society, and Conflict* (1975), and *Marketplace Behavior—Its Meaning for Management* (1978). Recent articles include "Autodriving: A Photoelicitation Technique," *Journal of Consumer Research* (1991); "The Disposition of the Gift and Many Unhappy Returns," *Journal of Retailing* (1992); "Giving Voice to the Gift: The Use of Projective Techniques to Recover Lost Meanings," *Journal of Consumer Psychology,* (1993); and "Stalking the Amphisbaena," *Journal of Consumer Research,* (1996).

As a principal in Social Research, Inc., for many years, he directed and participated in research investigations on behalf of numerous organizations, including major corporations, media, and various public and private agencies.